On Being a Christian

Hans Küng

On Being a Christian

XPRESS REPRINTS

Translated by Edward Quinn from the German
Christ Sein published 1974 by R. Piper & Co.
Verlag, Munich

ISBN: 978-0-334-02517-7

First published in English 1977
Reissued 1991 by SCM Press Ltd

Reissued 1995 by
XPRESS REPRINTS
SCM Press Ltd
9–17 St Albans Place, London N1 0NX

Printed in Great Britain by
Antony Rowe Ltd
Chippenham, Wiltshire

Acknowledgments

This book is extra-ordinary in many respects and in many respects too it is the result of extraordinary assistance. I worked on it at all times, day and night, and several manuscript versions of a number of sections were followed by more than half a dozen typescript versions. Dr. Margaret Gentner was responsible for the arduous task of preparing the manuscript for publication and for finally checking the footnotes. She was assisted in Tübingen by Ruth Sigrist and—when necessary—in Sursee, my home in Switzerland, by Frau Marlis Abendroth-Knüsel. Dr. Christa Hempel read the galley proofs and checked some of the bibliographical information. Frau Annegret Dinkel saw to the duplication of copies of the manuscript. Together with Dr. Margaret Gentner, I have to thank most of all Dr. Hermann Häring and Karl-Josef Kuschel, my student for the doctorate: these two made an unparalleled effort in reading each new version of the manuscript, discussing and studying with me the problems which were continually arising and helping me with countless suggestions and corrections. Without the generous helpfulness of all my assistants in the Institute for Ecumenical Studies the book would never have been completed for the deadline. Nor can I praise sufficiently the attentions of Frau Charlotte Renemann, who constantly provided in my house all that was necessary for our physical survival and for a very pleasant atmosphere in which to work.

The assistance of various colleagues in Tübingen—without exaggeration, still one of the best theological centers in the world—was important in another respect. Without constant discussion with both Catholic and Protestant specialist theologians, particularly in the free air of Tübingen, it would scarcely have been possible to produce this book or even anything like it. Incidentally, it can scarcely be taken for granted that a colleague working in the field of German language and literature should get himself involved with a theological book. I am especially grateful therefore to Walter Jens for reading through the manuscript with a critical eye from the first line to the last, in many instances even several times. To him I owe many stylistic and material improvements. A systematic theologian who enters into such detail in regard to the New Testament particularly needs someone to check his exegeses and syntheses. Gerhard Lohfink, my colleague in New Testament exegesis, provided this aid and read the whole manuscript. It was the same with some chapters of Section D, where I—a dogmatic theologian—had to deal with ethical questions. These were read by my colleagues in theological ethics, Alfons Auer and Wilhelm Korff. I am grateful to all these for corrections and suggestions. I must also thank Professor Julia Ching (Canberra, Australia, now in Tokyo) and Professor Henri Dumoulin (Tokyo) for looking through the section on the world religions.

I may be permitted also to mention with gratitude here another colleague who was only indirectly involved with this book, but without whose constant loyal and friendly help—which became publicly evident especially when I had to answer the interview given by Jerome Hamer, Secretary of the Congregation for the Doctrine of the Faith—I would have been kept back even more from my proper work as a result of the infallibility debate. This is Johannes Neumann, who has shown in his often unknown work as a canonist how even in the Church the law exists for men and not men for the law.

I am grateful to Baden-Württemberg for the unusual concession of a whole term's study leave in winter 1973/74. Only in this way could the completion of this book avoid being indefinitely postponed.

Tübingen, 1 August 1974

Contents

List of Abbreviations

BL	*Bibellexikon*
DBS	*Dictionnaire de la Bible, Supplément*
DS	Denzinger/Schönmetzer, *Enchiridion symbolorum*
DTC	*Dictionnaire de Théologie Catholique*
EKL	*Evangelisches Kirchenlexikon*
LThK	*Lexikon für Theologie und Kirche*
RGG	*Die Religion in Geschichte und Gegenwart*
ThQ	*Theologische Quartalschrift* (Tübingen)
ThW	*Theologisches Wörterbuch zum Neuen Testament*

The Books of the Bible in Alphabetical Order of Abbreviation

Ac.	Acts
Am.	Amos
Ba.	Baruch
1 Ch.	1 Chronicles
2 Ch.	2 Chronicles
1 Co.	1 Corinthians
2 Co.	2 Corinthians
Col.	Colossians
Dn.	Daniel
Dt.	Deuteronomy
Ep.	Ephesians
Est.	Esther
Ex.	Exodus
Ezk.	Ezekiel
Ezr.	Ezra
Ga.	Galatians
Gn.	Genesis
Hab.	Habakkuk
Heb.	Hebrews
Hg.	Haggai
Ho.	Hosea
Is.	Isaiah
Jb.	Job
Jdt.	Judith
Jg.	Judges
Jl.	Joel
Jm.	James
Jn.	John
1 Jn.	1 John
2 Jn.	2 John
3 Jn.	3 John
Jon.	Jonah
Jos.	Joshua
Jr.	Jeremiah
Jude	Jude
1 K.	1 Kings
2 K.	2 Kings
Lk.	Luke

Lm.	Lamentations
Lv.	Leviticus
1 M.	1 Maccabees
2 M.	2 Maccabees
Mi.	Micah
Mk.	Mark
Ml.	Malachi
Mt.	Matthew
Na.	Nahum
Nb.	Numbers
Ne.	Nehemiah
Ob.	Obadiah
1 P.	1 Peter
2 P.	2 Peter
Ph.	Philippians
Phm.	Philemon
Pr.	Proverbs
Ps.	Psalms
Qo.	Ecclesiastes
Rm.	Romans
Rt.	Ruth
Rv.	Revelation
1 S.	1 Samuel
2 S.	2 Samuel
Sg.	Song of Songs
Si.	Ecclesiasticus
Tb.	Tobit
1 Th.	1 Thessalonians
2 Th.	2 Thessalonians
1 Tm.	1 Timothy
2 Tm.	2 Timothy
Tt.	Titus
Ws.	Wisdom
Zc.	Zechariah
Zp.	Zephaniah

Translator's Foreword

At the request of the author, footnotes (apart from an occasional explanatory note by the translator) have been relegated to the end of this book. The same applies to Scripture references. In this way it is possible to read on without being distracted by an array of footnotes which otherwise might well have occupied in some instances more than half a page. But the reader who wishes to pause in order to examine more closely the author's argument or his sources can easily turn to the notes at the end.

Scripture quotations—also at the author's request—are not taken directly from any published version of the Bible, but are translated from the author's own fairly free German renderings in the light of the original texts and contexts and the more important and up-to-date commentaries.

EDWARD QUINN

Those for whom this book is written

This book is written for all those who, for any reason at all, honestly and sincerely want to know what Christianity, what being a Christian, really means.

It is written also for those

who do not believe, but nevertheless seriously inquire;

who did believe, but are not satisfied with their unbelief;

who do believe, but feel insecure in their faith;

who are at a loss, between belief and unbelief;

who are skeptical, both about their convictions and about their doubts.

It is written then for Christians and atheists, Gnostics and agnostics, pietists and positivists, lukewarm and zealous Catholics, Protestants and Orthodox.

Even outside the Churches, are there not many people who are not content to spend a whole lifetime approaching the fundamental questions of human existence with mere feelings, personal prejudices and apparently plausible explanations?

And are there not today also in all Churches many people who do not want to remain at the childhood stage in their faith,

who expect more than a new exposition of the words of the Bible or a new denominational catechism,

who can no longer find any final anchorage in infallible formulas of Scripture (Protestants), of Tradition (Orthodox), of the Magisterium (Catholics)?

These are all people

who will not accept Christianity at a reduced price, who will not adopt outward conformism and a pretense of adaptation in place of ecclesiastical traditionalism,

but who are seeking a way to the uncurtailed truth of Christianity and Christian existence, unimpressed by ecclesiastical doctrinal constraints on the right or ideological whims on the left.

This is not to say that what is offered here is merely a new adaptation of a traditional profession of faith or even a miniature dogmatic theology with

the answer to all old or new disputed questions; and it is certainly not an attempt to propagate a new Christianity. If there is anyone who can make the traditional articles of faith intelligible to modern man better than the present author, he is most welcome to do so. The author will reject no suggestion which may help to make his meaning clear. To this extent all doors remain open to greater truth. The present work is simply an attempt by someone convinced of the cause of Christianity, without proselytizing zeal or theological lyricism, without stale scholasticism or modern theological Chinese, to produce a relevant and opportune introduction
to *being* a Christian: not only to Christian
teaching or doctrine, but to
Christian existence, action,
conduct.
It is *only* an introduction: for only each one, for
himself alone, quite
personally, can be or
not be a Christian.
It is merely *one* introduction: other introductions
of a different character
are not to be ostracized,
but on the other hand a
little tolerance is
expected for this one.

What then is the aim of this book, which in fact has become a kind of small "Summa" of the Christian faith?
It is an attempt, in the midst of an epoch-making upheaval of the Church's doctrine, morality and discipline, to discover what is permanent: what is different from other world religions and modern humanisms; and at the same time what is common to the separated Christian Churches. The reader will rightly expect us to work out for him in his practice of Christianity, in a way that is both historically exact and yet up to date, in the light of the most recent scholarship and yet intelligibly, what is decisive and distinctive about the Christian program:
what this program *originally* meant, before it was covered with the dust and debris of two thousand years, and
what this program, brought to light again, can offer *today* by way of a meaningful, fulfilled life to each and every one.
This is not another gospel,
but the same ancient gospel
rediscovered for today!

This book was written, not because the author thinks he is a good Christian, but because he thinks that being a Christian is a particularly good thing. A book like this could and really should be the work of a lifetime. And even then it would not be complete. But if it is to serve as a guide in the present difficult situation of Church and society—to be, so to speak, a positive counterpart to my book on infallibility—then it must appear now and not sometime in the next three or thirty years.

A. THE HORIZON

I. The Challenge of Modern Humanisms

A direct question: *Why should one be a Christian?* Why not be human, truly human? Why, in addition to being human, should we be Christians? Is there something more to being a Christian than to being human? Is it a superstructure? a substructure? Just what does it mean to be a Christian, what does it mean to be a Christian today?

Christians ought to know what they want. Non-Christians ought to know what Christians want. Faced with the question, "What does Marxism want?", a Marxist will be able to give a concise and firm, if no longer undisputed, answer: world revolution, the dictatorship of the proletariat, the socialization of the means of production, the new man, the classless society. But what does Christianity want? The answer given by Christians is frequently muddled, sentimental, general: Christianity wants love, justice, a meaning to life, being good and doing good, humanity . . . But don't non-Christians want these things too?

The question of what Christianity wants, what Christianity is, has undoubtedly become far more acute. Today others are not simply saying something different, but often the same thing. Non-Christians too are in favor of love, justice, a meaning to life, being good and doing good, humanity. And in practice they often go further than Christians in this respect. But if others say the same thing, what is the point of being a Christian? Today Christianity is involved everywhere in a *double confrontation:* with the great world religions on the one hand and with the non-Christian "secular" humanisms on the other. And today the question is thrust even on the Christian who has hitherto been institutionally sheltered and ideologically immunized in the Churches: compared with the world religions and modern humanisms, is Christianity something essentially different, really something special?

This question cannot be answered merely theoretically or only in a general way. It must be investigated and answered as concretely and practically as possible within the horizon of our time, bearing in mind the experiences and conditions of our century, of our present world and society, of modern man. In this first section of the book of course there can be no question of a comprehensive analysis of our times. But there must certainly be a critical examination of Christianity itself in connection with competing ideologies, trends, movements. The present world and society will not be described and analyzed in themselves: on this there is an immense literature. But the meaning of Christianity in its relationship with this modern world and society will certainly be examined and defined afresh. The modern world and society are not the direct object of our study, but neither are they wholly irrelevant: in fact, they are constantly present as the background or reference point of our inquiry.

1. *Turning to man*

Are we mistaken in thinking—contrary to all appearances—that the very development of the *modern world itself*, its science, technology and culture, clarifies the question of being human in such a way as to make it, not more difficult, but easier to answer the question about being a Christian?

Are we mistaken in thinking—contrary to all appearances—that in the course of this modern development *religion* has by no means had its day, that man's ultimate questions have been neither solved nor—still less—liquidated, that God is less dead than ever, that—despite our incapacity to believe—we are conscious of a new need of faith?

Are we mistaken in thinking—contrary to all appearances—that *theology*, also shaken by the many crises of the human mind, is by no means at the end of its wisdom, by no means bankrupt, but—as a result of the immense labors of generations of theologians through two centuries—is in many ways better prepared than formerly to give a new answer to the question of being a Christian?

Secular world

Man today wants above all to be human. Not a superman, but equally not a sub-man. He wants to be completely man in a world as human as possible. Is it not surprising how man has got the measure of the world, has ventured on the leap into outer space just as he had previously ventured on the descent into the depths of his own psyche? Is it not surprising that he has consequently taken under his control much—indeed, almost everything—for which God, superhuman and supramundane powers and spirits were supposed to be responsible, and has truly come of age?

This in fact is what is meant when people speak of a "secular," a "worldly" world. Formerly "secularization"[1] meant primarily merely the transference—in a legal-political sense—of ecclesiastical property to worldly uses by individuals and states. But today it seems that not only certain items of ecclesiastical property, but more or less all the important spheres of human life—learning, economy, politics, law, state, culture, education, medicine, social welfare—have been withdrawn from the influence of the Churches, of theology and religion, and placed under the direct responsibility and control of man, who has himself thus become "secular."

It is the same with the word "emancipation," which originally meant the release in a purely legal sense of the child from paternal authority or of the slave from the master's power. But then it came to mean, in a derivative, political sense, the civic equality of all who were in a position of dependence on others: self-determination as opposed to alien determination of peasants, workers, women, Jews, blacks, Hispanies, national, denominational or cultural minorities. Finally "emancipation" has come to mean man's self-determination as such, as opposed to blindly accepted authority and unauthorized dominion: freedom from natural forces, from social constraint and from inward pressures on the person who has not yet found his identity.[2]

Almost at the same time as the earth ceased to be the center of the universe, man learned to regard himself as the center of the human world he had erected. In a complex process lasting for centuries which has been analyzed by Max Weber,[3] the great pioneer in the field of sociology of religion, man entered into his kingdom: experiences, knowledge, ideas, acquired originally in the light of Christian faith and linked with that faith, came under the control of human reason. The different spheres of life were seen less and less from the standpoint of a higher world. They came to be understood in themselves and explained in terms of their own immanent laws. Man's decisions and plans came to be based more and more on these intrinsic laws and not on the supposed will of supramundane powers.

Whether we like it or not, however we explain it, the fact is that even in the traditionally Catholic countries the remains of the Christian Middle Ages seem today to be largely liquidated and the secular fields largely withdrawn from the supremacy of religion, the control of the Churches, their dogmas and rites, and also from theological interpretation.

Is emancipation in fact the thread which runs through the history of mankind? Is this world really as secular in its depths as it appears on the surface? Does the last quarter of the twentieth century not indeed stand out as yet another new turning point in the history of ideas? Is a new awareness taking shape, a less rationalistic and less optimistic attitude perhaps to science and technology, economy and education, state and progress? In a word, are not man and his world anyhow more complex than they were thought to be by experts and planners in the different fields? These are open questions. What interests us first of all here is the place of the Churches and of theology in all this.

Surprisingly enough, Church and theology have not only—in the end—come to terms with the secularization process, but—particularly in the years since the Second Vatican Council—have even entered vigorously into the swing of it.

Opening out of the Churches

This secular world—formerly regarded as "this" world, the wicked world *par excellence*, a neopagan world—today is not only taken into account in Christendom, but largely consciously approved and assisted in its development. There is indeed scarcely a larger Church or a serious theology which does not claim to be "modern" in some sense, to recognize the signs of the times, to share the needs and hopes of modern man and actively to collaborate in solving the urgent problems of the world. At least in theory, the Churches today no longer want to be backward subcultures, organizations out of touch with the prevailing mentality, institutions proscribing advances in knowledge and productive curiosity: they want to break out of their self-imposed seclusion. The theologians want to leave traditional orthodoxy behind them and to make a more serious attempt to bring scholarly integrity to bear even on dogmas and the Bible. The faithful are expected to display something of this new freedom and frankness, in regard to doctrine, morality and Church order.

It is true that the different Churches have not settled a number of their *internal* problems: overcoming Roman absolutism in the Catholic Church, Byzantine traditionalism in Eastern Orthodoxy, the phenomena of disintegration in Protestantism. It is true that, despite endless "dialogue" and innumerable commissions, they have found no clear, practical solutions for a number of comparatively simple *inter-Church* problems: reciprocal recognition of ecclesial ministries, of the eucharistic community, common use of church buildings, common religious instruction and other questions on "faith and Church order." On the other hand, agreement has been easier with reference to *extra-Church* problems, in their demands on society. Both in Rome and in Geneva, in Canterbury, Moscow and Salt Lake City, it has been possible—at least in theory—to approve the following humane program: development of the whole man and all men; protection of human rights and religious freedom; the struggle to remove economic, social and racial injustices; promotion of international understanding; limitation of armaments; restoration and maintenance of peace; the struggle against illiteracy, hunger, alcoholism, prostitution and the drug traffic; medical aid, health service and other social services; help for people in distress and the victims of natural catastrophes (earthquakes, volcanic eruptions, cyclones, floods).

Should we not be glad at this progress on the part of the Churches? Naturally. And sometimes even a smile may be permitted. Both for papal encyclicals and for documents of the World Council of Churches it seems that the classical rule of politics holds: to find relief from the burden of the uncongenial and often fruitless "internal policy" of the Churches by seeking successes in an apparently congenial "foreign policy," which demands less from oneself than from others. In all this it is impossible completely to conceal a number of inconsistencies in the official attitude of the Churches: outwardly progressive, in regard to others; conservative to reactionary within their own sphere. The Vatican, for instance, vigorously defends social justice, democracy and human rights for the world outside, but continues to maintain internally an authoritarian style of government, the Inquisition, the use of public monies without public control. And the World Council of Churches boldly defends freedom movements in the West, but not those in the Soviet Union; concentrates its efforts for peace in the Far East without producing peace within its own sphere, between the Churches.

And yet we can sincerely approve the openness of the Churches toward the great needs of the present time. The Churches had neglected for too long their critical function as the moral conscience of society, had upheld for too long the union between throne and altar and other unholy alliances with the ruling powers, too long acted as guardians of the political, economic and social status quo. For too long they maintained an attitude of opposition or reserve toward all more fundamental changes in the system, under both democracies and dictatorships were concerned less with men's freedom and dignity than with their own institutional positions and privileges, afraid to make an explicit protest even against the murder of millions of non-Christians. It was not the Christian Churches—not even those of the Reformation—but the "Enlightenment," often apostrophized by Church and secular historians alike as "superficial," "dry" or "insipid," which finally brought about the recognition of human rights: freedom of conscience and freedom of religion, the abolition of torture, the ending of persecution of witches, and other humane achievements. It was the Enlightenment moreover which demanded intelligible religious services, more effective preaching and more up-to-date pastoral and administrative methods for the Churches—reforms widely extended in the Catholic Church only from the time of Vatican II. If we were to believe the church history manuals, the great ages of the Catholic Church in particular were those of reaction to the modern history of freedom: the Counter-Reformation, the Counter-Enlightenment, the Restoration, Romanticism, Neo-Romanesque, Neo-Gothic, Neo-Gregorian, Neo-Scholasticism. It was a Church therefore in the rearguard of mankind, compelled by its fear of anything new always to drag its heels, without providing any creative stimulus of its own to modern developments.

It is only against the background of this very dark past that the present development can be properly understood. In this plea particularly on the part of conservative Churches for more humanity, freedom, justice, dignity in the life of the individual and society, as opposed to all racial, class and national hatred, it is a question of a somewhat tardy but extremely significant *turning to man*. And, even more significantly, it is not merely through proclamations of Church leaders and theologians that more humanity is demanded of society. This humanity is practiced and lived unobtrusively by innumerable unknown people in innumerable places in the world. It is practiced and lived in line with the great Christian tradition, but at the same time with a new alertness, by all these innumerable anonymous Christian messengers of humanity, pastors and laypeople, men and women in a variety of familiar and even very unfamiliar situations: in the northeastern industrial area of Brazil, in the villages of southern Italy and Sicily, in mission stations in the African bush, in the slums of Madras and Calcutta, in the prisons and ghettos of New York, in the heart of Soviet Russia and in Islamic Afghanistan, in innumerable hospitals and homes for all needs of this world. It cannot be denied that active Christians took the lead in the struggle for social justice in South America, for peace in Vietnam, for the rights of blacks in the U.S.A. and South Africa, and also—it should not be forgotten—for the reconciliation and unification of Europe after two world wars. While the great figures of terror in our century—Hitler, Stalin and their deputies—were programmatic anti-Christians, the notable peacemakers and signs of hope for the nations on the other hand were professing Christians—John XXIII, Martin Luther King, John F. Kennedy, Dag Hammarskjöld—or at least men inspired by the spirit of Christ like Mahatma Gandhi. But, for the ordinary individual, those truly Christian people with whom he has come into personal contact in the course of his life are more important than the great leaders.

All these things and a number of other signs of positive movement in modern Christendom have captured the attention even of many people who are in no way committed to a particular Church. And both constructive discussion and practical co-operation between Christians on the one hand and atheists, Marxists, liberals, secular humanists of the most varied types on the other are no longer rare events. Perhaps Christianity and Churches are not really such an insignificant factor as they were assumed to be by some Western futurologists, only concerned with mankind's technological progress. Certain post-Christian humanists still feel the need of course to write on "the poverty of Christianity,"[4] just as Christians for their part have seized the opportunity as often as possible to write gleefully about "the poverty of humanism."

In fact the *poverty of Christianity* and the *poverty of humanism* are connected. Only frivolous Christians have ever disputed the fact that things go on in Christianity in a human, a very human way. At best they have tried to cover up and suppress the human, all-too-human scandals—great and small—in Christendom, mostly without success. On the other hand even post-Christian humanists should not really question the fact that they are still influenced—at least covertly—by Christian scales of values. But secularization cannot be understood merely as the legitimate consequence of the Christian faith, as some theologians like to think.[5] Nor can it be explained, as philosophers[6] try to explain it, only from its own deep roots. The modern idea of progress, for instance, is not merely a secularization of Christianity's eschatological interpretation of history; nor has it arisen from its own philosophical origins. The development took place in fact in dialectical exposition. For not only the Christian, but also the post-Christian, cultural heritage is not homogeneous. And what is really human, and humane—as recent history with all its cruelty shows—is not always easy to define without the Christian element in the background. And so too only very frivolous humanists will question the fact that modern post-Christian humanism, in addition to its debt to all the other sources (particularly the Greeks and the Enlightenment), owes an enormous amount to Christianity, whose human values, norms, interpretations have often been more or less tacitly adopted and assimilated, not always with due acknowledgment. Christianity is everywhere present in Western (and thus largely also global) civilization and culture, its men and institutions, needs and ideals. It is part of the air we breathe. There are no chemically pure secular humanisms.

We may state therefore as a provisional conclusion: *Christianity and humanism are not opposites.* Christians can be humanists and humanists can be Christians. We shall later show reasons why Christianity cannot properly be understood except as radical humanism. But it is clear even now that, wherever post-Christian humanists (of liberal, Marxist or positivist provenance) have practiced a better humanism than Christians—and they did this very frequently throughout the whole of modern times—this is a challenge to those Christians who have failed, not only as humanists but also as Christians.

2. *Christianity for sale?*

Christianity is challenged by modern post-Christian humanism not merely as a matter of fact. There is also a question of principle which has quite shattering consequences both in theory and in practice and which must be kept clearly in mind.

Has Christianity lost its soul?

If the Christian Churches at least in theory have become or are attempting to become so human, if they stand for all those human values for which others also stand, why do they not *quite* openly overcome all sectarian isolation? For this is the current trend. Numerous "Catholic" trades unions, sporting associations, student groups, in the post-conciliar period have given up their separate existence. "Catholic" parties have become "Christian," "Christian" parties "democratic." Why then is there a Church at all, claiming to have a special place in the world of men? If it is now so modern, progressive, emancipatory, why is it still at any point conservative, traditionalist, or at any rate covertly tied to the past? To put it briefly and clearly, *if it is now so human, what is the point of calling it Christian?*

This is an urgent question for many within the Churches. Unwavering fundamentalists and nervous pietists in the Protestant Churches are afraid that Christianity may be coming to an end. Conservative Catholics and in particular those belonging to the generation of the Montini Pope, disappointed by post-conciliar trends, see already "the Trojan horse in the City of God"[7] and brood sadly like Jacques Maritain, the Thomist philosopher, in the guise of a "peasant of the Garonne."[8] But even open-minded and knowledgeable Catholic theologians have issued warnings: Hans Urs von Balthasar temperately,[9] Louis Bouyer wittily and sarcastically analyzing the "breakdown of Catholicism."[10] And if the reaction of these men does not make an impression, it should be noted that level-headed observers even outside the Church are asking what is going on in Christendom today. The editor of *Der Spiegel*, for instance, scarcely to be classed as a conservative, long before he produced his book on Jesus, wrote a leading article[11] which culminated in the question: "What then is the point of the Church?" According to him, the conservatives have in their favor at least one argument which no progressive, however shrewd, can invalidate: "If what the most active innovators assert is true, then the Christian Churches are being liquidated ('liquefied' says Friedrich Heer), not only in the sense of losing their solidity, but in the sense of becoming superfluous." As far as I know, this question has not yet been thoroughly answered by any reformer.

We must therefore ask very seriously whether the whole modernization and humanization of Christianity—contrary to the best intentions of its advocates—is not bound to lead finally to a sellout of the Christian reality. It is typical of clearance sales that the façades—used for publicity—at first remain intact and even give the impression that business is flourishing, *although the substance itself is being sold.*

To what is all this leading? It may seem like a caricature, but there is considerable truth in the picture of uncommonly *open-minded Churches* which go in for action instead of prayer, get actively involved everywhere in society, subscribe to all manifestoes, identify themselves with all possible enterprises and—whenever possible—take part in revolutions, at least by supporting them in words from a distance; meanwhile, nearer home, the churches are becoming emptier, the sermon is acquiring a new function and the Eucharist is more and more forgotten, with the result that community worship—deliturgized and detheologized—degenerates into a socio-political discussion and action group or the conventicle of a "basic group."* All things considered, we have a Church in which contributions—even though smaller—are still received and money is paid out, but to whose gatherings in the last resort scarcely anyone comes: it is an "agglomeration" of individual Christians, each living his own life, but it can scarcely be called a "Church" (=*ecclesia*=congregation=assembly).

Is there perhaps a similarly *progressive theology* to match this sort of open-minded Church? Again, a certain amount of caricature may clarify the picture. Instead of the Neo-Scholastic Denzinger theology† from the last century, now abandoned, whose weakness was demonstrated at Vatican II, are we to have something like an adapted, up-to-date mixed cocktail theology which also lacks any Christian substance? A theology advancing in all directions at once, helplessly and without a plan, getting involved in everything and able to unite disappointed Christians of all denominations? Or we might ask, are Catholic Neo-Scholastics, grown weary of applying themselves to the exegesis of medieval theologians and papal encyclicals, subsequently to enjoy the novel experience of dabbling in the human sciences, late in life becoming also psychologists, also economists, also ecologists? Existentialist theologians, formerly considered modern, frustrated by a verbal theology forgetful of the world and blind to the future, politicize their thinking, show their social interest, orient themselves toward the future and, after the jargon of right-wing propriety, practice that of left-wing impropriety. And the descendants of Protestant pietists, tired of biblicism, are converted to post-idealistic ideological criticism and demand anti-authoritarian partisanship for social action and at least verbal revolution.

* *Kerngruppe, Basis-Gemeinde, communauté de base,* usually means a Christian group built up freely as a result of personal initiative as distinct from institutionalized Church structures. In spirit it may range from strict orthodoxy to the wildest experiments (which inevitably attract the greatest publicity). But it could also be a local parish or—for example—a university chaplaincy where the Christian commitment, going beyond Mass attendance and reception of the sacraments, is more determined than usually. (Translator.)

† Denzinger theology: dogmatic theology, as presented until recently in seminary textbooks, in the form of a number of theses drawn from the documents of the Church's teaching in H. Denzinger, *Enchiridion symbolorum, definitionum et declarationum de rebus fidei et morum* (first published 1854, frequently revised and brought up to date by various editors, the latest being A. Schönmetzer, published by Herder, Freiburg/Barcelona, Rome, New York; the edition used in the present translation is that of 1963, referred to as DS followed by the paragraph number).

Each thesis was followed by selected quotations from these documents, then "proved" with the aid of quotations from Scripture and the Fathers, perhaps also with "reasons" admitted to be persuasive rather than conclusive. (Translator.)

Such a theology—admittedly both traditional theology with all its odd propositions on faith and morals in a technical jargon for the initiated and likewise this modern theology with all its concern for the "world"—would be marked by *decentralization:* if a label is required, "centrifugalism" would be an ugly word for an ugly thing. What is wrong is not keeping one's eyes open and very closely examining men, the world, society, the present or even the past, tradition, history—if only this were done better, more thoroughly, more concretely, more realistically. The danger is that people may fail to see themselves in the world, abandon their critical dissociation, forget where they stand, lose their center. In that case theology is engaged in what Karl Barth rightly called *allotria,* alien fooleries, dons dancing in the carnival of Mardi gras: a *Carnaval des animaux* (*théologiques*), lacking however for the most part the musical humor of a Saint-Saëns. This sort of theology talks distractedly, in an uncontrolled, unconcentrated way, as soon as it has to speak of *something else,* when it really *must* speak of other things. It does not know why it is talking, what is the point of its talking, what is the aim of its talking. And out of this "theo-logy"—"talk of God" practiced in view of man, world, society, history—there emerges a modern or traditional, a learned and sometimes even very naïve "theological" *causerie* about all possible things: a theology which has degenerated to an ideology, speaking of everything "relevant" but not of God, seeking the "world" "concretely" more than the truth; it is more concerned with consciousness of time than with the message of salvation, practicing self-secularization instead of self-assertion.

Is it perhaps true what a number of people suspect? Self-alienation of theology in the name of enlightenment, actuality, interdisciplinarity of the human and mental sciences? Self-liquidation of the Church in the name of adaptation, of modernity, of dialogue, of communication, of pluralism? Self-abandonment of Christianity in the name of worldliness, maturity, secularity, solidarity and humanity? A leisurely ending without terror?

Of course this is not the case. Nor, we hope, will it be true in future. But even caricatures bring out the truth. And should we perhaps, blind to problems on the right, in fear of seeming not sufficiently modern or even of being too conservative, leave these and similar questions to the Pope and the conservatives? "Has the Church lost its soul?" was the title of a well-argued *Newsweek* analysis in 1971.[12] Has the Church lost its soul, its identity? The question was concerned with the Catholic Church which under John XXIII and Vatican II achieved the boldest change of course in modern Church history, but which is suffering in the post-conciliar period from a vacuum of intellectual leadership in Rome and in the episcopate as a whole in a way that reminds us of the age of the Reformation. The same questions however will have to be faced in this confused period of great change by all the Christian Churches, both the more progressive and the more conservative. For a Church can lose its soul by being so progressive that it fails to remain what it is in all the change *or* by being so conservative in remaining unchanged that it does not become anew what it ought to be. It is possible to endanger our life through overwork and being continually on the move, but also through surfeit and motionless repose.

No return

What we have just said cannot be misunderstood. We take nothing back. A turning to man, to the "world," to society, to the modern sciences, was overdue. Even conservative Christians cannot overlook the way in which the Church, particularly in modern times, has increasingly compromised and distorted the Christian message. In former epochs the Church in a critical-creative spirit helped to give shape and form to an age, but lately the Church has responded to new developments mainly by denunciation, reaction and if possible by attempting to restore the past. It thus became more and more remote from the men who were pressing modern history toward greater freedom, rationality, humanity: a Church encapsulated and on the defensive against the modern outlook, outwardly tied up with the ruling powers, inwardly traditionalist, authoritarian and often totalitarian.

It is possible to reject as inappropriate the programmatic *term* "political theology,"[13] which has been theologically and politically overburdened from the time of Constantine to that of Carl Schmitt,[14] who prepared the way for the *Führerstaat;* the term "social-critical theology," which can be understood more as functional than as programmatic, is to be preferred. But we must emphatically agree with the *intentions* of "political theology" if it is meant to bring out the intrinsic social relevance of the Christian message and thereby make clear the fact that the Church as a historical-social phenomenon has always been politically active and that its declared neutrality and abstinence from public comment in many cases only served to cover up the existing dubious political alliances. Theoretical discussion with the human sciences was and is just as urgent as practical social involvement—both practiced in an exemplary way particularly by young theologians, despite all difficulties from right and left. However much the Church will retain its place in society as the center of a great tradition, it must equally reject the idea of being simply the bulwark of the existing order. A great many of the difficulties in the Catholic Church and in Catholic theology spring today from the excessive pressure of problems which an authoritarian congestion of centuries has produced. A great deal of the confusion particularly among the faithful is not caused by theological criticism, which only uncovers what is already there. It comes from the Church leadership and its court theologians who for a long time have failed to prepare the faithful for the continually necessary reforms in teaching and practice and even systematically immunized them against such reforms, who have not introduced people to critical freedom but always preached to them with the emphasis only on unity, prayer and obedience.

This Church has certainly sinned more than other Churches against human fellowship and solidarity even in recent decades, in the name of dogmas and legal axioms; it has refused dialogue with Christians, non-Christians and particularly with its own "loyal opposition," has condemned, suppressed and neglected the conclusions of the natural and historical sciences. But the turning of this Catholic Church to the "world," to man, to society, was not—as some in Rome still think—an accident, a mishap partly connected with "good Pope John." It was simply a *historical necessity* with its roots in a completely changed society, prepared by a whole generation of theologians and laymen who refused to be discouraged, released by a great charismatic personality who was both warmly human and full of evangelical fervor, finally set in motion by a Church council. The bishops present there—advised and prompted by theologians —spoke a lot at that time about the breathing of the Holy Spirit; but under another Pope they returned to their old surroundings and the papal curia tried to correct the mistakes of the new Pope's predecessor and to consolidate afresh its tottering rule over the Roman Empire.

In view of the post-conciliar "backlash," which was not unexpected, it would be a pity if all too many who prepared and brought about the turning were to stop short in their progressiveness now that they have grown older, instead of proving their progressiveness by progressing. Church history goes on anyway and even the theology produced by Vatican II and its interpreters will not be final. But a return to the pre-conciliar Church is no longer possible. So much has become evident in the post-conciliar period: the point of no return has been reached and there are no alternatives. The escape routes which allured the nineteenth century—the romantically glorified Middle Ages, Neo-Romanesque, Neo-Gothic, Neo-Gregorian, Neo-Scholasticism, Neo-Ultramontanism—are no longer there. They have all been tested and found wanting. In the long run it is impossible even for the Catholic Church to serve, for the delight of a few aesthetes and philanthropists, inside and outside the Church, as a museum of Christendom (containing among its treasures Latin as the language of worship, Byzantine ceremonial, medieval liturgy and legislation, and post-Tridentine theology). Today the Church will not allow itself to be reduced to a mere center for worship.

We stand therefore by what we have said. Right along the line, as we hope to make clear in this book, there is an unbiased *open-mindedness* for what is modern, extra-Christian, non-Christian, human, and for relentless criticism of our own positions, for dissociation from all ecclesiastical traditionalism, from dogmatism and biblicism. Nevertheless, there is no place for uncritical ecclesiastical or theological *modernism.* Both lovers and scorners of Christianity among the educated classes may appreciate the fact that here from the very beginning we shall give unmistakable expression to the principle that a humanization of the Church was necessary and remains necessary, but on the one condition that there is no sellout of the Christian "substance."[15] The diamond is not to be thrown away, but polished and—if possible—made to sparkle. The meaning of the Christian reality must not be blurred in this turning to man, but made more precise, more relevant, more decisive: there must be a sense of proportion and a critical dissociation in regard to *all* movements of our time, in regard to secular Utopias, illusions, conformisms of right *and* left. Hence the title of this section—the challenge of modern humanisms—is to be understood actively and passively: the challenging modern humanisms are themselves being challenged.

3. *No abandonment of hope*

Theologians have been denigrating the world for so long that it would be surprising if they did not now feel the temptation to make amends for everything at once. There is a swing from Manichaeistic damnation of the world toward secular glorification of the world: both being signs of theological unworldliness. Do not untheological "men of the world" often see the world more discriminatingly, more realistically, in regard to both its positive and negative aspects? What is called for is common sense without illusions, since even in the present century far too many theologians have allowed themselves to be blinded by the spirit of the age and even provided a theological substructure for nationalism and war propaganda and moreover totalitarian party programs in shades of black, brown and finally red. In this way theologians too can easily become ideologists or champions of ideologies. *Ideologies* are understood here, not as if they were neutral in value, but critically as systems of "ideas," concepts and beliefs, of standards of interpretation, motifs and norms of action, which—controlled mostly by particular interests—reproduce the reality of the world in a distorted form, cover up the real abuses and replace rational arguments with an appeal to the emotions.

Is the solution simply to invoke the human factor? *Humanisms* too are subject to rapid change. What remains of Renaissance humanism after man's great disillusionment through a series of humiliations? The first came when Copernicus showed that man's earth was not the center of the universe; the second when Marx showed how dependent man is on inhuman social conditions; the third when Darwin described man's origin from the subhuman world; and the fourth was Freud's explanation of man's intellectual consciousness as rooted in the instinctive unconscious. In the very diverse images of man produced by physics, biology, psychoanalysis, economics, sociology, philosophy, what is left of the former homogeneous image? The humanism of the *honnête homme* of the Enlightenment, the academic humanism of the "humanities," the existentialist humanism of the individual existence (*Dasein*) hurled into nothingness: all these have had their day. This is to say nothing of fascism and Nazism, which—fascinated by Nietzsche's superman—at first likewise claimed to be human and social, but produced the insane ideology of "People and *Führer*," "Blood and Soil," which cost mankind an unparalleled destruction of human values and millions of human lives.

In view of this situation, after so many disappointments, a certain skepticism in regard to humanism is understandable. Many secular analysts today frequently restrict their work in philosophy, linguistics, ethnology, sociology, individual and social psychology to making some sense out of the illogical, confused, contradictory and unintelligible material by not attempting to give it a meaning at all, but by proceeding as in the natural sciences to establish the positive data (Positivism) and the formal structures (Structuralism) and being satisfied with measuring, calculating, controlling, programming and prognosticating the individual sequences. The crisis of secular humanism—which made itself felt at an early stage in interpretative art, in music and in literature—is perhaps most clearly evident at the point where hitherto humanism was at its strongest and had a broad basis of support among the masses: in technological-evolutionary humanism and in politico-social revolutionary humanism. After subjecting the situation of the Christian Churches to a relentless criticism, we shall not be accused of ideological bias if we try to clarify our own position by an equally relentless critical analysis of the ideologies prevailing today. It is not our intention to produce a pessimistic academic criticism, but a realistic appraisal of the present, which in East and West contains innumerable impulses toward better things but perhaps still needs a strong push in order to bring about a really better human society.

Humanity through technological evolution?

The *ideology of a technological revolution leading naturally to humanity* seems to be shaken. "It has been observed that if the last 50,000 years of man's existence were divided into lifetimes of approximately 62 years each, there have been about 800 such lifetimes. Of these 800, fully 650 were spent in caves. Only during the last 70 lifetimes has it been possible to communicate effectively from one lifetime to another—as writing made it possible to do. Only during the last six lifetimes did masses of men ever see a printed word. Only during the last four has it been possible to measure time with any precision. Only in the last two has anyone anywhere used an electric motor. And the overwhelming majority of all the material goods we use in daily life today have been developed within the present, the 800th, lifetime."[16] The upheaval of our lifetime therefore must be regarded as the second great break in the history of mankind, the first being the invention of agriculture in neolithic times and the transition from barbarism to civilization. Now, in our times, agriculture, which constituted the basis of civilization for thousands of years, has lost its dominance in one country after another. And at the same time the industrial age, begun two centuries ago, is passing. As a result of automation, in the progressive countries, manual workers are also rapidly becoming a minority and a superindustrial culture appears on the horizon, perceptible only in outline. Does this mean the fulfillment of what so many had been thinking and hoping: the optimism of the French Encyclopedists with their philosophy of history, Lessing with his "Education of the Human Race," Kant with his idea of an "eternal peace," Hegel with his theory of history as "progress in the consciousness of freedom," Marx with the Utopia of the "classless society," Teilhard with his idea of evolution to the "omega point"?

The progress of modern science, medicine, technology, industry, communication, culture is unparalleled: it surpasses the boldest fantasies of Jules Verne and other former futurologists. And yet this evolution still seems far away from the omega point and often even to lead away from it. Even someone who does not share the total criticism of the present social "system" on the part of the New Left and does not set all his hopes on a total transformation of the advanced industrial society, the longer he considers the situation, the less he can avoid the disturbing observation that something is wrong in this fantastic quantitative and qualitative progress. In a very short time the sense of *not being at ease* with technical civilization has become universal: many factors—not to be analyzed here—have contributed to this state of mind.

Particularly in the most progressive Western industrial nations people are becoming increasingly doubtful about the dogma they had believed for a long time: that science and technology are the key to man's universal happiness and that progress results inevitably and—as it were—automatically. It is no longer the danger—still very real, but diminished through the political arrangements of the superpowers—of an atomic destruction of civilization which most disturbs people. What are really disturbing are the great contradictions of international politics and economics, the wage and price spirals, the inflation which cannot be controlled either in America or in Europe, the insidious and often acute world currency crisis, the increasing gap between rich and poor nations: all the problems which, on the national level, are too much for governments and indicate a lack of stability even on the part of Western democracies—not to speak of the military dictatorships in southern Europe and South America. Most disturbing of all are the problems on the spot, as they are seen—for instance—in a city like New York, where the menace looming over all urban agglomerations is strikingly displayed: behind the most imposing skyline in the world an apparently infinitely expanding urban landscape with ever increasing air pollution, putrid water, rotting streets, traffic congestion, shortage of dwelling space, rising rents, the noise of traffic and all the uproar of civilization, health hazards, mounting aggression and crime, larger ghettos, more acute tensions between races, classes and national groups. In any case this is hardly the "secular city" which theologians dreamed up at the beginning of the sixties.

Are the negative results of technological development merely accidental? Wherever we look—in Leningrad and Tashkent, just as in Melbourne and Tokyo, and even in the developing countries, in New Delhi or Bangkok—the same phenomena stand out. They cannot simply be noted and accepted as in the inevitable darker side of great progress. Some undoubtedly are due to hasty reactions and abuses. But, taken as a whole, all these things arise out of the ambivalent character of progress itself, for which there has been so much longing, planning, laboring: progress which, if it continues in this way, will at once develop and destroy true humanity. The categories of "growth," "augmentation," "progression," "size," "social product" and "increasing dividends," once regarded as so positive, now seem more dubious. For they now express an inescapable "must," the pressure for ever increasing growth (of production, consumption, wastage). A feeling of lost freedom, of insecurity and fear of the future, is spreading particularly in the highly developed welfare states. Only now does the technological process seem really to have got into its swing and thus at the same time to escape any sort of control—particularly through the often clumsy and complicated workings of the democratic systems. The promise of a "Great Society" (L. B. Johnson)—assuming that man is by nature good if only his environment is good, and the environment becomes good if only the government invests sufficient money in it—proved impossible to fulfill even in the United States. It would have been impossible even if there had been no inhuman Vietnam war. The well-known gloomy computer analyses of an MIT team,[17] commissioned by the "Club of Rome," into growth (not only linear, but also exponential) and its consequences in the form of shortage of raw materials, overpopulation, scarcity of foodstuffs, environment pollution, offer the prospect not only of social unrest and the collapse of industry but of a veritable extinction of mankind at the latest by the year 2100. Although the underlying data and certain extrapolations are questionable, although newly emerging technological developments, planned counteraction and especially human behavior in the future are neglected, and consequently the total prognosis remains open to dispute, it was nevertheless rightly understood generally as a warning that the catastrophe is at least possible even if it is not inevitable.

And so the apocalyptic book titles mount up today: *Doomsday Book; Planned Confusion; After Us the Stone Age. The End of the Technical Age; No Place for Man. Programmed Suicide; Earth: Candidate for Death. Programmed Suicide Through Uncontrolled Progress; Endangered Future.*[18] Authors like Karl Steinbuch, who were promoting a technological euphoria as recently as 1968 with such titles as "Falsely Programmed,"[19] now demand in 1973 a "Corrective Price Adjustment," "An Agreed Clarification of the Norms of Our Social Life": admittedly, the author explains that he means by this only "a simple agreement on the principles according to which we want to live together."[20] But behavior investigators also, of the rank of a Konrad Lorenz, put before us "Civilized Man's Eight Deadly Sins": overpopulation, devastation of the environment, man's race against himself, entropy of feeling, genetic decay, the break with tradition, indoctrinability, nuclear weapons.[21] For some the oil crisis of 1973, with all its political and economic consequences, finally confirmed their worst fears and showed how easily the whole economic-social system of the West can be shaken both on a large and on a small scale and how rapidly the end of the affluent society may come.

The *Neo-Marxist social criticism* of these conditions—in particular the "critical theory" of the Frankfurt School (T. W. Adorno, M. Horkheimer, Herbert Marcuse), but also of Ernst Bloch—is obviously not disposed of with the failure of the "Prague spring" and the student revolutions.[22] The picture which emerges[23] is of a continually wealthier, greater, better society with an overwhelming capacity for achievement and a constantly rising standard of living. Yet at the same time and for that very reason it is a society also of consummate prodigality, of peaceful production of the means of vast destruction. Here is a technological universe with the possibility of total annihilation and thus still a world full of want, suffering, wretchedness, need, poverty, violence and cruelty. Progress must be considered from both sides. Dependence on persons has been abolished, but it is replaced by dependence on things, institutions, anonymous powers. With the liberation—or, better, "liberalization"—of politics, learning, sexuality, culture, a new enslavement has emerged in the form of pressure to consume. With increasing productive achievement has come integration into a gigantic apparatus. The multiplicity of commodities offered for sale has led to the maximizing of individual demands for consumer goods and the manipulation of these demands by the people who plan our requirements and by anonymous seducers in the advertising world. The greater rapidity of traffic plunges man into greater turmoil. With improved medicine we are faced with more psychic ailments and the prospect of longer but often not more meaningful life. Increasing prosperity brings in its train more depreciation and wastage. Man's dominion over nature has meant the destruction of nature. The perfection of the mass media has brought about functionalization, curtailment and impoverishment of language and indoctrination on the grand scale. With increasing international communication there is more dependence on multinational concerns (and soon also trades unions). The spread of democracy means more streamlining and social control on the part of society and its rulers. With a more elaborate technology there has emerged the possibility of more skillful (perhaps even genetic) manipulation. Alongside thoroughgoing rationality in detail there is a lack of meaning to the whole.

The list might be extended almost *ad libitum* and the slogans are well known: "culture as machinery," "art as commodity," "the writer as producer of texts," "sex as commercial value," "technology as personalization." This is a "hominized," but by no means humanized world, in a singular harmony of freedom and oppression, productivity and destruction, growth and regression, science and superstition, joy and misery, life and death. But these brief suggestions, which anyone can confirm with plenty of examples from his own experience, may suffice to make clear how much the progressive ideology of a technological evolution leading naturally to humanity has been shaken: a progress working destructively, a rationality bearing irrational features, a humanization leading to inhumanity. In a word, this is an evolutive humanism with the unintended factual consequence of *man's dehumanization.*

Are we painting too simple a picture in black and white? Obviously not. But there is black *and* white, and they merge into what is a gray, uncertain future even for someone who is not by nature inclined to pessimism. A book like Marcuse's *One-Dimensional Man* is shattering, particularly if in the last resort one does not agree with it and is not led by the impossibility of revolution to adopt a mood of resignation. Its fascination for the younger generation, which has grown up with progress and affluence, is unintelligible only to someone who has not read it and yet discusses it (as people often do with famous books) or who himself in this heartless and helpless world has become so heartless and helpless that he can no longer understand youth's protest (thus becoming himself a proof of Marcuse's thesis). This consciously accusing knowledge cannot be avoided by taking refuge in a philosophy of existence and ultimately of being, oriented to the private sphere, in the style of the earlier or later Heidegger. Nor can it be avoided with the aid of a philosophical-theoretical or historical hermeneutic (science of understanding), wanting to understand everything but deciding nothing and changing nothing. Nor perhaps with the aid of a Positivism bearing the imprint of the natural sciences or of a "critical rationalism" (K. Popper, H. Albert), claiming to avoid the extremes of authoritarian-dogmatic and anti-authoritarian radical thinking. But this critical rationalism too, with its completely dogmatic trust in a universally applied rationality of the natural sciences, stands alongside linguistic analysis and its formal "language games," apparently accused of being the scientific factor mainly responsible for the one-dimensionality of human existence.[24] The question is whether the "critical theory" of the New Left itself leads beyond one-dimensionality.

And yet, do we have to abandon hope when we abandon ideology? The baby must not be poured out with the bath water. What has to be given up is the *ideology of technological progress,* controlled as it is by vested interests, which fails to take account of the true reality of the world and with its pseudo-rationality creates the illusion of a manageable world. This is not to say that we must give up our concern for science and technology and thus with human progress. What we must abandon is only *faith in science as a total explanation of reality* (a *Weltanschauung*), in *technocracy* as a cure-all *substitute religion.*

The *hope* is not to be abandoned therefore *of a meta-technological society,* of a new synthesis between controlled technical progress and a human existence freed from the constraints of progress: a more human form of work, more closeness to nature, a more balanced social structure and the satisfaction also of non-material needs, of those human values, that is, which alone make life worth living and yet cannot be expressed in monetary terms. In any case mankind is fully responsible for its own future. Is nothing to be allowed to change? Perhaps through a radical, even violent, transformation of the social order, its representatives and values: that is, through revolution?

Humanity through politico-social revolution?

The *ideology of a politico-social revolution, leading naturally to humanity,* also appears to be shaken. This judgment forms the counterpoint to what we have just discussed. As in the previous section we made no attempt to belittle the importance of science, technology, progress, so too in what follows we are not going to condemn Marxism out of hand as undemocratic, inhuman and un-Christian when it claims to be the most influential revolutionary theory of society.

Christians too must recognize and understand what *humanistic potential* is concealed in *Marxisms.* This holds not only—as some think[25]—for the young Marx of the philosophical *Early Writings,*[26] influenced by Hegel and Feuerbach and making use of a humanistic terminology (man, humanity, alienation, liberation and development of man). It holds also for the mature Marx who spoke differently, avoiding ineffectual humanistic terms and phrases in the socio-economic work *Das Kapital.*[27] But the humanistic intention had been maintained. Instead of the inhuman conditions of the capitalist society, truly human conditions were to be created. There must no longer be a society where great masses of men are degraded, despised, impoverished, exploited: where the supreme value is commodity value, where money (the commodity of commodities) is the true God and the motives of action are profit, self-interest, selfishness; where in fact capitalism functions as a substitute for religion. But there must be a society where every man can be truly man: a free being, walking upright, dignified, autonomous, realizing all his possibilities. In a word, there must be an end of man's exploitation by man.

The humanity of conditions, of structures, of society and thus of man himself: this and nothing else, according to Marx, is what the proletarian revolution is about; this is the meaning of doing away with the division of labor, abolishing private property, establishing the dictatorship of the proletariat. This and nothing else is the nature of the future classless, Communist society at which Marx cautiously hinted and of which he provided no more than an outline. It would not be an earthly paradise, not a Utopia without existential problems; but it certainly had to be a realm of freedom and of human self-development, where—despite all individual peculiarities—there would be no inequality in principle and no oppression of men, classes or nations and where the exploitation of man by man would be at an end, so that the state would lose its political function as controlling power and religion would become superfluous. All things considered then, a socialized and democratized humanism.

So much for the program.[28] In regard to its realization, it might be better not to look immediately to Moscow or Peking. Perhaps more was done to maintain and develop Marx's original intentions by certain Yugoslav or Hungarian theorists[29] than by the great orthodox (Marxist-Leninist) systems which have actually prevailed and, as the powerful official bearers of Marxism, help to determine the course of world history. Marxism today must allow itself to be judged by what these official exponents have done, just as Christianity is judged by the realization of the Christian program on the part of the great Christian Churches which also help to decide the course of history. For the program cannot be completely separated from the history of its effectiveness, even though it is possible to raise critical questions about the program itself in the light of that history and the institutions emerging out of it.

Nevertheless, the fact that it is badly realized is not in itself an argument against a good program. If we concentrate immediately on the negative aspect, we can easily overlook what Russia (by comparison with the Czarist regime, cut off from the people by the Church and the nobility) owes to Lenin, what China (by comparison with the pre-revolutionary Chinese social system) owes to Mao Tse-tung, and indeed what the whole world owes to Karl Marx. Important elements of the Marxist theory of society have been adopted generally, even in the West. Is not man seen in his social character today quite differently from the way in which he was regarded in liberal individualism? Do we not concentrate—quite otherwise than in idealist thought—on concretely changing the social reality, on the factual alienation of man in inhuman conditions, on the necessity of finding practical proof of every theory? Are not work and the process of working seen now as of essential importance for the development of mankind and is not the influence of economic factors on the history of ideas and ideologies examined in detail? Is not the connection of socialist ideas with the advancement of the working classes and the relevance of all this to world history also recognized in the West? Have not even non-Marxists become sensitive to the contradictions and the structural injustices of the capitalist economic system and, for their analyses, do they not use the critical tools supplied by Marx? And, as a result, was not unrestrained economic liberalism—for which the maximizing of private gain is effected by satisfying wants—finally eliminated by more social forms of economic organization?

Wherever freedom of criticism exists and Marxism does not prevail as a dogmatic system, the *weaknesses* of Marx's theory of history and society as a total explanation of reality (as it is unfortunately claimed to be in all communist states) are of course recognized. It is not merely a matter of "bourgeois" prejudice to observe simply and objectively that Marx was mistaken in his basic assumption of the impossibility of improving the lot of the proletariat without revolution. Despite all the accumulation of capital, it has not been proved in practice that this would lead to a total proletarianization of an enormous reserve army of workers and that, from this army, in a dialectical reversal, the revolution was bound to proceed as transition to socialism and then to communism and to the reign of freedom. The theory of surplus value (produced by the worker, siphoned off by the capitalist) behind this assumption, at least for popular Marxism the corner pillar of Marxist economics, is in fact still repeated by orthodox Marxists but is set aside by other Marxist economists and completely rejected by non-Marxist economists. The theory of the struggle of two classes has proved too simple as a scheme of interpretation for the course of mankind's history and particularly for the analysis of the complex social classification of the present time (when the proletariat has largely become bourgeois and we can speak in the plural of middle classes). The theory of history of historical materialism rests to no small extent on false presuppositions and on subsequent artificial reconstructions of history.

The collapse of the capitalist system, particularly in the highly industrialized countries (England and Germany), which Marx expected at first in 1848, then in the fifties, then in the seventies, and which Engels prophesied for the turn of the century—as a result of which the communist mode of production was to follow in a dialectical leap—did not occur. On the contrary, it is significant that the socialist revolution was successful only in the backward agrarian countries. But capitalism proved to be open to correction to a large extent. It not only produced empirical social analysis and thus a system of control and correction, but at the same time realized far-reaching social reforms, from the prohibition of child labor to legally guaranteed provision for old age and various forms of participation in industry. Thus it was possible to free large groups of people from the pressure of poverty and lead them to a comparatively secure and in fact previously unimaginable material prosperity. Hitherto therefore, neither in the West nor in the East, neither in scientific theory nor in political practice, has a different economic and social system been developed which could remove the defects of capitalism without producing other and worse evils. Neither the orthodox centrally planned economy nor a soviet democracy, still less the very short-lived and shortsighted empty economic formulas expressing the wishful thinking of individual radicals, have produced any proof of being able better to guarantee freedom and democracy, justice and prosperity.[80] There is no sign in the heavens of the advent of the classless, free, communist society. On the contrary, there is the threat —quite otherwise than in the West—of the overwhelming power of the state: as a result of the identification of state and society, a socialist centralization at the expense of the working population. Individuals are put off with fair promises of a distant future happiness for mankind and obliged to increase production figures in an unmerciful system and with harsh work norms.

It remains true that a good program is not refuted by being badly carried out; things might have turned out differently. But it may be asked whether the problems arising from its realization are not perhaps due to the Marxist program itself. Nothing has done more to discredit Marxist theory than that centralized system which most often invoked it: *Soviet communism.* The longer it continued, the less could the Soviet Union—which even under Stalin had announced the transition from socialism to communism—serve left-wing critics of society as a shining example of the spirit of Marxist humanism.[81] What is regarded even by convinced socialists as the real original sin is the glorification of the party identified with the state and its oligarchic leadership and—linked with this—the ontologizing and dogmatizing of Marxist doctrine. This orthodox communism now indicted as Stalinism—for which Lenin shares responsibility—and the imperialistic policy toward the socialist "brother nations" reveal a highly organized system of domination by men over men, which has nothing to do with a humanistic socialism, and a suppression of freedom of thought, speech and action, from Magdeburg to Vladivostok, which is unparalleled in world history: totalitarian, bureaucratic, state-capitalist dictatorship at home; nationalistic imperialism abroad.

Soviet communism appears as a new alienation of man with a "new class"[82] of managers, with religious features (Messianism, absolute sacrifice) and "ecclesiastical" aspects (canonical texts, quasi-liturgical formulas, creed, infallible hierarchy, a people kept in tutelage, Inquisition and sanctions); the same holds too of Chinese Maoism. Half a century after the October Revolution there have to be death zones covering hundreds of kilometers to prevent millions fleeing from this "workers' paradise" (with concentration and prison camps), while—despite all structural parallels between Western and Eastern state centralization—there is no danger of a mass flight from West to East. The reaction of the Soviet government to the publication of Alexander Solzhenitsyn's *Gulag Archipelago* (1974) provides disturbing evidence of the fact that this economically, socially and ideologically immobile system, despite its policy of *détente* abroad, has no thought of making any decisive change at home in the immediate future to promote man's freedom.[33]

When the Christian Churches set up an authoritarian or totalitarian rule of power, burned human beings and sacrificed them to the system, they were clearly acting—as even their opponents admit and as we cannot sufficiently emphasize—unquestionably in a way contrary to the Christian program, to Jesus of Nazareth. But is a communist party going against its program, against the *Communist Manifesto* and Karl Marx himself, when it uses force on a large scale, establishes the dictatorship of the one class and the one party, mercilessly liquidates all opponents and strikes down "counterrevolutions" regardless of the victims?

In 1968 came the tragedy of "socialism with a human face." The attempt in Czechoslovakia to set up a humanist-pluralist Marxism broke down when confronted by orthodox Marxist-Leninism which could not permit any such pluralism and could not but fear the dissolution of the established power structure of its empire. In the same year Neo-Marxism in the West entered on a profound crisis as a result of the student revolts, first in America, then in Europe and Japan. Under the conditions we have described of the highly industrialized Western countries (but rapidly becoming characteristic also of the Eastern countries) and under the catalyzing effect of the Vietnam war, it was not surprising that Neo-Marxism began to exert its fascination on young people dissatisfied with the bourgeois society.[34] It had been recognized that man's alienation no longer arose simply from pauperization as in Marx's time, but from the constraints of the present-day welfare society.

At the same time the leaders of the student revolts had been inspired to a large extent by the theory of the New Left (Marcuse, Adorno, Horkheimer, Habermas). But this "critical theory" had not been able to cope adequately with both aspects of the double task before it. It explained very well what had to be changed in human society but less well what had to be preserved. The objectives of the change also remained vague. When therefore the transition came from the concept of revolution to revolutionary praxis, which had not been foreseen by the teachers, the latter felt that they had been misunderstood and had to take a stand against the "unconsidered and dogmatic application of the 'critical theory' to praxis in the changed historical reality."[85] In prefaces, postscripts, footnotes, interviews, they had subsequently to make clear that their theory of "negative dialectic," of "qualitative change," "catastrophic transformation," "practical emancipationism" had never implied direct transposition into praxis and still less immediate revolutionary violence. The students, who felt that they had been betrayed by these dissociations, responded with accusations of "abstraction," "inconsistency," "hostility to change," and did not hesitate even to use force against their teachers.

One thing however was now clear. Despite its basic insights, Neo-Marxist philosophy, in its attempt to find a way out of the logic of power, the efficiency-orientated society and technological constraints, had reached a dead end. Had it solved its central problem of bringing theory to bear on practice, truth on action, knowledge on decision, rationality on commitment, of reconciling present facts and future possibilities? The test case was the use of *force*. Force in the class war was approved by Marx (at that time in the name of the proletariat as the "vast majority") and by Lenin (now in the name of a minority as the "higher type of social organization of work"), also at a later stage by Rosa Luxemburg (who, however, rejected Lenin's policy of terror) and finally used by Stalin and Mao, involving millions of victims. This soon became also the great question for the student movement: force as counterforce against the structural force of the social system, subversive or open force, force against things or against persons? They appealed to Marx, according to whom the revolution had to use only the same amount of force as the opposition on the part of the ruling classes brought against it.

Disenchantment set in when the first deaths resulted from violence on both sides and when—particularly in France, but also up to a point in the United States—the police quelled the student revolts by force. A large number of students came to see that Marxist-Leninist theory permitted no rights to the class enemy and no pluralism or tolerance until the fall of the one class: that consequently—and this was confirmed in Prague—a pluralistic, non-violent Marxism was contrary to the ideas of Marx and Lenin. They shared in the social rebellion and approved the politicizing of thought. But the greater part of the students and the democratic public rejected blind faith in authority, antipluralistic intolerance, undemocratic and ultimately totalitarian attitudes—demanded in the name of an elitist privileged knowledge ("true awareness") and of dogmatic partisan thinking—just as they rejected attempts to realize these things by violence and terror. Only small groups, with a political credo expressed more in terms of Michael Bakunin's anarchism, South American urban guerrillas, Palestinian liberation fighters and Vietcong tactics, than of Karl Marx, turned in despair to terrorism. Deluded by political error and ideological blindness, they were bound to be condemned as criminals. But the great majority of activists entered on the "long march through the institutions," the end of which is not yet in sight.

What was said at the beginning about the important humanistic potential of Marxism remains beyond dispute. But even to many convinced socialists it became clear through these developments that not only orthodox Marxism-Leninism, ridden to death in the East, but also the "revolutionary humanism" (Habermas) of Western Neo-Marxism had collapsed as a total explanation of reality seeking to revolutionize society. Nor had revolutionary humanism been able anywhere hitherto to realize the much proclaimed humanization of society and the better world, without exploitation or domination. It is also a fact that its neglect of economic problems in favor of ideological and aesthetic problems produced a somewhat poverty-stricken concrete program. The question of the economic, social and political possibility of realizing the theories remained unanswered; the idea of a society free from domination, brought about as a result of revolutionary upheaval and the evolution from socialism to communism, remained as vague as it had been for Marx himself and came more than ever under suspicion as an ideology.

It is however possible to give a more positive judgment on the theory and practice of Marxism in its different forms. Certainly the manifold possibilities of realizing the critical attitude of mind and the humanistic impulses of socialism for a better society must not be underestimated. Our (necessarily curtailed) discussion, which anyone can easily supplement from his own knowledge of the political situation, is intended merely to show how much the ideology even of a violent political-social revolution, supposedly leading naturally to humanity, has been shaken. Is it not in fact a criticism which is self-destructive, which cannot be carried into practice: a practice which betrays its own aims by violence and oppression; a revolution which proves to be "opium of the people"; a humanizing therefore which leads again to inhumanity? In a word, here too, a revolution whose unintended, actual consequence is the *de-humanizing of man?*

Naturally the representatives themselves of the New Left also see the difficulties. Marcuse's analysis and accusation—by no means anti-technical in principle—is so shattering because he himself, after looking to East and West, finally admits in all sincerity that he can offer no remedy. In a mood of resigned "hopelessness" at the end of his book he professes his faith in "the negation" which "appears in the politically impotent form of the 'absolute refusal'" and in being "loyal to those who, without hope, have given and give their life to the Great Refusal."[36] It is the same with Jürgen Habermas, who has recently rejected any theoretical justification of a revolutionary class-struggle strategy, since for him there can be no theory which reckons from the very beginning with possible victims of a revolution and which involves men's deaths as part of the plan. This theory proves to be even more helpless in regard to the blows of fate which can affect any human life: "In view of the risks of an individual life of course no theory is even *conceivable* which could explain away the facticities of loneliness and sin, sickness and death. With these we have to live, in principle without consolation."[37]

Here again however the question arises: do we have to abandon hope when we abandon ideology? Here too the baby must not be emptied out with the bath water. What has to be given up is the *ideology of revolution*, which pursues social subversion with violence and sets up a new system of domination by men over men. This is not to say that every kind of Marxism or every effort for a basic change of society has to be given up. What must be abandoned is *Marxism as a total explanation of reality* (a *Weltanschauung*), *revolution* as a cure-all *substitute religion*.

The *hope* is not to be abandoned therefore of a meta-revolutionary society: beyond stagnation and revolution, beyond uncritical acceptance of the facts and total criticism of the existing order. Would it not be superficial and dangerous to consider the insights of Marxism and Neo-Marxism invalidated with the collapse of a more humane Marxism in Prague or with the ending of student revolts? It is not sufficient to trace back historically—so to speak—the ideas of the revolution to its spiritual fathers, who are rightly or wrongly invoked by young people in the West. For something quite specific found its expression here: the great disappointment in the progress which had been so much extolled, a social indignation at unjust conditions old and new, a protest against the constraints of the technological-political system, a deep desire for scientific analysis and enlightenment. It was tantamount to a cry for a really contented existence, for a better society, a realm of freedom, equality and happiness, a meaning in one's own life and a meaning in the history of mankind.

Out of all this there arises the serious question: is the Great Refusal of avant-garde youth to be answered with a Great Refusal of the establishment? Is the answer to the revolution to be the status quo? Is discontent to be further repressed, are we to continue playing at progress, is the system again only to be slightly improved? Are freedom, truth and happiness, therefore, to remain mainly advertising slogans for the dubious consumer goods of the advanced industrial society? Or should there still be opportunities for changing the meaningless life of man and society into one that is meaningful? Should we look for a qualitative change which will not again produce violence, terror, destruction, anarchy and chaos?

To put it quite clearly: it should not be assumed from the two foregoing critical analyses of our time that the ardently progressive technocrat or the revolutionary Marxist—still less socialist—cannot be a Christian. What matters is the place we assign to science and technology, how we value them and more particularly what we do with them. What matters is what we mean by Marxism (and still more, socialism). Marxism in particular is sometimes understood simply as the tendency toward positive social science or as ethical, economic, communal, scientific—and in this sense "revolutionary"—humanism, which by no means excludes belief in God. A Christian then can perhaps be a (critical!) "Marxist," although of course it is not only the Marxist who can be a Christian.[38] And a Christian can perhaps be a (critical!) "technocrat," although of course it is not only the technocrat who can be a Christian. Certainly the only "Marxist" who can seriously call himself a Christian is one for whom the Christian faith and not Marx is ultimately decisive on questions like the use of force, the class struggle, peace and love. And the only "technocrat" who can seriously call himself a Christian is one for whom the Christian faith and not scientific teleology is ultimately the decisive criterion on questions like technology, organization, competition, manipulation.

There are numerous technocrats who by no means make science and technology their religion. And there are also more and more Marxists in the West and even in the East who do not make their Marxism a religion. The longer we consider it, the more clearly does it appear that total rejection *or* total acceptance of technological evolution, as also total rejection *or* total acceptance of politico-social revolution, are false alternatives. Does not the evolution of society in the West and in the East also call for a new synthesis? In a more distant future cannot the two perhaps be linked together: the longing of a politico-revolutionary humanism for a fundamental change of conditions, for a better, juster world, for a really good life, and at the same time the demands of a technological-evolutive humanism for the possibility of concrete realization, for avoidance of terror, for a pluralistic order of freedom open-minded toward problems and not imposing a particular belief on anyone? Has not the Christian in particular something to contribute to this?

Between nostalgia and reformism

Now that the great ideologies have been shaken, it is not easy to find our bearings in the present contradictory and constantly changing world. Fashions change so rapidly and people are so ready to put up with everything at once, in body and soul, that we can scarcely speak any longer of fashion at all. Who can say what tomorrow will be? Who can tell even what is today? In this respect even the historian close to the contemporary scene—and there are few so knowledgeable and time-conscious as Golo Mann—has difficulty in finding his way: "We are living in an age of capitulation. We allow ourselves to be talked into doing whatever a couple of clever dicks or even one manipulator of a clever vocabulary want to persuade us to do. I have now lived attentively through a couple of historical epochs, or at any rate what are known as 'epochs,' but not yet one which has been so dominated by superficial intellectual fashions as the present, nor one in which people have so industriously sawn at the branches on which they were sitting. Poets against poetry, philosophers against philosophy, theologians against theology, artists against art and so historians or ex-historians or sociologists against history lessons."[39]

In the last century the Great Revolution was followed by the epoch of Romanticism. It lasted for a long time. In the last third of the present century the wave of revolts has been followed by a wave of nostalgia. For how long? To the end of the century, the end of the millennium? Is it simply a mood once more of surfeit, overrefinement, decadence and skepticism, at the end of the present millennium as it was at the end of the past century? In any case feeling is again predominant: rationality is played out and washed out by sensitivity. There is no more elucidation of the present —of which we have had enough—but instead the *glorification of a past* of which we always want more. Are we in for a new Philistinism, to some extent even supported by the Left? Perhaps it is often more a question of simple resignation. And even among the representatives of the Critical Theory there is a longing for what no longer exists. Already we are ridiculing those who tried to be progressive and bought a ticket to revolution years ago and now have to admit that the train has left for a different future.

It is completely understandable in an epoch of radical upheavals in all spheres of life that very many are longing for peace and security, for the apparently more stable conditions of former times. It is understandable in a technocratic, thoroughly rationalized world, at a time of unparalleled emotional impoverishment, that there should be a nostalgia for the apparently cloudless "good old times," particularly the "golden twenties": in fashion and coiffure, in films and literature, in illustrated papers and magazines, advertising and housing, furniture and music, old records and old possessions. Instead of imagining Utopias we take refuge in melancholy, instead of political aggressiveness we now have unpolitical sentimentality, instead of finished technique a taste for old junk, instead of revolutionary effort dilettantism.

In the midst of the Vietnam war, Erich Segal's *Love Story* was the first token of a reaction, in itself understandable, attentively recorded and delightedly propagated by such periodicals as *Time* and *Der Spiegel*.‡ Instead of protests and peace marches we now have the idylls of private happiness. Even in the most modern literature the old preferences are again evident: for narrative, biography and autobiography, for stories generally. In theater and opera—after all cultural revolution, agitation and provoca-

‡ *Love Story* was published in 1970 simultaneously in America and England, became a best seller and was made into a film. The blurb indicates why it marks a turning point: "Unlike most contemporary fiction dealing with young people, *Love Story* makes no claim to showing where it's at. Rather, it simply shows how it feels." (Translator.)

tion, insulting the public and driving away the public—the old works of the great authors are slowly returning, without disrespectful attempts to make them relevant or to graft into them social-critical moral verses for minors. Is all this meant to overcome the crisis in the theater? At the same time everything has been tried out once again: from the tango, old hits and stars, and numerous symbols of a time when it seemed we were serenely happy, up to the Marilyn Monroe cult, to yoga and superstition, drugs and transcendental meditation. And, above all, a touch of religion. The consciousness industry, as usual, lost no opportunity of marketing all this: sentimentality and ancient longings; feelings as commodities, wrapped in ecstasy. The business of nostalgia is flourishing. For how long?

All these fashions, waves, attitudes should not be taken too seriously, nor should the longing for the past. Even if we are not addicted to conservatism, might we not need a little more continuity? Might we not need more links with the past at a time of often frantic repression of history in school and society: as a balance to the striking deficiency of historical consciousness for which people try in vain to compensate with an excess of up-to-date ideology, paraded with an air of omniscience?

Why not then an unromantic, serious *meditation on the past?*

Might it not help us to be somewhat more modest, less arrogantly modern and infallibly omniscient, to get away a little from the present and to decide prudently just where we stand?

Might it not help us to understand the phenomena of the present in the light of their origin, to discern and classify the opportunities and limits of political action, to appreciate the course of coalitions and conflicts, the ambivalence of decisive situations, the difference between personal intentions and objective aims, between secondary consequences and remote effects?

Might it not help us to recognize society's stability and capacity for resistance, but also its mutability and capacity for change, despite all objective constraints, so that we can avoid both ruthless technocratic planning and ineffectual radical protests, both total criticism and the total resignation which easily ensues on it?

Might it not therefore help us to take a longer and more discerning view of day-to-day and party politics and thus to get rid of many rigidly held opinions, to be less surprised by young people who merely seem to be worse than ever before, to remain open-minded and not entirely without hope for a new future, so that we can get away from the false alternatives and polarizations of modern society into which we are frequently unwillingly drawn and which present us with numerous unnecessary conflicts?

In brief: let us have history, historical knowledge, not as in the last century as the primary basis of orientation or still less the stabilizing substitute religion of educated people, but as a very important aid to orientation for the present time and as enlightenment in the best sense of the word, so that we can reach a concrete judgment and concrete action, that effective policy which—according to Max Weber—is "a strong, slow drilling through hard boards with both passion and cool judgment."[40]

It thus becomes overwhelmingly clear that meditation on the past must simply *not* be a new, fashionable form of selfish indifference to history: not a sentimental backward glance at the past, resulting in a *turning back to the past, away from the present.* Is it likely to be possible in the long run simply to live on the old stocks? Can we creep back into the past when we are summoned to a new future? The vast problems of present and future will scarcely dissolve in the air if we turn our back on them. We must accept the challenge. Wistfulness is no substitute for daring.

No amount of wallowing in nostalgia will relieve us of the necessity of living life today and finding some way of mastering it. Admittedly, the activism of the revolutionary years is no longer in demand. But we can scarcely avoid the task of actively *reforming* the existing order. Between nostalgic or even merely conservative system upholders and revolutionary-illusionary system destroyers, the system reformers in today's society have again more chances of being heard. For something really must happen. What?

Most people today are glad if anything at all happens. And there are some who add together all the things that happen or at least could happen. This too is some consolation. But is man's good will sufficient—as the author of the book *The Future Has Already Begun*[41] somewhat prematurely assumed—to bring about a conversion, a new society, and even the "millennial man"?[42] We have nothing against new ways of life, tested in communal living, large families, experimental schools, new forms of vocational communities among architects, theater people, young film makers, social workers, agricultural and industrial communes. Nor have we anything against creativity studies which can discover the buried sources of imagination in every man. Nothing against group dynamics with their new understanding of human interaction and nothing against system analysis which teaches us again to grasp the totality without losing sight of details.

And yet we must ask if man can be assumed to be naturally good in view of all the madness and cruelty—both on a large and on a small scale—of which he has shown himself abundantly capable right up to the present time. Can we at least take for granted his good will and therefore his capacity to improve his human nature? Can the individual, can a government or a society make these assumptions? Or must not the changes emerge at a much deeper level, if the different forms of emancipation are not again to go wrong? The examples are obvious: an emancipation from the natural environment which turns into an exploitation of nature; sexual emancipation which degenerates into a wave of pornography; the struggle for a society free from domination which results in chaos and terror; experiments in living together in communes which lead to psychoses or even to premature breakdowns; emancipated hippies who end up having withdrawal treatment or as beggars in Katmandu.

Yet so often only compromises are offered. For example, perhaps because of the lack of a convincing alternative to the capitalist economic system, a compromise between *traditional* capitalism and *pure* democracy, in which neither the one nor the other principle can be realized to everyone's satisfaction.[43] In regard to such a realistic view, it is undoubtedly correct that neither criticism of the opposite position nor the better presentation of one's own standpoint is sufficient, that compromises are possible and necessary against all extremisms, that a practical compromise must be reached between capitalism and democracy even in industry. It must therefore be a just compromise: not indeed complete justice, but more equality; not indeed participation by everyone in all affairs, but more widely extended co-operation at the places of work; not the abolition of private property, but its further restriction; not the collectivization of the means of production, but a better balance between private production and public service. From such a standpoint it is assumed that the idea of the tasks, the responsibility and proper initiative of the employer must change.

But—and this is the decisive objection to this sort of compromise—the motives for such a change remain the same as ever: they amount simply to egoism (in this case on the part of the employers). "Those very people who are in fact specialists in self-interest in their purely economic functions do not act sufficiently in their own interest outside their properly economic functions—not because they are unselfish, but because they are not enlightened enough. I think they should be quite clear about the fact that self-interest and not some lofty moral norm requires them to meet the increasing demands for equality in a way that is fair to the other side, to make concessions in the form of practical measures. History shows that such defensive action, taken in advance, is a way of looking after one's own interests and not an expression of magnanimity."[44] What is involved therefore is the old egoism, this traditional human attitude, the thought of profit in the widest sense of the term, which is by no means restricted to the employer.

Despite all the emphasis on social dynamism, have we not here abandoned hope of a change in man? With all the many reforms are we not merely painting over the surface and not getting at the causes of evil? We seem to be engaged less in necessary radical reform than in that bustling, flustered *reformism* which in various spheres of life (university, industry, Church, education, state legislation) has produced a great deal of change and little improvement. At any rate there has been no change in man himself, no different basic attitude, no new humanity. But can we be content with less, in view of all man's wretchedness between inactive longing and ineffectual desire for reform? Ought we not to look in a different way quite dispassionately, at the human situation and judge it in the light of human existence with all its depths, which superficial nostalgists and reformists scarcely suspect?

Resignation has led to many a change of front. Liberal reformers and disappointed revolutionaries meet one another at the grave of their expectations. For some Ernst Bloch's "principle of hope" has been eliminated by the "principle of despair"–in different forms and in different degrees. After this great squandering of hope, in the changed conditions, after the individual's possibilities of change have proved arduous, those of mankind impossible, and those of the structures abrasive, how shall we be able still to think of conversion, change and resistance?

II. The Other Dimension

Neither nostalgia nor reformism offers a genuine alternative to the great ideologies of technological progress and politico-social revolution. Is disorientation all that finally remains of them? "The world has lost its bearings. Not that ideologies are lacking, to give directions: only that they lead nowhere," admitted Eugène Ionesco, founder of the theater of the absurd, at the opening of the Salzburg Festival in 1972,[1] which was subsequently carried out with all the old splendor. "People are going round in circles in the cage of their planet, because they have forgotten that they can look up to the sky. . . . Because all we want is to live, it has become impossible for us to live. Just look around you!"[2] Is this true? Perhaps half true.

1. *Approach to God*

Must we then indeed give up that hope of a meta-technological society which has progress under its control and has made possible a life worth living, freed from the constraints of progress, in a pluralistic order of freedom open-minded toward problems?[3] Must we also give up that hope of a meta-revolutionary society which produces a really contented existence in a realm of freedom, equality and justice, and gives a meaning to the history of mankind?[4]

Transcendence?

Today we do not want merely to go round in circles. It is absolutely necessary to free ourselves, to break out of the *one-dimensionality* of our modern existence, to "transcend" it. Marcuse's term, "one-dimensionality," is a very apt description of the existence of modern man, lacking genuine alternatives. Technological evolutive humanism—which only became aware of its one-dimensionality at all as a result of the radical criticism of the New Left—was the first to examine the problem, but up to now has produced no alternative. Social-revolutionary humanism exhibits a permanent awareness of problems and crises, but has not yet produced in either East or West a practicable way of liberation.[5]

In both cases man—as individual and as society—remains incapable of mastering his world, because he tries to cope with everything except himself. As he seems to be gaining the whole world, he is threatened with the loss of his own soul: in routine, bustling activity, endless talk, in disorientation and futility. This has little to do with the wickedness of man or of particular individuals. It is the legal constraints of the technocratic society itself, as we have seen, which threaten to crush man's personal dignity, freedom and responsibility.

In order to save man's humanity, it is obviously not sufficient to get rid of all ecclesiastical and theological dominating factors, to enlarge the competence of secular authorities, to give an autonomous instead of a religious basis and direction to the planning of life and the standardizing of action. In theory and practice there must be *genuine transcending*, a genuinely qualitative ascent to a real alternative away from one-dimensional thinking, talking and action in the existing society.

But even its theorists are resigned to the fact that there is just no prospect of this transcending in the present situation. In fact, the course of recent history has made it clearer than ever that a linear and, where possible, revolutionary transcending does not lead us out of one-dimensionality. Instead—as in other Utopias—we are in danger of taking intramundane, finite factors as final emancipation and the result is the totalitarian rule of men over men. This rule is no longer in the name of "the nation," "the people," or "the race," still less "the Church"; but the talk may well be of "the working class" or "the party," or—since we can no longer identify ourselves with the working class turned bourgeois or with a totalitarian party—"the true awareness" of the small elitist group of intellectuals. And here too the experience is repeated of man finally becoming dependent precisely on the forces and powers which he released when he came of age and claimed autonomy: thus his freedom is imprisoned by the world and its mechanism which he himself liberated. In this one-dimensional world of unfreedom man—both the individual and the group, nations, races, classes—is constantly forced to be distrustful, to be afraid of others and even of himself, to hate and thus to suffer endlessly. This is just not a better society, not justice for all, not freedom for the individual, not real love.

In view of this human situation therefore, must we not conclude—perhaps with a pious assurance of our horror of all metaphysics—that the *really other dimension* cannot be found on the plane of the linear, the horizontal, the finite, the purely human? Does not genuine transcending presuppose genuine transcendence? Are we not now perhaps more open-minded about this question?

The Critical Theory *starts out from its understanding of the social contradictions and the experience of unavoidable suffering, misfortune, pain, age and death in the life of the individual, which cannot simply be apprehended conceptually and "canceled" (in the Hegelian sense, as the first stage in a negative dialectic). It thematizes only indirectly the question of transcendence and thus the question of religion; but even this amounts up to a point to a* theologia negativa, *proceeding from the hope of perfect justice, the unshakable "longing for the other."*[6]

Marxism-Leninism *is beginning to be more discriminating in its discussion of the questions of meaning, sin and death in human life. The current* orthodox *answers—that meaning, happiness, fulfillment of life lie solely in work, militant solidarity and dialogic existence*[7]*—cannot silence the depressing "private questions" of progressive Marxists in East and West: where do we stand on individual guilt, personal fate, suffering and death, justice and love for the individual? In the light of all this the potential significance of religion is revealed afresh.*[8]

In the natural and humane sciences *some recognize better today the inadequacy of the materialist-Positivist world picture and understanding of reality and are beginning to relativize the absolute claim of their own methodology.*[9] *Responsible scientific-technical activity involves the question of ethics, but ethics in turn involves the question of discovering a meaning, of a scale of values, of models, of religion.*[10]

Depth psychology *has discovered the positive significance of religion for the human psyche, its self-discovery and its healing.*[11] *Modern psychologists have established a significant connection between the decline in religiosity and increasing disorientation, lack of standards, loss of meaning, the typical neuroses of our time.*[12]

Yet no less important than the new orientations in science and culture are the movements to be noted among the *younger generation,* to whose religious manifestations we shall have to return. In this respect East and West coincide. On the one side progressive Marxists like Machoveč demand from orthodox party Marxism "morally inspiring *ideals, models and standards of value*";[13] on the other side are the demands made on the capitalist system and formulated—for instance—by Charles A. Reich for the younger generation. Whether or not an empirical and systematical distinction can be made between the voices of "Consciousness I and II and III" in modern America,[14] it cannot be denied that they represent an attempt to cope with the great problems of modern society for which previous solutions were inadequate. And although Reich may have overrated the features of the counterculture in his analysis of the consciousness of the "new generation,"[15] the liberals and radical revolutionaries whom he criticizes have certainly neglected the decisive factor in the solution of these problems and the greatest and most urgent requirement of our time:

a new awareness of *transcendence*. What is needed in the midst of this technological world is a liberating breakaway from present conditions through the choice of a *new life-style*: the development of new powers to control the technological machinery, of a new independence and personal responsibility, of sensitivity, of aesthetic sentiment, of the capacity for love, the possibility of new ways of living and working together. And Reich rightly demands therefore a *new definition of values and priorities* and thus a new reflection on religion and ethics, so that a really new man and a new society becomes possible: "The power [of the new consciousness] is not the power of manipulating procedures or the power of politics or street fighting, but the power of new values and a new way of life."[16]

The future of religion

In the nineteenth and at the beginning of the twentieth century there were some who had expected, hoped for, proclaimed the end of religion. But no one had shown that this expectation, hope, proclamation had any foundation. Nor did the proclamation of the death of God become any more true by being constantly repeated. On the contrary, the persistent repetition of this prophecy, which obviously had not been fulfilled, made even many atheists skeptical about the prospects of ever bringing about the end of religion. In this connection Arnold Toynbee, the British historian, wrote:

> *In my belief, science and technology cannot survive as substitutes for religion. They cannot satisfy the spiritual needs for which religion of all kinds does try to provide, though they may discredit some of the traditional dogmas of the so-called "higher" religions. Historically, religion came first and science grew out of religion. Science has never superseded religion, and it is my expectation that it never will supersede it. How, then, can we arrive at a true, and therefore lasting peace? . . . For a true and lasting peace, a religious revolution is, I am sure, a* sine qua non*. By religion I mean the overcoming of self-centredness, in both individuals and communities, by getting into communion with the spiritual presence behind the universe and by bringing our wills into harmony with it. I think this is the only key to peace, but we are very far from picking up this key and using it, and, until we do, the survival of the human race will continue to be in doubt.*[17]

The fact that so many atheists never got away from religious problems, that the most radical atheists—Feuerbach and Nietzsche, who thought they had been liberated by their open profession of atheism—remained until the very human end of their life really fascinated by God and the problems of religion: all this seems—though we have no wish to gloat but only dispassionately to observe—to say less for the death than for a remarkable vitality of what is so often said to have died.

Marx, however, with his Utopia of a fading away of religion after the revolution, inspired by Feuerbach, was most clearly disavowed by developments particularly in the *socialist states.*

In the first place, not being confident that religion would automatically die out, the Soviet state (itself still very much alive) made militant-aggressive atheism part of its doctrine and exposed religion and Churches to the Stalinist terror aimed at their extermination and to the post-Stalinist repression. Nevertheless, almost sixty years after the October Revolution and indescribable persecutions and vexations of Churches and individuals, Christianity is more of a growing than a declining factor in the Soviet Union. According to the latest (perhaps exaggerated) statistics, every third adult Russian (Russians represent about half of all Soviet citizens) and every fifth adult Soviet human being is said to be a practicing Christian.[18]

In the West also however a number of prognoses have turned out to be mistaken. The *secularization process*—the reader may recall the reservation mentioned at the very beginning of this book[19]—has been overestimated by both sociologists and theologians, or they have failed to discriminate between its varied expressions.[20] Theologians of religionless secularity, who played the overture to the "Death of God theology," are now once more professing religion and even the religion of the people.[21] Often behind one-sided theories there lay not only an inadequate critical dissociation from the spirit of the age and its seductions, but also a very definite ideological interest: either nostalgia for the golden age (hypothesis of decline) or utopian expectation of a coming age (emancipation hypothesis). Often, instead of exact empirical studies, magnificent *a priori* theories were elaborated.

Even for futurologists however it proved more difficult to extrapolate the development of the phenomenon of religion than it was to deal with phenomena in other fields. What is there to be measured and counted here (for example, in the practice of faith and prayer and the motives of action) which would provide final and conclusive information about religion? The historically marked and socially objectivized religious reality—this sum total of doctrines and rites, modes of behavior, habits, rhythms of life and social structures—is in fact merely the tip of the iceberg of religion. The "total reality of religion," with all its impulses and inspirations, its beliefs and attitudes, its endowment of meaning and power of integration, the faith, hope and love which make these possible, is infinitely more. And religion, as old as humanity itself, has always managed throughout all millennia to capture man's mind afresh. Certainly old rites and customs may lose their religious significance and very often create instead scope for new forms of religious behavior: for instance, old virtues disappear and thus give way to new ones at first not recognized as such (decency, impartiality, fairness, a sense of responsibility, a critical spirit, solidarity).[22] After all our experiences so far, therefore, skepticism is called for at least as much in regard to the future of specific forms of irreligion as to the future of the Churches.

Various models for interpreting the secularization process have thus proved to be too much of the same type. Can secularization be identified with a decline in church membership? There still remains the whole field of non-ecclesiastical, non-institutionalized religion. Or can it be identified with rationalizing disenchantment? Rationalizing in one sphere of life does not exclude a sense for the non-rational or more-than-rational in another sphere. Or is it to be identified with desacralization? Religion can by no means be reduced to the sacral sphere.

On the future of religion, in principle, *three prognoses* are *possible* today:[23]

a. Secularization can be reversed, either by religious restoration or by religious revolution. The irreversibility of the secularization process has not been proved and—since the future can never be without surprises—such a development cannot *a priori* be excluded. But in the present situation it is not very likely.

b. Secularization continues without interruption. The Churches then become increasingly no more than legally recognized minorities. This prognosis is more probable, but—as we shall see—there are strong counterarguments.

c. Secularization continues, but in a modified form: it splits up the religious spectrum into ever new hitherto unknown social forms of religion, within the Churches or outside them. This prognosis perhaps contains the greatest probability.

The real experts on sociology of religion, from Max Weber and Emile Durkheim up to those of today, agree that there will always be religion as there will always be art. And religion—through all its changes—will remain of fundamental importance for humanity. It may be an integrating factor of society in Durkheim's sense (involving membership of a community) or a factor giving meaning and rationalizing values in Weber's sense (embedded into a system of interpretation). In less sacral forms, it may be important for interpersonal human relationships (Thomas Luckmann, Peter Berger), or, without abandoning the sacral forms, also indirectly for social institutions and structures (Talcott Parsons, Clifford Geertz). Or it may unite the functions of integrating and giving meaning by the formation of progressive elites in the pluralistic societies (Andrew Greeley).

Former studies in the sociology of religion often concentrated on statistics of church attendance and other religious practices. But there can be no doubt that even groups apparently remote from religion maintain an interest in the subject: contrary to some arbitrary assumptions and prejudices, this has been confirmed by recent statistics.[24] Certainly religion has lost its extensive control over other fields: it has less and less direct influence—for instance—on science, education, politics, law, medicine, social service. But can we conclude from all this that the influence of religion on the life of the individual and of society as a whole has declined? Instead of the former extensive control and guardianship, it may now have a more intensive and indirect moral influence.

The tacit moral influence of religion on the great economic, political and educational institutions of the United States, for instance, had been investigated by sociologists for a long time. A number of people have been surprised by the influence of the Churches in new ways on the civil rights and peace movements and the movements in the Third World, particularly in the struggle against poverty and in the struggle for national independence in Africa and South America. The fact that youth culture is affected to no small extent by a new religiosity will be shown later: it holds both for the Jesus movements and for the trends toward Eastern religiosity and mysticism. Negative symptoms reveal also much repressed religiosity, which has been driven underground: from the inoffensive forms of astrology, by way of all kinds of superstition, right up to constantly new, virulent forms of devil worship.

The *ideology* of *secularism* tried to make out of genuine and necessary secularization a *Weltanschauung* without faith: the end of religion or at least of organized religion, or at any rate of the Christian Churches, had come. As a result of the modern development, just described, sociologists are now more discriminating in their approach to the secularization process. They speak not so much of a decline of religion as of its *change of function*. It is recognized that society has become continually more complex and more differentiated and that, after the original far-reaching identity of religion and society, there had to be a separation of religion from the other structures. That is why T. Luckmann speaks of a detachment of institutional spheres from the cosmos of religious symbolism; T. Parsons of an evolutionary *differentiation* (division of labor) between the different institutions. Like the family, so too religion (or the Churches) has been liberated through the progressive differentiation of secondary (for instance, economic and educational) functions and could now concentrate on its proper task.

In that sense this secularization or differentiation offers a great opportunity. Within the system of man's interpretation of the world and himself, new and great questions have been raised by Christianity about the origin and definition of man and about the totality of the world and of history. Since then these great questions about the whence and whither have never come to rest and have fundamentally determined all subsequent time. This thrust and pressure of problems continue unchecked also in the new, secular age. And even though there was no continuity of answers, the continuity of the questioning at least remained. And yet modern man's secular sciences, despite all their successes, have proved notoriously inadequate in their answers to these great questions.[25] Pure reason seems here to be overtaxed.

Without entering further into the prognoses in regard to the future of religion, it can be said that the elimination of religion by science has not only not been proved, but is a methodologically unjustified extrapolation into the future based on an uncritical faith in science. Since there is now increasing skepticism in regard to the progress of reason and science, it becomes more than questionable whether science will or can play the part of a substitute for religion.

But all this is still far from substantiating belief in God: the question of God is an open question. Belief in God is challenged to give a reasoned account of the relation of its statements to reality and not to avoid the problem of verification.

Proofs of God?

It seems here as if we had been rushed into a dilemma, into an inescapable situation. *Either* belief in God can be proved and how is it then faith? *Or* it cannot be proved and how is it then reasonable? This is the perennial dilemma between reason and faith, particularly in the question of the knowledge of God, which some solve in favor of faith and the others in favor of reason—or even do not solve it at all.[26]

a. *Some* say that man knows God only if God makes himself known, that is, if he reveals himself. God has the initiative and encounters me solely in the word of *biblical revelation*. Sinful man therefore has no knowledge of God without God's gracious revelation: there is no human proof of God, but only God's proof of himself. What is expected from man is not dispassionate scrutiny, but trusting faith in virtue of the message: a *credo ut intelligam*, "I believe in order to know."

This—against the background of Luther's skepticism in regard to the seductive "whore reason"—is the position of Karl Barth's "*dialectical theology*"[27] and—in this question—also Rudolf Bultmann's,[28] together with their large following in evangelical theology.[29] This dialectical theology wants to secure God's divinity and his revelation, against all "natural theology" of Roman Catholicism and of anthropocentric Neo-Protestantism in the style of Friedrich Schleiermacher. Between man and God—the wholly other—is an infinite distance, which can be bridged only by God himself, "dialectically" through his revelation. Theology therefore cannot be formulated from man's requirements (*Bedürfnistheologie*): the word of God is not to be trimmed to man's needs.

But at this point a number of questions arise. Should it not be possible in principle to carry on the discussion about God with everyone? Cannot the other person's experiences be brought into the discussion? Is the truth of belief in God to remain merely an assertion? Where do I begin in the light of experience to be able to prove God? Is God then to be conjured up more or less magically? Is "revelation" an unsubstantiated assumption and thus perhaps merely an illusion or an ideological superstructure? Or is it simply an external law which man must accept forthwith, whether he understands it or not? Am I simply to dispense with my reason, simply to sacrifice my understanding? These questions, these demands for proof of belief in God seem to be justified:

Faith must not be blind, but responsible. Man ought not to be mentally coerced, but rationally convinced, so that he can make a justifiable decision of faith.

Faith must not be void of reality, but related to reality. Man ought not to have to believe simply, without verification. His statements should be proved and tested by contact with reality, within the present-day horizon of experience of man and society, and thus be covered by the concrete experience of reality.

b. *Others* say that man can believe in God only if he has first known God by reason. God's "supernatural" revelation in the word of the biblical proclamation presupposes the "natural" revelation of God in creation. The createdness of the world is not assumed in order to perceive the existence of the Creator (involving us, as some critics have maintained, in a vicious circle). But a reflection on the world as it is permits God to be shown clearly as the cause and goal of all things. Thus rational proofs of God are drawn from the reality of the world.

This—against the background of the theology of St. Thomas Aquinas[30] —is the position of the "*natural theology*" of Catholic Neo-Scholasticism and—with some reserve—of the First Vatican Council in 1870.[31] While Aquinas defends in principle the demonstrability of God,[32] Vatican I admittedly maintains in principle only the knowability of God (only a "possibility," a *potentia* of knowledge of God). This "natural theology"[33] seeks a middle way between a rationalism which reduces faith to reason (rejecting everything "supernatural") and a fideism which reduces all reason to faith (rejecting all "natural" knowledge of God). According to this view, despite all the dissimilarity between God and man, there is a similarity, an analogy, which makes possible an analogical argument—affirming, negating, transcending—for God. There is then a dual order of knowledge: "above" the "natural" sphere, which is known by reason, there is a "supernatural" sphere, which is known by faith. This has been described as a "two-story" theory, which makes it possible to do justice both to the phenomenon of philosophy (particularly philosophy of religion) and also to the phenomenon of religion (particularly the world religions). This is a theory which excludes contradictions between the "natural" and "supernatural" planes, between reason and faith. And here too there is no question of a theology adapted to requirements. Man's needs must not be the standpoint dominating everything, but certainly the methodical starting point. The order of knowledge where man begins is not identical with the order of being where God begins.

But a number of questions may be raised also against this conception. We may leave aside the specifically theological objections: that God's gracious action is left out of consideration and the one idea of God is split up into a "supernatural" and a "natural" God; that what is known in this way is not the one true Christian God, but an idol, the projection of man's imaginative view of the world. Quite general objections are raised today against the proofs of God.

a. Can a *proof* prove God? Can we proceed in questions of real life as we do in specialized, technical or scientific questions? Can we get anywhere at all in real-life questions with a purely rational thought sequence, linking together logically propositions already known in order to infer something unknown? Is it possible to prove in particular the existence of God by a process of logical reasoning, so that at the end we have not only a probable but a logically coercive understanding of the existence of God? Does not such a proof at best become an ingenious thought structure for philosophical and theological specialists which, however, for the average man remains abstract, impenetrable and uncontrollable, unconvincing and without binding force?

b. Can God still be *God* in a proof? Is not God reduced by such a process of reasoning to a mere thing which could be inferred, discovered, with a little human ingenuity? Does he not become an object, something set opposite the subject, to be fetched—so to speak—out of the hereafter externally and by a logical chain of reasoning? Is a God objectivized in this way still God at all?

c. Can *man's reason* reach so far? Since Kant's critique of pure reason, has it not become largely accepted that the range of our theoretical reason is restricted? Does it not remain tied to the horizon of human experience, so that any attempt to go beyond the limits of possible experience would be illegitimate? Have not the proofs of God's existence been knocked out of our hands by Kant's methodical criticism of the ontological, cosmological and teleological (physico-theological) proofs of God by theoretical reason? Is reason capable within the metaphysical field—and Kant does not deny this much—of doing more than regulating and arranging, without being able to draw conclusions about reality itself? Here in fact lies the real problematic of the proofs of God, as they were set down by Plato and Aristotle, given a place in Christian theology by Augustine, comprehensively systematized by Aquinas, freshly thought out by Descartes, Spinoza, Leibniz and Wolff (taking up again what had been the new "ontological" approach of Anselm of Canterbury), finally subjected as a whole to a radical critique by Kant and speculatively reinterpreted by Fichte and Hegel.

These objections can scarcely be ignored and it must be admitted:

As a discussion with nihilism makes clear,[84] *there is* no perceptible substructure *of reason which could form a basis for faith. It is not only at the "supernatural" superstructure that doubts are possible. They begin already with the uncertainty of human existence and of reality as a whole.*

The reality of God, if he should exist, is not directly involved *in the existence of the world. A God so involved is not God at all. He is not among the objects which present no problems of discovery within our experience. There is no direct experience of God. Nor is there any immediate intuition (as claimed in the "ontologism" of N. Malebranche, V. Gioberti, A. Rosmini).*

Without recourse to empirical experience (=a priori), *solely from the* concept *of God (as a necessary or absolutely perfect being), it is impossible to infer his necessary* existence. *The "ontological" proof of God (Anselm of Canterbury, Descartes, Leibniz), avoiding the digression by way of experience of the self and the world, presupposes a complete identity between the conceptual and the real order.*

With all proofs of God from experience (=a posteriori) *the question always arises whether they effect the transition from the "visible" to the "invisible," to the transcendence beyond experience. It is doubtful whether the different variants of either the cosmological (God as efficient cause) or the teleological (God as final cause) proof of God really reach an ultimate cause or goal not identifiable with me, society or the world (or whether they exclude an infinite regress).*

Belief in God cannot be proved if the existential components of a person are neglected, with the result that he is dispensed from belief instead of being summoned to it. In the light of previous experiences there is no purely rational demonstration of God's existence which could carry universal conviction. Proofs of God *turn out in fact* not to be coercive *for everyone, whatever may be thought of the abstract "possibility" of knowledge of God as taught by Vatican I. There is not a single proof that is generally accepted.*

Is there then no way out of the dilemma? Is there no middle way between a purely authoritative assertion of God in the sense of "dialectical theology" and a purely rational proof in the sense of "natural theology"?

More than pure reason

Even *Kant*, the "demolisher" of the proofs of God, never thought that God did not exist. And ought we not to agree with Kant at least in the sense that a middle way must be sought? There must be a way between a dogmatic assertion and a proof by theoretical reason, on the level of which the existence of God—according to Kant—cannot be proved, but also cannot be refuted.

How then does Kant establish the existence of God? In this respect Kant appeals—rightly, in principle—not to "pure," but to "practical" reason, which is manifested in man's action: it is a question, not of pure knowledge, but of human action. Kant argues from man's self-understanding as a moral, responsible being. His argument differs therefore from the purely rational proofs of God insofar as he rightly refuses to reduce man's actual existence to a neutral factor in the process of proof. That is why he speaks of a "postulate": God is "postulated" by morality (which is unconditionally commanded) and the striving for happiness (which must be adapted to morality), "postulated" as the condition of their possibility, evident only to practical reason. Kant speaks in this connection of "a faith," "purely rational faith."[35] Even in the critique of practical reason of course Kant does not look "outwards" or "upwards" into a beyond (a "transcendent"), but behind himself, backwards and inwards (to the "transcendental"): to the condition of the possibility of morality and happiness. Together with freedom and immortality, God is one of the three great ideas which no rational proof attains and which are nevertheless the essential presuppositions of moral action.

Kant's transcendental argument naturally came up against justifiable criticism, in two respects. In regard to the *first* ground of his argument: Is it legitimate to proceed from an unconditional "ought," from a categorical imperative? Does not the unconditional moral law hold only when a person has faced the question of what behavior is right? Must we really assume within ourselves the fact of an unconditional moral obligation, which as such postulates the existence of God (=a supreme good which unites morality and happiness)? Does not the assumption of an apodictically certain moral law within us—as expressed in the categorical imperative ("thou shalt")—itself presuppose the moral impulse, the question about morality or even the decision in regard to a moral life, which—as Nietzsche proves—may also turn out to be negative? Is not Kant therefore arguing in a circle here? Is not the unconditionality of the obligation of the "thou shalt" itself postulated and thus the postulate of the existence of God is founded on another postulate?

In regard to the *second* ground of his argument: The striving for happiness is certainly proper to all men. But what reasons have we for assuming that duty and inclination are bound to be in harmony? Why must someone who obeys the moral law necessarily gain happiness?

The concept of "postulate" itself points to the fact that the recourse to God is theoretically impossible without presuppositions, but that God himself must be presupposed if we want to live morally at all in a meaningful sense. In the midst of the modern secularization—and emancipation—process, it is a great idea of Kant that God is understood as the condition of the possibility of moral autonomy. He rightly refuses to let the contradictions, the antinomies, of pure reason break into the sphere of actual human existence or to let man drown in the unfathomable depths of absurdity. But ought there not to be an attempt to reach further back and to start out on a broader front?

Here at any rate we shall not assume the existence in us of a moral obligation, a stern moral law, a rigorous categorical imperative. Instead, we shall start out—as hitherto—from the whole reality of the world and of man, as it is concretely experienced, and then ask about the condition of the possibility of this wholly and entirely uncertain reality. Kant demolished the proofs of God as coercive arguments. But he did not liquidate their religious content. We shall not attempt to deduce God by theoretical reason from the experience of this reality of the world and of man, to demonstrate the reality of God in a process of syllogistic reasoning. But certainly the experience of reality accessible to every man will be inductively elucidated, in order—so to speak, on the lines of "practical reason"—to place him before a rationally responsible *decision* which claims more than merely pure reason, which claims in fact the whole man.

This is therefore not a purely theoretical, but a wholly practical function of reason: a meditative reflection, accompanying, opening up, elucidating the concrete experience of reality. Should it not be possible, in the light of this concrete reality of world and man, to attempt an account of belief in God which can stand up to criticism? Can we not talk of God in terms of the concrete experience of reality, proving our talk to be correct in the same terms and thus to be credible? In all this may we not be aware that there are not a few who are able to believe in God, but cannot justify their belief in the same way?

2. *The reality of God*

In our reflections so far we have left open the question whether God in fact exists. It will be answered in two phases, so that we can examine the specifically Christian understanding of God in the light of today's questions and ideas.[36] We cannot completely relieve the reader who gets involved in this question from a strenuous effort of conceptual thinking, if only because our answer must be stated in the most succinct, systematic form. But anyone for whom the existence of God is a certainty of faith may easily, if he wishes, pass over this more or less philosophical train of thought.

Today less than ever can it be assumed that people—whether atheists or Christians—know what they mean by God. First of all, we have no alternative but to start out from a preconception, a *preliminary notion* of God which will be clarified—up to a point—only in the analysis itself: for the questions of the fact that God is and of what he is are intimately connected. The preliminary notion of God is what people commonly understand by God but express in different ways: the mysterious and unshakable ground of what is—despite everything—a meaningful life; the center and depth of man, of human fellowship, of reality as a whole; the final, supreme authority on which everything depends; the Opposite, beyond our control, source of our responsibility.

The hypothesis

The ultimate questions, which—according to Kant—combine all the interests of human reason,[87] are also the first questions, the commonplace questions. "What can I know?" sums up questions about truth. "What ought I to do?" questions about the norm. "What may I hope?" questions about meaning. "Functional" and "essential" questions, technical-rational and total-personal questions, can all be distinguished, but are linked together in concrete life. "Calculating" thought, which—in Heidegger's sense—is concerned with what is feasible, computable, accurate, cannot be separated in ordinary life from "meditative" thought, which is concerned with meaning and truth. But the essential questions about meaning and truth, norms and values can be covered up and suppressed—more than ever under the soporific influence of the welfare society—until they emerge again as a result of reflection or even more as a result of "fate" in great things or in small.

In order to answer the question of the existence of God, it must be assumed that man accepts in principle his own existence and reality as a whole: that he therefore does not regard this undoubtedly profoundly uncertain reality and particularly his own profoundly uncertain existence *a priori* as meaningless, worthless, vain, as nihilism asserts; that he regards this reality, despite its uncertainty, as in principle meaningful, valuable, actual. Thus he brings to reality—as he is free to do—not a fundamental mistrust, a basic lack of confidence, but a *fundamental trust*, a basic confidence.[88]

Even for someone who so accepts in basic trust the reality of the world and man, the complete uncertainty of reality of course still persists in its ontic, noetic and ethical aspects. Trust in uncertain reality does not eliminate its radical uncertainty. And it is here that the question of God arises: reality, which can justify a basic trust, seems itself to be mysteriously unsubstantiated, sustaining though not itself sustained, evolving but without aim. Reality is there as a fact, yet remains enigmatic, without any manifest ground, support or purpose. Thus at any time the question can arise again of reality and unreality, being or not being, basic trust or nihilism.

Fundamentally, it amounts to the question: *where* is the explanation to be found of utterly uncertain reality? What makes it possible? What then is the *condition of the possibility* of this uncertain *reality?* The question therefore is not merely: what is the condition of the possibility of this utter *uncertainty?* This way of stating the question neglects the reality which persists in all uncertainty.[39]

If man is not to abandon any attempt to understand himself and reality, then these ultimate questions—which are likewise primary and which call inescapably for an answer—must be answered. At the same time the believer is in competition with the unbeliever, as to who can interpret more convincingly the basic human experiences.

A. From the quite concrete experience of life's insecurity, the uncertainty of knowledge and man's manifold fear and disorientation, which does not have to be set out in detail here, there arises the irrecusable question: what is the *source* of this radically *uncertain reality*, suspended between being and not being, meaning and meaninglessness, supporting without support, evolving without aim?

Even someone who does not think *that* God exists could at least agree with the *hypothesis* (which of course does not as such decide his existence or non-existence) that, *if* God existed, then a fundamental solution *would be* provided of the enigma of permanently uncertain reality, a fundamental answer—which would emerge naturally and would need interpretation—to the question of the source. The hypothesis may be set out in a succinct form:

If God existed, then the substantiating reality itself would not ultimately be unsubstantiated. God would be the primal reason *of all reality.*

If God existed, then the supporting reality itself would not ultimately be unsupported. God would be the primal support *of all reality.*

If God existed, then evolving reality would not ultimately be without aim. God would be the primal goal *of all reality.*

If God existed, then there would be no suspicion that reality, suspended between being and not being, might ultimately be void. God would be the being itself *of all reality.*

This hypothesis may be given more exact expression, positively and negatively:

a. *positively: If* God existed, then it could be understood

why ultimately in all the disruption a hidden unity can be confidently assumed, in all the meaninglessness a hidden significance, in all the worthlessness a hidden value: God would be the *primal source, primal meaning, primal value* of all that is;

why ultimately in all the emptiness a hidden being of reality can be confidently assumed: God would be the *being* of all that is.

b. *negatively: If* God existed, then on the other hand it could also be understood

why ultimately substantiating reality seems to be without substantiation from itself, supporting reality without support in itself, evolving reality without aim for itself;

why its unity is threatened by disruption, its significance by meaninglessness, its value by worthlessness;

why reality, suspended between being and not being, is suspected of being ultimately unreal and void.

The basic answer is always the same: because uncertain reality is itself *not God*; because the self, society, the world, cannot be identified with their primal reason, primal support and primal goal, with their primal source, primal meaning and primal value, with being itself.

B. In view of the particular uncertainty of *human existence*, a hypothetical answer might be formulated in this way: *if* God existed, then the enigma also of the permanent uncertainty of human existence *would be* solved in principle. It can be stated more exactly as follows: if God existed,

> *then, against all threats of fate and death, I could justifiably affirm the unity and identity of my human existence: for God would be the first ground also of my life;*
>
> *then, against all threats of emptiness and meaninglessness, I could justifiably affirm the truth and significance of my existence: for God would be the ultimate meaning also of my life;*
>
> *then, against all threats of sin and rejection, I could justifiably affirm the goodness and value of my existence: for then God would also be the comprehensive hope of my life;*
>
> *then, against all threats of nothingness, I could justifiably affirm with confidence the being of my human existence: for God would then be the being itself particularly of human life.*

This hypothetical answer too can be negatively tested. *If* God existed, then it would be understood also in relation to my existence why the unity and identity, truth and significance, goodness and value of human existence remain threatened by fate and death, emptiness and meaninglessness, sin and damnation, why the being of my existence remains threatened by nothingness. The fundamental answer would always be one and the same: because man is *not God*, because my human self cannot be identified with its primal reason, primal meaning, primal goal, with being itself.

In sum: if God existed, then the condition of the possibility of this uncertain reality would exist, its "whence" (in the widest sense) would be indicated. If! But from the hypothesis of God we cannot conclude to the reality of God.

Reality

If we are not to be rushed into a premature conclusion, we must again proceed step by step. How are the alternatives to be judged and how can we reach a solution?

a. One thing must be conceded to atheism from the very beginning: it is *possible to deny God.* Atheism cannot be eliminated rationally. It is unproved,[40] but it is also irrefutable. Why?

It is the experience of the radical *uncertainty* of every reality which provides atheism with sufficient grounds for maintaining that reality has absolutely no primal reason, primal support or primal goal. Any talk of primal source, primal meaning, primal value, must be rejected. We simply cannot know any of these things (agnosticism). Indeed, reality is perhaps ultimately chaos, absurdity, illusion, appearance and not being, just nothing (atheism tending to nihilism).

Hence there are in fact no positive arguments against the *impossibility* of atheism. If someone says that there is no God, his claim cannot be positively refuted. In the last resort neither a strict proof nor a demonstration of God is of any avail against such an assertion. This unproved assertion rests ultimately on a *decision* which is connected with the basic decision for reality as a whole. The denial of God cannot be refuted purely rationally.

b. On the other hand, atheism is also incapable of positively excluding the other alternative: as it is possible to deny him, so also it is *possible to affirm* God. Why?

It is *reality* in all its uncertainty which provides sufficient grounds for venturing not only a confident assent to this reality, its identity, significance and value, but also an assent to that without which reality ultimately seems unsubstantiated in all substantiation, unsupported in all support, aimless in all its evolving: a confident assent therefore to a primal reason, primal support and primal goal of uncertain reality.

Hence there is no conclusive argument for the *necessity* of atheism. If someone says that there is a God, his claim too cannot be positively refuted. Atheism for its own part is ultimately of no avail against such confidence imposed by reality itself. The irrefutable affirmation of God also rests ultimately on a *decision* which here too is connected with the basic decision for reality as a whole. For this reason it is also rationally irrefutable. And of course the affirmation of God is also impossible to prove by purely rational arguments. Stalemate?

c. The alternatives have become clear. And it is just here—beyond "natural," "dialectical" or "morally postulating" theology—that the essential difficulty lies in solving the question of the existence of God:

> If *God is, he is the answer to the radical uncertainty of reality.*
>
> That *God is, can however be accepted neither stringently in virtue of a proof or demonstration of pure reason nor absolutely in virtue of a moral postulate of practical reason, still less solely in virtue of the biblical testimony.*
>
> That *God is, can ultimately be accepted only in a confidence* founded *on reality itself.*

This trusting commitment to an ultimate reason, support and meaning of reality is itself rightly designated in general usage as "belief" in God ("faith in God," "trust in God"). This is belief in a very broad sense, insofar as it does not necessarily have to be prompted by Christian proclamation but is also possible for non-Christians. People who profess this faith—whether Christians or not—are rightly called "believers in God." On the other hand, atheism as a refusal to trust in God is again quite rightly described in general usage as "unbelief."

Hence man simply cannot avoid a *decision*—free but not arbitrary—both with reference to reality as such and also with reference to its primal reason, primal support and primal meaning. Since reality and its primal reason, primal support and primal meaning are not imposed on us with conclusive evidence, there remains scope for human freedom. Man is expected to decide, without intellectual constraint. Both atheism and belief in God are ventures, they are also risks. Any criticism of proofs of God is aimed at showing that belief in God has the character of a decision and—on the other hand—that a decision for God has the character of belief.

The question of God therefore involves a decision which must in fact be faced on a deeper level than the decision—necessary in view of nihilism—for or against reality as such. As soon as the individual becomes aware of this ultimate depth and the question arises, the decision becomes unavoidable. In the question of God too, not to choose is in fact a choice: the person has *chosen* not to choose. To abstain from voting in a vote of confidence in regard to the question of God means a refusal of confidence.

Yet unfortunately the "depth" (or "height") of a truth and man's certainty in accepting it are in inverse ratio. The more banal the truth ("truism," "platitude"), the greater the certainty. The more significant the truth (for instance, aesthetic, moral and religious truth by comparison with arithmetical), the slighter the certainty. For the "deeper" the truth is for me, the more must I first lay myself open to it, inwardly prepare myself, attune myself to it intellectually, willingly, emotionally, in order to reach that genuine "certainty" which is somewhat different from assured "security." A *deep* truth, for me outwardly uncertain, threatened by doubts, which presupposes a generous commitment on my part, can possess much more cognitive value than a certain—or even an "absolutely certain"—*banal* truth.[41]

Yet here too it does not follow from the possibility of affirming or denying God that the choice is immaterial. Denial of God implies an ultimately *unsubstantiated* basic trust in reality (if not an absolutely basic mistrust). But acceptance of God implies an ultimately *substantiated* basic trust in reality. A person who affirms God knows *why* he trusts reality. There can be no talk therefore, as will soon be made clear, of a stalemate.

d. If *atheism* is not nourished simply by a nihilistic basic mistrust, it must be nourished by a basic trust—but one that is ultimately *unsubstantiated*. By denying God, man decides against an ultimate reason, support, an ultimate end of reality. In agnostic atheism the assent to reality proves to be ultimately unsubstantiated and inconsistent: a freewheeling, nowhere anchored and therefore paradoxical basic trust. In less superficial, more consistent nihilistic atheism, radical mistrust makes an assent to reality quite impossible. Atheism anyway is unable to suggest *any condition for the possibility* of uncertain reality. For this reason it lacks a radical rationality, although this is often concealed by a rationalistic but fundamentally irrational trust in human reason.

The price paid by atheism for its denial is obvious. It is exposed to the danger of an ultimate lack of reason, of support, of purpose: to possible futility, worthlessness, emptiness of reality as a whole. If he becomes aware of it, the atheist is also exposed quite personally to the danger of an ultimate abandonment, menace and decay, resulting in doubt, fear, even despair. All this is true of course only if atheism is quite serious and not an intellectual pose, snobbish caprice or thoughtless superficiality.

For the atheist there is no answer to those ultimate and yet immediate, perennial questions of human life, which are not to be suppressed by simply being prohibited: questions which arise not merely in borderline situations, but in the very midst of man's personal and social life. Keeping to Kant's formulation of them:

> *What can we* know? *Why is there anything at all? Why not nothing? Where does man come from and where does he go to? Why is the world as it is? What is the ultimate reason and meaning of all reality?*
>
> *What ought we* to do? *Why do what we do? Why and to whom are*

we finally responsible? What deserves forthright contempt and what love? What is the point of loyalty and friendship, but also what is the point of suffering and sin? What really matters for man?

What may we hope? *Why are we here? What is it all about? What is there left for us: death, making everything pointless at the end? What will give us courage for life and what courage for death?*

In all these questions it is all or nothing. They are questions not only for the dying, but for the living. They are not for weaklings and uninformed people, but precisely for the informed and committed. They are not excuses for not acting, but incentives to action. Is there something which sustains us in all this, which never permits us to despair? Is there something stable in all change, something unconditioned in all that is conditioned, something absolute in the relativizing experienced everywhere? Atheism leaves all these questions without a final answer.

e. Belief in God is nourished by an ultimately substantiated basic trust: when he assents to God, man opts for an ultimate reason, support, meaning of reality. In belief in God assent to reality turns out to be ultimately substantiated and consistent: a basic trust anchored in the ultimate depth, in the reason of reasons. Belief in God as radical basic trust can therefore point also to the *condition of the possibility* of uncertain reality. In this sense it displays a radical rationality—which is not the same thing as rationalism.

The price received by belief in God for its yes is likewise obvious. Since I confidently decide for a primal reason instead of groundlessness, for a primal support instead of unsupportedness, for a primal goal instead of aimlessness, I have now reason to recognize a unity of the reality of world and man despite all disruption, a meaning despite all meaninglessness, a value despite all worthlessness. And, despite all the uncertainty and insecurity, abandonment and exposure, menace and decay of my own existence, I am *granted* in the light of the ultimate primal source, primal meaning and primal value an ultimate certainty, assurance and stability. This is no mere abstract security, isolating me from my fellow men, but always involves a concrete reference to the human "Thou": how is man to learn what it means to be accepted by God, if he is not accepted by any single human being? I cannot simply take or create for myself ultimate certainty, assurance and stability. It is ultimate reality itself in a variety of ways which challenges me to accept it, with which—so to speak—the "initiative" lies. Ultimate reality itself enables me to see that patience in regard to the present, gratitude in regard to the past and hope in regard to the future are ultimately substantiated, despite all doubt, all fear and despair.

Thus those ultimate and yet immediate religio-social questions of man, not to be suppressed by simply being prohibited, which we summed up under Kant's leading questions, receive in principle at least an answer with which man can live in the world of today: an answer from the reality of God.

f. How far then is belief in God *rationally justified?* Faced with the decision between atheism and belief in God, man cannot be indifferent. He approaches this decision with a mind already burdened. Essentially he would like to understand the world and himself, to respond to the uncertainty of reality, to perceive the condition of the possibility of uncertain reality: he would like to know of an ultimate reason, an ultimate support and an ultimate goal of reality.

Yet here too man remains free. He can say "No." He can adopt a skeptical attitude and ignore or even stifle any dawning confidence in an ultimate reason, support and goal. He can, perhaps utterly honestly and truthfully, declare his inability to know (agnostic atheism) or even assert that reality—uncertain anyway—is completely void, without reason or goal, without meaning or value (nihilistic atheism). Unless a person is prepared for a confident acknowledgment of God, with its practical consequences, he will never reach a rationally meaningful knowledge of God. And even when someone has given his assent to God, he is continually faced with the temptation to deny him.

If however man does not isolate himself, but remains completely open to reality as it is revealed to him; if he does not try to get away from the ultimate reason, support and goal of reality, but ventures to apply himself and give himself up to it: then he knows that—*by the very fact* of doing this—he is doing the right thing, in fact the most sensible thing of all. For in the very act of acknowledging what he perceives (in carrying out his *rationabile obsequium*) he experiences that which cannot be stringently proved or demonstrated in advance. Reality is manifested in its ultimate depth. Its ultimate reason, support, goal, its primal source, primal meaning and primal value are laid open to him as soon as he lays himself open. And at the same time, despite all uncertainty, he experiences an ultimate rationality of his own reason: in the light of this, an ultimate confidence in reason appears not as irrational but as rationally substantiated.

There is nothing in all this of an *external rationality*, which could not produce an assured *certainty*. The existence of God is not first rationally and stringently proved or demonstrated and then believed, as if the rationality of belief in God were thus guaranteed. There is not first rational knowledge of God and then confident acknowledgment. The hidden reality of God is not forced on reason.

What is implied is *an intrinsic rationality* which can produce a basic certainty. Despite all temptations to doubt, in the practical realization of this venturesome trust in God's reality man experiences the rationality of his trust: based on the perceptible ultimate identity, significance and value of reality; on its primal reason, primal meaning and primal value now becoming apparent. This then is the rationally justified venture of belief in God through which—despite all doubts—man reaches and must constantly maintain—despite all doubts—an ultimate certainty: a certainty from which no fear, no despair, no agnostic or nihilistic atheism can drive him, even in borderline situations, without his consent.

g. The *connection between basic trust and belief in God* is now obvious. From a material standpoint basic trust relates to reality as such and to one's own existence, while belief in God relates to the primal reason, primal support and primal meaning of reality; but, from a formal standpoint, basic trust and belief in God ("trust in God") have an analogous structure which is based on the material connection (despite the difference) between the two. Like basic trust, belief in God is

a matter not only of human reason, but of the whole, concrete, living man: with mind and body, reason and instinct, in his quite definite historical situation, in his dependence on traditions, authorities, habits of thought, scales of values, with his personal interest and his social involvement. Man cannot speak of this "matter" while remaining outside the "matter";

therefore super-rational: as there is no logically stringent proof that reality is real, neither is there such a proof of God. The proof of God is no more logically stringent than is love. The relationship to God is one of trust;

not however irrational: there is a reflection on the reality of God emerging from human experience and calling for man's free decision. Belief in God can be justified in face of a rational critique. It is rooted in the experience of the uncertainty of reality, which raises ultimate questions about the condition of its possibility;

thus not a blind decision, devoid of reality, but one that is substantiated, related to reality and therefore rationally justified in concrete existence. Its relevance to both existential needs and social conditions becomes apparent from the reality of the world and of man;

realized in a concrete relationship with our fellow man. Without the experience of being accepted by men, it seems difficult to experience acceptance by God;

not taken once and for all, for every case, but constantly to be freshly realized. Rational arguments never render belief in God unassailable and immune from crises in face of atheism. Belief in God is continually threatened and—under pressure of doubts—must constantly be realized, upheld, lived, regained in a new decision. Even in regard to God, man remains in insoluble conflict between trust and mistrust, belief and unbelief.

h. Looking back then on our reflections, what "help" can be given to the atheist? Not a rationally stringent proof of God, not an appeal to an unconditional "thou shalt," not an apologetic intended to be intellectually coercive, not a dogmatic theology decreeing from above. But:

First of all—at least where an appeal to the biblical message is not directly fruitful—*joint reflection* on the reality of the world and of men, aided by common experiences in regard to those ultimate and primary questions: that is, not simply getting people away from the point where they are standing, but staying with them and first considering and opening up their world, discovering the great questions of life in the everyday questions—all this, not in instruction, but in conversation.

At the same time—and perhaps more important—*trust shown in practice*, which elicits trust, a living venture as an invitation to the same venture: a leap into the water which "proves" in practice the possibility of being sustained and at the same time calls on the other to make a similar leap, that is, a testimony of belief in God confirmed by practice.

Finally—and really this is all that can help—*our own venture of trust.* We can learn to swim only by swimming ourselves. Like other experiences, this basic experience is brought to light only in its realization.

Ambiguity of the concept of God

If we want to give a name to what we have described here as primal reason, primal support and primal goal, as primal source, primal meaning and primal value, we shall not be able to dispense with *the term* "God." "God" is in fact, as Martin Buber explains in his moving meditations on the "Darkness of God," "the most loaded of all human words."[42] None has been so misused, defiled and mauled. Men have torn it apart into religious factions, have killed for it and died for it: there is no comparable term to designate the supreme reality and yet it is so often used to disguise the worst impieties. But just because it means so much for man—even for atheists, who reject God and not merely a nameless something—it cannot be given up. We may respect someone who avoids it: the term cannot be cleared of its dubious associations. But neither can it be forgotten. It can however be taken up and freshly considered—with all its consequences for man—and obviously also defined in other words. So, instead of talking no longer of God or instead of talking of him in the same way, the important thing today is to learn to speak with great care in a new way of God. If a theology were not logos of God, but were to speak only of man and human fellowship, it would have to be described honestly—as it was by Ludwig Feuerbach—as anthropology.

Of course, even for belief in God in the sense described, the term "*God*" *remains ambiguous.* Even to belief, God is nowhere present immediately and directly, objectively and explicitly. It is only contrary to the appearances of the world, beneath the surface and unobjectively, that God appears from the depths to be grasped by faith in the superficially perceptible phenomena, while remaining at the same time the incomprehensible. In any case, what is grasped is not present as clearly ascertainable and completely unambiguous: it is not only easy to overlook or to question, but can also be very diversely interpreted. Even if belief is an empirical intuition of the whole, this intuition is open to extraordinarily diverse conceptual interpretations. And man must constantly strive through conceptual reflection to extend, clarify and secure the fully living but perhaps also superficial and often one-sided experience of belief. Only in thoughtful reflection is the total experience given conceptual expression, made logically transparent and so too made clearly conceptually communicable to others. Reflection is nourished by experience. But experience needs the critical illumination and assurance of reflection.

All *philosophy* from the pre-Socratics to Hegel, and even the subsequent anti-theologies of Feuerbach and Marx, Nietzsche and Heidegger, revolve around the question of God, which, as W. Weischedel has explained at length, constitutes the central complex of problems of the history of philosophy.[43] In this connection it becomes clear how the meanings given to the name "God" are certainly very varied, but not wholly disparate nor indeed unrelated: "The 'divine' of the early Greek thinkers, immediately present in the world, is not the same as the Creator-God of philosophical theology under the influence of Christianity. God as Aristotle conceives him, as the final end of all striving in reality, is different from Kant's God guaranteeing the moral law and happiness. The God of Aquinas or Hegel, apprehensible by reason, is different from the God of Denis the Areopagite or Nicholas of Cusa, withdrawn into the realm of the ineffable. The merely moral God too, attacked by Nietzsche, is not the God of metaphysics as understood by Heidegger: the supreme Existent, upholding reality. And yet always and everywhere the meanings given to the name 'God' are related: the underlying theme is that God is that which determines all reality as its permeating and supreme principle."[44]

The universal concept of God is ambivalent, ambiguous. The history of philosophy itself cries out for a clarification. But this very history raises doubts as to its power to produce such a clarification. It seems to belong to the nature of this God of the philosophers, known in this way, to remain *in the last resort undetermined*.

Hence the different *religions* always sought to be more than philosophy. Religion certainly does not arise from a strictly rational proof of God and not at all from even the most circumspect conceptual reflection. Nor of course does religion emerge merely from man's irrational, subintellectual psychological strata. It is based, as the psychology of religion makes clear, on an empirical unity of knowing, willing and feeling, which is understood not as our own achievement but as a response to an encounter with God in whatever form or as an experience of God. Most religions appeal to a manifestation of God, who as such is hidden and therefore ambiguous. For this reason we naturally turn now to a consideration of the concrete religions which attempt to give a concrete answer for theory and practice to the question of the understanding of God and the understanding of man.

In turning our attention to the concrete religions of course we must not fall back to a stage before the Enlightenment, which Kant described as "man's emergence from his self-inculpated tutelage,"[45] nor must we forget the results of coping with the modern criticism of religion. If we are to speak honestly of God at the present time, we must keep in mind the *modern outlook* which enables both believers and unbelievers to purify and deepen their understanding of God and which will be summarized here in the form adopted by Heinz Zahrnt.[46]

a. The present-day understanding of God presupposes the modern *scientific explanation of the world:* weather and victories in battle, illnesses and cures, fortune and misfortune of individuals, groups and nations are no longer explained by the direct intervention of God, but by natural causes. This extrusion of God from the world provides an *opportunity:* it thus becomes clearer what God is not, that he cannot simply be equated with natural and historical processes. Do we recognize that this withdrawal from the realm of secondary causes is the possible precondition for a more personal, inward encounter with God? Or, after the Enlightenment has deprived nature of its gods, are we trying to deify the finite in new forms?

b. The present-day understanding of God presupposes the modern *understanding of authority:* no truth is accepted without being submitted to the judgment of reason, merely on the authority of the Bible or tradition or the Church, but only after a critical scrutiny. The fact that belief in God has ceased to be merely imposed by authority, to be merely a traditional or denominational affair and so taken for granted as part of a world view, provides an *opportunity:* man, as befits his dignity and God's glory, receives a new challenge to make the faith of the Fathers his own. Do people use the scope made available for human autonomy, so that they behave like adults, trusting God with their whole hearts and not like slaves with no will of their own, accepting God against their reason as true? Or, after the Enlightenment has demythologized authority, do we perhaps deliver ourselves up merely to other powers?

c. The present-day understanding of God presupposes *ideological criticism:* uncovering social misuse of religion by state or Church, exposing rationally the vested interests of persons or groups—exercising power on a greater or smaller scale—who invoke the Lord, as protector and guarantor of the largely unjust, existing order, to justify their divine right. This exclusion of God from involvement in social-political power relationships also provides an *opportunity:* man can go on his way, before his God as before political rulers, walking upright, without undignified cringing, as partner and not as subject. Has modern man understood the twilight of the gods, which came with the Enlightenment, in such a way that God is not a projection of man's selfish needs but really the Other? Or does he still try again to incorporate God ideologically into some kind of world process?

d. The present-day understanding of God presupposes the modern *shift of awareness from the hereafter to the here and now:* as a result of the process of secularization, the autonomy of earthly systems (science, economy, politics, state, society, law, culture) is increasingly not merely known in theory but also realized in practice. But this very abandonment of the mere promise of a hereafter and the closer concentration on the here and now provides an *opportunity:* life, which perhaps has lost something of its depth, might now gain in intensity. Have we recognized how God in this very life thus comes closer to man, challenges him now in the midst of his secularity? Or have we simply turned secularizing into secularism, into a world view, and lost sight of God as the One with whom we are involved unconditionally at all times in the present life: the immanent Transcendent?

e. The present-day understanding of God presupposes a modern *orientation to the future:* man today looks not so much longingly upwards or even merely backwards to past history, but as far as possible forwards. The deliberate incorporation of the dimension of the future, the active planning and shaping of the future, provides an *opportunity:* in this way the future dimension also of the Christian proclamation can be newly discovered and taken seriously. Is God taken seriously as the one who is to come and as the true future of man and the world? Or shall we perhaps completely forget the past, give up our memories of decisive moments of history and thus lose our bearings in the present?

The dangers of modern developments must therefore be considered, but at the same time the opportunities offered must be resolutely exploited. If we take seriously the history of man's enlightenment, we shall have to look for a future understanding of God expressed more or less in these terms:

not a naïve, anthropological projection: God as "supreme being" dwelling, in a literal or spatial sense, "above" the world.

not an "enlightened," deistic projection: God "outside" the world in a spiritual or metaphysical sense, living in a realm beyond this world ("hinterworld"), as an objectivized, hypostasized Opposite.

but a coherent understanding of reality: God in this world and this world in God; God not only as part of reality—a (supreme) finite alongside finite things—but the infinite in the finite, the absolute in the rela-

tive. God as the here-hereafter, transcendent-immanent, most real reality in the heart of things, in man and in man's history.

Against this background certain things become clear now which are relevant to our later consideration of the *Christian* understanding of God. A Christian understanding of God would have to go beyond a primitive, anthropomorphic biblicism or even a merely apparently superior, abstract theological philosophy and make sure that the "God of the philosophers" and the Christian God were not brought into a facile and superficial harmony (as with the old or new apologists and the Scholastics), nor on the other hand dissociated (as with the philosophers of the Enlightenment or the biblicist theologians). The Christian understanding of God "cancels and preserves" (*aufhebt*, in the best Hegelian sense of the word) the God of the philosophers in the Christian God, negatively, positively, eminently: critically negating, positively elevating, eminently surpassing. In this way then the completely *ambiguous* concept of God as understood generally and in philosophy would become in the Christian understanding of God unmistakably and unconfusedly *unambiguous*.

To achieve this certainly demands considerable effort on the part of Christian theologians.

The task of theology

"There is one thing I would like to tell the theologians: something which they know and others should know. They hold the sole truth which goes deeper than the truth of science, on which the atomic age rests. They hold a knowledge of the nature of man that is more deeply rooted than the rationality of modern times. The moment always comes inevitably when our planning breaks down and we ask and will ask about this truth. The present bourgeois status of the Church is no proof that men are really asking about Christian truth. This truth will be convincing when it is lived." The words are those of Carl Friedrich von Weizsäcker, physicist and philosopher, and they are addressed to theologians.[47]

a. First let us look back over the road we have traveled—theologically—up to now. The complex questions of theological method cannot be discussed here, but—at least for those interested in theology—some demarcation lines may be drawn. Despite all our dialectical theological statements, we cannot be accused of practicing "dialectical theology"[48] in the traditional sense—so to speak, vertically, from above. Our method has been to start out each time as consistently as possible "from below," from man's first questions, from human experience. All this was in view of a rational justification of faith today. For *in face of nihilism, we cannot appeal to the Bible in order to dismiss the basic problems of the uncertainty of reality as a whole and of human existence;*

in face of atheism, we cannot appeal to the Bible in order merely to assert the reality of God.

The phenomena of religion, of philosophy, of the universally human preconception required an adequate answer. Of course this is not our whole answer. What has been analyzed in the light of human experience can and must later be given a critical theological interpretation in the light of the Christian message. But in all this have we not been practicing "natural theology"? Certainly only theologians, in this case particularly Protestant theologians, can raise this question. But, although we started out with man's natural questions and needs, we have *not* been practicing "natural theology"[49] in the traditional Catholic sense—so to speak, in the basement. For

we do not take for granted the autonomy of reason, assuming that it is capable of demonstrating stringently the bases of faith, as if these had nothing to do with faith itself. On the contrary, we have shown that even the preliminary questions of faith—the reality of uncertain reality and the reality of God—cannot be known by pure reason, but only in a believing trust or in a trusting belief (in the wide sense of the term).

there is then no continuous, gradual, rational "procession" of man to God. But it is a question of a constantly new venture and of confidently taking a risk.

we are not upholding any highhandedness on man's part, with man taking possession of God. On the contrary, what is required of man is to lay himself open to reality, to respond to its challenge and claim, to accept its identity, significance and value, to recognize its ultimate reason, support and goal.

all things considered, therefore, we are not discussing any praeambula fidei *as a rational substructure of dogmatics based on rational arguments of pure reason. We are in fact seeking out "the" modern man in the place where he is actually living in order to relate the knowledge of God to the things that stir him.*

In this way we can make a fair criticism of the diverse "world views" held by non-Christians, without reinterpreting them theologically: both the position of the nihilistic atheists and that of the non-nihilistic (agnostic) atheists, as also ultimately the position of non-Christian believers in God, whether in a secular context or in that of the world religions.

Also in the theological interpretation envisaged here—it may be noted in anticipation—God will retain the primacy and the Gospel will remain the decisive criterion for the Christian. In the light of the Christian message it will be made clear

(i) that God is perceived as real in the reality of the world, since he discloses himself. The hidden God has the initiative: it is possible to know God because God makes himself known. Encounter with God, wherever and however it takes place, is God's gift. Man's "demonstration" of God's reality is always based on God's self-demonstration in reality for man.

(ii) that what is expected from man is not a neutral reaction, but a recognition in trust of the truth of God as it discloses itself to him. In this sense any believing trust on man's part, wherever and however it appears, is an effect produced by God operating in the reality of the world. And this always means for man a kind of conversion: turning away from his own selfishness, turning to the wholly Other.

(iii) that the Gospel will remain the decisive criterion. It does not simply provide an answer to our human questions, but even transforms this human, all-too-human questioning. It is an answer to these questions in their new form. In this sense it is a criticism, purification and deepening of human requirements. Hence Christian theology is in any case more than a theology adapted to these requirements.

b. In taking account of the modern outlook, does it still need to be stressed that theology may not pass over the other sciences and attempt itself to give *a total explanation of reality*. This is perhaps what representatives of "critical rationalism" fear, allergic as they are to the "theological heritage of philosophy," "theories of redemption," and to theology as a whole.[50] That such fears are groundless may be seen from the fact that our theology has

nothing against the ideals of accuracy, precision and efficiency, as upheld by the natural sciences, as long as the latter do not attempt without more ado to extend their methods from watches and computers to man's mind, which is neither a watch nor a computer.

nothing against science's objectivity, neutrality and freedom from values, as long as neither its presuppositions nor its social obligations and consequences are ignored and commitment is not excluded.

nothing against mathematization, quantifying and formalizing of problems, as long as no one is so lacking in a sense of humor as to assume that these methods serve to provide an exhaustive explanation of such phenomena as love and grace.

obviously nothing against natural science as the basis, not only of technology and industry, but also of the modern world picture as a whole, as long as the methods proper to other sciences are permitted at the same time—the social and cultural sciences for instance and perhaps even philosophy and theology.

in brief, nothing against critical rationality in science as a whole and in theology in particular, if this does not mean a certain kind of "critical rationalism," a rationality uncritical toward itself: a rationalism, that is, which makes a mystery of the rational, which seeks to deal with all questions of politics, aesthetics, morality and religion, only by methods appropriate to the natural sciences; and for this very reason, despite all its insistence on fallibility and revisability in regard to solutions of individual problems, it represents as a whole that kind of total dogmatic interpretation—claiming to be critical—with which it is always ready to reproach theology and which for its own part is no less open to the suspicion of ideology.

Should not theologians too be aware of their debt to the "tradition of critical thinking"?[51] The boldest of them in antiquity, the middle ages and modern times have had no small part in the enlightenment of mankind in regard to mythologies, ideologies and obscurantism of all kinds. Yet they have little use for making a mystery of reason. Even according to Adorno-Horkheimer's "Dialectic of Enlightenment," the supposedly very intelligent social technicians are in fact anything but true enlighteners. They have made the principle of thinking behind the Enlightenment into an instrument of social organization and with its aid have set up that technological system of control which negates the very thing which the Enlightenment intended by way of freedom, equality and happiness. It should be added that the great initiators of the Enlightenment—philosophers like Descartes, Spinoza and Leibniz, Voltaire also, Lessing and Kant, then natural scientists like Copernicus, Kepler, Galileo and Newton—would never have thought of forthrightly denying any dimension beyond that of mathematical-natural scientific reason. In this sense these great rational thinkers—by no means members of a professional substructure, which also exists—are wrongly called "rationalists," representatives of an "ism," blind to the wholeness of reality.

"Critical rationalism" overlooks the complexity of reality. "The real can be met with in a variety of ways and consequently take on a very different character. The reality of the atomic physicist is different from that of the Platonic philosopher, the reality of ordinary life different from that of religious experience. Considered in regard to its content, reality is fissured; differences appear with every change of focus. Evidently there is not simply *one* solid reality, but many different planes of reality. But this means that we cannot and may not turn a particular aspect into absolute reality: that would only lead to a mutiny of the other aspects."[52]

c. Obviously the development of the secular world and secular science presents an enormous *challenge to theology*: a challenge to critical theological introspection. The task today, which surpasses the powers of one generation of theologians, is no easier than that of the Greek and Latin Fathers of the second and third centuries or of Scholasticism confronted with Aristotelianism in the thirteenth century or of the Reformers of the sixteenth century. Today also the task can be effectively accomplished—as we are striving to do here—only against the background of this present world, as it really is, with the aid of the sciences and experiences of the present time, with an eye on the practice of the individual, of the Church, of society. The more therefore the theologian knows of this world, through the natural sciences, psychology, sociology, philosophy and—today less than ever to be forgotten—history, but most of all through his own experience, so much the better will he be able to fulfill his theological task.

Serious theology does not claim any elitist, privileged access to the truth. It claims only to be a scholarly reflection on its object with the aid of a method appropriate to this object, a method whose usefulness—as in other sciences—is to be proved by results. Theology can never be content to be graciously tolerated within a field where conclusions are notably inexact and lacking in binding force, as if "religious truth" were similar to "poetic truth." The rules of the game in theological science are not in principle different from those of the other sciences. It should not be thought that irrationality, unjustifiable reactions, subjective decisions are permissible here: arguments, information, facts, are not to be shut out; existing intellectual and social situations are not to be unconditionally authorized; there must be no partisan justification of certain dogmas, ideological structures, even forms of social domination. For serious theology it is not a question of rewarding simple faith or cementing an ecclesiastical system, but—always and everywhere—of seeking the whole and entire truth.

On the other hand, serious theology does not claim any complete, total possession of the truth, any monopoly of truth. It claims to be no more than scholarly reflection on its object from *one* particular standpoint, which is anyway one *legitimate* standpoint among others. Theology can never be a comprehensive, systematic world view, worked out down to the smallest details and rendering ultimately superfluous any further reflections of sociologists, psychologists, economists, jurists, medical experts and natural scientists. In theological science we cannot appeal to any authorities whatsoever to relieve us of the duty of attending to critical arguments, to evade the competition of ideas, to suppress temptations to doubt, to exclude the possibility of error on the part of certain persons or in certain situations. No science—theology no more than any other science—can take as its object *all* aspects of human life and action. But if, for scholars in other fields but likewise concerned with man, it is a question mainly of analysis of dates, facts, phenomena, operations, processes, energies, norms, for the theologian it is a question of *ultimate* interpretations, objectives, values, ideals, norms, decisions, attitudes. The often tormenting but perhaps nevertheless liberating questions about an ultimate why and wherefore, whence and wither, cannot—as we saw—be classified as emotional reactions and therefore not the legitimate object of our science. Hence the questions of theology do not touch merely a *part* of what men are and do.

They touch the most fundamental *aspect* of *all* that men are and do. From this *one* aspect theology examines *all* the strata of human life and action; from the one basic aspect *everything* can find expression, from this aspect the theologian must face *all* questions.

The theologian must not permit anyone to hold him back from this task, not even the leaders of his Church to whom he feels bound in loyalty. In disputed questions the tendency is to refer Catholic theologians to the Church's "teaching office," just as diplomats are referred to the "foreign office" for comments in certain cases. In fact this ecclesiastical "teaching office" in recent times, particularly from Rome, has taken a stand—fallibly or infallibly, after invoking the Holy Spirit—on all possible questions, but with a preference for sins and very special dogmas. I have dealt with this subject elsewhere.[53] But if this "teaching office" mostly knew *a priori* and without too much study "what is not permitted," it spoke for the most part only very generally and abstractly about "what is" positively "permitted." In the last five hundred years—to go no further back—no solemn doctrinal statement has been issued by Rome on the critical question of what Christianity really means, what the Christian message really implies, any more than on the Mafia or on the force of the seventh commandment in its own country. Evidently they are less concerned in Rome with some things than with others, as one may observe—perhaps with a rueful smile—after the experience of so much attention roused there from the very beginning by one's books.

For his part, the theologian can only perform his duty and exercise his responsibility of struggling unobtrusively to find an answer which he can justify before Church and society. This he should do undauntedly, in freedom, even if it means once again receiving from his headquarters, not help, but shots in the back—which might once have been fatal. He does not go on this way—as elderly prelates constantly fear—"alone." Even though a few "lone wolves" could not damage Catholic theology, the author is not vicious enough to be one of them. He wants to be in the "vanguard" and not an "outsider": one with his community, bound by its great tradition, united with its leaders and its teachers. In this way precisely he will be more and more involved in "the cause," the great cause of Christianity, without ever being able to claim infallibility for himself.

In this basic attitude we must now again broaden our horizon: after the challenge of the humanisms, we want first to face the challenge of the world religions before presenting against the total horizon of the modern world the *Christian* message, in order to show what it means to be a Christian today.

III. The Challenge of the World Religions

Christianity claims to be more than simply "religion." Christian theologians, following the example of Karl Barth and "dialectical theology," have protested vigorously against the conception of the Christian faith as "religion" and even—like Dietrich Bonhoeffer—demanded a "non-religious" interpretation of biblical concepts.[1] There is a great deal of truth in all this, as will become clear in our exposition of the New Testament message. But, whatever attitude we adopt to the theological question, from the standpoint of the comparative study of religion, Christianity does seem to be one religion among others: in this sense—we may perhaps paraphrase, since the concept can scarcely be unequivocally defined in view of the diversity of religions—it is a particular social realization of a relationship to an absolute ground of meaning, to an absolutely final concern, to something with which I am unconditionally involved.

1. Salvation outside the Church

For the first time in world history, it is impossible today for any one religion to exist in splendid isolation and ignore the others. Today more than ever, Christianity too is brought into contact, discussion and confrontation with other religions. To the extension of the geographical horizon of religion at the beginning of modern times there has been added in our own time an enormous extension of the historical horizon.

Revalued religions

The great world religions are recognized as a fact in Christendom today and—at least provisionally—as a permanent fact. This is not something that could always have been taken for granted. But the breakdown of the Christian missions in the countries of the Asian higher religions—in which a decisive part was played by catastrophic, quasi-infallible, wrong decisions by Rome, shamefacedly corrected centuries too late, but also by the equally long Protestant absenteeism—was cruelly brought home after the

Second World War to missionaries of the post-colonial age from North Africa to Korea. Unfortunately, in view of the minimal proportion of Christians, particularly in Asia (probably only .5 per cent in China and Japan, a little more—2 per cent—in India), this situation is likely to persist.

Is it not a fact that the more significant the religion of a country was, the less significant was the missionary success? The greater from the start the political weight of a country, the more difficult the Christian mission? May not those Asians perhaps be right who regard the four hundred years of the Christian missions in Asia—the home of all great religions—as merely one episode in the rich history of these highly gifted peoples over thousands of years? Was even that episode perhaps possible only as a result of the alliance of the clergy with the colonial powers at a time of political and cultural weakness? Is it now past, together with the end of Western colonial rule—shamelessly exploited to a degree by the Churches—and the end of the political, economic and legal privileges of the Christian missionaries?[2] Nor do recent developments particularly of the higher religions akin to Christianity lead us to expect much by way of sensational progress in the immediate future. However much Muslims and Jews are in political conflict with each other, they are not thereby brought any closer to Christianity. And the tremendous political revaluation which both Nehru's new India and particularly Mao's China—and finally, as a result of the oil crisis, the Arab states—have experienced makes the Christian mission in the Near, Middle and Far East still more difficult, if not altogether impossible.

Only now is it becoming clear how the epochal mistaken decisions (in liturgy, theology, church discipline) and faulty developments particularly in the Catholic Church—contrary to the better understanding of the Jesuit missionaries at the time—are almost irreparable. If Christendom at the time had not been so narrow-mindedly Western, if the missionaries had enjoyed the same freedom as the first Christian missionaries in the Hellenistic Roman Empire, the history of Asia and its religions might have taken a slightly different course. The Japanese Catholic Shusaku Endo in his novel *Silence*[3] presents dramatically the whole complex of problems of the missions in the seventeenth century with reference to the historic apostasy of Christovao Ferreira, missionary to Japan and Jesuit provincial. The conclusion must be that the tree of a Hellenized Christendom cannot simply be uprooted from Europe and replanted in the "swamp" of Japan, which has a completely different culture. It is surprising how vigorously Japanese Christians discuss all this even today.

Meanwhile—as a result of Vatican II[4] and the new missionary awareness on the part of the World Council of Churches[5]—the attitude within Christianity toward the world religions has become somewhat more positive, although with few signs of repentance for the past or acknowledgment of guilt: instead of the former contempt, esteem, at least in principle; instead of neglect, understanding; instead of propaganda, study and dialogue. Several centuries too late, with official blessing, the attempt is being made to liberate Christianity from its European-American, Latin-Roman wrappings: now at last we have as far as possible native clergy and bishops, more appropriate pastoral methods, the vernacular in worship, African Masses, services with prayers of the Islamic Sufis, Indian dance forms. Of course all this seems to succeed in the Church more in practice than in theory: up to now neither proclamation nor theology has become Chinese to the Chinese, Japanese to the Japanese or Indian to the Indians. But the fact cannot be overlooked that from Rome and Paris to Bangalore, Calcutta, Colombo, Tokyo and Canberra individuals and whole working groups are striving to discover and evaluate the true inspiration, the great concerns, the wealth of Islam, Buddhism, Hinduism, Confucianism and Taoism, and make them fruitful for Christian proclamation and theology.

The theological consequences of this rethinking are obvious. We are evaluating afresh the universal perspectives of the Bible (in Genesis, Romans, Acts, John's prologue): that God is Creator and Conserver of all men, that God operates everywhere, that he has made a covenant with all men (the "cosmic covenant," with Noah), that—according to the New Testament—he wills the salvation of all men without respect of persons and that non-Christians too as observers of the law can be justified.[6] In fact, then, there is salvation outside the Church. In addition to particular, there can be seen a general, universal salvation history.[7]

The other religions were regarded formerly as lies, works of the devil and—at best—vestigial truth. Now they count as a kind of ("relative") revelation through which innumerable individuals of ancient times and of the present have experienced and now experience the mystery of God. Formerly they seemed to be ways of damnation. Now they are recognized as ways of salvation—whether "extraordinary" or "ordinary" is a matter of dispute among scholars—for innumerable persons, perhaps indeed for the majority of mankind. They are therefore "legitimate" religions and represent in fact all the religion that is possible in a particular social situation, with forms of belief and worship, concepts and values, symbols and ordinances, religious and ethical experiences, which have a "relative validity,"[8] "a relative, providential right to exist."[9]

Wealth of the religions

If any Christian—particularly a strictly Evangelical theologian—wants to raise objections at this point, he should reflect calmly on the fact that every religion in the concrete is certainly a mixture of faith, superstition and unbelief. But can a Christian overlook the devotion and concentration with which people in the world religions have tirelessly sought—and also found—the truth? Do not all religions—or, if not the nature religions, at least the ethically higher religions—start out from the same perennial questions which open out behind what is visible and palpable and beyond one's own lifetime? Whence come the world and its order, why are we born and why must we die, what decides the fate of the individual and of mankind, how are moral awareness and the existence of ethical norms explained? And do not all religions seek to do more than interpret the world, to find in practice a way to salvation out of the misery and torment of existence? And do they not all regard lying, theft, adultery and murder as sinful and defend as a universally valid practical criterion something like the "golden rule" (Do not do to others what you would not have done to yourself)? No one who has the slightest knowledge of the world religions can dispute these facts:[10]

> *Not only Christianity, but also the world religions are aware of man's* alienation, enslavement, need of redemption: *inasmuch, that is, as they know of man's loneliness, addiction, abandonment, lack of freedom, his abysmal fear, anxiety, his selfish ways and his masks; inasmuch as they are troubled about the unutterable suffering, the misery of this unredeemed world and the sense and nonsense of death; inasmuch as they therefore await something new and long for the transfiguration, rebirth, redemption and liberation of man and his world.*
>
> *Not only Christianity, but also the world religions perceive* the goodness, mercy and graciousness *of the Divinity: inasmuch, that is, as they know that the Divinity, despite its closeness, is distant and hidden, that the Divinity itself must bestow closeness, presence and revealedness; inasmuch as they tell man that he may not approach the Divinity as a matter of course, confident in his own innocence, that he is in need of purification and reconciliation, that he needs sacrifice for the remission of sin, that he gains life only by passing through death; in fact, that in the last resort man cannot redeem and liberate himself, but is thrown back on God's all-embracing love.*
>
> *Not only Christianity, but also the world religions rightly heed the* call of their prophets: *inasmuch, that is, as they receive from their great prophetical figures—models of knowledge and behavior—inspiration, courage and strength for a new start toward greater truth and deeper understanding, for a breakthrough toward revival and renewal of the traditional religion.*

It is unfair to compare simply the great founders and reformers of the world religions with Christianity. Their work of reform and restoration can be seen in its proper light only by comparing their achievements with the religious situation as they found it. Then Hinduistic Brahmanism can be seen as "reformed" Vedic polytheism, Buddhism as reformed Brahmanism, Islam as reformed Arabic Animism. And the question then may be thrust on us once more: were not Buddha, Confucius, Lao-tse, Zarathustra, Muhammad, impelled by the same great, final questions to which we have just been alluding? Are not the Hindus perhaps seeking in Brahman (not the personal God, Brahman), the Buddhists in the Absolute, the Chinese in the Tao and the Muslims in Allah one and the same mystery of mysteries, one and the same ultimate reality? Naturally each religion has at the same time its own character and its own riches which are often not noticed by Christians. A few comments may help to throw light on this.[11]

a. The religions which originated in *India*—particularly Hinduism and Buddhism—are permeated by a primitive experience and a primitive hope of this subcontinent, so wealthy and yet so unspeakably poor and so often visited by catastrophe: that life is suffering and new life engenders new suffering and that nevertheless a conquest of suffering, a liberation and a redemption must be possible.

Hinduism: the "eternal," ancient, indigenous religion of India, which was not instituted but simply grew and to which no special god can be assigned. It is impressive in its basic mystical attitude, its unlimited open-mindedness and tolerance, its recognition and assimilation of alien ideas, its striving for infinity and capacity for development, which have produced —alongside primitive, mythological polytheism and orgiastic rituals—also intensely strict asceticism and meditation (Yoga) and such lofty philosophies as that of Sankhya. It is an open, growing religious system: a living unity in an amazing variety of views, forms and rites. All this with but firm, universally valid, dogmatic teaching on God, man and world; also without Church or mission, and yet with unbroken continuity and indestructible vitality. The goal sought through the most diverse forms of asceticism and meditation is redemption from the cycle of births in the absorption of the self into the cosmos or unity with the Absolute.

Buddhism: certainly the strongest counterpart to Christianity. It has existed since 500 B.C. in India, but is now largely outside that country, in a great variety of forms from Ceylon to Japan, where it permeates the Shintoistic state cult. It is impressive in a way different from Hinduism, as the "middle way" between the extremes of sensual passion and self-torment, between hedonism and asceticism. Buddha's "four noble truths"—the central point of his sermon in Benares—are meant to lead to an understanding of why we suffer, in order thereby to remove the cause of suffering and suffering itself. The cause of suffering is nothing other than selfishness, self-assertion, thirst for life, which leads from rebirth to rebirth. By recognizing and extinguishing this thirst for life we are able to conquer suffering which makes up life. Untroubled by such questions as that of the ultimate origin of the world, man should tread the eightfold path to the annihilation of suffering: right views, right willing, right speech, right action, right living, right effort, right recollection, right meditation.

Man is not to do nothing, but to remain untouched by anything he does or experiences. Instead of Hindu asceticism there has to be an insight into nothingness. In this way release is possible: release from selfishness, self-assertion, blindness; release therefore from suffering by deliberately not piling up life's positive and negative data (karma); finally release from the endless cycle of births of the phenomenal world of life through extinction or liberation in the infinite. Thus even the older, classical Hinayana Buddhism—the "lesser vehicle" of enlightenment toward complete liberation from suffering and passion—rightly or wrongly described as "atheistic" from the Western standpoint, seeks to answer man's final questions, to be a way of salvation. Admittedly, it was able to conceive this salvation —in a reverential *theologia negativa*—only as nirvana ("extinction"). This is nothingness, inasmuch as it means a liberation from all suffering, all sensuality, all limitation. An emptiness without images and without desire, which at the latest in Mahayana Buddhism—the "greater vehicle"—acquires a positively theological content and is identical with the Absolute and happiness, so that a strong awareness of transcendence, a richer worship and probably also a more perfect form of meditation become possible. This is a monastic world-denial which quite frequently turned out to be a mastery of the world, as is shown by the great cultural achievements of Buddhism in India, Indonesia and Japan.

b. *Chinese religion:* from the beginning of this century it has often been called Chinese Universism, since it centers on the harmony of the universe. About 500 B.C. it split up into two branches, Confucianism and Taoism, represented by the two opposed philosophers Kung Fu-tse and Lao-tse, both supposedly contemporaries of the Buddha. Today Chinese religion, insofar as it has been able to survive at all in the Maoist system, is a syncretist construction made up of Confucian, Taoist and Buddhist elements.

Confucianism, which grew out of the earlier Chinese religion, more pragmatic, concentrating on interpersonal relationships, says little about relations with a superhuman reality and is often understood as pure humanism, attaching importance only to the cultivation of human values —especially love (benevolence=*jen*), but also honor, duty, tact, taste—and secular ordinances. But the presupposition of its realization of a natural humanity, the basis of its prosaic, rational ethic and the meaning of all moral regulations is that in all his actions man should adapt himself to the eternal world order. He is expected to adapt himself harmoniously to the cosmic-moral law: a moral law *in* man, in which the "way" (*tao*) of heaven is made known. Man unites in himself the polar forces of the world: yang and yin, male and female principles which represent heaven and earth. The five basic human relationships between prince and subject, father and son, elder and younger brother, husband and wife, friend and friend, are given special consideration. The basic ethical attitude must be piety. And also both the cardinal virtues (benevolence, integrity, propriety, wisdom and sincerity) and the "golden rule": all these things were already known in this pre-Christian ethic.

Thus the Confucian conception of the harmony of man with heaven has profound theological implications. Wisdom consists in knowing the will of heaven. The noble person should feel reverence not only toward great men and the words of the saints, but primarily toward the commands of heaven. Confucianism then, like Hinduism and Buddhism, exhibits all the external characteristics of a religion: sacrifice to the gods and ancestors and an abundance of sacral actions for man's welfare. The state itself is seen as a religious institution and the ruler as representative of heaven (emperor worship). But heaven is understood as the personification of the cosmic and moral world order and as supreme spiritual power, directing the fate of men, and described also with personal features as "supreme ruler." A papal bull in the "rites controversy" (which was much more than a controversy on rites) forbade the early Jesuit missionaries to equate "heaven" or the "supreme ruler" with God.

While the humanistic ideology of Confucianism in practice emphatically makes man the measure of all things, raising him up out of nature, *Taoism* by contrast—stressing its superiority in metaphysical depth—demands man's integration into the cosmos, an attitude which encouraged both cosmological-ontological and natural-scientific questions and at the same time closely linked ontology and ethics. Instead of advanced culture, patriarchal society and self-confident knowledge, Taoism advocated a return to unspoilt nature, spontaneity, mysticism, to the ideals of a time before Confucius' enlightened epoch. Man had to find again his natural greatness or smallness and the measure of the cosmos was again to be the measure of man. This precisely is the way in which man will overcome death. Philosophical speculation and rules for rejuvenation exercises (breathing exercises, dietetics, sexual rules) are intermingled here. Finally personality will be submerged again into the formless and have eternal life. Taoism and Buddhism were found in China, but today—together with Confucianism—are largely—finally?—covered over by Maoism, which has many of the features of a substitute religion.

c. *Islam:* in the immense spaces between Morocco and Bangladesh, the steppes of Central Asia and the Indonesian islands, the religion of Muhammad prevails. It is the youngest, simplest, but also least original of the world religions, and arose in Arabia in the seventh century after Christ. And yet it possessed as scarcely any other religion did the formative power of a faith which has shaped its adherents into a uniform type. A simple profession of faith—dependent on Judaism and Christianity—

forms the object of Islamic dogmatics: there is no God but God and Muhammad is his prophet. Five simple basic duties or "pillars" of Islam form the object of a very highly developed Islamic jurisprudence: besides the profession of faith, the daily ritual prayer, taxation to help the poor, fasting in the month of Ramadan and the pilgrimage to Mecca. The idea of surrender to God's will permeates everything and suffering too must be accepted as the result of his irrevocable decision: "Islam" means submission, devotion, to God. The result of all this is a basic equality of all men before God and a supranational Muslim sense of community: a brotherliness which—at least in principle—could overcome racial differences and even the Indian caste system.

Apart from the division into three denominations in the generation after Muhammad, of which two remain today (the Sunnis as the great majority and a small number of Shiahs mainly in Persia), Islam in its long and embattled history, by contrast with other religions, has had no significant cleavages or schisms nor has it had to face competition from any newly founded religion (there have of course been setbacks—as in other religions—notably in Spain, Sicily and Eastern Europe). All this has strengthened the Muslim claim to be the final and definitive religion which, together with others, recognizes Abraham, Moses and particularly Jesus as prophets, but sees Muhammad as the last and greatest, the "seal of the prophets." Islam has also produced great achievements in theology, mysticism, poetry and culture in the past (in the Middle Ages) and extraordinary missionary successes in the present (in Central and Eastern Africa). Without sacraments, cult images, without holy orders or an infallible central authority, it is a religion easy to grasp and has an amazing power of resistance (as in the Soviet Union), cohesion (among the Arabs) and expansion (already more than half the Africans are Muslims). This is a religion to be reckoned with, even in politics, particularly in view of the national rebirth of the Arab states.

This is the world of the religions. It is only in the religions that we really find "religion." And, if we want to speak about religion, we need to know the religions. Yet we have to break off at this point. What could be said about Christianity if there were only a few lines to say it in? The depths and riches of man's religious experiences, as they find expression in the innumerable forms, shapes and ideas of the great religions, are ineffable. We can neither pin down the particular religions in their different stages (foundation, development, stabilization, eventually dissolution) nor—which is more important for the comparative study of religions—even merely indicate their convergences, affinities, meeting points, mutual influences and intermingling.

2. *Bewildering consequences*

It is typical of Christianity's new self-understanding that we are prepared today to take note of this immense ocean of religion, to explore it and even to find in it not only ways to perdition, but—as we saw—up to a point ways to life, even to man's all-embracing well-being, to "salvation." Some—and not only Christian missionaries—are however asking anxiously about the consequences for Christianity as the one way of salvation, if the other religions can in some sense at least also be ways of salvation. Are not these consequences confusing and dangerous?

Anonymous Christianity?

It was fifty years before the discovery of America when the Council of Florence (1442) defined what had become, from the time of Origen and particularly Cyprian, the traditional teaching of "*no* salvation outside the Church."[12] The council in fact made use of the strong words of Augustine's disciple, Fulgentius of Ruspe: "The holy Roman Church firmly believes, professes and proclaims that none of those who are outside the Catholic Church—not only pagans, but Jews also, heretics and schismatics —can have part in eternal life, but will go into eternal fire, 'which was prepared for the devil and his angels,' unless they are gathered into that Church before the end of life."[13] That is to say: all those outside are a *massa damnata*, an abandoned heap, excluded from salvation.

Five hundred years later and certainly none too soon, the Second Vatican Council conceded freedom of religion and belief. In a specific declaration on the subject it commended the world religions and in the Constitution on the Church acknowledged that all men of good will—that is, Jews too, Muslims, adherents of other religions, and even atheists ("who, without blame on their part, have not yet arrived at an explicit knowledge of God")—"can attain to everlasting salvation,"[14] at least in principle. Formerly it was thought that only baptized and practicing Christians gained salvation. Then it was admitted that individual non-Christians had a chance of salvation. Now apparently the religions as such are also regarded as possible ways to salvation.

If we compare the old and the new teaching, we cannot fail to notice an epoch-making reversal of the attitude to those outside the "holy Roman Church." What has happened here? Not much, some Catholic theologians soothingly claim, only a new "interpretation" of the infallible, ancient dogma: "Church" no longer means as at Florence "the holy Roman Church," but "properly speaking," "rightly understood," "fundamentally," *all* men of good will, who all "somehow" belong to the Church. But is not the whole of good-willed humanity thus swept with an elegant gesture across the paper-thin bridge of a theological fabrication into the back door of the "holy Roman Church," leaving no one of good will "outside"? The formula, "no salvation outside the Church," is then as true as ever, because all in fact are in the Church from the very beginning: not as formal, but as "anonymous" Christians[15] or—as we ought logically to say—"anonymous Roman Catholics."

Does this solve the problem? Are the masses of the non-Christian religions really marching into the holy Roman Church? Or is this going on only in the theologian's head? Anyway, in reality, they—Jews, Muslims, Hindus, Buddhists and all the others, who know quite well that they are completely "unanonymous"—remain outside. Nor have they any wish to be inside. And no theological sleight of hand will ever force them, against their will and against their desire, to become active or passive members of this Church—which in fact still seeks to be a free community of faith. The will of those who are outside is not to be "interpreted" in the light of our own interests, but quite simply respected. And it would be impossible to find anywhere in the world a sincere Jew, Muslim or atheist who would not regard the assertion that he is an "anonymous Christian" as presumptuous. To bring the partner to the discussion into our own circle in this way closes the dialogue before it has even begun. This is a pseudo-solution which offers slight consolation. Is it possible to cure a society suffering from a decline in membership by declaring that even non-members are "hidden" members? And what would Christians say if they were graciously recognized by Buddhists as "anonymous Buddhists"?

It must be admitted that a pseudo-orthodox stretching of the meaning of Christian concepts like "Church" and "salvation" is no answer to the challenge of the world religions. It is an evasion of the challenge and we may easily be caught by it from behind. Are we not thus in danger, without noticing it, of diminishing the reality of Christianity merely to save an infallible formula? Without wanting to do so, are we not making the Church equivalent to the world, Christendom to humanity? Does not Christianity thus become a religious luxury and the Christian ethos superfluous? As a result of such a conception, does not Jesus in the last resort become all too easily an avatar for the Hindus, a bodhisattva for the Buddhists, one of the prophets for the Muslims? All these are questions raised by many older missionaries which are not always answered by progressive young men and their teachers. Incidentally, this too is an illustration of the fact that opinions claiming to be progressive may not be adopted uncritically. Partisan thinking and toeing the party line are out of place in a theology which is concerned with the truth. And if the conservatives in the Church are not always right with their answers, they are however very often right with their questions.

Superior ignorance?

The challenge remains. Whatever is said positively and rightly about the religions may not subsequently be withdrawn and manipulated to the credit of the Church or Churches. Salvation outside the Church: why not honestly admit it, if this is in fact what we assert? This is the only way to take the other religions quite seriously, only in the light of this assumption can we take a realistic view of the problems.

Thus anyway the main question has been set out so much more clearly. If the Christian proclamation—otherwise than formerly—affirms the riches instead of the poverty of the religions, what has it to offer itself? If it perceives obvious light everywhere, to what extent does it want to bring "the light"? If all religions contain truth, why should Christianity in particular be *the* truth? If there is salvation outside the Church and Christianity, what is the point of the Church and Christianity at all?

In this respect too there are pseudo-solutions. Here it is not enough to make assertions. Least of all can we merely decree in dogmatic, "dialectical theology"—following in the footsteps of Luther, like the earlier Barth,[16] Bonhoeffer,[17] Gogarten,[18] and (less radically) E. Brunner[19] and H. Kraemer[20]—without a closer knowledge and analysis of the real world of the religions, that religion is nothing other than "natural theology," self-important, sinful revolt against God and unbelief; that Christianity is not a religion since the Gospel is the end of all religions. Nor can the problem as a whole be dismissed—as it is by other Protestant theologians—with a supercilious "we don't know," as if it were no concern of theirs. If Christian theologians have no answer to the question of the salvation of the greater part of mankind, they cannot be surprised when people react again as they have done in the past: Voltaire pouring out his scorn for the Church's presumption in claiming to be the sole way of salvation; Lessing content with an enlightened indifferentism, with his fable of the three rings, all supposed to be genuine and yet perhaps none of them really belonging to the father. It is all too easy to reverse the assertion of "dialectical theology," that the world religions are merely human projections, and declare that Christianity itself is a pure projection, the expression of absolutist-exclusive wishful thinking.

There is no mistaking the fact that the problem has become more acute. With the development of gigantic new continents, the world religions were mainly an external, quantitative challenge to Christendom. But now they have become an internal, qualitative challenge, not only for a few rationalists but for the Christian Churches themselves. It is no longer merely the fate of the world religions which is in question, as in the colonial epoch. Now the fate of Christianity itself is in question.

In saying this of course we are already approaching the other aspect of the problematic. The challenge of the world religions must be understood both actively and passively. For the world religions themselves are also challenged.

3. *Challenge on both sides*

The situation of the world religions has not become any easier as a result of modern developments. This fact too must be considered completely dispassionately. Christianity may not belittle other religions in order to be seen to be great itself. Yet neither can an idealizing of the world religions—easier from a distance than close at hand—help to clarify the position. Our systematic outline of the main points of the different religions must not be allowed to conceal their negative side: their quite concrete defects, weaknesses, errors; their actual remoteness from their original positions; their very mixed and contradictory structures (Islam's large-scale veneration of saints and use of amulets; popular Taoism's magic, alchemy, elixirs of life, immortality pills; a Chinese anniversary celebration made up of archaic, Confucian, Taoist and Buddhist elements; Hinduism in which almost anything is possible).

No leveling down

Lots of *parallels* between the different religions are noted as a matter of course in works on the phenomenology of religion[21] or in studies of universal history like those of Arnold Toynbee:[22] parallels in doctrine, ritual and life. And perhaps the concrete life of a religion is more important than abstract teaching. If, for example, all those beings venerated by invocations and oblations are designated "gods," then we must admit that polytheism is practiced, not only in the other religions but also in Christianity. Or may we judge them by different standards more or less from the very beginning? Is it permissible to see on the one hand only the lofty ideal and, on the other, the reality falling short of the ideal? In the fabulous golden temple of the Sikhs at Amritsar, at the sacred Ganges in Benares, in Buddhist Kandy or even Bangkok, the Christian is impressed but scarcely tempted to convert to a non-Christian religion. But on the other hand could a Sivite Hindu be expected to perceive a call to Christianity as a "monotheistic revolution,"[23] overthrowing the old gods, in a Neapolitan or Bavarian baroque church or even at St. Peter's in Rome? It would be easier to perceive such a call in a small North African mosque at the edge of the Sahara.

But, despite all parallels—positive or negative—the *differences* cannot be smoothed out, even on the purely phenomenological plane, although the temptation to do so was understandable at the beginning of the modern comparative study of religions. Even the phenomenologist of religion distinguishes in principle between a primitive and a highly developed religion, between one that has simply grown and one that has been founded, between a mythological and an enlightened religion, and particularly between an expressly monotheistic and expressly polytheistic or even pantheistic religion. As a result of the premature joy of discovery, in the concrete comparison of parallels and preliminary stages, it very often happens that only the similarities and not the contrasts are brought out. But identical concepts ("sacred meal," "baptismal bath," "sacred scripture") are misleading and obscure the very wide range of meaning. The relative value of the phenomenon ("prophet," "veneration of saints") within the whole is the decisive factor. For less sensitive noses incense and sandalwood may smell equally pleasant or unpleasant. Bible and Koran feel the same when handled, a sacrifice in any form is still a sacrifice. But the universal concept of sacrifice is equivocal and covers completely dissimilar things: the most lofty aspirations *and* the most dreadful aberrations, for some unselfish devotion and for others insane slaughter. And the fact that we do not have to wash our hands before reading the Bible creates a highly significant difference between ourselves and Islam: in the last resort Christianity is not a "book religion." And neither for Jews nor Christians was the Jordan ever a sacred river as the Nile, Euphrates and Tigris were for other religions. Nor does Christianity have a holy city in the same sense as Jerusalem was holy for the Jews or Mecca for the Muslims. The Christian Crusades were not only un-Christian, but unnecessary.

And how different are the "prophets" of the nations when we look beyond the externals: an ascetic in India or an itinerant thinker in China, a philosopher in Greece or a nabi in Israel. How different are the ideas of final liberation and salvation: elevation to the Idea or absorption in meditation, experience of nirvana, harmony with the Tao or submission to God's will. "Love of man" is not the same for Master Confucius as for the Master from Nazareth. And even the evil spirit is not the same for Zarathustra (Mazdaism, Indian Parseeism) and in the Old and New Testament. The even greater differences from the primitive religions cannot be listed here; but the fact, for instance, that the very gentle, peaceable Fiji Islanders no longer eat human beings in this century as they did in the last cannot be inessential—at any rate for visitors to the islands. All too frequently people overlook the differences particularly here. Because of the striking failure of the Christian missions and, for instance, the dissolving of ancient tribal cultures in Africa,[24] they overlook the immense enlightenment and liberation from the fear of demons, from magic, natural forces, irrationality, cruelty, impersonal, unsocial and unhistorical attitudes, brought by the Christian missions: undoubtedly a demythologizing and de-demonizing, a spiritualization and a humanization on the grand scale.

Hence, although the truth in other religions can be recognized, it cannot be disputed that there are substantial differences between the fearsome grimacing gods of Bali—the marvelous island of the gods—and a wall with icons of Orthodox saints in Zagorsk; between sacred temple prostitution and Christian consecration of virgins; between a religion whose symbol is the lingam (stone phallus), reproduced a thousandfold in the same temple, and another whose symbol is the cross; between a religion proclaiming a holy war against the enemy and a religion which makes love of enemies an essential part of its program; between a religion of human sacrifice (at least twenty thousand human beings sacrificed within four days at the consecration of the main temple in Mexico in 1487) and a religion of everyday self-sacrifice for men. Even the cruelties of the Spanish *conquistadors* and the Roman burning of heretics—not in fact in accordance with the Christian scheme but contradicting it, not Christian but unequivocally anti-Christian—do not cancel out these differences.

With all respect then for the magnanimously tolerant reformed Hinduism of Sarvepalli Radhakrishnan, president of the Indian state, who was influenced just as much by nineteenth-century European theological liberalism as by Vedanta, everything is not ultimately one and everything is not simply identical. The enlightenment and liberation, demythologizing and de-demonizing, the spiritualization and humanization which the Christian faith can bring must be apparent to some degree to anyone who knows India's concrete reality or even merely reads accounts of the disastrous influence of Hindu religion in its concrete forms on the situation of the subcontinent: the catastrophic economic and social effects even today of the worship of the cow, which even Gandhi supported, of the caste system which no legislation can overcome, of the shocking superstition and the charlatanry of many gurus, among other things.[25] In view of the radical contradictions between the religions, it is altogether too simple to compare them—as in an old and oft-quoted Buddhist parable—to a number of blind beggars each touching the same elephant: one grasps a foot and thinks it is a tree trunk, another an ear and takes it for a palm leaf, a third the tail and thinks it is a rope, but none of them gets the whole elephant.[26] And what if somebody blindly takes a tree trunk for an elephant? In the infinite variety of religions, in their ideas, forms and languages, Radhakrishnan with others rightly notes a genuine spiritual experience of the Absolute, rightly too a hidden agreement which makes possible a radical intellectual communication between the different religions. But the agreement must not be simplified, the differences must not be smoothed out, the utterly ambiguous inward religious experience must not be made absolute, as if all the religious statements that can be articulated, all revelations and creeds, authorities, Churches, rites and manifestations were irrelevant by comparison with this inward religious experience.

Radhakrishnan can be so tolerant only because—despite all syncretisms —his is a very qualified and in fact specifically Hindu tolerance (based on the authority of Vedanta). Eastern religions like Hinduism and Buddhism, predominantly mystically oriented, for which the experience of absorption is central, also represent in their own way an absolute claim to exclusiveness: unlike the prophetical religions (Judaism, Christianity, Islam), for which the event of revelation and God's authority are central, the very fact that they do not exclude other religions involves a claim to include them all.[27] Hinduism absorbs all other religions. Buddhism as supreme doctrine of salvation accepts other religions as lower grades for the ordinary man: it is more a resigned acceptance and tolerance than a readiness to recognize the validity of doctrines opposed to its own. In a later existence—it is assumed—the person now involved in error will come to the right belief.

Undoubtedly, in the course of history, there have been a number of "archetypal men." According to Karl Jaspers, Buddha, Confucius, Socrates, Jesus (not Moses, whose influence was too limited, and not Muhammad, whose originality was too slight) revealed ultimate human possibilities and thus set up irrefragable standards for human existence, with the result that they have influenced men's mental attitudes to an extraordinary extent and at an extraordinary depth for thousands of years.[28] Undoubtedly the essential content of their questions and answers is the same for each one. Common features can be seen in their proclamation and their way of life, in their position in regard to man and world, but also in the mythicizing in connection with their birth, vocation, temptation, as well as their "elevation" after death. But it is likewise indisputable that these different "archetypal men" cannot simply be integrated into a totality of truth: "they stand beside each other disparately; they cannot be combined into a single man who would more or less follow all their ways at once."[29] Only a naïve ignorance of the facts makes it possible to overlook or assimilate the distinctive qualities of each one. A decision can scarcely be avoided.

Any sort of cheap feeling of superiority, of aloofness from all religions and their alleged hairsplitting—possible not only on the part of philosophers, but also of theologians—leads for those who have lost sight of the central contents of faith to complete indifference. No amount of leveling down, abstracting, generalizing takes us anywhere. Obscuring the differences by bringing all religions under one umbrella has hitherto left the different religions completely unaffected. We know too much about the individual religions for a Christian dogmatic theologian to venture to declare openly that they are merely arbitrary, human fabrications, a Hindu universalist that they are all substantially the same or a secular humanist that they are all merely opium of the people.

Can we afford to dispense with intellectual discussion, quite dispassionately and modestly, with a readiness on both sides to listen? Not only among the Western religions, but also among those of the East, the *question of truth* cannot be left out or trivialized. The centuries-old rivalry—often very cruel and again virulent today—between Hinduism and Islam (as with India and Pakistan), Hinduism and Buddhism, Buddhism and Neo-Confucianism, confirms this. Even in the Asian religions not everything is a matter of indifference.

Certainly the question of truth and the question of salvation are not to be confused, as they were formerly in Christian theology. The modern Christian "theology of religions" is right in saying that people can attain salvation in other religions and in this sense the latter can reasonably be called "ways of salvation." But the question of salvation does not make the question of truth superfluous. If Christian theology today asserts that all men—even in the world religions—can be saved, this certainly does not mean that all religions are equally true. They will be saved, not because of, but in spite of polytheism, magic, human sacrifice, forces of nature. They will be saved, not because of, but in spite of all untruth and superstition. To this extent the world religions can be called ways of salvation only in a relative sense, not simply as a whole and in every case. However much truth they exhibit in certain respects, which Christians must affirm, they do not offer *the* truth for Christians. The Christian could not agree that he might just as well be a Buddhist, Hindu, Confucian or Muslim. When, for instance, Christians accept Yoga or Zen Buddhism ("Christian Yoga" or "Christian Zen"), it is not as a religion or ultimate belief, but as a method or a way of "illumination": a Zen detached from its religious foundations, attractive to many modern men because of its stress on the non-intellectual and on a mysticism which does not involve any flight from the world, on repose and silence, on the dynamic opening up of the deep strata of the human mind—interesting alike to theologians and philosophers and to psychiatrists and psychotherapists.[30]

Admittedly, we are not yet saying what the truth is for Christians, but certainly that there must be that critical, self-critical discussion with the world religions the criterion of which cannot be compassion but only truth: a searching diagnosis of the world religions which seeks not to judge but to help.

Helpful diagnosis

The world religions today then are challenged, in Toynbee's sense of "challenge and response": summoned to answer. Encounter with Christianity means for the Asian religions an impetus of unforeseeable extent, to critical introspection, to purification and deepening of the foundations of their own faith, to fertilization with Christian ideas and the development of fruitful possibilities. The analysis of Neo-Hinduism by comparison with classical Hinduism holds analogously for other religions: strengthening of monotheism, suppression of idolatry and elimination of crude corruptions, ethicizing of religion, support for social reforms and a modern system of education, new interpretation of the Upanishads and the Bhagavadgita; interest even in the figure of Jesus, although detached from his historical manifestation (John's Gospel is interpreted in a mystical sense), and serious consideration of the "eternal principles" proclaimed in the Sermon on the Mount.[81] We may also recall the influence of the Christian idea of peace—despite the failure of Christian practice—on the peace propaganda of Buddhism (peace pagodas in Rangoon and Hiroshima). The whole process of reform and renewal—and this means concentration, deepening, spiritualizing and in this very way simultaneously opening up and unifying —in which Christendom to the widest extent is involved today, represents a considerable challenge to those religions which on the whole—despite all new self-consciousness in the newly awakened nations, despite all Buddhist world councils, pan-Islamic conferences, a number of deepenings and counteradvances—have been unable to develop any similar spiritual dynamism (to say nothing of the African tribal religions).

If there is to be fruitful discussion on the same plane, it is urgently desirable for the world religions to develop scientific theologies in the modern sense which would be on a par with Christian theology: not merely an elevating meditation, but a self-critical reflection. Christian theology was the first to take up modern methodical-scientific thinking and indeed has helped considerably to produce such thinking. Genuine dialogue is possible only when there is a genuine plurality of theologies. This is not to say that Christian theology should or even could directly provide a scientific Hindu, Buddhist, Confucian, Taoist or Islamic theology. But Christianity can provoke a serious discussion by working out objectively and without prejudice a history of religion, phenomenology of religion, psychology, sociology and theology of religion.[82] To controversial theology between the Christian denominations there must be added a controversial theology between the different religions. Or, better, an ecumenical theology in the broadest sense of the term.

The world religions attempted in a variety of ways to get out of discussion with Christianity by mental encapsulation. While in the West a merciless analysis of the religious crisis prevails, in the East there is still apologetic self-assertion. But are isolation and demarcation any less impossible the longer they are maintained in the midst of modern traffic links and means of communication? The intellectual immobility and the often centuries-old rigidity even of the great Asian religions were perhaps less dangerous in quieter times. But today these religions, whether they want to or not, have to come to terms not only with Christianity but also with the hurly-burly of modern secular developments. These developments, coming from America, Europe and the Soviet Union in a thousand ways, with their great fascination and suggestion, are taking hold irresistibly of the countries of the Near and Far East and have already—as in China and Japan—flooded them with industry, science, culture, technology and politics. In a variety of ways this means a secularization of the religious, but often too a new sacralizing of the secular, which is the presupposition for substitute religions or quasi-religions: that elevation to the absolute of the nation, the social class, or science, or even a person, which scarcely brings happiness either to nations or to individuals. Atheistic, dialectical materialism in particular, in the form of missionary Communism—Marxism-Leninism or Maoism, given the stamp of "science"—is everywhere in competition but also in not unfruitful conversation with Christianity *and* world religions. The manifold failure of Christianity *and* the world religions in regard to the humanizing of man, to involvement in the struggle for justice, peace and freedom, and their influence—more divisive than unitive—on mankind as a whole form the somber background before which the whole development goes on.

"Modernity" for all these countries means not only a flood of economic and social structural changes, but a completely new form of awareness. In this respect it is not so important if some "sacred cows" and other religious specialities—against which even the All-Indian Congress has hitherto been largely powerless—have to be sacrificed to this development. The development becomes disastrous only where the religions concerned—apart from individual attempts as on the part of Indian reformed Hinduism or Japanese Zen Buddhism—have scarcely produced convincing answers to the new, basic questions, momentous for the future of both individuals and nations. In order, in this respect too, to put it quite concretely in the form of a helpful diagnosis—obviously again without any claim to completeness or thoroughness in terms of the history of religion—we shall refer to some critical points which must be taken seriously at least as questions and which demand a thorough discussion with Christianity.[33]

a. Even Islam, although oriented to Judaism and Christianity, thinks completely *unhistorically* in regard to its own proper revelation. Its foundation, the Koran, from the first to the last sura, is said to have been dictated to the prophet by an angel directly from a book kept in heaven: it is inspired even to the very word (verbal inspiration) and therefore infallible in every sentence (inerrancy, infallibility). That is why a person has to wash his hands before reading the Koran, but not before reading the Bible. The Koran is in no way the word of man, but directly God's word. In Islam the book takes the place of Christ: Koranology replaces Christology.

Yet the question—which might also be applied to the sacred writings of Hinduism or Buddhism—remains: will Islam in the long run be able to shut itself off from the intensive Western study of the Koran? Will it be possible to admit what no Muslim scholar—not only in Afghanistan—can openly say today, that the Koran contains a great deal of later, adventitious material and also includes a very human history? Is there any point then in claiming to find already outlined in the Koran—which, because of God's omnipotence, really recognizes no laws of nature—all modern developments up to electricity, microbes and satellites and to come across even the conquest of the moon, Islam's sacred symbol (admittedly of comparatively recent, Turkish origin)? Have not scientific-technical developments and state authority (particularly in Turkey) from the beginning of this century largely deprived the Koran of its force as a book of law and imposed an adaptation of religion at many levels (we need only recall the position of woman and the harem, and the civil and penal code as a whole)? How could Islam, with a theology highly developed in the Middle Ages but now unproductive, build into its system modern scientific, technical, economic, cultural, political achievements which had their origin elsewhere? Would not the Islamic equation of the will of Allah or the Koran with the secular legal system have to be abandoned? Would not law, the natural, historical and social sciences have to be developed independently of any foundation in the Koran, even if this were to lead to a tremendous upheaval of the authoritative traditions? Would not states under the influence and bearing the mark of Islam (Arab states, Pakistan, Afghanistan) then have to become neutral in religion (like Nehru's India) and "holy wars" have to cease? Can the internal unrest and deep crisis of adaptation, which have taken hold of Islam like other religions, be overcome in the long run by remaining rigidly on the defensive, by Islamic, conservative renaissance and an appeal to the achievements of their own past? Is there not necessary here too a new spiritual effort and a new attempt to come to terms with its own history, with Western civilization as a whole, and thus also with Christianity?

b. The great religions of the East, especially Hinduism, Buddhism and also Indian Jainism, think in circles: they have a *cyclical world picture*, in the light of which everything—both the course of the world and the life of the individual—is predetermined.

But here too the questions arise: Is not this belief the reason for that individual fatalism and social determinism which present one of the main obstacles to the social betterment of the masses, particularly in India? Will the Asian peoples, in taking over and digesting modern science and technology, be able to avoid coming to terms in a spirit of self-criticism with the idea of a linear or dialectical progress of history, as maintained by the Jewish-Christian tradition, then by Islam and finally by modern consciousness as a whole, including Marxism? A view of history which—quite unlike these religions—takes the unique individual person, his life and his work, absolutely seriously? What is an exuberantly fantastic cosmogony, world history and mythology supposed to mean today? What is to be made of the idea of continual new births in accordance with the law of karma, of action, the automatic recompense of all life's deeds—doctrines taken over by Buddha as self-evident dogmas from Upanishad Brahmanism?

c. The conception of return and rebirth is linked in Hinduism (essentially a collection of religions) with the *religious caste system*, which however was always decisively rejected by Buddhism and Sikhism (a monotheistic Indian-Islamic mixed religion). A man is born for his whole life (that is, each time) into the caste—in India there are about three thousand of them, with four basic types. His occupation, marriage partner and whole style of life are in principle decided by his caste.

The questions: Is not such a conception in flat contradiction to the view beginning to prevail all over the world of the basic equality of all men? Is not the apparently ineradicable caste system in India—although legally abolished, especially for the "untouchables," the pariahs without a caste—together with the economically and socially devastating cow worship, still the greatest burden for the new, democratic India? Is it not the reason why Hinduism, unlike Buddhism, apart from special cases, remains restricted to India? Does it not contradict the modern spirit of occupational mobility, the idea that it simply does not matter what or where one is and that everything—including a person's domicile—can change and change again? Is not the religious caste system—hitherto the protecting and supporting framework of the different syncretist forms of religion—in the process of dissolution in the great cities like Bombay, Delhi, Madras and Calcutta, and can this remain without repercussions on the religious consciousness?

d. According to the originally monastic conception (priority of the monastic community, with laypeople attached to the monasteries) represented not only by strict Buddhism, but also by the most influential Hindu philosophy—Sankhya's classical Vedanta system—earthly reality, life, joy, love, personality, self, the world as a whole, are ultimately nothing but insubstantial, *unreal appearance* (*maya*).

Questions: How could such a conception of the unreality of the world be lived credibly in a technocratic civilization, by men in a very real world of turning lathes, assembly lines, laboratories, computers, administrative buildings? Does the doctrine of the double truth offer a way of escape from reality as it is? And can the far-reaching cosmic *pessimism* of Buddhism—always criticized on this account by Chinese Neo-Confucianism—resulting from the mutability and triviality of all earthly things, linked as it is with supreme *indifference toward the social needs* of men, be an answer to the new hopes of the emerging nations of eastern

Asia? Will not Buddhism in its propaganda for peace and justice have to adapt itself still more to secular events or to the originally Christian slogans? And is not this same ethical *passivity* also the weak point of the individualist-quietist mysticism of Chinese Taoism, to which a speculative philosophy of nature and silent absorption without desire into the source of things are more important than all the social virtues? Could the laudable, passive Eastern tolerance ever go so far as to be unable any longer to produce the prophetic "No" to coarse and superstitious forms of religion, to adulteration and degeneration of belief in God, to social abuses and inhuman conditions?

e. By contrast with Buddhism and Taoism, Chinese Confucianism stresses the priority of ethics over metaphysical speculation. Although in Neo-Confucianism (from the twelfth century), which looks for heaven in man, ethics becomes metaphysical and metaphysics ethical, Confucianism nevertheless remained perhaps the "most secular" religion of the East, interested more in the harmony of men with one another and with the cosmos than in the hereafter or nirvana. Could Confucianism perhaps be Asia's religious future?

Here too however counterquestions arise: Do not Confucianism and Neo-Confucianism in particular hold to an almost unparalleled *traditionalism:* ancestor worship, overvaluation of age, priority of classical education, structure of state and society based on the model of the patriarchal family? Contrary to the original pluralism of Chinese thinking, does not this mean the ideological support of a rigid social system of unique duration? Does it not amount to the anti-progressive state ideology of the "kingdom of the mean," of isolated, ancient China: one of the most conservative ideologies of world history, which has been called the codification of the order of subordination? Is not this the reason why Chinese Confucianism, weakened as a result of the fall of the emperor in 1912—just as the Russian Orthodox Church, the most traditional branch of Christendom, likewise closely linked with the former political system, lost power in 1917—came under the jurisdiction of Communism in 1949 and since then, together with Taoism, has been regarded as the enemy of all progress and restricted by the Communists as much as possible in its opportunities of exercising any influence? Indeed, did not Maoism as it replaced the religious by the Marxist content become for many in practice the successor of Confucianism: for all its positive intentions and genuine achievements, taking over the system of state orthodoxy and from time to time also the old Chinese isolationism and raising the divine emperorship to life in a new form?[34]

4. Not exclusiveness, but uniqueness

Unhistoricity, circular thinking, fatalism, unworldliness, pessimism, passivity, caste spirit, social disinterestedness: the concrete questions to be put to the world religions in order to provide a diagnosis, so far as this is possible here, may be summed up under these headings. They are not however to be understood as relieving Christianity of its own burdens. For most sociologists the American racial system, particularly as represented by very biblically minded Protestants, is merely a variant of the caste system. And the notorious social backwardness of Catholic countries and their susceptibility to Communism can scarcely be ascribed to Confucian traditionalism. Christian Europe—Christian only in name, according to Gandhi, and in reality worshiping Mammon—and the aggressiveness, the lust for power and profit, of Christian countries in Asia, Africa and South America have compromised the Christian message for a long time ahead. But we shall be continually coming across the problems of Christendom. Here meanwhile, to clarify the situation, it should be stated that the great world religions are now seen to be not less but more open to question than Christianity. The countries of Asia and Africa today are under the utmost pressure as a result of the rapid transition from pre-industrial culture to modern industrial society: a pressure which is quite different from that which capitalism exerted in its early stages in Europe. Because of the shockingly low standard of life and the constantly increasing population, because of international competition and national independence, the level of production is being extended and raised as rapidly as possible, industrialization and technical training consequently pushed forward and pre-technical structures removed. The result will be a new consciousness, an unavoidable secularization and thus too a destruction of religious traditions, values, institutions, the desacralization of which has in fact scarcely begun.

Christian existence as critical catalyst

None of this means that the traditional religions must disappear. They too undergo change and can slowly adapt themselves. The absorbent power of the Eastern religions is enormous and we may have to reckon—as in the Arab states—not so much with a decline as with a renaissance of the world religions in the post-colonial age. Perhaps we must also expect missionary drives outside Asia, although these may scarcely have any greater success than formerly. In the European Renaissance and classical period there was an affinity with Greek antiquity, in the Enlightenment with Confucian China. Today there are some (as earlier in Romanticism) who feel a certain affinity (always selective) with Indian spirituality, others with Zen Buddhism. But the significance of such phenomena—partly a matter of fashion—must not be exaggerated. What is more important for the future is the fact that the world religions are imperiled in a way they have never been before: by being ignored when their traditionalism breaks down, attacked when they attempt to resist, but in any case inwardly eroded and outwardly manipulated (Islam, for instance, as a useful tool for pan-Arabic or at least anti-Israeli policy). If under these circumstances they come up at all against religious indifference (especially in countries like Egypt and India where industry is just beginning) or inward aversion (among many educated people in highly industrialized Japan), or open aggression (in Communist China), the non-Christian religions too will not be able to avoid a basic rethinking of their position and thus a renewed and still more serious discussion with Christianity.[35]

As a result of their history, Western science and technology have accumulated far too many elements from the Jewish-Christian tradition to be taken over by other peoples without further questioning of their own religious positions. We have seen that the influence of Western civilization led to far-reaching changes of attitude on the part of Hinduism and Buddhism, particularly toward material goods, social justice, world peace and the meaning of history. But what of the importance of history, of progress, of the world, the significance of the individual, of woman, of human labor, individual freedom, fundamental equality, social commitment? On these and so many other questions now thrust on the non-Christian religions, Christian theology has been producing ideas methodically and systematically throughout the whole of the modern era. For the other religions, with modern scientific theologies still in their initial stages, these ideas might be no less useful than the achievements of Western natural science and technology for the industrial and cultural development of these countries. These possibilities may become a little clearer in the present book, without having constantly and explicitly to refer to the other religions.

What then are we to strive for, in accordance with the results of this compressed analysis in the light of Christianity?

Not the arrogant domination of a religion *claiming an exclusive mission and despising freedom. This danger, although unintended, arises as a result of the dogmatic repression of the problem of religion by Karl Barth and "dialectical theology." We do not want a narrow-minded, conceited, exclusive particularism which condemns the other religions in toto, a proselytism which carries on unfair competition and takes too restricted a view not only of the religions but also of the Gospel.*

We do not want the syncretist mingling of all religions, *however much they contradict one another, harmonizing and reducing and thus sup-*

pressing the truth. This danger, again unintended, arises from the liberal solution of the problem of religion, advocated by Toynbee and a number of experts in comparative religion. This is a crippling, dissolvent, agnostic-relativistic indifferentism, approving and confirming the other religions indiscriminately, which at first seems to be liberating and creative of happiness, but finally becomes painfully monotonous, since it has abandoned all firm standards and norms.

What we must strive for is an independent, unselfish Christian ministry to human beings in the religions. *We must do this in a spirit of open-mindedness which is more than patronizing accommodation; which does not lead us to deny our own faith, but also does not impose any particular response; which turns criticism from outside into self-criticism and at the same time accepts everything positive; which destroys nothing of value in the religions, but also does not incorporate uncritically anything worthless. Christianity therefore should perform its service among the world religions in a dialectical unity of recognition and rejection, as* critical catalyst and crystallization point *of their religious, moral, meditative, ascetic, aesthetic values.*

Seen in this way, Christian *missionary activity* would make sense. It would clearly be concerned not only with religions but with believers. But this would not mean that it was directed primarily to winning the greatest possible number of converts. The real aim would be to enter into genuine dialogue with the religions as a whole, giving and taking, in which the most profound intentions of the latter could be fulfilled. Thus it would not again come to a pointless, fruitless collision, with the Christian self-confidently but unsuccessfully attempting to prove the superiority of Christianity. There would be a genuine and fruitful encounter in which the other religions would be encouraged to bring out what is best and deepest in them. The truth of the other religions would be acknowledged, honored and appreciated; but the Christian profession of faith would not be relativized or reduced to general truths. In a word, then, there would be neither arrogant absolutism, not accepting any other claim, nor a weak eclecticism accepting a little of everything, but an inclusive Christian universalism claiming for Christianity *not exclusiveness, but certainly uniqueness.*

Common quest for truth

The religions of Asia, largely isolated in the course of history, could certainly learn a lot from such a critical-constructive encounter. But on the other hand Christian faith too could only gain from it. For example, in view of the excessive complexity of its dogmatics and the frequent preference of Christian piety for secondary matters and even secondary gods, Christianity might learn something from the strict simplicity of Islam, from its steady, unshakable concentration on the decisive reality of faith: the one God and his legate. Christianity could correct its all-too-anthropomorphic ideas of God the Father in the light of the reverent, more or less transpersonal (better than "impersonal") understanding of God on the part of the Asian religions: an understanding which made a lasting impression on Goethe, German Idealism, Schopenhauer, Jung, Huxley and Hesse—and rightly so. Christianity, still too much oriented to the "hereafter," might learn to appreciate the profound and concrete humanity of Chinese thought, the faith in the perfectibility and educability of man which was taken over from Confucianism into Maoism. Again it could learn from Islam possible solutions of the racial problem and the way to handle prudently relations with primitive peoples. Comparisons—for instance—between the Christian idea of the kingdom of God and the Buddhist nirvana, between our ethos and theirs, could be very fruitful.

Certainly Christianization must never again mean Latinization, Romanization, Europeanization, Americanization. Christianity is not simply the religion of the West. In the early days of the Christian Church there was a Palestinian and Greek, Roman and African, Coptic and Ethiopian, Spanish and Gaulish, Alemannic and Saxon, Armenian and Georgian, Irish and Slav Christianity. According to the Christian theology of the second century (especially Justin) and the third (especially the Alexandrians Clement and Origen), the divine Logos (*logos spermatikos*, "seminal word") was active everywhere from the beginning. But if the pagans Plato, Aristotle and Plotinus, or later—for others—even Marx and Freud could be "pedagogues" leading men to Christ, why not also the philosophers and religious thinkers of other nations? Does not the East offer forms of thought and organization, structures and models, within which Christianity could be conceived and lived just as easily as in Western forms?[36] As Gandhi pointed out, is not Jesus an Eastern figure, perhaps more open to an Eastern interpretation? Is not the personality of Jesus being intensively studied and freshly interpreted by important non-Christian thinkers in India?[37] Ought we not to distinguish in principle and practice between what is unacceptable to Christians in the religious aspects and what is completely acceptable in the cultural aspects of Hinduism, Buddhism, Confucianism, Taoism, Islam? Have not certain forms of Hinduism, Buddhism, Islamic mysticism grasped at a far deeper level than the Greeks—and still more than the "Critical Theory"—the New Testament truths of God's love, of peace, of vicarious suffering, even of justification by faith (Amida Buddhism)? Could not therefore all that which otherwise exists perhaps isolated and scattered, fragmentarily and sporadically, distorted and disfigured, be brought to its full realization in Christianity: without a false, antithetic exclusiveness, but with a creative rethinking, resulting in a new, inclusive and simultaneously critical synthesis? What then are the requirements for a Christianity of the future?

We need a genuine Indian, Chinese, Japanese, Indonesian, Arabic, African Christianity.

We need an oikoumene, *no longer in the narrow denominational-ecclesiastical, but in a universal-Christian sense: no longer based on missionary conquest of the other religions, but listening to their concerns, sharing their needs and at the same time giving a living testimony of its own faith in word and deed.*

We need a mission which, while fully alert to syncretist indifferentism, includes tolerance: while claiming absolute validity, ready to revise its own standpoint wherever this turns out to be in need of revision.

Criticism of the religions includes therefore—and this is often overlooked—self-criticism on the part of Christianity. The English translator and editor of the Japanese novel *Silence*, already mentioned, draws attention to this mutual theological giving and taking: "If Hellenistic Christianity does not fit Japan, neither does it (in the opinion of many) suit the modern West; if the notion of God has to be rethought for Japan, . . . so has it to be rethought for the modern West; if the ear of Japan is eager to catch a new strain in the vast symphony, the ear of the West is no less attentive—searching for new chords that will correspond to its awakening sensibilities."[38] In a number of points the self-critical reflection of Christian theology today is largely open to such an interchange of ideas: for instance, in its criticism of a solidly Hellenistic-physicistic understanding of Jesus' divine sonship. The same is true of the criticism of the mythological idea of a sin transmitted through physical generation, an idea spread in the Western Church since Augustine's time, but one which a Confucianist believing in man's goodness could never properly understand. There is further evidence of this openness in the stress now laid on a "hierarchy of truths," permitting the center of the faith to stand out as central and peripheral statements (like the Vatican dogmas on Mary and the Pope) as peripheral.

The fact should be stressed therefore that many problems in the dialogue with the non-Christian religions lie within Christian theology itself. It is of course understandable that not all the distinguished specialists for Islam; Taoism; Caodaism; Jainism; Hinayana, Mahayana and Matrayana Buddhism; and the still more numerous Hindu systems can follow with equal intensity the new and often very rapid developments of Christian theology. But, despite the difficulty that normally the theologian cannot also be a specialist in comparative religion nor the expert in comparative religion a specialist in systematic theology, we must still stick to this principle: if we are not to be talking at cross-purposes from the beginning in the dialogue between Christianity and the world religions, if we really want to meet one another, then in all our comparisons and confrontations we must *continually subject both factors in the comparison to a critical examination.* In a comparison, for instance, of the concept of "trinity," instead of merely dwelling on the exact interpretation of the Hindu "Trimurti" (Brahma as Creator, Vishnu as Preserver, Siva as Destroyer) or of the "Trinity of the Three Pure Ones" in religious Taoism, we ought at the same time to question critically the Christian doctrine of the Trinity. We should have to ask whether Greek and particularly Latin speculation on the Three-in-One—Augustine's psychological interpretation, refined by Aquinas' doctrine on relations, with the triangle symbol because of the "one nature"—really corresponds, as it attempts to do, to the biblical statements on the relationships of Father, Son and Spirit. Perhaps after such reciprocal questioning it would be easier to talk to an overtolerant Indian polytheist than to a strict Arabian monotheist. The same holds for comparisons with reference to incarnation, virgin birth, miracles, eternal life.

Thus even Christendom within its own field would *not simply* remain in *possession* of the known truth, *but would be in search* of the ever greater and so constantly new unknown truth: engaged in free discussion, bound by its own tradition but without dogmatic fixation, open to any good argument. Precisely by this means Christendom could more easily find its way back to the simple and unique grandeur of its message. With this message it convinced the world at the beginning and this is the message required of it again today.

But, with all our comparisons and all our efforts, both for an understanding of other religions and for a truly ecumenical Christianity, one thing must not be forgotten: it is a question *more of human beings* and their living experiences *than merely of concepts, ideas or systems.* In practice this means:

a. The modern world religions must not be understood or reconstructed in an archaic sense, *merely* in the light of the classical texts. They cannot simply be pinned down to the sterile, backward-looking elements in their tradition. Modern religions must be understood also as they see themselves today, when--for example—most Asians think of God far less impersonally than could be expected in the light of the ancient systems of Sankhya and others. Religions are not historical monuments which can be studied and understood only by scholars with the aid of texts. They are living faiths which are constantly freshly experienced by real men in the course of the history of religion. They are therefore to be intrepreted in a forward-looking spirit. They are open to new questions and are constantly raising new questions themselves.

b. A truly Indian, Chinese, Japanese, Indonesian, Arabic, African Christianity cannot be devised in the study. We should greatly overrate the resources of European-American theology if we thought its scholarly reflection, exegetical, historical and systematic analyses and comparisons could provide a concrete translation of the Christian message into other cultures. For this there is needed, as formerly for its translation into the world of Hellenism, the living experiences of concrete human beings from these cultures themselves.[89] Without such experiences, creative rethinking is impossible, a new ecumenical synthesis remains pure theory and a truly universal Christianity a beautiful postulate. European-American theology can of course create the conditions for such a translation. It can attempt to make clear, in a self-critical, scientific reflection on its own traditions with reference to other traditions, what is not essentially Christian from its very origin and what is essentially Christian. In the rest of this book we hope in this sense to make a modest contribution also to the discussion with the world religions: on the one hand to bring out, without dogmatic bias and with the utmost possible historical exactitude, the figure of Jesus and the original Christian message; on the other hand to make suggestions which should stimulate the comparison—often neglected—with other great figures in the history of religion.

And so now, after surveying as far as possible in a brief space the horizon of modern Christianity, we shall turn to the central question, the answer to which we have hitherto largely taken for granted: if there is supposed to be a difference both between Christianity and the world religions and between Christianity and the modern humanisms, in what does this difference consist? Christian? What is really Christian?

B. THE DISTINCTION

I. What Is Special to Christianity?

1. *The Christ*

The word "Christian" today is more of a soporific than a slogan. So much—too much—is Christian: Churches, schools, political parties, cultural associations, and of course Europe, the West, the Middle Ages, to say nothing of the "Most Christian King"—a title conferred by Rome, where incidentally they prefer other attributes ("Roman," "Catholic," "Roman Catholic," "ecclesiastical," "holy") which they can then without more ado simply equate with "Christian." Inflation of the concept of "Christian" leads—like all inflation—to devaluation.

Dangerous memory

It is a fact too rarely remembered today that this word—which arose in Antioch, according to the Acts of the Apostles[1]—was first used within the context of world history more as a term of abuse than as an honorable title.

It was so used about 112 by Pliny the Younger, Roman governor in the province of Bithynia in Asia Minor, when he consulted the Emperor Trajan about "Christians" accused of various crimes: his investigation had shown that they did in fact refuse to worship the emperor, but otherwise only recited a hymn (or perhaps a creed) to Christ as to a god and bound themselves not to commit theft, brigandage, adultery, breaches of faith.[2]

A little later, Cornelius Tacitus, a friend of Pliny, working on a history of imperial Rome, gave a more or less exact account of the great fire of Rome, generally ascribed to the Emperor Nero himself, who however shifted the blame onto the "Christians": the name was derived from someone executed by Pontius Pilate during the reign of Tiberius, a certain "Christus," after whose death this "pernicious superstition," like everything vicious and shameful, spread to Rome and there gained an immense number of followers.[3]

A little later again, but far less accurately, Suetonius, the emperors' biographer, reports that Claudius expelled the Jews from Rome, since they were continually creating disturbances at the instigation of Chrestus (*impulsore Chresto*).[4]

Finally, the earliest Jewish testimony is provided, about A.D. 90, by Flavius Josephus, the Jewish historian who was in Rome at that time. He mentions with obvious reserve the stoning in 62 of James, "the brother of Jesus, the so-called Christ."[5]

So much for the earliest pagan and Jewish testimonies. A great deal would have been achieved if it were remembered today also that Christianity is obviously not some sort of world view nor a kind of idealist philosophy, but has something to do with a person called Christ. But *memories* can be painful, as many politicians have discovered when they wanted to revise a party program. In fact, memories can even be *dangerous*. Modern social criticism has again drawn our attention to this fact: not only because generations of the dead control us, have their part in determining every situation in which we are placed and to this extent man is predefined by history,[6] but also because recollection of the past brings to the surface what is still unsettled and unfulfilled, because every society whose structures have grown rigid rightly fears the "subversive" contents of memory.[7]

Christians, Christian Churches, without remembrance. It seems to be precisely the opposite way round. The Christian Churches appear to be chained to the past. If they suppress history at all, it is the always sinister future which they dismiss in order to concentrate on the present state of the Church, assumed to be eternal, in dogma, worship, discipline, piety. We comfort ourselves with memories of the past, positively cultivate them in the Churches, in order to sustain the present. Cultivation in a general sense: we "cherish" age, honor what is old, old people, the elders; we venerate tradition and traditions; we restore churches, chapels, statues, pictures, hymns, theologies. But there is also cultivation in the special sense of "cult": Christian worship is essentially recollection. Is not this the reason why we have been reading aloud from the same book, continuously, for almost two thousand years? Is not this the reason why we have celebrated uninterruptedly the same meal—this is obviously what Pliny was talking about—which has been called from the earliest times *anamnesis* (recollection, remembrance), *memoria Domini* (commemoration of the Lord), and in which millions still take part on Sunday all over the world?

Oddly enough this very cult of remembrance has contributed to no small degree to wiping out the memory of the past. The texts were read aloud, often mumbled or sung in an unintelligible, ancient language and without any sort of explanation, in order to keep up the old custom and carry out a duty. The meal was celebrated, often scarcely recognizable beneath the ostentatious ceremonial, in order to satisfy religious needs. People cherished the past to avoid facing the challenge of the present and the future. The great tradition was acclaimed but confused with ideas which just happened to be handed down. The old were honored and the young forgotten, antiquity esteemed and the modern world neglected, restoration was taken in hand only to result—often unnoticed—in degeneration. Paper flowers were dusted when roses might have been cultivated.

Memory in itself could be a great opportunity, a springboard, flexible, with a free end permitting an immense leap. Memory can awaken past terrors as a warning, but it can also—more dangerously—rouse hopes which have not been fulfilled. Memory can curb the excessive power of the factual, can divert the pressure of existing facts, can break through the wall of reality, of what has been effected, can get rid of the present and open the way to a better future. Merely as recollection, it can do this at least for brief moments. Really *activated,* it can do this permanently. It can do so particularly stubbornly whenever it has remained undischarged.

Christianity means the *activation of memory.* As J. B. Metz—here linking up with Bloch and Marcuse—rightly insists, it is the activation of a "dangerous and liberating memory."[8] This indeed was originally the intention behind the reading of the New Testament writings, the celebration of the memorial meal, life lived in imitation of Christ, the whole, multifarious involvement of the Church in the world. Memory of *what?* The first pagan and Jewish accounts of Christianity, already quoted, belonging to the time of the later New Testament writings, bear the mark of this obviously disturbing memory. But the account of these world-transforming memories is found mainly in the Christian testimonies themselves. Memory of *what?* This basic question arises for us today in the light of both the New Testament and Christian history as a whole.

Firstly: the diversity, contingency and up to a point the inconsistency of the writings contained in the New Testament collection are often and rightly stressed. There are detailed, systematic, didactic writings, but also answers—showing little sign of planning—to questions from the addressees. They include a brief letter, scarcely two pages long, written for the occasion, to the master of a runaway slave, and the more long-winded description of the acts of the first generation and their chief figure. There are gospels, mainly giving an account of the past, and prophetical epistles directed to the future. Some are in an easy-flowing style, others are carelessly written; language and ideas show that some are by Jews, others by Hellenists; some were written at an early date, others almost a century later.

We are certainly justified in asking what really holds these very different twenty-seven "books" of the New Testament together. The answer, according to the testimonies themselves, is amazingly simple. It is the memory of one Jesus, called in New Testament Greek *Christos* (Hebrew *mashiah,* Aramaic *meshiah:* Messiah=Anointed).

Secondly: the rifts and breaks, the contrasts and inconsistencies in tradition and in the *history of Christendom* as a whole are likewise often and rightly stressed. For centuries Christians formed a small community, for centuries afterwards a large-scale organization; for centuries they were a minority, then became a majority for long ages; the persecuted became the powerful and even quite often the persecutors. Centuries of an underground Church were followed by those of a state Church; centuries of martyrs from the time of Nero by those of court bishops from the time of Constantine. There were ages of monks and scholars and—often intertwined—those of ecclesiastical politicians; centuries of the conversion of the barbarians and the rise of Europe were succeeded by centuries of the Holy Roman Empire, newly founded and again ruined by Christian emperors and popes; there were centuries of papal synods and centuries of councils aimed at reforming the papacy. After the golden age of both Christian humanists and secularized Renaissance men came the ecclesiastical revolution of the Reformers; then came the centuries of Catholic or Protestant orthodoxy and again of evangelical awakening. In sum: there were times of adaptation and times of resistance, dark ages and the Age of Enlightenment, centuries of innovation and centuries of restoration, periods of despair and periods of hope.

Again it is not surprising that people ask what really holds the very oddly contrasting twenty centuries of Christian history and tradition together. And again there is no other answer than this: it is the memory of the one Jesus, called also throughout the centuries "Christ," God's last and decisive ambassador.

This however really amounts to a first answer to our opening question: admittedly very provisional and sketchy, but remarkably concrete insofar as it relates to this person. And now that we have not been sparing in our criticism of the Christian position, but slow to give our own answers, we shall perhaps be expected to follow this up with equally clear, positive statements about Christianity. Self-criticism is of little interest unless it includes a modest degree of self-confidence; yet it is just the latter which many Christians, insisting on trust in God, seem to lack, although it is the very thing expected of them by people who hold different views.

Taking concepts at their face value

The outlines will have to be filled in later. But at a time of theological confusion and conceptual obscurity plain speaking is necessary. The theologian is doing no service to Christians or non-Christians if he does not call things by their true names and take concepts at their face value.

As we saw,[9] Christianity today is confronted with the *world religions* which likewise reveal truth, are ways to salvation, represent "legitimate" religions and can indeed also be aware both of the alienation, enslavement and unredeemed state of men and of the presence, the grace, the mercy of the Divinity. The question is thrust upon us: if all this is so, what is there special about Christianity?

The answer—still sketchy but exactly to the point—must be: according to the earliest testimony and that of tradition as a whole, according to the testimony of Christians and non-Christians, the special feature of Christianity—it will eventually become clear that this answer is far from being banal or tautologous—is this *Jesus himself*, who is known even today by the ancient name of *Christ*. Isn't this so? None of the other religions, great or small, however much they may occasionally venerate him even in a temple or in their holy book, would regard him as ultimately decisive, definitive, archetypal for man's relations with God, with his fellow man, with society. The special feature, the most fundamental characteristic of Christianity is that it considers this Jesus as ultimately decisive, definitive, *archetypal* for man in these various dimensions of his. And this is just what was meant from the beginning by the title of "Christ." It is not without reason that this title, together with the name of "Jesus," developed even then into a proper name.

As we also saw,[10] Christianity is confronted at the same time with the *post-Christian humanisms*—evolutionary or revolutionary—which likewise stand for all that is true, good and beautiful, which uphold all human values and fraternity together with freedom and equality, and which often intervene more effectively for the development of the whole man and of all men. On the other hand, the Christian Churches and theologies also are seeking in a new way to be human and philanthropic: modern, relevant, enlightened, emancipatory, dialogic, pluralist, involved, adult, worldly, secular—in a word, human. The question is inescapable: if all this is so, or at least ought to be so, what is there special about Christianity?

The answer—again only sketchy, but still quite precise—here too must be: according to the earliest testimony and that of tradition as a whole, the special feature of Christianity is again this *Jesus himself* who is constantly freshly known and acknowledged as *Christ*. Here too there is a countertest: none of the evolutionary or revolutionary humanisms, however much they may occasionally respect him as man and even set him up as an example, would regard him as ultimately decisive, definitive and archetypal for man in all his dimensions. The special feature, the most fundamental characteristic of Christianity is that it considers this Jesus as ultimately decisive, definitive, *archetypal*, for man's relations with God, with his fellow man, with society: in the curtailed biblical formula, as "Jesus Christ."

From both perspectives the conclusion emerges that, if Christianity seeks to become relevant, freshly relevant, to men in the world religions, to the modern humanists, it will certainly not be simply by saying later what others said first, by doing later what others did first. Such a parrot-like Christianity does not become relevant to the religions and the humanisms.

In this way it becomes irrelevant, superfluous. Actualization, modernization, involvement, *alone*, will not make it relevant. Christians, the Christian Churches, must know what they want, what they have to say to themselves and to others. For all their unreserved open-mindedness toward others—this is not to be stressed again here—they must speak of what is their own, bring it home, make it effective. Hence Christianity can ultimately be and become relevant only by activating—as always, in theory and practice—the *memory of Jesus as ultimately archetypal:* of Jesus the Christ and not only as one of the "archetypal men."[11]

If then today the North American theologian, occupied mainly with psychology, sociology, politology, the intellectual as a committed Christian in France, Spain, Germany or Holland, the students' chaplain in Islamic Jakarta, the missionary in Africa or India, or even a Catholic-educated Roman *contessa* helplessly asks what is really Christian, what on the whole distinguishes Christianity from other religions or quasi-religions, philosophies or world views, it is because they are looking for the answer in some sort of abstract axioms, concepts, principles, ideas. But they cannot find it there, since Christianity—as its name alone suggests—cannot in the last resort be reduced to any kind of eternal ideas, abstract principles, human attitudes. The whole of Christianity is left hanging in mid-air if it is detached from the foundation on which it is built: this Christ. An abstract Christianity is of no importance to its followers or to the world. In point of fact Christians ought to know this. But they often assume with astonishing naïveté that they also know already who and what this Jesus Christ is. So they do not expect any answer from that quarter. They look for it elsewhere: in some kind of philosophy or world view, in youth culture, in black culture, in India, in a romantic Third World or any other cultural or ideological refuge of modern times, in psychoanalysis or in sociology, in cybernetics, linguistics, behavior study, in the very latest wave of science. But the question remains: how does one know so certainly as a Christian who and what this Jesus Christ is? Is he perhaps precisely the unknown in Christendom and outside it, himself making Christianity the great unknown?

For the time being we may point out once again quite briefly that it seems possible to answer the questions urgently raised on all sides by Christians about the *distinctive feature of Christianity* only by reference to the person of this Christ. This claim can be tested by a few examples.

First: Is a meal celebrated with deep faith in God by Christians and Muslims in Kabul, in which prayers from the Christian and Sufi traditions are used, a celebration of the Christian eucharist? Answer: Such a feast can be a very genuine, even very laudable religious service. But it would be a Christian eucharistic celebration only if it specifically recalled the person of this Jesus Christ (*memoria Domini*).

Second: If a very devout Hindu with faith in God bathes in the Ganges at Benares, is this equivalent to Christian baptism? Answer: From a religious standpoint bathing in this way is certainly a very significant and salutary rite of purification. But it would become Christian baptism only if it took place in the name of Jesus Christ.

Third: Is a Muslim in Beirut who upholds everything said of Jesus in the Koran—and that is a great deal—already a Christian? Answer: He is a good Muslim as long as the Koran remains binding on him and in this way he may gain salvation. But he becomes a Christian only if Muhammad is no longer *the* prophet with Jesus as his precursor, but if this Jesus Christ becomes authoritative for him.

Fourth: Is the defense of humanitarian ideals, human rights and democracy in Chicago, Rio, Auckland or Madrid Christian proclamation? Answer: This is a social commitment urgently required of individual Christians and the Christian Churches. But it becomes Christian proclamation when what is to be said in the light of this Jesus Christ is brought home practically and concretely in modern society.

Keeping in mind the clarification already given in the first part of this book and anticipating the concrete details to be discussed in this second and in the third and fourth parts, in order to avoid confusion and unnecessary misunderstandings, without discriminating against other views, with conviction but without undue emphasis, we can and must venture to make the following plain demarcations:

> Christian *does not mean everything that is true, good, beautiful, human. Who could deny that truth, goodness, beauty and humanity exist also outside Christianity? But everything can be called Christian which in theory and practice has an explicit, positive reference to Jesus Christ.*
>
> A Christian *is not just any human being with genuine conviction, sincere faith and good will. No one can fail to see that genuine conviction, sincere faith and good will exist also outside Christianity. But all those can be called Christians for whom in life and death Jesus Christ is ultimately decisive.*
>
> Christian Church *does not mean just any meditation or action group, any community of committed human beings who try to lead a decent life in order to gain salvation. It could never be disputed that commitment, action, meditation, a decent life and salvation can exist also in other groups outside the Church. But any human community, great or small, for whom Jesus Christ is ultimately decisive can be called a Christian Church.*
>
> Christianity *does not exist wherever inhumanity is opposed and humanity realized. It is a simple truth that inhumanity is opposed and humanity realized also outside Christianity—among Jews, Muslims, Hindus and Buddhists, among post-Christian humanists and outspoken atheists.*

But Christianity exists only where the memory of Jesus Christ is activated in theory and practice.

Now all these are primarily distinguishing formulas. But they are not merely theoretical, still less empty formulas. Why?
They refer to a very concrete person.[12]
They have behind them the Christian beginnings and the great Christian tradition.
They provide a clear orientation for both present and future.
They are therefore helpful to Christians and yet can also win the agreement of non-Christians, whose convictions are respected in this way and whose values are expressly affirmed without being appropriated by dogmatic sleight of hand for Christianity and Church.

Just because the concepts of what is Christian are not diluted or arbitrarily stretched, but precisely grasped, just because the concepts are taken at their face value, two things are possible: to maintain open-mindedness for all that is non-Christian and at the same time to avoid all un-Christian confusion. In this sense these distinguishing formulas—however sketchy they must seem for the time being—are of great importance. Provisional as they are, they serve to distinguish what is Christian.

Against all well-meant stretching, blending, misinterpreting and confusing of the meaning of Christian, things must be called by their true names. The Christianity of the Christians must remain Christian. But it remains Christian only if it remains expressly committed to the one Christ, who is not any sort of principle, or an intentionality or an evolutionary goal, but—as we shall later see more closely—a quite definite, unmistakable, irreplaceable person with a quite definite name. In the light of this very name Christianity cannot be reduced or "raised" to a nameless—that is, anonymous—Christianity. To anyone who thinks a little about the two words anonymous Christianity is a contradiction in terms, like wooden iron. Being humanly good is a fine thing even without the blessing of the Church or theological approval. Christianity however means a profession of faith in this one name. Nor can Christian theologians spare themselves the question: what or who is really concealed behind this name?

2. *Which Christ?*

The Christ of piety?

Philosophers have taken more trouble with the Platonic dialogues, to find out who Socrates really was and what he wanted, than quite a few

Christian theologians have done with the original Christian documents, to discover what lies behind the name of Jesus Christ. They think they can take it for granted that Christians know all about him and all that they have to do is to speculate more deeply on this knowledge, apply it in practice and make it freshly relevant for man and society today. Why, how can they—so naïvely, we must say—take this knowledge for granted? If for the time being we set aside an understanding gained without much reflection from the Bible, it must be assumed that knowledge of Christ comes mainly from Christian piety and Christian dogma.

Christian experiences of the one Christ however can be very different. And the same experiences can be for some the reason why they have kept the Christian faith, for others the reason why they have given it up. There are Christians who got to know Christ at an early date as the pious, ever friendly divine Saviour and have never parted from this "sweet Jesus": consequently the social-critical Jesus of Pasolini's film on St. Matthew's Gospel leaves them anxious and disturbed. Others, perhaps in the youth movement between the two world wars, got to know him as the great leader and still sing as enthusiastically as ever "Follow me, says Christ our hero," even though it is not always clear today in which direction they are to go. Others again were touched by his gentle and humble heart, so that for them "the Sacred Heart" became a proper name, whereupon the theologians began to develop a sublime theology of the "personal center." For very many the name reminds them of Christmas and the "holy infant so tender and mild": every year they sing the old hymns and forget it all promptly by New Year's Eve at the latest. Others again recall his name and think simply of God on earth and ignore the fact that the Father is not the Son and the Son is not the Father. And yet again for others this is the name of the divine Son of a much more human and lovable virgin mother, more close to us, who can then become so important that she stands on our altars—as at Lourdes—even without her Son.

We could go on in this vein, but we really have no wish to hurt anyone's most sacred feelings. The author too likes to celebrate Christmas and sings "Silent Night, Holy Night" without too many inhibitions. He also appreciates poetry. But he thinks that poetry and reality should not be confused. This holds not only for songs about the moon—particularly blatant in this cosmic age—but also for the praises sung—recently more than formerly by very different kinds of singers—of the Star, indeed the Superstar of life.

Innumerable hymns have been sung in all the languages of the world over the past two thousand years, particularly to him, and to him more than anyone. Innumerable images of this one man have also been painted, struck, cut and cast, in a thousand ways. And this is not the least that can be said about him. And yet this very diversity of images, which cannot be traced back—as with the Buddha, who always looks the same—to a very few formalized basic postures, raises the question: which is the true image of Christ?[13]

Is it the beardless, young-looking, kindhearted shepherd of the early Christian art of the catacombs *or* is it the bearded emperor and ruler of the world, in the image forms of the imperial cult of late antiquity, in courtly-rigid inviolability and menacing majesty before the gold background of eternity? Is it the *Beau-Dieu* of Chartres *or* the German *Miserikordien-Heiland* (man of sorrows)? Is it Christ the King and Judge of the world, enthroned on the cross, on Romanesque portals and apses *or* the cruelly realistic suffering Christ in Dürer's *Christus im Elend* and in the last Grünewald crucifixion still preserved? Is it the handsome Christ untouched by suffering in Raphael's *Disputa* or Michelangelo's Christ, suffering a human death? Is it the sublime sufferer of Velázquez *or* the tormented-quivering Christ of El Greco? Is the true image conveyed by the smooth "Enlightenment" salon portraits of Rosalba Carriera and of a Fritsch presenting the elegant popular philosopher Jesus *or* by the sentimental Sacred Heart pictures of Catholic late baroque? In the eighteenth century is it Jesus the gardener or apothecary dispensing virtue powder *or* later the classicist Saviour of Thorwaldsen which offended his Danish compatriot, Kierkegaard, by eliminating the scandal of the cross? Is it the meek and mild human Jesus of the German and French Nazarenes and the English Pre-Raphaelites *or* the Christ—pointing to quite different dimensions—of the twentieth-century artists: Beckmann, Corinth, Nolde, Masereel, Rouault, Picasso, Barlach, Matisse, Chagall?

The *theologies* lying behind the pictures are no less varied. Which Christology then is the true one?

In *antiquity* is it the Christ of Bishop Irenaeus of Lyons or of his disciple Hippolytus (anti-Pope to Calixtus), is it that of the brilliant Greek thinker Origen or that of the Latin stylist and lawyer Tertullian? Is it the Christ of the Constantinian court bishop and historiographer Eusebius or that of the Egyptian desert Father Anthony, that of Augustine the greatest Western theologian or that of Leo the most outstanding Pope of the first five centuries? Is it the Christ of the Alexandrians or that of the school of Antioch, that of the Cappadocians or that of the Egyptian monks?

In the *Middle Ages* is it the Christ of the Neo-Platonic speculative thinker John Scotus Erigena or of the ingenious dialectician Abélard, that of Peter Lombard's *Sentences*—on which so many commentaries were written—or that of the sermons by Bernard of Clairvaux on the Song of Songs? Is it the Christ of Thomas Aquinas or that of Francis of Assisi, that of the powerful Pope Innocent III or that of the heretical Waldensians and Albigensians whom he opposed? Is it that of the brooding apocalyptist Joachim of Flora or that of the daring thinker Cardinal Nicholas of Cusa, that of the Roman canonists or that of the German mystics?

In *modern times* is it the Christ of the Reformers or that of the Roman popes, that of Erasmus of Rotterdam or that of Ignatius of Loyola, that of the Spanish inquisitors or that of the Spanish mystics whom they persecuted? Is it the Christ of the Sorbonne theologians and the French crown lawyers or the Christ of Pascal, is it that of the Spanish scholastics of the baroque age or that of the German theologians of the Enlightenment, that of Lutheran and reformed orthodoxy or that of the older or modern Free Churches? Is it the Christ of the philosopher-theologians of German Idealism—Fichte, Schelling, Hegel—or is it that of Kierkegaard, the opponent of these philosopher-theologians? Is it that of the historical-speculative Catholic school of Tübingen or that of the Neo-Scholastic Jesuit theologians of Vatican I, that of the Protestant revival movements in the nineteenth century or that of the liberal exegesis of the nineteenth and twentieth centuries, that of Romano Guardini or that of Karl Adam, that of Karl Barth or that of Rudolf Bultmann, that of Paul Tillich, of Teilhard de Chardin or of Billy Graham?

It seems there are as many images of Christ as there are minds. Even today piety provides very diverse answers to the question: "Which Christ? What does he mean for me?" As the latest investigations[14] among all possible classes, callings, denominations show, some acknowledge him within the Church in prayer and acclamation, sacraments and liturgy, as Son of God, Redeemer, Risen Lord and Founder of the Church. Others he meets as a fellow human being, in ordinary life "outside," in social commitment as friend, elder brother, champion, instigator of unrest, enthusiasm and true humanity. Personal experiences of conversion, spontaneous professions of faith in him, are opposed by dogmatic formulas, doctrines restated in catechism style and in rigid forms. For some he signifies love, meaning, support, ground in life, and is the embodiment of happiness, calm and consolation even in disappointments, in despair and suffering. For others he is harmless, means little, cannot help. And if he challenges some to reflection, meditation, adoring contemplation, others respond tersely, are even irritated, avoid the issue or are simply at a loss.

The Christ of dogma?

It would be wrong to get the impression that in these images, theologies, interpretations, experiences of Jesus everything is equally important or equally correct, still less that nothing is correct or important. What must be made clear is that apparently we cannot so simply and naïvely assume that what lies behind the name of Christ is known from Christian piety, literature, art and tradition. Too many diverse and—where possible—touched-up photographs of one and the same person make detective work difficult. And Christian theology to a considerable extent is constantly detective work, often an extremely absorbing and exhausting work of discovery.

Yet this is just what some theologians would deny. What could be discovered about this person has been discovered once and for all and private detectives are not wanted. It is a question here of something more than Christian piety, experience, literature, art, tradition. It is a question of the *Church's teaching*—to be more precise, the official teaching of the ecclesiastical magisterium.[15] The true Christ is the Christ of the Church. Perhaps it is not *Roma locuta* that counts here, but certainly *Conciliis locutis*: what the ecumenical councils of the Church from the fourth to the eighth century have pronounced, defined, marked out, against heresies of right and left. In the light of all this who then would the true Christ be?

In any case, even according to the councils, he would not be simply "God." Certainly, as a result of an educationally inadequate, superficial religious instruction and a liturgy and art which overexalted him, the answer of believers and (therefore) of unbelievers is often unfortunately "Jesus= God." And how often do we see children pointing to a crucifix and saying: "That is God, hanging on the cross." But, however much they may be due to the influence of the Church's dogmatic definitions emphasizing the divinity of Jesus, these are misunderstandings: they produce an irresponsible dilution, superficiality, simplification and even a heretical one-sidedness of the well-thought-out and secure teaching of the early councils. "God in human form" is Monophysitism. "God suffering on the cross" is Patripassianism. No early council ever simply identified Jesus with God in the way that the Germanic tribes a little later were converted from the God Wotan to the God Jesus: it is for this reason that the name of Jesus is omitted from the *Confiteor* in the Frankish-Roman Mass and that he is addressed directly in other prayers, without reference to the Father.

Even according to the first ecumenical Council of Nicea (325, in the imperial summer residence), Jesus is only "consubstantial with the Father."[16] And, according to the counterbalancing Council of Chalcedon (451, near Constantinople), he is "consubstantial with us men": one person (a divine hypostasis) in whom are united two natures—a divine and a human—without confusion or change, without division or separation.[17] This is the classical answer in terms of the "hypostatic union" and the "God-man" which has been repeated since then in innumerable theological textbooks and catechisms of the different Churches of East and West.

And yet, is it so simple? As Athanasius, the leading figure at Nicea, testifies, the ecumenical councils at the beginning made no claim to propositional infallibility.[18] This venerable conciliar history is not without fluctuations and—up to a point—even contradictions. This is evident at least to anyone who knows a little more than is contained in the theological manuals about Nicea I and II, Ephesus I and II, Constantinople I, II, III and IV.[19] And the great Council of Chalcedon itself was also the occasion of the first great and lasting schism in the Church—not yet overcome—between the Chalcedonian Churches and others which stood by Ephesus II. Chalcedon then had by no means solved the problem permanently. A few years later a dispute of exceptional violence broke out on the question opened up by Chalcedon, whether Christ—being God—could suffer at all. And this "Patripassianist, Theopaschite" controversy dominated from then onwards the whole sixth century and turned in the seventh century into the "Monothelite" dispute (one will or two wills in Christ, one divine and the other human?).[20]

For us today the problem lies deeper. Only too often behind the Christ image of the councils there can be perceived the unmoving, passionless countenance of Plato's God, who cannot suffer, embellished with some features of Stoic ethics. The names of these councils show that they are exclusively Greek. But Christ was not born in Greece. Both for these councils and the theology behind it the work of translation must be continued. The whole doctrine of the two natures is an interpretation in Hellenistic language and concepts of what Jesus Christ really means. The importance of this teaching should not be belittled. It has made history. It gives expression to a genuine continuity of Christian faith and provides important guidelines for the whole discussion and for any future interpretation. But on the other hand no one should get the impression that Christ's message today could or should be stated only with the aid of these Greek categories—unavoidable at the time but inadequate—only with the aid of the Chalcedonian two-natures doctrine, only with the aid, that is, of what is called classical Christology. What is a Jew, a Chinese, a Japanese or an African, or even the average European or American today, to make of those Greek ciphers? Recent attempts—both Catholic and Protestant—at a solution of the Christological problem go far beyond Chalcedon.[21] And the New Testament itself is infinitely richer.

The Chalcedonian formula therefore must be regarded—as Karl Rahner puts it in a well-known phrase—more as a beginning than as an end.[22] Here we shall merely summarize briefly the roots from which the different *objections* to the traditional solution of the Christological question—two natures in one (divine) person—have grown:[23]

a. The two-natures doctrine, using terms and ideas which bear the imprint of Hellenistic language and mentality, is no longer understood today. In practice therefore it is avoided as much as possible in the proclamation of the Church's teaching.

b. The two-natures doctrine did not solve the difficulties even *at that time*, as is evident from the post-Chalcedon history of dogmas. On the contrary it led to ever new logical dilemmas.

c. The two-natures doctrine, in the opinion of many exegetes, is by no means identical with the *original* New Testament message about Christ. Some regard it as displacing or—up to a point—even corrupting the original message, others as at least not the sole possible and certainly not the best interpretation.

Very similar objections can of course be raised also against the traditional Protestant triple office doctrine of Jesus as prophet, priest, king, developed by Calvin and later adopted by Catholic theology. Is this doctrine, in such a brief, systematic form, founded in the New Testament? And are these three—of all titles—still supposed to have any meaning for man in our secularized society?[24]

Certainly it is thanks to the Christian tradition in piety, literature and art that the memory of this Christ remained alive, that he himself did not become a monument of the past, but again and again proved to be relevant to the concerns of a new age. Without the continuity of a believing community, if perhaps we had been forced to rely only on a book, there would be no living message of Christ and no living faith in Christ. Each generation appropriated the recollection of him in a new form. Any theologian who neglects this great tradition will pay dearly for it. It is right to honor even today the professions of faith of the ancient councils, which were both brief summaries and defensive demarcations. They are not merely antiques and curiosities. They are signs of the stability of the Christian faith throughout the centuries of change. We shall have to return to them later.

At the same time it must not be forgotten that this great tradition is surprisingly complex. The testimonies to one and the same Christ are very varied, full of contrasts, often disparate and contradictory. And truth and poetry particularly at this point need a close theological scrutiny. Even traditionally minded theologians must admit that not everything in this tradition can be equally true, not everything can be simultaneously true.

The great conciliar tradition too therefore raises the question: which Christ is the true one? And particularly anyone who cherishes a Christological tradition in theology and piety, declared to be exclusively orthodox, will have to ask himself whether just this "orthodox" Christ, lodged in a very fine Church, hospitalized, domesticated, is the true Christ. For not only dust, but also too much gold, can cover up the true figure.

The Christian message aims at making intelligible what Jesus Christ means and is for man today. But does this Christ become really intelligible for man today if we simply start out dogmatically from established teaching on the Trinity? Can he be understood if we simply take for granted the divinity of Jesus, the pre-existence of the Son, and then merely ask how this Son of God could unite to himself, could assume, a human nature, frequently leaving the cross and resurrection to appear as something which happened purely as a result of his "becoming man"? Can modern man understand if we emphasize the title of Son of God and suppress as much as possible the humanity of Jesus, denying him existence as a human person? Will he understand if Jesus is more adored as divinity than imitated as earthly and human? Would it not perhaps correspond more to the New Testament evidence and to modern man's historical way of thinking if we started out like the first disciples from the real human being Jesus, his historical message and manifestation, his life and fate, his historical reality and historical activity, and then ask about the relationship of this human being Jesus to God, about his unity with the Father. In a word, therefore: can we have less of a Christology in the classical manner, speculatively or dogmatically "from above," but—without disputing the legitimacy of the older Christology—more of a historical Christology "from below," in the light of the concrete Jesus, more suited to modern man?[25]

The Christ of the enthusiasts?

JESUS CHRIST
Wanted—*For Sedition, Criminal Anarchy—*
Vagrancy, and Conspiring to Overthrow
the Established Government

Dresses poorly. Said *to be a carpenter by trade. Ill-nourished, has visionary ideas, associates with common working people, the unemployed and bums.* Alien—*believed to be a Jew.* Alias: *"Prince of Peace," "Son of Man," "Light of the World," etc., etc. Professional Agitator, Red Beard, marks on hands and feet the result of injuries inflicted by an angry* mob *led by respectable citizens and legal authorities.*

So runs the now well-known "warrant" which first appeared in a Christian underground newspaper in the United States.

Charismatic *Jesus movements* have existed at all times, on the margin or outside of the established Churches: non-conformist appeals to the original, true Christ against the Christ appropriated by the Churches. These fanatical movements were often wildly revolutionary, aggressive, violent; often gentle, introverted, mystical. Even in the early Church there were various apocalyptic enthusiasts. Then came the "spirituals," flagellants and apostolic brethren, of the Middle Ages, the enthusiasts and Anabaptists of Reformation times. Later came radical pietism in Germany, Independents, Quakers and Plymouth Brethren in England, the various revival movements in the United States. Finally, there is the Pentecostal movement which made its entry in a quite orthodox way into the Catholic Church after Vatican II. All these are possible forms of charismatic movements.[26]

Often too there were simply lone wolves who followed their own, often scarcely orthodox Christ: these too were active in early, medieval and modern Christendom, producing books, pamphlets, novels, or simply adopting a special way of life. The list of those who ignored their Church but loved their Christ would be a very long one: among them were quite notable great minds, theologians, writers, painters. There were also Jesus disciples, clowns, freaks, beatniks in wild variety, but at least they were not as boring as the orthodox Latin and Greek Christology of the second millennium after the close of the great controversies in the East. And there was the Jesus clown of our millennium, acknowledged by all the Churches: Francis of Assisi.

No one familiar with history therefore need be surprised that even today —after so much talk of secularity, evolution and revolution—this Jesus has again become popular and, it seems, for secular evolutionaries and revolutionaries alike. And in America, now that the "death of God" itself is rapidly dying and Jesus after almost two thousand years still had the honor of "making" the cover story of *Time* magazine twice in one year,[27] those time-conscious theologians who always like to ride on the crest of the latest wave, hoping to reach a new shore, have noted that the wind has changed again: from secularity to religiosity, from publicity to interiority, from action to meditation, from rationality to sensitivity, from the "death of God" to interest in "eternal life." Perhaps as Christians—after Marx, Freud, Nietzsche and other bringers of salvation of our day—they find it *still* more important to be occupied with Jesus.

The present new orientation could be instructive also for the future. Whether any of these movements turns out to be enduring or brief, it should not be played off by the Church against revolutionary movements. They are frequently also a protest against the domesticated plaster Christ in the Churches who neither feels nor can feel pain. They are not always signs of conventionality and Church loyalty. Too many impulses from the revolutionary movement have been preserved: the attitude of protest against concentration on a successful career and acquisition of wealth, against the consumer- and efficiency-oriented society, the technologically automatized and manipulated world, uncontrolled progress, even the established Churches. In some of these movements too we find an expressionist style, a trend to romanticism, frequent irrationalism. What we said earlier about the cultural criticism of revolutionary humanism[28] has therefore by no means become superfluous.

The initial difficulties also of young people could remain the same for a long time: apart from the general situation of society, the problems with parents, teachers, superiors, often uninspiring work, and all kinds of dubious or even not so dubious pleasures, up to an inner void, boredom and despair. But for some the objectives of the search have changed again. After all the disturbances, manifestations and provocations, some are no longer looking for politico-revolutionary action, but for inward peace, security, joy, strength, love, a meaning to life. Charles Reich's "Consciousness III"[29] is more than ephemeral feelings of flower children and veneration of a fellow rebel. It means a different awareness, transcending the machine, rising above existing conditions to liberation; the choice of a new life-style, development of new human capacities, a new independence and personal responsibility; it means a new determination of values and priorities, a new man and for that very reason a new society. But the demands of the Jesus enthusiasts are less abstract than those involved in Consciousness III. Some of these skinheads or long-haired people have lost their fear of religion, even the fear of calling Jesus by his name. After they have tried everything—sex and alcohol, hashish, marijuana, LSD and other drugs which widen the field of consciousness—some seem to find Jesus the "greatest trip." "The Beatles are more popular than Jesus Christ": after this arrogant dictum of the Beatle John Lennon in 1966 came the song "My sweet Lord, I really want to know you" by ex-Beatle George Harrison in 1971. Bible, prayer—yes, even baptism—are in, at least for the time being.

The importance of all this must not be exaggerated. Much of it is merely fashion, business, kitsch, inflation by the news-hungry mass media and profit-hungry managers. It is part of the system that every protest against commercialization itself becomes commercialized. Nevertheless: if drugs now as before present the greatest problem to the American police (more than half the offenses against property are due to the influence of drugs), we can hardly be sorry that a way of release has been found for some of the hundred thousand or so (mainly young) addicts in New York alone.[80] Christianity as seen in the person of Jesus is certainly not a substitute for drugs: the opiates are not to be replaced by an "opium of the people," nor one ecstasy by another. But, for some drug addicts or those who are despairing of life altogether, Christianity as seen in Jesus *can* obviously provide a reliable opportunity of overcoming their paralysis and making fresh activity possible.

Critics, however, fear naïveté, romanticism, contempt for reason in these religious waves; they object to the childish trust in miracles, missionary enthusiasm, political and social apathy and escapism; even detect reaction, restoration and counterrevolution. All this can in fact be involved. The only question is, why? Why are such religious movements wrongly appropriated by the Right and then wrongly condemned by the Left? They are equally close to and remote from both sides. Many revolutionaries now as before also appeal to Jesus. But—and this is more important—such religious trends are a sign that neither the bourgeois ideology of progress nor a superficially revolutionary criticism of society can satisfy these young people: not prosperity culture nor its counterculture, not the noise and bustle of civilization nor drug-produced ecstasy, not evolutionary or revolutionary humanisms. And even those superficial "liberals" who see in mere "liberalization" a universal panacea must at least understand that this liberalized youth would now also like to know what really was the point of being liberalized. People like this think they have avoided the question of the place of the individual in the whole and are then immensely surprised and disgruntled when young people, already accustomed to a literature quite free of taboos, find even the obscenities boring (not every writer is a Henry Miller or D. H. Lawrence), turn to Segal's *Love Story* or again to Hermann Hesse's *Steppenwolf* or *Siddhartha* and—hostile to institutions, but not remote from religion—seek happiness in a different direction.

Against this background it is and remains in any case a surprising phenomenon, after all the fashions falling over one another—not forgetting, in addition to psycho and sensitivity training, the trend toward Far Eastern mysticism—that this Jesus is and becomes constantly freshly relevant, apparently as fascinating as ever. Nor is this any longer Jesus regarded exclusively as a fellow rebel in the fight against war and inhumanity: it is Jesus seen also as the victim abused by everyone, as the most constant and most available symbol for purity, joy, final surrender, true life. And, oddly as some of it may sound to the satisfied bourgeois, could not Jesus revolution, God trip, baptism or therapy of the Holy Spirit perhaps be a new expression of a primitive longing of mankind? Of a hunger for true life, true freedom, true love, true peace, which in the long run cannot be suppressed?

Who indeed would have thought that the secular closing message of the popular musical *Hair*—"Life can begin again inside you. Let the sun, let the sunshine in"—might be taken up in just this way? Jesus' presence there was only marginal: "My hair, like Jesus wore his. Hallelujah: I like it . . . Mary loved her Son. Why doesn't my mother love me?" Is it so surprising, in view of unsuccessful revolts and in view of the orgies and hippie murders which succeeded only too well, that some of the younger people think that "life"—so extolled in that song of the sun—is not worth living without another kind of inwardness and brotherliness, without unselfishness, purity of heart and that love which is more than sex. The question of the *meaning* of life—of a life that is successful, happiness-creating and happy, fulfilled and therefore right—cannot be suppressed, cannot be dismissed either through analyzing the psyche or through changing society. Quite a few today are again convinced that they can find precisely in Jesus the answer to the question thus formulated in *Hair:*

Where do I go?
Follow the river.
Where do I go?
Follow the gulls.
Where is the something,
Where is the someone
That tells me why
I live and die?

Follow my heart beat.
Where do I go?
Follow my hand.
Where will they lead me?
And will I ever
discover why
I live and die,
I live and die?

Nevertheless, despite all positive aspects of the charismatic Jesus movements, it would be quite wrong to link the future of Christianity with any sort of fashions or "waves," still more to base it on emotions, hysterias or ideologies of intoxication. Movements of religious enthusiasm to—often symbioses of rebel counterculture and conservative biblicism—are ambivalent. Sometimes even in the same individual they take the form of a mixture of dubious religiosity, genuine religion and—again something different—Christian faith. They have their time, are changed and often only their vestiges remain. Enthusiastic movements venerate their Christ and appropriate him at the same time. And the true Jesus Christ anyway is not the "Superstar" who could be "made," "built up," "composed," finally "staged" as desired, and then even "consumed." Christianity must not be confused with show business or the narcotics industry.

Not that there is anything against linking Christianity with fascinating music. How fruitful the association is can be seen in its history from Gregorian chant to Igor Stravinsky, Krzysztof Penderecki and the spirituals. Nor is there anything particularly against setting biblical themes to music in beat and rock rhythms. Others however may be left to judge the quality of the mixture that emerges from the Rolling Stones, Beatles, Serge Prokofiev and Richard Strauss. From the Gospels at any rate we cannot mix everything together for Jesus' last week—even guided by the highly accomplished Archbishop Fulton J. Sheen's *Life of Christ.*[31] And if the Christ of the devotional objects of a Christian piety and the God beyond this world of a Christological dogmatism have no support in the Gospels, then still less does the all-too-earthly idol of ecstatics and addicts. There is nothing against the authors of the song, of the long-playing record, of the musical and finally of the film *Jesus Christ Superstar*: the young Englishmen Lloyd Webber and Tim Rice, who yielded to the fascination of the "incredible drama" of the Jesus story and brought in for the stupendous, elaborate Broadway production of the profitable rock opera the shrewd and versatile director of *Hair* (T. O'Horgan: "The swing is back to the superrational consciousness").

It was suggested at the time that these people knew nothing about religion or Jesus, but the question may also be asked whether those who know more could make it intelligible for others and particularly for younger people. And anyone who says that this sort of thing is a sacrilegious distortion of the story of Jesus might well reflect how often in the past excessive piety has trivialized it. Critics who claim that only Jesus' humanity is portrayed here should remember how frequently his divinity alone was brought out in the Churches. The complaint that the resurrection is left out of these presentations may be countered by pointing out how often theologies treated the crucifixion as no more than an unfortunate incident between the incarnation and the resurrection.

In any case, *Jesus Christ Superstar* together with a number of similar productions gives very many people an opportunity to reflect a little more about this Jesus: which is at least no worse than reflecting on *My Fair Lady, Hello, Dolly!* or *Man of La Mancha.* Moreover, we may confidently hope that the "superb story" of this Christ is strong enough to shine out in its own light even through the multimedial glitter of a popular-ingenious Broadway spectacle. But what is this light?

The Christ of literature?

"If anyone could prove to me that Christ is outside the truth, and if the truth really did exclude Christ, I should prefer to stay with Christ and not with truth." Fyodor Mikhailovitch Dostoevsky wrote this shortly after his release from prison.[32] Measured not only by Dostoevsky's standard but also by the profound seriousness with which the problem of Jesus is treated in modern literature as a whole, the Jesus songs of the Beatles and others, as also the musical *Jesus Christ Superstar,* and even the more deeply penetrating *Godspell* (=gospel), seem very trivial.

What is *typical* of the attitude of contemporary literature to Jesus of Nazareth?[33] First of all, while religion is subjected to criticism and the Church largely ignored and rejected, the figure of Jesus is conspicuously "spared," with the result that an express rejection—as with Gottfried Benn and the later Rainer Maria Rilke,[34] understandable after reading their predecessor Nietzsche—occurs comparatively rarely. Above all, the attempt is made—so to speak—to edge toward the figure of Jesus, speaking of him only very indirectly and almost timidly. As the cave dwellers in Plato's allegory see only the silhouettes outlined by the sun, so modern writers see more of the shadows he casts than of himself in the light of day. Jesus is seen in his reflection. He is observed in the effects he produces in the people who come into contact with him. Jesus is not described, not furnished with predicates, not adorned with titles. He is approached as we pass by the place where he is standing: at one time this might have been described as a very "modest approach." This sort of thing—which must not be misunderstood—is evidence of enormous respect, of absolutely unique reverence toward this figure.

This new orientation also means of course that the time for a more or less orthodox, *conventional portrayal of Jesus in historical and psychological terms is past*. This may perhaps be a matter of regret for those who read Giovanni Papini's poetic *Story of Christ* (1921)[35] in their early years as students or—with even greater enthusiasm—the empathic twenty-four Nicodemus letters by the Polish author Jan Dobraczyński with the programmatic title *Give Me Your Cares* (1952);[36] the latter also went into almost innumerable editions and describes the figure of Jesus from the standpoint of a Jewish scribe, himself struck with his wife's sickness, who links together the problem of Job and the problem of the cross and thus solves them. It will also be regretted by those who recall Pär Lagerkvist's *Barabbas* (1950)[37]: the man burdened with guilt, doubting, seeking, unable to get away from Jesus who had been executed in his place. The same applies to the book *The Master* (1952)[38] by the Jewish author Max Brod (Kafka's executor). Here Jesus is described in the light of a first growing but finally waning sympathy between the nihilistic-existentialist Jason-Judas, a Greek official in the Roman administration in Jerusalem, and his almost Mary-like foster sister Susanna: he is an authentic human figure in the style of the great Jewish prophets.

All these literary portrayals of Jesus, like some earlier ones at the turn of the century,[39] were by no means lacking in aesthetic quality or theological depth. Not least when they were written by authors outside or on the margin of the Church. But they were based on a naïve and word-for-word reading of the Gospels. These writers, unburdened with recent exegetical and historical problems, made brilliant use of literary imagination and modern psychology in a tacit attempt to update the Gospels, reading into them what cannot be read out of them. They used the Gospel accounts as chronicles in need of embellishment and employed all the aids of history, psychology and aesthetics to produce a kind of fictional biography.[40] Taken together, these works may be regarded as the poetical counterparts of the historical lives of Jesus by the liberal (or orthodox) exegetes of the nineteenth and early twentieth centuries.

This indirect approach to Jesus on the part of modern writers finds support in the theological interpretation of the Gospels, which shows that they do not provide anything like a biography and simply cannot be used without more ado as historical sources (we shall have to look into this matter more closely here). It is also doubtful whether the stylistic aids and methods of literature are really adequate to give expression in words to the life of Jesus, his person and cause, the divine and human elements brought together in a historically concrete person.

Of course the conventional novels about Jesus were themselves meant to be more than history: it is not easy to be neutral and impartial when writing about Jesus. In one way or another they were testimonies to the religion of their authors. For the most part even the conventional portrayals of Jesus emerged out of an interest in bringing the divinely exalted, unworldly and thus irrelevant Christ of dogma, liturgy and theology down to earth, in making him again humanly intelligible "from below," challenging, inviting, and thus at the same time giving expression to our own individual and social problems.

While however the conventional novels about Jesus—despite their religious interest—had a more or less poetic character, the *new Jesus portrayals* are primarily critical. This holds particularly for those poetic-real Jesus portrayals which have a basis at least remotely in the context of the New Testament and where Jesus, even though alienated, appears as a real person. The very person of Jesus here constitutes a radical criticism of the different forms of Jesus kitsch and false Jesus piety. This approach breaks through the walls of the ecclesiastical-sacral sphere and deliberately seeks to bring down the exalted Christ as a divine cult figure. Jesus is to be freed from the rigidity of dogma and cult and liberated for men: an example of authentic human existence even to the extremes of ugliness, cruelty and brutality. Unlike the books on Jesus by earlier authors, the New Testament evidence here plays only a slight role. The more recent authors begin with modern man's horizon of experience and have no intention at all of providing an authentic image of Jesus.

Against this background it is not surprising that—apart perhaps from two novels which appeared in 1970, Günter Herburger's *Jesus in Osaka* and Frank Andermann's *The Great Countenance*[41]—there are now scarcely any Jesus portrayals in the form of larger literary works, in novels or plays, where Jesus is explicitly the "hero" at the center of events. On the other hand the literary *forms* are very *varied*: an abundance of ideas which frequently take form in religious genres and for their content are mostly linked with the key points of Jesus' life—birth, passion, death and resurrection. This is seen particularly in poetry: there are impressive examples in the work of Peter Huchel and Paul Celan.[42] But there are also short stories, for instance, by Friedrich Dürrenmatt and Peter Handke, plays like the Spaniard F. Arrabal's *Auto Cemetery* and short prose pieces as in Günter Grass's novel *The Tin Drum*.[43]

The literary *techniques* are as *varied* as the literary forms. As in other fields of contemporary literature, the traditional narrator's standpoint appears to be superseded, as the traditional verse and strophe forms are also superseded in poetry. Instead we have reflections, alienations, refractions, parodies, travesties, associations, evocations, transferences of familiar patterns of language and ideas into a different context or finally montages of linguistic forms of diverse provenance.[44] Here are three examples which are important also for their content.

Multiple refraction is used by Walter Jens to convey the presence of Jesus. From a novel, *Herr Meister*, he quotes a passage (subsequently deleted by the author) containing sentences from the Jesus analysis of the novel's hero: "You supported his steps, his sweat touched you; you smelt his blood-trail and heard his terrible moaning: at first far away, then coming closer, rattling and loud, then drowned by the street-criers or the shouting of people watching at their windows, slowly dying away. And if you didn't want to watch, if you were shut up in a room, hiding in cellars or courtyards, you must have seen his shadow glide past. The sun cast the shape of the cross upon the wall, the stones became eyes, all the walls picked up his reflection and nothing has been effaced."[45]

An example of the way in which his person is reflected in the people concerned with him is found in a short play by Ernest Hemingway. Three Roman soldiers, slightly drunk, come into a tavern late on a Friday evening. Brutally, but deeply impressed, they tell how they nailed him to the cross and lifted him up: "When the weight starts to pull on 'em. That's when it gets 'em." "It takes some of them pretty bad." "Ain't I seen 'em? I seen plenty of them. I tell you, he was pretty good in there today." The last sentence, repeated several times, runs like a refrain through the play.[46]

Alienation is achieved by Wolfgang Borchert through transference to another context. A soldier nicknamed Jesus has to lie down in graves to test their capacity for the bodies of the fallen. Despite the order he suddenly refuses to perform this service, "he won't put up with it any longer." "Why in fact do they call him Jesus . . . ? No particular reason. The chief always calls him that, because he looks so gentle. The chief thinks he looks so gentle. So they call him Jesus." " 'Yes,' said the sergeant as he got a new charge ready to blast the next grave, 'I'll have to report him, we can't do without graves.' "[47]

Finally the literary *themes and motifs* are as *varied* as the literary forms and techniques in present-day portrayals of Jesus. Throughout all the literary epochs of the century there persists of course the theme of the returning Jesus (*Jesus redivivus*), beginning with Balzac and Dostoevsky, continuing with Hauptmann and Rilke, up to Ricarda Huch and Günter Herburger.[48] "Why do you come to hinder us?" These words of Dostoevsky's Grand Inquisitor could be put up over practically all the contemporary portrayals of Jesus. Everywhere the time planes are telescoped in such a way as to depict Jesus as a disturbing factor of the first rank for the present-day ecclesiastical and social order: whether as in Dostoevsky he turns up in the Church as defender of human freedom or as in Hermann Hesse, the early Rilke and Bert Brecht,[49] he appears as brother and friend of the poor and oppressed. For others—from the naturalism of Arno Holz, by way of the left-wing expressionism of a Carl Einstein, to Erich Kästner —he appears as a social revolutionary.[50] For Andermann he is a resistance fighter or again for Dostoevsky, Hauptmann and the expressionists he is the model of all fools, clowns and lunatics, the sufferers and God-obsessed.

From here there is a direct line to the pop scene with which we are already familiar: Jesus as a marginal figure and an outcast from Church and society, precursor of all beatniks and hippies; dream figure and synthetic art figure, projected by modern longings (whipped up by Marx, Freud and Marcuse) for liberation from any form of coercion, for an unburdened, happy life. So, for instance, in Herburger we have a democratic "Everyman"-Jesus, emancipated on all sides (in relation to a Japanese combine, a Zen master, the Pope, a television woman theologian, the rich man of capitalist society). Does he represent the pop temper of a future generation? In any case these are no more than ambiguous, utopian outlines of the future without any clear result. Even with the Dadaist Hugo Ball, Jesus was one who made men become children again; now with Herburger the Jesus who finally identifies himself with children and children's partisans. This is a Jesus descended from the cross in order to be identified with men.

The crucified—or the empty cross? This is a central problem of the modern literature on Jesus which was stated long ago in Jean Paul's dreadful vision of a "speech of the dead Christ from the roof of the world that there is no God" (in *Siebenkäs*, 1796–97),[51] admittedly in the form of a merely hypothetical warning. But its influence can be seen in Romanticism in the works of all possible "monks of atheism" (Heinrich Heine) up to Dostoevsky's "demons." For Dostoevsky in particular the figure of this very crucified and forsaken Christ represented a colossal temptation. After his flight from Russia to Basle, he barely avoided an epileptic fit when looking at Holbein's dead, crucified Christ.[52] This picture plays an important part in the first part of *The Idiot*, written three months later in Geneva. Prince Myshkin cries out in horror: "Why, that picture might make some people lose their faith."[53] *The Idiot* provides the early classical example of a Jesus portrayal no longer direct but indirect, poetic-transfigural, in which the Jesus event is seen—so to speak—as the concealed basic pattern behind a person, an action, a set of circumstances or a conflict. In regard to this novel Heinrich Böll admits: "I still do not know any better literary portrayal of Jesus."[54] Dostoevsky never wrote the book he had planned on Jesus Christ. But when he was dying, he asked his wife to open at random the Gospel—which had scarcely ever left his side since his release from prison—and read a page to him. He dedicated to his wife his last and greatest work, *The Brothers Karamazov*. It carries as a motto what amounts to Dostoevsky's legacy:

> *Truly, truly, I tell you:*
> *if a grain of wheat that falls into the ground*
> *does not die, it remains alone;*
> *but if it dies, it yields much fruit.*[55]

Against the "blockheads" among the critics of *The Brothers Karamazov*, who "lack any understanding of the stubborn denial of God which I portrayed in the legend of the Grand Inquisitor and in the subsequent chapters of my novel," Dostoevsky says: "In Europe there is not and *never has been* so powerful an *expression* of atheism. Consequently I do not believe in Christ and I do not profess this faith like a child, but my hosanna has passed through the great *purgatory of doubt*, as the devil says of himself in my last novel."[56]

Here too perhaps this psychologically and theologically uncannily clear-sighted author saw more deeply than others the significance of Jesus. Certainly more deeply than Andermann, who has Jesus taken down alive from the infamous cross (a touching gesture on the part of a Jew after so much suffering in the Nazi and war period). More deeply too than Herburger, whose emancipated Jesus does not want to die, ostentatiously climbs down from the cross and has it burned, so that he can be wholly a man indistinguishable from the rest of men. To the cliché of the "empty cross" there corresponds in literature the cliché of the "resurrection in ourselves" or of the "unending crucifixion" (with Marie-Luise Kaschnitz, Kurt Marti, Kurt Tucholsky).[57] This approach helps to make clear how Jesus represents human existence lived and endured to its very roots and how the key points of Jesus' life can be understood also as the key points of our own existence. So for instance in the novel *The Greek Passion* by Nikos Kazantzakis,[58] whose life and work were stamped by the conflict between religious theory and ecclesiastical practice in Greece: the actors in a Passion play, presented before their un-Christian village priests and the newly arrived miserable refugees, begin to identify themselves with their roles as Christ and the apostles and are therefore themselves beaten and crucified.

The Christ-Jesus antithesis has frequently become a Jesus-God antithesis. Jesus as man and brother has been set up against the sinister, cruel, often incomprehensible God. It is not least in this connection—as we observed at the beginning of this section—that in all the radical theocriticism and criticism of religion Jesus is spared and even in the midst of all talk about the death of God in literature is roused again to new life.

After this brief survey, is it necessary to insist again on how much literature can help us to understand the Jesus event? Are not the writers often more alert, perceptive and sensitive than the theologians? Literature reveals areas of language and images which translate afresh, transpose, render intelligible the Jesus event. It opens up new possibilities of confronting and reconciling our human experiences with the message of this Jesus Christ. It enables us—so to speak—to take an outsider's view, to highlight the strangeness of what had once seemed familiar, to bring out the inexplicable in the commonplace.

A writer certainly does not want to draw an objective, historically accurate picture of Jesus, containing all the relevant details. What he seeks is to bring out and emphasize one aspect which he thinks important, to bring together a number of themes, to throw a clearer light on one point. Style is achieved by subjective emphasis. The writer as such is not interested in historically exact investigation. But in view of the many Christ images not only of the councils, of the devout and the enthusiasts, of theologians and painters, and also of the writers, it is the theologian who must answer the question: which portrait of Christ is the true one? To which of them should we cling in practice? The question therefore at the end of this chapter, even more than at the beginning, is: which Christ is the real Christ?

II. The Real Christ

Whatever the reason for it, the fact deserves careful consideration that, after the fall of so many gods in this century, this person, broken at the hands of his opponents and constantly betrayed through the ages by his adherents, is obviously still for innumerable people the most moving figure in the long history of mankind: unusual and incomprehensible in many respects. He is the hope of revolutionaries and evolutionaries, he fascinates intellectuals and anti-intellectuals. He requires the capable and the incapable. He constantly stimulates theologians and even atheists to think again. To the Churches he is an occasion for continual self-questioning as to whether they are monuments or living witnesses to him and at the same time he radiates beyond the Churches ecumenically into Judaism and the other religions. Gandhi said: "I tell the Hindus that their lives will be imperfect if they do not also study reverently the teaching of Jesus."[1]

The question of the truth now becomes so much more urgent: which Christ is the true Christ? The simple answer, "Be nice. Jesus loves you," is not sufficient. This can easily be uncritical fundamentalism or pietism in hippie clothing. And if we rely on feelings, the name can be changed as desired: instead of Che Guevara with the Jesus look we can have Jesus with the Guevara look, and again vice versa. The choice between the Jesus of dogmatism and the Jesus of pietism, between the Jesus of protest, of action, of revolution, and the Jesus of feelings, of sensitivity, of fantasy, raised as a question of truth will have to be expressed more precisely: The Christ of dreams or the Christ of reality? The *dreamed-up* or the *real* Christ?

1. Not a myth

What can prevent us from following a merely dreamed-up Christ, a Christ dogmatically or pietistically, revolutionarily or enthusiastically manipulated and staged? Any manipulation, ideologizing, even mythicizing of Christ reaches its limit in *history*. The Christ of Christianity—this cannot be sufficiently stressed against all old or new syncretism—is not simply a timeless idea, an eternally valid principle, a profoundly significant myth.

Only naïve Christians can rejoice over a Christ figure among the gods in a Hindu temple. The gracious acceptance of their Christ into a pantheon was opposed by the early Christians with all their powers and often enough they paid for their resistance with their lives. They preferred to be insulted as atheists. The Christ of the Christians is a quite concrete, human, historical person: the Christ of the Christians is no other than *Jesus of Nazareth*. And in this sense Christianity is essentially based on history, Christian faith is essentially historical faith. It is interesting to compare the synoptic Gospels with the best-known Hindu poem, *Ramayana* (beautifully depicted at night before the temple of Prambanan in Java and in innumerable temple frescoes). This describes in twenty-four thousand stanzas in Sanskrit how Sita, the wife of the noble-minded Prince Rama (Vishnu incarnate) was abducted to Ceylon by Ravana, king of the giants, and how Rama, assisted by an army of apes, had a bridge built across the ocean and rescued his faithful wife but finally cast her off. The difference is striking. It was only as a historical faith that Christianity was able to prevail at the very beginning against all the mythologies, philosophies and mystery cults.

In time and place

"And Christ?" Kafka bowed his head. "That is an abyss filled with light. We must close our eyes if we are not to fall into it."[2] But even though innumerable people have discovered superhuman, divine reality in Jesus and even though he was given high-sounding titles from the very beginning, there is no doubt that he was always regarded both by his contemporaries and the later Church as a *real human being*. Apart from the few and not very fruitful pagan and Jewish testimonies (even Talmud and Midrash fail us here), the New Testament writings are our only reliable sources and for all these Jesus is a real human being who lived at a quite definite time and in quite definite surroundings. But did he really live?

The *historical existence* of Jesus of Nazareth, like that of the Buddha and other apparently indisputable facts, has also been disputed. There was a great but unnecessary uproar in the nineteenth century when Bruno Bauer explained Christianity as an invention of the original evangelist and Jesus as an "idea." It was the same in 1910 with Arthur Drews's interpretation of Jesus as pure "Christ myth"[3] (the Englishman J. M. Robertson and the American mathematician W. B. Smith held similar views). But extreme positions have their advantages. They clarify the situation and mostly cancel themselves out. Since that time the historical existence of Jesus has not been disputed by any serious scholar. Obviously this has not prevented less serious writers from going on writing less serious things about Jesus (Jesus as psychopath, as astral myth, as son of Herod, as secretly married, and so on). But it is a little distressing to see a philologist ruining his reputation by interpreting Jesus as the secret designation of a hallucinatory fungus, Fly-Agaric (*Amanita muscaria*), supposedly used in the rites of the first Christians.[4] May we expect some even more original discovery in the future?

We know incomparably more that is historically certain about Jesus of Nazareth than we do about the great founders of the Asian religions:

more than we know of Buddha (died about 480 B.C.), whose image in the didactic texts (*sutras*) remains oddly stereotyped and whose life story is presented in the rigidly systematized legend less as historical than as an ideal type;

more certainly than we know of Buddha's Chinese contemporary, Confucius (died probably 479 B.C.), whose undoubtedly real personality cannot by any effort be precisely apprehended, because of the unreliability of the sources, and which was only subsequently linked with the Chinese state ideology of "Confucianism" (the word itself, unknown in Chinese, means in fact "teaching or school of the learned men");

more finally than we do of Lao-tse, a figure accepted as real by Chinese tradition but simply not comprehensible in biographical terms, again because of the unreliability of the sources from which—according to our choice—it would be possible to assign his life to the fourteenth, thirteenth, eighth, seventh or sixth century B.C.

A critical comparison in fact produces amazing differences:

The teachings of Buddha have been transmitted through sources which were recorded at least five hundred years after his death, when the original religion had already undergone a far-reaching development.

It is only since the first century B.C. that Lao-tse has been designated as the author of the Tao Tê Ching, the classical "Book of the Way and of Virtue," which is in fact a compilation of writings from several centuries, finally becoming decisive for the formulation of Taoist teaching.

Of the most important texts containing the Confucian tradition, the *Biography* by Szu-ma Chien is four hundred years and the *Analects* (Lun-yü, a collection of Confucius' sayings, attributed to his disciples and incorporated into situation accounts) about seven hundred years after the Master's death; they are scarcely reliable anyway. There are no authentically assured writings nor any authentic biography of Confucius (nor is it likely that the *Chronicle of the State of Lu* is by him).

European texts are in much the same state. The oldest extant manuscript of the Homeric epics is from the thirteenth century. The text of Sophocles' tragedies is based on a single manuscript of the eighth or ninth century. But the New Testament manuscripts in our possession are much closer in time to the original writings, more numerous and in closer agreement with each other than any other ancient book.[5] There are accurate manuscripts of the Gospels dating from the third and fourth century.

In recent times, particularly in the Egyptian desert, even older papyri have been discovered: the oldest fragment of the Gospel of John—the last of the four Gospels—now in the John Ryland's library in Manchester, belongs to the beginning of the second century and does not deviate by a single word from our printed Greek text. The four Gospels therefore already existed about the year 100; mythical enlargements and new interpretations (in the apocryphal gospels and so on) are found from the second century onwards. The road obviously ran from history to myth and not from myth to history.

Jesus of Nazareth is not a myth: his history can be *located*. It is not a legend which turns up in a number of places, like the story—regrettable as it may be for the Swiss—of the national hero William Tell. The events certainly took place in a politically insignificant country, in a marginal province of the Roman Empire. Nevertheless, this country of Palestine represents a very ancient civilization at the center of the "fertile crescent." Before the cultural-political balance was shifted to the two tips of the crescent, Egypt and Mesopotamia, about the seventh millennium B.C., there occurred here the great revolution of the early ice age, when the hunters and food gatherers settled down as agriculturalists and cattle breeders: thus for the first time in history men began to make themselves independent of nature, to dominate it as autonomous producers, until almost four thousand years later when the next revolutionary step took place at the two extremities of the crescent, Egypt and Mesopotamia. Now came the creation of the first advanced civilizations and the invention of writing; finally, five thousand years later we have what must be regarded as the last great revolutionary step for the time being, we are literally reaching for the stars.

Jericho, named in the parable of the Good Samaritan and again recently excavated, can be regarded as the oldest urban settlement in the world (7000–5000 B.C.). As a narrow land bridge between the kingdoms on the Nile, Euphrates and Tigris, an obvious battlefield for the great powers, Palestine in the time of Jesus was under the rule of the Roman military power, hated by the Jews, and the half-Jewish vassal-rulers nominated by Rome. Although some National Socialists tried to make him an Aryan, Jesus undoubtedly came from Palestine: to be more exact, from the northern region of Galilee with a population not wholly Jewish but mixed, which however—unlike Samaria, lying between Judea and Galilee—recognized Jerusalem and its temple as the main cult center. It was in any case a small sphere of action: between Capernaum on the pleasant lake of Gennesaret in the north and the capital city Jerusalem in the mountainous south it is only eighty miles as the crow flies, a week's journey in those days by caravan.

Jesus of Nazareth is not a myth: his history can be *dated*. It is not a supratemporal myth of the kind which was characteristic of the early civilizations. Not a myth of everlasting life as in Egypt. Not a myth of cosmic order as in Mesopotamia. Not a myth of the world as transformation as in India. Not a myth of the perfect man as in Greece. It is a question of the history of this one man who was born in Palestine at the beginning of our era under the Roman Emperor Augustus, appeared in public under his successor Tiberius and was finally executed by the latter's procurator, Pontius Pilate.

Uncertainties

Other more exact circumstances of place and time remain doubtful, but they are not particularly relevant.

a. *Where did he come from?* Jesus' birthplace is not mentioned by the evangelists Mark and John, while Matthew and Luke—deviating from each other in closer details—make it Bethlehem, perhaps for theological reasons (Davidic descent and the prophecy of Micah), although some scholars suggest Nazareth. It seems impossible to decide exactly where he was born. In any case it is quite evident from the whole of the New Testament that the real home town of the "Nazarene" was Nazareth, an insignificant place in Galilee. The genealogies of Jesus in Matthew and Luke coincide at David, but otherwise are so far apart that they cannot be harmonized. The more or less universal view of exegetes today is that the infancy stories, embellished with a number of legendary features, and likewise the edifying story of the twelve-year-old Jesus in the temple, recorded only by Luke, have a special literary character and are used as aids to the theological interpretation of the evangelists. Up to a point the evangelists have no inhibitions in talking about Jesus' mother Mary, his father Joseph, and also of his brothers and sisters. According to the sources, both his family and the people of Nazareth seem to have dissociated themselves from his public activity.

b. *When was he born?* If Jesus was born under the Emperor Augustus (27 B.C. to A.D. 14) and King Herod (27–4 B.C.), the year of his birth was not later than 4 B.C. We can deduce no more from the miraculous star—which is not to be equated with a particular constellation of stars—than from the census of Quirinius (A.D. 6 or 7), which was perhaps important for Luke as the fulfillment of a prophecy.

c. *When did he die?* If Jesus was baptized by John the Baptist—and this is generally accepted as a historical fact—according to Luke in the fifteenth year of the Emperor Tiberius (that is, A.D. 27/28 or 28/29), if he was about thirty years old according to Luke at this first public appearance and according to tradition as a whole (including Tacitus) condemned under Pontius Pilate (26–36), he must have met his death about the year 30. Even if we refer to the calendar of feasts of the Qumran community near the Dead Sea, it is impossible to be quite certain of the day of his death: the three first evangelists differ in this respect from John (15 or 14 Nisan).

If then the dates of Jesus' life—like many points of time in ancient history—cannot be established with final accuracy, it really is remarkable that he made such an impact on history. Within that adequately defined space of time, a man about whom there are no "official" documents, no inscriptions, chronicles or court files, who was active in public at the most for three years (according to the three Passovers reported by John), but perhaps only for one year (the Synoptics mention only one Passover), perhaps even merely for a few dramatic months, mostly in Galilee and then in Jerusalem, this one man has so changed the course of history that with good reason people began to date the years of the world from his birth (subsequently an embarrassment to the leaders of the French Revolution as also to those of the October Revolution and of the Hitler era). None of the great founders of religions lived in so restricted an area. None lived for such a terribly short time. None died so young. And yet how great his influence has been: every fourth human being, about a thousand million human beings, are called Christians. Numerically, Christianity is well ahead of all world religions.

2. *The documents*

Christian faith speaks of Jesus, but historiography also speaks of him. Christian faith is interested in Jesus as the "Christ" of the Christians, historiography in Jesus as a historical figure. As a result of modern scientific thinking and the development of a historical consciousness men today are more interested than in the Middle Ages or in antiquity in getting to know the personality of the human Jesus as it really was. But to what extent is Jesus of Nazareth accessible to the historian's questioning and study? Does the historian get anywhere near him?

More than a biography

Despite innumerable books on Jesus in the form of a novel, *one* thing has become clear. However easily his history can be located and dated, it is quite *impossible* to write a *biography* of Jesus of Nazareth. Why? The presuppositions are simply lacking.

There are the early Roman and Jewish sources, but these—as we saw—report scarcely anything that is useful beyond the fact of the historical existence of Jesus. And, in addition to the Gospels officially accepted in the Church from time immemorial, there are the considerably later "apocryphal" (=hidden) gospels, embellished with all kinds of strange legends and dubious reconstructions of the sayings of Jesus, which are not used in public worship and which—apart from a very few sayings—likewise produce nothing that is historically certain about Jesus.

There remain then those *four Gospels* which, according to the "canon" (=guiding principle, standard, list) of the early Church, were accepted for public use into the collection of New Testament Scriptures (analogous to those of the Old Testament), as original testimony to the Christian faith: a selection which—like the New Testament as a whole—has proved its worth by and large over the history of two thousand years. Nevertheless, these four "canonical" Gospels do not provide the course of Jesus' life with its different stages and events. On the infancy we know little that is certain, nothing at all about the time up to his thirtieth year. More importantly, in perhaps only a few months or at best three years of public activity, it is impossible to establish the very thing that would be needed for any biography: his development.

Certainly we know in a general way that Jesus' path led from his Galilean homeland to the Jewish capital, Jerusalem, from the proclamation of the nearness of God to the conflict with official Judaism and to his execution by the Romans. But the first witnesses were obviously not interested in a chronology or topology of this path. Nor were they any more interested in his inner development, in the genesis of his religious and particularly his messianic consciousness, or in his motives, still less in a "character study" of Jesus, his "personality" and "interior life." To this extent (and only to this extent) the nineteenth-century liberal quest of the historical Jesus failed in its attempt to work out the periods and motivations of Jesus' life, as Albert Schweitzer admits in his classical history of *The Quest of the Historical Jesus.*[6] An external and more particularly an internal psychological development of Jesus cannot be read out of the Gospels, but only read into them. How does this come about?

Even for non-theologians it is important and not without interest to know how the *Gospels emerged* in a process of about fifty to sixty years.[7] Luke speaks of this process in the opening statements of his Gospel. Surprisingly enough, Jesus himself did not leave a single written word and did nothing to secure the faithful reproduction of his words. The disciples at first passed on orally what he had said and done. At the same time, like any narrator, they themselves changed the emphasis, selected, clarified, interpreted, extended, in each case in the light of their own personal inclination and the needs of their hearers. There may have been from the beginning a straightforward narrative of the work, teaching and fate of Jesus. The evangelists—certainly not all directly disciples of Jesus, but witnesses of the original apostolic tradition—collected everything very much later: the stories and sayings of Jesus orally transmitted and now partly fixed in writing, not as they might have been kept in the civic archives of

Jerusalem or Galilee, but as they were used in the religious life of the early Christians, in sermons, catechetics and worship. All these texts emerged out of a particular "living situation" (*Sitz im Leben*), they already had behind them a history which had helped to shape them, had already been passed on as the message of Jesus. The evangelists—undoubtedly not merely collectors and transmitters, as people once thought, but absolutely original theologians with their own conception of the message—arranged the Jesus narratives and Jesus sayings according to their own plan and at their own discretion. They provided a particular setting as the background for a continuous narrative. The story of the Passion, related with striking unanimity by all four evangelists, seems to have been formed into a single narrative at a comparatively early date. The evangelists—themselves certainly actively engaged in missionary work and in catechizing—arranged the traditional texts to suit the needs of their communities. They interpreted them in the light of the Easter events, expanded them and adapted them where they thought it necessary. Hence, despite all their common features, the different Gospels each acquired a very different profile of the one Jesus.

In the midst of the upheaval between the first and second generation of Christians, shortly before the destruction of Jerusalem in the year 70, it was *Mark*—according to the most widely held view today—who first wrote a Gospel (this theory of the priority of Mark is opposed to the older traditional view that Matthew's Gospel came first). It represents a supremely original achievement: this Gospel, though scarcely written in literary language, constitutes a completely new literary genre, a form of literature which had never existed before that time.

After the destruction of Jerusalem, *Matthew* (probably a Jewish Christian) and *Luke* (a Hellenist writing for an educated public) used for their larger Gospels on the one hand Mark's Gospel and on the other hand a collection (perhaps more than one) of Jesus' sayings known as the Logia source, generally designated Q (for *Quelle*=source) by scholars in this field.[8] This is the classical "Two Source Theory" as it was worked out in the nineteenth century and meanwhile has proved successful in a variety of ways in the exegesis of particular texts. It assumes that each evangelist has also made use of his own material—special material as distinct from their common sources—a fact which is clearly manifested when the different Gospels are compared with each other. The comparison shows also that Mark, Matthew and Luke largely agree on the great structural plan, on the selection and arrangement of the material and very often even in the wording, so that they can be printed alongside one another to make comparison easier. They form a con-spectus: a "syn-opse." They are therefore called the "Synoptic" Gospels and their authors the Synoptists.

By comparison with these, the Gospel of *John*, writing in the Hellenistic area, has a completely different character in both the literary and theological sense. Because of Jesus' very different manner of speaking in John, the un-Jewish form of what amount to long monologues, and because of its content wholly oriented to the person of Jesus himself, the fourth Gospel provides an answer only in a very relative sense to the question of who the historical Jesus of Nazareth was: for example, with reference to the traditions of the Passion history and the events immediately preceding it. Seen as a whole, it is obviously more remote from the historical reality of the life and work of Jesus than are the Synoptic Gospels. Undoubtedly too it was the last Gospel to be written (as David Friedrich Strauss discovered early in the nineteenth century). It could have been written about the year 100.

Committed testimonies

From all this it is clear that the Gospels cannot be regarded as stenographic reports. They are not meant to give a historical account of Jesus nor to describe his "development."

From beginning to end, their aim is to proclaim him in the light of his resurrection as Messiah, Christ, Lord, Son of God. For "Gospel" did not originally mean a written Gospel, but—as is clear from Paul's letters—an orally proclaimed message: good, joyful news (*euangelion*). And "the gospel of Jesus Christ, the Son of God," first written by Mark, is intended to convey the same message of faith now in written form.

The Gospels then are not meant to be disinterested, objective, documentary accounts and still less neutral, scientific historiography. Nothing like this would have been expected at that time, since the meaning and influence of historical events was always described together with the facts. They are therefore accounts which, in one form or another, also counted as testimony and were strongly colored by the attitude of the author behind them. The historiographers Herodotus and Thucydides were just as much partisans for the Greek cause as Livy and Tacitus for the Roman. They made their attitude quite apparent and frequently even drew a lesson from the events they reported: they produced not merely a narrative or a reportage, but didactic-pragmatic historiography.

The Gospels however are genuine testimonies in a very much deeper sense. As the "Form-Critical School" made clear after the First World War by investigating individual sayings and stories of Jesus down to the slightest detail,[9] they are determined and characterized by the different forms of religious experience of the communities. They see Jesus with the eyes of faith. They are therefore *committed testimonies of faith meant to commit their readers:* documents not by non-participants but by convinced believers wanting to appeal for faith in Jesus Christ and which therefore take the form of an interpretation or even of a profession of faith. These accounts are at the same time sermons, in the broadest sense of the term. Their authors are witnesses so stirred by this Jesus as one can be stirred only in faith and they want to transmit this faith. For them Jesus is not only a figure of the past: he is living also today and has a decisive significance for the hearers of this message. In this sense the Gospels are meant not only to report, but to proclaim, to stir, to rouse faith. They are committed testimony or—as it is often expressed with the corresponding Greek word—"kerygma": proclamation, announcement, message.

This orientation and peculiar character of the Gospels do not merely render impossible a biography of Jesus. They make any dispassionate, historical interpretation of the texts more difficult. Of course no serious scholar assumes today, as people did at the beginning of Gospel criticism, that the disciples deliberately falsified the story of Jesus. They did not arbitrarily invent his deeds and words. They were simply convinced that they now knew better than in Jesus' lifetime who he really was and what he really signified. Hence they had no hesitation in following the custom of the time and placing everything that had to be said in regard to him under his personal authority: both by putting certain sayings into his mouth and by shaping certain stories in the light of his image as a whole. But the question arises quite seriously at least for our historical consciousness: how much in these Gospels is an account of what really happened and how much is interpretation? How do we distinguish between Jesus' own words and deeds and interpretation, supplementation, paschal exaltation or glorification by the community or the evangelists?

If we have to assume that the Gospels are primarily sources revealing the post-paschal faith in Christ on the part of the Christian communities, can they still be sources at all for what the pre-paschal, earthly, historical Jesus himself said and did? Karl Barth[10] and with him Bultmann[11] and Tillich,[12] as a result of the conclusions of the early liberal quest for the historical Jesus, took up an attitude of historical skepticism (which Schweitzer by no means shared) and linked this up with Kierkegaard's conception of faith, defending a faith that is historically uncertain (or dogmatically insured against history) as true faith.

Today, however, as a result of the new state of the exegetical problem, a far-reaching agreement in principle even between the more progressive German scholars and the more conservative Anglo-Saxon and French scholar is emerging. The Gospels are certainly testimonies of faith, documents of faith for faith (in this respect Barth, Bultmann and Tillich were right). But just as certainly they contain historical information. In any case, starting out from them, we can raise the counterquestion about the Jesus of history. Even Albert Schweitzer, frequently wrongly regarded as a skeptic (he was skeptical only in regard to the modernized liberal Jesus, the type who might at any time have intervened in the debate at a clergy conference), had asked about the historical Jesus and accordingly submitted his own attempt at a reconstruction: the Jesus—for him the original Jesus—of "consistent eschatology" (to be discussed later).

3. *History and faith's certainty*

The stories of Jesus lead us to ask for his real history: not indeed for a continuous biography, but certainly for what really happened. Despite all the difficulties, the preconditions for such an investigation have become easier. This is the result of the modern *historical-critical method*. If the New Testament can be described today as the best-investigated book in world literature—circulating in about fifteen hundred languages—this is the result of some three hundred years of comprehensive, scrupulously exact work on the part of whole generations of scholars. They have made use of textual and literary criticism, form and genre criticism, together with the history of concepts, motives and tradition, while wrestling over every sentence and even—as will become clear to the non-expert after a glance at the numerous commentaries and more particularly the monumental nine-volume theological dictionary of the New Testament—every word.[13]

What has *textual criticism* achieved for the investigation of the Gospels? With the aid of external and internal criticism, taking into consideration language and content, and examining the history of the texts, it has established the text of the Scriptures in the oldest attainable form with the greatest possible accuracy and exactitude.

And *literary criticism?* It has investigated the literary integrity of the Scriptures. It has brought out the diversity of the legal, religious and social conditions presupposed by the authors, the differences in language, chronology and historical data, in theological and moral views. By distinguishing between oral and written tradition as sources, it has thrown light on the possible state of the original text before new material was introduced. It has determined the age, origin, recipients and the literary character of the New Testament writings. It has compared them as literature with contemporary Jewish and Hellenistic literature and described their special features.

And *form and genre criticism?* It has raised the question of the situation of the text in the life of the community and the individual, of the literary form, of the framework of smaller literary units, of the original form, and has attempted in this way to determine afresh both the historical reliability and the content of tradition.

And finally the *history of tradition?* It has undertaken the examination of the pre-literary process, analyzed the oldest hymns, liturgical fragments, laws, etc., linked them with worship, preaching, catechesis and community life, and thus attempted to discover the decisive factors in the Church's origin and the first stage of its development.

Counterquestions about Jesus

With the historical-critical method in this comprehensive sense theology is provided with an instrument enabling the question about the true, real, historical Christ to be asked in a way that was simply not possible in former centuries.

The Gospels themselves assert the claim that the living Christ whom they proclaim is the same as the man Jesus of Nazareth with whom at least some of their witnesses had lived during his earthly activity. Certainly the testimonies of faith *are* not simply accounts, but they *contain* an account and are *based* on accounts of the real Jesus. But in what respect and to what extent? The reader of the Gospels would certainly like to know whether and how far there is or is not agreement between the Jesus of the Gospels and the Jesus of history: are they really true testimonies?

The counterquestion about Jesus is not irrelevant for the historian. *It is only by raising this question that the scholar concerned either with the ancient East or with the Roman Empire, either with the Jewish or with the Christian religion, can make any attempt to explain the amazing rise of Christianity.*

But neither is it irrelevant even for the believer. *This question alone can enable both the preacher and his hearers to know whether their faith is ultimately based on what happened, on history, or on a myth, on legends and assumptions, or perhaps simply on a misunderstanding. Whether therefore his Christian commitment in the world of today is ultimately substantiated and justified or not.*

It is not irrelevant even for the non-believer. *Only in the light of this question can the old Communist, the supporter of the New Left, the liberal atheistic humanist or positivist know what is ultimately the point of the dispute. Whether he is fighting against phantoms or against real opponents. Whether he is coming to grips not only with the political and social consequences of Christianity, not only with some sort of modern, medieval or ancient Christianity, but truly with the reality, the heart of Christianity itself.*

In *theology* today can the question of historical truth still be dogmatically suppressed, can history be slighted in principle in the name of faith? The wind of scholarship has changed direction in recent years, even though some older warriors would like to remain satisfied with an unsubstantiated "kerygma" and if necessary perhaps even with an irrational *Credo quia absurdum* ("I believe just because it seems absurd"). Pure kerygmatic theology has had its day. A scholarly answer to the question about the Jesus of history is again regarded as possible today in a new form and within certain limits: not only in Anglo-Saxon[14] and French[15] exegesis, but also once more in German and indeed—after Ernst Käsemann had given the signal to turn in 1953[16]—in the Bultmann school itself.[17] However justified the interpretation of all New Testament texts with reference to the "historicity" of human existence ("existential interpretation") and to the "decision" of the individual, it must not become so individualistic and introspective as to fade out real history (and thus the "world," society, the social relevance of the message, the future).

The kerygma of the community simply cannot be understood unless we begin quite concretely with the historical Jesus of Nazareth, as Bultmann's theology of the New Testament also proves. The proclamation of Jesus itself would not have been transmitted at all or finally recorded in the Gospels if it had not corresponded to the proclamation of the community. The post-paschal proclamation does not in fact mean an absolutely new start. Between the pre-paschal Jesus and the proclamation of the post-paschal community there is not only a break, but also a connection: *a continuity despite all discontinuity*. The alternative, kerygma (proclamation) *or* history (report), is a false alternative. *In* the Gospel message of faith is to be recognized that history in which the evangelists—themselves in the service of the proclamation—were obviously interested decades after the historical Jesus and the kerygmatic Pauline letters: and not merely in Jesus' "word," "kerygma," "proclamation" (Bultmann), but also in his deeds, his fight and his destiny of death.

Of course it would be unreasonable for an uncritical reader to assume that we could take for granted *a priori* the reliability of a piece of tradition, that we could without more ado therefore take the whole content of the Gospels (with that of the Old Testament) in one lump as historical facts. But it would likewise be unreasonable for a hypercritical reader to think that reliability is *a priori* exceptional, that practically nothing in the Gospels could be taken as historical fact. The truth lies between shallow credulity which is closely related to superstition and radical skepticism which is frequently linked with an uncritical belief in hypotheses. If we examine the state of the New Testament sources without prejudice, we shall describe the *Jesus tradition* historically as *relatively reliable*. This means when we come to interpret it that the transformations, developments and contrarieties of the New Testament tradition exclude the smooth assumption that Jesus himself or the Holy Spirit made provision for an exact retention and transmission of his words and deeds. We must allow for changes of perspective and shifts of emphasis, growth and regression, disclosures and closures, within these traditions.

As we saw, the Jesus of history is not identical with the Christ image of traditional dogmatics.[18] Nor is he identical with the speculative idea of Christ fostered by German Idealism with its orientation to the Gospel of John.[19] But neither is he identical with the "liberal" portrayals of Jesus in the nineteenth century, based on a preference for Mark.[20] Nor again is he identical with the Jesus image of "consistent eschatology" which saw in him simply the prophet of the imminent end of the world.[21]

In terms of *method*, this means that, if today we are to make statements which are historically certain about Jesus, we cannot start out from a particular image of him. But neither can we start out from what are possibly only post-paschal sovereign titles like Messiah, Christ, Lord or Son of God. We shall have to begin modestly with the individual, certainly authentic sayings (*logia*) and actions of Jesus. In this respect, methodically, the critical principle has come to prevail that we are more certain to come across the authentic touch of Jesus where something cannot be explained or deduced either from contemporary Judaism or from primitive Christianity. In this way it is possible to build up a minimum of authentic Jesus material. But even this pragmatic principle has its limits. It leads to a minimalistic contraction if it is forgotten that Jesus was a man rooted in his own time and undoubtedly had much in common also with contemporary Judaism and with primitive Christianity. Of course such common features can be ascribed to Jesus very cautiously only if they do not contradict what has been critically established as typical Jesus material but can be fitted into the dominant features. At the same time there is a relatively wide border area where it can scarcely be decided with any certainty whether Jesus himself is speaking or the community is interpreting him.

And should it not be possible in this way to restore the original delineation of Jesus by carefully taking off the different layers of paint imposed upon it? A comprehensive historical analysis of the Gospels makes it possible to bring out over a wide area what belongs to each of the *three different strata:* what is redaction by the evangelists (redaction history), what is interpretation, explanation or occasionally even reduction by the post-paschal *community*, and finally what are pre-paschal sayings and actions of *Jesus*, and hence what is Jewish in a general sense and what is typical for Jesus, what corresponds to the total context and what does not.

This means that an examination must be carried out saying by saying, narrative by narrative: all things considered, a difficult and delicate business. It presupposes a considerable skill and—like all historical research—an objectivity as free as possible from (denominational, historical, personal) bias.

Indubitable mathematical or scientific certainty is not to be expected from any historical argumentation. With Jesus as with Socrates, and in varying degrees with all historical personalities, it is often possible to reach only a more or less high degree of probability. Our knowledge—beginning with the question whether my legal father is my real father—is of course based to a large extent on such probabilities. And, in order to be defensible, faith no more needs a guaranteed infallible knowledge at its disposal than love does. Like all human knowledge, the knowledge of faith is also fragmentary. Only when faith remains aware of this does it remain free from arrogance, intolerance and false zeal.

Despite all difficulties then we can uphold the historical possibility and the theological legitimacy of a recourse to the Jesus of history. If we may sum up the perhaps rather brittle material in even more brittle terms, we are raising a methodical counterquestion from the testimonies of faith to the Jesus of history.

Why is it *possible?* Because, between the preaching of Jesus and the preaching of his herald, on the whole between the Jesus of history and the primitive Christian proclamation of Christ, despite all the discontinuity, there is a continuity. Why is it also *justified?* Because the primitive Christian proclamation of Christ could have emerged and can be understood only in the light of the history of Jesus. Why is it even *necessary?* Because it is only in this way that the primitive Christian and thus too the modern proclamation of Christ can be protected from the suspicion that it is not founded on a historical fact, but is merely an assertion, a projection of faith, or even a pure myth, an apotheosis.

The question is thus concentrated on the *content.* If today no biographical chronology, topography, psychology of the life of Jesus, certainly no "closed" (traditional, speculative, liberal or consistent-eschatological) image of Jesus, can be reconstructed, if the Gospels are to be regarded as committed testimonies of faith meant to commit their readers, *what* can still be reconstructed with the aid of a counterquestion?

First of all, a very general answer can be given: *the typical basic features and outlines of Jesus' proclamation, behavior and fate.* And it is just this which suffices and is decisive for the believer. Such a reconstruction can be carried out, even though what we call the authenticity of every individual saying of Jesus or the historicity of every individual narrative is not proved. A saying put into Jesus' mouth by the evangelist—and therefore "unauthentic"—can just as authentically reproduce the authentic Jesus as a saying which he himself really uttered—and therefore "authentic." In this connection what are more important than the historically proved authenticity of a particular saying are the ruling tendencies, the peculiar forms of behavior, the typical basic trends, the clearly dominating factors, what is not pressed into schemes and patterns but the "open" total picture. And in this respect we are not without an answer.

That is to say, an answer is possible if we avoid the danger of not seeing the wood for the trees, the consensus for the diversities of opinion—a danger to which scholars preoccupied with exegetical details are sometimes exposed. These discussions of exegetical details are about as important or unimportant as the question whether Bach's Brandenburg Concertos were originally written for the Margrave of Brandenburg (they were not) or whether the Second in F Major should be played with the trumpet or the horn (and which), and so on. Certainly these are important differences, at least for the musical scholar. But there is no doubt about the name of the work and everyone knows the melody, whether it is played with trumpet or horn. And, although there may be some doubt about the details of the score, there can be none at all about the existence of the work and about the score as a whole. In fact, we can hear and enjoy the Brandenburg No. 2, even without knowing the problems of the history of music, although a little knowledge helps us to get more out of listening to it. Need we take any further the comparison with the Gospels and their theme?

In the Gospel testimonies of faith the *history of Jesus himself* is related: memories still alive in the community, experiences, impressions, traditions of the living Jesus of Nazareth, his words, deeds and sufferings. Not directly, but certainly throughout the Gospel testimonies of faith, we can hear Jesus himself. That is to say, if anyone in face of this testimony raises not secondary but essential questions and raises them not merely casually but seriously, he will receive peculiarly harmonious, clear and original answers. They do not simply happen to combine different forms of theological treatment. Even though the authenticity of some individual feature may remain historically questionable, there is heard here the original word of Jesus, the original Jesus himself. At the same time we must be prepared for surprises. The original Jesus might be just as different from the traditional as the artist's original from his touched-up paintings. And we might then see all that the Church and theology have made out of this Jesus liturgically, dogmatically, politically, legally, educationally, and what they have done with him often without being aware of it.

Restoration, reconstruction, however, are terms which can be misunderstood. Only a positivist conception of history would be satisfied with the observation of facts and the reconstruction of the causal connections. In Christianity it is a question not merely of "Jesus as he really was," not merely of a "historical Jesus" remaining in the past. Christianity is interested in Jesus as he confronts us *here and now*, in what he has to tell us authoritatively in the present state of man and society. In this sense the "historical Jesus" and the "Christ of faith" cannot be set apart from each other as two diverse factors. Even in the liberal quest for the historical Jesus, historical research on Jesus and the examination of Christological problems cannot be completely separated: because of the new state of the problem, which we have described, this is less than ever possible today. But it remains of fundamental importance particularly for the present significance of Jesus. Today less than ever are we thrown back on assumptions and conjectures. Because of the work of so many generations of exegetes and the results of the historical-critical method, we are able today to know better than perhaps any former generations of Christians—except the first—the true, original Jesus of history.

But is our *faith* any better on this account? What does historical-critical research on Jesus mean on the whole for faith, for my faith?

Justifiable faith

Can historical-critical research on Jesus, can theological scholarship as a whole produce faith, the certainty of faith, as some hope? No, it *cannot provide reasons for faith.* For I do not believe "in" research, in theological scholarship, in the results of scholarship—which are often altered. Only the message in which I believe can provide reasons for faith. And even then it is not the message as such, as the word of man, but the person who speaks to me, who is proclaimed, in this message. I believe—first of all, to put it quite simply—in God as he addresses me in this Jesus.

On the other hand, however, can this research on Jesus, theological learning as a whole, perhaps destroy my faith, as others fear? No, it *cannot destroy faith.* Neither the conceit of the theologically educated nor the fear of the theologically uneducated is called for. As theology cannot provide reasons for faith, neither can it destroy faith. The ground of faith is not theology, but God himself. And, as long as I keep to this ground, even tendentious, false criticism may threaten but not destroy my faith. In the history of exegesis and theology this sort of criticism has constantly been overcome by genuine, objective criticism. And this again can only help my faith. In what way?

Theological learning, research on Jesus, with courage for critical thinking and respect for the facts, enable us to take stock of the tradition of faith, *to give an account of our faith* to ourselves and to others. Both uncritical credulity and critical skepticism can be shaken out of their false security. But faith itself can be purified from both inculpable superstition and ideologies inspired by vested interest. Thus impediments to faith can be removed and even readiness for faith awakened. Certainly, historical-critical research cannot and is not meant to provide me with proofs of faith. Faith presupposes my personal decision. If it could be proved, it would no longer be faith. It should however be a well-founded, responsible decision, made after reflection. But faith should not try to establish historical facts from its own resources. Certainties of faith may not be presented as scientific conclusions. An account of Christian faith must be given in such a way that people can be expected to respond and that it can be realized at the present time. We can demand of a person only that for which he can be held responsible.[22]

Purely "historical faith" then is not saving faith. The results of scholarship are not truths of salvation merely because they are historically certain.

But on the other hand "unhistorical faith" is not necessarily a sign of strong faith: sometimes it is a sign of feeble thought. The faith of a rational human being should at least not be irrational. Christian faith, according to its original testimonies, is a faith to be rationally understood and justified. But theology consists precisely in methodically circumspect, scholarly justification of any talk of and to God.[23]

As a concrete task this means that, from the history of this Jesus, from his words, from his conduct and his fate, the undiluted claim and the true meaning of his person can and should be made intelligible. It should be recognized from history how he then set and still sets ultimate questions before the individual and society in a way quite unparalleled in its criticism and promise, how in person he is invitation, challenge, encouragement to faith.

And what does it really mean *to believe?* To begin with, a summary description in question and answer form will suffice:

> *Is Christian faith a matter of understanding?*
> *To take faith simply as an act of understanding, as theoretical knowledge, as acceptance of the truth of biblical texts or ecclesiastical dogmas, even as an assent to more or less improbable assertions: this is the intellectualist misunderstanding of faith.*
> *Is Christian faith an effort of will?*
> *To understand faith simply as an act of will, as resolution of the will in face of inadequate evidence, as a blind venture, as a* Credo quia absurdum, *even merely as a duty of obedience: this is the voluntarist misunderstanding of faith.*
> *Is Christian faith a matter of emotion?*
> *To understand faith simply as an act of feeling, as a subjective emotion, as an act of faith* (fides qua creditur) *without any content of faith* (fides quae creditur), *where the fact of believing is more important than what one believes: this is the emotional misunderstanding of faith.*
> *Christian faith is none of these things. In absolute trust and complete reliance, the whole man with all the powers of his mind commits himself to the Christian message and to him whom it announces. It is simultaneously an act of knowing, willing and feeling, a trust which includes an acceptance of message and person as true.*

Hence I do not simply believe various facts, truths, theories, dogmas: I do not believe this or that. Nor do I believe merely in a person's trustworthiness: I do not simply believe this man or that. But I venture quite confidently to commit myself to a message, a truth, a way of life, a hope, ultimately quite personally to someone: I believe "in" God and in him whom God sent.[24]

Of course believing takes different forms in the different Christian

Churches. And it is in the strength of the different traditions that the weaknesses also lie. The specific danger of Protestant belief is biblicism, the danger of Eastern Orthodox belief is traditionalism, the danger of Roman Catholic belief is authoritarianism. All these are defective modes of believing. Against these dangers it must be clearly stated that

> *the Christian (the Protestant too) believes, not in the Bible, but in him whom it attests;*
> *the Christian (the Orthodox too) believes, not in tradition, but in him whom it transmits;*
> *the Christian (the Catholic too) believes, not in the Church, but in him whom the Church proclaims.*
> *What man can turn to as absolutely reliable for time and eternity are not the texts of the Bible, nor the Fathers of the Church, nor indeed an ecclesiastical magisterium, but it is God himself as he spoke for believers through Jesus Christ. The biblical texts, the statements of the Fathers and ecclesiastical authorities, are meant—in varying degrees of importance—to be no more and no less than an expression of this faith.*

Historical criticism—an aid to faith?

Can I be *certain* of my faith? A man never has his faith safely, so to speak, "in the bag." If I am resolved to believe—and genuine faith requires a decision—this is not a once-and-for-all decision for faith. And if I progress in knowing by faith—and genuine faith always implies knowledge and knowledge which progresses with experience of life—then my knowledge of faith is nevertheless everywhere followed by doubt as its shadow. There are and throughout life there always will be temptations to give up the faith, at the same time the challenge to maintain and deepen it despite everything. And I shall constantly have to put my faith into practice, to realize it and lay hold on it, despite all doubts, uncertainties and obscurities. Lay hold on it, since another lays hold on me, encompassing me, one who never coerces, but invisibly accords complete freedom in the whole visible world, so that man can live by the invisible and master the problems of the visible world. This sustaining reality of God is never granted to me intuitively, unequivocally, free of doubt, securely. I can always decide otherwise, I can live as if God did not exist. But I can also live by faith and then admittedly not be secure, yet wholly and entirely *certain*. The believer, like the lover, has no conclusive proofs to give him complete security. But the believer too, like the lover, can be completely certain of the Other by committing himself entirely to the Other. And this certainty is stronger than all the security established by proofs.

If then the ultimate reality of God is revealed only to trusting, committed faith, it is obviously not accessible to historical investigation. The external consequences of faith can be historically established at different times, among different nations and cultures. But what such faith ultimately means for the life of a man and the life of mankind in depth cannot—any more than love—be measured by statistics or grasped by scientific methods: it can only be experienced. But this should not prevent us from giving a clear answer to the remaining closing questions relating to historical-critical Jesus research and Christian faith.

a. Does historical-critical Jesus research presuppose faith? No. Even the unbeliever can carry out objective research on Jesus.

The unbeliever, like the believer, will certainly approach Jesus with a preconception. For Jesus is not simply unknown to him. But this preconception must not become a prejudice if the investigation is to be carried out objectively.

If a researcher takes up a negative attitude to Jesus, he will at least not regard his No as already a final conclusion.

If he takes up a positive attitude, his Yes must not pass over the problems of research.

If he takes up an indifferent attitude—if this is ever possible—this indifference too must not be elevated to a principle.

The presupposition of historical research therefore is not belief or unbelief, still less indifference, but certainly an open-mindedness in principle toward everything that comes to us from this frequently disturbing figure. A preconception certainly cannot simply be laid aside. But it can be suspended, as long as we are aware of it. And it can be corrected in the light of the figure we are to know.

b. On the other hand, does faith presuppose historical-critical Jesus research? No. There was faith even before Jesus research and today many believe without regard to the results of research.

Such a faith however must be described as naïve in the light of the present state of consciousness. Naïveté in matters of faith is not evil but at least dangerous. Naïve faith can miss the true Jesus and lead us with the best intentions to false conclusions in theory and practice. Naïve faith can lead the individual or a community to become blind, authoritarian, self-righteous, superstitious. Both at the beginning and also today faith should be an intelligent, justifiable faith. But intelligent, justifiable faith today presupposes—directly or indirectly—historical research, at least in its general results. If we do not take note of it or take note too late, then unexpected confrontations will lead to unnecessary crises of faith. It is very easy then for church leaders, who did nothing to enlighten the faithful, to shift the blame onto the theologians. But modern means of communication increasingly lead to the most important results of research becoming common property. Fortunately, they can no longer be kept secret.

c. A positive result emerges from the two answers. Christian faith and historical research are not mutually exclusive in one and the same person. The two Nos involve a Yes.

Christian faith can reveal new depths, perhaps the decisive depth, to the scholar. History entirely free of presuppositions is *a priori* impossible. But internal involvement promotes understanding. On the other hand a knowledge of history can reveal new prospects to the Christian believer, can give him insight and satisfaction, can inspire him in a variety of ways. Enlightenment—as history proves—can avert religious fanaticism and intolerance. Only faith and knowledge combined—a faith that knows and a knowledge that believes—are capable today of understanding the true Christ in his breadth and depth. After this long approach route, is it not time to turn to him in all his concreteness, in his concreteness and in his strangeness? The next section provides for the transition and a further clarification of what is distinctively Christian.

III. Christianity and Judaism

Jesus is by no means merely an ecclesiastical figure. Sometimes he is even more popular outside the Church than inside it. But, however popular he is, what is immediately evident—when we look at the real Jesus—is his *strangeness*. And historical analysis, however uncongenial, arduous or even superficial it may seem to some, can help to ensure that this strangeness will not be concealed: that he is not simply fitted into our personal or social requirements, habits, wishful thinking, cherished ideas, that he is not appropriated into the world outlook, moral theories, legal opinions, of Church authorities or theologians, not played down in the Church's rites, creeds and feasts. The all-important point is to let Jesus speak without restriction, whether this is congenial or not. Only in this way can he himself come closer to us in his strangeness. Obviously this does not mean the mechanical repetition of his words, the recital of as many biblical texts as possible, preferably in a long-familiar translation. Nevertheless an interpretation that is relevant in the proper sense of the word is possible only at a certain distance from him. Strictly speaking, I must at the same time keep at a distance from myself, from my own thoughts, ideas, valuations and expectations. Only when it becomes clear what he himself wanted, what hopes he brought for the people of his own time, can it also become clear what he himself has to say to the people of the present time, what hopes he can offer for mankind today and for a future world.

1. *The sufferings of the past*

What is there about this Jesus that seems strange to us? Here we shall be occupied first of all only with a single, but admittedly basic feature of his nature. Jesus was a human being, a fact which has always been more or less clearly asserted in Christendom. But there has not been the same readiness to admit that Jesus was a *Jewish* human being, a genuine Jew. And for that very reason he was only too often a stranger to both Christians *and* Jews.

Jesus the Jew

Jesus was a Jew, a member of this small, poor, politically powerless nation living at the periphery of the Roman Empire. He was active among Jews and for Jews. His mother Mary, his father Joseph, his family, his followers were Jews. His name was Jewish (Hebrew *Yeshua*, a late form of *Yehoshua*="Yahweh is salvation"). His Bible, his worship, his prayers were Jewish. In the situation at that time he could not have thought of any proclamation among the Gentiles. His message was for the Jewish people, but for this people in its entirety without any exception.

From this basic fact we can conclude without more ado that without Judaism there would be no Christianity. The Bible of the early Christians was the Old Testament. The New Testament Scriptures became part of the Bible only by being appended to the Old. The Gospel of Jesus Christ everywhere quite consciously presupposes the Torah and the Prophets. The Christians too hold that the same God of judgment and grace speaks in both Testaments. This special affinity was the reason why Judaism was not discussed in the earlier chapter on the non-Christian religions, although everything positive that was said there about these religions as ways of salvation holds to a far greater extent and in a very different way for Judaism. It is not with Buddhism, Hinduism and Confucianism, not even with Islam despite its influence there, but only with Judaism that Christianity has this unique relationship: a relationship of origin, resulting in numerous common structures and values. At the same time the question also immediately arises, why it was not Judaism—despite its universal monotheism—but the new movement starting out from Jesus—Christianity—which became a religion for all mankind.

It is precisely between those who are most closely related that the bitterest hostility can exist. One of the saddest features of the history of the last two thousand years is the hostility which has prevailed almost from the beginning between Jews and Christians. It was mutual, as so often between an old and a new religious movement. It is true that the young Christian community at first seemed to be no more than a particular religious trend within Judaism, professing and practicing a special conception of religion, but incidentally maintaining its connection with the Jewish national community. But the process of detachment from the Jewish people was rooted in the profession of faith in Jesus. It was very quickly set in motion with the formation of a Gentile Christianity free from the law. The Gentile Christians soon formed the overwhelming majority and their theology lost any immediate reference to Judaism. After a few decades the process was completed with the destruction of Jerusalem and the end of temple worship. In a dramatic history the Church had thus been changed

—quantitatively and qualitatively—from a Church of Jews into a Church of Jews and Gentiles and finally a Church of Gentiles.

At the same time the Jews who did not want to recognize Jesus began to be hostile to the young Church. For their part they thrust the Christians out of the national community and persecuted them, as is illustrated particularly by the story of Saul the Pharisee, who however as the Apostle Paul constantly upheld the special election of the people of Israel. It was perhaps already in the second century that the cursing of "heretics and Nazarenes" was included in the main rabbinical prayer, recited daily (*Shemoneh 'Esreh*). In short, at an early date Jews and Christians were at cross-purposes with each other. The intellectual discussion was reduced more and more to wrestling for proof-texts for or against the fulfillment of the biblical promises in Jesus.

A history of blood and tears

The rest was predominantly a history of blood and tears.[1] Once in control of power in the state, the Christians forgot only too quickly the persecutions by Jews and Gentiles which they had suffered. Christian hostility to Jews was not at first racial, but religious. It would be more correct on the whole to speak of anti-Judaism than of anti-Semitism (for Arabs, too, are Semites). In the Imperial Constantinian Church what had been pre-Christian, pagan anti-Judaism was given a "Christian" stamp. And although in subsequent times there were also examples of fruitful collaboration between Christians and Jews, the situation of the Jews became very much more difficult, particularly after the high Middle Ages. Jews were slaughtered in Western Europe during the first three Crusades and Jews in Palestine were exterminated. Three hundred Jewish communities were destroyed in the German Empire from 1348 to 1349; Jews were expelled from England (1290), France (1394), Spain (1492) and Portugal (1497). Later came the horrifyingly virulent anti-Jewish speeches of the elderly Luther. Persecution of Jews continued after the Reformation, there were pogroms in Eastern Europe, and so on. It must be admitted that, during these periods, the Church probably slew more martyrs than it produced. All of which is incomprehensible to the modern Christian.

It was not the Reformation, but humanism (Reuchlin, Scaliger), then pietism (Zinzendorf) and particularly the tolerance of the Enlightenment (with its declarations of the rights of man in the United States and in the French Revolution) which prepared the way for a change and up to a point also brought it about. The complete assimilation of European Jews at the time of their emancipation admittedly did not entirely succeed, but came nearest to doing so in America. It would be presumptuous to attempt to trace here the terrible history over many centuries of the suffering and death of the Jewish people, culminating in the Nazi mass insanity and mass murder which claimed a third of all Jewry as its victims. The word "deplore" in the Declaration of the Second Vatican Council—like a corresponding declaration of the World Council of Churches,[2] more a beginning than an end—sounded terribly weak and vague after all these horrors. Even this statement was nearly prevented by the Roman Curia, quick to get upset about Hochhuth's problem-charged *The Deputy* but still too concerned with political opportunism and persistent anti-Jewish feeling to give diplomatic recognition to the state of Israel.

In view of this situation—still far from being resolved—and of a veiled anti-Judaism in Rome and Moscow, unfortunately also in New York and elsewhere, it must be absolutely clearly stated that Nazi anti-Judaism was the work of godless, anti-Christian criminals. But it would not have been possible without the almost two thousand years' pre-history of "Christian" anti-Judaism, which prevented Christians in Germany from organizing a convinced and energetic resistance on a broad front.

Although some Christians were also persecuted and others—especially in Holland, France and Denmark—gave effective help to Jews, it must be noted in order to define more precisely the question of guilt that none of the Nazi anti-Jewish measures were new: special distinguishing clothing, exclusion from professions, prohibition of mixed marriages, expropriation, expulsion, concentration camps, massacres, burnings. All these things existed in what were called the "Christian" Middle Ages (see, for example, the measures adopted by the great Fourth Lateran Council in 1215) and at the time of the "Christian" Reformation. Only the racial argument was new, prepared by the French Count Arthur Gobineau and the British-born Houston Stewart Chamberlain and put into practice in Nazi Germany with horrifyingly thorough organization, technical perfection and a dreadful industrialization of murder. After Auschwitz there can be no more excuses. Christendom cannot avoid a clear admission of its guilt.

2. *Future possibilities*

Must the sufferings of the past, however, be the sufferings of the future? The awareness which started with the Enlightenment and had its effect particularly in the United States in the nineteenth century has meanwhile stamped itself on the whole of Christendom.

Increasing understanding

The most recent, most terrible catastrophe to affect the Jewish people and the re-emergence of the state of Israel—which Christians had not expected and which is the most important event in Jewish history since the destruction of Jerusalem and the Temple—have shaken anti-Jewish "Christian" theology: that pseudo-theology which reinterpreted the Old Testament salvation history of the Jewish people as a New Testament history of a curse on the Jewish people, overlooking the permanent election of this people asserted by Paul and relating it exclusively to Christians as the "new Israel." With the Second Vatican Council the new awareness also came to prevail in the Catholic Church.[8]

The idea of a collective guilt on the part of the Jewish people of that time or even of the present in regard to the death of Jesus was expressly rejected by the council. No one dares any longer to take seriously the old widespread prejudices that Jews are "money-men," "poisoners of wells," "Christ killers," "deicides," "cursed and condemned to dispersion."

It is easier now to perceive the psychological motives operative in anti-Judaism: group hostility, fear of being the odd man out, search for scapegoats, contrary ideals, personality structure disturbance, mass emotionalism.

The old excuses offered shamefacedly or shamelessly have become obsolete: "The Jews too have made mistakes"; "We must understand the spirit of the age in which these things happened"; "The Church itself was not involved"; "One had to choose the lesser evil."

We are beginning therefore to recognize that the Jews are in many respects an enigmatic community linked by a common destiny and with an amazing power of endurance: a race, a single-language community, a religious community, a state, a nation, and yet not really any of these. They are a community linked by a common destiny, involved in a religious mystery in which this "people of God" is acknowledged by devout Jews and devout Christians alike to have a special vocation among the peoples of the world. Christians must at least take note of the fact that within this perspective—despite the cruel sacrifices involved for Arabs who have lived in Palestine for centuries—the movement for their return to their "promised land" has a religious significance for many Jews.

Whatever Christians of Arab descent—for whom one must have sympathy—may think about the state of Israel, a Church which—as so often in the past—preaches love and sows hatred, proclaims life and yet prepares death, cannot invoke Jesus of Nazareth to support its attitude. Jesus was a Jew and all anti-Judaism is a betrayal of Jesus himself. The Church has stood too often between Jesus and Israel. It prevented Israel from recognizing Jesus. It is high time for Christendom not merely to preach "conversion" to the Jews, but to be "converted" itself: to the *encounter* which has scarcely begun and to a not merely humanitarian but *theological discussion* with Jews, which might be an aid not merely to a "mission" or capitulation, but to understanding, mutual assistance and collaboration.

Indirectly perhaps it might even help toward increasing understanding between Jews and Christians on the one hand and Muslims on the other, for we cannot ignore the fact that Muslims in virtue of their origin are closely linked with both Jews and Christians: through a common belief in God the Creator and in the resurrection of the dead with reference to Abraham and Jesus, both of whom have an important place in the Koran. After all that has happened, the conditions are more favorable than they have ever been for a genuine discussion between Christians and Jews, to whom Christianity, Islam and mankind as a whole owe the incomparable gift of strict monotheistic belief. These conditions must include an unreserved acknowledgment of the religious autonomy of the undoubtedly rigorous and exacting Jewish partner.

a. Long before Hitler's time, in *Christendom* as a whole and among exegetes particularly in German-speaking and Anglo-Saxon countries, a new open-mindedness had been established for the Old Testament in its autonomy and in its agreement with the New Testament. The importance of the rabbinical commentators for the understanding of the New Testament has likewise been recognized. We have begun to see that there are powerful aspects of Hebrew thought which can be compared with that of the Greek-Hellenistic world: greater historical dynamism, total alignment, devout and joyous acceptance of the world, the body and life, hunger and thirst for justice, orientation to the future kingdom of God. All this has helped to overcome the Neo-Platonic, Neo-Aristotelian, Scholastic and Neo-Scholastic incrustation of Christianity. For the official Catholic Church the declaration of Vatican II on the Jews became "the discovery or rediscovery of Judaism and the Jews both in their intrinsic value and in their meaning for the Church" (J. Oesterreicher).[4]

b. The mental situation of *Judaism* has likewise changed very much, particularly since the restoration of the state of Israel: the decreasing influence of casuistic legalist piety especially among the younger generation and the increasing importance of the Old Testament by comparison with the former universal validity of the Talmud. What is most typically Jewish has been brought home to Christians by the great minds of Jewry in this century: women like Simone Weil and Edith Stein, men like Hermann Cohen, Martin Buber, Franz Rosenzweig, Leo Baeck, Max Brod, Hans Joachim Schoeps, but also more indirectly Sigmund Freud, Albert Einstein, Franz Kafka, Ernst Bloch. And thus the way has been prepared today for a common investigation by Jewish and Christian scholars of both the Old Testament and the rabbinical works and also up to a point of the New Testament (as a testimony also of the history of the Jewish faith). This affinity has also been made clear in a more lively and original development in worship on both sides, an affinity which goes far beyond literary criticism and philology. There is no doubt about the fact that the Jew in virtue of his Judaism can discover aspects of the New Testament which often enough escape the Christian. All things considered, despite numerous inhibitions and difficulties, there is a growing awareness of a common Jewish-Christian *basis* which is not merely humanitarian but *theological*. Jews too are asking today for "a Jewish theology of Christianity and a Christian theology of Judaism" (J. Petuchowski).[5]

The theological discussion between Christians and Jews, however, has proved to be infinitely *more difficult* than that between separated Christians who have a common basis at least in the Bible. But the conflict between Christians and Jews cuts right across the Bible and splits it into two Testaments, of which the former prefer the New and the latter the Old. And can we ever overlook the real point of the controversy? The very person who seems to unite Jews and Christians also separates them abysmally: the Jew Jesus of Nazareth. Can Jews and Christians ever reach agreement about him? It seems that more is involved here than "two ways of faith" (M. Buber). For Jews to give up their unbelief in regard to Jesus seems just as unlikely as for Christians to cease to believe in Jesus. For then the Jews would no longer be Jews and the Christians no longer Christians.

Discussion about Jesus?

The dispute seems hopeless. Is there really any point in Jews and Christians discussing Jesus of Nazareth? But the question could be put in another way. Would there not be advantages to both sides if the Christian readiness for understanding were met on the Jewish side with a movement to break down mistrust, skepticism and rancor toward the figure of Jesus and instead to arrive at a more historical-objective judgment, to spread genuine understanding and perhaps even regard for his person? Immense progress has been made in recent times. A long list could be produced of authors and their books on Jesus of Nazareth published recently in the state of Israel.[6] There are undoubtedly numerous Jews who would at least accept the "Jesus of culture" even though they reject the "Jesus of religion."[7] The *cultural* significance of Jesus is therefore asserted. And it is in fact very difficult for a modern Jew to share fully in Western cultural life without constantly encountering Jesus, even if it is only in the great works of Bach, Handel, Mozart, Beethoven, Bruckner and of Western art as a whole.

This, however, still leaves open the question of the *religious* significance of Jesus. If today the religious significance of Judaism is being subjected by Christians to a new appraisal, should not Jews on the other hand face up to the question on the religious significance of Jesus? Jesus—the last of the Jewish prophets? Even in the nineteenth century there was a considerable Jewish tradition which attempted to take Jesus seriously, as a genuine Jew, even as a great witness of faith. And at the turn of the century Max Nordau, the faithful collaborator of Theodor Herzl, the founder of the Zionist movement, wrote: "Jesus is the soul of our soul, as he is flesh of our flesh. Who then would want to exclude him from the Jewish people?"[8]

In the first half of the present century there followed the first thorough studies of the figure of Jesus on the Jewish side: the various publications of Claude G. Montefiore[9] and especially Joseph Klausener's work,[10] certainly the best-known book on Jesus by a Jew and one which, as a result of its use of material from Talmud and Midrash, can be described as the beginning of the modern Hebrew quest for the historical Jesus. It was the important Jewish thinker Martin Buber who first described Jesus as the "elder brother," to whom "belongs an important place in Israel's history of faith," who "cannot be fitted into any of the usual categories."[11] The Jewish Jesus scholar David Flusser draws attention to the fact that in Jesus we have in the concrete a Jew talking to Jews: from him a Jew can learn how to pray, fast, love his neighbor, can learn what is the meaning of the Sabbath, of God's kingdom and the judgment.[12] Schalom Ben-Chorin's book *Brother Jesus. The Nazarene from the Jewish Viewpoint* is on these lines: "Jesus is certainly a central figure of Jewish history and the history of the Jewish faith, but he is also a part of our present and future, no less than the prophets of the Hebrew Bible whom we can also see not merely in the light of the past."[13]

Here however the *limit* to a Jewish acknowledgment of Jesus the Jew also becomes clear. For all his understanding of the figure of Jesus, Schalom Ben-Chorin writes in the same book: "I feel his brotherly hand which grasps mine, so that I can follow him," but adds, "It is *not* the hand of the Messiah, this hand marked with scars. It is certainly not a *divine*, but a *human* hand in the lines of which is engraved the most profound suffering . . . The faith of Jesus unites us, but faith in Jesus divides us."[14] But does not this very hand with its wounds call for an explanation, a deeper explanation?

It is not impossible that in the future more Jews will come with a struggle to acknowledge Jesus as a great Jew and witness of faith and even as a great prophet or teacher of Israel. The Gospels have a unique fascination for a number of Jews. They show to the Jew the possibilities lying within the Jewish faith itself. And cannot Jesus be understood almost as a *personal symbol of Jewish history?* The Jew Marc Chagall constantly depicted the sufferings of his people in the figure of the Crucified. We might see it in this way: does not the history of this people with its God, this people of tears and of life, of lamentation and confidence, culminate in this one figure, Jesus, and his history as a striking sign of the crucified and risen Israel?

In all this, however, there remains the one disturbing question: who is Jesus? More than a prophet? More than the law? Is he even the Messiah? A Messiah crucified in the name of the law? Must the discussion come to a complete end at this point? Here perhaps the Jew particularly could help the Christian to conduct the *discussion* on Jesus afresh, as we suggested, not from above, but *from below*. This would mean that we too would consider Jesus today from the standpoint of his Jewish contemporaries. Even his Jewish disciples had to start out first of all from Jesus of Nazareth as man and Jew and not from someone who was already obviously the Messiah or still less Son of God. It was only in this way that they could raise at all the question of the relationship of Jesus to God. And for them, even later, this relationship did not consist in a simple identification with God, which might have meant that Jesus was God the Father. Perhaps the Jew could also help the Christian to understand better those central New Testament statements on Jesus and particularly his honorific titles which have an eminently Hebraic background.

Be that as it may, if in what follows we start out from Jesus of Nazareth as man and Jew, we shall be able to go *a good part of the way together* with an unbiased Jew. And it may be that in the end the final decision for or against Jesus will yet look rather different from what the long Jewish-Christian dispute might have led us to expect. The only plea we are making at the moment is once more for open-mindedness which does not permit the unavoidable pre-conception—Christian or Jewish—to become a pre-judgment. We are not asking for neutrality but certainly for objectivity in the service of the truth. At a time of fundamental reorientation of the relationship between Christians and Jews, we shall have to remain open to all future possibilities.

For the time being, however, we seem to have said enough about the *distinguishing* Christian feature. Looking back, what makes Christianity to be Christianity? We may distinguish it from the modern humanisms, from the world religions or from Judaism: the distinguishing Christian factor is this Christ who, as we saw, is identical with the historical Jesus of Nazareth. Jesus of Nazareth as the Christ, finally authoritative, decisive, archetypal, is what makes Christianity what it really is.

But we must not merely provide a formal outline, which is what we have been doing up to now. We must now also determine the content. Looking ahead, therefore, we can sum it up in the fact that Jesus himself in person is the *program* of Christianity. That is why we said at the beginning of this chapter and say again at the close that Christianity consists in the activation of the memory of Jesus Christ in theory and practice. But, to determine the content of the Christian program, we must know what sort of a memory we have of him. "We must learn again to spell out the question: who is Jesus? Everything else is a distraction. We must measure ourselves against Jesus, not measure him against our churches, dogmas and devout church members . . . Their value depends entirely on the extent to which they point away from themselves and call us to follow Jesus as Lord."[15]

C. THE PROGRAM

I. The Social Context

If Jesus Christ himself is the distinctive feature of Christianity and if the same Jesus Christ is also the program of Christianity, the questions arise: Who is this Jesus? What did he want? For, whoever he was and whatever he wanted, Christianity is bound to seem different in the light of what each of us understands of his person and attitude. The questions have been raised not only in a modern context, but also in the total social, cultural-religious context of his own time and there they became finally questions of life or death. Jesus— What does he want? Who is he? Does he belong to the establishment or is he a revolutionary? Is he a guardian of law and order or a champion of radical change? Does he stand for a purely inward-looking spiritual life or does he advocate thoroughgoing worldliness?[1]

1. *Establishment?*

Jesus has often seemed to be "domesticated" in the Churches, turned almost into the representative of the religio-political system, justifying everything in its dogma, worship and canon law: the invisible head of a very clearly visible ecclesiastical machinery, the guarantor of whatever has come into existence by way of belief, morals and discipline. What an enormous amount he has been made to authorize and sanction in Church and society in the course of Christendom's two thousand years! How Christian rulers and princes of the Church, Christian parties, classes, races have invoked him! For what odd ideas, laws, traditions, customs, measures he has had to take the blame! Against all the varied attempts to domesticate him, therefore, it must be made clear: *Jesus did not belong to the ecclesiastical and social establishment*.

The religio-political system

Is this an anachronistic statement of the question? Not at all. In Jesus' time there was a solid religio-political-social establishment, a kind of theocratic ecclesiastical state which was to break him.[2]

The whole structure of power and dominion was understood to be authorized by God as supreme Lord. Religion, judiciary, administration, policy were indissolubly interwoven. The structure was dominated by the same men: a priestly hierarchy with higher and lower clergy (priests and Levites), inheriting office, unloved by the people, but, together with a few other groups, exercising dominion over the by no means homogeneous Jewish society. They were of course under the control of the Roman occupying power, which had reserved to itself political decisions, provision for peace and order, and—it seems—death sentences.

The ruling classes were represented by seventy men under the presidency of the high priest in the central governmental, administrative and judicial body, all-powerful in all religious and civil matters, the supreme council in Jerusalem (called in Aramaic Sanhedrin, Greek *synedrion*=assembly). The high priest, although appointed by the Romans, always remained the supreme representative of the Jewish people.

And Jesus? Jesus had nothing to do with any of the three groups wielding power. He had nothing to do with the "high" or "chief" priests (the officiating high priest and—apparently in a kind of consistory—the retired high priests, together with some other holders of high priestly offices). Nor was he connected with the "elders" (the heads of the influential non-sacerdotal, aristocratic families in the capital). Nor, finally, was he one of the "scribes" (jurist-theologians, mostly but by no means always sharing the Pharisaic outlook), who had also for some decades been members of the supreme council. All these groups were soon to be Jesus' enemies. It was clear from the beginning that he was not one of them.

Neither priest nor theologian

The Jesus of history was *not a priest*. We must not be misled in this respect by the letter to the Hebrews, where Jesus is described as the "eternal high priest": this is a subsequent, post-paschal interpretation. He was an ordinary "layman" and *a priori* suspect to the priests as the ringleader of a lay movement from which they dissociated themselves. His followers were simple people. Among the numerous figures appearing in Jesus' popular parables that of the priest turns up only once, not as an example but as a deterrent, since—unlike the heretical Samaritan—he passes by the man fallen among thieves. It seems that Jesus quite deliberately drew his material mostly from ordinary life and not from the sacral sphere.

And, although professors of theology may deplore the fact, the historical Jesus was *not a theologian*. An indirect proof of this may be found in the late "legend"* of the twelve-year-old boy in the temple, included in the

* "Legend": a literary genre used to explain the origins of a holy person; it is not necessarily unhistorical, but is meant more to satisfy the reader's interest in the hero's sanctity than to provide historical details. (Translator.)

Lucan infancy narratives.[3] Jesus was a villager and moreover—as his opponents pointed out—had not been through a course of study.[4] He could produce no evidence of a theological training; he had not spent the usual long years of study with a rabbi, had not been ordained and authorized as a rabbi by imposition of hands, even though many apparently addressed him by that title as a matter of courtesy. He did not pretend to be an expert on all possible questions of doctrine, morality or law, nor did he regard himself primarily as a guardian and interpreter of sacred traditions. Living as he did on the heritage of the Old Testament, he did not apply to it a scholastic exegesis as the scribes did, he scarcely invoked the authority of the Fathers, but put forward his own ideas directly and naturally with amazing freedom in method and in choice of subject.

He could perhaps be described as a public storyteller of the kind that can be seen even today addressing hundreds of people in the main square of an Eastern city. Jesus of course did not tell any fairy tales, sagas or miracle stories. He drew upon his own and others' experiences and turned them into the experiences of his hearers. His interest was expressly practical and he wanted to advise and help people.

Jesus' style of teaching is not professional, but popular and direct: if necessary, keenly argumentative; often deliberately grotesque and ironical, but always pregnant, concrete and vivid. He finds just the right word, uniting in a remarkable way close observation of facts, poetic imagery and rhetorical passion. He is not tied down to formulas or dogmas. He does not indulge in profound speculation or in erudite legal casuistry. He makes use of universally intelligible, catchy sayings, short stories, parables, drawn from the plain facts of ordinary life, familiar to everyone. Many of his sayings have become proverbs in every language. Even his statements about the kingdom of God are not secret revelations of conditions which are going to exist in heaven, nor are they profound allegories with several unknown factors, of the kind produced in abundance in Christendom after his time. They are sharply pointed likenesses and parables which set the very varied reality of God's kingdom in the midst of human life dispassionately and realistically observed. Despite the decisiveness of his views and demands, they do not presuppose any special intellectual, moral or ideological attitudes. People are expected simply to listen, to understand and draw the obvious conclusions. No one is questioned about the true faith or the orthodox profession of faith. No theoretical reflection is expected, but an urgent, practical decision.

Not with the rulers

The Jesus of history was *not a member or a sympathizer of the liberal-conservative government party*. He was not one of the Sadducees. The high priest was normally chosen from this party of the socially privileged class, whose name came either from that of the high priest Zadok (of Solomon's time) or from the adjective *saddik* (=righteous). As a clerical-aristocratic party, the Sadducees combined liberalism abroad with conservatism at home. They practiced a realistic "foreign policy" of adaptation and détente and respected unreservedly Rome's sovereignty, but internally they were concerned to maintain their own power, in order to save whatever could be saved of the clerical, ecclesiastical state.

Jesus was obviously not prepared to adopt the new-Hellenistic style of life in a spirit of apparent open-mindedness toward the world; but neither was he prepared to uphold the existing order or to set aside the great idea of the approaching kingdom of God. He rejected both that kind of liberalism and that kind of conservatism.

He had no sympathy for the conservative *view of the law* held by the leading groups. These latter certainly regarded only the written law of Moses as binding, but for that very reason rejected the later, often milder interpretations of the Pharisees. They wanted above all to maintain the temple tradition and therefore urged an uncompromising observance of the Sabbath and insisted on the strict penalties of the law. In practice, however, they frequently had to adapt themselves to the Pharisees' more popular view of the law.

Nor had Jesus any sympathy for the conservative *theology* taught by the priestly aristocracy of the Sadducees. It was a theology which insisted on the written word of the Bible and preserved orthodox Jewish dogmatics, maintaining that God now largely leaves the world and man to their fate and regarding belief in the resurrection as an innovation.

Radical change

Jesus was not concerned about the religio-political status quo. His thinking was wholly and entirely dominated by the prospect of the better future, the better future of the world and of man. He expected an imminent radical change in the situation. That is why he criticized in word and deed the existing order and radically called in question the ecclesiastical establishment. Temple liturgy and legalistic piety had been the two foundations of the Jewish religion and the national community since Israel's return from the Babylonian exile in the fifth century and the reform of the scribe Ezra: for Jesus they were not the supreme norm. He lived in a different world from that of the hierarchs and politicians, who were fascinated by Roman world power and Hellenistic civilization. Unlike the temple liturgists, he did not believe merely in the permanent lordship of God over Israel, in his ever existing, enduring world dominion, which is involved in the very fact of the creation of the world. Like many devout people of his time, he believed in the advent in the near future of God's rule over the world, which would bring with it the eschatological and final consummation of the world. "Your kingdom come" meant what in theological jargon are known as the *eschata*, "the last things," the "eschatological" rule of God: *the future kingdom of God at the end of time.*

Jesus was sustained therefore by an intense *expectation of the end.* For him the existing system was not final, history was moving toward its end. In fact the end was at hand, at that very moment. His own generation would see it: the turning point of all the ages and God's eschatological revelation[5] (Greek, *apocalypsis*). There is no doubt then that Jesus was under the spell of the "apocalyptic" movement which had gripped large sections of Jewry from the second century B.C. onwards, under the influence of anonymous apocalyptic writings ascribed to Henoch, Abraham, Jacob, Moses, Baruch, Daniel and Ezra. Jesus, it is true, was not interested in satisfying men's curiosity with mythical speculations or astrological predictions. Unlike the apocalypticists, he did not bother about dating and localizing the kingdom of God, nor did he reveal apocalyptic events and secrets. But he shared the belief that God would soon, within his lifetime, bring the course of the world to an end. What was anti-God and satanic would be destroyed. Hardship, suffering and death would be abolished; salvation and peace, as the prophets had proclaimed, would be established. This would be the turning point and judgment of the world, the resurrection of the dead, the new heaven and the new earth, the world of God replacing the existing increasingly evil world. In a word, God's kingdom would be present.

The expectation fostered by certain statements of the prophets and by the apocalyptic writings had mounted in the course of time and impatience had increased. For the man who was later to be called the *precursor* of Jesus this tense expectation had reached its climax. He proclaimed the approaching kingdom of God as judgment. It would not however be a judgment as generally understood by the apocalypticists: a judgment on the others—the pagans—and the destruction of God's enemies and the final victory of Israel. As maintained in the great prophetical tradition, it would be a judgment particularly on Israel: descent from Abraham would be no guarantee of salvation.

John's prophetic figure represented a living protest against the affluent society in the towns and villages, against the Hellenistic culture of the cities. In a spirit of self-criticism he confronts Israel with its God and, looking to God's kingdom, he demands a "penance" that amounts to more than ascetical practices and liturgical acts. He calls for repentance and a turning of one's whole life to God. That is the reason why he baptizes. It is typical of him that this *baptism of penance* is administered once only and offered to the whole nation, not merely to a chosen group. It cannot be derived either from the ritually repeated expiatory immersions of the Qumran community near the Jordan or from the baptism of

Jewish proselytes (a rite of reception into the community, required by law, only known in later times). Immersion in the Jordan becomes the eschatological sign of purification and election in view of the approaching judgment. This form of baptism seems to be an original creation of John. It is not without good reason that he is called the Baptist.

According to all the Gospel accounts, the *beginning of Jesus' public activity* coincides with the Johannine movement of protest and awakening. John the Baptist—whom some circles even in later New Testament times regarded as a rival of Jesus—constitutes for Mark "the beginning of the gospel"; and, if we disregard the prelude of the infancy stories in Matthew and Luke and John's prologue, this idea was consistently maintained in the later Gospels.

Even Jesus submits to John's baptism of penance.[6] This fact creates dogmatic problems, but for that very reason is generally accepted as historical. Jesus thus approves John's prophetical activity and, after the latter's imprisonment or even earlier, links up his own preaching with John's. He takes up John's eschatological call for penance and draws his conclusions from it with ruthless logic. It is not impossible that Jesus became aware of his own vocation at his baptism, even if the scene has been given Christological features (voice from heaven) and been adorned with legendary embellishments (the Spirit descending "as a dove").[7] All accounts agree anyway that he was aware from that time onwards of being possessed by the Spirit and authorized by God. The baptismal movement and particularly the arrest of John were signs for Jesus that the time was fulfilled.

So Jesus begins to proclaim the "good news" up and down in the country and to gather around him his own disciples, some at first perhaps from the Baptist's circle.[8] He announces: "The kingdom of God is close at hand, repent and believe the good news."[9] But, unlike the sinister threats of judgment uttered by the ascetical John, this from the beginning is a friendly, joyous message of the goodness of the approaching God and of a kingdom of justice, joy and peace. The kingdom of God does not come primarily as judgment but as grace for all. Not only sickness, suffering and death, but also poverty and oppression will come to an end. This is a liberating message for the poor, the miserable and those burdened with sin: a message of forgiveness, justice, freedom, brotherliness and love.

This very message, however, bringing joy to the people, is evidently not aimed at the maintenance of the established order as defined by temple worship and observance of the law. Jesus does not seem merely to have had certain reservations in regard to sacrificial worship.[10] He evidently assumed that the temple would be destroyed at the end-time, now imminent,[11] and he soon came into conflict with the law when he came to be regarded by the Jewish establishment as an extraordinarily dangerous threat to its power. The hierarchy and their court theologians were bound to ask if he was not in fact preaching revolution.

2. Revolution?

If by "revolution" we mean a fundamental transformation of an existing state of affairs, then the message of Jesus was certainly revolutionary. Of course the word is sometimes used merely to advertise a new product which is to replace the old and we speak—not entirely incorrectly—of a revolution in medicine, in business management, in education or in fashion. But such facile, ambiguous, general ways of speaking are not really helpful in the present context. Our question must be stated more precisely. Did Jesus want the social order, its values and representatives, to be suddenly and violently overthrown (*re-volvere* means "to roll back")? This is revolution in the strict sense (as in the French Revolution or the October Revolution), whether it comes from left or right.

The revolutionary movement

Like "establishment" this question is by no means an anachronism. The "theology of revolution"[1] is not an invention of our time. The militant apocalyptic or Catharist movements in antiquity, the radical sects of the Middle Ages (especially the political messianism of Cola di Rienzo) and the left wing of the Reformation (particularly Thomas Münzer) were all attempts to realize this theology of revolution in the history of Christendom. The thesis that Jesus himself was a politico-social revolutionary has been maintained from time to time, at first by the early pioneer of the historical-critical investigation of the Gospels, S. Reimarus (†1768),[2] then by the Austrian socialist leader K. Kautsky,[3] later by Robert Eisler,[4] whose work has been largely reproduced in our own time by J. Carmichael,[5] and most recently by S. G. F. Brandon.[6]

Now there is no doubt that Jesus' native country, Galilee, was particularly susceptible to calls for revolution and was regarded as the home of the *revolutionary movement of the Zealots* (Greek *zelotes*, meaning "enthusiast," with an undertone of fanaticism). Nor is there any doubt that at least one of Jesus' followers, Simon the Zealot,[7] had been a revolutionary; some have thought that the name of Judas Iscariot implies the same thing and that it was on this account that even John and James were called "sons of thunder."[8] Finally and more importantly, it should be observed that the term "King of the Jews"[9] played a decisive role in the process before Pontius Pilate, that Jesus was executed by the Romans for political reasons and that he had to suffer the death reserved to slaves and political rebels. These accusations might have been given a certain plausibility by such events as Jesus' entry into Jerusalem and the purification of the temple, at least in the way they are reported.[10]

No other people was as tenacious as the Jewish in its mental and political resistance to the alien Roman rule. The Roman authorities' apprehensions of revolution were only too well founded. They had been faced for a considerable time with an acute revolutionary situation in Palestine. Unlike the Jerusalem establishment, the revolutionary movement rejected any form of collaboration with the occupying power, even the payment of taxes; it had numerous lines of communication particularly with the Pharisee party and became increasingly influential.

Numerous Jewish nationalist partisans were active particularly in Jesus' homeland, and Herod—the Idumaean appointed as "King of the Jews" by the Roman Senate, at the end of whose term of office Jesus was born—was forced to have them executed. After the death of King Herod, who had ruled with firmness and cunning, disturbances broke out again and were ruthlessly suppressed by Roman troops under the Syrian supreme commander Quintilius Varus (later unsuccessful against the Germanic tribes). The real foundation of a revolutionary party came about in Galilee under Judas of Gamala (mostly known as "the Galilean"). It was soon after this that the Emperor Augustus in the year A.D. 6 had Herod's son, the brutal Archelaus, deposed as vassal ruler (no longer "king" but "ethnarch") of Judea. Judea was placed under direct Roman administration under a procurator and the whole population registered by the Roman supreme commander in Syria, now Sulpicius Quirinius, to secure a more effective system of taxation (Luke has a vague reference to it in connection with the birth of Jesus).[11] In Galilee—where the people under the other son of Herod, Herod Antipas, were only indirectly affected—the rebellious Zealots attempted a rising, the only result being that their leader Judas perished and his supporters were dispersed.

Yet, despite the absolute superiority of the Roman military power, the resistance groups were not liquidated. They had their bases mainly in the wild Judean mountains, and Josephus, the Jewish historiographer in the service of the Romans, complains about those whom he calls—like the Romans—simply "brigands" or "bandits": "And so Judea was filled with brigandage. Anyone might make himself king as the head of a band of rebels whom he fell in with, and then would press on to the destruction of the community, causing trouble to few Romans and then only to a small degree but bringing the greatest slaughter upon their own people."[12]

Forming a kind of town guerrilla, the resistance fighters disposed summarily of enemies and collaborators with a short dagger (Latin *sica*). For this reason the Romans called them appropriately *sicarii*, "stabbers." There was always a special danger on the great feast days, when large crowds of pilgrims turned up in Jerusalem. The Roman governor (procurator) then usually took the precaution of leaving his seaside residence at Caesarea to go to the capital. This is what Pontius Pilate did at the time when Jesus' conflict with the Jewish establishment had reached its climax. But, even apart from this, he had good reason to be there. For his constant provocations from the beginning of his period of office in the year 26 had created a mood of rebellion and an uprising could have broken out at any time. Among other things, contrary to all sacred traditions, which were respected even by the Romans, Pilate had caused the military standards adorned with the image of the emperor, the state cult divinity, to be brought overnight to Jerusalem. This led to violent demonstrations and Pilate gave way. But when he took money from the temple treasury to build an aqueduct to Jerusalem, he nipped the rising opposition in the bud. And, according to Luke,[13] for some reason or other, he had a number of Galileans slaughtered with their sacrificial animals when they came up to the temple in Jerusalem. Barabbas too, whom Pilate freed instead of Jesus, had taken part in a revolt involving murder.[14]

After Jesus' death, Pilate was deposed by Rome on account of his brutal policy in the year 36. It was not until thirty years later that the guerrilla war finally became the great national war which the Jerusalem establishment was unable to prevent. Here again a Galilean, John of Gischala, leader of the Zealots, played an essential part and, after a long conflict with other revolutionary forces, defended the temple area until the Romans broke through the three surrounding walls and the temple went up in flames. With the conquest of Jerusalem and the liquidation of the last resistance groups the revolution reached its cruel end. Even then one of the groups had been able to hold out for three years in Herod's mountain fortress, Masada, against the Roman besiegers. Masada, where the last resistance fighters finally committed suicide, is today a Jewish national shrine.[15]

Hope of a liberator

There is no doubt that the national expectation of a great liberator, an "anointed one" (Messiah, Christ) or king who was to come, an eschatological envoy and plenipotentiary of God, played a considerable part in the revolutionary movement. What attracted the people's faith was something the Jewish rulers preferred to pass over in silence and even the theologians did not like to mention. Under the influence of the apocalyptic writings and ideas, messianic expectation had frequently mounted up to enthusiasm. Anyone who now appeared on the scene with a claim to leadership raised the question of whether he was perhaps "the one to come" or at least the latter's forerunner.

Expectations of course varied greatly in detail. While some expected the Messiah to be the political descendant of David, others looked for the apocalyptic Son of Man, Judge and Saviour of the world. Even in A.D. 132, in the second and last great revolt against the Romans, the leader of the Zealots, Bar Kokhba, "Son of the Star," had been welcomed by Akiba, the most respected rabbi of his time, and by many other scribes as the promised Messiah, before he fell in battle and Jerusalem after a second destruction became for centuries a city forbidden to Jews. After this, rabbinic Judaism was little inclined to recall the memory of Bar Kokhba.

And Jesus? Was his message not *very close to the revolutionary ideology?* Would it not have had a strong appeal to the Zealot revolutionaries? Like the political radicals, he expected a fundamental change in the situation, the early dawn of God's rule in place of the human system of government. The world was not in order: there had to be a radical change. Jesus too sharply criticized the ruling classes and the rich landowners. He spoke out against social abuses, miscarriages of justice, rapacity, hardheartedness, and on behalf of the poor, oppressed, persecuted, wretched, forgotten. He spoke scathingly of those who wore soft clothing in the royal courts,[16] indulged in bitterly ironic remarks about the tyrants who assumed the title of benefactors of the people[17] and—according to the Lucan tradition—showed little respect for Herod, whom he called a fox.[18] He too preached a God who was not on the side of the rulers and the established authorities but a God of liberation and redemption. He too made the law more strict in some respects and expected from his followers unconditional allegiance and an uncompromising engagement. There was to be no looking back after putting one's hands to the plow,[19] no excuses on account of business, marriage or funeral.[20]

It has been observed that Che Guevara, the Cuban guerrilla, bore a remarkable facial resemblance to the conventional picture of Jesus. But, apart from this, is it so surprising that Jesus has exercised an influence on many revolutionaries right up to Camillo Torres, the Colombian priest-revolutionary? And there can be no doubt that the Jesus of the Gospels is not the sweet, gentle Jesus of an earlier or later Romanticism nor a solid ecclesiastical Christ. There is nothing in him of the prudent diplomat or the churchman ready for compromise and determined to maintain a balance. The Gospels present us with an obviously clear-sighted, resolute, unswerving, and—if necessary—also pugnacious and aggressive and always fearless Jesus. He had come in fact to cast fire on earth.[21] There was to be no fear of those who can kill the body but can do no more than this.[22] The time was at hand when swords would be needed, a time of the greatest distress and danger.[23]

Not a social revolutionary

Nevertheless, we cannot make Jesus a guerrilla fighter, a rebel, a political agitator and revolutionary or turn his message of God's kingdom into a program of politico-social action, unless we distort and reinterpret all the Gospel accounts, make a completely one-sided choice of the sources, irresponsibly and arbitrarily work with isolated texts—whether Jesus' own sayings or community creations—and largely ignore Jesus' message as a whole: in a word, we would have to use a novelist's imagination instead of adopting a historical-critical method.[24] Even though it is as much the fashion today to speak of Jesus, the rebel, the revolutionary, as it was in Hitler's time to speak of Jesus the fighter, the leader, the military commander, or in sermons of the First World War of Jesus the hero and patriot, it must be made unmistakably clear—for Jesus' own sake, regardless of the spirit of the age—that he was neither a supporter of the system nor a politico-social revolutionary.

Unlike the revolutionaries of his time, Jesus does not proclaim a national religio-political theocracy or democracy to be established by force with the aid of military or quasi-military action. It is possible to follow him without an explicitly political or social-critical commitment. He does not give the signal to storm the repressive structures, he does not work from either right or left for the fall of the government. He waits for God to bring about the cataclysm and proclaims as already decisive the *unrestricted, direct world dominion of God himself, to be awaited without violence.* This is an upheaval, not activated from below, but controlled from above, and people have to understand the signs of the time and be wholly and entirely prepared for it. It is this kingdom of God which must be sought in the first place and all the other things with which men are preoccupied will be given with it.[25]

He does not indulge in polemics or agitation against the Roman occupying power. The names are given of a number of villages and towns in Galilee where Jesus was active, but—oddly enough—neither Herod's capital and residential city, Tiberias (named after the Emperor Tiberius), nor the Hellenistic Sepphoris. Clearly rejecting any political misinterpretation, Jesus points out to Herod, "the fox," the true nature of his mission.[26] Jesus brusquely refuses to stir up anti-Roman feeling.[27] The Lucan sword imagery must be seen in connection with Jesus' rejection of the use of force.[28] He avoids all titles such as Messiah and Son of David which might be misinterpreted in a political sense. In his message of the kingdom of God there is no trace of nationalism nor of prejudice against unbelievers. Nowhere does he speak of restoring David's kingdom in power and glory. Nowhere does he show any sign of acting with a political objective, to seize worldly power. On the contrary, there are no political hopes, no revolutionary strategy or tactics, no exploitation of his popularity for political ends, no tactically shrewd coalition with particular groups, no strategic long march through the institutions, no tendency to accumulate power. What we do find is quite the reverse (and this is socially relevant): renunciation of power, forbearance, grace, peace; liberation from the vicious circle of violence and counterviolence, of guilt and reprisals.

If there is a historical core to the *story of the temptations*,[29] stamped as it is with biblical symbolism, this can only be that one easily comprehensible temptation to which the three can be reduced: the diabolic temptation of political messianism. This was a temptation which Jesus consistently resisted, not only on this occasion, but throughout his public life as a whole (this could be the implication of calling Peter Satan).[30] He remained between the fronts and did not allow himself to be appropriated by any group and made its "king" or head. On no account would he violently anticipate or bring about by force the kingdom of God. The obscure saying about the kingdom of heaven coming by violence and the violent trying to seize it by force[31] may well be an explicit rejection of the Zealot revolutionary movement. Perhaps too the invitation to wait patiently for God's hour as expressed in the parable of the seed which grows of itself[32] and the warning about false prophets[33] are evidence of anti-Zealot polemics which had become utterly irrelevant for the evangelists after the catastrophic year 70.

To the Romans, little interested in internal Jewish religious disputes but suspicious of all nationalist movements, Jesus must certainly have seemed like a political agitator and in the last resort a rabble-rouser and potential rebel. The Jewish accusation before Pilate was understandable and apparently justified. And yet it was deeply prejudiced and indeed—on this the Gospels unanimously insist—completely false. Jesus was condemned as a political revolutionary and this he was not. He gave himself up without resistance to his enemies. Serious scholars today are agreed on the fact that Jesus never appears as the head of a political conspiracy, does not talk like the Zealots of the Messiah-king who will crush the enemies of Israel, nor of Israel's world dominion. Throughout all the Gospels he appears as the unarmed, itinerant preacher and the charismatic physician who does not inflict wounds but heals them: one who relieves distress and does not exploit it for political ends, who proclaims not militant conflict but God's grace and forgiveness for all. Even his social criticism, reminiscent of the Old Testament prophets, was based not on a social-political program but quite definitely on his new understanding of God and man.

Non-violent revolution

Historical or not, the story of Jesus' entry into Jerusalem riding on a donkey[34] is typical: not the victor's white horse, not an animal symbolizing dominion, but the mount used by the poor and powerless. *The purification of the temple* is linked by the Synoptics with the entry into Jerusalem[35] and both events are played up by Matthew and John in contrast to Mark, but even Mark gives them an exaggerated importance for the sake of a vivid description. It could not in any case have amounted to a riot, which would immediately have brought about the intervention of the temple police and the Roman cohorts in the castle of Antonia at the northwestern corner of the temple forecourt.

Whatever the historical core of the narrative was—and its historicity is questioned by some exegetes, but with scarcely adequate arguments—it is clear from the sources that it was not an act typical of the Zealots, not an act of sheer violence and still less an open revolt. Jesus did not intend finally to expel all tradesmen, to take possession of the temple or to reorganize temple and priests, as the Zealots wanted to do. It was of course a deliberate provocation, a symbolic act, an individual prophetic sign in action, a demonstrative condemnation of these goings-on and of the hierarchs who profited by them: it was a blow for the holiness of the place as a place of prayer. This condemnation—perhaps linked with a threat to the temple or even a promise to the Gentiles[36]—must not be minimized. Undoubtedly it was a flagrant challenge to the hierarchy and the groups financially interested in the pilgrimage trade.

This again shows that Jesus did not belong to the establishment. All that was said above under this heading remains correct. He was not a conformer, not an apologist for the existing state of affairs, not a defender of repose and order. He invited a decision. It was in this sense that he brought the sword: not peace, but strife, reaching occasionally even to the heart of the family.[37] He raised fundamental questions about the religious-social system, the existing order of Jewish law and temple, and to this extent his message had political consequences. At the same time it must be noted that, for Jesus, *a politico-social revolution* is just not the *alternative* to the system, the establishment, the existing order. Che Guevara, romanticizing force and glorifying it as the midwife of the new society,[38] or Camillo Torres have less right than Gandhi or Martin Luther King to claim Jesus as their example.

The Zealot revolutionaries wanted to act, not merely to talk. As against the establishment's immobility and obsession with power, they wanted not only to give a theological interpretation of reality but to change it politically. They wanted to commit themselves, to pursue their aims with ruthless logic. Being and action, theory and practice had to correspond to each other. Being consistent, coherent, meant being revolutionary.[39] They wanted to grasp things "radically," at the root, the *radix*, actively to undertake responsibility for the world in order to bring it into harmony with the truth. In this radical spirit they strove for the final realization of the *eschaton*, of the kingdom of God, if necessary—in God's name—by armed force.

Jesus approved neither the methods nor the aims of this revolutionary radicalism of the Zealots, who regarded the overthrow of the anti-God Roman state as a divine obligation and who were seeking a restoration of the old order (a nationalistic re-establishment of the great kingdom of David). Jesus was different, provocative even in this respect. He did not preach a revolution, either of the right or of the left:

There was no call to refuse payment of taxes: give Caesar what is Caesar's—but do not give him what is God's.[40]

No proclamation of a war of national liberation: he accepted invitations to eat with the worst collaborators and set up as an example the Samaritan, the national enemy, hated almost more than the pagans.

No propagation of the class struggle: unlike so many militants of his time, he did not divide men into friends and enemies, into children of light and children of darkness.

No gloomy social-revolutionary abstemiousness: Jesus celebrated festive meals at a bad time of political subjugation and social need.

No abolition of the law for the sake of the revolution: he wanted to help, to heal, to save, not to force people to be happy in the way decided by individuals. First comes the kingdom of God and everything else will be given with it.[41]

Thus Jesus combines severe criticism of rulers who wield power ruthlessly with the call, not to tyrannicide, but to service.[42] His message does not culminate in an appeal to bring about a better future by force: anyone who takes up the sword will fall by the sword.[43] He appeals for renunciation of force: not to resist the evildoer,[44] to do good to those who hate us, to bless those who curse us, to pray for those who persecute us.[45] All this is for the sake of the future kingdom, in the light of which all existing systems, all ordinances, institutions, structures and indeed all differences between the mighty and the powerless, between rich and poor, appear from the very beginning to be relatively unimportant: the norms of this kingdom must be applied even now.

If Jesus had carried out a radical agricultural reform in Palestine, he would have been forgotten long ago. If he had behaved like the rebels in Jerusalem in the year 66 and set on fire the city's archives together with all the bankers' bonds or if—like Bar Giora, the leader of the Jerusalem revolution two years later—he had proclaimed the universal liberation of Jewish slaves, his action—like that of Spartacus, the heroic slave liberator, with his seventy thousand slaves and the seven thousand crosses on the Appian Way—would have remained merely an episode in history.

On the other hand, Jesus' "revolution"—if we want to use this ambiguous, inflammatory expression—was radical in a true and more clearly to be defined sense and has therefore permanently changed the world. He went beyond the alternatives of established order or social-political revolution, of conformism or non-conformism. We might also say that he was more revolutionary than the revolutionaries. Let us see more exactly what this means:

love of enemies instead of their destruction;
unconditional forgiveness instead of retaliation;
readiness to suffer instead of using force;
blessing for peacemakers instead of hymns of hate and revenge.

The first Christians followed out Jesus' teaching at the time of the great Jewish rebellion. When the war broke out, they did not make common cause with the Zealot revolutionaries but fled from Jerusalem to Pella on the other side of the Jordan. And in the second great revolt under Bar Kokhba they were fanatically persecuted. But it is significant that the Romans did not proceed against them until Nero's persecution.

Jesus then did not demand and still less did he set in motion a politico-social revolution. What he did set going was a decidedly *non-violent revolution:* a revolution emerging from man's innermost and secret nature, from the personal center, from the heart of man, into society. There was to be no continuing in the old ways, but a radical change in man's thinking and a conversion (Greek, *metanoia*), away from all forms of selfishness, toward God and his fellow men. The real alien powers, from which man had to be liberated, were not the hostile world powers but the forces of evil: hatred, injustice, dissension, violence, all human selfishness, and also suffering, sickness and death. There had to be therefore a changed awareness, a new way of thinking, a new scale of values. The evil that had to be overcome lay not only in the system, in the structures, but in man. Inner freedom had to be established and this would lead to freedom from external powers. Society had to be transformed through the transformation of the individual.

In view of all this, the question inevitably arises: is not this Jesus then in the last resort an advocate of retreat and encapsulation from the world, of a piety cut off from the world and an interiority remote from the world, of a monastic asceticism and absenteeism?

3. *Emigration?*

There is a political radicalism which presses for the total conquest of the world, if necessary by force of arms, for religious reasons: the total realization of God's kingdom in the world as a result of human effort. This is the radicalism of the Zealots. But there is a solution that is the very opposite of this, although equally radical: instead of active commitment for life or death, the paradox of the great refusal. This means: not rebellion but renunciation, not an attack on the world hostile to God but repudiation of this world, not mastering history but opting out of history.

Apolitical radicalism

This is the apolitical (even if only apparently unpolitical) radicalism of the monks, "those living in solitude" (Greek, *monachos*=solitary), or of the anchorites, "those who have fled" (into the desert).[1] This means segregation, withdrawal, *emigration* from the world on the part of the individual or the group: external-local or internal-mental, organized or unorganized, through encapsulation and isolation or through migration and new settlement. This, as quite generally understood, is the anchorite-monastic tradition in the history of both Christendom and Buddhism (with its eightfold way intended for a monastic community): the tradition of critical dissociation and retreat from the world. To this tradition belong individual ascetic recluses (hermits, of whom the classical example is Anthony, the Egyptian "Father of the Desert" in the third century, some being still found today on Mount Athos in Greece). In the same tradition also are the organized monastic communities later favored by the Church (the first of them founded by Pachomius in the fourth century) who lead a "common life" (Greek, *koinobion*, hence coenobitism). This tradition of "retreatism" lives on even today, occasionally in very secular forms: among the hippies of the sixties and in the diverse forms of Consciousness III, among young people hiking into the desert, to India, Nepal, Afghanistan and—up to a point—in the Jesus movement. In all this people constantly appeal to the example of *Jesus*. Are they right to do so?

They are certainly not entirely wrong. Jesus was anything but a conventional type. His way of life was not what is usually described as a "career." His life-style in some respects resembled that of the hippies. We do not know whether the account of his fasting in the desert, followed by the temptations, is historical. But we do know that the whole manner of his life was unusual. He was certainly not "socially adjusted." Although he was the son of a carpenter and apparently himself also a carpenter,[2] he did not follow any occupation. Instead, he led an unsettled, wandering life, preached and worked in public places, ate, drank, prayed and slept quite frequently in the open air. He was a man who had left his native country and cut himself off even from his family. Is it surprising that his relatives were not among his supporters? According to an ancient Marcan tradition, passed over in silence by Matthew and Luke, they even tried to fetch him back, saying that he was out of his mind.[3] The incident has led some dabblers in psychiatry to maintain that he was mentally disturbed, but without explaining his enormous influence. But even though the Gospels provide no insight into his psyche—their interest lies elsewhere—they do show that his outward behavior cannot exactly be described as "normal" in the light of the behavior patterns of his time.

Jesus did nothing for his livelihood. According to the Gospel accounts, he was supported by friends and a group of women cared for him. Obviously he did not have to provide for a family. If we do not read things into the Gospel,[4] we must conclude that he was unmarried, like the Baptist before him and Paul after him. For this people, for whom marriage was a duty and a divine precept, celibacy on the part of an adult Jew was unusual, even provocative, but—as we shall see shortly—not unknown. If the saying about becoming eunuchs for the sake of the kingdom of heaven, recorded only by Matthew, is genuine at all,[5] it would have to be understood also as self-justification. Obviously Jesus' unmarried state does not provide any argument for the law of celibacy. He issued no command even to the disciples, but—on the contrary—even in that single text of Matthew he insisted on the voluntary character of this renunciation: he who can take it, let him take it. Nevertheless, Jesus' celibacy, taken together with all the other features, makes it clear that only by doing violence to the texts can he be turned into a cultured, urbane pastor handing out moral teaching, as the liberal exegetes of the nineteenth century saw him. In this respect too Jesus was different. Was there not something unworldly, fanatical, almost clownish about him? Have not such a lot of Jesus freaks, Jesus fools, throughout the centuries, and particularly the monks, the ascetics, the religious orders, perhaps very rightly appealed to him as their model?

And yet it must be said that Jesus was *not an ascetic monk*, striving for perfection by turning away from the world and living in mental and if possible local isolation. This too is not an anachronistic observation.

Monasticism

Until recently little notice had been taken of the fact that there was a well-organized *Jewish monasticism* in Jesus' own time. It was known of course from the writings of both Flavius Josephus, the Jewish historiographer, and Philo, the Jewish philosopher and famous contemporary of Jesus in Alexandria, that there was a further group—the *Essenes*—in addition to the Pharisees, Sadducees and Zealots. The Essenes probably originated among the "devout" or "pious" (Hebrew, *Hasidim*) who had at first supported the Maccabean party of revolt. Later they dissociated themselves from these "devout" people and from the less apocalyptically and rigoristically inclined Pharisees. The division came when the Maccabees began to seek more political power and Jonathan—who was not of Zadokite descent and as a war leader constantly had to undergo ritual purification—took over the office of high priest in 153 B.C. According to Philo and Josephus, these Essenes to the number of about four thousand lived apart in the villages, and some also in towns, gathered together in solid communities, and had their center at the Dead Sea.

The real relevance of the Essenes to the study of the historical Jesus became clear however only in 1947 when an Arab goatherd came across a cave in the ruins (Khirbet) of *Qumran* on the steep eastern side of the desert of Judea, sloping down to the Dead Sea: there he found jars containing several scrolls. Thereupon hundreds of caves were examined and in eleven of them numerous texts and fragments of texts were discovered. Among these were biblical texts—in particular, two scrolls of the Book of Isaiah—a thousand years older than the manuscripts known up to that time (now exhibited with other Qumran manuscripts in the "Manuscript Temple" of the Hebrew University in Jerusalem). There are also Bible commentaries (especially that on Habakkuk) and finally non-biblical texts which are decisive for our question, among them the Rule of the Community of Qumran (1QS) with the shorter Rule of the Congregation (1QSa). All these constitute the remains of the library of what we must now regard as an extensive monastic settlement. The settlement itself with its main and neighboring buildings was excavated in the ruins in 1951–56, together with a cemetery containing eleven hundred graves and an ingeniously constructed water-supply system (with eleven different cisterns). The sensational discovery of the library and the Qumran community settlement, which produced a veritable flood of literature,[6] reveals one highly significant fact. At the time of Jesus there existed a Jewish monastic community which already comprised all the features of Christian coenobitism as it was founded by the Egyptian Pachomius, given a theological substructure by Basil the Great, brought to the Latin West by John Cassian and made the model for all Western monasticism in the form of the Benedictine rule by Benedict of Nursia. The essential features are "1. a common life in one center, dwelling, working and praying together; 2. uniformity in clothing, food and asceticism; 3. preservation of this community by a written rule, based on obedience."[7]

This monastic institution raises an important question: was Jesus perhaps an Essene or a Qumran monk? Were there any connections between

Qumran and the origins of Christianity? The two questions must be distinguished. In the first joy of discovery some investigators were inclined to see parallels at every point,[8] but the first question is now answered in the negative by all serious scholars.[9] The second question may be answered with a cautious affirmative, but the influence must be regarded as more indirect than direct. John the Baptist in particular may at first have had some connection with the community: according to tradition, he grew up in the desert and was active in the neighborhood of Qumran. In any case, the Teacher of Righteousness, the founder of the Qumran community, on the one hand and the Baptist and Jesus on the other were opposed to official Judaism and to the Jerusalem establishment. For all of them the division reached right to the heart of Israel. They all expected the end to come soon: this last generation they regarded as evil, judgment was imminent, a decision had to be made, serious moral demands were inescapable. But, despite these common features, there were differences which cannot be ignored.

It has in fact already been made clear that the repeated purifying baths of Qumran, meant only for the chosen saints, were something quite different from John's unique baptism offered to the whole people. Nor did John found a community centered on the observance of the law and segregated from the rest of the people: by his call for penance he wanted to orient the whole nation to what was to come. As for Jesus, apart from a few common terms, phrases, ideas and external similarities—not surprising among contemporaries—scarcely anything can be produced which might point to a direct connection on his part with the Essenes in general and with Qumran in particular. Neither the Qumran community nor the Essene movement is even mentioned in the New Testament; nor, on the other hand, is there any mention of Jesus in the Qumran writings.

Not a religious

It is of course much too vague to say that Jesus was not a monk or anything of that kind. In view of the later development of Christianity, it is of the greatest importance to decide what were the concrete differences between Jesus and the Essene monks of Qumran. To put it more plainly: when the rich young man asked what he had to do in order to be "perfect,"[10] why did not Jesus send him to the famous monastery at Qumran? Or, if the silence in the New Testament on Qumran and the Essenes is explained by their disappearance after the Jewish war in the year 70, why did not Jesus himself found a monastery? This is not a question to be suppressed by anyone—like the present writer—who for a variety of reasons finds monasteries attractive, has a high opinion of a number of religious communities and appreciates the great achievements of monasticism for

Christian missionary work, for Western colonization, civilization and culture, for education, nursing and pastoral care. If here too we are concerned about an unbiased analysis, we shall have to say that—despite all they have in common—there is a world of difference between Jesus and the monks. There was nothing eremitical or monastic about Jesus' community of disciples.

a. *No isolation from the world.* The Essenes cut themselves off from the rest of men in order to keep at a distance from all impurity. They wanted to be the pure congregation of Israel. Theirs was a mental emigration. This holds particularly for the people of *Qumran.* After a severe conflict with the officiating high priest (this must have been Jonathan, who is described in the documents merely as the "Wicked Priest"), a crowd of priests, Levites and laymen withdrew in protest to the bleak desert near to the Dead Sea. So there was also a local emigration. Here, far from the corrupt world, under the leadership of a now unknown "Teacher of Righteousness," they wanted to be truly devout: untainted by anything impure, segregated from sinners, observing God's commandments down to the smallest detail, in order thus to prepare the way of the Lord in the desert.[11] Not only the priests, but the whole community here observed the priestly regulations on purification and continually renewed their purity by daily cleansings, not merely washing their hands but bathing completely: a true community of saints and elect on the way of perfection, "being made blameless in their ways."[12] They formed a priestly people, living constantly as in the temple.

Jesus however demands neither local nor mental emigration. He requires no withdrawal from the ordinary business of the world, no world-forsaking attitude. For him salvation is not to be found in breaking down the self or in severing its ties with the world. Far Eastern teachings on absorption of the self are alien to the mind of Jesus. He does not live either in a monastery or in the desert. In fact, in one passage,[13] he expressly rejects the possibility of finding revelation in the desert. He is active in full public view, in the villages and towns, in the midst of men. He is in contact even with the socially disreputable types, with the legally "unclean" and those written off by Qumran; but he has no fear of scandal on this account. For him purity of heart is more important than all the regulations on purity.[14] He does not run away from the powers of evil, but enters into conflict with them on the spot. He does not turn away from his opponents, but tries to talk to them.

b. *No bipartition of reality.* Philo and Josephus give brief accounts of the theology of the Essenes in a more or less Hellenizing form (particularly with reference to the immortality of the soul). But we have a relatively exact knowledge of the theology of the *Qumran monks.* Despite the restraining influence of Old Testament monotheistic belief in a creator, this theology is dualistic. The community claims to be under the guidance of light and truth. But darkness prevails outside it, among the pagans and those Israelites who do not give their undivided loyalty to the law. There is no salvation outside Qumran. The sons of light, truth and righteousness are fighting against the sons of darkness, lies and iniquity. The sons of light are to love one another, but to hate the sons of darkness. From the beginning God chose for men the one destiny or the other and assigned to them two spirits, with the result that the whole of history is an unceasing struggle between the spirit of truth or light and the spirit of iniquity or darkness, the latter being able to confuse even the sons of light. Only at the end of time will God bring this strife to an end. This confrontation of two spirits is not in the Old Testament, but the idea may have been derived from Persian dualism, with its two eternal principles, one good and the other evil.

Jesus however is unaware of such a dualism: not even according to John's Gospel, where the antithesis between light and darkness plays an important part. There is no *a priori* division, from the very beginning, of mankind into good and bad: *everyone* has to repent, but everyone *can* repent. Unlike that of Qumran or even of John the Baptist, Jesus' preaching on penance does not start out from God's anger but from his grace. Jesus does not preach a judgment on sinners and the ungodly. God's mercy knows no limits. Forgiveness is offered to all. And for that very reason we should not hate even enemies, but love them.

c. *No legal fanaticism*. The *Essenes* practiced the strictest obedience to the law. That in fact is the reason why they dissociated themselves from the Pharisees, whom they regarded as far too lax. Their zeal for the law was seen particularly in their strict observance of the Sabbath. Food was prepared in advance. Not the slightest work—not even relieving nature—was permitted. With the *monks of Qumran* we find a similar strict observance of the law. Conversion, repentance, meant returning to the law of Moses. For them the way of salvation was the observance of the law. And this meant the whole law with all its provisions, without compromises or alleviations. Nothing could be carried on the Sabbath, not even medicaments; a cow could not be helped to calve, nor could a beast be got out of a ditch. Out of loyalty to the law and in opposition to the priests in Jerusalem, the Qumran people had even kept the old solar calendar and rejected the recently introduced (Seleucid) lunar calendar. Their scheme thus conflicted with the order of feasts in the temple in Jerusalem. The sacral language, pure Hebrew as the language of the law, was cultivated in the monastery. Not being able to offer sacrifice in the temple, they sought to atone for the sins of the people through prayer and uncompromising fidelity to the law.

To *Jesus* however this sort of zeal for the law is utterly alien. On the contrary, throughout all the Gospels, he displays an astonishing freedom in regard to the law. For the Essene monks, he was unequivocally a lawbreaker—particularly in regard to the Sabbath—and deserving of punishment. If he had been in Qumran, he would have been excommunicated and expelled.

d. *No asceticism.* The *Essenes* practiced asceticism as part of their striving for purity. In order to avoid becoming unclean through intercourse with women, the elite renounced marriage. There were of course also married Essenes. These were allowed to marry—after a three-year probation—solely for the purpose of procreation, intercourse being forbidden during pregnancy. The Essenes gave up their personal property to the community, where a kind of communism prevailed. They ate no more than was necessary to satisfy their hunger. In the *Qumran* monastery strict morality was the rule. Only in this way could the struggle against the sons of darkness be carried on. Here too, on entering the community, personal property was handed over to be administered by an overseer. The monks following the Rule of the Community (1QS)—that is, at least the members living in the monastery—had to be celibates. It is only in the shorter Rule of the Congregation (1QSa) that married members are envisaged (does this rule represent an earlier or a later phase in the history of Qumran or a provision for the community of Israel at the end of time?). The asceticism of Qumran was determined also by the needs of worship. Full members were expected to maintain vigil for a third of the night in order to read in the Book of Books, to study the law and to praise God together.

Jesus however was not an ascetic. He never demanded sacrifice for the sake of sacrifice, renunciation for the sake of renunciation. He did not impose any additional ethical requirements or special ascetical accomplishments, even for the sake of greater happiness hereafter. He defended his disciples who did not fast.[15] Sour-faced piety he found repulsive; he rejected any ostentatious devotion.[16] Jesus was not a glutton for sacrifice and did not demand martyrdom. He shared in the ordinary life of men, ate and drank, and accepted invitations to banquets. In this sense he was certainly not an outsider. Unlike the Baptist, he had to face the (undoubtedly historical) charge of being a glutton and a drinker.[17] For him there was nothing unclean about marriage: it had been willed by the Creator and his plan had to be respected. He did not impose a law of celibacy on anyone. Renunciation of marriage was voluntary: an individual exception, not a rule for his disciples. Nor was renunciation of material possessions necessary in order to follow him. By comparison with the more somber teaching of Qumran and John's call for strict penance, Jesus' message appeared in many respects as one of joy and liberation.

e. *No hierarchical order.* The *Essenes* had a strict order of precedence in four states or classes, each sharply distinguished from the others: priests, Levites, lay members, applicants. Each later entrant was subordinated even in the smallest things to the member who had entered immediately before him. Everyone had to comply with the directives of the leaders of the community. The monastic community of *Qumran* was rigidly organized in the same four classes. Both in discussions—at which a priest had to be present with each group—and at meals the diversity of ranks had to be respected. The precedence of the priest appears even at the messianic meal. Obedience of the lesser members to the higher was inculcated and imposed with severe penalties. For example, a quarter of the food ration might be withdrawn: for one year for a false declaration of one's property, six months for being naked unnecessarily, three months for a foolish remark, thirty days for sleeping during the full assembly or for stupid, loud laughter, ten days for interrupting a speaker. A particularly harsh measure was that of expulsion from the community: the expelled person had to find his subsistence, apparently like John the Baptist, in the open country.

Jesus however managed without any sort of list of penalties. He did not call disciples to follow him in order to found an institution. He demanded obedience to the will of God, and in that sense obedience consisted in becoming free from all other ties. He repeatedly condemned seeking for better places or positions of honor. He more or less reversed the customary hierarchical order: the lowly were to be the highest and the highest the servants of all. Subordination had to be reciprocal, expressed in mutual service.

f. *No monastic rule*. The course of the *Essenes'* day was strictly regulated: first of all prayer, then work in the fields; at midday washings and a common meal, afterwards work again; and in the evening another meal in common. Silence prevailed when the community assembled. Before a member was accepted, he had to go through a two- or three-year probationary period (novitiate). At the reception the obligation to observe the ordinances was solemnly imposed on him. He made a kind of vow in the form of an oath which culminated in a promise of loyalty, particularly to his superiors. At the common meal especially, all members and not only the priests had to wear the white robe which was the priestly costume, the dress of the pure. In *Qumran* the whole life followed a similarly strict rule: prayer, meals and deliberations had to be in common. Both the ceremonially regulated meals and the purifying baths had a religious significance. There was an intense liturgical life. Admittedly, no sacrifices were offered after the members had dissociated themselves from the temple and its calendar. But there were regular services of prayer, each with its own psalms: the rudiments—so to speak—of the Church's daily office of prayer.

With *Jesus* there is none of this: no novitiate, no initiation oath, no vow, no regular devotional exercises, no directives in regard to worship, no long prayers, no ritual meals or baths, no distinctive clothing. Instead of this, compared with Qumran, there is criminal irregularity, casualness, spontaneity, freedom. Jesus did not compose any rules or ordinances. Instead of rules for a dominion of men over men (often decked out with spiritual trimmings), he produced parables about the rule of God. When he demanded constant, indefatigable prayer,[18] he did not mean the unceasing service of prayer practiced in some monastic communities ("perpetual adoration"); he meant the constant attitude of prayer on the part of someone who at all times expects everything from God. Man may and should insistently press his claims on God. But he should not use a lot of words, as if God did not know already what it was about. Prayer should not become either a pious demonstration before others or an arduous achievement before God.[19]

Not for the elite, but for all

Once again it is clear that Jesus was different. He did not belong to the establishment nor to the revolutionary party, but neither did he want to opt out of ordinary life, to be an ascetic monk. Obviously he did not adopt the role which a saint or a seeker after holiness, or even a prophet, is frequently expected to play. For this he was too normal in his clothing, his eating habits, his general behavior. He stood out from others, but not by an esoteric-pious life-style. The really striking thing about him was his message. And this was the very opposite of the exclusive, elitist ideology of the "sons of light." A division between men cannot be drawn by men. God alone, who sees into men's hearts, can do this. Jesus did not proclaim a judgment of vengeance on the children of the world and of darkness, nor did he promise a kingdom for an elite who had achieved perfection. He proclaimed the *kingdom of unlimited goodness and unconditional grace, particularly for the abandoned and distressed.* Compared with the very gloomy doctrine of Qumran and the Baptist's stern call to penance, Jesus' message seems extraordinarily joyful. It is difficult to decide whether Jesus himself actually used the word "Gospel."[20] But what he had to say was certainly not a threatening message, but—in the most comprehensive sense of the term—a message of joy. And it was addressed particularly to those who were not an elite and knew it.

What then is meant by the imitation of Christ? The conclusion seems inevitable that the later anchorite-monastic tradition, with its detachment from the world and in the form and organization of its life, could appeal to the example of the monastic community of Qumran. But it could scarcely claim Jesus as a model. He did not demand either a mental or a physical emigration. What we call the "evangelical counsels" as a way of life—surrender of possessions to the community ("poverty"), celibacy ("chastity"), unconditional subordination to the will of a superior ("obedience"), all secured by oaths ("vows")—existed in Qumran, but not among Jesus' disciples. Now that these connections and distinctions are better known than they used to be, any Christian religious order is bound to face the question whether it can appeal more to Qumran as its model than to Jesus. There is certainly a place in Christendom even today for communities and basis groups of all kinds with a special commitment, in the spirit not of Qumran but of Jesus.

The serious, devout ascetics of the Qumran monastery must have heard of Jesus, at least of his crucifixion. In the light of what the prophets had announced, they even expected two Messiahs at the end of time, one priestly and the other royal, a spiritual and a secular leader of the community of salvation; in their rule they had even settled the order of places at the messianic meal. In this way they may have prepared for the coming of Jesus, but in the end they ignored him. They kept up their hard life in the burning desert and just about forty years later went themselves to their deaths. When the great war broke out the political radicalism of the Zealots and the apolitical radicalism of the anchorites were found side by side (exemplifying the saying: *les extrêmes se touchent*). In their solitude of course the monks had always been preparing themselves for the last battle; the "War Scroll" (1QM), also discovered at the time, gave precise directives for the conduct of the holy war. Hence the monks also took part in the revolutionaries' struggle, regarding it as the eschatological conflict. The tenth Roman legion under Vespasian (later emperor) advanced from Caesarea as far as the Dead Sea and toward Qumran in the year 68. It must have been at this time that the monks packed up their manuscripts and hid them in the caves. They never returned to collect them. They must have met their deaths at that time. For a while a post of the tenth legion was stationed in Qumran. During the Bar Kokhba revolt, after Jewish partisans had once again occupied the remaining buildings, Qumran was finally destroyed.

What remains after all this? If a person will not accept the establishment and yet will not commit himself either to the political radicalism of violent revolution or to the apolitical radicalism of devout emigration, then one choice alone seems to remain: that of compromise.

4. Compromise?

Both the politico-social revolutionaries and the monastic "emigrants" take God's rule quite seriously and accept its consequences. It is in this ruthless determination to get down to the roots, this consistent pursuit of wholeness and undividedness that their radicalism consists. They want therefore a tidy, unequivocal solution, political or apolitical, absolutely clear and final: world revolution or flight from the world. As opposed to such a solution, all that seems possible is ambiguity, duplicity, two-facedness, half measures: tactical maneuvering between the established order and the radicalisms, abandoning any attempt to remain absolutely faithful to the truth, to shape life according to *one* standard, really to attain perfection.

The devout

This would be the way of cheerful inconsistency, legal harmonization, diplomatic adjustment and moral compromise. *Compromittere* means to promise together, to come to an arrangement. Must man not perforce attempt a compromise between the absolute divine precept and his concrete situation? Is there not such a thing as force of circumstances? Are not politics—on a large or small scale—the art of the possible? Certainly, "thou shalt"—but within the framework of the possible. Is not this Jesus' way? The way of moral compromise is that of *Pharisaism*.[1] Pharisaism has been made out to be worse than it really was. Even in the Gospels, in the light of later controversy, the Pharisees are frequently presented indiscriminately as examples of hypocrisy, as pious dissemblers. We can see the reasons for this. The Pharisees were the sole party which had survived the great revolution against the Romans, when both the establishment and the radicals—political or apolitical—had been swept away. Pharisaism provided the foundation of subsequent Talmudic and also modern Orthodox Judaism. It was therefore Pharisaism which was left as the sole Jewish opponent of early Christendom and this fact found expression in the Gospels, written after the year A.D. 70. On the other hand, Flavius Josephus—by his very name a living compromise—is full of praise for the Pharisees: in his later pro-Jewish work, *Jewish Antiquities*, he wanted to compensate for his pro-Roman *Jewish Wars*.

The Pharisees then cannot simply be identified with the scribes. The priestly establishment too had its theological and legal—in fact, Sadducean—experts for all questions of legal interpretation, it had its court theologians. The name "Pharisees" does not mean "hypocrites" at all, but "separated" (Aramaic *perishaiia*, from the Hebrew *perushim*). They also liked to be called devout, righteous, God-fearers, poor. The name "separated," probably first used by outsiders, would also have suited the Essenes and the Qumran monks. Presumably these simply represented a kind of radical wing of the Pharisaic movement. As already explained, *all* the "devout" had turned away at an early stage from the power politics and worldliness of the Maccabean freedom fighters when they became established, from the Maccabean dynasty whose later descendant, Mariamne, was to be the founder of the new Herodian ruling family. The devout wanted to shape their lives according to the Torah, the Law of God. Some however did not want to share the radicalism of the others. Consequently the devout split up into Essenes and Pharisees. After a bloody struggle with the Maccabee Alexander Janneus (103–76 B.C.), who was the first to assume again the title of king, the Pharisees renounced all attempts to change the situation by force. They wanted to prepare themselves by prayer and a devout life for the turning point which God himself would bring about. This lay movement comprised about six thousand members, but could be very influential among a total population of perhaps half a million: they formed solid communities but lived with the rest of the people. Mostly craftsmen and tradesmen, they were grouped into "fellowships" under the leadership of the scribes. Politically, even in Jesus' time, the Pharisees were moderates, although a number of them sympathized with the Zealots.

It should not be forgotten that the Pharisee whom Jesus put forward as typical was not a hypocrite.[2] He was a sincere, devout man and spoke the simple truth. He had done all he said. The Pharisees were of exemplary morals and consequently enjoyed the respect of those who could not reach their standards. In fulfilling the law, they regarded two things as particularly important: the purity regulations and the obligation of tithes.

Although comparatively few of them were in fact priests, they required all members even in ordinary daily life to observe the *purity regulations* intended for the priests. In this way they let it be known that they regarded themselves as the priestly people of the end-time.[3] It was not for the sake of hygiene and propriety therefore that they washed their hands, but for the sake of cultic purity. Certain kinds of animals, blood, contact with a corpse or a carcass, bodily discharges and other things led to a loss of cultic purity. It had to be regained by a bath of purification or even a period of waiting. They had to have clean hands to pray. That is why it was so important to wash one's hands before every meal. It is also the reason why they insisted on keeping drinking vessels and dishes clean.

The *tithe* precept—to give 10 per cent of all earned or acquired income to maintain the priestly tribe of Levi and the temple—was largely neglected among the people. The Pharisees therefore took it all the more seriously. From everything that was at all suitable, even from vegetables and potherbs, 10 per cent was set aside and supplied to the priests and Levites.

The Pharisees regarded all these things as matters of precept. But they undertook voluntarily more than was commanded. Christian moral theology, taking up again Pharisaic ideas, later described such voluntary acts as *works of supererogation:* good works not strictly required, but complementary, superfluous, which could be counted against a person's offenses in the great final settlement, so that the scales of God's justice would be weighted on the side of good. Works of penance, voluntary fasting (twice in the week, on Mondays and Thursdays, to atone for the sins of the people), alms (charitableness pleasing to God), punctual observance of the three daily periods of prayer (observed wherever one happened to be at the time) were all eminently suitable for keeping the balance sheet straight. Is all this really so very different from what Christendom (particularly Catholic Christendom) later claimed to be distinctively "Christian"? Could Jesus—placed between the establishment on the one hand and the radicalisms on the other—do otherwise than opt for this party, the party of the truly devout?

Moral compromise

Oddly enough, Jesus seems to have had difficulties with this devout morality. Compromise is its typical feature. In themselves God's commandments are taken terribly seriously. In fact, people do more than is required or commanded. Observance is painfully exact and a whole pile of additional precepts is built up around God's commandments, as an assurance against the ever present menace of sin, for the application of the law to the smallest details of ordinary life, to decide in all cases of uncertainty what is or is not sin. For people must know exactly what they have to do to keep the law: how far they can walk on the Sabbath, what they can carry around, what work they can do, whether they can marry, whether they can eat an egg laid on the Sabbath. Within the framework of a single regulation a whole web of detailed regulations could be woven. There is no question, for instance, simply of washing one's hands: it has to be done at a quite definite time, right up to the wrist, with the hands in the correct position, the water poured twice (first to remove the uncleanness, secondly to absorb from the first pouring the drops which have become unclean).

This is how they learned to strain out a gnat: an elaborate technique of piety. Precepts were heaped on precepts, regulations on top of regulations: a system of morality which could embrace the whole life of both the individual and society. Here was the zeal for the *law*, but on the other hand a dread of sin lurking everywhere. In the Scriptures the law in the narrower sense (=the five books ascribed to Moses=the Pentateuch=Torah), in which ethical and ritual precepts were regarded as of equal value, was considered more important than the prophets. And to the written law, the Torah, was added oral tradition, *halakhah*, the "tradition of the Fathers," the work of the scribes. This tradition was to be venerated equally with the Scriptures: *pari pietatis affectu*, as the Council of Trent was to say later.[4] In this way it was possible to develop a firm doctrine of the resurrection, against the Sadducees. And in all this the importance grew of the teaching office of the scribes, who were occupied with the complicated application of particular precepts and could say in every case what the ordinary person had to do. This skill in applying the law to every possible case was to be known later as "casuistry" and large volumes by Christian moral theologians are full of it. The whole of daily life from morning to night was divided up and encapsulated into legal cases.

Incidentally this seemed like a friendly service to humanity in the eyes of many Pharisees. The scribes really wanted to help. They wanted to make the law *practicable* by skillfully applying it to the conditions of their own time. They wanted to relieve man's conscience, to give him security. They wanted to indicate exactly how far it was possible to go without committing sin, to offer solutions in particularly difficult circumstances. They provided (to use the expression of John XXIII when addressing Catholic canonists) a tunnel through a whole mountain of precepts, piled up between God and man. Strictness was thus combined with leniency, rigid traditionalism with practical realism. It was possible to insist on the law while providing excusing causes and dispensations. The law was taken literally, but the letter was given an elastic interpretation. The way of the law was to be followed, but byways were also marked out. Thus the law could be kept and sin avoided. Work was forbidden on the Sabbath (the scribes had drawn up a list of thirty-nine forbidden works), but an exception could be made and the Sabbath profaned if there was a danger to life. Nothing could be carried outside the house on the Sabbath, but the yards of several houses might be understood as a common house precinct. An ox which had fallen into the pit on the Sabbath could be got out (this was forbidden in Qumran). It is easy to understand the gratitude of the people for this interpretation which softened the harsh Sadducean law of the temple priests continually insisting on the Sabbath observance. The Pharisees —unlike the Sadducean hierarchs in the distant temple, but close to the people in the towns and villages, close to the synagogue, the house of teaching and prayer—were more or less like the leaders of a people's party. They did not regard themselves as conservative reactionaries (these resided in the temple), but as a moral renewal movement.

They showed harshness only toward those who did not know or did not want to know the law. Here "segregation" was inevitable. It was necessary, not only in regard to the Hellenizing Jerusalem establishment, but also in regard to the *'am ha-arez*, the "peasants," who were not versed in the law and consequently did not observe it or as hard-working people *could* scarcely be bothered about cultic purity. There had to be "segregation" particularly from all types of public sinners who did not *want* to keep the law: prostitutes of course, but likewise tax farmers. For the occupying powers handed over the tax offices to the highest bidders, who could then indemnify themselves by extorting more than the official tariffs. "Tax collectors" became a synonym for rogues and swindlers: people with whom it was impossible to sit at the same table. All these impious people were regarded as holding up the advent of the kingdom of God and the Messiah. If the whole nation would keep the law faithfully and exactly in purity and holiness, like the Pharisees, then the Messiah would come, gather the scattered tribes of Israel and set up the kingdom of God. For the law was the sign of election, it was grace.

Not a pious legalist

Jesus seemed *close* to the Pharisees and yet was infinitely *remote* from them. He too tightened the law, as is evident from the antitheses of the Sermon on the Mount: anger alone implies murder,[5] adulterous desire is already adultery.[6] But was this casuistry? On the other hand Jesus was amazingly lax. He seemed to be undermining all morality when he made the abandoned and disreputable son finally come off better with his father than the upright son who had stayed at home.[7] It was the same with the tax swindler who was supposed to count for more before God than the devout Pharisee, who really was different from other people, particularly these tricksters and adulterers.[8] This sort of talk—including the stories of the lost sheep and the lost coin[9]—would have seemed morally subversive and destructive and offensive to every decent Israelite.

The conflict with the Pharisees was bound to come to a head, since there was so much in common between the two sides. Like the Pharisees, Jesus dissociated himself from the priestly establishment in Jerusalem, rejected both the Zealot revolution and local or mental "emigration." Like the Pharisees, he wanted to be devout in the midst of the world; he lived, worked and entered into discussions among the people; taught in the synagogue. Was he not rather like a rabbi, repeatedly a guest in a Pharisee's house[10] and warned of Herod's snares precisely by the Pharisees?[11] Like the Pharisees, he kept to the law in principle or at any rate did not deliver a frontal attack on it by demanding its abolition or repeal. He had come, not to annul the law, but to fulfill it.[12] Was he not perhaps—as a number of Jewish scholars today try to see him[13]—simply a Pharisee of a particularly liberal kind, fundamentally a devout moralist, faithful to the law, even though extraordinarily magnanimous in his outlook? Are there not parallels to some of his statements among the rabbinical sayings? And yet the counterquestion arises: why did hostility to Jesus continue to increase even among Pharisee circles?

His sayings are in fact paralleled frequently in Judaism and sometimes in Hellenism. But one swallow does not make a summer and an isolated statement of a single rabbi is not the whole story. This is obvious enough, particularly when the one statement is contrasted with a thousand statements by others, as for instance on the question of the Sabbath. For us here it is a matter of secondary importance to know who said what and when he said it. It is of primary importance to know in the light of what presuppositions, in what total context, how radically something was said and what were the consequences for the speaker and his hearers. It cannot be accidental that just this one Jew made history and fundamentally changed the course of world history and the position of Judaism.

Anyway it must be said quite categorically, to distinguish his message from that of Judaism or a re-Judaized Christianity, that Jesus was not a pious legalistic moralist. However much the historical Jesus lived on the whole in complete fidelity to the law, there can be no doubt that he never hesitated to act against the law when it seemed important to do so. For, if he did not abolish the law, he placed himself in fact *above* it. We must fix our attention on three facts, admitted by the most critical exegetes.[14]

He recognized no ritual taboos. *He said that nothing coming into a man from outside can make him unclean: he is made unclean only by what comes out of himself.*[15] *To say this is not merely to criticize—as, for instance, the monks of Qumran criticized—an externalized practice of purity which does not come from the heart. He did not tighten the purity regulations—as again they did in Qumran. What he said was unparalleled in Judaism and was bound to be understood as a grave attack on all who were intent upon ritual exactitude. Even if he was speaking within a particular situation and not stating a policy (more against the oral tradition on purity than against the purity regulations of the Torah itself), he did set aside all purity regulations as meaningless and he rendered obsolete the Old Testament distinction between clean and unclean animals and foods. Jesus was not interested in cultic purity and ritual correctness. For him, purity before God alone meant purity of heart. Here in the last resort was a challenge to the distinction taken for granted in Old Testament cult and by the religions of the ancient world as a whole: the distinction between a profane and a sacral sphere.*[16]

He did not advocate an asceticism of fasting. *The Baptist did not go around eating and drinking, but Jesus did—the accusation of being a glutton and a drunkard was connected with this question of fasting. He was never accused of failing to fast on the Day of Atonement and other days of mourning. But he did not practice voluntary private fasting as —like the Pharisees—John's disciples apparently did: the people at the wedding—he claimed—do not fast as long as the bridegroom is with them.*[17] *This enigmatic saying means that now is the time of joy and not a time to fast: fasting is turned to feasting, because the feast expected at the end of time is already beginning. Jesus was bound to give great offense by this teaching. It was obvious that he attached little importance to this sort of penance, self-denial, self-punishment, as a means of obtaining God's favor and gaining merits. It was an open attack therefore on surplus good works, works of supererogation, which —in the parable of the Pharisee and the tax collector—Jesus showed to be incapable of justifying a person.*[18]

He was not scrupulous about Sabbath observance. *There is even more evidence of this than of other infringements of the law. It became a kind of test case: Jesus notoriously violated the Sabbath rest. He not only allowed his disciples to pluck the ears of corn on the Sabbath,*[19] *but also repeatedly healed on that day.*[20] *He thus violated the commandment to which devout Jews even today are most sensitive and which at that time was firmly upheld both by the temple establishment on the one hand and by the Zealots, Essenes and Qumran monks on the other. It was the mark distinguishing Israel from the pagan world. Yet he infringed this commandment, not only when life was endangered, but on occasions when he could easily have acted differently: any of his cures could easily have been effected on the next day. Here too Jesus was not interested in particular interpretations—whether strict or lax—or in all the "ifs" and "buts" of casuistry. It was not a question merely of recognizing exceptions to the rule: the rule itself was challenged. He assured men of freedom in principle in regard to the Sabbath in the undoubtedly authentic saying that the Sabbath exists for man and not man for the Sabbath.*[21]

To Jewish ears a statement of this kind must have sounded scandalous in the highest degree. They regarded the observance of the Sabbath as the supreme act of worship: it existed, not for man, but for God, and Jesus' contemporaries thought that God himself with all his angels observed it in heaven with ritual exactitude. If some rabbi at some time somewhere said that the Sabbath had been entrusted to the Jews, not the Jews to the Sabbath, this is one of those solitary swallows that do not make a summer: the statement is not one of principle; its purpose was different and there was no question of a critical attitude toward the Sabbath. But for Jesus the Sabbath is not a religious end in itself: man is the end of the Sabbath. It is not a question of not doing anything on the Sabbath, but of doing the right thing: if even beasts can be saved, then still more human beings.[22] *But in this way it is left in principle to man to decide when he will keep the Sabbath and when not. This is important also for the observance of the other commandments. Certainly the law is not opposed, but in practice man is made the measure of the law. For the orthodox Jew this would seem to mean turning things upside down.*

So much must belong to the historical core of the tradition. The offensiveness of Jesus' whole attitude to traditional piety can be appreciated from the way in which tradition got round his sayings about the Sabbath. Some are omitted: Matthew and Luke are silent about the revolutionary statement that the Sabbath was made for man. Secondary arguments are added: quotations and references to the Old Testament examples, which in fact did not prove what they were meant to prove.[23] Or the texts are given a Christological significance: Mark already suggests that it is not man as such, but the Son of Man, who is lord of the Sabbath.[24]

Against self-righteousness

It is difficult to decide how many of the other accusations leveled against the Pharisees were made by Jesus himself.[25] The Pharisees are accused of delivering 10 per cent of potherbs but ignoring God's great demands for justice, mercy and loyalty; they strain out gnats but swallow camels.[26] They fulfill in minute detail the purity regulations but they remain inwardly impure: beautifully whitened graves, full of dead men's bones.[27] Furthermore, they make a show of missionary zeal but ruin the people they convert: proselytes who become children of hell, twice as evil as themselves.[28] Finally, they give money to the poor, carefully observe the times of prayer, but their piety only serves their craving for recognition and their vanity: a theatricality which has already had its reward.[29] To a large extent, when Jesus accuses the scribes, the Pharisees too are included: they impose heavy burdens on men but will not raise a finger to help.[30] They look for honors, titles, adulation, and put themselves in God's place.[31] They build monuments to the former prophets and kill those of the present time.[32] In a word, they have knowledge but do not live in accordance with it.

More important than these particular accusations is the attitude of mind behind them. What has Jesus really against this kind of piety? He does not proclaim a kingdom of God which can be set up, brought about, constructed and extorted by the exact fulfillment of the law and better morals. No kind of moral rearmament can produce it. Jesus proclaims a *kingdom that is created by God's liberating and gladdening act*. God's kingdom is God's work, his dominion one that liberates and gladdens. Jesus is not by any means merely ironical about the seriousness of moral effort. It is true that his use of the terms "sin" and "sinning" is noticeably rare. He is not a pessimistic preacher denouncing sin in the style of an Abraham of Sancta Clara. But neither is he a liberal optimist like Rousseau, assuming that man is by nature good and discounting all sense of sin and the need for moral exertion. On the contrary, he maintains that his opponents *make light of sin*. In two ways:[33]

> *By their* casuistry *they* isolate *the individual sin. The requirement of obedience to God is split up into detailed, individual actions. Their primary concern is not with false basic attitudes, basic trends, basic dispositions, but with individual moral lapses, with drawing up lists of sins. These individual acts are registered and catalogued: against each commandment there are grave and venial offenses, sins of weakness and sins of malice. The dimension in depth of sin is never brought to light.*
>
> Jesus *disposes of casuistry by the very fact of going to the roots: not*

only to the act of murder but to the angry disposition, not only to the act of adultery but to adulterous desire, not only to perjury but to the untrue word. He shows that what really make a person impure are the sins of the tongue, belittled by his opponents. He never marks out an area within which there is sin, while outside it there need be no fear of sin. He gives examples, but does not define particular cases in which we ought to proceed in this way or that. He is not interested in cataloguing sins, not even in the distinction between slight and serious, still less between pardonable and unpardonable sins. While some rabbis regard murder, unchastity, apostasy, contempt for the Torah, as unpardonable sins, Jesus recognizes only one such, the sin against the Holy Spirit:[84] *all that is unforgivable is the rejection of forgiveness.*[85]

For the Pharisees sin is compensated by the consideration of merit. The weight of merits is balanced against the weight of sin and can even cancel out the latter. Not only our own merits, but also those of others (the Fathers, the community, the whole nation) can be appropriated without difficulty. With this business of loss and gain all that matters is to avoid showing a final deficit and to have capitalized as much merit as possible for heaven.

For Jesus there is no question of merit at all.[86] *If he speaks of reward—and he does so very often, adopting the usage of his time—he does not mean what is earned, not a reward for achievement to which man has a claim in virtue of his merit, but the reward of grace which God by his own will bestows on man, without any claim on man's part. What counts here, as the parable of equal pay for all the laborers in the vineyard vividly shows,*[87] *is not the calculation of merits but the rules of God's mercy which—contrary to all bourgeois justice—gives each one the full amount, whether he has worked for a short or a long time: more than he deserves. Man should therefore be content to forget the good he has done.*[88] *Even when he thinks he has earned nothing, he is recompensed.*[89] *God really does recompense people: that is what is meant by talking about reward. Even any gift of a cup of water, which has been forgotten, has its reward. A person who talks of merit is looking to his own achievement; to talk of recompense is to look to God's fidelity.*

Someone who makes light of sin by casuistry and the consideration of merit is uncritical in regard to himself: self-satisfied, self-assured, self-righteous. And this also means: hypercritical, unjust, harsh and unloving toward others who are different, the "sinners." He compares himself with these others. He wants to be a match for them, to be recognized by them as devout and moral; he dissociates himself from them. Here and not merely at the surface lies the root of the accusation of hypocrisy generally directed against the Pharisees. Anyone without self-criticism takes himself too seriously and his fellow men and especially God too lightly. This is how the son who remained at home estranged himself from his father.[40] So too Simon the Pharisee knows about forgiveness, but does not know what forgiveness is.[41]

What is it really that stands here between God and man? Paradoxically, it is man's own morality and piety: his ingeniously devised moralism and his selective technique of piety. It is not—as people at that time thought—the tax swindlers who find it most difficult to repent, not being able to remember all those whom they have cheated or how much they would have to restore. No: it is the devout who find it most difficult, being so sure of themselves that they have no need of conversion. They became Jesus' worst enemies. Most of the sayings on judgment in the Gospels apply to these, not to the great sinners. Those who finally sealed his fate were not murderers, cheats, swindlers and adulterers, but the highly moral people. They thought that in this way they were doing a service to God.

The Pharisaic spirit was maintained. In the great conflict Rome was the military victor. Zealotism broke down, Essenism was eradicated, Sadduceeism left without temple or temple ministry. But Pharisaism survived the catastrophe of the year 70. Only the scribes remained as leaders of the enslaved people. Thus out of Pharisaism there emerged the later, normative Judaism which was kept alive—despite all the hostility—in virtue of its "separateness," very much modified and adjusted, in the midst of the world and which set up again the Jewish state after almost two thousand years. But Pharisaism lives on also—and sometimes more so—in Christianity. But it is contrary to the spirit of Jesus himself.

Provocative on all sides

Establishment, revolution, emigration, compromise: for Jesus there seems to be no way out of the quadrilateral. And these four reference points still retain their meaning today, even in an absolutely different historical situation. Even the theologian must not speak in a merely abstract way about social relativity—as often happens in connection with Jesus and particularly when the attempt is made to emphasize the social significance of the Christian message. That is why it was important to see Jesus of Nazareth as he really was, in his social context, as concretely as possible within a brief space. But at the same time we must see him as he is: that is, as he can become significant—despite his strangeness—today even in our social context. Such a systematic localization largely avoids two errors: placing him in an irrelevant historical situation or trying to make him relevant, regardless of history. Positively speaking, it allows for both *historical distance in time* and *historical relevance at all times*. It is thus possible to discover important constants despite all variables.

We seem to have reached some odd conclusions. Jesus apparently cannot be fitted in anywhere: neither with the rulers nor with the rebels, neither with the moralizers nor with the silent ascetics. He turns out to be provocative, both to right and to left. Backed by no party, challenging on all sides: "The man who fits no formula."[42] He is neither a philosopher nor a politician, neither a priest nor a social reformer. Is he a genius, a hero, a saint? Or a religious reformer? But is he not more radical than someone who tries to re-form, reshape things? Is he a prophet? But is a "last" prophet, who cannot be surpassed, a prophet at all? The normal typology seems to break down here. He seems to have something of the most diverse types (perhaps more of the prophet and reformer than of the others), but for that very reason does not belong to any one of them. He is on a different plane: apparently closer than the priests to God, freer than the ascetics in regard to the world, more moral than the moralists, more revolutionary than the revolutionaries. Thus he has depths and vastnesses lacking in others. It is obviously difficult both for friends and enemies to understand him, still less wholly to penetrate his personality. Over and over again it becomes clear that *Jesus is different*. Despite all parallels in detail, the historical Jesus in his wholeness turns out to be completely unique—in his own time and ours.

As a secondary conclusion to this chapter, it should be noted how superficial it is to place all "founders of religions" in a series, as if fundamentally they could not only be interchanged but also substituted for one another. Quite apart from the fact that Jesus of Nazareth did not intend to found any religion, it must now be clear that the historical Jesus cannot be interchanged either with Moses or with Buddha, either with Confucius or with Muhammad.

To sum it up briefly, Jesus was not someone brought up at court as Moses apparently was, nor a king's son like Buddha. But neither was he a scholar and politician like Confucius nor a rich merchant like Muhammad. The very fact that his origins were so insignificant makes his enduring significance all the more amazing. How *different* indeed is Jesus' message

from the absolute validity of the continually expanded written law (*Moses*);
from the ascetic retreat into monastic silence and meditation under the rules of a religious community (*Buddha*);
from violent revolutionary world conquest by fighting against unbelievers and setting up theocratic states (*Muhammad*);
from the renewal of traditional morality and established society in accordance with an eternal cosmic law in the spirit of an aristocratic ethic (*Confucius*).

Obviously this is a question, not merely of some more or less contingent possibilities, but of some supremely important *basic options* or *basic positions*. Within the framework of possibilities open to Jesus in his own time some of the universally *religious* basic positions seem to be reflected which, as such or in a transmuted form as *secularized* basic positions, have been maintained to the present time.

The truth of other religions must find a place and even be given a new emphasis in Christianity. Nothing of this can be taken back. After all, Christianity has learned something from Plato, Aristotle and Stoicism, even from the Hellenistic mystery cults and from the Roman state religion, but scarcely anything from India, China and Japan. Nevertheless, no one who invokes this Jesus can justify a mingling of all religions. In this respect we must confirm what we said before. The great individual figures cannot be interchanged: their ways do not start out equally from one and the same person, do not envisage at the same time world annulment (Buddha) and world becoming (Confucius), world dominion (Muhammad) and world crisis (Jesus).[48] Jesus of Nazareth cannot serve as a cipher for all kinds of religion; he cannot be used as a label for an ancient or modern syncretism.

And yet it is only a negative outline of the figure of Jesus that emerges from what we have said up to now. The positive question has been stated more or less indirectly. Now we have to ask: What really impelled him? What is his center?

II. God's Cause

We are not asking here about Jesus' consciousness or his psyche. We have stressed the fact on a number of occasions that the sources disclose nothing about these things. But it is possible to raise the question of what is central in his proclamation and in his behavior. What did he stand for? What did he really want?

1. The Center

It will become clear only later how fundamental these questions are. Jesus does not proclaim himself. He does not thrust himself to the front. He does not come saying: "I am the Son of God; believe in me." He is not like those itinerant preachers and men of God described by Celsus, who were still turning up in the third century with the claim: "I am God (or a son of God, or a divine Spirit). And I have come. Already the world is being destroyed . . . Blessed is he who has worshiped me now!"[1] The person of Jesus is subordinated to the cause he represents. And what is this cause? It can be described in one sentence: *Jesus' cause is the cause of God in the world*. It is fashionable now to insist that Jesus is wholly and entirely concerned with man. This is true. But he is wholly and entirely concerned with man because he is first of all wholly and entirely concerned with God.

God's kingdom

He speaks of this cause as the approaching kingdom of God (*malkut Yahweh*).[2] This term is at the center of his proclamation, but is never defined. In his parables, however—the foundation stone of the Gospel tradition—he constantly describes it in different ways to bring home its meaning to everyone. It is clear from the texts that he is speaking of the kingdom of God and not of the Church. "Kingdom of heaven" in Matthew is certainly a secondary form, adopted because of the Jewish aversion to using God's name and having the same meaning: "heaven" stands for God. "Kingdom" here does not mean a territory or a sphere of dominion. It means God's reign, the activity of ruling which God will take over: "God's rulership." "God's kingdom" thus becomes "the designation for God's cause."[3]

This expression, extremely popular in Jesus' time, acquires a more exact meaning when it is used to silence his opponents. What is the kingdom of God for Jesus? Briefly summed up, in the light of what we have already said:

It is not merely God's continuing rule, existing from the dawn of creation, as understood by the religious leaders in Jerusalem, but the future eschatological kingdom of God.

It is not the religio-political theocracy or democracy which the Zealot revolutionaries wanted to set up by force, but the immediate, unrestricted rule of God himself over the world, to be awaited without recourse to violence.

It is not the avenging judgment in favor of an elite of the perfect, as understood by the Essenes and the Qumran monks, but the glad tidings of God's infinite goodness and unconditional grace, particularly for the abandoned and destitute.

It is not a kingdom to be constructed by men through an exact fulfillment of the law and a higher morality in the sense understood by the Pharisees, but the kingdom to be created by God's free act.

More positively, what kind of kingdom will this be?

It will be a kingdom where, in accordance with Jesus' prayer,[4] God's name is truly hallowed, his will is done on earth, men will have everything in abundance, all sin will be forgiven and all evil overcome.

It will be a kingdom where, in accordance with Jesus' promises,[5] the poor, the hungry, those who weep and those who are downtrodden will finally come into their own; where pain, suffering and death will have an end.

It will be a kingdom that cannot be described, but only made known in metaphors: as the new covenant, the seed springing up, the ripe harvest, the great banquet, the royal feast.

It will therefore be a kingdom—wholly as the prophets foretold—of absolute righteousness, of unsurpassable freedom, of dauntless love, of universal reconciliation, of everlasting peace. In this sense therefore it will be the time of salvation, of fulfillment, of consummation, of God's presence: the absolute future.

This future belongs to God. The prophetic faith in God's promises is made decidedly concrete and intensified by Jesus. God's cause will prevail in the world. This is the hope that sustains the message of God's kingdom. It is opposed to the mood of resignation which assumes that God belongs to the hereafter and that the course of world history is unchangeable. This hope does not arise out of resentment at the distress and despair of the present time, projecting the image of a completely different world into a rosy future. It arises from the certainty that God is already the creator and hidden lord of this contradictory world and that in the future he will redeem his word.

Apocalyptic horizon

May his kingdom come: like that whole apocalyptic generation, Jesus expected the kingdom of God, the kingdom of justice, freedom, joy and peace, in the *immediate future*. We saw from the very beginning how his understanding of God's kingdom differed from the static interpretation of the temple priests and others:[6] the present system is not final, history is moving toward its end; this very generation in fact is the last and will actually experience the now threatening end of the world together with its renewal. But it was all to be different, very different.

In the light of the sources we might speculate at length without reaching any certain conclusion as to whether Jesus expected the advent of God's kingdom at his death or immediately after it. It is quite clear that he expected the kingdom of God in the immediate future. It would be an error in method for us to take the easy way of excluding just the most difficult and embarrassing texts from Jesus' proclamation and ascribing them without more ado to later influences.

Jesus never means by "kingdom" (*basileia*) God's continual rule over Israel and the world, but always the future rule at the consummation of the world. There are numerous sayings which expressly announce or assume the closeness of the (future) kingdom of God.[7] It is true that Jesus refuses to give an exact date.[8] But there is not a single saying of Jesus which postpones the end-event to the distant future. On the contrary, it is clear from the oldest stratum of the Synoptic tradition that Jesus expects the kingdom of God in the immediate future. The classical texts referring to this "immediate expectation"[9] would have been such a stumbling block to the subsequent generation that there can be little doubt about their authenticity. They defy any attempt to make them innocuous. Jesus and to some extent the primitive Church speaking with him, and clearly also the Apostle Paul, reckoned with the advent of God's reign in their lifetime—on this it seems, the leading exegetes are largely in agreement.

Admittedly, with the passing of time, even in the New Testament, an unmistakable process of *softening and displacement of these statements* can be observed. At the earliest stage in the history of the formation of the tradition it is "this generation,"[10] in a later stratum only "some" of Jesus' hearers,[11] who will see the coming of God's kingdom. Still later, the third evangelist places at the center Jesus' entry on the scene as itself the fulfillment of the time of salvation;[12] unlike the earlier evangelists, he says nothing about Jesus' Jewish judges living to see the advent of the Son of Man.[13] The last phase of this shifting of perspectives can be seen in the later books of the New Testament. This is the case particularly in John's Gospel, where the end-event—apart from a few texts on the last judgment,[14] which some say are interpolated—is assumed to be already here: judgment is passed now, at the hearing of the word; now is the transition from death to life. On the other hand, in the second letter of Peter, perhaps the last of the New Testament writings, the disturbing delay of the day of the Lord is explained by a quotation from the Psalms: with the Lord one day is like a thousand years, a thousand years like one day.[15] A process of self-interpretation and self-demythologizing is perceptible therefore already in the New Testament itself.

This development within the New Testament simply underlines the fact that Jesus himself did not speak of the imminence of God's rule merely with a kind of "prophetic intensity," but really believed in the immediate proximity of the kingdom. This belief alone can explain his extraordinarily urgent sayings about not being concerned for security of life, food and clothing,[16] about prayer being heard,[17] the faith that moves mountains,[18] the decision that cannot be deferred;[19] the imagery of the great banquet and even the Our Father and the Beatitudes.

The parables of the kingdom confirm this interpretation. It is generally held that most of the parables belong to the basic stock of the Jesus tradition, since they cannot have emerged either from later Judaism or from the post-paschal community. These parables are not meant to be obscure but to prepare the way for the coming kingdom of God. For this kingdom, for which it is worth giving up everything—as for the expensive pearl or the treasure in the field[20]—is always the kingdom of the *future*, as is clearly assumed in the parables of the fish net[21] and the darnel in the wheat.[22] The picture of the seed growing spontaneously[23] does not mean simply that the kingdom is present already and developing, but that it comes "of itself." And the point of the two parables of the mustard seed[24] and the leaven[25] is not the natural process of growth, but the tremendous contrast between the insignificant beginning and the astounding end. They are parables, therefore, not of development, but of contrast.[26] The thoroughly exotic character of Jesus' whole proclamation of the kingdom is undeniable.

The question thus becomes so much more urgent: is not this proclamation of the kingdom of God in the last resort simply a form of late Jewish apocalyptic? Is not Jesus ultimately an apocalyptic fanatic? Was he not under an illusion? In a word, was he not mistaken? Strictly speaking, we need not have any dogmatic inhibitions about admitting this in certain circumstances. To err is human. And if Jesus of Nazareth was truly man, he could also err. Of course there are some theologians who are more afraid of error in this connection than they are of sin, death and the devil. This fear of error can go so far as to lead to the alteration of the very words of Scripture, particularly in regard to the present question. The preparatory theological commission of Vatican II twisted the statement of the letter to the Hebrews to the effect that Jesus "was tempted in all things as we are, but without sin"[27] to mean almost its very opposite: "without sin or ignorance."[28] In the final version the reference was dropped completely. If anyone therefore feels that he must speak of "error" in connection with Jesus' expectation of an imminent end, let him do so. In terms of cosmic knowledge it was an error. The question remains however as to whether the term "error" is completely adequate in this connection.[29]

Demythologizing inevitable

The problem is not solved simply by saying that the primitive Church is largely responsible for the description of the course of end-events even in the early Marcan apocalypse:[30] desecration of the temple, appearance of false prophets, war, natural disasters, hunger, persecution of Jesus' followers, judgment. Certainly it cannot be overlooked that this "Synoptic apocalypse" (it is not in John) contains material from the apocalyptic tradition and from interpretations of later experiences (of the Jewish war, for instance, particularly in the Lucan redaction). The tendency to produce a kind of apocalyptic timetable with the greatest possible exactitude in detail—which is due to the influence of apocalyptic on the literary composition—can be seen in such phrases as "let the reader understand."[31] It is generally admitted that Jesus, unlike the apocalypticists, was not interested in satisfying human curiosity, in exactly dating and localizing the kingdom of God, in revealing apocalyptic events and secrets, or in foretelling the exact course of the apocalyptic drama. The concentration of his proclamation therefore on what is really decisive is unmistakable. Nevertheless, the question remains: was he not in fact mistaken if, as it seems from the undoubtedly authentic material, he expected an early end to the world?

For the sake of comparison, however, another question may be raised: was the narrator of the creation of man and the world in six days mistaken, since he was contradicted by the later scientific account of the origin of things? Yet, although the new account disturbed many Christians when they first heard it, most of them take it for granted today. Has not this process of factual "demythologizing" preserved and the stripping of ideological veils made even clearer the *reality* with which the author was concerned: God as origin of all things, without any competition from an evil principle; the goodness of all created things and the grandeur of man?

The fact that our planet with our humanity has a beginning and end is confirmed by a number of the conclusions of the natural sciences, and this is of no slight importance for our understanding of the world and of ourselves. The term "error" used in this connection seems therefore too vague and even inappropriate.

The Bible starts with creation and sees the end as the consummation of God's work on his creation. Neither the "first things" nor the "last things," neither the dawn of time nor the end of time, are *directly accessible to experience.* There are no human witnesses. World creation and world consummation can be described and narrated only in *images:* poetic images and narratives for what is fundamentally ineffable. As biblical protology cannot be a report or a history of events which took place at the beginning, neither can biblical eschatology be an anticipated report or prognosis of events which are to take place at the end. And, as the biblical narratives of God's creative work were drawn from the surroundings of the author's own time, so too the narratives of God's final work were drawn from contemporary apocalyptic. Certainly no one today could hold the naïve opinion that the Synoptic account of the end of the world is a scientific account of what will happen: stars falling from heaven, the sun darkened and the angels blowing trumpets. What is announced, with the aid of imagery familiar at the time, is the eschatological-definitive revelation of God's rule which is brought about solely by God's power and which—as we know better today—transcends all our ideas and imagery.

With reference both to the "first things" and to the "last things," therefore, we cannot dispense with *demythologizing, not to eliminate but to interpret:* a translation of the message in terms of the situation, the understanding of reality, the mythological world picture, of that time into the terms of our situation today, of the present understanding of reality, of the modern world picture.[82] All this for the sake of men today *and* of the message itself. The interpretation and demythologizing beginning in the New Testament itself must be made explicit and consistently developed. We must insist again that the narratives and images are not to be eliminated or reduced to precise concepts and ideas for proclamation today. But they must be correctly understood. It is of primary importance to distinguish between the *framework of understanding or ideas* and the *reality* portrayed which must now be *freshly understood.*

Jesus naturally made use of the apocalyptic imagery and ideas of his own time. And even though—as we pointed out—he expressly rejected any exact calculations of the eschatological consummation and—by comparison with early Jewish apocalyptic—restricted to the utmost any picturesque description of the kingdom of God, in principle he remained within the framework of understanding of immediate expectation which seems strange to us today, within the horizon of apocalypticism. This framework of understanding has been rendered obsolete by historical developments, the apocalyptic horizon has been submerged: this must be clearly recognized. In the light of today's perspectives we have to say that what is involved in this immediate expectation is not so much an error as a time-conditioned, time-bound world view which Jesus shared with his contemporaries. It cannot be artificially reawakened. Nor indeed should the attempt be made to revive it for our very different horizon of experience, although there is always a temptation to do so particularly in what are known as "apocalyptic times." The apocalyptic framework of ideas and understanding of that time is alien to our mentality and today would only conceal and distort the reality behind it.

What really matters today is whether Jesus' basic idea, the *reality* with which he was concerned in the proclamation of the future kingdom of God, still makes sense in the completely transformed horizon of experience of men who in principle have come to terms with the fact that world history is continuing—at least for the time being. Or we may rightly ask positively how Jesus' message has remained so inspiring even after his death and although the world has not yet come to an end. Indeed, why did it become inspiring only after his death? This has in fact something to do with his death, which represented a very definite end. But it also has to do with his life and teaching. Here some new distinctions must be introduced.

Between present and future

However intelligible in their particular form, the parables contain a mystery: "the mystery of the kingdom of God."[33] The suggestion that these words are addressed only to Jesus' disciples and not to the people at large—who are to remain in their blindness—is a subsequent interpretation by the evangelists.[34] The parables themselves prove the opposite. And even the evangelist later states expressly that Jesus spoke to the people in many such parables, in a way that they could understand.[35] What then is the *mystery* of the kingdom of God which is announced in the parables?

We told only half the truth when we spoke above of contrast in connection with the parables of growth. This much is certain: Jesus had no thought of an organic development of the kingdom of God, still less of identifying it with the Church. The kingdom comes by an act of God. But —despite the contrast between the small beginning and the magnificent end—there is the promise of the mighty tree in the grain of mustard seed, of bread for many in the little leaven in the meal, of the great harvest in the inconspicuous seed: of the glorious end in the slight beginning. And where is the beginning to be made if not with Jesus himself? Who is in fact the sower who scattered a little seed on good soil and produced a hundredfold?[36] In Jesus' unassuming talk and action—in his word calling to the poor, hungry, weeping, downtrodden; in his deeds giving aid to the sick, suffering, possessed, those burdened with sin, the hopeless—there is already the promise of the kingdom where sin, pain, suffering and death will have an end: the kingdom of absolute righteousness, freedom, love, reconciliation and eternal peace, God's absolute future. In Jesus God's name is already sanctified, God's will is already done on earth, all sin is forgiven and all evil overcome; in him here and now the time of fulfillment, of salvation, of redemption, has come, the kingdom of God has itself dawned—"in your midst."[37] In him therefore is founded the "mystery of the kingdom of God" announced in the parables. He is himself the end. With him the consummation of the world, God's absolute future, has already dawned—even now. With him God is present.

If we really do take seriously Jesus' expectation of an early advent of the kingdom, we must for this very reason recognize that beginning and end, present and future, cannot be torn apart—as they are if we pursue only *one* trend in the Synoptic proclamation, excluding everything else as unauthentic or leaving it aside as insignificant. Neither purely futurist "thoroughgoing" or "consistent" eschatology (A. Schweitzer), which has nothing to say about the present, nor the purely presentist "realized" eschatology (C. H. Dodd), which overlooks the outstanding future, represents the *whole* Jesus. Jesus' proclamation is not merely a form of late Jewish apocalyptic, concerned solely with future realities and demanding nothing for the present. But still less is it an interpretation merely of the present and of life here and now, having nothing to do with apocalyptic and an absolute future.

Statements about the future *and* about the present, both of which are found in the Gospels, must be taken seriously and linked together in different ways. They are not to be understood (psychologically) as different "moods" in the psyche of Jesus (W. Bousset), nor (biographically) as different "stages" in Jesus' life (P. Wernle, J. Weiss); but neither do they represent, as we have already seen (in the light of the history of the tradition), merely different "strata" in the Synoptic tradition (C. H. Dodd). If we want to avoid arbitrary postulates and fabrications, the present and the future must be seen in an essential tension which cannot be relaxed. It is precisely against the background of the immediate expectation of the end that the *polarity* of the "not yet" and "but even now" holds: unequivocally the future kingdom of God which, through Jesus, is a power and begins to exert an influence even for the present time. Jesus' sayings about the future must not be understood as apocalyptic information, but as eschatological promise.[38] There can be no talk therefore of the future kingdom of God without consequences for present-day society. But neither can there be any talk of the present and its problems without looking to the absolute future by which they are determined. If anyone wants to talk about the future in the spirit of Jesus, he must also speak of the present and vice versa. The reasons for this are clear.

> God's absolute future *throws man back on the* present. *The future cannot be isolated at the expense of the present. The kingdom of God cannot be merely a consoling promise for the future, the satisfaction of pious curiosity about the future, the projection of unfulfilled promises and fears (as Feuerbach, Marx and Freud thought). It is precisely in the light of the future that man ought to be initiated into the present. It is by hope itself that the present world and society are to be not only interpreted but changed. Jesus did not want to provide information about the end of time, but to issue a call for the present in view of the approaching end.*

The apocalypticists asked about the kingdom of God, the absolute future, in the light of the present situation of man and the world. That is why they were so concerned about the exact date of its arrival. Jesus takes the very opposite line: he asks about the present situation of man and the world in the light of the imminent advent of God's future kingdom. That is why he is not concerned about the time or manner of the arrival of God's kingdom. But he believes in the absolutely certain fact of the imminent consummation. It is precisely by looking to the end that we can see clearly what is coming next. The future is God's call to the present. Life even now is to be shaped in the light of the absolute future.

> *The* present *directs man to* God's absolute future. *Our present time must not be made absolute at the expense of the future. The whole future of God's kingdom must not be frittered away in our preoccupation with the present. The present with its poverty and sin is and remains too sad and too discordant to be already the kingdom of God. This world and society are too imperfect and inhuman to be already the perfect and definitive state of things. God's kingdom does not remain at its dawn, but must finally break through. What began with Jesus must also be finished with Jesus. The immediate expectation was not fulfilled. But this is no reason for excluding all expectation.*

The whole New Testament—and in this respect the futuristic interpolations in John's Gospel are important, if they really are no more than "interpolations"—for all its concentration on the dawning of God's rule in Jesus, clings firmly to the still outstanding future consummation. Jesus' cause is God's cause and therefore can never be lost. As the primal myths are to be distinguished from the primal event of creation, so the end myths are to be distinguished from the end-event of consummation. And just as the Old Testament placed the primal myths in a historical setting, linked them with history, so did the New Testament with the end myths. Even though history has outstripped the time-bound immediate expectation, it has not thereby set aside all expectation of the future. The polarity of the "not yet" and "but even now" constitutes the tension of human life and of the history of mankind.

God is ahead

Jesus' message of the kingdom of God retained its attraction. The end of the world did not come. Nevertheless, the message kept its meaning. The apocalyptic horizon of the message was submerged. But the eschatological message itself, the cause with which Jesus was concerned, remained relevant even within the new framework of understanding and ideas. Whether it comes tomorrow or after long ages, the end casts light and shade before it. Can we close our eyes to this fact? The world does not last forever. Human life and human history have an end. But the message of Jesus tells us that, *at this end*, there is not nothing, there is *God*. As God is the beginning, so too he is the end. God's cause prevails in any case. The future belongs to God. It is with this future, God's future, that we have to reckon: we do not have to calculate days and hours. In the light of this future of God we must shape the present, both of the individual and of society. Here and now.

This is not then an empty future, but a future to be revealed and fulfilled. It is not a mere future happening, an event still to come, which futurologists might construct by extrapolation from past or present history —without, incidentally, being able completely to exclude its surprise effect. It is an *eschaton*, that ultimate reality of the future which is something really different and qualitatively new, which admittedly announces its coming in anticipation. We are concerned then, not merely with futurology, but with eschatology. An eschatology without a true, still outstanding, absolute future would be an eschatology without true hope, still to be fulfilled.[80]

This means that there are not only provisional meanings which men can attach to each particular situation. There is an *ultimate meaning of man and the world* which is freely offered to man. All alienation can be removed. The history of man and the world is not exhausted—as Nietzsche thought—in an eternal return of the same thing, nor does it finally and in some vague, absurd emptiness. No. The future is God's and therefore there is fulfillment at the end.

The category *Novum* (E. Bloch) acquires its importance in this connection. And the hope of a different future is one which unites not only Israel and the Christian Churches, but also Christians and Marxists. This really different, absolute future cannot be identified—as it is in one-dimensional technical thinking—with the automatic technical-cultural progress of society, nor even with the organic progress and growth of the Church. Still less can it be identified—as in the existentialist interpretation of Heidegger and others—with the possibility of existence open to the individual and the continually new futurity of his personal decision. This future is something qualitatively new which at the same time stimulates a fundamental transformation of present conditions. It is of course also a future which cannot be identified with a coming socialist society.

In all these *false identifications* the fact is overlooked that it is a question of the future, of *God's* kingdom.[40] Neither the solidly institutionalized Church of medieval and Counter-Reformation Catholicism nor Calvin's Genevan theocracy was the kingdom of God; nor was it the apocalyptic kingdom of revolutionary, apocalyptic fanatics like Thomas Münzer. Theological idealism and liberalism were also wrong in identifying God's kingdom with an existing order of wholesome morality and consummate bourgeois culture. And certainly it was not the thousand-year political Reich, based on ideologies of nation and race, as propagated by National Socialism. Nor, finally, was it the classless realm of the new man which Communism has hitherto striven to realize.

In the light of Jesus' teaching, against all these premature identifications, it must be observed that the kingdom of God—the consummation—*does not come about either through social* (intellectual or technical) *evolution or social revolution* (of the right or left). The consummation comes by *God's action*, which cannot be foreseen or extrapolated. It is an action of course which does not exclude but includes man's action here and now, in the individual and the social sphere. At the same time, just as formerly a false "interiorizing" of God's kingdom had to be avoided, today there must be no false "secularizing" of God's kingdom.

It is a question then of a *really different dimension:* the divine dimension. We are speaking of *transcendence*, but not of transcendence understood primarily in a spatial sense as in the older physics and metaphysics, where God was *above* or *outside* the world. On the other hand, it certainly does not mean an idealist or existentialist interiorization: God *in* us. Transcendence is to be understood as Jesus spoke of it, primarily in a temporal sense: God *before* us.[41] God is not simply the timeless, eternal reality behind the one regular flow of coming to be and passing away of past, present and future, as understood particularly from Greek philosophy: *he is the future reality, the one who is to come, who bestows hope*, as he can be known from Israel's promises of the future and from Jesus himself. His divinity is understood as the power of the future making our present appear in a new light. The future is God's: which means that, wherever the individual human being goes, in life or death, God is there. In whatever direction mankind as a whole evolves, rising or declining, God is there. He is there as the first and last reality.

What does this mean for man? That *he cannot take existing things* in this world and society *as definitive*. That for him neither the world nor he himself can be the first and last. That the world and he himself simply as such are utterly relative, uncertain and unstable. That he is therefore living in a critical situation, however much he likes to close his eyes to it. He is pressed to make a final decision, to accept the offer to commit *himself to the reality of God*, which is ahead of him. It is a decision in which everything is at stake: an either-or, for or against God.

Despite the submergence of the apocalyptic horizon, *the appeal has lost none of its urgency*. A *conversion* is peremptorily thrust upon him. A new way of thinking and acting is urgently required. This is an absolutely final choice: a reinterpretation of life, a new attitude to life, a new life as a whole. Anyone who asks how much time he has left to live without God, to postpone conversion, is missing the future and the present, because by missing God he misses also himself. The hour of the finally definitive decision is here and now, not at an end-time—calculable or incalculable—of man or of mankind. And it is wholly personal for each and every one. The individual cannot be content—as he often can be in psychoanalysis—without enlightenment about his behavior, without having to face any moral demands. Nor can he shift the decision and the responsibility to society, its defective structures and corrupt institutions. He himself is pressed here to commit himself, to give himself. In metaphorical terms the question of the precious pearl,[42] the treasure in the field,[43] becomes wholly personal for him. So, even now, everything—life and death—is at stake. Even now, through self-sacrifice, he can gain himself. Even now it is true that he who will gain his life will lose it and he who will lose it will gain it.[44]

This conversion is possible only by relying confidently on the message, on God himself, with that confidence which will not be put off and which is called *faith*. It is a faith which can move mountains,[45] but which shares in the promise even in the most meager form of a grain of seed, so that man can always say: "I believe, help my unbelief."[46] It is a faith which never becomes simply a possession, but remains a gift. With regard to the future, this faith has the dimension of hope. In hope faith reaches its goal; on the other hand, hope has its permanent ground in faith.

This hope in God's future must serve, not only to interpret the world and its history and to throw light on the individual's existence, but also to criticize the present world and thus to transform society and existence. The maintenance of the status quo for time and eternity therefore really cannot be justified in the light of Jesus' teaching. But neither can violent, total social upheaval at any price be justified. The implications of conversion by faith may become clearer in what follows. Here—assuming that it has become intelligible up to a point today—it is sufficient to quote what the earliest evangelist provides, admittedly in his own formulation, as a brief summary of Jesus' message: "The time has come and the kingdom of God is near. Be converted and believe the good news."[47]

2. *Miracles?*

Jesus did not merely talk, he also acted. His *deeds* were as provocative as his words. In fact, many of these very deeds present modern man with more difficulties than all his words. The miracle tradition is much more disputed than the word tradition. Miracle, "dearest child of faith" according to Goethe, in the age of natural science and technology has become the weakest child of faith. How are we to overcome the tension which exists between the scientific understanding of the world and belief in miracles, between rational-technical world organization and the experience of miracles? Admittedly, even Fathers of the Church along with modern apologists have regarded miracles as restricted essentially to the time of the Church's origin. What J. S. Semler in his day called the "principle of economy" is used today with reference to miracles in the course of the Church's history. In regard to miracles of the present time people seem always to have more inhibitions than they do in regard to those of the past. But this only shows their embarrassment with regard to miracles as such.[1]

Concealing embarrassment

The term "miracle" is almost as vague as "revolution." We can speak of the "economic miracle" and miracles of technology, miracles of atomic energy and miracles of deep sea research: all these are miracles which man (or "nature"), but certainly not God, has produced. This may make things easy for theologians. The concept of miracle can be given such a broad meaning that it becomes completely inoffensive. There are some therefore who think they can get round the problem of miracles by seeing these everywhere: for them all that happens in the world is or becomes miraculous, inasmuch as all that happens is permeated by divine activity or is perceived as such. But is a pit disaster in which dozens are killed supposed to be a miracle in the sense that the rescue of buried miners is often described as a miracle? In this view why should God be supposed to be more involved in the second event than in the first? By what right do we give God the credit for accidents which turn out well and not blame him for fatal accidents? The concept of miracle is completely emptied of meaning by our imposing subsequently a religious meaning on all that happens in the world.

All this however is a graceful way of concealing the real problematic of New Testament miracles: that is, whether the miracles ascribed to Jesus, which, as far as the text is concerned, were contrary to the laws of nature, were historical facts or not. Neither modern religious talk of miracles being present everywhere nor talking in an archaic and equally evasive way of God's "great deeds" or "deeds of power," nor even a straightforward "narration" of the miracle stories, gets rid of the question raised by David Hume and John Stuart Mill: are miracles—supernatural interventions—conceivable if they are understood, not in a vague, but in a strict, modern sense as breaches of the laws of nature by God? As Christians must we believe *such* miracles? What does critical historical science say about that which natural science regards as impossible?

If we speak of *having to believe,* something is wrong. We *may* believe *good* news. But how then are all the miracle stories of the Gospels to be judged? What is to be said of the healing miracles (fever, paralysis, consumption, haemorrhage, deafness and dumbness, blindness, epilepsy, deformity, dropsy, healing of the high priest's servant's ear), the expulsion of demons, raising to life three dead persons, the seven nature miracles (walking on the water, stilling the storm, Peter's draught of fishes, the coin in the fish's mouth, cursing the fig tree, feeding the crowds in the desert, changing water into wine)?

For some people, even today, none of this creates any problem. In all Churches there are devout people to whom Jesus means so much and the world picture of science and technology and all historical difficulties so little that they have no inhibitions about accepting all miracles literally as having happened exactly as they are described. Such readers may pass over the following pages and go on to the next chapter. But there are others who have difficulties about the New Testament accounts of miracles. Accounts of miracles, as Lessing long ago pointed out, are no longer "proofs of the spirit and of power"; they are not present-day miracles. Those people then who ask what really happened and who cannot be dismissed as rationalists can be helped only by complete historical and theological truthfulness. For:

a. Critical minds will scarcely be helped by those theologians who perhaps even today, while not asserting in a fundamentalist spirit that the historicity of the miracle accounts is a matter of faith, think that they can prove this apologetically in every individual case. The time must really be gone forever when quite a few thought they could demonstrate the possibility even of Christ's walking on the lake.

b. Critical minds will scarcely be helped forward either by those theologians who talk only about Jesus' message and pass over his miracles in silence. The miracle stories as a whole (not each individual story) belong in fact to the oldest elements of the Gospel tradition. From the standpoint of literary criticism the evidence for Jesus the miracle worker is just as certain as that for Jesus the preacher. And no one who wants to be taken seriously as a historian can eliminate half even of Mark's Gospel as a result of ideological prejudice.

c. Finally, critical minds will not be greatly helped by those theologians who adjust their whole interpretation of the miracle stories to the fact that Jesus repeatedly refused to verify his message by miracles.[2] Jesus does not in fact adopt a critical attitude in principle to miracles. He refuses a sign, not to suggest that miracles are impossible, but because they are misleading. He does not reject belief in miracles, but the demand and the craving for miracles: not miracles as such, but spectacular miracles. Man should believe Jesus' word even without proof from miracles.

Anyway, people in Jesus' time, including the evangelists, were just not interested in the point which so interests modern man, the man of the rational and technological age: the laws of nature. People then did *not* think *in terms of* natural science and therefore did not regard miracles as a breach of the laws of nature or as a break in the otherwise uninterrupted causal sequence. Even in the Old Testament no distinction was made between miracles which correspond to the laws of nature and those which breach the laws. Any event through which Yahweh reveals his power is regarded as a miracle, a sign, as Yahweh's great or mighty deed. God, the primal reason and creator of the world, is active everywhere. Human beings can experience miracles everywhere: from the creation and conservation of the world to its consummation, in both great things and small, both in the history of the nation and in the rescue of the individual from great distress.

Both in New Testament times and in pagan antiquity the *fact* that there can be and are miracles everywhere is simply taken for granted. Miracles were understood, not as something contrary to natural laws, but as something that rouses admiration, that transcends ordinary human powers, that is inexplicable for man, behind which another power—God's power or even an evil power—is concealed. The fact that *Jesus* also worked miracles is important for the evangelists and their time. But neither the historical nor the natural sciences had been developed at that time. And why should not modes of representation and means of expression like epics and hymns, myths and sagas, be appropriate to testify to the activity of the living God? No one thought then of a scientific explanation or a subsequent investigation of a miracle. The Gospels never describe how the miraculous event came about. There is no medical diagnosis of the sickness nor any information about the therapeutic factors. And why should there be? The evangelists do not want to thrust themselves into the event they report. They elevate it. They do not explain but exalt. The miracle narratives are not meant to provide a description but to rouse admiration: these are the great things that God has done through a man. There is no attempt to demand faith in the existence of miracles as such or in the fact that this or that event is really a miracle. What is expected is faith in God who acts in the man doing these things and of whose activity the miraculous deeds are signs.

What really happened

The starting point for the interpretation of the miracle accounts in the Gospels therefore must be the fact that they are not eyewitness reports, not scientifically tested documentation, not historical, medical or psychological records. They are simply unsophisticated popular narratives which are meant to call forth admiring belief. As such they are wholly at the service of the proclamation of Christ.

Under these conditions however can the historian still be expected to say anything about Jesus' miraculous works? Can he get at the reality concealed behind the popular narratives at all? The individual miracle story simply does not appear to yield enough information to enable a literary-historical analysis to reach the real "event." And yet there is no question here of all or nothing, of everything being legendary or nothing being legendary. There is no need at all either to accept *all* miracle stories in an uncritical, fundamentalist spirit as historical facts, and, regardless of contradictions, to "believe" in them, or on the other hand in a spirit of narrow-minded rationalism to refuse to take *any* miracle stories seriously.

The hasty conclusion is a result of putting all miracle stories on the same plane. The most recent form-critical investigation has examined the literary form of the miracle stories very closely. The variations noted in the New Testament include: Old Testament models (especially the miracles at the exodus from Egypt and those of the prophets Elijah and Elisha); narrative styles common to Jewish, Hellenistic and New Testament miracle stories; certain tendencies to heighten the miraculous element (particularly in John) or occasionally to restrain it (in Matthew, by comparison with Mark). The New Testament miracle stories themselves therefore urgently demand a *discriminating consideration*, following closely the individual accounts and not getting confused by the redactional summaries (collected accounts) of the evangelists,[8] which give the impression of a continuous, widespread miracle-working activity on the part of Jesus.

However skeptical they may be in regard to individual miracle stories, even the most critical exegetes today agree that the coverage of miracles as a whole cannot be dismissed as unhistorical. Despite numerous legendary features in detail, certain facts are generally accepted:

a. There must have been *cures of varied types of sickness* which were amazing at least to people at that time. To some extent it will have been a question of psychogenetic afflictions, among them certain psychogenetic skin diseases all presumably listed in ancient times under the title of "leprosy." The accusation of magic (expulsion of devils by the archdevil, Beelzebub), frequently leveled against Jesus and not arbitrarily invented in the Gospels because of its offensiveness, was conceivable only if provoked as a result of real happenings. The historically indisputable conflicts about the Sabbath were also linked with cures. There is no reason for striking the therapeutic element from the tradition.

Even today there are some cases which are still medically inexplicable. And modern medicine, which has recognized more than ever the psychosomatic character of a large number of illnesses, is aware of amazing cures as a result of extraordinary psychological influences, of an infinite trust, of "faith." On the other hand, the earliest Gospel tradition includes cases in which Jesus could not work a single miracle—as in his home town of Nazareth—since faith and trust were lacking.[4] Such things are received only by the believer. Jesus' cures have nothing to do with magic and sorcery, where the person is overpowered against his will. They are an appeal for faith,[5] which itself sometimes appears to be the real miracle by comparison with which the cure is of secondary importance.[6] The healing stories of the New Testament must be understood as stories of faith.

b. Cures of "possessed" people in particular must have occurred. Nor is there any reason to exclude this exorcistic element from the tradition. Sickness was frequently linked with sin, and sin with devils. And particularly those illnesses which lead to serious personality disorders, mental illnesses with very striking symptoms (for example, foaming at the mouth as in epilepsy), were ascribed at that time and for many centuries afterwards to a devil who had taken up residence in the sick man. But, in the absence of institutions for the insane, people were confronted in public more often with the mentally ill, those who were obviously not in control of themselves. The cure of such illnesses—for instance, a raving lunatic in the synagogue[7] or an epileptic[8]—was regarded as a victory over the devil who had dominated the sick person.

Not only Israel, but the whole ancient world was filled with belief in devils and fear of devils. The more distant God seemed, so much the greater was the need of intermediate beings—good and evil—between heaven and earth. People often speculated about whole hierarchies of evil spirits under the leadership of a Satan, Belial or Beelzebub. In all the different religions everywhere there were sorcerers, priests and doctors who strove to exorcise and repel devils. The Old Testament had been very reserved in regard to belief in devils. But between 538 and 331 B.C. Israel belonged to the Persian Empire, with its dualist religion of a good god from whom all good proceeds and an evil god, the source of all evil. The influence of this belief is unmistakable and thus belief in devils clearly appears in the religion of Yahweh as a late, secondary element; but it ceased to play a part in later and particularly modern Judaism.

Jesus himself, living in the very midst of this period of solid belief in devils, shows no sign of a disguised Persian dualism with God and the devil fighting on the same plane for world and man. He preaches the joyful message of God's rule and not the threatening message of Satan's rule. He is manifestly not interested in the figure of Satan or the devil, in speculations about the sin and fall of the angels. He does not develop any doctrine of devils. With him there are no sensational gestures to be seen, no special rites, no incantations or manipulations, as with the Jewish or Hellenistic exorcists of his time. He links with devils sickness and possession, but not all possible evils and sins, world political powers and their rulers. Jesus' exorcisms and expulsions of devils are a sign that God's rule is at hand and that an end is being prepared for the devil's rule. That is why, according to Luke, Jesus sees Satan falling like lightning from heaven.[9] Understood in this way, the expulsion of devils and man's liberation from the devil's spell just do not amount to any sort of mythological act. They constitute the beginning of a de-demonizing and demythologizing of man and the world and a liberation for true creatureliness and humanity. God's kingdom is creation healed. Jesus liberates the possessed from psychical constraints and breaks through the vicious circle of mental disturbance, devil religion and social ostracism.

c. Finally other miracle stories may at least have been *occasioned by historical facts.* The story of calming the storm, for instance, may have originated in a rescue from distress at sea after prayer and a call for help. The story of the coin in the fish's mouth may be based on Jesus' request to catch a fish in order to pay the temple tax. Obviously these are merely conjectures. It is no longer possible to reconstruct the actual occasion, since the narrator was just not interested in it. What mattered for him was the testimony, the most impressive testimony possible for Jesus as the Christ.

What was transmitted

From this standpoint is it surprising that what actually happened was expanded, embellished, heightened in the course of forty to seventy years of oral tradition? It is not only in the East that this sort of thing is normal when stories are repeatedly told.

a. There can scarcely be any doubt that there have been *further developments* of the original tradition. A comparison of the texts with one another, as they have been transmitted—which cannot be carried out here[10] —reveals a number of such developments: accounts are duplicated (two miraculous draughts of fish, crowds fed on two occasions); numbers are increased (one blind man—two blind men; one possessed man—two possessed men; four thousand and then five thousand fed, seven and then twelve baskets left over); miracles are magnified (as can be seen by comparing together the different Synoptic accounts and these again with the parallels in John, or by comparing the three accounts of raising the dead); finally, Jesus' miracles are generalized (collective account). Jesus frequently appears as the Hellenistic "man of God" (*theios aner*), endowed with wonderful powers. There may have been linguistic misunderstandings: the Aramaic *ligyona* can mean "legion" (a legion of devils) or "legionary" (a devil with the name of "legionary"); the same word can be used in Greek for walking "at (near) the lake" or "on the lake." Other features can be ascribed to the joy of embellishing and heightening the effect—as happened, for instance, in the Old Testament with reference to Israel's passage through the Red Sea: according to Mark, at the arrest of Jesus the ear of the high priest's servant was cut off; according to Luke, it was also immediately restored. The story of the wonderful catch of fish might be a preliminary symbolic portrayal of the "fisher of men"; in any case it was reproduced by Luke as the story of the calling of the disciples and by the author of the supplementary chapter of John's Gospel as the story of a resurrection appearance.

b. Of course the primitive Christian communities shared their contemporaries' enthusiasm for miracles and the possibility cannot be excluded that they transferred to Jesus *themes and material from outside* Christianity, in order to emphasize his greatness and authority. This sort of thing happened with all the great "founders of religions," whose fame was enhanced by miracle stories. At any rate, we cannot simply distinguish between the pagan and Jewish miracles on the one hand and New Testament miracles on the other by asserting that the latter are historical while the former are not. Numerous cures are attested by votive tablets (existing even today) in the Asclepius shrine at Epidauros and elsewhere. Rabbinic and particularly Hellenistic miracle stories of cures, metamorphoses, expulsions of devils, raising the dead, calming storms were circulating in abundance.

Certainly there are important differences: with Jesus there are no self-help miracles, spectacular miracles, penal miracles, no miracles by way of reward, honorarium or profit. But there are no less important similarities. The coin (or pearl) in the fish's mouth is a widespread motif of fables in both Judaism and Hellenism (for instance, the ring of Polycrates). The changing of water into wine—recorded, oddly enough, only in John—is a well-known feature of the Dionysius myth and cult. Both Tacitus and Suetonius relate the cure of a blind man with the use of spittle by Vespasian.[11] Lucian tells of a man carrying away his bed after being cured.[12] There is a remarkable similarity even in detail between the raising from death of a young bride before the gates of Rome,[13] ascribed to

Apollonius of Tyana, a contemporary of Jesus, and the raising of the young man at Nain.[14] Any Jew would have enjoyed the grotesque story of the expulsion of the devil, "Legion," which is said to have cost the owner an enormous herd of two thousand ("unclean," forbidden!) pigs. But it is scarcely possible to believe that Jesus worked such a miracle. The episode could have been based on a story of a Jewish miracle-man in the unclean Gentile country (with the motif of the cheating or cheated devil).

The gift of seeing into men's hearts—a notable feature of John's Gospel—has a parallel in Qumran. From this it appears to be the expression, not of a mythological omniscience, but of messianic authority: an authority not meant for an admiring public but as a "judgment" for the person concerned.[15] There are miracle stories which might seem to owe more to the Hellenistic type of "man of God" or "divine man" than to Old Testament figures like Moses and Joshua, David and Solomon, Elijah and Elisha.

c. Over and above this, however, it has to be remembered that the Gospels are written in the light of the risen and exalted Lord. For this reason the possibility cannot be excluded that some miracle stories offer *anticipated portrayals of the risen Christ:* epiphany stories, which frequently have an obvious point and—for the community—a symbolic meaning (rescue from the "storm" of tribulation and so on). Such miracles anticipate the glory of the risen Christ. Among these may be included the story of Jesus' transfiguration on the mountain,[16] likewise those of walking on the lake[17] and the feeding of the five thousand (or four thousand).[18] Among them should be included especially the stories of the raising of Jairus' daughter from the dead,[19] and—despite their sensational character, recorded notably only by Luke and John—the raisings of the young man of Nain[20] and Lazarus.[21] All these accounts are meant to present Jesus as the Lord of life and death, as Son of God. Christian and non-Christian motifs can intersect in the same story. Any close analysis reveals the fact that very many narratives and particularly those of the storm and walking on the lake, the multiplication of the loaves and raising the dead have been developed and stylized in accordance with Old Testament motifs (particularly from the Psalms).

Christian science

There is no more that historical investigation can reveal, even if it starts out free from any *a priori* assumption of the impossibility of miracles. We are not concerned here with the possibility or impossibility of miracles as a whole. But the onus of proof is on anyone who wants to accept miracles in the strict sense. And miracles in the strictly modern sense of breaking through the laws of nature cannot be historically proved. Consequently it is better today for the most part to avoid the ambiguous expression "miracle." The result will be a large measure of agreement with the New Testament itself. The Greek word for miracle (*thauma*), used since the time of Homer and Hesiod, does not appear once; nor does the Latin Vulgate use the term *miraculum* in the New Testament. It is better—and again following the New Testament and particularly John—to speak of "signs" or "significant deeds." It is a question of charismatic (not medical) therapeutic-exorcistic acts which have the character of signs but admittedly do not distinguish Jesus from other similar charismatics. These actions cannot be shown to be without analogies in the history of religion. They cannot be ascribed uniquely, incomparably, unmistakably, to Jesus alone and to no other person. But they were astonishing at least to the people of his own time. So astonishing that they thought him capable of more, indeed of everything, and particularly after his death in the light of the distance in time they could not praise him enough.

Was Jesus then something of a *healing practitioner*, putting into practice a doctrine, a science of healing? The "Christian Science" movement regards Jesus of Nazareth in fact as the first teacher and practitioner of Christian science. Jesus is portrayed as the model of a new method of healing by the power of faith. Was this then the conquest of all that is imperfect, all that has to do with sickness and suffering—ultimately characterized as illusion—by way of mind and spirit, without any external intervention?

This would be a *misunderstanding* of Jesus' charismatic deeds. The cures and the expulsions of devils are by no means regular occurrences, still less do they follow a plan. Jesus often withdraws from the people and imposes silence on the person cured.[22] Jesus was not a miracle-man, a Hellenistic "man of God," wanting to make as many people well as possible. The older Palestinian stratum—as form-critical analysis has shown—refrains from the Hellenistic stylization which characterizes the pagan accounts of miracles. The topics and technique of these stylized miracle accounts display the following stereotype features: exposition of the horror of sickness and vain attempts to cure it, description of the cure (by gesture, word, spittle, etc.), finally demonstration (the lame person carries his bed, etc.) and reaction of the witnesses (closing chorus: cries, astonishment, fear among the eyewitnesses). The older Palestinian miracle narratives—as, for instance, the healing of Peter's mother-in-law[23]—are brief and without literary pretensions. They refrain from embellishment and from secular motifs. Stylistic features penetrate only slowly.[24]

The original, straightforward narratives place Jesus' divine authority in the center. Jesus saw his vocation, his fullness of the Spirit, his message, all confirmed in his charismatic deeds and on that account came into conflict with his family and with the theologians.[25] The important thing was not the negative but the positive aspect. The Gospels were not interested in a breach of nature's laws, but they were interested in the fact that in these deeds God's power itself was breaking through. Jesus' charismatic cures and expulsions of devils were not an end in themselves. They were *at the service of the proclamation of God's kingdom.* They interpret or confirm the words of Jesus. A paralytic is healed in order to prove that Jesus is justified in forgiving sin.[26] They do not occur regularly and certainly not in an organized way—the transformation of the world remains God's affair. They occur as examples, as signs—God is beginning to transform the curse of human existence into blessing.

More important than the number and extent of the cures, expulsions of devils and wonderful deeds is the fact that Jesus turns with sympathy and compassion to all those *to whom no one else turns:* the weak, sick, neglected, social rejects. People were always glad to pass these by. Weaklings and invalids are burdensome. Everyone keeps his distance from lepers and "possessed." And the devout monks of Qumran (and similarly up to a point the rabbis), faithful to their rule, excluded from the very beginning certain groups of men:

> *No madman, or lunatic, or simpleton, or fool, no blind man, or maimed, or lame, or deaf man, and no minor, shall enter into the Community, for the Angels of Holiness are with them.*[27]

Jesus does not turn away from any of these, he rejects none of them. He does not treat the sick as sinners, but draws them to himself to cure them. "Clear the way for the strong, the healthy, the young": these are not the words of Jesus. He has no cult of health, youth or achievement. He loves them all, as they are, and so is able to help them: to the sick in body and soul he gives health; to the weak and aged strength; to the unfit fitness; to all those whose life is impoverished and hopeless he gives hope, new life, confidence in the future. And are not all these actions—even though they do not infringe any law of nature—very unusual, extraordinary, astonishing, marvelous-wonderful? The Baptist, in prison, does not know what he is to make of Jesus. According to the tradition, Jesus answers with a picture of the kingdom of God which in its poetic form does not present an exact list of miracles (some of them may have occurred in the presence of the messengers), but a messianic hymn in striking contrast to Qumran:[28]

> *The blind see and the lame walk,*
> *the lepers are cleansed and the deaf hear,*
> *the dead are raised to life*
> *and the poor receive the good news.*

Which means: the wonderful effects of the coming kingdom of God are perceptible even now. God's future exercises its influence even on the present time. That is not to say that the world itself is already transformed—God's kingdom will come first. But its power radiates already from Jesus, from his words and deeds; in him a beginning has been made. If he cures the sick, if he drives out devils by the Spirit of God, then *in him and with him* the kingdom of God has already come.[29] Jesus did not establish the kingdom of God by his deeds there and then. But he certainly set up *signs* in which the coming kingdom already flashes its light. These are significant, corporeal, typical advance portrayals of that definitive and comprehensive well-being of body and mind which we call man's "salvation." In that sense he could say: "The kingdom of God is in your midst."[30]

Indications, not proofs

Jesus' significant deeds are *not unequivocal arguments of credibility*, adequate in themselves to justify faith. Miracles alone prove nothing. Even for Jesus' contemporaries they were ambiguous. Each one's attitude to Jesus and his person decided whether one and the same deed was the effect of God's power or a diabolic snare. This attitude decided whether he would allow himself to be convinced or would evade the challenge, whether he worshiped or cursed. The historicity of miracles therefore is not the crucial question for Christian faith. In itself the acceptance of historicity is no more a proof of faith than is its rejection a proof of unbelief. The crucial question for *Christian* faith is the question about this Christ himself: what think you of him? We must also ask: what think you of God?

Jesus' charismatic deeds are merely hints, indications, which become credible because of the person who performs them. They are not proofs which in themselves could verify the reality and truth of revelation. In face of his opponents Jesus himself rejects any demonstration of his power, any proof of his authority. He refuses "signs" such as the Pharisees demand and as the apocalypticists too expect of the Messiah.[31] As John's Gospel especially—in the spirit of the Synoptic temptation accounts—clearly shows,[32] such a demand is a challenge to God and therefore the very opposite of genuine faith. Jesus was not concerned with propaganda, but with man's salvation.

The real evil, both of the supernaturalistic conception of miracles (as divine interventions contrary to the laws of nature) and of the universally religious interpretation (everything in the world, in harmony with the laws of nature, is miraculous), is the detachment of the statements on miracles from Jesus and his word. The key to the understanding of the New Testament miracle accounts is not the breach of the laws of nature (which cannot be verified historically) and not God's universal government of the world (which is not to be questioned), but Jesus himself. It is only *in the light of his word* that his charismatic deeds acquire their *unequivocal meaning.* That is why in the answer to John the enumeration of the signs of the coming kingdom culminates in the preaching of the Gospel[33] and ends with declaring blessed those who are not scandalized at his person.[34] The charismatic deeds elucidate Jesus' words, but on the other hand they need Jesus' words to interpret them. Only in the light of Jesus' words do they gain their credibility.

Neither Jesus' words nor his deeds can be separated from his person. This is made clear from the miracle narratives in John's Gospel, which are so vivid and yet in the last resort symbolic, emerging probably from a special source: the multiplication of the loaves is a sign of Jesus as "the bread of life,"[35] the cure of the blind man a sign of Jesus as "the light of the world,"[36] the raising of the dead a sign of Jesus as "the resurrection and the life."[37] He himself, announcing the kingdom of God in word and deed, is really the unique sign of the coming kingdom which is being given to men. It is wholly and entirely a secondary question—which need not disturb anyone's faith—whether with the progress of science what was thought to be a miracle has found or may still find a scientific explanation. Jesus himself remains the sign which announces the future in word and deed and which justifies faith. What is demanded is not faith in miracles, but *faith in Jesus* and in him whom Jesus has revealed. In this sense—as again John's Gospel makes clear—the believer can dispense with miracles entirely: "Blessed are those who have not seen and yet believe."[38]

What then do we learn from the New Testament miracle accounts?

> *Jesus would be misunderstood if he were regarded as a practitioner of healing and a specialist in miracles, burdening himself methodically with all man's frailties. His activity must not be misinterpreted in a scientistic sense.*
>
> *Jesus would likewise be misunderstood if he were regarded merely as a pastor and confessor, concerned only with man's soul and spirit. His activity must not be misinterpreted in a spiritistic sense.*

Hence the message of God's kingdom is aimed at man in all his dimensions, not only at man's soul but at the *whole* man in his mental and material existence, in his whole concrete, suffering world. And it holds for *all* men: not only the strong, young, healthy, capable, whom the world so likes to exalt, but also the weak, sick, old, incapable, whom the world so likes to forget, to overlook, to neglect. Jesus did not merely talk, but also intervened in the field of sickness and injustice. He has not only the authority to preach, but also the charism of healing. He is not only *preacher* and *adviser.* He is at the same time *healer* and *helper.*

Even in this respect he was again different from the priests and theologians, the guerrilla fighters and the monks: he taught like one having power.[39] What is this? A new teaching full of power? According to Mark, this is what people asked and said after the first miracle.[40] In him there dawned something which was very forcefully rejected and even condemned as magic by some but which gave others the impression of an encounter with divine power: the kingdom of God, which consists not merely in forgiveness and conversion, but also in the redemption and liberation of the body and in the transformation and consummation of the world. So Jesus appears not only as the preacher, but also in word and deed as guarantor of the coming kingdom of God. But what, it must now be asked, is its norm?

3. *The supreme norm*

Whatever limits may be imposed on our treatment of the Christian reality, one question is still thrust upon us: to what must man really hold fast? If someone does not want to tie himself to the establishment or—on the other hand—to support the cause of revolution, if he will not decide for local or mental emigration and yet rejects moral compromise, what does he really want? Here are four possibilities. As with the four corners of a quadrilateral, it seems there cannot be a fifth. Which way is he to turn? What law will he follow? What indeed is supposed to be the norm here? What is the supreme norm? This was a question of fundamental importance at that time as it is now. What counted for Jesus as the supreme norm?

No natural law

The supreme norm is not a law of natural morality: *not a natural moral law*. To make this clear, at least briefly, is not entirely irrelevant at a time when an important papal encyclical, invoking the authority of Jesus Christ, has claimed that the reasons for the immorality of "artificial" contraception are to be found in such a natural law. The fact that Jesus does not justify his demands by starting out from an allegedly certainly recognizable and unchangeable essential nature uniting all men cannot be ascribed merely to a lack of theological reflection. He is just not concerned with an abstract human nature, but with the concrete, individual human being. He speaks quite naturally and at the same time most impressively of man's world: of the birds of the air and the lilies of the field, grapes and figs, thorns and thistles, seedtime and harvest, sun and rain, weather, rust and moths . . . Nothing is denigrated, but neither is anything romanticized; everything is accepted as it is. He also speaks quite concretely of man in this world, in his living reality: the children in the market square and the father with his family, the woman at home, the worker in the vineyard, the shepherd with his sheep, the farmer in the field, the judge and the accused, the king and the slave. Again nothing is dyed black, but neither is anything seen through rose-colored spectacles; man is viewed realistically and often—as we can easily see, reading between the lines—described with wit and irony.

In Jesus' mind therefore the world and man are God's world and man. Jesus is not—like Confucius, for example—influenced by belief in an eternal cosmic law in accordance with which man is expected to act. He scarcely uses even the word "creation" and never "nature," a word derived from Greek thought. The concept of a common, unchangeable human nature is of no interest to him. Unlike the Stoics, he does not start out from an idea of man, as if man as such were something holy. In particular he does not think of deducing from some sort of permanent and unchanging structures of human nature universally binding, unchanging basic laws of action: first principles from which other principles are more or less directly deduced and which then all together provide an unequivocal answer for all possible cases in moral theology (with reference to private property, family, state, sexuality, divorce, death penalty, etc.).

Certainly world and man are of importance to Jesus. For him creation tells of the Creator who makes his sun rise on good and evil and the rain fall on the just and unjust. The grass of the field and the sparrows bear witness to God's solicitude which makes any anxious concern for himself on man's part seem superfluous. Sowing, growth and harvest recall God's promise; lightning, rain and storm his judgment. For Jesus all creation is bathed in the light of God and becomes a symbol pointing to him who is its Creator and Finisher. But Jesus neither reasons from creation to the existence of God nor does he deduce by natural reason from nature and its structures an ontologically substantiated system of norms and doctrine which would have to be a foundation for every other law.

If Jesus did not defend any "ethics of natural law" in the scholastic sense (under the influence of Greek philosophy), neither did he—on the other hand—defend a "formal ethics of duty" such as Kant later expounded. Even the "golden rule" of the Sermon on the Mount, utilized by Kant—do to others what you would have them do to you[1]—is not a formal principle, not a categorical imperative, from which all concrete ethical requirements could be deduced. Nor, finally, did Jesus uphold a "material value ethic" as developed especially by Max Scheler. He does not set up any scale of values nor does he justify a gradation of intrinsic values by way of vital, aesthetic and intellectual to moral and religious values. Even the concept of righteousness—which becomes significant in Jesus' proclamation through the redaction of Matthew—is not meant to be the supreme value, but stands alongside other no less important universal concepts. And even love does not function as supreme value from which all the rest in their entirety might be deduced. Jesus is not at all interested in completeness. He scarcely mentions the state and says nothing at all about economics, culture, education and many other things. Obviously there was much that simply lay outside the horizon of his times. But this does not explain everything. The limitations are not merely those imposed by the conditions at the time, but there is a deliberate limitation and concentration. A great deal that may be important in other respects is obviously not important to him. What then is important? Before we give a positive answer, there is a second demarcation line to be drawn.

No revealed law

Nor is the supreme norm a positive revealed law: *it is not a revealed law of God.* Jesus is not—like Moses, Zarathustra and Muhammad—a representative of a typical legalistic religion. For him the determining factor in ordinary life is not an eternal cosmic law (as in Chinese or Stoic thought); nor is it a revealed law governing all spheres of life such as Islam finds in the form of a book (Koran) pre-existing in God's presence, and which had been made known to the nations by other prophets before Muhammad, although in an adulterated form until Muhammad as the last prophet after Jesus—as the "Seal of the Prophets"—restored the primitive revelation.

It is true that Jesus has constantly been presented in Church history as the "new lawgiver" and the Gospel as the "new law." And Jesus did not by any means reject the Old Law as such when he attacked the Pharisaic (early Jewish) legalism. Even in his own time legalistic piety should not be equated with the widespread legalism.[2] In itself the law manifests God's ruling will. In itself it manifests God's goodness and fidelity, it is a document and proof of his grace and love to his people and demands not only individual acts but the heart. Jesus did not want to replace it by his own message. As we saw, he came to fulfill and not to annul. He was not a defender of an anarchistic lawlessness.

Nevertheless, for him the law was not the supreme norm permitting no dispensation. Otherwise he would not have been able to set himself above it. But in fact—as we also saw—it is clear that Jesus did set himself above the law: not only above tradition, the oral tradition of the Fathers, the *halakhah*, but above Scripture itself, the sacred law of God, the Torah, recorded in the five books of Moses (=Pentateuch).[3] He rejected completely the binding force of oral tradition. In word and deed he attacked the regulations of cultic purity and fasting and particularly the Sabbath regulations. All of which, as we explained, earned him the fierce hostility of the Pharisees. But their hostility is also explained by the fact that the rejection of oral tradition involved also the Torah itself, the Mosaic Law, which the traditions of the Fathers were supposed merely to interpret: we need only recall the prescriptions of the Torah on clean and unclean food[4] or the Sabbath precept.[5] But Jesus directly opposed the Mosaic Law by prohibiting divorce,[6] oaths,[7] reprisals,[8] and by commanding love of enemies.[9]

Jesus' criticism of the law was further strengthened by his criticism of the temple worship. For Jesus the temple is not everlasting, as it is for most of his fellow countrymen. He expects its demolition,[10] the new temple of God is even now ready and will replace the old in the time of salvation.[11] In the meantime Jesus does not merely stress in a general way the secondary importance of sacrifice.[12] There must be reconciliation before offering sacrifice.[13]

We cannot make light of Jesus' criticism of the Old Testament law. He did not merely interpret the law differently on certain points: the Pharisees also did this. Nor did he merely make the law more strict or more radical on certain points (making anger equivalent to murder, adulterous desire the same as adultery): the "Teacher of Righteousness" in the Qumran monastery also did this. What Jesus did was to set himself above the law with a disconcerting independence and freedom, whenever he thought it right to do so. Even if Jesus did not use the exact formulas—although only an excessively skeptical criticism can doubt this—both the "But I say to you" in the antitheses of the Sermon on the Mount and the "Amen"—never used by anyone else at the beginning of a series of statements—provide an exact expression of his radicalization, criticism, and even compensatory reactivation of the law. At the same time they give rise to the problem of the authority which he claims: an authority which seems to go far beyond that of the legal theologian or even of a prophet. Even if someone accepted the whole Torah as from God, but asserted that an odd verse or two was from Moses and not from God, he would be regarded by his contemporaries as despising the word of Yahweh. Could there then be a "more abundant justice"[14] than that of the law? At the very beginning of the earliest Gospel we are told that Jesus' hearers were perplexed by the fact that he did not teach as the scribes did.[15]

God's will instead of legalism

What then did Jesus want? This has already been made clear: to defend God's cause. This is the meaning of his message of the coming of God's kingdom. But, in Matthew's version of the "Our Father," the petition that God's name should be hallowed and his kingdom come is supplemented by the sentence: "Your will be done." What God wills in heaven is to be done on earth. This then is the meaning of the message of the coming of God's kingdom if it is understood as a demand made on man here and now: let what God wills be done. This holds for Jesus himself, even when it leads to his own passion: may his will be done.[16] God's will is the measure. This is to hold also for his followers: he who does God's will is his brother, sister, mother.[17] It is not by saying "Lord, Lord," but by doing the Father's will that we get to heaven.[18] There cannot then be any doubt —and it is confirmed throughout the whole of the New Testament—that the supreme norm *is the will of God.*[19]

For many devout people "doing God's will" has become a pious formula. They have identified it with the law. The fact that this is a very radical watchword becomes clear only when we see that God's will is not simply identical with the written law and still less with the tradition which interprets the law. Although the law can declare God's will, it may also be used as a shelter in which to hide from God's will. The law thus easily leads to an attitude of legalism: an attitude widespread in Jesus' time, despite rabbinic statements on the law as expression of grace and of God's will.

A law provides security, because we know exactly what we have to keep to: just this, no less (which can sometimes be irksome) but no more (which is sometimes very congenial). I have to do only what is commanded. And what is not forbidden is permitted. And there is so much we can do or omit in particular cases before coming into conflict with the law. No law can envisage all possibilities, take into account all cases, close all gaps. It is true that we constantly try to give an artificial twist to former legal regulations (on morals or doctrine) which once had a meaning but have lost it in the meantime, to adapt them to new conditions or to deduce from them conclusions applicable to the changed situation. This seems to be the only way if the letter of the law is identified with God's will: interpreting and explicating the law until we have an accumulation of laws. In the Old Testament there were said to be 613 regulations (in the Roman Code of Canon Law there are 2414 canons). But the finer the net is woven, the more numerous are the holes. And the more precepts and prohibitions are set up, the more the decisive issue is concealed. Above all, it is possible that the law as a whole or even particular laws are kept only because they are laid down and the consequences of breaking them are to be feared. We would not do what is required if it had not been prescribed. On the other hand it is possible that much is not done that really should be done, merely because there is no law about it and no one can bind us to it. Like the priest and the Levite in the parable, we saw the victim and passed by. Thus both authority and obedience are formalized: something is done simply because the law requires it. And in that sense every precept or prohibition is in principle equally important. It is not necessary to distinguish between what is important and what is not.

The *advantages of legalism* both then and now are immense. It is easy to see why so many people in their relations with other *human beings* prefer to keep to a law rather than make a personal decision. How much more would I have to do which is not prescribed, how much omit that is not forbidden? The law does at least lay down clear limits. In particular cases there is still always room for discussion: Was there really an infringement of the law? Was it really adultery? Was it forthright perjury? Was it murder in the proper sense of the term? And even though adultery is forbidden by the law, this is not the case with everything that leads to it. If perjury is against the law, this does not include all the more harmless forms of untruthfulness. Murder may be illegal, but not all evil thoughts, which—as is well known—are duty-free. What I do on my own, what I think, desire and want in my heart is my own affair.

It is also easy to see why so many people prefer to keep to a law even with reference to *God* himself. For in this way I know exactly when I have done my duty. If I achieve something, I can expect a corresponding reward; or even an extra allowance if I have done more than my duty. Thus my debits and credits can be accurately calculated, moral deficits compensated by special works of supererogation and perhaps finally penalties canceled out by rewards. The accounts are clear and we know where we stand with God.

It is precisely this legalistic attitude however to which Jesus gives the *deathblow*.[20] He aims, not at the law itself, but at legalism, from which the law must be kept clear: at *compromise*, which is typical of this legalistic piety. He breaks through man's protective wall, one side of which is God's law and the other man's fulfilling of the law.[21] He does not allow man to take refuge from the law in legalism and he strikes man's merits out of his hand. He measures the letter of the law against God's will itself and thus places man, liberated and gladdened, immediately before God. Man's relationship to God is not established by a code of law, without his being personally involved. He must submit himself, not simply to the law, but to God: to accept, that is, what God demands of him in a wholly personal way.

That is why Jesus does not attempt to talk learnedly of God, to proclaim universal, all-embracing moral principles, to present man with a new system. He does not give directives for all spheres of life. Jesus is *not a legislator* and does not want to be one. He neither binds people again to the old legal system nor issues a new law, embracing all spheres of life. He does not compose either a moral theology or a code of conduct. He issues neither moral nor ritual instructions as to how people are to pray, fast, observe sacred times and respect sacred places. Even the "Our Father," not recorded at all by the earliest evangelist, is not reproduced as a single, binding form of words, but in different versions in Luke (probably original) and Matthew. Jesus is not concerned about repeating a prayer in the same words. And the commandment of love particularly is not to become a new law.

Quite concretely, without any casuistry or legalism, unconventionally and with a sure aim, Jesus lays hold on the individual and summons him to *obedience to God*, who is to embrace his whole life. These are simple, transparent, liberating appeals, dispensing with arguments from authority or tradition, but providing examples, signs, tokens, for transforming one's life. They are great, helpful directives, often in the form of deliberate overstatements, without any ifs and buts: If your eye leads to sin, pluck it out! Let your speech be "Yes, Yes," and "No, No"! First be reconciled with your brother! Each one must find for himself the application to his own life.

The meaning of the Sermon on the Mount

The *Sermon on the Mount*,[22] in which Matthew and Luke collected Jesus' ethical requirements—short sayings and groups of sayings mainly from the logia-source Q—aims at taking God's will absolutely seriously. It has constantly presented a fresh challenge to Christians and non-Christians: to the Jacobins of the French Revolution and the Socialist Kautsky, as well as to Tolstoy and Albert Schweitzer. What is the object of the Sermon on the Mount?

One possibility can be excluded from the beginning. The Sermon on the Mount is certainly not meant to be a *stricter legal ethic*. It has occasionally been described in a misleading way as the "law of Christ." But the Sermon on the Mount deals with the very things which cannot be the object of legal regulation. Talk of "more abundant justice" or of "perfection" does not mean a quantitative increase in requirements. Jesus—as the antitheses of the Sermon on the Mount make clear—just does not put into practice that obedience to the dots or crosses of the letter of the law which a Jewish-Christian logion, cited by Matthew,[23] demands. This would mean depriving obedience of its force, not in a liberal but in an ultra-conservative sense.[24] His message is anything but a sum of precepts. Imitating him does not mean carrying out a number of regulations. There are good reasons why the Sermon on the Mount should open with promises of happiness for the unhappy. The gift, the present, grace, are prior to the norm, the demand, the directive: everyone is called, to everyone salvation is offered, without any prior achievements. And the directives themselves are the consequences of his message of God's kingdom. His reaction is expressed only in examples and signs. But none of this suffices to make clear the import of the Sermon on the Mount.

Is it a two-class ethic? *Does it imply a minimal, normal righteousness, based on the commandments, for the people as a whole, and a "higher righteousness" or "perfection" for the disciples or for the chosen few?*

This was traditional Catholic teaching before Vatican II. But the Sermon on the Mount is not a monastic rule. What are known as the "counsels" or "evangelical counsels" are addressed to all. No one gets to heaven without fulfilling precisely this higher righteousness, which —even according to Matthew—is therefore required of everyone.[25]

Is it a penitential ethic, *impossible to fulfill? Is the Sermon on the Mount purely and simply a call to penance, providing as it were a list of faults on which we ought to examine ourselves and intended to draw us out of the powerlessness of our sinful state toward the good. This was Martin Luther's opinion. Certainly the Sermon on the Mount holds a mirror before man and reveals to him what he is. But it requires a totally new way of acting in a new situation. There is no repentance without doing God's will, without good works, without acts of love. Nowhere are we told that Jesus fulfills the absolute demands of the Sermon on the Mount in our place.*

Is it a pure dispositional ethic? *Is it sufficient to mean well, to be good at heart? This was the view of Kant, of philosophical idealism and of liberal theology in past centuries. Certainly the deed itself is given only a relative importance in the Sermon on the Mount, the motive is ultimately decisive, the how and why are more important than the what. But it is not sufficient to have willed the good. The Sermon on the Mount insists on action. The act is by no means irrelevant. What happens is that the will is taken for the deed, but obedience must be continued right up to the concrete action. Heart and action are not to be separated.*

Is it a new social ethic? *Is it a new social order to be observed to the letter, an order of love and peace, of Christ's kingdom on earth, for which political power and legal system, police and army, are no longer necessary? In the course of Church history this view has been held by many (peaceful or revolutionary) fanatics and in the present century both by Count Leo Tolstoy and quite a few religious socialists. Certainly the Sermon on the Mount cannot be understood in a purely private sense as concerned only with personal and family relationships. There are unjust, oppressive, dehumanizing conditions which must be exposed and attacked in the light of the Sermon on the Mount, where love must intervene. Nevertheless, the kingdom of God is not founded on men's moral actions. And the Sermon on the Mount is never presented as the basic law of a new society, with the aid of which the world is to be freed from all evils. As the Sermon on the Mount cannot be restricted to individual and family relationships, neither can it be simply expanded to form a social program.*

Is it a short-term interim ethic? *Does it represent "emergency legislation" for the end-time? Are its radical demands such that they could be fulfilled only for a short time before the approaching end of the world, but have now become meaningless? This is what J. Weiss and A. Schweitzer thought. Undoubtedly the Sermon on the Mount is set within the framework of the message of kingdom of God which is to come soon. But it cannot be explained exclusively in the light of the apocalyptic glow of the approaching end. Jesus' demands—love of neighbor, for instance—are motivated not simply by the approaching end of the world, but in principle by the will and nature of God. What are required are not extraordinary heroic deeds (giving up all possessions, martyrdom), but very ordinary acts of love. It is precisely by doing the will of God that our constant readiness for the approaching kingdom of God is proved. It is true of course that God's will appears clearly and purely in the "Last Days," divorced from all "human statutes." God's closeness gives Jesus' demands an extraordinary urgency, but also the joyous certainty that they can be fulfilled.*

This is the common denominator of the Sermon on the Mount: *God's will be done!* The time for relativizing God's will is past. What is required is not pious enthusiasm or pure interiority, but obedience in disposition and deed. Man himself must accept his responsibility in face of the closely approaching God. Only through resolutely, unreservedly doing God's will does man come to share the promises of the kingdom of God. But God's liberating demand is radical. It permits no casuistic compromise. It transcends and breaks through secular limitations and legal systems. The challenging examples of the Sermon on the Mount[26] are just not meant to impose a legal limit, as if to say: "Offer only the left cheek, go only two miles, give merely your cloak, and that's the limit of good fellowship." God's demand appeals to man's magnanimity, it is a demand always for more. Indeed, it reaches to the absolute, the infinite, the whole. Can God be satisfied with a limited, conditional, formal obedience—related only to what is specifically commanded or forbidden? This would mean leaving out one final reality which cannot be brought under any amount of minute legal regulations and prescriptions and which nevertheless decides man's attitude. God wants more: he lays claim not to half the will, but the whole. He demands not only external acts which can be observed and controlled, but also internal responses which cannot be controlled or checked. He demands man's heart. He wants not only good fruits, but the good tree:[27] not only action, but being; not something, but myself—and myself wholly and entirely.

This is what is meant by the amazing antitheses of the Sermon on the Mount, confronting the law with the will of God. Not only are adultery, perjury, murder contrary to God's will, but also those things which simply cannot be brought under the law: even an adulterous disposition, untruthful thinking and talking, a hostile attitude. To use the word "only" in any sense in interpreting the Sermon on the Mount means curtailing and weakening the unconditional will of God. There is no question of "merely" a better fulfillment of the law, "merely" a new disposition, "merely" an examination of sin in the light of Jesus who alone is righteous, "merely" for those called to perfection, "merely" for that time, "merely" for a short period.

How difficult it was for the later Church to uphold Jesus' radical demands is evident from their *softening*[28] even in Matthew's (Palestinian-Syrian?) community. According to Jesus any sort of anger should be kept down;[29] according to Matthew at least certain offensive expressions, such as "empty-headed" and "godless," should not be used.[30] According to Jesus we should do without oaths altogether and get through life with a simple "Yes" or "No";[31] according to Matthew at least certain forms of oath should be avoided.[32] According to Jesus we should point out his fault to our neighbor and, if he avoids it, we should forgive him;[33] according to Matthew there must be a proper legal procedure.[34] According to Jesus, for the protection of the wife, who was at a legal disadvantage, divorce should be absolutely forbidden to the husband;[35] according to Matthew an exception can be made, at least if the wife is guilty of flagrant adultery.[36]

Are all these merely attempts to soften the law? We must see in them also at least an effort to maintain the permanent validity of Jesus' absolute demands when ordinary life goes on, unaffected by the immediate expectation of the future kingdom. Take *divorce*, for example.[37] In a quite un-Jewish way, contrary to the patriarchal-Mosaic law,[38] Jesus strictly forbade divorce on the conclusive ground that God welds marriages together and will not have men unbind what he has bound. The question was hotly debated between the schools of Shammai on the one hand and Hillel on the other, whether a wife could be dismissed only for a sexual lapse (Shammai) or for practically any reason, such as even a burnt meal (Hillel, whose view—according to Philo and Josephus—reflected the usual practice). These debates were of no importance to Jesus. He was concerned with essentials. Admittedly, the question which had become urgent in view of the delay of the end of all things, which Jesus had not answered, now had to be answered: what had to be done if, despite God's absolute requirement, a marriage did break down and life had to go on? Jesus' unconditional appeal to maintain the unity of marriage now came to be understood as a legal rule which had to be more and more precisely defined. To the prohibition of dismissal and remarriage of the wife there was added —in view of the Hellenistic legal situation—the prohibition of divorce on the wife's part, together with exceptional rules for mixed marriages[39] and the prohibition of remarriage for either party;[40] and yet adultery had also to be admitted as an exceptional ground for a divorce.[41] The question might be asked whether a solution could have been found without again making use of casuistry and laying down the law for particular cases.

Jesus himself anyway, not being a lawyer, made his unconditional appeals and left it to others to realize them in particular situations. This is evident from the example of *property*. Jesus, as we shall see later, did not prescribe for everybody either renunciation of possessions or common ownership. One will sacrifice everything to the poor,[42] another will give away half his possessions,[43] a third will help with a loan.[44] One gives all he has for God's cause,[45] others are active in serving and caring for the needy,[46] someone else practices apparently foolish prodigality.[47] Nothing here is legally regulated. Hence there is no need of exceptions, excuses, privileges or dispensations from the law.

The Sermon on the Mount of course by no means aims at a superficial situation ethic, as if only the law of the actual situation could be the dominating factor. The situation cannot decide everything. What is decisive in the particular situation is the absolute demand of God himself, claiming total possession of man. In view of the ultimate and definitive reality, the kingdom of God, a fundamental transformation is expected of man.

III. Man's Cause

A fundamental transformation is expected: something like a new birth of man himself, which can be understood only by one who actively takes part in it. It is therefore a transformation which does not come about merely through progress in right thinking for the sake of right action (as with Socrates) or through the education of man who is fundamentally good (as with Confucius). Nor is it a transformation through enlightenment, as the ascetic Siddhartha Gautama passed by way of meditation through enlightenment (*bodhi*) to become Buddha, the Enlightened, and in this way to reach an understanding of suffering and finally extinction in nirvana. According to Jesus, a fundamental transformation is achieved through man's surrender to God's will.

1. *Humanization of man*

Jesus expects a different, a new man: a radically changed awareness, a fundamentally different attitude, a completely new orientation in thought and action.

The changed awareness

Jesus expects no more and no less than a fundamental, *total orientation of man's life toward God:* an undivided heart, in the last resort serving not two masters but only one. Awaiting God's rule, in the midst of the world and among his fellow men, man should give his heart in the last resort simply and solely to God: not to money and possessions,[1] not to rights and honor,[2] nor even to parents and family.[3] In this respect, according to Jesus, we cannot simply speak of peace: here the sword rules. Even the closest bonds must be set aside as of secondary importance beside this basic decision. Imitating Christ in this way takes precedence even over family ties: anyone who wants to be a disciple of Christ must "hate" father, mother, brothers and sisters, wife and children, even himself. Even himself! I know by experience that the real enemy of such a transformation is my own self. It follows immediately therefore that anyone who tries to preserve his own life will lose it and he who loses it will gain it.[4] Is this a hard saying? It is a rich promise.

The meaning now becomes clear of a term we have already come across and which is of central importance: *metanoia*,[5] "conversion," or—as it was formerly misleadingly translated—"repentance." It is not a question of "doing penance" externally, in sackcloth and ashes. It is not an intellectually determined or strongly emotional religious experience. It is a decisive change of will, an awareness changed from the roots upwards, a new basic attitude, a different scale of values. It is therefore a radical rethinking and re-turning on the part of the whole man, a completely new attitude to life. Nevertheless, Jesus does not expect an acknowledgment of sin, a confession, from the person who wants to change his ways. He is not very interested in the latter's problematic past, which of course has to be abandoned. All that matters is the better future, this future which God promises and gives to man, to which the latter must turn irrevocably and unreservedly, without looking back, now that his hand is on the plow.[6] Man can live on forgiveness. This is conversion based on that imperturbable, unshakable confidence in God and in his word which even in the Old Testament was known as *faith*.[7] It involves a believing trust and a trustful faith, which is something very different from Buddha's insight (based on Indian philosophy), or Socrates' dialectic of thought (as understood in Greek philosophy), or Confucius' piety (in the Chinese tradition).

God himself, by his Gospel and his forgiveness, makes possible a conversion inspired by faith, a new beginning. Heroism is not required of man: he can live in the trusting *gratitude* of the man who found the treasure in the field, who received the precious pearl.[8] He should not be placed under new legal pressures or forced to accomplish something new. Certainly he will do his duty and think nothing of himself merely for doing this.[9] But his model will be the child rather than the faithful servant: not because the child's supposed innocence is to be made into a romantic ideal, but because the child—helpless and small—takes it completely for granted that he is to be helped, to be given presents, that he must surrender himself single-mindedly and full of confidence.[10] What is required therefore is childlike gratitude, not looking for a reward—not even the reward of grace—not like the son who remained at home had been doing for years and yet was left out in the end.[11] Man should not act for the sake of reward or punishment. Reward and punishment should not be made the motive of moral action: Kant's reaction to primitive eudaemonism was justified. But in his actions man should certainly be aware of his responsibility: that, with all his thoughts, words and works, he is approaching God's future, God's final decision. And whatever a person has done—even merely giving a cup of water to someone who is thirsty,[12] but also even uttering an idle word[13]—remains present to God, even though it is long past for man.

Accepting this responsibility has nothing to do with the cheerlessness of devout observers of the law. Jesus' call to conversion is a call to *joy*. It should not be assumed that the Sermon on the Mount begins with a new list of duties. It begins in fact with a list of blessings.[14] A sad saint is for Jesus just a sad saint.[15] Because God is generous, the wage earners in the vineyard are told, that is no reason for being envious.[16] The very correct brother of the prodigal son should have rejoiced and been happy.[17] Aversion from the sinful past and the return of the whole man to God is a joyful event for God and men. And for the person concerned it is a true liberation. For no new law is imposed on him. The weight is light and the burden easy[18] and man can bear it gladly if he submits to God's will.

Once again, however, we are thus faced by a question which has hitherto been constantly present, but which now—after so much talk about God's will as the supreme norm of human action and life—should be expressly stated and answered: just what is the will of God? What does God really want?

What God wills

God's will does not waver. Nor can it be manipulated. From all that we have said hitherto, from the concrete requirements of Jesus himself, it should already have become clear that God wills nothing for himself, nothing for his own advantage, for his greater glory. God wills nothing but man's advantage, man's true greatness and his ultimate dignity. This then is God's will: *man's well-being*.

From the first to the last page of the Bible, it is clear that God's will aims at man's well-being at all levels, aims at his definitive and comprehensive good: in biblical terms, at the salvation of man and of men. God's will is a helpful, healing, liberating, saving will. God wills life, joy, freedom, peace, salvation, the final, great happiness of man: both of the individual and of mankind as a whole. This is the meaning of God's absolute future, his victory, his kingdom, which Jesus proclaims: man's total liberation, salvation, satisfaction, bliss. And this very radical identification of God's will and man's well-being, which Jesus took up from the standpoint of God's closeness, makes it clear that there is no question of putting a new patch onto old clothing or of pouring young wine into old wineskins. Here we are actually faced with something new and it is going to be dangerous to the old.

What to some people might seem like an autocratic and arbitrary use of freedom on Jesus' part now becomes clearly its great and potent consistency. God is not yet seen apart from man, nor man apart from God. We cannot be for God and against man. If we want to be devout, we cannot behave in an inhuman way. Was that so obvious then? Is it obvious now?

Certainly God is not interpreted by Jesus in terms of human fellowship, he is not reduced to fellow feeling. Idolizing man dehumanizes him no less than enslavement. But man's friendliness for man is based on God's friendship for man. That is why the universal and final criterion must be: God wills man's well-being.

A number of things then appear in a different light. Since *man himself is at stake,*

Jesus, who is generally completely faithful to the law, does not hesitate to act in a manner contrary to it;

he repudiates ritual correctitude and taboos and demands purity of heart instead of external, legal purity;

he rejects an asceticism of fasting and, as a man among men, prefers to be called a glutton and a drunkard;

he is not scrupulous about Sabbath observance, but declares that man himself is the measure of the law.[19]

Relativized traditions, institutions, hierarchs

Is it not obvious that all this would seem *scandalous* to any devout Jew? This is an immense relativization. Here is someone who is indifferent to the most sacred traditions and institutions of the nation. Does not this fact alone explain the irreconcilable suspicion and hatred especially on the part of the priests and theologians? Here is someone shaking the *hierarchy* to its foundations by his relativizing of the legal system and the cultic ordinances.

> *Jesus* relativizes the law *and this means the whole religio-political-economic order, the whole social system. Even the law is not the beginning and the end of all God's ways. Even the law is not an end in itself, it is not the final court of appeal.*
>
> *Therefore there is to be no more of the old-style legalistic piety. Possession of the law and correct observance of the law do not guarantee salvation. In the last resort the law is not decisive for salvation. This sort of self-reliant legalistic religion is abolished, even though it is not denied that the law is God's good gift. But what holds now is the proposition, obvious in itself and yet revolutionary as opposed to the traditional view: the commandments are for man's sake and not man for the sake of the commandments.*[20]

This means that *service to man* has *priority over observance of the law.* No norms or institutions can be made absolute. Man may never be sacrificed to an allegedly absolute norm or institution. Norms and institutions are not simply abolished or annulled. But all norms and institutions, all laws and precepts, edicts and statutes, regulations and ordinances, dogmas and decrees, codes and clauses, must be judged by the criterion of whether they exist for man or not. Man is the measure of the law. In the light of this, is it not possible critically to discriminate between what is right and what is wrong, what is essential and what is irrelevant, what is constructive and what is destructive, what is good or bad order?

God's cause is not law, but *man*. Man himself therefore replaces a legal system that has been made absolute. *Humanity* replaces legalism, institutionalism, juridicism, dogmatism. Man's will, it is true, does not replace God's will. But God's will is made concrete in the light of the concrete situation of man and his fellow men.

Jesus relativizes the temple *and this means the whole order of cult, the liturgy, worship of God in the strict sense of the term. Even the temple is not the beginning and the end of all God's ways. Even the temple will have an end, it is not eternal.*

Therefore there is to be no more of the old-style temple piety. Possession of the temple and correct observance of the order of worship do not guarantee salvation. In the last resort the temple is not decisive for salvation. This sort of self-satisfied temple religion is abolished, even though it is not denied that the temple is God's good gift. But what holds now is the proposition, once again obvious in itself but likewise revolutionary as opposed to the traditional view: be reconciled first with your brother and then come and offer your gift.[21]

This means that *reconciliation and everyday service to our fellow man have priority over service to God* and observance of the times of cult. Cult, liturgy, service to God, likewise, cannot be made absolute. Man may never be sacrificed to an allegedly absolutely obligatory rite or pious custom. Cult and liturgy are not simply abolished or annulled. But all cult and all liturgy, rites and customs, practices and ceremonies, feasts and celebrations are to be judged by the criterion of whether they exist for man or not. Man is the measure even of service to God. In the light of this, once again, is it not possible critically to discriminate between what is right and what is wrong also in cult and liturgy, what is important and what is unimportant, what is good and what is bad service to God?

God's cause is not cult, but *man*. Man himself therefore replaces a liturgy that has been made absolute. *Humanity* replaces formalism, ritualism, liturgism, sacramentalism. Service of man, it is true, does not replace service of God. But service of God never excuses from service of man: it is in service to man that service to God is proved.

If it is said that God and therefore the service of God is the decisive thing for man, we must then at once recall that man with his world is the decisive thing for God. God's directive is meant to help and serve man. Consequently we cannot take God and his will seriously without at the same time taking seriously man and his well-being. Man's humanity is demanded by the humanity of God himself. Injury to man's humanity closes the way to true service of God. Humanizing man is the precondition of true service of God. Hence it is true that service of God cannot be reduced simply to service of man nor service of man simply to service of God. But it can and must be said that true service of God is already service of man and true service of man also already service of God.

If we reflect on all that has been said here about changed awareness, the will of God and the revolutionary relativizing of the most sacred traditions and institutions, we shall understand how essential—quite in the tradition of the Old Testament prophets—the *combative*[22] element is to the make-up of Jesus. Jesus cannot by any means be understood merely as a soft, gentle, unresisting, good-natured and humbly acquiescent figure. Even the Jesus image of Francis of Assisi has its limits, and still more does the pietistic and to some degree also the hierarchistic Jesus image of the nineteenth and twentieth centuries. Nietzsche, a pastor's son, rightly rebelled against this feeble Jesus image of his youth, which he could not associate with the Gospel statements about Jesus as the pugnacious critic of the hierarchs and theologians. In his *Antichrist* therefore he arbitrarily explained—without any support in the sources—this pugnacious Jesus as the creation of the pugnacious primitive Christian community which needed an aggressive model. But the sources themselves make it clear how much Jesus combined unselfishness and self-assurance, humility and severity, gentleness and aggressiveness. Nor was this merely a question of the iron hand in the velvet glove. Even Jesus' tone was often extremely severe. We scarcely ever find him using honeyed words, but he could certainly speak bitterly. Whenever Jesus had to assert God's will in face of the resistance of the powerful—persons, institutions, traditions, hierarchs—he did so aggressively, with no holds barred. He spoke in this way for the sake of men, on whom no unnecessarily heavy burdens were to be imposed.[23] That is why he relativized the most sacred institutions and traditions *and their representatives:* for the sake of God who wills man's total well-being, his salvation.

How little Jesus' message has to do with that decadent weakness which Nietzsche loathed so much becomes clear if we introduce a word which Nietzsche likewise regarded with suspicion and which we have hitherto—in complete harmony with the Jesus of history—used very sparingly, so much has it been misused by Christians and non-Christians and cheapened by the pious and impious: the word "love."

2. Action

Apart from the formulation of the chief commandment, drawn from the Old Testament, Jesus in the Synoptic Gospels uses the words "love" and "loving" in the sense of love of neighbor, like the word "neighbor" itself, very sparingly. Nevertheless, love of one's fellow man is present everywhere in Jesus' proclamation. Evidently, where love is concerned, actions speak louder than words. It is not talk, but action, which makes clear the nature of love. Practice is the criterion. What then is love, according to Jesus?

Both God and man

A *first* answer is that, according to Jesus, love is essentially *love of both God and man*. Jesus came to fulfill the law by making God's will prevail, and God's will aims at man's well-being. That is why he can say that all the commandments are summed up in this dual commandment of love. Judaism had already spoken sporadically of love in this dual sense. But Jesus achieves simply and concretely an unparalleled *reduction* and *concentration* of all the commandments into this dual commandment and combines love of God and love of man in an indissoluble unity. Since then it has been impossible to play off God and man against each other. Thus love becomes a requirement which can encompass without restriction the whole life of man and yet is involved in a distinctive way in each individual case. It is typical of Jesus that love thus becomes the criterion of piety and of a person's whole conduct.

For Jesus however love of God and love of man are *not the same thing*, since for him quite obviously God and man are not the same. It is not God who loses, but man, when either God is humanized or man idolized. God remains God. God remains the one Lord of the world and of man. He cannot be replaced by human fellowship. Where is the man so free of limitations and faults that he could become God for me, the object of a completely unconditional love? The romanticism or mysticism of love can conjure up an idealized picture of the other person, can conceal or postpone but not eliminate conflicts. In the light however of the unconditional love of God who embraces all, our fellow man too can be loved quite radically, as he is, with all his limitations and faults. There is no doubt that Jesus gives *to God the absolute primacy*, precisely in man's interest. That is why he claims man as a whole: his whole will, his heart, his innermost core, the person himself. And that is why, when someone is converted, comes back to him in trustful faith, he expects no more and no less than love, wholehearted, undivided love: you must love the Lord your God with your whole heart, with your whole soul and your whole mind; this is the first and greatest commandment.[1]

But this love does not mean a mystical union with God, in which someone tries to withdraw from the world, to be isolated from men and one with God. In the last resort, a love of God without love of man is no love at all. And if God must keep his inalienable primacy and God's love can never become a means or a symbol for love of man, *neither* can *love of man* ever become a means or a *symbol for love of God*. It is not only for God's sake, but for his own sake, that I must love my fellow man. I must not keep looking over my shoulder at God when I turn to my fellow man, nor indulge in pious talk when I am supposed to be helping somebody. The Samaritan helps without dragging in religious reasons: the need of the man fallen among thieves is sufficient for him and at that moment his whole attention is concentrated on the victim.[2] Those declared blessed at the last judgment had no idea that they had met the Lord himself in those whom they had fed, to whom they had given drink, whom they had sheltered, clothed and visited. On the other hand those who are condemned show that, at best, they would have loved their fellow men for the Lord's sake.[3] This is not only false love of God, but also false love of men.

Yet love of man is still too general a description. We are speaking certainly of universal humanity, but we must be more precise. In Jesus' way of speaking there is not even a hint of "embracing millions," of "a kiss for the whole world," as in the poem by Schiller, turned by Beethoven in the Ninth Symphony into a great hymn to joy.* A kiss of that kind costs nothing: it is not like kissing this one sick, imprisoned, underprivileged, starving man. Humanism costs so much less, the more it is directed to all mankind and the less it is open to the approach of the individual man with his needs. It is easier to plead for peace in the Far East than for peace in one's own family or in one's own sphere of influence. The humane European can more easily identify with the Negroes in North America and in South Africa than with immigrant workers in his own country. The more distant our fellow men, the easier it is to profess our love in words.

The person who needs me here and now

Jesus however is not interested in universal, theoretical or poetical love. For him love does not consist primarily in words, sentiments or feelings. For him love means primarily the great, courageous deed. He wants practical and therefore concrete love. Hence our *second* answer to the question

* Seid umschlungen, Millionen!
Diesen Kuss der ganzen Welt!

on love must be stated more precisely: according to Jesus, love is *not simply love of man but essentially love of neighbor*. It is a love, not of man in general, of someone remote, with whom we are not personally involved, but quite concretely of one's immediate neighbor. Love of God is proved in love of neighbor, and in fact love of neighbor is the exact yardstick of love of God. I love God only as much as I love my neighbor.

And *how much* love shall I give my neighbor? Jesus recalls an isolated formula from the Old Testament[4]—referring however only to the members of one's own nation—and answers forthrightly and without any qualification: *as yourself*.[5] It is an obvious answer and, for Jesus, at once covers everything without more ado: it leaves no loopholes for excuses or subterfuges and at the same time lays down the direction and measure of love. It is assumed that man loves himself. And it is just this obvious attitude of man toward himself which should be the measure—in practice, beyond measure—of love of neighbor. I know only too well what I owe myself and I am no less aware of what others owe me. In everything that we think, say and feel, do and suffer, we tend quite naturally to protect, shield, advance ourselves, to cherish ourselves. And now we are expected to give exactly the same care and attention to our neighbor. With this all reserves are broken down. For us, who are egoists by nature, it means a radical conversion: to accept the other person's standpoint; to give the other exactly what we think is due to ourselves; to treat our fellow man as we wish to be treated by him.[6] As Jesus himself shows, this certainly does not mean any feebleness or softness, any renunciation of self-confidence, any annihilation of self in devout meditation or strenuous asceticism in the Buddhist or supposedly Christian sense. But it certainly does mean the orientation of ourselves toward others: an alertness, an openness, a receptivity for our fellow man, a readiness to help without reserve. It means living not for ourselves, but for others: in this—from the standpoint of the person who loves—is rooted the indissoluble unity of undivided love of God and unlimited love of neighbor.

The *common denominator* of love of God and love of neighbor therefore is the *abandonment of selfishness* and the *will to self-sacrifice*. Only when I no longer live for myself can I be quite open for God and unreservedly open for my fellow man whom God accepts just as he accepts me. Loving my fellow man does not complete my task of loving God. I remain directly responsible to God and none of my fellow men can take this responsibility away from me. God however encounters me, not exclusively, but—since I am myself human—primarily in my fellow man and expects my self-surrender at that point. He does not call me out of the clouds, nor merely indirectly in my conscience, but above all through my neighbor: a call which is never silenced, but reaches me afresh each day in the midst of my ordinary secular routine.

But *who* is my neighbor? Jesus does not answer with a definition or a more precise qualification, still less with a law, but—as so often—with a story, an exemplary narrative. According to this, my neighbor is not merely someone who is close to me from the very beginning: a member of my family, my circle of friends, my class, my party, my people. My neighbor can also be a stranger, a complete stranger, anyone who turns up at this particular juncture. It is impossible to work out in advance who my neighbor will be. This is the meaning of the story of the man fallen among thieves: my neighbor is *anyone who needs me here and now.*[7] At the beginning of the parable the question is asked: "Who is my neighbor?" At the end it is significantly reversed: "To whom am I neighbor?" The important thing in the parable is not the definition of "neighbor," but the urgency of the love required just from me, in the concrete case, in the concrete need, quite aside from the conventional rules of morality. Nor are the needs lacking. Matthew in the discourse on judgment repeats four times six of the works of love which were relevant then as they are now.[8] This does not mean that there is to be a new legal system. As in the case of the Samaritan, what is expected is an active, creative approach, fertile imagination and decisive action in each individual case in the light of the particular situation.

What God really wants then becomes clear in love. What is involved in the commandments also becomes clear. In any case it is not only, as in Islam, a question of an obedient "submission" (=*islam*) to the will of God revealed in the law. In the light of love the *commandments* acquire *a uniform meaning,* but they are also *restricted* and occasionally even *abolished.* Anyone who understands the commandments legalistically and not in the light of love is constantly faced with a conflict of duties. But love puts an end to casuistry: man no longer observes precept or prohibition more or less mechanically, but adapts himself to what reality itself demands and makes possible. Thus every precept or prohibition has its intrinsic criterion in love of neighbor. The bold Augustinian saying, "Love and do what you will," has its basis here. That is how far love of neighbor goes.

Even enemies

Does it not perhaps go too far? If my neighbor is anyone who needs me here and now, can I stop at that? According to Jesus, I certainly should not. And, after our first two answers to the question on love, we must now make our *third* and final answer even more pointed. According to Jesus, love is not merely love of neighbor but essentially *love of enemies.* And it is this love of enemies, not love of man or even love of neighbor, which is *typical for Jesus.*

It is only with Jesus that we find the requirement of love of enemies set out as part of a program. Even Confucius, though he does not speak of "love of neighbor," at least mentions "love of man," but means by this simply deference, magnanimity, sincerity, diligence, kindness. As we observed, there are sporadic references in the Old Testament also to love of neighbor. Like most of the great religions, Judaism too had its "golden rule," presumably derived from Graeco-Roman pagan sources, both in a negative and—as in the Jewish *diaspora*—in a positive form: to treat one's fellow men as one would wish to be treated oneself. The great Rabbi Hillel (circa 20 B.C.) described this golden rule—admittedly in a negative form—as being almost the sum total of the written law. But this rule could also be understood as a shrewd, selfish adaptation, one's neighbor simply as a fellow national, as a member of the same party, and love of neighbor as one precept among a mass of other religious, moral and ritual precepts. Even Confucius was aware of the golden rule in a negative form, but expressly rejected love of enemies as unfair: we should repay goodness with goodness, but wrong must be repaid with justice, not with goodness. And in Judaism hatred of enemies was considered more or less permissible: personal enemies formed an exception to the obligation of love. The devout monks of Qumran even expressly commanded hatred toward the outsiders, the sons of darkness.

Does not all this show once more how the numerous parallels between statements in Jesus' proclamation on the one hand and sayings of the Jewish wisdom literature and of the rabbis on the other must be seen within the total context of their respective understanding of law and salvation, of man and his fellow men? The superiority of Jesus becomes apparent, not in the often completely comparable individual statements, but in the unmistakable originality of the whole teaching. The programmatic "love your enemy" is Jesus' own expression and is typical of his love of neighbor, which now really does know no bounds.[9]

It is typical of Jesus *not to recognize the ingrained frontier and estrangement between those of one's own group and those outside it.* It is true, as we have said, that he restricted his mission to the Jews:[10] otherwise there would not have been such bitter controversy about the mission to the Gentiles in the primitive community. But Jesus shows an openness which in fact bursts through the immovable frontiers between members of different nations and religions. For him, it is not the fellow national or the co-religionist who counts, but the neighbor who can confront us in any human being: even in a political or religious opponent, rival, antagonist, adversary, enemy. This is Jesus' concrete, *practical universalism.* It is an openness, not only for members of one's own social group, one's own stock, one's own nation, race, class, party, Church, to the exclusion of others, but unlimited openness and overcoming of demarcation lines wherever they are drawn. The practical breaking down of existing frontiers—between Jews and non-Jews, those who are near and those who are far away, good and bad, Pharisees and tax collectors—and not merely isolated achievements, charitable works, "Samaritan deeds," is the object of the story of the Good Samaritan. After showing the failure of the priest and the Levite, the Jewish ruling class, it sets up as an example, not—as Jesus' hearers might have expected—the Jewish layman, but the hated Samaritan, the national enemy, half-breed and heretic. Jews and Samaritans cursed each other publicly in religious services and would not accept assistance from one another.[11]

In the final antithesis of the Sermon on the Mount Jesus expressly *corrects the Old Testament commandment,* "You shall love your neighbor," and the Qumran precept, "You shall hate your enemy." Instead, he declares: "But I say to you, 'Love your enemies and pray for those who persecute you.'"[12] According to Luke, this holds also for those who are hated, cursed, insulted: "Do good to those who hate you, bless those who curse you, pray for those who treat you with contempt."[13] Isn't all this too exaggerated, isn't it taking things too far for the average man? *Why* does Jesus talk like this? Is it perhaps on account of our common human nature? Is it the result of a philanthropy which finds something divine even in misery? Perhaps it expresses a universal compassion for all sufferers and serves to ease a conscience troubled by the infinite suffering of the world. Or is he expounding an ideal of a universal moral perfection?

Jesus has a different motive: the perfect imitation of God. God can be rightly understood only as the Father who makes no distinction between friend and foe, who lets the sun shine and the rain fall on good and bad, who bestows his love even on the unworthy (and who is not unworthy?). Through love human beings are to prove themselves sons and daughters of this Father[14] and become brothers and sisters after being enemies. God's love for all men is for me then the reason for loving the person whom he sends to me, for loving just this neighbor. *God's love of enemies* is itself therefore the *reason for man's love of enemies.*

It may therefore be asked on the other hand: is not the *nature of true love* made clear in face only of an opponent? True love does not speculate on its requital, does not balance one deed against another, does not expect a reward. It is free from calculation and concealed self-seeking: it is *not egoistic, but completely open for other persons.*

Can we say therefore: not *eros,* but *agape?* not *amor,* but *caritas?* It is not as simple as that. Both words mean "love." It is true that theologians have been at great pains to distinguish between *eros*—love as desire, in the Greek sense—and *agape*—love that gives, in Jesus' sense.[15] In this respect they were able to conclude from the quite remarkable lexical evidence that the noun *agape* scarcely appears in Greek secular literature and the verb *agapan* ("to love") only marginally. On the other hand, the word *eros* does not appear at all in the New Testament and only twice in the Greek Old Testament—in a negative sense, in the Book of Proverbs.[16] Evidently the word had been compromised by its connection in Greek usage with morbid eroticism and purely instinctive sexuality, manifested also in the pagan cults.

Obviously there is a distinction between desirous love, seeking *only* its own, and self-giving love, seeking the advantage of the other: the distinction, that is, between selfish love and the true love which Jesus had in mind. Nevertheless, the *distinction between selfish love and true love is not identical with the distinction between "eros" and "agape":* as if only *agape* and not also *eros* could be true love. Could not someone desire another person and yet be able at the same time to give himself? And, on the other hand, is not a person who gives himself also permitted to desire the other? Is there to be nothing lovable, nothing worth loving, in either lover or beloved? Does not the God of the Old Testament—for instance—desire his people Israel passionately, "jealously," as the prophets say, like a man who loves his faithless wife? Is not God's covenant with his people thus represented in symbols of *eros* as marriage and the people's desertion as adultery? Was not the Song of Songs, a collection of sensual love songs, admitted to the Old Testament canon? And has not God's love in the New Testament very human features: the love of a father who wants his prodigal son back?

It is striking that the Greek Old Testament speaks quite naturally of a husband's *agapan* for his wife and of husband and wife for their children. And Jesus, according to the Greek New Testament, uses the same verb for both love of friends and love of enemies.[17] Jesus in the Gospels appears as wholly and entirely human, cuddling children,[18] allowing women to anoint him,[19] aware of a bond of "love" between himself and Lazarus and his sisters:[20] evidently this "love" does not exclude *eros*. Jesus calls his disciples "friends."[21] Obviously neither the Old nor the New Testament is interested in the distinction between a "heavenly" and an "earthly" love. God's love is described in a pleasantly human way and elemental human love is in no way denigrated. Genuinely human love of husband and wife, father, mother, child, is not opposed to love of God but set within the context of that love. But when *eros* and *agape* are regarded not only as distinct, but as mutually exclusive, this is at the expense of both *eros* and *agape*.[22]

Then *eros* is devalued and condemned. Passionate love desiring the other for oneself is restricted to sex and thus both eroticism and sexuality are depreciated. *Eros* is then regarded with suspicion even when it appears not simply as uncanny, overpowering, blind, sensual passion, but—as for instance in Plato's *Symposium*—as a drive toward the beautiful and as creative force, which becomes a pointer to the supreme, divine Good (in Plotinus a longing for reunion with the One). Education hostile to *eros* and more especially religious attitudes opposed to *eros* and sexuality have caused an enormous amount of harm. But why should loving desire and loving service, the game of love and the fidelity of love, be mutually exclusive?

When *eros* is depreciated, however, *agape* is overvalued and dehumanized. It is desensualized and spiritualized (then falsely called "Platonic love"). Vitality, emotion, affectivity are forcibly excluded, leaving a love that is totally unattractive. When love is merely a decision of the will and not also a venture of the heart, it lacks genuine humanity. It lacks depth, warmth, intimacy, tenderness, cordiality. Christian charity often made little impression just because it had so little humanity.

Should not all that is human be echoed in all love of man, love of neighbor and even love of enemies? This sort of love does not become selfish, seeking only its own, but strong, truly human, seeking with body and soul, word and deed, what is for the good of the other. In true love all desire turns, not to possession, but to giving.

True radicalism

In equating God's cause and man's cause, God's will and man's well-being, service of God and service of man, and in the resultant relativizing of law and cult, of sacred traditions, institutions, hierarchs, it becomes clear where Jesus stands within the *quadrilateral* of establishment, revolution, emigration and compromise. It becomes clear why he cannot be classified either with the ruling classes or with the political rebels, either with the moralizers or with those who have opted for silence and solitude. He belongs neither to right nor left, nor does he simply mediate between them. He *really* rises *above* them: above all alternatives, all of which he plucks up from the roots. This is his *radicalism:* the radicalism of *love* which, in its blunt realism, is fundamentally different from the radicalism of an ideology.

It would be completely false to connect this love only with great deeds and great sacrifices: for example, in particular cases, a necessary break with relatives, renunciation of possessions in particular circumstances, even perhaps a call to martyrdom. In the first place and for the most part it is a question of behavior in *ordinary life*: who is first to greet the other,[23] what place we seek at a feast,[24] whether we are quick to condemn or judge compassionately,[25] whether we strive for absolute truthfulness.[26] Just how far love goes particularly in ordinary life can be seen under three headings which serve to define this radical love in a very concrete way, as it exists between individuals or between social groups, nations, races, classes, parties, Churches.

a. *Love means forgiving:* reconciliation with one's brother comes before worship of God. There is no reconciliation with God without reconciliation with one's brother. Hence the petition of the Our Father: forgive us our trespasses as we also forgive those who trespass against us.[27] This does not mean that God expects special efforts from man to obtain forgiveness. It is sufficient for man to turn confidently to God, to believe and accept the consequences of his belief. For if he himself is dependent on forgiveness and has received it, he should be a witness of this forgiveness by passing it on. He cannot receive God's abundant forgiveness and for his own part refuse a slight forgiveness to his fellow man, as the parable of the magnanimous king and his unmerciful servant clearly explains.[28]

It is typical of Jesus that readiness to forgive has no limits: *not seven times, but seventy-seven times, that is, constantly, endlessly.*[29] *And it is for everyone, without exception. In this context likewise the prohibition of judging*[30] *is typical of Jesus, again in contrast to the general Jewish theory and practice. The other person is not subject to my judgment. All are subject to God's judgment.*

Jesus' requirement that we should forgive is not to be interpreted juridically. Jesus does not mean that there is a law requiring us to forgive seventy-seven times, but not the seventy-eighth time. It is an appeal to man's love: to forgive from the very beginning and constantly anew.

b. *Love means service:* humility, having the courage to serve, is the way to true greatness. This is the meaning of the parable of the wedding feast: abasement follows self-exaltation—the embarrassment of demotion —and exaltation follows self-abasement—the honor of promotion.[31]

It is typical of Jesus to demand self-denying service, regardless of rank. *It is significant that the same saying of Jesus on service is recorded in a variety of forms (at the dispute among the disciples, at the Last Supper, at the feet-washing): the highest should be the servant (waiter at table) of all.*[32] *Hence, among Jesus' disciples, there can be no office established merely by law and power and corresponding to the office of those who hold power in the state; nor can there be an office established simply on the basis of knowledge and worth, corresponding to the office of the scribes.*

Jesus' requirement of service is not to be understood as a law forbidding any super- or subordination among his followers. It is however a decisive appeal for service even on the part of superiors toward subordinates, that is, for reciprocal service on the part of all.

c. *Love means renunciation:* there is a warning against exploitation of the weak.[33] A resolute renunciation of all that hinders readiness for God and neighbor is required. Expressed forcibly, it means even cutting off one's hand if it leads to temptation.[34] Jesus however expects renunciation, not merely of negative things—of lust and sin—but also of positive things —of rights and power.

> *Typical of Jesus is voluntary* renunciation without accepting anything in return. *This can be expressed in concrete examples:*
>
> *Renunciation of rights in favor of the other person: going two miles with someone who has forced me to go one mile with him.*[35]
>
> *Renunciation of power at my own expense: giving my cloak also to someone who has already taken my coat.*[36]
>
> *Renunciation of counterforce: presenting the left cheek to someone who has struck me on the right.*[37]
>
> *These last examples especially show more clearly than ever that Jesus' requirements must not be understood as laws. Jesus does not mean that, while there can be no reprisals for a blow on the left cheek, it may be right to hit back after a blow in the stomach. Certainly these examples are not meant to be taken merely symbolically. They are very typical borderline cases (frequently formulated in a somewhat exaggerated Eastern style) which might at any time become reality. But they are not to be understood in a legal sense, as commands to do just this and to do it constantly. Renunciation of force does not mean* a priori *renunciation of any resistance. According to the Gospel accounts, Jesus himself certainly did not present the other cheek, but protested when he was struck. Renunciation must not be confused with weakness. With Jesus' requirements, it is not a question of ethical or still less ascetic achievements which might make sense in themselves, but of blunt requests for the radical fulfillment of God's will in each particular case to the advantage of our fellow man. All renunciation is merely the negative aspect of a new positive practice.*

From this standpoint even the Ten Commandments of the Old Testament[38] seem to be—in the Hegelian threefold sense—"canceled" (*aufgehoben*): discarded and yet preserved, elevated to a higher plane through the radical "higher righteousness" proclaimed by Jesus in the Sermon on the Mount.[39]

> *We must certainly not only have no other gods beside him, but must love him with our whole heart, our whole soul and our whole mind, and our neighbor and even our enemy as ourselves.*
>
> *We must not only not use God's name pointlessly, but we must not even swear by God.*
>
> *We must not only make the Sabbath holy by resting, but must be active in doing good on that day.*
>
> *We must not only honor father and mother in order to have a long*

life on earth, but—for the sake of the true life—show them respect even by leaving them.

We must not only not kill, but we must refrain even from angry thoughts and words.

We must not only not commit adultery, but we must avoid even adulterous intentions.

We must not only not steal, but we must even renounce the right to reparation for the wrong we have suffered.

We must not only not bear false witness, but we must be so absolutely truthful that "Yes" means simply "Yes" and "No" means "No."

We must not only not covet our neighbor's house, but we must even put up with evil. We must not only not covet our neighbor's wife, but we must even refrain from seeking a "legal" divorce.

Was not the Apostle Paul right—here too in striking agreement with the Jesus of history—to claim that love is the fulfilling of the law?[40] And, according to Augustine, it may be stated more forcibly: "Love and do as you will." There is no new law, but a new freedom from the law.

But, precisely in the light of all this, the question arises: was Jesus himself content with words, with appeals? Did he prefer a congenial, non-committal, inconsequential, pure theory to practical action? What did Jesus do in the last resort? Did he put his own theory into practice?

3. *Solidarity*

Even Jesus' *words* were eminently *deeds*. His word alone demanded total commitment. And it was through his word that the decisive event occurred: the *situation* was *fundamentally changed*. Neither people nor institutions, neither the hierarchs nor the norms were ever again the same as they had been before. Both God's cause and man's found expression in his liberating words. He thus opened up to men completely new possibilities, the possibility of a new life and a new freedom, of a new meaning in life: a life according to God's will for man's well-being, in the freedom of love, outstripping all legalism. It meant the end of legalism in all its forms: both the legalism of the established order of things (law and order) and the legalism even inherent in violent revolutionary or ascetic, world-forsaking radicalisms, and finally the legalism of casuistic morality steering a middle course.

Jesus' words therefore did not amount to any sort of pure "theory": he was, in fact, not particularly interested in theory at all. His proclamation was wholly related, oriented, to practice. His demands required a free response, but imposed new obligations and had consequences—as we shall see later—of life or death, both for himself and for others. But this is not the whole story.

Partisan for the handicapped

Jesus' words really were eminently deeds. But that is not to say that what he did can be reduced to his word, his practice to preaching, his life to proclamation. Theory and practice, for Jesus, coincide in a much more comprehensive sense: his *whole behavior* corresponds to his proclamation.[1] And, while his verbal proclamation substantiates and justifies his conduct, his actual behavior clarifies his proclamation in the light of practice, makes it unassailable: he lives what he says and this gains for him the minds and hearts of his hearers.

We have already seen this displayed in one small part of his inspired behavior.[2] Jesus turned in word and deed to *the weak, sick and neglected.* This was a sign, not of weakness, but of strength. He offered a chance of being human to those who were set aside by society's standards at the time: the weak, sick, inferior, despised. He helped them in body and soul, gave health to many a physically and mentally sick person, gave strength to the many who were weak and hope to all the misfits. All these things were signs of the approaching kingdom of God. He existed for the *whole* man: not only for his intellectual life, but also for his material and secular interests. He existed for *all* men: not only for the strong, young, healthy, but also for the weak, aged, sick and crippled. In this way Jesus' deeds elucidate his words and his words interpret his deeds. But this alone would not have created the amount of scandal which was in fact created. More was involved.

The fact that he was so determined to receive the sick and "possessed" was unusual, but this could be tolerated: miracle-men are needed at all times to satisfy the craving for miracles. All the same, even this interest created problems. At that time the sick were regarded as responsible for their own misfortune, sickness was the punishment for sin: the possessed were driven by the devil; lepers, bearing already the mark of death, did not belong to the fellowship of the living. Whether it was fate, sin or simply the prejudices of their time, the reason is not important: they were all social outcasts. But Jesus took up an essentially positive attitude to all of them and—in this respect we can rely on John[3]—rejected in principle any causal connection between sin and sickness and also social ostracism.

In addition to all this—even though it is not a decisive factor—it must certainly be noted that, regardless of manners and customs, he had already brought suspicion on himself by *the company he kept.*

Women, *who did not count in society at that time and had to avoid men's company in public. Contemporary Jewish sources are full of ani-*

mosity toward women who, according to Josephus, are in every respect inferior to men.[4] *Men are advised to talk very little even with their own wives, still less with other women. Women lived as far as possible withdrawn from public view; in the temple they had access only to the women's forecourt and in regard to the obligation of prayer they were in the same category as slaves. Whatever may be the historical status of the biographical details, the evangelists have no inhibitions about speaking of Jesus' relationships with women. According to them, Jesus had got away from the custom of having no contact with women. Not only does he display no contempt for women, he is surprisingly at ease with them: women accompanied him and his disciples from Galilee to Jerusalem;*[5] *personal affection for women came naturally to him;*[6] *women attended him as he was dying and saw to his burial.*[7] *The legally and humanly weak position of woman in the society of that time was considerably upgraded by his prohibition of divorce, which had hitherto been possible if the husband alone simply issued a writ of divorce.*[8]

Children, *who had no rights. Jesus gave them preferential treatment and defended them against his disciples, fondled and blessed them.*[9] *In a very un-Jewish way they were presented as an example to adults because they could accept a gift without calculating its worth and without ulterior motives.*[10]

People ignorant of religion, *the numerous small people who could not or would not bother about the law. These "simple" ones are commended: the uneducated, backward, immature, irreligious, those who are not at all clever or wise,*[11] *the "little" or "lowly,"*[12] *even "least" or "lowest."*[13]

This then is not an aristocratic morality for "superior" individuals set apart—for instance, by Confucius—from the common people. Nor is it an elitist monastic morality for the "intelligent" who might be suitable for a community of Buddhist monks. And it is certainly not a morality of the higher "casts" in the Hindu sense, which permits pariahs in society, subject to all the remaining discriminations.

Which poor?

The poor, little people: Jesus proclaimed his message in a provocative way as good news for the *poor*. His first appeal, exhortation, call to salvation, his first beatitude, were meant for the poor. Who are these poor?

The question is not easy to answer, since the first beatitude is understood in different ways even in the Synoptic Gospels. Matthew[14] evidently understands it in a religious sense: the poor "in spirit," the *mentally* poor, are identical with the humble of the third beatitude who are aware of their spiritual poverty, aware that they are beggars in the sight of God.

But Luke[15]—omitting Matthew's qualification—understands the expression in the sociological sense: the really poor people. Jesus himself may well have meant it in this sense: at least as recorded in the shorter and probably more original Lucan version,[16] the first, second and fourth beatitude of Matthew's expanded version[17] go back to him. It is a question of the *truly* poor, mourning, hungry, those who have had a raw deal, those on the fringe of society, the deprived, the outcasts, the oppressed of this world.

Jesus himself was poor. Whatever the historians may say about the stable at Bethlehem, as a symbol it is absolutely to the point. As Ernst Bloch rightly says: "The stable, the carpenter's son, the fanatic among the humble people, the gallows at the end, all this is the stuff of history, not the gold of fable."[18] This does not mean of course that Jesus belonged to the proletariat, the broad masses of the lowest stratum of society: even then craftsmen were more or less upper class, petit bourgeois. But in his public activity Jesus was completely unassuming and undoubtedly led a free, vagrant life. And his preaching was addressed to all, especially to the lowest classes. His followers, as we heard, belonged to the "little"[19] or "simple"[20] people, the uneducated, the ignorant, the backward, whose religious knowledge left as much to be desired as their moral behavior and who were contrasted with the "prudent and wise." But Jesus' opponents belonged particularly to the small petit bourgeois middle class (Pharisees) and the thin (mainly Sadducee) upper class who were disturbed by his message, not only in their religious, but also in their social conscience.[21]

No amount of discussion can conceal the fact that Jesus was a *partisan for the poor*, the mourning, the hungry, the failures, the powerless, the insignificant. The rich who heap up for themselves treasures which rust and moths consume and which thieves can steal, who give their heart to wealth, he presents in all their miserliness as a shocking example.[22] Success, social advancement mean nothing to him: anyone who exalts himself will be humbled—and vice versa.[23] He has no interest in the people who are secure and sheltered, attached to the transitory goods of this world. We have to decide, we cannot have two gods. Whenever—with large or small savers—possessions come between God and man, whenever anyone is a slave to money and makes money his idol,[24] the curse holds of "woe to the rich," which Luke himself contrasts with the blessing promised to the poor.[25] Jesus' warning is crystal-clear: it is easier for a camel to go through the eye of a needle than for a rich man to get into God's kingdom.[26] All artificial attempts to modify the saying (a small gate instead of a needle's eye, a ship's rope instead of a camel) are of no avail. Wealth is extremely dangerous to salvation. There is nothing evil about poverty. In principle Jesus is on the side of the poor.

Nevertheless, Jesus does not propagate *dispossession of the rich* nor a kind of "dictatorship of the proletariat." He demands, not revenge on the exploiters, not expropriation of the expropriators nor repression of the oppressors, but peace and the renunciation of power. And, unlike the Qumran monastery, he does not require the surrender of possessions to the community. Anyone who renounces his possessions is expected, not to transfer them to the community, but to give them to the poor. But he did not require all his followers to renounce possessions. Here too, as we have seen, there was no law. A number of his followers (Peter, Levi, Mary and Martha) speak of houses as their own. Jesus approves Zacchaeus' distribution of only half of his possessions.[27] What he demanded of the rich young man,[28] if the latter wanted to follow him, he did not require generally and rigidly from everyone in every situation. Certainly anyone who wanted to go with him had necessarily to leave everything behind, but could not anyway live on nothing. What in fact did Jesus and his disciples live on in their vagrant life? The Gospels make no secret of it. He was supported by those of his followers who had money, especially by the women who followed him.[29] Sometimes he accepted invitations: both from rich Pharisees and from rich tax collectors. Luke however subsequently idealizes conditions in the primitive community and justifies them with an appeal to Jesus' sayings against possessions in the rigorist and severe form in which he himself had recorded them (as a comparison with Mark and Matthew shows). In reality there was no renunciation of possessions even in the primitive community.[30]

Jesus then was not a naïve enthusiast in economic matters, making a virtue of necessity and adding a touch of religion to poverty. Poverty may teach men to pray, but it also teaches them to curse. Jesus glorifies poverty no more than sickness; he provides no opium. Poverty, suffering, hunger are misery, not bliss. He does not proclaim an enthusiastic spirituality which suppresses all thought of injustice or provides a cheap promise of consolation in the hereafter. On the other hand, he was not a fanatical revolutionary, wanting to abolish poverty by force overnight and thus mostly only creating more poverty. He displayed no animosity toward the rich, brutal as they were in the East at that time. He was not one of those violent men offering happiness to the people who merely give a further twist to the spiral of violence and counterviolence, instead of breaking through it. Certainly he in no way agreed with social conditions as they existed. But he saw definitive solutions in a different way. To the poor, the suffering and the hungry, in the midst of their misery, he called: "Salvation is yours," "You are blessed, happy."

Happiness for the poor? Happiness for the unhappy? The beatitude is not to be understood as a universal rule, obvious to everyone, valid everywhere and at all times: as if all poverty, all suffering, all misery automatically guaranteed heaven and even heaven on earth. It should be understood as a promise: a promise which is fulfilled for the person who does not merely listen in a neutral spirit, but confidently makes it his own. For him God's future is already breaking into his life and bringing even now consolation, inheritance, repletion. Wherever he may go, God is ahead: he is there. By his confidence in this God ahead of him, his situation is already changed. Even now he can live differently, he becomes capable of acting in a new way, capable of unhesitating readiness to help, without thought of prestige or envy of those who have more. For love does not mean purely passive waiting.

Just because the believer knows that his God is ahead, he can commit himself actively and at the same time in all his activity and commitment he can display an astonishingly superior indifference: unconcerned—like the birds of the air and the lilies of the field—trusting to God's providence and looking to the joyous future, he does not worry about food or clothing or at all about the next day.[81] It was this aspect of Jesus, this "simple" life, which impressed even a Henry Miller. It had of course a somewhat different meaning in Jesus' own country and in his time. Because of the agrarian culture and the climate, little clothing was required, finding a home presented no great problem, food could be obtained if necessary in the fields. It really was possible to live practically from hand to mouth and to pray: "Give us today our daily bread."[82] Francis of Assisi and his first brothers tried to follow this out literally.

If however the text is expanded, as Matthew expands it, it is a question of a demand imposed on *everyone*, even if the early end of the world is not expected. Poverty "in spirit" is required as a basic attitude of *simplicity and trust, content with frugal provision and freedom from care*. It is directed against all pretentious, immodest arrogance and anxious concern, which can be found even among those who are materially poor. Poverty in spirit then means *inward freedom from possessions*, which must be realized differently in different situations. But in any case the economic values can no longer be supreme and a new scale of values is imposed on us.

Jesus did not want to address merely a particular group or class and certainly not only those groups who had assumed the honorary religious title of "the poor" ("the humble" according to the prophets and the Psalms). With his radical demands he infiltrates every social stratum and reaches everyone, both the grasping rich and the envious poor. He had compassion on the people and not merely for economic reasons. To live on bread alone is a temptation that comes to everyone. As if man had not another, quite different need. In John's Gospel—as in the story of the multiplication of the loaves—it is just this mistaken demand for bread alone that precipitates the great controversy, at the end of which the majority turn away from Jesus: the masses are not seeking him, but only food and repletion. Jesus did not preach either a welfare society or a soup-kitchen Communism. His message is not, as in the Brechtian phrase, "first feeding, then morality,"[83] but "first God's kingdom, then all the rest."[84] Even to those abandoned by this world he preaches that there is something more important, that, even when their economic needs are satisfied, they are still poor, wretched, exploited, needy, in a very much deeper sense.

In brief, every man constantly stands as a "poor sinner" before God and men, as a beggar who needs mercy and forgiveness. Even the humble servant can be as hardhearted as the great king.[35] Centuries earlier for Isaiah, whom Jesus quotes in answer to the Baptist, the poor (*anawim*) are the oppressed in the comprehensive sense: the afflicted, bruised, dependent, despairing, wretched. And Jesus calls to himself all the distressed and abandoned in material need (Luke) or mental anguish (Matthew), all indeed who are careworn and burdened, even those burdened with sin. He is the advocate of all these people. And it is here that the real scandal lies.

The moral failures

The absolutely unpardonable thing was not his concern for the sick, the cripples, the lepers, the possessed; not the way he put up with women and children around him; nor even his partisanship for the poor, humble people. The real trouble was that he got involved with *moral failures*, with obviously *irreligious and immoral people*: people morally and politically suspect, so many dubious, obscure, abandoned, hopeless types existing as an ineradicable evil on the fringe of every society. This was the real scandal. Did he really have to go so far? This attitude in practice is notably different from the general behavior of religious people: different in particular from the elitist (monastic, aristocratic or caste-tied) ethic of the Eastern religions and most of all from the strict morality of the properly legalistic religions (Judaism, Mazdaism, Islam).

It may have been the community which, as a result of hindsight, produced the general and programmatic formula: Jesus came to seek and to save what was lost,[36] to call not the just but sinners.[37] But, whatever may be the historical value of particular sayings, even the most critical exegetes do not dispute the fact that he associated with moral failures, people without religion or morals: those at whom men pointed the finger of scorn, who were marked out with horror as "sinners." The insulting epithet already mentioned, used by Jesus' opponents and certainly not invented by the community, "glutton and drunkard," was supplemented by a much more serious accusation: "friend of tax collectors and sinners."[38]

Tax collectors: these were the downright sinners, miserable sinners in the proper sense of the term, practicing a proscribed trade, odious cheats and swindlers, grown rich in the service of the occupying power, afflicted with permanent uncleanness as collaborators and as traitors to the national cause, incapable of repentance because they simply could not remember how many they had cheated or how much was involved. And such professional swindlers were the very people with whom Jesus had to get involved. Here too it is not important to establish in detail the historical accuracy of the stories of the scandalous junketings with Zacchaeus, the chief tax collector,[39] or of the reception of the tax collector Levi into the circle of Jesus' disciples.[40] Although they cannot be accepted *a priori*, neither can they be *a priori* excluded (this is particularly the case with the calling of Levi, son of Alphaeus, recorded already by Mark). It is striking enough that the Gospels mention by name no less than three tax collectors among Jesus' followers. It is in any case generally recognized as a historical fact that his opponents accused him of receiving sinners and eating with them.[41]

He did not refuse to receive *sinners*, the lawless and the lawbreakers, although of course the righteous also came to him. He stayed with tax collectors and notorious sinners. "If this man were a prophet, he would know what sort of woman is touching him and who she is": it is no longer possible to define the character of this account of the wholly unconventional homage of the sinner known in the city—most probably a prostitute—whom he did not restrain when she washed his feet with perfumed oil.[42] It is the same with the moving story in the Johannine tradition of the woman discovered in the very act of adultery and saved by Jesus from arrest by the guardians of the law.[43] These may be legends or recollections or both in one, presented as typical accounts.

Among the most certain elements of the tradition in any case is the fact that Jesus displayed a provocative partiality for sinners and identified himself with people who had neither religion nor morals. With him the wasters and the outcasts had a future. It was the same with the sexually exploited—and yet for this reason despised—women, all victims of a society of "righteous" people. On such occasions he hit on just the right word: "Her many sins are forgiven because she has loved much. Let the one who is without sin among you throw the first stone."[44]

It cannot be denied then that Jesus was "in bad company."[45] Dubious characters, delinquents, are continually turning up in the Gospels: types from which decent people would do better to dissociate themselves. Contrary to all expectations cherished by his contemporaries of the preacher of God's kingdom, Jesus refused to play the part of the pious ascetic, keeping away from feasts and not mixing with certain types of people. It would certainly not be right to romanticize Jesus' undeniable "downward bent." There was no question of "like to like." Jesus displayed no desire for the *dolce vita*, no partiality for the demimonde. He did not justify the "milieu." He never excused sin. But, from the Gospel accounts, there can be no doubt that, in the face of all social prejudices and reservations, Jesus *rejected any social disqualification* of particular groups or unfortunate minorities.

Was the novelist Günter Herburger right to portray Jesus as among the immigrant workers in Osaka? Undisturbed by all the talk behind his back, undisturbed by all the open criticism, Jesus got himself involved with the types on the fringe of society, the social outsiders, religious outcasts, the underprivileged and the downgraded. He made common cause with them. He simply accepted them. He not only preached a love open to all men, he also practiced it. Certainly he did not ingratiate himself, he did not by any means share in the activities of disreputable groups. He did not sink down to their level, but drew them up to himself. But he did not simply enter into discussion with these notoriously bad people, but—quite literally—*sat down with them*. Many were indignant: he was regarded as impossible.

Did he not realize what he was doing? Did he not realize how much sharing a meal—then as now—can compromise a person? When we are invited, we consider carefully who is inviting us—and also who must be avoided at all costs. This should have been particularly obvious to an Oriental: *fellowship at table* meant more than mere politeness and friendliness. It meant peace, trust, reconciliation, fraternity. And this—the devout Jew would add—not only in men's eyes, but also in God's. Even today in Jewish families the father breaks a piece of bread with a blessing at the beginning of a meal, so that each has a share through the broken fragment in the blessing invoked. Could God approve of fellowship at table with sinners? Just that? As if the law did not provide the most exact criterion to decide with whom one could be in fellowship, who belonged to the community of devout believers.

For Jesus this fellowship at table with those whom the devout had written off was not merely the expression of liberal tolerance and humanitarian sentiment. It was the expression of his mission and message: peace and reconciliation for all, without exception, even for the moral failures. The morally upright felt that this was a transgression of all conventional moral norms, in fact as a destruction of morality itself. Rightly?

The law of grace

The God of Judaism too could forgive. But whom is he to forgive? The person who has changed his ways, who has made full restitution, done penance, redeemed his debt of sin by his efforts (fulfillment of the law, vows, sacrifices, alms) and has shown that he is leading a better life. In brief, forgiveness is for the person who was a sinner and has now become righteous. But there is no forgiveness for those who remain sinners: the sinner faces judgment, punishment. This is justice.

Is the rule no longer to hold that the sinner must first make an effort, do penance, then receive grace? Is this whole system to lose its force? Must it not be made completely clear—as in the Old Testament books of Deuteronomy and Chronicles—that fidelity to the law is rewarded by God and lawlessness punished? According to this friend of tax collectors and sinners, is God, the holy God, supposed to *forgive sinners as such*, the unholy? But such a God would be a God of sinners: a God who loves sinners more than the *righteous*.

Here, clearly, *the very foundations of religion* are being shaken. Traitors, swindlers and adulterers are put in the right as against the devout and righteous.[46] The depraved good-for-nothing is preferred to his brother who has worked hard at home.[47] The hated foreigner—and, what is more, a heretic—is set up as an example to the natives.[48] And at the end then all will get the same reward.[49] What are all the great discourses in favor of the wastrels supposed to mean?[50] Are the sinful supposed to be nearer to God than those who remained righteous? It is scandalous if there is to be more joy in heaven over one sinner doing penance than over ninety-nine righteous who need no penance.[51] Righteousness seems to be turned upside down.

Will not someone who is so sympathetic to outlaws and lawless men also break the law himself? Will he not fail to observe both ritual and disciplinary regulations, as these are set down according to God's commandment and the tradition of the Fathers? This is a fine purity of heart! Feasting instead of fasting! Man the measure of God's commandments! Celebration instead of punishment! Under these circumstances it is not surprising if prostitutes and swindlers are supposed to enter God's kingdom before the devout,[52] unbelievers from all parts before the children of the kingdom.[53] What kind of lunatic justice is this which in fact abolishes all sacred standards and reverses all order of rank, making the last first and the first last?[54] What kind of naïve and dangerous love is this, which does not know its limits: the frontiers between fellow countrymen and foreigners, party members and non-members, between neighbors and distant people, between honorable and dishonorable callings, between moral and immoral, good and bad people? As if dissociation were not absolutely necessary here. As if we ought not to judge in these cases. As if we could always forgive in these circumstances.

Yes, Jesus did go so far: *we may forgive*, endlessly forgive, seven and seventy times.[55] And all sins—except the sin against the Holy Spirit, against the reality of God himself, when the sinner does not want to be forgiven.[56] Evidently an *opportunity* is offered to *everyone*, independently of social, ethnic, politico-religious divisions. And the sinner is accepted even before he repents. First comes grace, then the achievement. The sinner who has deserved every punishment is freely pardoned: he need only acknowledge the act of grace. Forgiveness is granted to him, he need only accept the gift and repent. This is a real amnesty—gratis. He need only live confidently in virtue of this grace. *Grace* then counts *before law*. Or, better, what holds is the law of grace. Only in this way is a new, higher righteousness possible. It begins with unconditional forgiveness: the sole condition is trust inspired by faith or trusting faith; the sole conclusion to be drawn is the generous granting of forgiveness to others. Anyone who is permitted to live, being forgiven in great things, should not refuse forgiveness in little things.[57]

Of course anyone who understands his critical situation knows also that the decision brooks no delay. When his very existence is threatened with moral ruin, when everything is at stake, it is time for bold, resolute and prudent action. Offensive and provocative as it may seem, this is evident from the example of the unjust steward, without illusions, making the most of the little time that remains.[58] It is not just any sort of opportunity: it is the chance of a lifetime. Anyone who wants to gain his life will lose it, and anyone who loses his life will find it.[59] The gate is narrow.[60] Many are called, few are chosen.[61] Man's salvation remains a miracle of grace, possible only to God, with whom indeed everything is possible.[62]

So the great feast is ready: ready for all, even the beggars and cripples on the byways, not to speak of those on the highways.[63] And what sign could have shown more clearly that forgiveness is offered to all than those *meals* of Jesus, with all who wanted to be present, including those who were not admitted to decent houses? So these people who were otherwise excluded received the invitation with no slight joy: here they received consideration instead of the usual condemnation. A merciful acquittal instead of a quick verdict of guilty. Grace surprisingly instead of universal disgrace. A true liberation! A true redemption! This is a very practical demonstration of grace. Hence these meals of Jesus remained in the memory of the early Christian communities and were understood after his death at a still deeper level: as an astonishing picture, as—so to speak—a preliminary celebration, an anticipation of the eschatological banquet announced in the parables.[64]

The question however remains: *how* can *such grace*, forgiveness, liberation and redemption for the sinner be *justified?* The explanation is clear from the parables of Jesus. His defense consists first of all in counterattack. Are the righteous who do not need penance really so righteous, are the devout so devout? Are they not giving themselves airs about their morality and piety and, for that very reason, becoming sinners?[65] Have they any idea of what forgiveness is?[66] Are they not merciless toward their brothers who lapse?[67] Are they not pretending to obey, but in reality not doing so?[68] Are they not refusing to respond to God's call?[69] Even the innocent are not without guilt if they think they owe nothing more to God. And the guilty become innocent when they abandon themselves, in their abandonment, completely to God. This means that the sinners are more truthful than the devout, since they do not conceal their sinfulness. Jesus puts them in the right as compared with those who will not admit their sinfulness.

Nevertheless, Jesus' real justification and answer is different. Why may we forgive instead of condemning, why does grace come before law? Because *God himself* does not condemn, but *forgives.* Because God himself freely chooses to put grace before law, exercises his right to give grace. Thus, throughout all the parables, God appears in constantly new variations as the one who is generous: as the magnanimous, merciful king,[70] as the lender generously canceling a debt,[71] as the shepherd seeking the sheep,[72] as the woman searching for the lost coin,[73] as the father rushing out to meet his son,[74] as the judge hearing the prayer of the tax collector.[75] Again and again he is seen afresh as the God of infinite mercy and all-surpassing goodness.[76] Man ought—so to speak—to copy God's giving and forgiving in his own giving and forgiving. Only in this light can the petition of the Our Father be understood: "Forgive us our debts as we also have forgiven our debtors."[77]

All this Jesus proclaims—as always—in an untheological way, without working out a profound theology of grace. The word "grace" does not occur either in the Synoptics—except in Luke, where in most cases it is not in the original context—or in John (apart from the prologue). "Forgiveness" appears mostly as a formula in connection with baptism and "mercy" as a noun is completely lacking in the Gospels.* It is otherwise with verbs, words denoting activity: "forgive," "release," "bestow." This indicates the decisive factor: Jesus speaks about "grace" and "forgiveness" mainly *in the sense of accomplishment.* The fact that no judgment is passed on the prodigal son, that the father interrupts his confession of sin, falls on his neck, has festive clothing, ring and sandals brought, the fatted calf slaughtered and a feast held: this is grace in its accomplishment. This too is how the servant, the moneylender, the tax collector, the lost sheep experience generosity, forgiveness, compassion, grace. Acceptance is absolute, without inquiry into the past, without special conditions, so that the person liberated can live again, can accept himself—which is the most difficult thing, not only for the tax collector. This is grace: a new chance in life.

The parables of Jesus then were more than mere symbols of the timeless idea of a loving Father-God. These parables expressed in words what occurred in Jesus' actions, in his acceptance of sinners: forgiveness. The forgiving and liberating love of God for sinners became an event in Jesus' words and deeds. *Not punishment of the wicked, but justification of sinners:* here already is the dawning of God's kingdom, the approach of God's justice.

Through all that he taught and practiced, Jesus put in the wrong all those who—though devout—were less magnanimous, compassionate and

* In English versions our Lord is frequently described as "having mercy" or "compassion," but in the Greek (except in Matthew 9:13, which is a quotation from Hosea 6:6) only the verbal form is used. (Translator.)

good than he was. It must then have been a great scandal to these less magnanimous, devout people when Jesus did not merely announce grace, mercy and forgiveness in a general way, but invoked this God whose love is given to sinners, who prefers sinners to the righteous, and boldly anticipated God's right to dispose of grace. He took it on himself—even the most critical exegetes admit this as a historical fact[78]—*to assure the individual sinner directly of forgiveness.*

According to the earliest Gospel, the first typical confrontation which Jesus has with his opponents turns on such an assurance of forgiveness: "My son, your sins are forgiven."[79] The devout Jew also believes that God forgives sins. But this man presumes to promise forgiveness quite definitely here and now to this particular individual. He personally accords and guarantees forgiveness of sins. By what right? *By what authority?* The reaction is swift: "What is he talking about? He is blaspheming. Who can forgive sins but God alone."[80]

Undoubtedly Jesus shares this assumption. It is *God* who forgives. That is precisely what is meant by the passive form of the assurance as it is handed down to us ("are forgiven"). But it is obvious to his contemporaries that here is someone who dares to do what no one hitherto—not even Moses or the prophets—has dared. He boldly announces God's forgiveness, not only as the high priest did to the whole people in the temple on the Day of Atonement, following the highly detailed order of reconciliation appointed by God. He dares to assure any moral failures quite personally in their concrete situation, "on earth"—so to speak, on the street—of forgiveness: thus he not only preaches grace, but exercises it himself authoritatively here and now.

Is this supposed to mean therefore that we have now an arbitrary justice of grace as the opposite of an arbitrary lynch justice? It does seem as if a human being is here anticipating God's judgment. Contrary to all Israel's traditions, someone is doing what is reserved to God alone, intruding and encroaching on God's most innate right. Even if God's name is not cursed, it is still *blasphemy:* blasphemy arising from arrogance. Who does this man think he is? His claim, which is quite unparalleled even in other respects, culminates in something that must provoke indignation and passionate protest: in the claim to be able to forgive sins. Conflict has become inevitable: a conflict of life and death with all those whom he has put in the wrong, whose wrong attitude he has laid bare. At a very early stage—immediately after the accounts of the forgiveness of sin, the banquet with tax collectors, the neglect of fasting, infringement of the Sabbath rest—Mark's Gospel[81] notes the deliberations of Jesus' opponents, the defenders of law, right and morality, on how they can liquidate him.

IV. The Conflict

Skandalon: a small stone over which one might stumble. Jesus in person, with all that he said and did, had become a stumbling stone, a continual scandal. There was his oddly radical identification of God's cause with man's: to what tremendous consequences in theory and practice this had led. He had been aggressive on all sides, now he was attacked on all sides. He had not played any of the expected roles: for those who supported law and order he turned out to be a provocateur, dangerous to the system. He disappointed the activist revolutionaries by his non-violent love of peace. On the other hand he offended the passive world-forsaking ascetics by his uninhibited worldliness. And for the devout who adapted themselves to the world he was too uncompromising. For the silent majority he was too noisy and for the noisy minority he was too quiet, too gentle for the strict and too strict for the gentle. He was an obvious outsider in a critically dangerous social conflict: in opposition both to the prevailing conditions and to those who opposed them.

1. The decision

Here was an enormous claim, but with so little to back it up: lowly origin, no support from his family, without special education. He had no money, held no office, had received no honors, had no retinue, he was not backed by any party or authorized by any tradition. How could a man without power claim such authority? Was not his situation hopeless from the very beginning? Who in fact was for him? But, while his teaching and his whole conduct exposed him to fatal attacks, he was also offered spontaneously trust and love. In a word, he represented for many a parting of the ways.

Those who were for him

On his side were *the people:* hard to define and never constant. In his Galilean homeland Jesus had created a considerable stir. Even though the individual narratives were fitted by the evangelists into schemes to suit their own intentions, these accounts undoubtedly contain historical material in regard to the attention, astonishment and praise of the masses. This people, a flock without a shepherd, feeling misunderstood by both the establishment and the rebels, despised alike by the pharisaical devout individuals of the towns and villages and by the ascetics of the desert, useless for either temple or military service, incapable of exact observance of the law and still less of major ascetic achievement: this is the people on whom Jesus has compassion.[1] These humble, unassuming, not very refined people, poor wretches of all kinds, these who are called blessed, who are not enfranchised, who can be neglected and abused with impunity at all times by the ruling parties and authorities: these must feel that he understands them. They are for him. But how many of them and for how long?

Undoubtedly his *closest followers* are for him. These too are small people: men and women who go around with him, who have left house and family, calling and homeland, and spend days and nights—often under the open sky—with him; who quite literally "follow" him. It is to these and not to his family that he feels tied—tied more than Buddha, Confucius, Socrates or Muhammad, who were married; although marriage and family probably played a role only in Muhammad's activity. Jesus' young men, "adherents," "disciples," then are not simply those who hear and accept Jesus' words and occasionally follow him around out of curiosity or for other reasons. The disciples formed the narrower circle around Jesus—which was not unusual with a skilled teacher in Israel. But how was an untrained person to train others? Jesus had an exceptionally short time—by comparison, for instance, with Buddha or Muhammad—to form a group of disciples. He formed them in his own way.

The better-known rabbis too had disciples who followed them. The terms "rabbi" (master, teacher), "disciple" (pupil), "follow" were current in Judaism.[2] But how different was the circle around Jesus. What was lacking—as it was also lacking to the group around John—was anything in the nature of a "school." But—unlike John's disciples, some of whom joined Jesus' circle—the ascetic element was also lacking. For all the hardships, this was an unforced, free, vagrant life, under the banner of a joyous message. But the distinction between this group of disciples and others lay elsewhere.

The stories of the calling of the disciples[3]—undoubtedly fitted by the redactors into their own schemes—say nothing about the presuppositions of individual psychology and still less about a process of group dynamics. They bring out the fact—which is exemplary for discipleship generally—that the master here chooses the pupils and not, as in the rabbinical schools, the pupils the master.[4] It is therefore not a free option on the part of the disciple, but a sovereign call by the master, with whom the initiative lies and remains. The disciples are not received into a teacher-pupil relationship, but called into a community of life and destiny. They are not introduced to an understanding of the law, but initiated into doing God's will. This is not training for a time, but formation for a lifetime. The disciple here never becomes a master. One is to be the master, all the others brethren: for this reason in Matthew's community even the adoption of the title of rabbi—as also the forms of address, father or teacher—is rigorously forbidden.[5]

Once again it becomes clear that Jesus did *not* think of training an ascetic elite. There are many sayings of Jesus—the Sermon on the Mount, for instance—where it is simply impossible to decide whether they are directed to the narrower circle of disciples or to all; obviously not only the evangelist, but also Jesus and the community, were scarcely interested in such a distinction. Why?

The kingdom of God is to come for all *and the requirements of repentance, of a new way of thinking, of a new attitude to life, of doing God's will, of love, forgiveness, service, renunciation, are in principle the same for all. And this alone is the decisive factor.*

Jesus did not expect everyone *to give up family, calling and homeland, to go around with him and undertake a special task: he never rejected in principle family, calling, homeland. In particular—if the saying about eunuchs for the sake of the kingdom of God, recorded only by Matthew,[6] goes back to Jesus—renunciation of marriage is not required from all his followers, but only exceptionally, in order to be free for the special needs and tasks arising from the imminent end of the world.*

Membership of the special circle of disciples therefore is not a condition of salvation. There are so many in the Gospels who hear the word and believe, so many—the sick who have been cured, sinners, tax collectors—who are affected by him, become his witnesses, but remain completely within their own sphere of life. Wherever Jesus proclaims his message, he leaves behind him supporters who with their families await God's kingdom and who receive him and his disciples. None of these are reproved for being perhaps irresolute or imperfect, still less excluded from God's kingdom. They are all for him.

"He who is not with me is against me."[7] This saying is directed against those who fail to stand up resolutely and unequivocally for Jesus and his message and so scatter instead of gathering. But it is not directed against those who do not join the narrower circle of disciples. The truth may sound like a paradox. But there it is.

"He who is not against us is for us."[8] This is directed against his disciples' claim to be an exclusive group. He takes under his wing a man who is outside the circle of disciples—"outside the Church," as it were—who acts charismatically in the name of Jesus and who must not be forbidden to do so. According to one account, Jesus even expressly forbids someone he has healed to follow him and leaves him to proclaim the message in his family and home.[9]

The following of Christ therefore is not a privilege of the group of disciples. This is important. Being a disciple does not mean belonging to an elite: it is not for the sake of asceticism that they have to leave all things. It is for the sake of a special task that they *may* leave all things. It is a special task; a special destiny, a special promise; a special opportunity which is missed by the young man whose riches prevent him from following Jesus.

Task, destiny and promise become particularly clear in the *accounts of sending out* the disciples recorded in all three Synoptic Gospels.[10] Despite all post-paschal elaboration and adaptation, these accounts with their Palestinian coloring must have a pre-paschal core. It is striking that their proclamation mandate does not include proclaiming Christ. It is no longer possible to trace how much of the portrayal of the disciples, their sending out, their deeds in the power of the Spirit and their return is supplemented from the analogous experiences of the primitive community. But the possibility cannot be excluded that the historical Jesus himself gave his disciples a share in his authority to preach, heal and help. In this sense Jesus—unlike Buddha—did more than point the way.

The disciples had a *special task:* to be fishers of men; to catch men, as it is vividly and clearly stated in connection with the calling of the first disciples,[11] which is linked in Luke with the legendary narrative of the miraculous catch of fish.[12] They are to catch men in the name of Jesus himself for the coming kingdom.[13] They had therefore to be actively at his side, "with him": not only to receive the message but to pass it on, to share in the announcement of the coming kingdom and its peace, to let its healing forces become charismatically effective even now.[14] This is a joyous message which becomes a judgment only on those who reject it.

The disciples had a *special destiny:* being with Jesus means leaving everything behind and going around with him from place to place. This means breaking the old ties and entering into a new commitment to his person. It means also—like him—to have nothing, nowhere to lay one's head,[15] unprotected and defenseless, to share poverty and suffering with him.[16] For the disciple is not above his master, the servant not above his lord.[17] Such a commitment must certainly be well considered, just as building a tower or starting a war must be carefully considered.[18] What is required is absolute involvement, without looking back for any reason at all: "Let the dead bury their dead."[19]

The disciples had a *special promise:* no hierarchical honors are promised, no places to right or left.[20] The promise is different: anyone who confesses Jesus on earth, Jesus himself will confess him at the judgment. The peril matches the promise.[21]

Is it surprising that the *later Christian community* saw itself reflected in the disciples who followed Jesus on his way? Is not every believer in *his* way called to the way that Jesus went? Has not everyone his task of proclamation, his destiny with Jesus, his promise? In the light of this it is understandable that the name of "disciple" came to be the name of believers as such. In this light it can be understood that a scene like the calming of the storm is regarded by Matthew as a symbol of the following of Christ and of discipleship[22] and that particularly in the Johannine farewell discourses the pre- and post-paschal situations of the disciples are seen as one.[23]

Discipleship is the *opposite of hierarchy:* hierarchy means "sacred dominion," discipleship means service with nothing sacral about it. The unfortunate term "hierarchy" stems from an anonymous writer who adopted the pseudonym of Paul's disciple, Denis the Areopagite, almost five hundred years after New Testament times; he understood the term, however, not only of officeholders, but of the whole Church in all its grades (as a reflection of the heavenly hierarchy). The New Testament communities, however, consistently avoid giving Jesus' disciples any titles associated with civil or religious officialdom. These expressions all designate a relationship between ruler and ruled. And this is just what discipleship is not. Discipleship is not constituted by law and power; it has nothing in common with the office of those who hold power in the state.[24] Nor of course is discipleship a matter of knowledge and worth: it does not correspond to the office of the scribes, conscious of their knowledge.[25] No. Discipleship is a call, not to rule, but to *service*.

It is therefore not merely accidental that the young community, instead of the usual terms for "office," should have chosen a completely "non-sacral" term to define a special function of the individual in the community: in Greek *diakonia*, in English the completely secular "waiting at table." Where was the difference between master and servant more vividly expressed than at meals, when the noble masters reclined at table wearing their long robes while the servants attended them with their clothes girded. It came as a great reversal of roles when Jesus said: "If anyone wants to be great among you, let him wait on you at table; and if anyone wants to be first, let him be the servant of all."[26] This saying of Jesus must have made a deep impression on the disciples since it appears six times in the Synoptic Gospels and John's Gospel takes up the theme of service at table in a most emphatic way in the narrative which replaces the account of the Last Supper.[27] Jesus washes the dirty feet of his followers, the most menial service to another human being and not—for instance—a religiously trimmed and stylized cultic act of condescension, performed once a year by someone who at other times is always the noble lord.

Discipleship therefore means the opposite of a dominion (often very piously described as "ministry") of men over men. Discipleship means an unpretentious service of men to men, active and proving itself in small things, in quite ordinary, banal daily life. This is certainly not an unreal life, without subordination or superordination: these are necessary and helpful in any human society, as long as they remain oriented, not to titles and positions, but both to the diverse gifts and tasks of the individual and to the benefit of the community. But it is a life free from prejudice without domination or enslavement: talking, acting, also suffering, with one another, free from domination, for the sake of the reign of God.

But is Jesus' discipleship no more than merely an unforced co-operation of all with all, no more than a gathering, a movement? Did Jesus then not found a Church? Buddha set up a monastic community, Confucius founded a training school, Muhammad established a strong, expansionist Islamic state. And Jesus?

A Church?

Jesus proclaimed the kingdom of God, which for him was certainly not identical with a Church. It has even been questioned whether Jesus himself selected precisely *twelve*[28] from the group of disciples. But, from an ancient creed, quoted by Paul in the spring of 55 or 56,[29] it is evident that the twelve existed at the time immediately after the death of Jesus. The most obvious explanation is that given by the Gospels themselves, although little can be said about the exact historical point of time or circumstances: it was the historical Jesus himself who called, "made," the twelve.[30]

Would Judas Iscariot otherwise have been counted among the twelve, a fact which was bound to be an extraordinary burden to the early Church (and for Jesus himself, who seems to have been very seriously deceived in Judas)? Would the traitor have been allowed to share in the promise that the twelve would sit on thrones judging the tribes of Israel?[31] Would there have been a "by-election" for Matthias to take his place, the account of which in the Acts must have some historical basis?[32] These inconvenient facts are a guarantee that the twelve were called by Jesus himself. None of the more circumstantial attempts at an explanation can provide a convincing answer as to when, where and how, in so short a time, the circle of the twelve could have been formed.

As far as posterity is concerned, the twelve of course as individuals are faceless men. Even their names are not absolutely certain: the lists[33] differ from each other, particularly with reference to Thaddaeus or Simon. The evangelists do not seem interested in the pre-history and the characters of individuals. Obviously there are some very unimportant people among them: fishermen; a tax collector (Matthew, presumably identical with Levi[34]) and a Zealot (Simon, the Canaanite[35]), as such, deadly enemies; perhaps also some peasants or workmen. Only two stand out (the two "Sons of Thunder," John and James, remain very sketchy figures): Judas

Iscariot and Simon, with the nickname—perhaps given by Jesus himself—of "Cephas" or "Petros" (rock).[86] The latter, a fisherman from Bethsaida, married in Capernaum, passionately devoted to Jesus but wavering at the end, was indisputably spokesman for the other disciples—even if his role was subsequently stylized—and was later important as the first witness of the risen Christ and leader of the primitive community. The ambivalent figure of Peter in particular clearly shows that the two first Gospels at least do not attempt to idealize the disciples: they are normal, erring and sinful men, not heroes or geniuses. Their incomprehension, their pusillanimity, their unreliability and finally their flight, are reported without extenuation. Only Luke—who idealizes also the primitive community as a model—tones down and sometimes even removes offensive features. He passes over the saying addressed to Peter after his confession, assimilating him to Satan, curtails the Gethsemane scene to show the disciples in a more favorable light, suppresses the account of their flight and makes amazingly positive statements about Peter and the disciples.[87]

More important however than the question about individual members of this circle is the question of its significance. Did Jesus foresee Peter and the twelve as the foundation of a Church which he would establish? Certainly no one will dispute the fact that the New Testament Church traced itself back to Jesus as the Christ ("the Church of Jesus Christ") and that the apostles were of fundamental importance for it. But these connections, to which we shall have to return, must not be simplified and—above all—not pre-dated.

As we have seen, the historical Jesus counted on the consummation of the world and its history in his lifetime. And he certainly did *not* want to prepare for the coming of God's kingdom by founding *a special community distinct from Israel* with its own creed, its own cult, its own constitution, its own ministries. In all his proclamation and activity, Jesus never turned to a special group in order to set it apart from the people—in the style, for instance, of the Essenes, the Qumran monks or the Pharisees. Never did he speak—again unlike Qumran and some other separatist groups with reference to themselves—of a "holy remnant" of Israel which would be God's pure community of the elect. Jesus will have no isolation or segregation. He does not think he is sent to the assembly of the "just," "devout," "pure," but to the assembly of *all* Israel, which must include the neglected, inferior and poor, the sinners, written off by the remnant communities: a great *collective eschatological movement*. He rejects the premature separation of good and bad fish, wheat and darnel.[88] Despite all failures, he constantly turns again to the whole Israel. He sees this totality of Israel and not only a holy remnant community as called to be the people of God of the end-time.

And it is just this people of God of the end-time of which the twelve are the sign. Symbolizing the twelve tribes of Israel,[89] they show forth the disciples as God's people of the end-time. In view of the early approach of the kingdom, they have been chosen to represent the full number of Israel now to be restored from its scandalously reduced state (only two and a half tribes—Judah, Benjamin and half of Levi—had constituted the people of Israel from the time of the conquest of the northern kingdom in 722 B.C.). Neither the circle of disciples nor still less those Israelites prepared to repent are organized into a closed community. In the earliest Gospel these twelve are not given the title of apostles at the time of their calling.[40] Here too it is Luke who first mentions that Jesus himself called just these twelve "apostles."[41] But in the Pauline letters others, in addition to the twelve, are called "apostles" (Andronicus, Junias, Barnabas, perhaps also Silvanus and James, the brother of the Lord). The twelve therefore can by no means be *a priori* identified with the apostles.

All this means that Jesus did *not found a Church* during his lifetime.[42] It says much for the fidelity of the tradition—evidently not embellished by the primitive Church—that the Gospels make no mention of any saying of Jesus addressed to the general public which calls men programmatically to a community of the elect or announces the foundation of a Church or a new covenant. The parables of the fish net and of the leaven, of sowing and growth, describe the future kingdom of God, which cannot be identified with the Church. Jesus never required membership of a Church as a condition of entry into God's kingdom. The obedient acceptance of his message and the immediate and radical submission to God's will sufficed.

The word "Church" occurs only twice altogether in the Gospels and only once in the sense of the whole Church: "You are Peter and on this rock I will build my Church."[43] This is one of the most controverted texts in the New Testament. It is only now that a consensus between leading scholars of the different Churches is beginning to take shape. Even Catholic exegetes today admit that the logion, Matthew 16:17–19, found oddly enough only in Matthew (and unknown to Mark and Luke), does not fit in—despite its Semitic character—with Jesus' proclamation, characterized as this is by the early expectation of the end. It is a very ancient post-paschal construction by the Palestinian community or by Matthew, presupposing a Church already institutionally consolidated, equipped with powers of teaching and jurisdiction.[44]

But however this logion—almost every word of which is contested—is to be understood in detail, even if it stems from the original Jesus, it was not addressed to the general public and it clearly assigned the building of a Church, not to the present, but in every individual formulation to the future. Neither the supporters of Jesus who are simply prepared to repent nor the disciples called in a special way to follow him—the twelve—are set apart from Israel by Jesus as the "new people of God" or the "Church" and contrasted with the ancient people of God. It was only after the death and resurrection of Jesus that primitive Christendom spoke of a "Church." The "Church" in the sense of a special community distinct from Israel is quite clearly a *post-paschal factor*.

Hence Jesus is *not* what is generally understood as the founder of a religion or of a Church. He did not think of the creation of a large religious structure to be founded and organized by himself. He regarded himself from the very beginning as sent only to the children of Israel.[45] Neither for himself nor for the disciples did he think of a mission among the pagan nations: the missionary command is post-paschal.[46] But he does seem to have thought of the eschatological pilgrimage of the pagan nations to the mountain of God as described by the prophets.[47] According to a strange and archaic saying, it would be at this hour of the Gentiles when unnamed people would stream in from East and West and recline at table in the kingdom of God, while the children of the kingdom were thrust out.[48] But God's promise must first be fulfilled and salvation offered to Israel. Successfully?

However much Jesus turned to *all*, however much he addressed *all* Israel (universal *de jure*) and however little he excluded the Gentiles from the kingdom (universal *de facto*), his whole manifestation provoked a painful separation. The words he spoke, the deeds he performed, the demands he raised confronted people with a final decision. Jesus left no one neutral. He himself had become the great question.

Without office or dignity

What attitude is one to take up to this message, to this behavior, to this claim and in the last resort to this person? The question could not and cannot be avoided. It runs as a pre-paschal question through the post-paschal Gospels and it has not ceased to be raised up to the present time. What do you think of him? Who is he? One of the prophets? Or more?

What sort of a "role" does he play in connection with his message? What is his attitude toward his "cause"? Who is he, who in any case is not a heavenly being disguised for a time as a man, but a completely human, vulnerable, historically palpable human being, who as head of a group of disciples is not unreasonably addressed as "rabbi," "teacher"? Someone who as preacher of the approaching kingdom of God appeared to some as a "prophet," perhaps even as the prophet expected at the end of time and about whom his contemporaries were obviously not agreed among themselves?[49] It is striking that there is nothing in the Gospels about a definite experience of being called as a prophet, as Moses and the prophets were called, or even Zarathustra or Muhammad, or of an illumination like that of Buddha.

To some Christians the statement that Jesus is the Son of God appears to be the center of the Christian faith. But we must look more closely at this. Jesus himself placed the kingdom of God at the center of his proclamation and not his own role, person or dignity. No one questions the fact that the post-paschal community, while constantly maintaining the full humanity of Jesus of Nazareth, gave to this man the titles of "Christ," "Messiah," "Son of David," "Son of God." And the fact can be understood and will later be explained that they sought out and transferred to Jesus the most important and richest titles from their Jewish and later Hellenistic environment, in order in this way to give expression to his meaning for faith. In view of the nature of our sources it cannot simply be taken for granted that Jesus himself assumed these titles. This is very questionable and must be examined without prejudice.

The very fact that we are here concerned with the center of the Christian faith—with Jesus as the Christ—requires us to be doubly cautious, so that wishful thinking does not supersede critical reasoning. Here particularly it must be remembered that the Gospels are not purely historical documents, but written records of the practical proclamation of faith: they are meant to provoke and confirm faith in Jesus as the Christ. It is just here that the frontier is particularly hard to define between historical happenings and interpretation of history, between historical account and theological reflection, between pre-paschal sayings and post-paschal knowledge.

The early Christian communities, however, their worship and their proclamation, their discipline and mission, and also the redactors of the Gospels, may have exercised an influence not only on the sayings of the risen and exalted Lord, but even on the sayings of the earthly Jesus, particularly the Christological statements about himself. For the interpreter this means that the most orthodox theologian is not the one who regards as *many* as possible of Jesus' sayings in the Gospel tradition as genuine. But neither is the most critical theologian the one who regards as *few* as possible of the Gospel sayings of Jesus as genuine. Both uncritical faith and skeptical criticism are equally irrelevant to this central question. As we have said, true criticism does not destroy faith nor does true faith prevent criticism.[50]

Must we not allow for the possibility that the profession of faith and the theology of the communities have affected the *messianic* stories in particular?

This could have happened, for instance, in the *genealogies*, already mentioned, which seek to announce Jesus as Son of David and child of promise, but which are notably absent from the earliest Gospel and—apart from their coincidence at David—are so little in harmony in Matthew and Luke;

or in the *infancy stories* arranged in legendary form, which describe the mystery of this origin, but which are likewise found only in Matthew and Luke and at the same time offer little that can be historically verified;

or in the *baptism and temptation stories* which likewise have a special literary character and attempt to present Jesus' mission in the form of didactic narratives;
or in the *story of the transfiguration* which even in Mark includes different strata of tradition and which uses various epiphany motifs in order to make clear Jesus' eschatological messianic role and dignity.

Obviously it should not be claimed that all these stories are *merely* legends or myths. They are frequently linked with historical events—as, for instance, the baptism of Jesus. But it is often scarcely possible to establish the historical element and in any case it cannot simply be assumed that the messianic statements were originally linked with it. These messianic stories have their meaning, but we shall miss just this and get into contradictions if we try to understand them sentence by sentence as historical reportage.

Every serious exegete today stresses the fact that the faith and theology of primitive Christendom exercised an influence particularly on the *messianic titles*. A closer investigation—of which only the results can be reproduced here[51]—would reveal the following facts:

In one of the two main sources of the Synoptic Gospels, known as the logia-source or Q (for Quelle=*"source"), the title of Messiah is completely lacking.*

In the narrative tradition Jesus permits others to use messianic predicates of him, without either expressly approving or rejecting them. Both Peter's confession ("You are the Messiah"[52]) and the high priest's interrogation of Jesus ("Are you the Son of the Blessed One?"[53]) must be regarded as the reflection of the Christ confession of the later community, as also those two unique Synoptic texts which speak of "the Son"[54] in a way that recalls John's Gospel but not the historical Jesus.

According to the Synoptic Gospels then—naturally John's is different, speaking of "Son" and "Son of God" in terms of theological reflection—Jesus never himself assumed the designation of Messiah or any other messianic title.

The earliest evangelist still treats Jesus' messianic claim as a mystery hidden from the public at large: known to the heavenly and infernal powers (devils), but on these as on the people who are cured, on Peter after his confession and on those present at the "transfiguration" of Jesus, silence is imposed, although this would obviously be impossible to maintain in reality; only Easter makes it possible to understand Jesus' hidden messianic activity.

Jesus' proclamation and practice would not in any case have corresponded to the usual messianic expectation (of the Pharisees, Zealots, Essenes).

On the basis of these findings, which can easily be substantiated in detail, even more conservative exegetes conclude that Jesus himself did not assume any title implying messianic dignity: not "Messiah," nor "Son of David," nor "Son," nor "Son of God."[55] But, after Easter, looking back, the whole Jesus tradition was seen in a messianic light—and rightly, as will become clear—and in that light the messianic confession was brought into the presentation of the Jesus story. The redactors of the Gospels too look back and talk *in the light of the paschal faith,* for which the Messiahship —now quite differently understood—is no longer a problem. But previously it had been a problem, a real problem.

There is only one title on which there is still serious discussion as to whether Jesus himself used it. The mysterious, apocalyptic title "Son of Man," which here means decidedly more than "man," turns up for the first time in the book of Daniel: in the vision of the four animals and of him who comes on the clouds of heaven, who is like a "Son of Man," given power, honor and dominion, so that all nations serve him in an everlasting kingdom which will never be destroyed.[56] In other apocalyptic writings[57] also the Son of Man—understood no longer as in Daniel as the people of Israel, but as an individual figure—plays an important role. Looking from this standpoint at the New Testament, two points strike us:

On the one hand, both the Greek-speaking Church before Paul and Paul himself avoid this title, evidently because of the possibility of misunderstanding (as a designation of human origin) and do not make use of it even in the primitive Christian creeds.

On the other hand, it is only in the four Gospels themselves that the title retains its place. It is found there eighty-two times and never in any statement by others about Jesus, but always exclusively on his lips. Is there any explanation other than the fact that the title was rooted inviolably in the tradition of Jesus' sayings from the very beginning and thus some at least of the earliest sayings about the Son of Man—others are recognizably secondary when the Synoptics are compared with one another—go back in essentials to Jesus and were used by him presumably in the sense of Jewish apocalyptic.[58]

These findings however become extraordinarily complicated as a result of the fact that Jesus constantly speaks in a detached way, in the third person, of the Son of Man, and that some of these sayings speak of the coming, others of the suffering and still others of the present, earthly Son of Man: the three different groups can scarcely be linked with each other. The end of this discussion is not yet in sight.[59]

For some exegetes the title of Son of Man is purely and simply community theology. But this theory dismisses too easily the remarkable textual evidence that "Son of Man" is always Jesus' self-designation, never a form of address, a confession or a simple statement.

For others Jesus himself used this mysterious title to register his messianic claim. But are there any texts at all which suggest that Jesus wanted to provoke reflection with this ambiguous secret name, which could also be understood simply as "man" without any messianic reference?

Again for others Jesus did not see himself as the present but as the future Son of Man and judge of the world. But where in the Synoptics is there any mention of such a definition or designation, of his being taken up or exalted to be the Son of Man coming to judge?

Finally, for a fourth group, Jesus speaks of another figure whom he expects as Son of Man. He is said to have used this apocalyptic idea in order to make the verdict at the last judgment by the Son of Man coming from heaven dependent on a man's present profession of faith in himself.[60] But is there anything in the texts to suggest that Jesus ever regarded himself as no more than a precursor and why is his relationship to this Son of Man allegedly distinct from himself nowhere defined?

We cannot assert anything here very apodictically. Probably Jesus did not describe himself as Son of David, Messiah (Christ) or Son of God (Son). It is also possible that he did not use the term "Son of Man" of himself, at least not in an unequivocally messianic sense for his own time. All that is really certain is that for the post-paschal community Jesus is identical with the Son of Man: for them Jesus is the apocalyptic man who is to come for the judgment and for the redemption of his followers. Is this a negative result? Yes, possibly; yes, with reference to the use of the titles by Jesus himself. No, certainly no, with reference to Jesus' claim. For obviously *his claim does not stand or fall with his titles,* not even the title "Son of Man." On the contrary, the great questions of what and who he is are not settled by this evidence, but only raised in a more acute form. What and who is this man who is not supported by any special descent, family, education, retinue, party and who possibly attaches no importance to special titles and dignities and yet—as we have seen—raises a stupendous claim?

It must not be forgotten that the titles in question here were—each in its own way—encumbered with the different traditions and the more or less political expectations of his contemporaries. This Jesus was just not a "Messiah," a "Son of David," a "Son of Man," in the sense generally expected. And, from all appearances, he certainly did not want to be anything of this kind. Apparently none of the familiar concepts, none of the usual ideas, none of the traditional offices, none of the current titles were appropriate to express his claim, to define his person and mission, to reveal the mystery of his nature. The messianic titles of majesty themselves make it clearer than the human, all-too-human roles assigned to the Messiah by the priests and theologians, the revolutionaries and ascetics, the religious or irreligious small people, that this Jesus is different.

And for this reason he left no one indifferent. He had become a public person and had provoked a conflict with the milieu. Confronted by him, the people and particularly the hierarchy found themselves before an inescapable final choice. He provoked a final *decision;* but not a yes or no to a particular title, to a particular dignity, a particular office, or even to a particular dogma, rite or law. His message and community raised the question of the aim and purpose to which a man will ultimately direct his life. Jesus demanded a final decision for God's cause and man's. In this cause he is completely absorbed, without seeking anything for himself, without making his own role or dignity the theme of his message. The great *question* about his *person* was raised only *indirectly* and his avoidance of all titles deepened the mystery.

The advocate

It has constantly been a source of amazement that the Gospel accounts of the trial cite so little to explain the motivation behind the condemnation of Jesus of Nazareth to death. For if anything is certain in this life story it is his violent death. But even if one does not regard the high priest's question about Jesus' Messiahship as a post-paschal interpretation, if he only reads the story of the Passion, the condemnation of Jesus to death will remain largely unintelligible to him. There were some claimants to Messiahship, but no one was condemned to death for this claim.

Was it perhaps simply a tragic judicial error which could be annulled by a retrial, as some well-meaning Christians and Jews now demand? Was it indeed the deliberate wickedness of a stubborn people, bearing a moral guilt which would cost the lives of innumerable Jews through twenty centuries of Christendom? Was it simply one of those well-known arbitrary acts of the Roman authorities who were ultimately responsible, which would mean the exoneration of the Jews? Or could it have been a deliberate plan of the Jewish leaders to stir up the innocent people and—as the evangelists suggest to exonerate the representative of Rome—to use the Romans, who were convinced of Jesus' innocence, as an involuntary tool? According to Mark, Pilate's question, "What evil has he done?", is answered only by the resounding cry, "Crucify him."[61]

We may however see it from the other side and ask what evil must he really have done to provide adequate reasons for his condemnation. Is the justification of Jesus' condemnation perhaps so brief in the Passion story because the Gospels as a whole provide a comprehensive and really adequate explanation of it? In the light of this, it seems, the *charge* would not be difficult to formulate.

Or must it be repeated once more that this man had offended against almost everything that was sacred to this people, this society and its representatives: that, without bothering about the hierarchy, he set himself in word and deed above the cultic taboos, the fasting customs and particularly the Sabbath precept; that he fought not only against certain interpretations of the law ("traditions of the Elders"), but against the law itself (unambiguously in forbidding divorce, in forbidding reprisals, in the commandment to love one's enemies); that he not only interpreted the law differently and not only tightened it at certain points, but changed it, indeed set himself above it with a disconcerting independence and freedom whenever and wherever it seemed right to him for the sake of human beings; that he proclaimed a "higher righteousness" than that of the law, as if such a thing were possible and as if God's law were not the final authority.

Even if he did not announce it as part of his program, did he not in practice question the existing order of the Jewish law and thus the whole social system? Even if he did not want to abolish them, did he not in fact completely undermine the existing norms and institutions, the prevailing precepts and dogmas, ordinances and statutes, inasmuch as he questioned their absolute validity by asserting that they existed for man's sake and not man for theirs? The question naturally arose: is this man greater than Moses who gave us the law?[62]

And again, although this too was no part of his program, did he not in fact question the cult as a whole, the liturgy? And, even though he had no wish to abolish all rites and customs, celebrations and ceremonies, did he not in practice erode them by putting service of man before service of God? The question may be put more concisely: is this man greater than Solomon who built the temple?[63]

Finally, did he not make man the measure of God's precepts by identifying God's cause with man's, God's will with man's well-being? Did he not in this way impose a love of man, of neighbor, of enemies, which disregards the natural frontiers between members and non-members of the family, between fellow countrymen and foreigners, party members and non-members, between friends and enemies, neighbors and those far away, good and bad? Did he not relativize the importance of family, nation, party and even law and morality? Was he not bound to incur the hostility of rulers and rebels, the silent majority and the loud minority? Did not preaching endless forgiveness, service without regard to rank, renunciation without compensation, mean the abandonment of all recognized distinctions, useful conventions and social barriers? As a result he was bound—contrary to all reason—to take the side of the weak, sick, poor, underprivileged and therefore to oppose the strong, healthy, rich and privileged; contrary to sound morals, to be soft with women, children, small people; even—contrary to all laws of morality—to compromise with really irreligious and immoral people, outlaws and lawbreakers, with fundamentally godless people and to favor these as against the devout, moral, law-abiding people who believe in God. Had not this friend of public sinners—men and women—the audacity to propagate pardon instead of punishment for the wicked and even, here and now, with colossal presumption, directly to assure individuals of forgiveness for their sins, as if the kingdom of God were already present and he himself the judge, the final judge of man? Finally, the question must be faced: is this man greater than Jonah,[64] who preached penance, more than a prophet?

Jesus then shattered the foundations, the whole theology and ideology of the hierarchy. And again the amazing *contrast* should be noted: just an average man from Nazareth—from which nothing good could come[65]—of inferior origin, from an insignificant family, followed by a group of young men and a couple of women, a man without education, money, office or dignity, not empowered by any authority, not authorized by any tradition, not backed by any party—and yet such an unparalleled *claim*. An innovator, putting himself above law and temple, above Moses, king and prophet, using the word "I" with suspicious frequency—not only in John, but also in the Synoptics in contexts from which it cannot be eradicated by literary criticism. To this there correspond—even if one were to be hypercritical and trace them back, not to Jesus, but to the community—both the "I say to you" of the Sermon on the Mount and the "Amen," oddly used at the beginning of many sentences, implying a claim to an authority which goes beyond that of a rabbi or even of a prophet.

Nowhere does he substantiate this claim, which in the Gospels raises a question with reference to both his words and his deeds. Indeed, in the discussion about authority, he refuses to give any justification.[66] He simply assumes authority. He has it and gives effect to it, talks and acts in the light of it, without appealing to a higher authority. He asserts a completely underived, supremely personal authority. He is not merely an expert or a specialist, like the priests and theologians, but one who—without appealing to any source or argument for his authority—on his own account proclaims in word and deed God's will (=man's well-being), identifies himself with God's cause (=man's cause), is wholly devoted to this cause and thus, without any claim to title or authority, becomes the supremely personal, public *advocate of God and man.*

An advocate of God and man? "Blessed is he who is not scandalized in me!"[67] But are we not bound to be scandalized?

Is a teacher of the law who sets himself up against Moses not a false teacher?

Is a prophet who does not belong to the succession from Moses not a lying prophet?

Is someone claiming to be above Moses and the prophets, who even assumes the function of a final judge in regard to sin, thus intruding in a sphere that belongs to God alone, not—this must be clearly stated—a blasphemer?

Is he not anything but the innocent victim of a stubborn people and in fact a fanatic and heretic, as such supremely dangerous, very seriously threatening the position of the hierarchy, disturbing the existing order, stirring up unrest, seducing the people?

Only against this background does the absolutely secondary importance of Jesus' assumption or non-assumption of special titles become clear. The subsequent attribution of these titles might not be the obvious thing to do after his death and failure, but it would fit in with his whole activity. All that he did or permitted had raised a claim surpassing that of rabbi or prophet and completely equivalent to that of a Messiah. Rightly or wrongly, in practice, in word and deed, he acts as God's advocate for man in this world. Thus it becomes clear at the same time how false it would be simply to deny any messianic character to the story of Jesus and to say that this character was only subsequently imposed. Jesus' claim and influence were such that messianic expectations were roused by his proclamation and activity as a whole and were believed, as the saying recorded of the disciples on the way to Emmaus clearly expresses: "We had hoped that it would be he who would redeem Israel."[68] Only in this way is it possible to understand the absolute call to follow him, the calling of the disciples and the selection of the twelve, the stirring of the whole people and certainly the violent reaction and permanent irreconcilability of his opponents.

As the public advocate of God and man, Jesus had become in person the great sign of the times. By his whole existence he confronted men with a decision: for or against his message, his activity, and indeed his person. To be scandalized or to be changed, to believe or not to believe, to continue as before or to repent. And, whether one said "Yes" or "No," he was marked for the coming kingdom, for God's final judgment. In his person God's future throws its shadow, its light for man, in advance.

If he was right in claiming to be the advocate of God and man, the former age would really have passed away and a new age dawned. Then a new and better world would be on the way. But who is to say whether he is right? It is as a powerless, poor and insignificant *human being* that he enters on the scene with such a claim, such authority, such significance, sets aside in practice the authority of Moses and the prophets, and claims for himself the authority of *God*. How could the accusation of false doctrine, lying prophecy, and indeed of blasphemy and misleading the faithful, fail to be justified?

Certainly he invokes God in all that he does and says. But again, what sort of God would this be if he were right? Jesus' whole proclamation and action raises the question of God as final and inescapable: what he is like and what he is not like, what he does and what he does not. In the last resort the whole conflict centers on God.

2. *The debate on God*

We must recall the debate on God as it stood at that time,[1] but we must bring to it a fresh outlook. We must see it now in the light of different assumptions. The new scientific explanation of the world, the different conception of authority, ideological criticism, the switching of consciousness from the hereafter to the present, man's orientation to the future have had an enormous influence on our understanding of God and cannot be reversed today merely by an appeal to what Jesus said.

As explained earlier, the modern understanding of God must start out from a coherent understanding of reality: God in this world and this world in God. This is a God who is not merely part of reality, a (supreme) finite alongside the finite, but the infinite in the finite, the absolute in the relative, the hidden-close, the present-hereafter, transcendent-immanent, ultimate reality at the heart of things, in man and in the history of mankind. He is the God who does not operate merely in some sort of "supernatural" realm or exclusively within the periods of salvation history: in emergencies as a helper in need in history or a stopgap in the cosmos: that is, only at the point where man's natural resources fail, where he cannot make further progress. God is the most real reality, active in all reality: everywhere and at all times providing the world and men with a final point of reference, a unity, value and meaning. There is no action of God *alongside* world history, but only *in* the history of the world and of man's activity.

Should it not be possible also to understand the God of Jesus against such a modern horizon? Should it not be possible to bring what is decisive from Jesus' standpoint within this horizon? And on the other hand should it not be possible to answer and to answer unequivocally—particularly from Jesus' standpoint—what necessarily had to remain—as we saw—equivocal, vague, open, in man's general or philosophical understanding of God?[2] We cannot avoid a more wide-ranging investigation of this problem.

Not a new God

Of course, Jesus did not want to proclaim anything like an ambiguous private God or an indeterminate pseudo-modern belief in God: that unassuming God of bourgeois mediocrity who corresponds exactly to our very selective, favorite moral ideas, having no disturbing features and making no inconvenient demands; a God who simply takes people as they are and allows them to continue in their selfish ways; who is more than satisfied when we acknowledge his existence and who will never hurt anyone, since he understands and therefore pardons everything. In brief, this is a God who harms no one and is useful to no one, but also thus makes possible a kind of "religion" which disturbs nothing and imposes no obligation.[3]

Is this God a kind of household God? No. Jesus does not proclaim such an innocuous product of wishful thinking, which would be practically a model for the projection theory of Feuerbach and Freud. He proclaims no God other than the not very congenial *God of the Old Testament*.[4] Jesus had no desire at all to found a new religion or proclaim a new God. Nor was he doing anything like Akhenaton of the Eighteenth Dynasty of the Pharaohs: this "heretic" king, husband of the famous beauty Nefertiti, was an idealist who got himself involved in an unparalleled monotheistic revolution to replace the Egyptian state god Amon by the one God Aton, whose visible embodiment was said to be the sun; he failed after incurring the hatred of the priesthood and the hostility of the people.

When Jesus speaks of God he means the ancient God of the patriarchs Abraham, Isaac and Jacob: Yahweh, the God of the people of Israel. For him this is the *one* and *sole* God, beside whom there are not simply no greater, equal or lesser gods, but—and this had been characteristic of the religion of Moses—*no other gods* at all. This one God is not merely competent for certain areas of life, like the pagan gods: fertility gods for the fields, the war-god Ares for victory and Aphrodite for love. This one God is competent for all areas: he gives everything, all life, all goodness. In accordance with Israel's first commandment, Jesus confirms the strict faith in this one God, of whom there can be no images and who can demand man's complete devotion, complete love.[5]

Faith in one God is common to *Jews, Christians and also Muslims*. Faith in the one God active in history, attested of Abraham in both Old and New Testaments and also in the Koran, forms the common reference point between Judaism, Christianity and Islam. It could form the basis for a better understanding and deeper solidarity between the three great religious communities which were so often hostile to one another in the past. None of them can understand its own nature without reference to the other two and therefore should never regard the others as "infidels," "apostates" or "obsolete," but as "fathers" and "sons," "brothers" and "sisters," under one and the same God.

This faith in one God, although providing no social program, has incisive social consequences: it demythologizes the divine world powers in favor of the one God. It prevents the deifying of political powers and rulers, the idolizing of natural forces, and breaks through the constantly recurring cosmic dying and coming to be. It means a radical rejection of all the many gods, not called such but—even in our apparently atheistic age—still worshiped by men; it rejects all earthly agencies with divine functions on which everything is thought to depend, in which men hope and which they fear as they fear nothing else in the world. They sing

Holy God, we praise thy name;
Lord of all, we bow before thee

and it is of little importance whether the words are addressed—sometimes by monotheists, at others by polytheists—to the holy God Mammon or to the holy God Sex, to the holy God Power or to the holy God Science, to the holy God Nation or to the holy God Party.

For Israel and for Jesus therefore this one God and not the many gods is the *unequivocal answer* to those pressing questions of human life facing all of us which human and particularly philosophical thinking cannot easily avoid, but to which they also cannot provide a clear answer. He is clearly not a primal cause which is ultimately perhaps a dark, fatal chasm, as some Gnostics surmised; not a primal sense which is ultimately great nonsense. But he is clearly a God of benevolence and salvation.

This one God was known to Israel from a long *history*: from the time when insignificant groups of slaves, perhaps nomads, kept in Egypt as a cheap labor force for Pharaoh's building works, came to believe in one God who promised them liberation. They had trusted to his guidance through the desert, until they finally settled down. And new generations—groups, the nation, individuals—again and again were to know him as liberator and savior. Thus this God and his action were experienced and attested in a wholly concrete way in the course of history: through innumerable narratives and finally through historical works covering quite surprisingly long periods of time. We may recall the "Pentateuch" (five books—Genesis, Exodus, Leviticus, Numbers, Deuteronomy—for a long time ascribed to Moses), which emerged out of a variety of traditions in a redactional process lasting for centuries, the Deuteronomic historical work (the books of Joshua, Judges, 1–2 Samuel, 1–2 Kings), and finally the historical work of the Chronicler (1–2 Chronicles, to which the books of Ezra and Nehemiah are added).[6]

History therefore came to be understood in Israel as the interplay of events between God and his people. Thus certain experiences of individuals and groups, and even of the whole nation, showing God's activity for believers, were related and extolled both in religious services and elsewhere: by parents for children, priests for pilgrims, public storytellers and traveling singers for their hearers. In this way in the course of time a unique, extensive, thoroughgoing, *historical way of thinking* developed in Israel. The past remained present and helped people both to endure the present and to see into the future. Israel's credo is not a philosophical-speculative, but a historical credo, centered on the God of liberation who "led Israel out of Egypt,"[7] who is perceptible not to neutral, aloof historians, but to those who see God at work in the historical facts. And this primitive confession of the Yahweh worshipers' community of faith and cult, which only very much later became a political community, is a confession of praise. The Old Testament as a whole is full of the *praise* of God and his deeds: from what was probably the oldest hymn of Yahweh, who threw the Egyptian horses and chariots into the seas,[8] right up to the second Isaiah's songs of praise, promising liberation at the time of the Babylonian exile,[9] and both the psalms of praise by the people or individuals and the great hymns to God the Creator.

But is not this merely one side of the picture? Israel's and Jesus' understanding of God is not to be optimistically trivialized. There is no empty jubilation in the Old Testament. Besides praise there is always *complaint*. Modern man's anxieties about God—his absence, incomprehensibility, inactivity—are also to be found in the Old Testament. The suffering both of the nation and of the individual—that great counterargument against God and his goodness—is continually present and often cries to heaven. When the earliest Gospel gives us Jesus' last words to his God in the form of an inarticulate cry,[10] there is in it the echo of all the crying of a constantly suffering and oppressed and also guilt-laden people. They cried to God in Egypt when they scarcely knew him. The people cried to him and individuals cried, when they had settled in the promised land, then in the Babylonian exile and finally under the alien Roman power—in all possible situations of distress and sin.

The fact that one can cry to him in every situation amounts almost to a definition of this God. And where in ancient times has this cry been more challenging than in what is one of the great works of world literature, written between the fifth and second century B.C., the story of the completely isolated and wretched Job—counterpart of Jesus, the other suffering servant of God—incessantly torn hither and thither, suffering endlessly and without reason, between rebellion and submission? In him is manifested more acutely than anywhere else the basic attitude of the man of the Old Testament toward his God. This suffering, doubting, despairing man—so closely related to modern man in face of nihilism and atheism—does not find his ultimate support with the key of pure reason, attempting to solve the riddle of suffering and evil. He does not find it in psychological, philosophical or moral arguments, which seek to transform the darkness of suffering and evil into light and which again are too abstract and too general to provide much help in concrete suffering. Nor does he find it in the optimistic logic of a rational apologetic and "justification of God" (known as "theodicy" since the time of the great Leibniz) which seeks to satisfy curiosity and get behind God's mystery and world plan.

Suffering, doubting, despairing man finds his ultimate support only in the forthright admission of his inability to solve the riddle of suffering and evil. He is content to renounce any pretensions to be a neutral and presumably innocent censor passing judgment on God and his world. He decisively rejects even the slightest, inarticulate mistrust, any thought that the good God is not really good to man. Positively he relies on that certainly insecure and yet liberating venture of giving an *absolute and unreserved trust* simply and forthrightly to the incomprehensible God: in doubt, suffering and sin, in all mental distress and all physical pain, in all fear, anxiety, weakness, temptation, in all emptiness, comfortlessness, indignation. He clings to God even when utterly empty and burnt out, even in the most desperate situation, when all prayer dies out and no words come to his lips. This is a basic confidence of the most radical character, which does not superficially appease but encompasses and embraces anger and indignation and which also endures God's perpetual incomprehensibility.

Only by saying "Amen" ("So be it") explicitly or implicitly—despite everything—can suffering be endured if not explained. "Saying 'Amen'" is the translation of the Old Testament noun "belief" (*heemen*). The world with its enigma, its evil and suffering, can be affirmed because of God. Not otherwise. The mystery of the Incomprehensible in his goodness embraces also the misery of our suffering.

Is such an absolute and unshakable faith and trust really so easy? It is seen in a new light in the New Testament. Yet it remains true that this is the one God and this is faith in him as understood also by Jesus in the light of the dramatic history of his people, moving between complaint and praise, sin and pardon, decline and new beginning, anger and grace. This is God as he is attested in the most varied forms and modes of speech: in poetry and prose, in self-portrayals and historical narratives, legal statutes and cult rubrics, prophetic threats and promises, hymns and lamentations, sagas and legends, stories and parables, oracles, proverbs and theological propositions. All these different literary genres obviously bear the mark of their quite concrete "living situation" (*Sitz im Leben*) and were formed at a quite definite place: in the larger family circle, in worship or in legal practice, at court, in war or in the theological schools. However and wherever this may have come about, God is increasingly clearly attested as the one who is as he wills to be: the liberating Lord and Ruler of history, the legislator, the Creator of the world and finally its judge and finisher.

This nation however continually falls short of the claim of its God. *Mediators* appear continually at God's call, to act between God and his people. First comes Moses, followed by the charismatic leaders ("judges") of the people. Then the *prophets*, at the time of the institutionalized kingdom until the fall of the northern and later of the southern kingdom, the destruction of the temple and the exile to Babylon. Solitary, powerless, not getting a hearing and apparently unsuccessful, these prophets remain without followers and fail to carry with them an enthusiastic movement. The lamentations of the prophets from Elijah to Jeremiah provide abundant evidence of the loneliness, exhaustion, despair of the misunderstood and worn-out messengers of the one God. The tensions between their human weakness and the mandate imposed on them, between inability and obligation to speak, threaten to tear them apart.

Jesus belongs to the tradition of these prophets. In his time the spirit which the prophets had aroused was thought to be extinguished. People were expecting a new and final mediator in the person of the Messiah or Son of Man. At the same time, in Babylon, the second Isaiah was producing the astounding songs of the "Servant of God" whose vicarious suffering for the many—a feature not associated with any prophet—would lead to his death but would also be rewarded by God after death.[11]

Jesus did not want to found a new religion. Whenever he speaks of God's kingdom and God's will, he does so in the light of the Old Testament understanding of God. He no more provides a theoretical proof of the one God than the prophets did. Nor does he make God a moral "postulate." What he does is simply to take for granted the reality of God in practice and constantly to speak about him in new ways. He does not show the same hesitation as many Jews of his time about using the term "God," even though he does not avoid the use of other titles like "highest" or "king." When Jesus proclaims the message of the irrevocable closeness of God and his kingdom, he is not giving any new revelations of God's nature, any new concept of him. He does not reflect or reason on God's inner being. Like the Old Testament—but also like Buddha, Confucius, Muhammed—Jesus shows no interest in either a knowledge of nature or in metaphysical speculations. He does not bother about a theory of what God is "in himself" or about theological propositions on the divine essence and attributes. As we saw, Jesus speaks of God in parables: God for him is not the "object" of speculative, meditative or argumentative thinking in quest of a single origin and goal of all things, but the concrete partner of his trustful faith and devout obedience. The profession of faith in a Yahweh whom man is expected to love wholeheartedly is expressly confirmed by Jesus in the chief commandment.

This of course is the fundamental difference between the idea of God on the part of Israel and Jesus on the one hand and on the part of the great Asian and even Greek religions on the other. It may be worthwhile to reflect a little on these differences, even though the reader who is less interested in the history and philosophy of religion may perhaps prefer to pass over the following section.

The God with a human face

However much there is in the ideas of God in ancient Greece and in the Eastern religions—particularly in Buddhism, which in this respect is the religious opposite pole to Christianity—and however much can be learned from them, they remain inadequate. Even today the differences are important.

The God of Israel and Jesus is *different from the impersonal divinity of Eastern religions. Hinduism* and *Buddhism* also accept a supreme reality. And yet, at least at their higher levels of reflection, they are largely indifferent to a personal creator of the world. The supreme reality—Brahman—is above the god Brahma who, according to Brahmanic theology, created the world and glories in the fact.

This supreme reality is frequently understood—as in the classical Hindu philosophy of Sankhya—in a strictly monistic way, as an absolute unity of being. While atheism believes only in the world and not in God and normal theism in God and the world, so philosophically oriented Hinduism and Buddhism believe—supratheistically—only in God. This absolute, impersonal, one being here too however is by no means nothingness without content, but in fact pure being. And human qualities, even the noblest, are still too feeble and inadequate to serve as a way of describing it. Thus the absolute remains undefinable: it escapes any demarcation in a clearly outlined anthropomorphic concept. That is why there are a great number of truly religious standpoints, of approaches to the absolute, modes of worship.

While Jesus then promises entry into the kingdom of God and thus a personal and universal salvation, Hinduism and Buddhism promise entry into nirvana and thus extinction in an eternal repose without desire, without suffering, without consciousness. The original meaning of nirvana, according to Buddha himself, is difficult to understand exactly, but none of the Buddhist schools has understood it as nothingness. By contrast with the older Hinayana Buddhism, which understood nirvana more negatively as the removal of all suffering (and of rebirth) and as an indescribable, unknowable, unchangeable state, the more developed Mahayana Buddhism reaches a very much more positive definition of nirvana, which is now understood as absolute bliss. And even if here too we do not reach a world creator, world ruler, world finisher, we do find Buddha figures bringing salvation which are manifestations of the original Buddha. Indeed, in the influential Amithaba Buddhism—in Japan, as Amida Buddhism the most widespread form of Buddhism—there is mention even of a paradise of personal beatitude, of the "pure land," which we enter not by our own efforts as in the older Buddhism, but by trusting in the promise and power of Buddha, the Buddha of light and compassion.

The tension between a more personally oriented and a more impersonal religiosity therefore also pervades the history of Buddhism. But, even though nirvana has generally no cosmological function for Buddhism—the world is not God's world but has emerged through man's avarice and stupidity—"on the other hand, we are told that Nirvana is permanent, stable, imperishable, immovable, ageless, deathless, unborn and unbecome, that it is power, bliss and happiness, the secure refuge, the shelter, and the place of unassailable safety; that it is the real Truth and the supreme Reality; that it is the *Good*, the supreme goal and the one and only consummation of our life, the eternal, hidden and incomprehensible Peace. Similarly, the Buddha who is, as it were, the personal embodiment of nirvana, becomes the object of all those emotions which we are wont to call religious."[12]

A whole system of ritual and religious expressions is thus linked with an Absolute, rationally understood as such. What can scarcely be given logical expression functions in practice through the centuries. Thus both Buddhism and Hinduism also tolerate polytheism: all kinds of divinities are worshiped. In this way the personal factor, neglected in philosophically oriented religion, finds abundant expression in concrete religion.

On the other hand, all this raises serious questions also for *Christianity*: for instance, whether the Christian cult of saints does not in fact largely amount to the same thing as polytheism. But, more seriously, we must ask if God is rightly understood as personal at all, if he is rightly even called "person." Jesus does not use the term; it is never used of God in the Bible. Is it perhaps all-too-human? The Greek *prosopon* (Latin *persona*) means the mask worn by the actor, the role he plays—in a more general way, the visage. Whatever meaning this concept had for the theater in antiquity, it had little for ancient philosophy. It was only the early Christian doctrines of the Trinity and the Incarnation which gave it a new importance.

The controversy went on endlessly in Greek and Latin, becoming more and more confused in the process of interpreting the terms, as to whether and how far the concept of person (*persona, prosopon, hypostasis*)—now increasingly understood as intellectual individuality—can be applied to God. According to orthodox Trinitarian theology, as it finally came to prevail, God is not one person, but one nature in three persons (Father, Son, Spirit). On the other hand, Jesus Christ is one (divine) person in two natures (divine and human). But in recent years this terminology has become increasingly open to misunderstanding and even unintelligible. The reason for this is not least because "person" is no longer understood ontologically but mainly psychologically: person as self-consciousness and personality, the person as shaped by his behavior in the course of his history as an individual. In the light of all this "person," "personal," "personality," have acquired a variety of meanings. And the traditional teaching on the three persons in popular understanding has come to mean largely a doctrine of three gods (tritheism). We shall have to return to this point later.

We should therefore not quarrel about words, either with Hindus and Buddhists or with modern agnostics—or even with Christians. God is certainly not person as man is person: the All-embracing and All-pervading is never an object from which man can dissociate himself in order to make statements about it. The primal reason, primal support and primal meaning of all reality, who determines every individual existence, is not one individual person among other persons, is not simply a superman or a superego. And he is certainly not an infinite, still less a finite, *alongside* or *above* finite things. He is the infinite *in* all that is finite, being itself in all that is. Out of reverence for the divine mystery, the Eastern religions and a number of recent thinkers insist on this fact against all-too-human "theistic" ideas of God. Christian theologians too recognize it when they speak of God as the divinity, the supreme good, truth, goodness, love itself, being itself, sun, ocean. Even the most positive human attributes are in fact inadequate for God. Whenever they are affirmed, therefore, they need at the same time to be denied and to be translated into the infinite. God then cannot be confined even within the concept of person: God is *more than a person.*

This however also means that if the positive human attributes are affirmed in such a way that their finiteness is excluded and if they are raised to infinity, they can be predicated of God. Only in this way does the Absolute not remain for us a nothingness without content. And therefore we must also say that if God is more than a person, anyway *not less than a person*, God is not a "thing"; he is not transparent, controllable, open to manipulation; he is not impersonal, not sub-personal. Or are we to say that a God without mind and understanding, freedom and love, is still God? Would such a God be able to explain mind and understanding, freedom and love, in the world and in man? Would the God who gives meaning to persons not himself be personal? Is not the ancient Israelite saying true: "Should he who planted the ear not hear? Should he who formed the eye not see?"[13]

God is not an ultimate reality which is indifferent to us and leaves us indifferent, but one which involves us unconditionally, liberating us and making demands on us. An unemotional geometry of the universe, subject to the necessity of natural law, as discovered by the physicist or mathematician with the aid of his particular and limited methods, cannot explain the whole. God is more than a universal reason, more than a vast, anonymous consciousness, more than a self-thinking thought drawn in upon itself, more than the pure truth of the cosmos or the blind justice of history. God is not a neuter, but a God of men who provokes a decision of faith or unbelief: he is spirit, creative freedom, the primal identity of truth and love, a partner encompassing and establishing all interpersonal relationships. If, with the religious philosophies of East or West, we want to call him being itself, then he is being itself manifesting itself personally with an infinite claim and infinite understanding. It is better however—if we are concerned about words—to describe him, not as personal or impersonal, but as *transpersonal, superpersonal.*[14]

Whatever words we use, the decisive thing is that God is not below our level. Even though we can speak *of* God only with the aid of analogical concepts, metaphors, images, symbols, we can still speak *to* him appropriately in human terms. We need not place the ultimate reality before ourselves in thought, but we should place ourselves before it. Man should not be deprived of speech before him, but the very opposite: he should do what is typically human, get up and speak to God.

From the first to the last page of the Bible there is talk not only of and about God, but constantly also to and with God, praising and complaining, begging and protesting. From the first to the last page in the Bible—Feuerbach undoubtedly understood this correctly—God is subject and not predicate: love is not God, but God is love. From first to last the Bible means by God a true *partner*, friendly to man and absolutely reliable: not an object, not a silent infinite, not an empty unechoing universe, not an indefinable, nameless depth in a Gnostic sense, not a dark, indeterminate void interchangeable with nothingness, least of all an anonymous, interpersonal something which could easily be confused with man and his (so very fragile) love. No. Where others perceived only an infinite silence, Israel heard a voice. Israel was permitted to discover that the one God can be heard and addressed, that he comes among men as one who says "I" and makes himself "Thou" for them: a "Thou" who talks to them and to whom they can talk. And when man is addressed by this "Thou," he discovers in his own self a dignity which no secular humanism can guarantee: a dignity which cannot permit men ever to be misused as cannon fodder, as material for experiment or as fertilizer for evolution.

Despite all successive corrections of the understanding of God, on this point there is no process of development in the Bible. "Spiritualizing" here would mean volatilizing, would take away the concrete basis from genuine prayer and worship. No matter how God is spoken of in the Bible, mythologically or unmythologically, imaginatively or conceptually, prosaically or poetically, the relationship to God as an approachable partner, as a "Thou"—whether called a person or not—is a basic, constant factor of biblical faith in God which can never be abandoned, even though it must constantly be interpreted afresh.

The God with qualities

Jesus too speaks naturally of God and to God. And for him this God is not ambiguous, a "God without qualities": God is unequivocally good and not evil. Nor has he any evil principle in competition with himself. Satan, emerging under Persian influence in early Jewish times, is quite clearly subordinated to him. God is not indifferent, but friendly to man. Jesus calls him good, alone good, merciful. But these qualities do not play any part as objective predicates. They are qualities of his activity for man and the world: they make God what he is, not intrinsically or independently, but for man and world, they explain how he acts on man and world. They are predicates, not of a being "in itself," but of his relationship to us. It is only in God's acts that his actuality is revealed: in action on man and world, so that to speak of God we must speak simultaneously of man.

For Jesus God does not merely act in a "supernatural" sphere, but rules in the midst of the world and provides for the great and small world of man. God's care thus renders superfluous man's anxious preoccupation with himself. Jesus does not reach God by a process of reasoning from the world, but sees the whole world in God's light, sees there a likeness which directs us simultaneously to its creator and finisher. The world is thus understood—without reference to causality or a concept of nature—in such a way that we can live in it in practice under the guidance of God's word, as it has been heard in history: the word which leads us to understand the world as God's, good in itself but spoilt by man.[15]

a. The God of Israel and of Jesus is *different from the remote God of classical Greek philosophy*. But he is certainly not close in the sense that God was close for the early Greek thinkers, the divinity directly present in the world as its origin and formative principle. Nor is he like the later Stoic divinity, pantheistically identified with the world. He does not belong simply to the world, he is not part of the world: neither as the natural ground of the world nor as world force or world law. He is not merely form, figure and order of reality. He is and remains the wholly Other.

Distinct as he is from the world, the God of Israel and of Jesus is not separated from the world like the God of classical Greek philosophy, which left such a mark on Christian theology. He is not like *Plato*'s idea of the good (and the world of ideas as a whole), which is separated by a sharp cleavage from the phenomenal, unreal world of sense and of evil matter, so that there is inevitably a fatal hostility to matter and the body. Nor is he like the God of *Aristotle*, who lives eternally apart from the world as a thinking thought which thinks only itself, neither knows nor loves the world, without causal efficiency, providence or moral authority. Nor, finally, is he like *Plotinus*' divine One, existing separately from that world which has emanated from its original unity and is therefore in decline: this is matter as evil, from which man must liberate himself.

Despite his distinction from man and the world, the *God of Israel and Jesus* is not remote, but *close*. He appears above all as creative will. He is the powerful and continually effective creator of the world, creating the world by his will as good and—as later Judaism consistently developed the idea—out of nothing. He is the sovereign lord of man, expecting obedience from his creature, good in itself but spoilt by its own evil will, from man in his wholeness without distinction between mind and sense. He is the wise lord of history, guiding the history of his people and of mankind as a whole from the beginning toward a goal: not arbitrarily, but according to his plan, so that every detail, even suffering and death, acquires its place and meaning in a history of salvation which speaks to man and provides him with both instruction and warning. Finally, he is the just judge who brings world history to its end, passes judgment and establishes his kingdom. All this is presented in the Old Testament, not in the form of a cosmological or theological theory, but of a historical narrative or—better—narratives, not intended to give man philosophical insights, but to make him aware of his utter dependence on God and rouse in him the courage to believe.

This God then is here *and* hereafter, distant *and* near, above the world *and* within the world, future *and* present. God is oriented to the world: there is no God without a world. And the world is wholly ordered to God: there is no world without God. The contradiction therefore is not, as with the Greeks, between a spiritual God and a material world as such, but between God and the sinful world turned away from him. And redemption is not expected as the overcoming of the Platonic dualism of God and world, spirit and matter, but as liberation of the world from sin, misery, death, and as fellowship with God.

b. The God of Israel and of Jesus is *different from the apathetic divinity of classical Greek philosophy*. Certainly he is not moved in the sense understood, for instance, by the early Greek thinker Heraclitus: a God coming to be, as world soul and world reason permeating like a living fire the eternally flowing universe, its conflicting elements and all its enigmatic and ambiguous phenomena. Nor is he moved in the way described in myth: like those human—all-too-human—Homeric gods in conflict with each other, who were subjected to severe criticism particularly by Xenophanes and Plato.

Yet, for all his constancy, permanence and identity with himself, the God of Israel and of Jesus is not unmoved in the same way as that God of classical philosophy which emerged out of the reaction against mythology and the philosophy of becoming and which was far too often a model for Christian theology. He is not unmoved in the same way as *Plato*'s sun (conceived under the influence of Parmenides, the antipode of Heraclitus), intelligible, existing outside history, outside space and time: the supreme idea of the Good, enthroned above the hierarchy of the eternal-unchangeable world of ideas, which is self-sufficient as an eternal, absolutely unmoving and unchangeable first principle. He is not unmoved in the same way as *Aristotle*'s divine mind: the unmoved first mover who is so rigidly immobile and immutable that he knows only himself and cannot sustain any action in regard to others. Nor is he unmoved like the One of *Plotinus* which, as supreme being in a system of emanating and diversified grades of being, itself remains fixed in absolutely rigid immutability, so that it cannot be regarded as living at all. With this classical triple constellation of philosophy then God not only does not come to be or perish, but he is absolutely immobile and immutable: qualities which Parmenides in opposition to Heraclitus ascribed, not indeed to God, but certainly to being as such.

Despite the fact that the *God of Israel and of Jesus* never comes to be nor perishes, he by no means appears as immobile and immutable, but as a *living* God. We must not be deceived by the Bible's often naïve, mythological, anthropomorphic, human modes of speech. It is not simply a question of a more primitive, retarded understanding of God. Certainly there is a tendency to spiritualize God even in the Old Testament and the Septuagint in particular—the old Greek translation—reinterpreted the primitive text in an attempt to modify or even eliminate as far as possible certain anthropomorphic, human-style statements. But the parts which contain anthropomorphisms do not by any means belong only to the strata of a more primitive tradition, as it was once assumed. They are found also in the later prophets. They are signs, not of an undeveloped, childish way of thinking, but of a very precise and in its way mature thinking.

This God of Israel and of Jesus is neither an elemental first principle nor a metaphysical reality, neither a dumb force nor an anonymous power. He is the living Creator-God. He is certainly not an all-too-human God with playful moods, but a God of freedom who makes possible and guides world and history, knows them, loves them and makes them good, down to the smallest detail.

His *eternity* must not be understood as Platonic timelessness, but as powerfully living simultaneity with all time;

his *ubiquity* is not inactive extension in the universe, but sovereign dominion over all space;

his *spirituality* is not exclusive opposition to matter which is regarded as evil, but power infinitely superior to all created things;

his *goodness* toward the world and men is not a natural radiation of the good, but freely loving, gracious attention;

his *immutability* is not a rigid, elemental, dead immobility, but essential fidelity to himself in all his abounding life;

his *justice* is not a distribution of rewards and reprisals based on a timeless idea of order, but a merciful, salvation-creating justice, rooted in fidelity to the covenant with men;

his *incomprehensibility* is not the abstract lack of qualities of a nameless "whence" of our uncertain existence, but the otherness, uncontrollability, unforeseeability which are demonstrated in his action.

These predicates, deduced by the Greeks by a process of reasoning from the existing world, are therefore not irrationally rejected in the Bible but concretely surpassed. God is more than the superlative of human nature and human possibilities.

God therefore should not be conceived as an abstract idea remote from man, but as concrete reality which is by no means indifferent to him but absolutely involves him and imposes claims on him. He is not a God who remains immovable in (or outside) a moving world, but the God who acts within the scope of human history, makes himself known in human happenings, reveals himself in a human way, makes possible encounter, conversation, association, with himself. He is then not a God who keeps out of everything and remains exalted in a transcendence untouched by the world's suffering, but one who actively takes part and becomes involved in this somber history. He is not a God of solitude, but a God of partnership, of the covenant. He is not an apathetic, unfeeling, impassible, but a sympathetic, compassionate God. In brief, he is a *God with a human face.*

All Yahweh's words and deeds, recorded in the Old Testament from Genesis onward, show that this God is the very opposite of apathetic. He is a God who speaks, commands, promises, rages, seeks, concedes, forgives. He is a God who feels joy and sadness, pleasure and horror, love and anger, zeal and hatred, revenge and repentance; who makes demands and practices clemency, who can permit himself to repent but also to repent of his repentance. Even the attributes he possesses *negatively* are not to be understood in a primitive sense as human, all-too-human passions and feelings.

God's *jealousy* is not the result of envy and fear, but the expression of his uniqueness which permits no other gods beside himself, the consequence of the will of him who insists absolutely on his directives for man's good.

God's *anger* (hatred, horror, revenge) is not an irrational outburst, not a selfish inappeasability, but the other side of his love, of his holy will, the expression—that is—of his aversion from all that is evil and of his displeasure in the sinner.

God's *repentance* is not the consequence of ignorance and later insight, but a sign of the fact that man is not subject to an unalterable fate, that human history for God is not an empty, indifferent spectacle, that God does not persist unchanged in face of changed circumstances and does not show his pleasure or displeasure blindly and arbitrarily but justly.

All these *anthropomorphisms*[16] are by no means meant simply to reduce God to man's state. God must remain God. The fact is also stressed in the Old Testament that God is not man and does not have to repent. But the anthropomorphisms are meant to bring the living God closer to man. They are intended to bring out and preserve genuinely human feeling, thinking, willing, in regard to God. They are meant to provoke genuinely human listening, responding, questioning, trusting, obeying, praying, praising, thanking. Abstract philosophical definitions of the divine nature leave man cold. The divine being in all its passionate agitation must enter into man's consciousness, so that he can encounter God as intensely and concretely as he encounters another human being: a face that lights up as we approach, a hand that guides us. But what finer, greater, deeper images, codes, symbols, ideas, concepts, than these human ones has man at his disposal in order to find his way to God—as explained—affirming, denying, transcending? Only in this way does God appear as more than merely the ultimate cause of all that happens, as a power, that is, which determines man in his whole concrete reality.

It has now become very much clearer that the *God of the philosophers* and the *God of Israel and of Jesus* cannot be brought into a superficial harmony.[17] As opposed to all "natural theology," Pascal, Kierkegaard and Karl Barth had the right view of this. But, as the great Catholic tradition has always rightly held as against "dialectical theology," neither is the distinction perfectly simple. The relationship must in fact be seen in a genuinely dialectical way: the "God of the philosophers" is—in the best Hegelian sense of the term—"canceled-and-preserved" (*aufgehoben*)* positively, negatively and supereminently in the "God of Israel and of Jesus."

What is important today therefore, when we attempt to understand Jesus and his God, is to take seriously both the modern development of the understanding of God and the decisive element of the biblical faith in God in a new understanding of *God's historicity*.[18] This is a God who is a living God in contrast to a God existing in an unhistorical way—a superearthly ruler of the world or a supratemporal steersman of history—who *has and founds a history* and is demonstrated to the world and man as *primal historicity* and *power over history*. This then is an understanding of God which does not dwell on biblical terminology in order to pass over the conclusions of Greek and modern philosophy. Nevertheless, it does not postulate an abstract God of which we would have to complain with Heidegger: "This is a God to whom man can neither pray nor offer sacrifice. Before the *causa sui* man cannot fall on his knees in awe, nor can he sing and dance before this God."[19]

Revolution in the understanding of God

The knowledge of the one, sole God emerged from Israel's history, from the experiences of men who heard his voice and addressed him in their answers and questions, prayers and curses. There was never (nor is there today between Jews and Christians) any need to dispute the fact that this God is close to us, a living God with a human face. It might even be said that Jesus merely grasped Israel's understanding of God in its purest form and in all its consequences. Is this all?

* Cf. G. R. G. Mure, *An Introduction to Hegel*, Oxford University Press, 1940, p. 135. (Translator.)

Certainly Jesus' originality must not be exaggerated: this is important in discussion with Jews today. People have often assumed and still assume that Jesus was the first to call God "Father" and men his children. As if God had not been called "Father" in the most diverse religions, even by the Greeks whom we have just mentioned: as far back as Homer's epics there are genealogies in which Zeus, son of Chronos, appears as father of the family of gods. In Stoic philosophy the notion of God was elucidated in cosmological terms: the divinity was regarded as the father of the reason-permeated cosmos and of the children of men, endowed with reason, who were related to him and cared for by him.

It is however this very evidence from the history of religion which makes clear how *problematic is the use of the name "Father"* as applied to God, particularly in the age of women's emancipation. Should we without more ado apply to God a name implying sexual differentiation? Is God a man, masculine, virile? Are we not making God in the image of man, to be more exact of a male human being? In the history of religion the gods appear generally as sexually differentiated, although perhaps at the beginning there were bisexual or sexually neutral beings and even later they continue to display features of both sexes. But there is food for thought in the fact that the "Great Mother" in matriarchal cultures, from whose womb all things in all their variety emerged and to which they return, takes the place of the Father-God. The question is still debated among historians, but if matriarchy turns out to be older than patriarchy, the cult of the Mother-Goddess—which in Asia Minor, for example, had some influence on the later cult of Mary—would have preceded chronologically that of the Father-God.

However this historical question is decided, the designation of God as Father is not determined solely by Yahweh's uniqueness. It appears to be also sociologically conditioned, bearing the imprint of a male-oriented society. In any case God is not forthrightly male. Even in the Old Testament, in the prophetical books, God has also feminine, maternal features. But, from the modern standpoint, a clearer view is necessary. The designation "Father" will be misunderstood unless it is regarded, not in contrast to "Mother," but symbolically (analogously): "Father" as patriarchal symbol —also with matriarchal features—of a transhuman, transsexual ultimate reality. Today less than ever may the one God be seen merely within a masculine-paternal framework, as an all-too-masculine theology used to present him. The feminine-maternal element in him must also be recognized. To address God as Father can then no longer be used as the religious justification of a social paternalism at the expense of woman or in particular for the permanent suppression of the feminine element in the Church (or ministry).[20]

God appears in the Old Testament differently from the way in which he appears in other religions. He is not the physical father of gods, demigods and heroes. But neither is he simply the father of all men. Yahweh is the father of the people of Israel, which is called God's first-born son.[21] He is especially the father of the king and the latter is regarded as pre-eminently God's son: "You are my son, today I have begotten you."[22] This is a "decree of Yahweh" when someone succeeds to the throne and means, not a miraculous earthly begetting, but the installation of the king taking over his rights as son. In later Judaism it is promised that God will be the father of the devout individual[23] and of the chosen people of the end-time: "They will observe my commandments, and I shall be their father and they will be my children."[24] It is clear from all this that the father symbol in its indispensable positive aspects has no sexual implications and has nothing to do with religious paternalism: it is an expression signifying power, but at the same time closeness, protection, care.

At this point however important differences appear in *Jesus'* way of speaking about the Father. A number of sayings of Jesus, as recorded, could in themselves be paralleled in the wisdom literature. As so often, it is difficult to prove positively that they are sayings of Jesus himself. But, whether they are Jesus' own words or not, they acquire their special tone from the whole context. In the first place, it is striking that Jesus never connects God's fatherhood with the people as such. For him, as for John the Baptist, membership of the chosen people is no guarantee of salvation. Still more striking is the fact that Jesus, quite unlike John, relates this fatherhood to the wicked and unrighteous and in the light of this perfect fatherhood of God justifies that love of enemies which is so typical of his teaching.[25] What is going on here?

Certainly references to the Father always point first of all to God's active providence and care for all things: he is concerned about every sparrow and every hair on our heads,[26] knows our needs before we ask him,[27] makes our anxieties seem superfluous.[28] He is the Father who knows about everything in this utterly unredeemed world and without whom nothing happens: the practical answer to the question of theodicy about life's riddles, suffering, injustice, death, in the world. He is a God whom we can absolutely trust, on whom we can wholly rely even in suffering, injustice, sin and death. He is not a God at an ominous, transcendent distance, but close in incomprehensible goodness. He is a God who does not make empty promises for the hereafter nor trivialize the present darkness, futility and meaninglessness, but who himself in the midst of darkness, futility and meaninglessness invites us to the venture of hope.

But more than this is involved. What breaks through here is the same as what is so incomparably portrayed in that parable where the main figure is not the son, nor the sons, but the father. This is the father who lets his son go freely, without fuss, without chasing or following him, but then runs toward him on his return from exile, seeing him first and interrupting his admission of guilt, accepts him without demanding an explanation, a period of probation or preliminary conditions, and provides a great feast—to the scandal of the upright son who remained at home.[29]

What then is meant here by "father"? Evidently, not only that we misunderstand God if we think we have to protect our freedom from him; not only that God's rule and man's activity, theonomy and autonomy are not mutually exclusive; not only that the problem—so much discussed by theologians—of the reconciliation of divine predestination and human freedom, of the *concursus* of the divine and the human will, is not a real problem. It meant just what this "friend of tax collectors and sinners," who thought he had to seek and to save the abandoned and the disreputable, also expressed in other parables: speaking of God—as we have seen—as the woman(!) or the shepherd, rejoicing at finding what had been lost, as the magnanimous king, the generous lender, the gracious judge. As a result he got himself mixed up with moral failures, irreligious and immoral people, gave them preferential treatment and even assured them of forgiveness on the spot. What does all this mean if not that Jesus presents God quite expressly as father of the "prodigal son," as *Father of the abandoned?*

This then for Jesus is the one true God, beside whom there can be no other gods, however holy. This is the God of the Old Testament—better understood. He is a God who is evidently more than the supreme guarantor of a law to be accepted without question, even though it can perhaps be adroitly manipulated. He is a God who is also more than that omniscient being, dictating and centrally directing everything from above, who strives relentlessly to achieve his plans, even by "holy wars" on a great or small scale and by the eternal damnation of his opponents. This Father-God is nothing like the God feared by Marx, Nietzsche and Freud, terrifying man from childhood onward into feelings of anxiety and guilt, constantly moralizingly pursuing him: a God who is in fact only the projection of instilled fears, of human domination, lust for power, arrogance and vindictiveness. This Father-God is not a theocratic God who might serve as an excuse—if only indirectly—for the representatives of totalitarian systems, whether pious-ecclesiastical or impious-atheistic, who attempt to take his place and exercise his sovereign rights. These men become holy or unholy gods of orthodox teaching and absolute discipline, of law and order, of dictatorship and planning, regardless of the claims of other human beings.

No. This Father-God is a God who meets men as a God of redeeming love. He is not the all-too-masculine God of arbitrary power or law. He is not the God created in the image of kings and tyrants, of hierarchs and schoolmasters. But he is the good God—it is difficult to find less trite formulas—who identifies himself with men, with their needs and hopes. He does not demand but gives, does not oppress but raises up, does not wound but heals. He spares those who impugn his holy law and thus attack himself. He forgives instead of condemning, liberates instead of punishing, permits the unrestricted rule of grace instead of law. He is therefore the God who turns, not to the righteous, but to the unrighteous. The God who prefers the sinner: the prodigal to the one who stayed at home, the tax collector to the Pharisee, the heretics to the orthodox, the prostitutes and adulterers to their judges, the lawbreakers and outlaws to the guardians of the law.

Can it still be said that the name of father, as used here, merely echoes our experience of fatherhood in this world? Is it a projection which simply serves to transfigure the circumstances of earthly fatherhood and dominion? No. *This* Father-God is different. He is not a God of the hereafter at the expense of the here and now, at the expense of man (Feuerbach). He is not a God of the ruling classes, of empty promises and a distorted consciousness (Marx). Not the product of resentment, not the guardian of the wretched loafers' morality of good and evil (Nietzsche). Not a tyrannical superego, the product of wishful thinking based on the illusory needs of early childhood, a god of compulsive ritual arising out of a guilt and father complex (Freud).

In order to justify his scandalous talk and behavior, Jesus appeals to a very different God and Father: a unique, even dangerous, a really impossible God. Can we actually take all this? That God himself justifies infringements of the law? That he ruthlessly sets himself above the righteousness of the law and has a "higher righteousness" proclaimed? That he himself therefore permits the existing legal order and thus the whole social system—even the temple and all divine worship—to be called in question? That he himself makes man the measure of his commandments; through forgiveness, service, renunciation, through love, cancels the natural frontiers between comrades and non-comrades, strangers and neighbors, friends and enemies, good and bad, and thus places himself on the side of the weak, sick, poor, underprivileged, oppressed, and even of the irreligious, immoral and godless? This would certainly be a new God: a God who has set himself free from his own law, a God not of the devout observers of the law but of the lawbreakers, in fact—we must speak hyperbolically in order to bring out the contradictions and the scandal—not a God of God-fearers, but a *God of the godless*. This would be a truly unparalleled *revolution in the understanding of God*.

There seems here to be a "revolt against God," not indeed in the sense of ancient or modern atheism, but certainly a revolt against the God of devout believers. Can we in fact assume, may we really believe that God himself, the true God, is behind such an unprecedented innovator, someone who is more revolutionary than all the revolutionaries, setting himself above law and temple, above Moses, king and prophet, even making himself judge over sin and forgiveness? Would God not be contradicting himself if he had such an *advocate*? Could such a person rightly claim God's authority and will against God's law and temple? Could he rightly assume authority for such talk and action? Could there be a God of the godless, with a blasphemer as his prophet?

Not an obvious form of address

Jesus never tires of attempting by every means to make it clear that God really is like this, that he really is the Father of the abandoned, really a God of the moral failures and the godless. Should not this be an enormous liberation for all who are burdened with troubles and sin? Should it not be an occasion of joy and hope for all? It is not a new God that he proclaims: now as always it is the God of the Covenant. But it is this old God of the Covenant in a decidedly new light. This is not *another* God, but he is *different*. He is not a God of law, but a God of grace. And, retrospectively, in the light of the God of grace even the God of law can be better, more profoundly and in fact more graciously understood: the law itself as expression of grace.

All this of course is not obvious to man. A rethinking with all its consequences is required, a really new awareness, a true inner conversion, founded on that unswerving confidence which is called faith. Jesus' whole message is a single appeal not to be worried but to be converted: to rely on his word and trust the God of grace. His word is the sole guarantee given to men that God really is like this. Anyone who does not believe this word will suspect that his deeds are the work of devils. Without his word, his deeds remain equivocal. Only his word makes them unequivocal.

Anyone however who commits himself to Jesus' message and fellowship becomes aware in Jesus who it was whom he addressed as "my Father." With the use of "Father" as he understood the term (not in contrast to "mother") he got to the heart of the whole dispute. The linguistic evidence provides a notable confirmation of this.[30]

With the great abundance of ways of addressing God at the disposal of ancient Judaism, it is surprising that Jesus chose just this form of "my Father." Isolated statements about God as Father are found in the Hebrew Old Testament.[31] But up to now it has not been possible anywhere in the literature of ancient Palestinian Judaism to point to the personal Hebrew form of addressing God as "my Father." Only in the Hellenistic field, certainly under Greek influence, is there some slight evidence of addressing God with the Greek *pater*.

The evidence however of the use of the Aramaic form, *abba*, for "Father" is more extraordinary. It seems from the available testimonies[32] that Jesus constantly addressed God as *abba*. Only in this way can the subsequent usage—even in Greek-speaking communities—of this unusual Aramaic form of addressing God be explained.[33] On the other hand in all the extensive literature of prayer—both liturgical and personal—in Judaism from ancient times up to the Middle Ages there is not a single example of the use of *abba* as a form of addressing God. How is this to be explained? Hitherto only one explanation has been found: *abba*—like our "Daddy"—is originally a child's word, used however in Jesus' time also as a form of address to their father by grown-up sons and daughters and as an expression of politeness generally to older persons deserving of respect. But to use this not particularly manly expression of tenderness, drawn from the child's vocabulary, this commonplace term of politeness, to use this as a form of addressing God, must have struck Jesus' contemporaries as irreverent and offensively familiar, very much as if we were to address God today as "Dad."

For Jesus however this expression is no more lacking in respect than it is when used as the child's familiar way of addressing his father. For familiarity does not exclude respect. Reverence remains the basis of his understanding of God. But not its center. Just as a child addresses its earthly father, so according to Jesus should man address his heavenly Father: reverently, ready to obey, but above all securely and confidently. Jesus teaches his disciples also to address God with this confidence, which includes reverence: "Our Father in the heavens."[84] To address God as "Father" is the boldest and simplest expression of that absolute trust with which we trust in God for good, for all good, with which we trust him and trust ourselves to him.

The Our Father is a prayer of petition wholly expressed in the non-sacral language of everyday life which has reached us in two versions, one shorter[85] and one longer.[86] There is no insistence on the exact words and no compulsion to use a particular form. It involves no sort of mystical immersion or purification, and certainly it makes no claim to reward (except on condition of one's own readiness to forgive).[87] It is easy to find parallels to the individual petitions in Jewish prayers: for instance, in the Eighteen Benedictions. But as a whole the Our Father in its brevity, precision and straightforwardness is quite unique. It is a new, non-sacral prayer, not in the sacred, Hebrew language, but in the Aramaic vernacular, without the customary ritual addresses and obeisances to God. It is a very personal prayer which nevertheless brings those praying closely together in the opening words: "Our Father." It is a very simple prayer of petition, but wholly concentrated on essentials, on God's cause (that his name be kept holy, his kingdom come, his will be done) which appears to be inextricably linked with man's cause (his bodily needs, his sin, temptation and the power of evil).

All this provides an exemplary realization of what Jesus said about verbose prayer: not to want to get a hearing by babbling on as if the Father did not already know what we need.[88] We are not asked to omit the prayer of petition and restrict ourselves—as the Stoics concluded from

God's omniscience and omnipotence—to praising and glorifying God. We are invited to insist tirelessly, conscious of God's closeness, in unswerving confidence, in a wholly human way, on our needs, like the importunate friend in the night,[39] like the undaunted widow before the judge.[40] The question of unheard prayer never occurs: a hearing is assured.[41] If it seems that prayer has not been heard, this should lead not to silence but to renewed petition: always however assuming that his will, not ours, should be done.[42] Here lies the mystery of prayer being heard.

Jesus recommended prayer far away from the public gaze, even in the seclusion of an ordinary storeroom.[43] Jesus himself prayed in this way. Even if most of the texts on this scheme in the Synoptic Gospels are Luke's redactional additions to Mark's Gospel,[44] the latter does relate that Jesus prayed for hours in solitude outside the times set for liturgical prayer.[45] Jesus himself gave thanks. Even if the authenticity of the Johannine-sounding conclusion on the mutual knowledge of Father and Son is disputed, there can be little doubt about the immediately preceding prayer of thanksgiving, praising the Father—despite all setbacks—for concealing "these things" from the wise and prudent and revealing them to the infants, the uneducated, the unimportant and unassuming people.[46]

At this point however a new and surprising feature can be observed. Jesus frequently speaks of "my Father" (in heaven) and then of "your Father." But nowhere in the Gospels is there a single passage in which Jesus associates himself with his disciples in an "our Father." Is this fundamental *distinction between "my" and "your" Father* the Christological style of the community?[47] It is at least just as possible to assume that this particular linguistic usage is so constant in the whole of the New Testament because —as the Gospels clearly imply—it was characteristic of Jesus himself: as the expression of his mission.[48] It would be going too far if we were to take the one enigmatic logion of Matthew 11:27 (and par.), with its Johannine overtones (no one has yet explained how this "thunderbolt from the Johannine sky" could have fallen into the Synopsis), as indicating a unique revelatory event (presumably at Jesus' baptism), even if it is very freely translated: "My Father has given me all things (=the full revelation). *Just as* only a father knows his son, *so* only a son (really) knows his father and anyone to whom the son chooses to reveal him."[49] But, on the other hand, can it be denied that Jesus' whole message of God's kingdom and will is oriented to God as to the "Father"?

In view of the familiar usage of the word, we should not read too much into *abba* as a form of addressing God. Jesus certainly never designated himself simply as "the Son." Indeed he absolutely and directly rejected a direct identification with God, a deification: "Why do you call me good? No one is good but God alone."[50] But on the other hand he never said, like the Old Testament prophets: "It is the Lord who speaks" or "the word of Yahweh." Instead he speaks with an emphatic "I" or even "But I say to you"—which are without parallels in the Jewish world of his time and are rightly attributed to the pre-paschal Jesus. On the basis of the sources, is it possible to deny that this herald of the Father-God lived and worked in virtue of an unusual intimacy with him? Can we deny that his message of God's kingdom and will was sustained by a special experience of God? Are his tremendous claim, his supreme certainty and natural directness conceivable without a very singular immediacy to God, his Father and our Father?

Evidently Jesus is *God's advocate* not only in an external legal sense, not only a deputy, agent or attorney for God. But he is an advocate in a deeply intimate-existential sense, a personal ambassador, trustee, confidant, friend of God. In him, without any compulsion, but inescapably and immediately, man was confronted with that ultimate reality which challenges him to decide what he is ultimately seeking, where he is ultimately going. Jesus seems to be driven on by this ultimate reality in all his life and action: in regard to the religio-political system and its upper stratum, in regard to law, cult and hierarchy, in regard to institution and tradition, family bonds and party ties; but also in regard to the victims of this system, people of all kinds who were suffering, thrust aside, downtrodden, involved in sin and failure, whom he defended with compassion.

His life seems to be pervaded by this ultimate reality: when he proclaims God as Father, when he rises above the religious fears and prejudices of his time, when he identifies himself with the people who are ignorant of religion. It is the same when he refuses to treat the sick as sinners or to see God the Father suspected as an enemy to life, when he liberates the possessed from psychical compulsions and breaks through the vicious circle of mental disturbance, belief in devils and social ostracism. He seems to live wholly and entirely in virtue of this reality: when he proclaims the rule of this God and does not simply accept the circumstances of human dominion, when he will not have women abandoned in marriage to the whims of men, when he defends children against adults, poor against rich, small people as a whole against great. It is again the same when he defends even people with a different religion, those who are politically compromised, the moral failures, the sexually exploited, those forced to the edge of society, and assures them of forgiveness. Living then by this reality he makes himself accessible to all groups and does not simply accept what the representatives of official religion and their experts declare to be infallibly true or false, good or bad.

It is therefore in this ultimate reality—which he calls God, his Father and our Father—that his basic attitude is rooted, an attitude which can be described in one word: his *freedom*, which is infectious and opens up for the individual and for society in their one-dimensionality a *really different dimension*, a real alternative with different values, norms and ideals. It means a truly qualitative ascent to a new awareness, to a new goal and way of life and so also to a new society in freedom and justice.

This question of Jesus' relationship to his Father brings us to the ultimate mystery of Jesus. The sources give us no insight into his mind and soul. Neither psychology nor mental philosophy are of any use here. This much however may be said: although Jesus himself did not expressly claim the title of "Son" and although a post-paschal Son of God Christology cannot be imposed on the pre-paschal texts, the fact cannot be overlooked that the post-paschal designation of Jesus as "Son of God" has a real foundation in the pre-paschal Jesus. In all his proclamation and behavior Jesus was interpreting *God*. But, seen from the standpoint of this God whom he proclaimed so differently, was not *Jesus* himself bound to appear in a different light? Anyone who commits himself to Jesus with unswerving trust finds that what he has hitherto understood as "God" is changed in an unsuspected and liberating way. But if anyone commits himself through Jesus to this God and Father, must not that person too be changed whom he has hitherto known as "Jesus"?

There it is. The peculiarly new proclaiming and addressing of God as Father also threw a new light on the person who proclaimed and addressed him in this peculiarly new way. And, as it was impossible even then to speak of Jesus without speaking of this God and Father, so it was difficult subsequently to speak of this God and Father without speaking of Jesus. When it was a question of the one true God, the decision of faith was centered, not on particular names and titles, but on this Jesus. The way in which someone came to terms with Jesus decided how he stood with God, what he made of God, what God he had. Jesus spoke and acted in the name and the power of the one God of Israel. And for this God finally he let himself be slain.

3. *The end*

On almost all important questions—marriage, family, nation, relations with authority, dealings with other individuals and with groups—Jesus' ideas were different from those commonly accepted. The conflict about the system, law and order, cult and customs, ideology and practice, the prevailing norms, limits to be respected and people to be avoided; the dispute about the official God of the law, the temple, the nation, and about Jesus' claim: all this had to be brought to an end. It had to be made clear who was right. It was now a conflict of life and death. The fighter who had been so challenging in his magnanimity, spontaneity and freedom now became a silent sufferer.

In face of death

From the very beginning all the Gospels are marked by a foreboding of death. Was this due to a post-paschal tendency to turn the history into a history of suffering? As against the former imaginative historicizing and psychologizing study of the life of Jesus, there is now agreement on one point. Jesus did not enjoy a "Galilean spring," filled with success, before the catastrophe in Jerusalem. Any sort of "spring romanticism" would have been disturbed by the determination of his opponents to have him put to death, which is recorded at the very beginning of the earliest Gospel.[1] But the temptation stories, recorded at the beginning of the Gospels, also make it clear that Jesus' life and activity were never free from temptations, tribulations and doubts.

Moreover, it has been discovered that the temporal and geographical framework[2] even of Mark's Gospel—activity in Galilee, starting out from Capernaum, brief stay in pagan country, Peter's confession and the beginning of the road to Jerusalem, entry, stay and Passion—has a literary function and the details cannot be taken *a priori* as historical. Most of the narratives can be switched around, as can be seen from the slightly different arrangement in Mark and Luke. Peter's confession cannot be taken as historically certain, nor can the temporary flight from Herod Antipas into the area of Tyre in Phoenicia, northwards into the neighborhood of Caesarea-Philippi and into the "Decapolis" under direct Roman military administration, on the far side of the lake of Gennesaret (near the present-day Golan Heights). Of course an unrecorded journey through pagan territory cannot be excluded. There is however no doubt that Galilee was the main center of Jesus' activity and that the turning point in his life came when he went up to Jerusalem (once only, according to the Synoptics). The Gospel account that Jesus experienced from the very beginning approval and rejection, strong support and bitter hostility, can also be regarded as historically accurate.

If Jesus wanted to announce his message to the whole nation, he had to establish himself above all in the religious center: in Israel's city of destiny, the holy city of God and the city of the great king.[3] Here at the last hour the nation was to be confronted with the message of God's kingdom and will. As Luke frequently reports,[4] the disciples hoped that the journey to Jerusalem would lead to the appearance of the kingdom of God. Here then the decision had to take place.

The suggestion that Jesus went to Jerusalem only in order to die there could be a later interpretation. This holds also for the ancient Palestinian Judaeo-Christian *announcement of the suffering and resurrection* of the "Son of Man," repeated three times in Mark,[5] the third announcement amounting to a veritable summary of the Passion and resurrection. Distributed deliberately over the story in the course of the redaction, they are meant to give expression to God's mysterious plan, to Jesus' wonderful foreknowledge and finally to his voluntary suffering and his obedience to Scripture. In the style of Jewish apocalyptic, they are *vaticinia ex eventu:* prophecies constructed on the basis of their fulfillment, formulated after and in the light of the events. The technical term is used for a literary genre which occurs frequently in the Old Testament and in ancient literature generally. These announcements are aids to proclamation, to the *kerygma,* and therefore are not prophecies or predictions in the strict sense. They are "kerygmatic formulas" which enable Jesus' way of the cross to be seen as the fulfillment of God's plan of salvation and not the consequence of blind fate. They are not sagacious prognoses by Jesus himself, but interpretations of the Passion by post-paschal Christendom.

Does this mean that Jesus never thought that he might lose his life? This is a different question. Would he have been so naïve as not to have had any presentiment of what finally happened to him? A Christological interest must be allowed for everywhere in the Gospels, but historical skepticism can become uncritical. No supernatural knowledge was required to recognize the *danger of a violent end,* only a sober view of reality. His radical message raised doubts about the pious self-reliance of individuals and of society and about the traditional religious system as a whole and created opposition from the very beginning. Consequently Jesus was bound to expect serious conflicts and violent reactions on the part of the religious and perhaps also the political authorities, particularly at the center of power. Accusations of infringing the Sabbath, contempt for the law, blasphemy, had to be taken seriously. The move of the heretical "prophet" from the province to the capital, confusing and upsetting the credulous people, in any case meant a challenge to the ruling circles. Even as late as John's Gospel we can read: "Search and you will find that no prophet comes from Galilee."[6] The entry into Jerusalem, interpreted symbolically and given a legendary touch with the reference to the peaceable mount used on that occasion, perhaps did not have the triumphal character subsequently attributed to it. But anyone who was suspected of working miracles by demonic power, of being a false prophet or a blasphemer, had to reckon with the possibility of the death penalty. To incur the death penalty it was sufficient deliberately to break the Sabbath after a single warning in the presence of witnesses (this comes out clearly in Mark, where there is a warning after the first infringement of the Sabbath and plans to kill him immediately after the second).[7]

It seems—although some dispute this—that a Jewish court could not carry out death sentences in Judea and Samaria: the *jus gladii* was apparently in the hands of the Roman occupying power. But—apart from the fact that the leading Jewish circles had interests in common with the

Romans in certain cases, as for instance against popular agitators and popular risings, and were by no means disinclined to collaborate—the situation in Galilee at least was different. The Jewish ruler there, by grace of Rome, could pronounce and carry out death sentences. It is historically certain that Herod Antipas had John the Baptist arrested and beheaded at the fortress of Machaerus, either because John had disapproved of Herod's marriage with his sister-in-law, Herodias,[8] or—more probably—because Herod took John's activity to be political and feared the possibility of a revolt.[9] For Jesus, who undoubtedly knew about it and evidently was frequently regarded as John's successor, it was in any case an extremely serious warning.

To the authorities even a non-political mass movement could seem politically dangerous. The background of the warning—notably ascribed to the Pharisees—that Herod was seeking his life[10] was only too real. But Jesus' sensational entry into Jerusalem could only increase the danger. And the prophetical act of cleansing the temple—which certainly has a core of historical truth—likewise put his life in danger, since it was an act of arrogance in the sanctuary itself. The fate of the prophets must have given Jesus food for thought:[11] at least Isaiah, Jeremiah, Amos, Micah and Zechariah were regarded as martyrs and in his own time monuments were being built as atonement for their murder. The same could perhaps be said also of the fate of the Servant of God in Deutero-Isaiah, who was sacrificed for many.[12] If Jesus had to allow even for the possibility of a violent death, then he might also have sought an interpretation of this death. For this reason some regard as basically an original saying of Jesus the words about the Son of Man coming not to be served but to serve, and to give his life as a ransom for many,[13] which are also confirmed by the tradition of the Last Supper.[14]

In view of these facts it is difficult critically to eliminate all the material on the suffering Jesus was to undergo: not only the prophecies of suffering, but also the numerous threats and charges against the murderers of God's messengers, against the builders of prophets' tombs, against those who seek the prophet's death, against Jerusalem as murderer of the prophets, against the traitor. It is the same with the sayings about Jesus' fate, his homelessness, the coming separation, the fate of the Baptist and the prophets, the paschal lamb, the chalice and the criminal's grave (which was not exactly what happened). Finally there are all the metaphors and enigmatic sayings about the murdered shepherd and the scattered flock, the bridegroom snatched away, the ransom, chalice and baptism, the temple keystone, the coming age of the sword . . .[15] Even if we maintain a critical reserve, we cannot deny a historical core to what is perhaps the shortest, most vague and linguistically the oldest variant of the prophecies of the Passion:[16] that Jesus will be delivered up to men. And the saying to

Peter about Satan,[17] within the context of the announcement of the Passion, can hardly have been invented.

Whatever attitude we adopt to the authenticity of any particular saying, we may take it as certain that Jesus, having frequently risked his life by his talk and actions, must have reckoned with a violent end. That is not to say that he directly provoked or willed his death. But he was *living face to face with death.* And he accepted death freely, with that freedom which united fidelity to himself and fidelity to his mandate, responsibility and obedience, since he recognized in it the will of God. It was a question, not only of suffering death, but of yielding up and sacrificing his life. This we must keep in mind constantly as we look at that scene on the eve of his execution to which is traced back the specifically Christian religious service maintained throughout the whole two thousand years: the Last Supper.

A last meal

Critical exegesis today generally accepts the fact that Jesus like some at least of his disciples was *baptized,* but that neither he himself nor—according to the Synoptic Gospels[18]—his disciples baptized before Easter; also that the Risen Lord's command to baptize contains nothing historically verifiable.[19] Today also it is however generally admitted that there was no initial stage in the Church without baptism and that baptism began in the primitive community soon after Easter. Is there a contradiction here? The explanation lies in the fact that the community, even without definite instructions or still less "institution" of a baptismal rite, could believe that they were fulfilling the will of Jesus when they baptized. They could recall Jesus' approval of John's baptism. They could also recall the baptism itself of Jesus and of the disciples. It was therefore a response, not to certain mandatory words of Jesus, but to his message as a whole, which calls for conversion and faith and promises forgiveness of sin and salvation. The community therefore baptized in the mind and spirit of Jesus: in fulfillment of his will, in response to his message and therefore in his name.[20]

Was it perhaps similar with the *Last Supper?* Is it possible that Jesus himself did not celebrate such a meal, but the post-paschal community did celebrate one "in memory of him," in the mind and spirit and thus according to the mandate of Jesus? The Church's celebration of the eucharist might then be justified in the same way as that of baptism. But the evidence here is more complex. Baptism and eucharist cannot simply be put on the same plane historically. Of course it is open to doubt whether Jesus "instituted" a supper. The twice repeated order to recall it, as found in Paul, is lacking even in Mark. But, in the light of the sources, it is not so easy to doubt that Jesus *celebrated* with his disciples a parting meal, a last supper.

The fact that Jesus celebrated a common meal with his disciples is recorded in four different readings.[21] It is clearly attested by Paul for the beginning of his missionary activity in Corinth in the forties of the first century.[22] But at the same time he appealed to a tradition which, according to himself, goes back to the Lord: which he received in Damascus, Jerusalem or at the latest Antioch, that is, directly or indirectly from the primitive community, and of which there were eyewitnesses still alive. The second main strand of the tradition, contained in the accounts of Mark and then of Luke—in individual Semitic turns of phrase perhaps more original, but in the final version certainly more recent—deviates too much in language from the Pauline account to be drawn from the same Greek source. On the other hand, this Marcan account agrees in substance so closely with the Pauline that both must go back to a common Aramaic or Hebrew source. The age, the extent and definiteness of the tradition of the Last Supper—the Lucan version is a mixed type drawn from the Pauline and the Marcan forms—in any case scarcely allow any scope for doubt about the *facticity* of a last meal of Jesus with his disciples. The real problem—made much more difficult as a result of the liturgical forms imposed on the accounts—lies in the determination of the *significance* of this last meal.

One thing should be obvious. We cannot without more ado ascribe to Jesus himself ideas about the Last Supper held by the primitive community, the Hellenist communities, still less those of later dogmatic theology in the Church. In the controversies on the eucharist originating in the Middle Ages any understanding of Jesus' supper was largely blocked because the disputants started out from the interpretative words over the bread and wine, considered in isolation from the Last Supper itself. The fundamental importance of the common meals for Jesus' proclamation as a whole has been overlooked: how—as a result of not excluding even those suffering from discrimination and degradation—they acquired meaning as signs of the coming kingdom and the grace and forgiveness offered in advance. For the Baptist the baptism of penance was a typical sign in action; for Jesus and his message the sign took the form of feasts held in an atmosphere of joy, in which people celebrated their common membership of the future kingdom. The stories of the multiplication of the loaves also provide indirect testimony of this.[23] A last meal, a parting meal of Jesus can be properly understood only against the background of this long *series of meals*, which were continued by the disciples even after Easter.

In the light of all this it is at once clear that Jesus did not intend to make this meal the foundation of a new liturgy. The table fellowship was to be realized once more with those who had gone around, eaten and drunk with him. Expecting the coming kingdom and his own departure,

Jesus wanted to have this meal with his followers. If there is one statement in the account of the Last Supper which goes back to Jesus himself, it is that about not drinking of the fruit of the vine until the day when he would drink with them the new wine in the kingdom of God:[24] a statement not taken up in the later liturgical tradition, not even in Paul's account.

It is of secondary importance whether this meal was a ritual Passover meal (as Mark says, but only in the narrative framework, not in the account of the meal itself) or not (which is John's view). There are reasons for both opinions. But it is mainly the weakness of the evidence, the improbability of the convocation of the court and the execution on the Passover feast which make the Johannine dating more probable and suggest that the Passover dating is to be ascribed to the community, who wanted to understand Jesus' Last Supper as a substitute for the Passover meal. But even if the meal had been celebrated the night before, it would have been under the influence of the Passover.

Whether or not it was a Passover meal, the particular *words of Jesus* did not fall—so to speak—from heaven as sacred words of institution, as was once assumed by those who interpreted these words in isolation from the rest. They fitted easily into the ritual laid down—and still observed up to a point in modern Jewish families—for a festive Jewish meal. The words over the bread follow the grace before the main meal when the head of the family gives praise over the round, flat bread, breaks it and distributes the pieces of the one bread to the guests. The words over the wine come after the thanksgiving at the end of the meal, when the head of the family lets the cup with wine circulate and each one drinks from it. This is a gesture of fellowship which anyone in ancient times could understand, even without accompanying words.

Jesus therefore had no need to invent a new rite, but only to link an announcement and a new interpretation with an old rite. He interpreted the bread and—at least according to the Marcan version—the wine with reference to himself. In face of his imminent death he interpreted bread and wine—so to speak—as prophetic signs of his death and thus of all that he was, did and willed: of the sacrifice, the surrender of his life. Like this bread, so would his body be broken; like this red wine, so would his blood be poured out: this is my body, my blood. In both cases what is meant is the whole person and his sacrifice, wholly and entirely. And as the head of the family gives a share in the blessing of the meal in the form of bread and wine to those eating and drinking, so Jesus gives to his followers a share in his body given up in death ("body" or "flesh" in Hebrew or Aramaic always means the whole person) and in his blood shed for "many" (with the "inclusive" meaning=the sum total, consisting of many).

The disciples are thus taken up into Jesus' destiny. The meal becomes a sign of a new, permanent communion of Jesus with his followers: a *new covenant* is established. The (more original?) Pauline version, "This chalice is the new covenant in my blood,"[25] brings out better than the Marcan the idea of the new covenant. This is the covenant prefigured (and sealed by the sprinkling of blood and a meal) in the covenant at Sinai,[26] which Jeremiah predicted for the time of salvation,[27] and which played an important part in Jesus' own time also in Qumran, where there was a daily community meal with a blessing of bread and wine. The blood of Jesus shed, the body given up are therefore signs of the new covenant made between God and his people.

It could be a post-paschal interpretation which makes Jesus understand his death as a *vicarious* atonement for the many: in the sense, that is, of the innocent, patiently borne, voluntary suffering and death of the Servant of God in Isaiah 53,[28] willed by God and therefore vicarious atonement. The idea that the death of the innocent, the innocent shedding of blood, counts as atonement was of course not unknown in the Jewish thought of the time.

The question however is certainly irrelevant which was debated at the time of the Reformation, about the meaning of "is," since neither the community nor Jesus himself had our concept of a substance. People did not ask what a thing was, but what it was for: not in what it consisted, but what was its function. Paradoxically enough, the originally Aramaic sentence was most probably formulated without even using the word with which the centuries-long controversy was concerned. In the original language Jesus would have said: "This—my body."[29]

The *ancient community* is thus confirmed by the action and the word of the meal and at the same time a *new community* is promised: *koinonia, communio*, with Jesus and with one another. The Master's departure is announced to the group of disciples and yet the communion with him and with each other remains established until their table fellowship is renewed in the kingdom of God. They are to remain united even during his absence. It is not without reason that the idea of the Church was later linked with Jesus' Last Supper.[30]

Stages

This is not the place to deliver a paper on the *Passion story*. It is easier to look it up in one of the Gospels, perhaps first of all in Mark.[31] John, it seems, must have used an older Passion account and agrees for once with the three Synoptics on the sequence of events: Judas' betrayal, a last meal at which the traitor is designated, arrest and interrogation, proceedings before Pilate and crucifixion. In addition to these sections, which appear in the same place also in John, there are the Gethsemane scene and Peter's denial together with its announcement.

The community had understandably the greatest interest in the facts connected with the arrest, trial and execution. Hence the Passion story is worked out in greater detail than all that went before it. Mark extends it even into the pre-history, so that his Gospel has been described, not entirely incorrectly, as a "Passion story with a circumstantial introduction." The meaning of the Passion comes out clearly here and is underlined by the calm and dispassionate way in which it is related. From the very beginning the story must have been told with its individual stages closely linked: as used in religious services, in instruction, with some pieces perhaps added on other occasions. But while Mark sees the revelation properly so-called in the cross and the acceptance of being forsaken by God, Matthew emphasizes the majesty and the authority of Jesus, and Luke the suffering of the just one as example for the disciples. At the same time, with all the Gospels, there is a visible tendency to use the Passion story to protect the community from temptation and apostasy.[82]

All this however makes it clear that what we have before us is not a police report or a record of the trial such as the dossier on Joan of Arc. There was never any intention of producing a neutral and disinterested report of this trial. The writers believed in the person who had gone on this dreadful road and this faith was to be made completely evident in the narrative as an *appeal to faith*. Historical recollections and post-paschal experiences of faith cannot be separated. That is why they did not hesitate to introduce even legendary material, miraculous events, cures, angelic appearances, even cosmic-apocalyptic miracles, in brief, all that could make the meaning of this story evident: that even in these shattering events and particularly here God had a hand. That in them it was God's plan and providence which prevailed. That men in all their waywardness and sin really remain the instruments of God. And above all that this Jesus was not refuted through this shameful last road, but even confirmed as Messiah.

This appeal to faith is helped by the unobtrusive style of the accounts, the peculiar, lofty-solemn and yet realistic language oriented to the Old Testament, which—as in the musical structure of the Passions of J. S. Bach—renders the significance of the event perceptible even down to the commonplace, brutal, inhuman details. Numerous allusions and explicit quotations from the Old Testament—especially from Psalms 22, 31 and 69, and from the Servant Songs—also serve as aids to this appeal for faith.[83] From the entry into Jerusalem, linked with Zechariah's saying about the king riding humbly on an ass's foal to the Daughter of Sion,[84] right up to the disposal of his clothing by lot and the insults at the foot of the cross, for which Psalm 22 is cited, Jesus is made to appear as the one in whom God's counsels are carried out and Scripture is fulfilled, in accordance with the motto: "The Son of Man is going away as it was written of him."[35] So the whole absurd story becomes comprehensible as the expression of God's mysterious imperative, as the Risen Christ himself according to Luke interprets to the disciples going to Emmaus "all that relates to him in all the Scriptures": "Did not Christ have to suffer all this in order to enter into his glory?"[36] These constant references to the Old Testament greatly helped the first communities to sustain the almost intolerable story of their Lord and Master.

The stylization of the narratives, while revealing the author's sensitivity and involvement, and producing the same effects on the reader, may be helpful to the preacher, but creates all the more difficulty for the historian: how much is reportage and how much interpretation? In these narratives what is *history* and what is proclamation, how can we distinguish between the historical record and its theological interpretation? We know less that is certain about the last section of Jesus' life, narrated so circumstantially and coherently, than we might have assumed at the first reading of the Gospels. On the other hand, it would be dogmatic arbitrariness to assume that the proclamation has completely covered up the history and that we can no longer know what really happened. Here too the serious interpreter cannot avoid the effort of distinguishing between the one and the other.

In some cases a mere comparison of the texts shows how a narrative acquires legendary features. According to Mark someone who happened to be standing by draws a sword and cuts off the ear of the high priest's servant. According to Luke—who is generally more interested than the others in miraculous phenomena—Jesus heals the wounded man. Finally, John even gives the name of the disciple and the servant.[37] Again, according to Mark and Matthew, there is no angel present at the agony in the Garden of Gethsemane. According to Luke there is an angel and Jesus' sweat comes in drops of blood which fall to the ground.[38] There are other examples.

On the other hand, however, there are small, irrelevant details which show that the narratives to some extent ultimately go back to eyewitnesses, some of them still known to the narrator. There is, for example, the inglorious scene—not otherwise worth mentioning—of the young man who had to leave his clothes behind and flee naked as Jesus was being arrested.[39] Or the naming of Alexander and Rufus, sons of Simon from Cyrene who was forced to carry the condemned man's cross (probably the crossbeam),[40] whom Matthew and Luke no longer regard as worth mentioning.[41] There is also the naming of the Galilean women standing by the cross, while the name of Jesus' mother is strangely lacking.[42] Even Old Testament quotations can point indirectly to historical facts. The disposal by lot of Jesus' clothes at the foot of the cross was read into Psalm 22:19,[43] but it could also correspond to a regular practice at an execution. The shame of Jesus' death between two criminals is made bearable with the aid of a quotation from Isaiah 53:12; but it might well have happened like this, since the presence of the Roman governor in Jerusalem would probably serve as an opportunity to get several pending cases settled together.[44] The people who mocked Jesus, nodding their heads, are described in terms of Psalm 22:8; but their behavior is psychologically quite understandable.[45] A supporting reference to the Old Testament therefore is not *a priori* an argument against historicity.

These details are mentioned only to make clear that, with caution and discrimination, questions about history as it happened can be asked in the light of history as it is proclaimed. Making allowance for all the legendary elaborations, differences in the accounts, borrowings from the Old Testament and subsequent Christological interpretations, it is possible to know at least in outline—quite adequately for our purposes—what really happened in the different phases. We can also often discover a quite surprising agreement between the accounts of a variety of witnesses about the different conflict situations between Jesus and the Jewish and Roman authorities and even between Jesus and his disciples.

The outbreak of the conflict. According to all the evidence the immediate occasion for the arrest was Jesus' sensational *entry into Jerusalem* shortly before the great Passover feast, the feast of Israel's liberation from bondage in Egypt. Did this Galilean heretic have to come to Jerusalem, expecting the kingdom of God, at the very moment when immense crowds of pilgrims from Galilee were streaming into the capital and the Roman governor was arriving with military reinforcements to maintain security? Did he and his band have to accept the cheers of a crowd of dubious followers just when apocalyptic national hopes of the coming of the kingdom and liberation from Roman rule were being revived and incidents were frequent? Did he have to claim authority even—most probably—in the temple precincts and make bold to cleanse the sanctuary in anticipation of the advent of the kingdom? Did he have to attempt to defend his claim and his authority in the way described in the "conflict stories"[46]—the time and place of which may sometimes be arranged differently[47]—and apparently at the same time to announce the destruction of Jerusalem and the temple?[48] All this amounted to an open challenge to the system and its representatives and more or less provoked the great trial of strength.

We do not know what in particular Jesus was expecting. On the basis of the textural evidence, some think that he did not distinguish between the coming of the kingdom (*parousia*), the resurrection and the rebuilding of the temple; that the distinction between resurrection, ascension and second coming, as successive events, is a post-paschal systematization.[49] But the whole affair of Jesus' appearance in the religious center proves that he was seeking a decision in his cause. On the other hand, his opponents had to attempt to unmask him now as a heretic or a false prophet, as an enemy of the law, of the temple, or even of the Roman rule.

The betrayal. In the already tense situation it seemed to the Jewish (and perhaps also the Roman) authorities that quick action was called for. He had to be dealt with summarily. In view of a possible people's uprising the case would have to be settled *before the feast*. This important note in Mark[50] shows two things:

a. The *Johannine chronology* is probably correct, since it is only in line with this that the case could have been settled before the feast. This would mean that the Last Supper took place a whole day before the eve of the Passover (=Thursday), then the execution on the eve of the Passover, when the lambs were being slaughtered in the temple (on 14 Nisan=Friday), finally the Passover feast on the day after the execution (=Saturday). In any case Mark and John agree in placing Jesus' execution on the Friday of the Jewish Passover week in Nisan (corresponding more or less to our April), whether this was the Passover feast day (15 Nisan) or its eve (14 Nisan).[51] Astronomical calculations suggest that the Johannine date would fall on 7 April in the year 30.

b. The distinction between the *Jewish people* and *their leaders* was originally important. While the Synoptists distinguish Jesus' opponents according to the groups to which they belong, John's Gospel speaks in a very general and mostly negative way of "the Jews." The word "Jew" occurs seventy-one times in John's Gospel, but only eleven times in the other three Gospels taken together.

The seizure of Jesus "by guile," taking him—so to speak—by surprise at dead of night, made possible the offer—according to all the evidence—of a man of whom we know nothing except the one decisive fact that he was a disciple of Jesus, even one of the twelve. Just what he disclosed and whether there was a betrayal properly so called, we do not know. Only Matthew[52] suggests avarice as *Judas'* motive and even, probably inspired by a saying of Zechariah, mentions the sum of thirty silver pieces.[53] Some think that "Iscariot" does not mean "man from Kerioth," but that it is a mutilated form of the Latin *sicarius*, meaning "dagger man" or "assassin." Judas, it is claimed, impelled by Zealot enthusiasm, was disappointed and made contact with Jesus' enemies in order to force him to act. But such explanations are pure hypotheses and others, appearing in fictional lives of Jesus, are pure fantasies. The legendary touch which makes Judas an agent of the devil can be seen in the later Gospels[54] and the idea is developed by Dante, who places him with Brutus, the murderer of Caesar, in the lowest depths of hell. The designation of the traitor at the supper could well be historical,[55] but the framework, Jesus' foreknowledge and Mark's usual emphasis on the disciples' lack of understanding are probably theological interpretation.

The arrest. The arrest took place just before the feast, according to all the accounts outside the city on the far side of the Kedron valley on the Mount of Olives in a garden called *Gethsemane*. There were no witnesses to Jesus' tribulation there and his struggling in prayer:[56] it is impossible therefore to discover anything about the historical facts. It is very important however for the history of dogma that Jesus' fear and horror are explicitly described, in a way quite unlike Jewish and Christian stories of martyrdom. The sufferer here is not an aloof Stoic, still less a superman. He is a man in the fullest sense, tempted and tried, but not understood at all by his closest friends, who even went to sleep during his agony.

In a surprise action during the night, led by Judas, who was familiar with his habits, Jesus was arrested by a gang of his opponents. Judas' kiss with the disciple's form of address, "Rabbi," difficult to explain historically, remains a symbol of the meanest betrayal. It is not clear *who* gave the order or who took part in the arrest. Almost certainly there would be a detachment sent by the temple priests, under pressure from the high priests in contact with the Sanhedrin. But there may have been a prior arrangement between the Jewish and the Roman authorities. This would explain both the mention of the Roman cohort (probably together with the Jewish temple police) by John, who otherwise plays down the Roman involvement, and the prompt sentencing by Pilate, who was not particularly notable for his compliance. There can be no doubt about the later collaboration of the Jewish and the Roman authorities. But, according to all the accounts, Jesus was first taken into custody by Jewish officials.

It is significant that the arrest took place without any resistance on the part of Jesus or his disciples. The clumsy and absurdly ineffective sword blow by an unknown person and the legend of the healing of the injured ear only underline this fact. From then onwards Jesus was completely isolated, without followers of any kind. The *flight of the disciples*—like the arrest itself—is very briefly reported, without excuses. Only Luke attempts to gloss over this painful fact, at first by silence and afterwards by mentioning the friends watching from a distance. John for apologetic reasons exaggerates the voluntary character of Jesus' acceptance of it all, turning the account almost into mythology: the bloodhounds fall back as if in the presence of divinity and then seize him after he has dismissed his disciples.[57]

There is a particularly clear contrast between Jesus' fidelity (before the court) and the infidelity (before a girl) of that disciple who had emphatically sworn his loyalty even to death. The story of *Peter's denial*, forthrightly and credibly told in all the Gospels, originally probably a coherent piece of tradition related for its own sake, could have been passed on by the disciple himself to the community. In any case—apart from the dramatic conclusion, probably added by Mark, with the second cock-crow (hens were apparently forbidden in Jerusalem)*—it may well correspond to the historical facts, since there is no evidence of any aversion to Peter in the community.

The trial. Despite the closest critical investigation,[58] since we have neither official records nor statements of eyewitnesses, it is no longer possible to reconstruct the details of Jesus' trial.

Several things are still not clear. Was he judged according to the older Sadduceic or the newer Pharisaic law (as recorded in the later Mishnah)? Were there two sessions of the Sanhedrin (one at night and a second in the morning) or only one, during the daytime (as Luke says, with greater probability)? Did the witnesses for the prosecution tell the truth or not with reference to Jesus' words about the temple? Was the Sanhedrin allowed to pronounce and carry out death sentences and could such a sentence have been passed even at night and within the space of a single day? Was anyone ever condemned to death by the Jewish authorities for asserting messianic claims and in the case of condemnation for blasphemy (in Jesus' time certainly not merely malicious use of God's name) was not the penalty stoning instead of crucifixion? Was a formal death sentence pronounced—as Luke implies, without saying anything explicitly—or was there merely an agreement to hand him over to Pilate? Was there in fact a regular trial at all or merely a hearing to define more exactly the charges before the Roman governor?

At any rate it is *clear* that the whole inquisitorial process before the Sanhedrin—and, according to John, still more that before Pilate—has been arranged in the form of a *community profession of faith in Christ:* according to the deposition of many witnesses, the messianic testimony of Jesus himself at the center and as a consequence the condemnation to death for blasphemy.[59]

The silence of Jesus, frequently stressed in the Gospels, is meant to bring out his will to suffer, his yes to the will of the Father. What is behind the "many" charges, of which only one is cited (a fact which is not often observed), must be gathered (as we have largely tried to do) from the Gospels as a whole. In view of the fact that "Son of God" was not a messianic title, the direct question about *divine sonship* is scarcely probable. Exaltation and parousia too never appear together except in the answer ascribed to Jesus.[60] The odd combination of "sitting" (on the right of God's power) and "coming" (with the clouds of heaven) could have arisen from linking together two Old Testament statements.[61] As far as we know, no one was prosecuted solely for claiming to be the Messiah: something

* Cf. V. Taylor, *The Gospel According to St. Mark*, London/New York, 1952, p. 550: "Either the threefold denial will take place before a cock crows twice or, more probably, the reference is to the beginning of the fourth watch when the signal known as *gallicinium* ('cock-crowing') was given by a bugle call." (Translator.)

else had to be involved. In this connection of course the saying, probably of Jesus himself, about the *destruction* (and rebuilding) *of the temple*[62] may have played a part. Josephus also tells of a prophet—Jesus, son of Ananias—who announced the fall of the temple and was therefore handed over by the Jews to the Romans, whipped by them and then set free.[63] How much embarrassment this saying of Jesus created for the community can be seen from the way in which it was rendered harmless: according to Mark it is plainly a false testimony, according to Matthew it means only that the temple could be destroyed, Luke simply leaves it out and in John it is interpreted allegorically. What all the evangelists make absolutely clear is that Jesus was innocently condemned. The titles of majesty appearing alongside one another at a central point in the account of the trial—Messiah, Son of God and Son of Man—are the community's profession of faith in the condemned man.

Furthermore, whatever may be the details of the inquisitorial process, it is clearly established as an indisputable fact that Jesus was handed over by the Jewish authorities *to the Roman governor, Pontius Pilate*, and that he was not stoned in accordance with the Jewish custom but crucified in accordance with the Roman. All the sources agree[64] that it was the Jewish leaders—high priests and elders—who handed him over to the Romans as a political suspect. At the hearing, whatever form it took, no doubt the charges were investigated which could lead to proceedings by the Roman authorities. In view of their constant fear of mass uprisings and demonstrations, the latter would react very promptly to the charges that this man was politically dangerous and—as his entry into Jerusalem and his cleansing of the temple might show—had messianic ambitions. It is relatively unimportant whether a formal sentence of death was pronounced by the Sanhedrin or there was merely an agreement to surrender him to Pilate (with all the consequences), or even merely a suggestion that Jesus was dangerous as a pretender to messianic claims and therefore a potential rebel.

Although never used later by the community as a messianic title, according to all the accounts the term "King of the Jews"[65] played the main role in the trial. This is confirmed by the undoubtedly historical fact of the inscription (*titulus*), customary at Roman crucifixions, indicating the offender's crime: "King of the Jews" reproduces in Graeco-Roman form the meaning of the charge brought by his Jewish accusers, for messianic ambitions could be understood by Pilate, the Roman, only in a political sense. Although Jesus had never raised such a political claim, as we saw, it was natural for outsiders to cast him in this mold.

Jesus was *condemned to death* as a result of the collaboration between spiritual and political authorities. According to all the accounts, the charge created some embarrassment for Pilate since he could scarcely find any material facts on which to base it, although he did regard him as a Zealot leader. Even allowing for the tendency of the evangelists to set up Rome's representatives as witnesses to Jesus' innocence and to relieve them of guilt, it is quite likely that he tried to get Jesus amnestied—as an individual case, since an annual custom is improbable. But finally, at the wish of the people incited by their leaders, he released the Zealot revolutionary Barabbas ("son of Abbas"). This much at least the sources unanimously report, while Pilate's wife's intercession is mentioned only by Matthew,[66] the inconclusive hearing before Herod Antipas only by Luke,[67] the hearing before the former high priest Annas and the exhaustive interrogation by Pilate only by John.[68] But, by condemning this Jesus—who had never claimed any messianic title—as "King (=Messiah) of the Jews," paradoxically enough, Pilate made him in the eyes of the general public a crucified Messiah. This was to become important for the post-paschal faith and its understanding of the pre-paschal Jesus. The irony of the inscription on the cross could have been deliberately intended by the Roman. The dispute about the formula shows that this was how it was taken by the Jews, for whom a crucified Messiah was a monstrous scandal.[69]

The execution. Before the execution—there are also historical parallels for this—Jesus was exposed to the mockery and ridicule of the Roman soldiery. The ridiculing of Jesus as a mock king confirms the view that he was condemned for messianic pretensions. The terrible flogging with leather whips into which pieces of metal were inserted was customary before a crucifixion.[70] Jesus' collapse on the way under the burden of the crossbeam and the enforced assistance of Simon from Cyrene in North Africa —apart from the mention of Simon's sons—are highly probable. The way of the cross is not of course what is known today as the "Via Dolorosa." More probably it would have led from Herod's palace—this and not the fortress of Antonia was Pilate's residence in Jerusalem—to the place of execution on a small hill outside the city wall at that time, called Golgotha ("skull"), presumably on account of its shape.

The execution could not be more tersely described than it is by the evangelists: "And they crucified him."[71] Everyone at that time knew only too well the horrible Roman form of execution (but probably invented by the Persians) for slaves and political rebels. The condemned man was nailed to the crossbeam which was then secured to a stake already driven into the ground, the feet being fastened by nails or ropes. The inscription which the criminal bore on the way to execution, giving the reason for his condemnation, was then fixed to the cross, visible to all. It was often only after a long time (sometimes only on the next day), after the bloody beating and the hanging, that the victim bled to death or choked. It was a form of execution both cruel and discriminating. A Roman citizen might be beheaded but not crucified.[72]

Nothing is embroidered in the Gospels. Even Mark's count of the six hours on the cross (which does not agree with John's timing) might well, within the scheme of three times three hours, be pointing more or less symbolically to the significance of this death and to God's plan behind it all. This holds still more for the two *apocalyptic signs* cited by Mark but not mentioned by John. The sun is darkened (impossible at the time of the spring full moon), a sign also noted at the death of Caesar and other great events in antiquity and announced in particular by the prophet Amos in connection with "mourning for an only son."[78] The second is the tearing of the temple curtain, as a sign probably of the end of the temple worship which comes with Jesus' death. These signs become even more miraculous in later writings like the Nazarene Gospel or the Gospel of Peter. There we have the shattering of the gigantic lintel of the temple, darkness as in the night, massive tremors as the corpse is laid in the earth, conversion of thousands of Jews who perceived their error at the reappearance of the sun.

All these are obviously not historical, but theological statements as aids to understanding this otherwise uncannily prosaic, unsentimental narrative. No pains or torments are described, no emotions or aggression aroused. There is no intention of describing Jesus' behavior in undergoing this death. Instead, what is to be brought out by every means—Old Testament quotations and allusions, wonderful signs—is the significance of this death: the death of this one man who had roused so many expectations and who was now liquidated and mocked by his enemies and left completely in the lurch by his friends and even by God himself. At the same time, in Mark, everything leads up to the question of faith: In this terrible, shameful death does one see, like the mockers, the death of a misguided, broken-down enthusiast who cries in vain for Elijah to save him? Or, like the Roman centurion—the first pagan to bear witness to him—the death of the Son of God?

Why?

What the Gospels appear to present as the goal and consummation of the earthly life of Jesus of Nazareth was bound to seem to his contemporaries like the end of everything. Had anyone promised more than he did? And now this complete fiasco of an ignominious death!

Anyone who thinks that all religions and their "founders" are alike will see the *differences* which appear if he compares the deaths of such men. Moses, Buddha, Confucius, all died at a ripe old age, successful despite many disappointments, in the midst of their disciples and supporters, their "span of life completed" like the patriarchs of Israel. According to the tradition, Moses died in sight of the promised land, in the midst of his people, at the age of 120 years, his eyes undimmed, his vigor unfaded. Buddha died at the age of eighty, peacefully, his disciples around him, after he had collected in the course of his itinerant preaching a great community of monks, nuns and lay supporters. Confucius returned in old age to Lu—from which he had once been driven out when Minister of Justice—after he had spent his last years in training a group of mainly noble disciples, to preserve and continue his work, and in editing the ancient writings of his people, to be transmitted to posterity only in his version. Muhammad, after he had thoroughly enjoyed the last years of his life as political ruler of Arabia, died in the midst of his harem in the arms of his favorite wife.

Here on the other hand we have a young man of thirty, after three years at most of activity, perhaps only a few months. Expelled from society, betrayed and denied by his disciples and supporters, mocked and ridiculed by his opponents, forsaken by men and even by God, he goes through a ritual of death that is one of the most atrocious and enigmatic ever invented by man's ingenious cruelty.

Historical questions about the way to the cross are of secondary importance by comparison to the reality that is ultimately involved here. Whatever the immediate occasion of the outbreak of open conflict, whatever the motives of the traitor, whatever the exact circumstances of the arrest and the procedures at the trial, whoever the individual culprits, where and when precisely the stages of this way occurred: the death of Jesus was not an accident, not a tragic error of justice nor a purely arbitrary act, but a historical necessity—which included the guilt of those responsible. Only a complete rethinking, a real *metanoia* on the part of those affected, a new awareness, an abandonment of preoccupation with their own activity, giving up all legalistic self-assurance and self-justification, and a return to radical trust in the God of unconditional grace and abounding love proclaimed by Jesus could have averted this disaster.

Jesus' violent end was the *logical conclusion of his proclamation and his behavior*. Jesus' passion was the reaction of the guardians of the law, of justice and morality, to his action. He did not simply passively endure death, but actively provoked it. His condemnation is explained only by his proclamation. His suffering is elucidated only by his action. Only his life and work, taken together, make clear what distinguishes the cross of this one man from those crosses of the Jewish resistance fighters which the Romans set up in masses a few decades after Jesus' death, in sight of the walls of the encircled capital. It is his life which distinguishes his cross from the seven thousand crosses of Roman slaves set up on the Appian Way after the unsuccessful revolt of Spartacus (not crucified himself, but killed in battle); and indeed from the innumerable crosses great and small of all those who have been tormented and oppressed from the dawn of history.

Jesus' death was the penalty he had to pay for his life. But it was quite different from Brutus' murder of Julius Caesar, the politician, after he had failed to make himself king, as recorded by Plutarch with historical and poetical flair and turned by Shakespeare into drama. The death of the unresisting Jesus of Nazareth, not seeking political power but standing only for God and his will, was on another plane. And the Passion story of the Gospel does not need to be turned into drama or history, but itself in its austere sublimity leads to the question why just this person was allowed to bear this unbounded suffering.

If however we take the Gospels as a whole and not only the Passion story—which can really be understood only against the background provided by the Gospels—it is completely clear why this point was reached, why he did not die by a heart attack or accident, but was murdered. Or should the hierarchy have let this radical go who arbitrarily proclaimed God's will without giving any reasons or justification?

This *heretical teacher* who regarded the law and the whole religious and social order as irrelevant and brought confusion into the minds of the people who were ignorant of religion or politics?

This *false prophet* who prophesied the fall of the temple and relativized its cult as a whole and plunged particularly the traditionally devout into the most profound uncertainty?

This *blasphemer* who, in a love that knew no bounds, accepted among his followers and friends irreligious and morally unstable people; who thus, in his underground hostility to law and temple, degraded the sublime and just God of this law and temple and reduced him to the God of these godless and hopeless people; who in his monstrous arrogance even encroached on God's most essential sovereign rights by personally assuring and guaranteeing forgiveness here and now?

This *seducer of the people* who in person presented an unparalleled challenge to the whole social system, a provocation of authority, a rebellion against the hierarchy and its theology: all of which might have resulted, not only in confusion and uncertainty, but in real disturbances, demonstrations, even a new popular revolt, the always threatening great conflict with the occupying army and the armed intervention of the Roman imperial power?

From the theological and political standpoint, the enemy of the law was also an enemy of the people. John's shrewd observation of the intervention of the high priest Caiphas in the decisive session of the Sanhedrin was not an exaggeration: "You do not understand at all: you do not reason that it is better for you if one man dies for the people than for the whole nation to perish."[74]

The political trial and execution of Jesus as a political offender by the Roman authorities, therefore, was not by any means a misunderstanding or a pointless happening, the result merely of a trick or a blatantly trumped-up charge. The existing political, religious and social conditions provided a certain amount of excuse for the political charge and the execution. Under these conditions *a simple separation of religion and politics* was impossible. There was neither politics without religion nor religion without politics. Anyone who started a disturbance in the religious sphere also disturbed the political order. Jesus represented a security risk for both the religious and the political authorities. *Nevertheless*, if Jesus' life and death are not to be misrepresented, *the political element must not be put on the same plane* as the religious. The political conflict with the Roman authority was only a consequence (not inevitable as such) of the religious conflict with the Jewish hierarchy. Here we must clearly distinguish between the religious and the political charge.

The *religious charge* that Jesus assumed a sovereign liberty in regard to law and temple, that he questioned the traditional religious system and claimed an absolutely unparalleled authority by proclaiming the mercy of God the Father and giving his personal assurance of forgiveness of sins: this charge was *true*. According to all the Gospels it seems to be justified. From the standpoint of the traditional religion of the law and temple, the Jewish hierarchy had to act against the heretical teacher, false prophet, blasphemer and religious seducer of the people, if they were not to undergo a radical conversion and put their faith in the message with all its consequences.

But the *political charge* that Jesus sought political power, called people to refuse to pay taxes to the occupying power and to revolt, that he saw himself as political Messiah-king of the Jews: this charge was *false*. According to all the Gospels it takes the form of a pretext and a calumny. It became clear in every detail in the section on Jesus and revolution[75] and it was confirmed throughout the following chapters that Jesus was not an active politician, not an agitator or social revolutionary, not a militant opponent of Roman power. He was condemned as a political revolutionary, although he was not one. If Jesus had been more of a politician, his chances of success would have been better.

The political charge was a cover for the religious hatred and envy of the hierarchy and their court theologians. Messianic pretensions did not even constitute an offense according to the existing Jewish law. The issue could be decided by their success or failure. But they could be presented in a way that made it very easy for the Romans to twist them into a claim to political dominion. Such a charge must have seemed plausible to Pilate and would have been apparently justified in the conditions at the time. Nevertheless it was not only profoundly biased, but essentially false. That is why the title "King of the Jews" simply could not be used in the community as a Christological title of majesty. From the standpoint of the Roman power Pontius Pilate did not by any means have to act against *this* "King of the Jews" and the governor's delaying tacts as generally reported confirm this. According to the sources then, even in the political conflict, there was no question of a continual political "dimension" in the story of Jesus. It was apparently only at the last moment and not on their own initiative that the Roman authorities entered into the plan: brought into it, according to all the Gospels, only as a result of the denunciation and concerted political intrigues of the Jewish hierarchy.

The religious conflict of Jesus with the law, temple and hierarchy (either Christ or the tradition of the law) therefore could not before Easter have been raised to the level of a full-scale political conflict with the emperor and the imperialistic Pax Romana (either Christ or Caesar): it could not have provided a basis for drawing conclusions without more ado and all too directly for a "political theology."[76] Jesus' Gospel particularly was not "highly political," although it was certainly not "unpolitical" in the sense of being concerned only with strictly personal religion. Jesus had no directly political, but a thoroughgoing "religious" message and mission, which of course later had incisive "political" implications and consequences. To be exact, Jesus' message and mission were *indirectly political* and this could have consequences for a "political theology."

This is confirmed by the historical influence of the Crucified. The young Christian community was soon being persecuted for religious reasons by the Jewish authorities, but was left in peace by the Romans until Nero's time—when there were other grounds for persecution. Obviously there had always been a religious opposition between Jewish and Roman *belief*. In this sense "Either Yahweh or Caesar," a proposition naturally affirmed by Jesus (and the later Christians), still counted. It was not only faith in Christ but faith in Yahweh which questioned from a religious standpoint the Roman state gods and especially the cult of deified emperors; and this questioning could have political implications. But this religious questioning did not seem to the Romans to be a reason for proceeding against the Jewish hierarchy. The religious opposition between Jewish (Christian) and Roman belief did not necessarily have to turn into a political opposition between Jewish and Roman *power*, as the message and behavior of Jesus himself clearly showed. In the political sphere what counted for Jesus was not the Zealot "either-or" of political radicalism, but the discriminating "Give to Caesar what is Caesar's and to God what is God's."[77] It was only when Caesar demanded from Christians what belonged to God that the conflict arose with the Roman state and its gods and the opposition emerged between Christ and emperor, Church and Rome.

It is really superfluous to decide who had the greater guilt for Christ's death. Both Jewish and Roman authorities were involved in it. There should never have been any talk of a collective guilt of the Jewish people at that time (why not also of the Roman people?), still less of a collective guilt of the Jewish people (and the Roman people?) today. The exactitude of the earlier Gospels in speaking of the really responsible authorities, officials, leading circles, particular groups is wholly to be preferred to the global talk of "the Jews" favored in John's Gospel. Those responsible were a small group who of course thought that they represented the people. Given the circumstances at the time and the relations between the two powers, the Roman governor was a tool of the Jewish hierarchy. For its own part, in its inquisitorial, legalistic zeal, the Jewish hierarchy was a tool of the law.

It was the law which sought his death, not simply the priests or high priests, elders or scribes as individuals. Even if the statement is not strictly historical, there is objective truth in John's version of what the Jews said to Pilate: "We have a law and according to the law he ought to die."[78] The law therefore killed him and Christians later drew the obvious conclusion. Since that time the one who was crucified in the name of the law has divided Jews and Christians. But at the same time he also binds them indissolubly into a history of solidarity, which ought never to have been denied by either side. It is absurd to charge the Jews today with guilt for the death of Jesus: a charge that has brought immense suffering on this people. Would modern society or Church have coped more easily with a figure like Jesus or indeed do they today cope more easily with the person himself? But what remains is not guilt, but the promise of grace. The crucified Jesus can at any time be brought home, not to the Jewish law which crucified him, but to the Jewish people who remain the chosen people. Who looks more like the original figure of the Jewish people, persecuted in the world and condemned to untold suffering, than the crucified Jew, Jesus of Nazareth? The people who should today consider themselves guilty of Jesus' crucifixion and death are all those, whether Jews or Christians, who have little or nothing to learn from the representatives of legality (effective in such a variety of forms) of that time. They crucify Jesus again.

In vain?

For that time the death of Jesus meant that the law had conquered. Put in question radically by Jesus, it retaliated and killed him. Its rightfulness had been proved again. Its power had prevailed. Its curse had struck. "Anyone hanged on a tree is cursed by God." This Old Testament aphorism for criminals strung up on a post after being executed[79] could be applied to him.[80] Being crucified, he is a man cursed by God. For any Jew, as Justin's Dialogue with the Jew Tryphon shows,[81] this was a decisive argument against Jesus' Messiahship. His death on the cross was the *fulfillment of the curse of the law.*

His unresisting suffering and helpless death, accursed and dishonored, for his enemies and even his friends, was the unmistakable sign that he was finished and had nothing to do with the true God. He was wrong, wholly and entirely: in his message, his behavior, his whole being. His *claim* is now *refuted*, his authority gone, his way shown to be false. Who could overlook the fact that the heretical teacher is condemned, the prophet disowned, the seducer of the people unmasked, the blasphemer rejected. The law has triumphed over this "gospel." There is nothing in this "higher righteousness," based on a faith which is opposed to the righteousness of the law based on righteous works. The law—to which man must submit unconditionally—and with it the temple are and remain God's cause.

The one crucified between the two crucified criminals is visibly the condemned embodiment of illegality, unrighteousness, ungodliness: "counted among the wicked,"[82] "made sin,"[83] *sin personified*. He is literally the representative of all lawbreakers and outlaws, whom he has defended and who really deserve the same fate: the *representative of sinners* in the worst sense of the word. Both the scorn of his enemies and the flight of his friends seem to be justified. For the latter this death means the end of the hopes settled on him, the refutation of their faith, the victory of futility.

This is the picture of a failure that was not accidental but inevitable. The question cannot be suppressed: *Did he die in vain?* If we can assume that Jesus expected his violent death, we still do not know exactly what he thought and felt as this death came upon him. According to Mark, there were none of Jesus' followers at the foot of the cross, who might have passed on his last words; only some Galilean women, without Jesus' mother, watched from a distance. The flight of the disciples is again confirmed here.[84] It would have been natural to fill in these gaps in our information with impressive or touching details in the style of Jewish and Christian legends of the martyrs. In fact this did happen later and indeed in a way that was completely suitable: in Luke the prayer for his enemies, not knowing what they were doing, and the conversion of one of the criminals crucified with him, who is to be that very day with him in paradise;[85] in John the parting with loving care from his mother and the beloved disciple.[86]

There is nothing of all this in the earliest Passion account. There are no edifying embellishments, no touching words or gestures, no reference to an unshakable inward resignation. His death is described briefly and with staggering simplicity: "Then Jesus uttered a loud cry and expired."[87] This loud, inarticulate *cry* corresponds to the fear and trembling before death, mentioned by all three Synoptists[88] and toned down only by Luke[89] with a reference to an angelic manifestation, as a sign of God's closeness. Is this the cry of someone praying confidently or of someone despairing of God?

It is striking how this terrible cry is offset in the later tradition by consoling and triumphalist expressions. Luke articulates the inarticulate cry with the aid of the verse of the Psalm: "Into thy hands I commend my spirit."[90] John replaces the cry with an inclination of the head and the fine words: "It is consummated."[91] By comparison with these modifications, the words of the Psalm used by Matthew and Mark to interpret Jesus' death, quoted in Aramaic or Hebrew, may come nearer to the reality: "My God, my God, why hast thou forsaken me?"[92] This is not a "hymn of trust" as some have held, oversimplifying the text in the light of later verses of the Psalm. But neither is it a "cry of despair" as others have thought as a result of disregarding the fact that it *is* an appeal to God. It is a death not simply accepted in patience, but endured screaming to God: God remains the final support in death, a support however which is incomprehensible to the one who is abandoned unsupported to suffering.

Here is the peculiarity of this death. Jesus died *not merely*—and this is toned down in Luke and John—*forsaken by men, but absolutely forsaken by God.* And it is only here that the most profound depth of this death finds expression: that which distinguishes this death from the "beautiful death"—so often compared with it—of Socrates, who had been charged with atheism and corrupting youth, or of some Stoic sage. Jesus was utterly abandoned to suffering. There is no mention in the Gospels of serenity, inward freedom, superiority, grandeur of soul. This was not a humane death, coming gently by hemlock poisoning, after seventy years, in ripeness and repose. It was a death coming all too soon, breaking off everything, totally degrading, in scarcely endurable misery and torment. A death not characterized by lofty resignation, but by absolute and unparalleled abandonment. And yet, for this very reason: is there a death which has shaken but perhaps also exalted mankind in its long history more than this death so infinitely human-inhuman in the immensity of its suffering?

The death of the heretic and blasphemer, the false prophet and politically suspect seducer of the people might perhaps have been one to be endured in a stoically heroic attitude. The decisive thing—not as a psychological but as a public fact—was rather different. Jesus found himself left alone, not only by his people, but by the one to whom he had constantly appealed as no one did before him. Left absolutely alone. Once again, we do not know what Jesus thought and felt as he was dying. But it was obvious to the whole world that he had proclaimed the early advent of God in his kingdom and this God did not come. A God who was man's friend, knowing all his needs, close to him, but this God was absent. A Father whose goodness knew no bounds, providing for the slightest things and the humblest people, gracious and at the same time mighty; but this Father gave no sign, produced no miracles. *His Father* indeed, to whom he had spoken with a familiarity closer than anyone else had known, with whom he had lived and worked in a unity beyond the ordinary, whose true will he had learned with immediate certainty and in the light of which he had dared to assure individuals of the forgiveness of their sins: this Father of his did not say a single word. God's witness was left in the lurch by the God to whom he had witnessed. The mockery at the foot of the cross, reported in a variety of ways, underlines vividly this wordless, helpless, miracle-less and even God-less death.

The unique communion with God which he had seemed to enjoy only makes his forsakenness more unique.[93] This God and Father with whom he had identified himself to the very end did not at the end identify himself with the sufferer. And so everything seemed as if it had never been: in vain. He who had announced the closeness and the advent of God his Father publicly before the whole world died utterly forsaken by God and was thus publicly demonstrated as godless before the whole world: someone judged by God himself, disposed of once and for all. And since the cause for which he had lived and fought was so closely linked to his person, so that cause fell with his person. There was no cause independently of himself. How could anyone have believed his word after he had been silenced and died in this outrageous fashion?

The Crucified was not left to be covered over with earth as executed Jews usually were. Roman custom permitted the body to be handed over to friends or relatives. It was not a disciple—we are told—but an individual sympathizer, who appears only at this juncture, the councilor Joseph of Arimathea, apparently not later a member of the community, who had the body buried in his private grave. Only a few women were witnesses.[94] Mark at an early stage attaches importance to the official notification of death.[95] And not only Mark, but also the ancient profession of faith, transmitted by Paul,[96] stresses the fact of the burial which is beyond doubt. But although there was a great religious interest at that time in the graves of the Jewish martyrs and prophets, oddly enough there never arose a cult at the grave of Nazareth.

V. The New Life

We have reached the most problematic point of our study of Jesus of Nazareth. Even some of those who have followed the discussion sympathetically up to now might hesitate here. The reason for this sensitivity is that the most problematic point of our own existence is also involved.

1. The beginning

It is the point where all prognosis and planning, interpretation and identification, action and passion come up against an absolute, unsurmountable frontier: death, which is the end of everything.

Introduction

The end of everything? Or was Jesus' death perhaps not the end of everything? Here particularly we must exercise great caution. We must not confirm Feuerbach's suspicion that we are merely projecting our own needs: that the resurrection is nothing more than the satisfaction of man's longing for a direct assurance of his personal immortality. Nor may we by a theological sleight of hand now deny that Jesus of Nazareth really died a human death at all. His God-forsaken *death may not be reinterpreted,* turned into a mystery or a myth, as if it were only half true. Concern for Jesus' divine immortality led the early Gnostics to raise doubts about any sort of real death; for similar reasons the medieval scholastics more or less nullified the God-forsakenness of his death by making the unbiblical assertion of a simultaneous beatific vision of God; today again, on the basis of dogmatic presuppositions, some exegetes overhastily interpret Jesus' death as being-with-God and his death cry as a hymn of trust. Death—the very opposite of Utopia[1]—thus itself becomes Utopia. Yet Jesus' death was real, his abandonment by men and God obvious, his proclamation and his action repudiated, his failure complete: a total break, which death alone can achieve in the life and work of a man.

Even the non-Christian historian will not now dispute the fact that it was *only after Jesus' death* that *the movement invoking his name really started.* At least in this sense his death was not the end of everything: his "cause" continued. And even anyone who wants to understand merely the course of world history, only to interpret the beginning of a new epoch, simply to explain the origin of that world-historical movement which is known as Christianity, will find himself faced with inescapable and interconnected questions.

How did a new beginning come about after such a disastrous end? How did this Jesus movement come into existence after Jesus' death, with such important consequences for the further destiny of the world? How did a community emerge in the name of a crucified man, how did that community take shape as a Christian "Church"?

To be more precise:

How did this condemned heretical teacher become Israel's Messiah, the Christ? How did this disowned prophet become "Lord," how did this unmasked seducer of the people become "Saviour," this rejected blasphemer "God's Son"?

After leaving this man to die in complete isolation, how did it come about that his followers not only clung to his message under the impact of his "personality," his words and deeds, not only summoned up their courage some time after the catastrophe to continue to proclaim his message of the kingdom and the will of God—for instance, the "Sermon on the Mount"—but immediately made this person himself the essential content of the message?

How did they come to proclaim, therefore, not only the Gospel of Jesus, but Jesus himself as the Gospel, unintentionally turning the proclaimer himself into the content of the proclamation, the message of the kingdom of God into the message of Jesus as the Christ of God?

What is the explanation of the fact that this Jesus, the man who was hanged, not despite his death but precisely because of it, became himself the main content of their proclamation? Was not his whole claim hopelessly compromised by his death? Did he not want the greatest things and yet hopelessly failed to get what he wanted? And, in the religio-political situation at the time, could a greater psychological and social impediment to the continuance of his cause have been devised than this disastrous end in public shame and infamy?

Why was it possible then to link any sort of hope with such a hopeless end, to proclaim as God's Messiah the one judged by God, to explain the shameful gallows as a sign of salvation and to turn the obvious bankruptcy of the movement into its phenomenal new emergence? Had they not given up his cause as lost, since his cause was bound up with his person?[2]

Where did they get their strength from: these men who came forward as his apostles so soon after such a breakdown, the complete failure of his plans; who spared no efforts, feared neither adversity nor death, in order to spread this "good" news among men, even to the outposts of the Empire?

Why did there arise that bond to the Master which is so very different from the bonds of other movements to the personalities of their founders, as for instance of Marxists to Marx or enthusiastic Freudians to Freud? Why is Jesus not merely venerated, studied and followed as the founder and teacher who lived years ago, but—especially in the worshiping congregation—proclaimed as alive and known as the one who is active at the present time? How did the extraordinary idea arise that he himself leads his followers, his community, through his Spirit?

In a word then, we are faced with the *historical enigma of the emergence,* the beginning, the origin, *of Christianity.* How different this was from the gradual, peaceful propagation of the teachings of the successful sages, Buddha and Confucius; how different also from the largely violent propagation of the teachings of the victorious Muhammad. And all this was within the lifetime of the founders. How different, after a complete failure and a shameful death, were the spontaneous emergence and almost explosive propagation of this message and community in the very name of the defeated leader. After the disastrous outcome of this life, what gave the initial impetus to that unique world-historical development: a truly world-transforming religion emerging from the gallows where a man was hanged in shame?

Psychology can explain a great deal in the world, but not everything. Nor do the prevailing conditions explain everything. In any case, if we want to interpret psychologically the initial stages of Christianity, we may not merely presume, postulate, work out ingenious hypotheses, but we must consult without prejudice those who initiated the movement and whose most important testimonies have been preserved for us. From the latter it becomes clear that this *Passion story* with its disastrous outcome—why should it ever have entered into the memory of mankind?—was transmitted only because there was also an *Easter story* which made the Passion story (and the story of the action lying behind it) appear in a completely different light.

But, far from ceasing, the *difficulties* only really begin at this point. For if someone wants to accept what are known as the resurrection or Easter stories literally with simple faith, instead of trying to find a psychological explanation, that will not be the end of it. A little reflection, any kind of reasoning, will bring him up against almost unsurmountable obstacles. Historical-critical exegesis only increases the embarrassment, as it has done ever since the most acute polemicist of classical German literature—Gotthold Ephraim Lessing—two hundred years ago brought to the notice of a bewildered public those "Fragments by an Anonymous Person" (the Hamburg rationalist H. S. Reimarus, died 1768) among which were "The Aims of Jesus and His Disciples" and "Concerning the Story of the Resurrection." If, as men of the twentieth century, we want to believe in some sort of resurrection not only halfheartedly, with a bad conscience, but honestly and with conviction, the difficulties must be faced squarely and without prejudices of faith or unbelief.[3] But it is just at this point that the *reverse side* of the difficulty is revealed. These are surmountable difficulties.[4]

First difficulty. What is true of the Gospels as a whole is particularly true of the Easter stories: they are *not unbiased reports* by disinterested observers but depositions in favor of Jesus submitted in faith by supremely interested and committed persons. They are therefore not so much historical as theological documents: not records of proceedings or chronicles, but testimonies of faith. The Easter faith, which characterized the whole Jesus tradition from the very beginning, obviously determined also the Easter accounts themselves, thus creating extraordinary difficulties from the start for a historical scrutiny. It is *in* the Easter stories that we must ask about the Easter message.

The reverse side of this difficulty is that this is the very way in which the central importance of the Easter faith to primitive Christendom becomes clear. At least for primitive Christendom, Christian faith stands or falls with the evidence of Jesus' resurrection, without which there is no content to Christian preaching or even to faith. Thus Easter appears—opportunely or inopportunely—not only as the basic unit, but also as the permanent, constitutive core of the Christian creed. Even the earliest brief Christological formulas in Paul's letters, if they amount to more than a title, are concentrated on Jesus' death and resurrection.

Second difficulty. We tried to understand the numerous miracle stories of the New Testament *without assuming a "supernatural" intervention—which cannot be proved*—in the laws of nature. It would therefore seem like a dubious retrogression to discredited ideas if we were now suddenly to postulate such a supernatural "intervention" for the miracle of the resurrection: this would contradict all scientific thinking as well as all ordinary convictions and experiences. Understood in this way, the resurrection seems to modern man to be an encumbrance to faith, akin to the virgin birth, the descent into hell or the ascension.

The reverse side. It is possible that the resurrection has a special character preventing it from being placed without more ado on the same plane as other miraculous or even legendary elements of the primitive Christian tradition. Virgin birth, descent into hell and ascension are in fact listed together with the resurrection in the "Apostles' Creed," which stems from the Roman tradition of the fourth century; but in the New Testament itself, in contrast to the resurrection, they appear only in isolated passages and without exception in later literary strata. The earliest New Testament witness, the Apostle Paul, never mentions the virgin birth, descent into hell or ascension, but firmly maintains the resurrection of the Crucified as the center of Christian preaching. The resurrection message is not the special experience of a few enthusiasts, the special teaching of some apostles. On the contrary, it belongs to the oldest strata of the New Testament. It is common to all New Testament writings without exception. It proves to be central to the Christian faith and at the same time the basis of all further statements of faith. The question therefore may at least be raised as to whether in the resurrection we are faced with something absolutely final, an eschaton—something which does not face us in the virgin birth, descent into hell or the ascension—where it is no longer appropriate to speak of an intervention within the supernatural system against the laws of nature. We shall have to look into this more closely.

Third difficulty. There is *no direct evidence* of a resurrection. There is no one in the whole New Testament who claims to have been a witness of the resurrection. The resurrection is nowhere described. The only exception is the unauthentic (apocryphal) Gospel of Peter[5] which appeared about A.D. 150 and at the end gives an account of the resurrection in a naïve, dramatic fashion with the aid of legendary details: these—like so many apocryphal elements—entered into the Church's Easter texts, Easter celebrations, Easter hymns, Easter sermons, Easter pictures, and were thus mingled in a variety of ways with popular belief about Easter. Even such unique masterpieces of art as Grünewald's unsurpassed depiction of the resurrection in the Isenheim altar can be misleading in this respect.

The reverse side. The very reserve of the New Testament Gospels and letters in regard to the resurrection creates trust. The resurrection is neither depicted nor described. The interest in exaggeration and the craving for demonstration, which are characteristic of the Apocrypha, make the latter incredible. The New Testament Easter documents are not meant to be testimonies for the resurrection but testimonies to the raised and risen Jesus.

Fourth difficulty. A close analysis of the Easter accounts reveals insuperable *discrepancies and inconsistencies.* Attempts have indeed been made constantly to combine and harmonize them into a uniform tradition. But—to sum it up briefly—it is impossible to establish agreement about 1. the people involved: Peter, Mary Magdalene, the other Mary, the disciples, the apostles, the twelve, the Emmaus disciples, five hundred brethren, James, Paul; 2. the locality of the events: Galilee, a mountain there or the lake of Tiberias; Jerusalem, at Jesus' grave or a meeting place; 3. the whole sequence of appearances: morning and evening of Easter Sunday, eight days and forty days later. At every point harmonization proves to be impossible, unless we are prepared to accept textual changes and to minimize the differences.

The reverse side. Obviously no one at the time needed or wanted a uniform scheme or a smooth harmony, still less any sort of biography of the risen Jesus. The New Testament authors are not interested in any kind of completeness nor in a definite sequence and least of all in a critical historical investigation of the different pieces of information. From this it is clear that there is something more important to be stressed in the individual narratives: for Paul and Mark the calling and mission of the disciples; for Luke and John it is more the real identity of the risen with the pre-paschal Jesus (perception of the identity and ultimately proof of identity by the demonstration of his corporality and his sharing food, with a constantly greater emphasis on conquering the doubts of the disciples). At the same time it becomes clear that any how, when or where of the narratives is of secondary importance by comparison with the fact—of which there is no doubt in the different sources—of the resurrection which in every context is clearly not identical with death and burial. What is required is a concentration on the true content of the message and this in turn will make possible a renewed investigation into the historical discrepancies.

Clarifications

We have to go back from the Easter stories to ask about the Easter message. While the story of the empty tomb is found only in the Gospels, other New Testament books—especially the Pauline letters—attest the fact that Jesus is encountered as a living person by the disciples. While the Easter stories of the evangelists are presented in a legendary form, other New Testament testimonies take the form of a creed. And while the stories of the tomb are not covered by any direct witnesses, in Paul's letters (decades in advance of the Gospels) there are statements of Paul himself, speaking of "appearances," "revelations" of the risen Jesus. Even the creed already mentioned, expressly "adopted" by Paul and "transmitted" to the community in Corinth at its foundation, in the light of its language, authority, the persons involved, possibly stemming from the early Jerusalem community, at any rate from the time between 35 and 45, cites in its extension a list of witnesses of the resurrection which could be controlled by contemporaries: those by whom the Risen One "was seen," to whom "he appeared," to whom he "was revealed," by whom he was encountered, most of them still living and open to questions in the years 55 to 56, when the letter was written in Ephesus.[6]

In the list (reflecting the history of the primitive community?) of authoritative witnesses Peter appears at the head, oddly enough under his Aramaic name of Cephas. Just because he was the first witness of the risen Jesus, he may well have been also the "rock man,"[7] "strengthener of the brethren"[8] and "shepherd of the sheep."[9] But a reduction of all the appearances—to the twelve (the central controlling body in Jerusalem), to James (the brother of Jesus), to all the apostles (the greater circle of missionaries), to more than five hundred brethren, to Paul himself—to the one appearance to Peter, as if the former were merely to confirm the latter, is not justified either by these or other texts. The persons and events, time and place are too diverse; and the forms of the Christ proclamation are also too diverse, particularly with Peter, James and Paul.

Before bringing out the true content of the Easter message, however, it will be better to attempt some clarifications which may prevent unnecessary misunderstandings of the message from the very beginning. For various formulas and ideas are used in the New Testament for the Easter event which, rightly understood, can help in the question under discussion: "raising" and "resurrection," "exaltation" and "glorification," "taking up" and "ascension." How are all these to be understood?

Resurrection or raising? Today we speak perhaps too glibly of "resurrection" in the sense simply of Jesus' action by his own power. In the New Testament however "resurrection" is rightly understood as "raising by God." It is essentially a work of God on Jesus, the one crucified, dead and buried. Jesus' "raising" (passive) is probably therefore more original in the New Testament and certainly more universal than Jesus' "resurrection" (active).[10] "Raising" places God's whole action on Jesus at the center. It is only by God's life-creating action that Jesus' deadly passivity becomes new, vital activity. It is only as the one raised (by God) that he is the one who (himself) has risen. Throughout the New Testament resurrection is understood, not simply as Jesus' deed, but in the sense of raising as a work of the Father.[11] It is so expressed in an ancient formula: "God raised him, releasing him from the pangs of death."[12] The emphasis laid here on "raising" and the one "raised" is not meant to exclude other expressions, but to avoid any mythological misunderstanding which could otherwise easily creep in.*

Raising up as a historical event? Since according to New Testament faith the raising is an act of God within God's dimensions, it can *not* be a *historical* event in the strict sense: it is not an event which can be verified by historical science with the aid of historical methods. For the raising of Jesus is not a miracle violating the laws of nature, verifiable within the present world, not a supernatural intervention which can be located and dated in space and time. There was nothing to photograph or to record. What can be historically verified are the death of Jesus and after this the Easter faith and the Easter message of the disciples. But neither the raising itself nor the person raised can be apprehended, objectified, by histori-

* Since "raising" is less frequently used in English than *Auferweckung* in German, the latter term—like *Auferstehung*—will mostly be translated as "resurrection" except where the emphasis is clearly on God's action. (Translator.)

cal methods. In this respect the question would demand too much of historical science—which, like the sciences of chemistry, biology, psychology, sociology or theology, never sees more than *one* aspect of the complex reality—since, on the basis of its own premises, it deliberately excludes the very reality which alone comes into question for a resurrection as also for creation and consummation: the reality of God.

But just because it is God's action according to New Testament faith which is involved in the resurrection, this cannot be a merely fictitious or imaginary but in the most profound sense a *real* event. What happened is not nothing. But what happened bursts through and goes beyond the bounds of history. It is a transcendental happening out of human death into the all-embracing dimension of God. Resurrection involves a completely new mode of existence in God's wholly different mode of existence, conveyed visually and in need of interpretation. The fact that God intervenes at the point where everything is at an end from the human point of view, this—despite the maintenance of natural laws—is the true miracle of the resurrection: the miracle of the beginning of a new life out of death. It is not an object of historical knowledge, but certainly a call and an offer to faith, which alone can get at the reality of the person raised up.

Resurrection imaginable? People too easily forget that both "resurrection" and "raising" are metaphorical, visual terms. The picture is taken from "awakening" and "rising" from sleep. But, as an image, symbol, metaphor, for what is supposed to happen to the dead person, this can be both easily understood and easily misunderstood. It is the very opposite of returning as from sleep to the previous state of things, to the former, earthly, mortal life. It is a radical transformation into a wholly different state, into another, new, unparalleled, definitive, immortal life: *totaliter aliter*, utterly different.

To the question that people are constantly inclined to ask—how are we to imagine this wholly different life?—the answer is simple: not at all! Here there is nothing to be depicted, imagined, objectified. It would not be a wholly different life if we could illustrate it with concepts and ideas from our present life. Neither sight nor imagination can help us here, they can only mislead us. The reality of the resurrection itself therefore is completely *intangible* and *unimaginable*. Resurrection and raising are pictorial-graphic expressions; they are images, metaphors, symbols, which corresponded to the thought forms of that time and which could of course be augmented, for something which is itself intangible and unimaginable and of which—as of God himself—we have no sort of direct knowledge.

Certainly we can attempt to convey this intangible and unimaginable life, not only graphically but also intellectually (as for instance physics attempts to convey by formulas the nature of light, which in the atomic field is both wave and corpuscle and as such intangible and unimaginable). Here too we come up against the limitations of language. But then there is nothing left for it but to speak in paradoxes: to link together for this wholly different life concepts which in the present life are mutually exclusive. That is what happens in a way in the Gospel accounts of the appearances, at the extreme limit of the imaginable: not a phantom and yet not palpable, perceptible-imperceptible, visible-invisible, comprehensible-incomprehensible, material-immaterial, within and beyond space and time.

"Like the angels in heaven," Jesus himself observed, using the language of the Jewish tradition.[13] Paul speaks of this new life in paradoxical terms, which themselves point to the limits of what can be said: an imperishable "spirit-body,"[14] a "body of glory,"[15] which has emerged through a radical "transformation"[16] from the perishable body of flesh. By this Paul simply does not mean a spirit-soul in the Greek sense (released from the prison of the body), which modern anthropology can no longer conceive in isolation. He means in the Jewish sense a whole corporeal human being (transformed and permeated by God's life-creating Spirit), which corresponds much more closely to the modern integral conception of man and to the fundamental importance of his corporality. Man therefore is not—Platonically—released *from* his corporality. He is released *with* and *in* his now glorified, spiritualized corporality: a new creation, a new man.

Corporeal resurrection? Yes and no, if I may recall a personal conversation with Rudolf Bultmann. No, if "body" simply means the physiologically identical body. Yes, if "body" means in the sense of the New Testament *soma* the identical personal reality, the *same self* with its whole history. In other words, no continuity of the body: questions of natural science, like that of the persistence of the molecules, do not arise. But an identity of the person: the question does arise of the lasting significance of the person's whole life and fate. In any case therefore not a diminished but a finished being. The view of Eastern thinkers, that the self does not survive death and that only the works live on, is certainly worth considering in the sense that death means a transition into dimensions other than those of space and time. But it is inadequate. If God is the ultimate reality, then death is not destruction but metamorphosis—not a diminishing, but a finishing.

If then the resurrection of Jesus was not an event in human space and human time,[17] neither can it be regarded *merely* as a way of expressing the significance of his death.[18] It was admittedly not a historical event (verifiable by means of historical research), but it was certainly (for faith) a real event. Consequently the resurrection cannot mean *merely* that his "cause"[19] goes on and remains historically linked with his name, while he himself no longer exists, no longer lives, but is and remains dead. It is not like the "cause" of Monsieur Eiffel, which lives on in the Eiffel Tower though the man himself is dead; nor is there any similarity to Goethe, who "speaks even today," being remembered in his work. With Jesus it is a question of the living *person* and *therefore* of the cause. The reality of the risen Jesus therefore cannot be left out of consideration. Jesus' cause—which his disciples had given up as lost—was decided at Easter by God himself. Jesus' cause makes sense and continues, because he himself did not remain—a failure—in death, but lives on completely justified by God.

Easter therefore is not a happening *merely* for the disciples and their faith. Jesus does not live *through* their faith. The Easter faith is not a function of the disciples' faith. He was not—as some think—simply too great to die: he did die. But Easter is an event primarily for Jesus himself: Jesus lives again *through God—for their faith.* The precondition of the new life is God's action which is not chronologically but objectively prior to it, in advance of it. Thus that faith is first made possible, established, in which the living Jesus himself proves to be alive. Even according to Bultmann, the formula, "Jesus is risen into the kerygma (proclamation),"[20] is liable to be misunderstood. Even according to Bultmann, it does not mean that Jesus lives because he is proclaimed: he is proclaimed because he lives. It is therefore a very different situation in Rodion Shchedrin's oratorio, *Lenin in the Heart of the People,* where the Red Guardsman sings at Lenin's deathbed: "No, no, no! That cannot be! Lenin lives, lives, lives!" Here it is only "Lenin's cause" that continues.

Exaltation? In the older texts of the New Testament the "exaltation" or "taking up" of Jesus is simply a form of expression for Jesus' raising or resurrection, with a different emphasis. The fact that Jesus was raised means in the New Testament nothing more than that he was elevated to God by the very fact of being raised: exaltation as completion of the resurrection.[21]

But does not exaltation mean assumption into *heaven?* Metaphorically we can in fact speak of assumption into "heaven." At the same time it is clear that the blue firmament can no longer be understood as in biblical times as the external side of God's presence chamber. But it can certainly be understood as the visible symbol or image for the real heaven, the invisible domain ("living space") of God. The heaven of faith is not the heaven of the astronauts, even though the astronauts themselves expressed it that way when they recited in outer space the biblical account of creation. The heaven of faith is the hidden invisible-incomprehensible sphere of God which no journey into space ever reaches. It is not a place, but a mode of being: not one beyond earth's confines, but bringing all to perfection in God and giving a share in the reign of God.

Jesus then is taken up into the glory of the Father. Resurrection and exaltation, when linked with Old Testament phraseology,[22] mean accession to power (enthronement) on the part of him who has conquered death: assumed into God's sphere of life, he shares God's rule and glory and so can exercise his claim to universal dominion for man. The Crucified is *Lord* and calls men to follow him. He is thus installed in his heavenly, divine dignity, which again finds its traditional expression in a metaphor referring to the son or representative of the ruler: "Sits at the right hand of the Father." That is, he is nearest to the Father in authority and exercises it vicariously with the same dignity and status. In the earliest Christological formulas, as used for instance in the apostles' sermons in Acts, Jesus was indeed man in lowliness, but, after raising him, God made him Lord and Messiah.[23] It is only to the exalted and not to the earthly Jesus that Messiahship and divine sonship are ascribed.[24]

This is important for the Easter *appearances*, however they are ultimately to be understood. It is from this heavenly state of divine power and glory that he "appears" to those whom he will make his "instruments": this is what Paul learnt[25] and what is quite naturally assumed in the appearances in Matthew, John, and in Mark's supplement, where there is no mention of the whence and whither of the one who appears. Easter appearances are manifestations of the already exalted Jesus. It is always the exalted Jesus who appears, coming from God, whether it is Paul hearing the one who calls him from heaven or—as in Matthew and John—the risen Jesus appearing on earth.

In the New Testament then—apart from an exception to be discussed immediately—raising from death and exaltation to God are one. Whenever there is a mention only of the one, the other is implied. Easter faith is faith in Jesus as the Lord who is risen (=exalted to God). He is both the Lord of his Church, present in the Spirit, and the hidden Lord of the world (cosmocrator) with whose rule the definitive rule of God has already begun.

A *resurrection?* In the earliest stage of the Church there was no tradition of a visible ascension of Jesus in sight of the disciples.[26] But there is one exception. Luke is more interested than others from the start in demonstrating the corporeal reality of the risen Jesus and in the apostles as eyewitnesses: *unlike the other witnesses, he separates resurrection and exaltation in time.* He alone mentions a separate ascension in Bethany, which closes the time of Jesus' appearances on earth (before the heavenly appearance to Paul) and definitely opens the period of the Church's world mission lasting until Jesus' second coming.[27] This is particularly clear in the Acts of the Apostles which follows on Luke's Gospel (after 70) and was probably first written between 80 and 90. In the conclusion added subsequently to Mark, stemming from the second century, this idea of a separate ascension is adopted, under the influence both of the phraseology used to describe the taking up of Elijah[28] and of the words of the Psalm about sitting on the right hand of the Father.[29]

Obviously Jesus did not go on a journey into space. In which direction would he have ascended, at what speed, and how long would it have taken? An ascension in these terms is inconceivable to modern man, but it was familiar enough to people at that time. We hear of an ascension, not only in connection with Elijah and Enoch in the Old Testament, but also with other great figures of antiquity like Hercules, Empedocles, Romulus, Alexander the Great and Apollonius of Tyana. It was a question of being carried up, not of a "journey to heaven," neither the way to heaven nor the arrival there being described, but only the disappearance from earth. In this respect the cloud signifies both the closeness and the unapproachability of God. The taking up pattern was therefore at Luke's disposal as ideal type and narrative form.

Presumably he himself turned the traditional exaltation-statement into a taking up story, for which all the essential structural elements were available in the earlier stories of the tomb and the appearances. Why? Luke was probably not concerned only with visualizing the statement of a non-visual exaltation. As in his whole Gospel, he was determined to correct quite firmly the still widespread expectation of the parousia, the second coming of Jesus, at an early date: instead of inactive waiting, there had to be the mission to the world. Jesus himself had gone to heaven and left the task to his disciples. It was the Holy Spirit who was now to come to equip the disciples for the imminent missionary age—the time of the Church in continuity with the time of Jesus—until at the end of time Jesus will return as palpably as before. Luke wants to say that only those have understood Easter who do not look up to heaven in amazement but bear witness to Jesus in the world.[80]

So the story of the ascension—especially in the subsequent version of Acts, with cloud and angels—seems almost like a parousia story in reverse. In Luke's Gospel as also in Mark's supplement the Easter appearances and the ascension seem to have taken place on the same Easter day. Only the Acts of the Apostles, which is later—obviously influenced by the sacred biblical number forty (Israel's forty years in the desert, forty days of fasting on the part of Elijah and Jesus)—mentions forty days between Easter and ascension: the symbolic figure for a time of grace. The ascension is *not* to be understood or celebrated as a *second "salvation fact"* after Easter, *but* as a specially emphasized *aspect of the one Easter event.*

Pentecost? It is again only from the late Lucan Acts of the Apostles that we learn of a Christian feast of Pentecost. *Pentekoste*[81] (=fiftieth day) had been a harvest festival for the Jews. Luke incorporates this feast from the Jewish calendar into the context of promise and fulfillment in the history of salvation. For him it is obviously the feast of the promised gift of the Spirit and the nativity of the universal Church. It is not easy to discover what are the historical facts behind it. On the first Pentecost after Jesus' death, when many pilgrims must certainly have come to Jerusalem, the first gathering of Jesus' followers—returning mainly from Galilee—and their constitution as the eschatological community (with enthusiastic-charismatic accompanying manifestations) may well have taken place. Luke perhaps made use of a tradition of the first occurrence of a mass ecstasy under the influence of the Spirit in Jerusalem at the first Pentecost.

Oddly enough, neither Paul nor Mark nor Matthew seems to know anything of a Christian Pentecost. For John Easter and Pentecost (gift of the Spirit)[32] expressly coincide.

In the whole of the New Testament *baptism*, which recalls Easter, is also the sacrament of the reception of the Spirit—apart from two exceptions, again in Luke's Acts of the Apostles,[33] which proves the rule. But many centuries later the second anointing after baptism, typical for Rome, developed independently in the Western Church as a proper rite for the reception of the Spirit, since the bishops in the West had reserved in practice this rite to themselves: *confirmation*. To justify this canonical development not only were these two texts of the Acts of the Apostles invoked (which refer to the unity of the Church and not to a special sacrament), but also the Lucan distinction between Easter and Pentecost (although even in the Pentecost narrative the new converts' reception of the Spirit is linked with baptism). From the modern standpoint we cannot recognize confirmation as a separate, autonomous and independent sacrament. But it can certainly be regarded as the closing phase—appropriate in connection with infant baptism—of the one rite of initiation (before admission to the eucharist): as unfolding, confirming and completion of baptism.[34]

A *Church's Year?* During the first three centuries *Pentekoste* did not designate a specific feast of Pentecost but the whole festal period lasting fifty days, which had begun with the Easter vigil: a continuous feast of the Lord—so to speak—to the glory of the risen Christ, during which people prayed only standing and not kneeling, when there was no fasting but abundant Alleluia singing in the liturgy.

But that mention by Luke of a Christian feast of Pentecost, unique in the New Testament, became so strongly established in the Church's consciousness that from the fifth century onwards, in addition to Easter and fifty days after Easter, a separate feast of Pentecost began to be celebrated. Soon also a separate feast of the ascension forty days after Easter was established. Instead of the fifty-day period of rejoicing, celebrating resurrection, ascension and the gift of the Spirit, a new *historicizing approach to the feasts* came to prevail. In a recourse to the biblical indications of time, as a result of extending the Easter feast to the whole year, the idea finally arose of the "Church year" (an expression first used in the sixteenth century): an annual liturgical cycle made up of feasts of the Lord, to which there were later added feasts of the saints. As late as the Middle Ages the year began at different times—Easter, the annunciation and especially Christmas, which had been celebrated as a feast since the fourth century—and only in modern times has the first Sunday of Advent come to be accepted as the beginning.

But—we may now ask summarily, after these clarifications—with all these developments and occasionally entanglements, what is the real content of this message which has kept faith and worship alive through two thousand years of Christendom, which is both the historical source and the objective foundation of the Christian faith?

The ultimate reality

The message with all its difficulties, its time-bound concrete expressions and amplifications, situational expansions, elaborations and shifts of emphasis is basically concerned with something simple. And—despite all discrepancies and inconsistencies of the different traditions in regard to place and time, persons and the sequence of events—the different primitive Christian witnesses, Peter, Paul and James, the letters, the Gospels and Acts, are agreed that the *Crucified lives forever with God, as obligation and hope for us.* The men of the New Testament are sustained, even fascinated, by the certainty that the one who was killed did not remain dead but is alive and that the person who clings to him will likewise live. The new, eternal life of the one is a challenge and real hope for all.

This then is the meaning of the Easter message and the Easter faith, completely unambiguous despite all the ambiguity of the different accounts and ideas of Easter. It is a truly revolutionary message, very easy to reject not only then but also today: "On this subject we will hear you again," said some skeptics to Paul on the Areopagus in Athens, according to Luke.[35] Not of course that this held up the victorious progress of the message.

It had been prepared already in *Judaism.* In Persian times after the Babylonian exile, people were becoming less and less satisfied with the ancient answer that all accounts were settled within the present life, between birth and death, in terms of appropriate rewards or reprisals. This was how Job's friends argued. Neither in the life of the people nor in that of the individual did good and bad seem to be adequately recompensed. Thus in the two centuries before Christ the expectation began to prevail more and more clearly—supported by some biblical texts on the possible intervention of God in any kind of distress or danger—that the comprehensive fulfillment was still to come: that God's justice would produce the great settlement in a last judgment.

Against the background of this expectation—for the first time in the Old Testament, probably under Persian influence, in the book of Daniel about the middle of the second century before Christ[36] and in the apocalyptic literature as a whole, especially in the non-canonical book of Enoch —faith had been roused in the universal resurrection of the dead or at least of the just. The resurrection was seen as the presupposition for carrying out the last judgment and for the completion of the history of mankind. These reflections were not directly concerned with the fate of the dead, about which there were very diverse opinions. What counted was the success of God's cause for the people and the individual in this very unjust world: resurrection was seen as part of God's self-justification, as an argument in theodicy. It is in this sense that the devout Jew confesses three times a day in the second benediction of the Eighteen Benedictions: "Blessed art Thou, O Lord, that quickenest the dead."

This Jewish faith, with its apocalyptic background, is taken for granted in the New Testament as a whole. The Christian faith on the other hand —which must of course be freed from purely time-conditioned apocalyptic ideas—includes that Jewish faith in a final concentration. Jews and Christians believe in the resurrection. The faith of Jews and Christians rests on the fact that for them the living God is the *unshakably faithful God* as we constantly encounter him in the history of Israel. He is the Creator who keeps faith with his creature and partner, come what may. He does not withdraw his yes to life, but at the decisive frontier itself adds another yes to his first yes. He is faithful in death and beyond death.

What however the Jews expect for all men in the future has come already for *Christians* in the One as sign of obligation and hope for all. The Jewish faith in a universal resurrection and the particular faith in Jesus' resurrection are therefore interrelated. The first Christians see the resurrection of Jesus against the background and in the light of the Jewish hope of a universal resurrection of the dead. But at the same time Jesus' resurrection confirms the Jewish faith in a universal resurrection and thus Jesus' unique significance for men becomes manifest: the raising of Jesus is the beginning of the universal awakening of the dead, the beginning of the new age, the beginning of the end of the present age.[87] Christians therefore do not merely say: "Since there is a universal resurrection of the dead, this one person in particular must have been raised up." But they say also with Paul: "Since this one person has been raised, there is also a universal awakening of the dead." Since this one person lives and has from God such a unique significance for all, all those will live who trustingly commit themselves to him. To all who share the lot of Jesus there is offered a share in God's victory over death: thus Jesus is the first fruits of the dead,[88] the first-born from the dead.[89]

The Crucified *lives.* What does "lives" mean here? What is concealed behind the diverse time-conditioned ideal types and narrative forms which the New Testament uses to describe it? We shall attempt to convey the meaning of this life with two negative definitions and one positive.

No return to this life in space and time. Death is not canceled but definitively conquered. In Friedrich Dürrenmatt's play *Meteor* a corpse (faked, naturally) is revived and returns to a completely unchanged earthly life—the very opposite of what the New Testament means by resurrection. Jesus' resurrection must not be confused with the raisings of the dead scattered about in the ancient literature of miracle workers (even confirmed with doctors' attestations) and reported in three instances of

Jesus (daughter of Jairus,[40] young man of Nain,[41] Lazarus[42]). Quite apart from the historical credibility of such legendary accounts (Mark, for instance, has nothing about the sensational raising of Lazarus from the dead), what is meant by the raising of Jesus is just not the revival of a corpse. Even in Luke's account Jesus did not simply return to biological-earthly life, in order—like those raised from the dead—to die again. No, according to the New Testament conception, he has the final frontier of death definitively behind him. He has entered into a wholly different, imperishable, eternal, "heavenly" life: into the life of God, for which—as we have seen—very diverse formulas and ideas were used in the New Testament.

Not a continuation of this life in space and time. Even to speak of life "after" death is misleading: eternity is not characterized by "before" and "after." It means a new life which escapes the dimensions of space and time, a life within God's invisible, imperishable, incomprehensible domain. It is not simply an endless "further": "further life," "carrying on further," "going on further." But it is something definitively "new": new creation, new birth, new man and new world. That which finally breaks through the return of the eternal sameness of "dying and coming to be." What is meant is to be definitively with God and so to have definitive life.

Assumption into ultimate reality. If we are not to talk in metaphors, raising (resurrection) and exaltation (taking up, ascension, glorification) must be seen as one identical, single happening. And indeed as a happening in connection with death in the impenetrable hiddenness of God. The Easter message in all its different variations means simply one thing: Jesus did not die into nothingness. In death and from death he *died into* and was *taken up* by that *incomprehensible and comprehensive ultimate reality* which we designate by the name of God.[43] When man reaches his eschaton, the absolutely final point in his life, what awaits him? Not nothing, as even believers in nirvana would say. But that All which for Jews, Christians and Muslims is God. Death is transition to God, is retreat into God's hiddenness, is assumption into his glory. Strictly speaking, only an atheist can say that death is the *end of everything.*

In death man is taken out of the conditions that surround and control him. Seen from the standpoint of the world—from outside, as it were—death means complete unrelatedness. But, seen from God's standpoint—from within, as it were—death means a totally new relationship: to him as the ultimate reality. In death a new and eternal future is offered to man, to man—that is—in his wholeness and undividedness. It is a life different from all that can be experienced: within God's imperishable dimensions. It is therefore not in our space and our time, not "here" and "now" "on this side." But neither is it simply in another space and another time: a "beyond," an "up there," an "outside" or "above," "on the other side." Man's last, decisive, quite different road does not lead out into the universe or beyond it. It leads—if we want to speak metaphorically—as it were into the innermost primal ground, primal support, primal meaning of world and man: from death to life, from the visible to the invisible, from mortal darkness to God's eternal light. Jesus died into God, he has reached God: he is assumed into that domain which surpasses all imagination, which no human eye has ever seen, eluding our grasp, comprehension, reflection or fantasy. The believer knows only that what awaits him is not nothing, but his Father.

From this negative and positive definition it follows that *death* and *resurrection* form a *differentiated unity*. If we want to interpret the New Testament testimonies in a way that does not run counter to their intentions, we may not simply make the resurrection into an interpretative device, a means by which faith expresses the meaning of the cross.[44]

Resurrection means dying into God: death and resurrection are most closely connected. *Resurrection occurs with death, in death, from death. This is brought out most clearly in early pre-Pauline hymns in which Jesus' exaltation seems to follow immediately on the crucifixion.*[45] *And in John's Gospel especially Jesus' "exaltation" means both his crucifixion and his "glorification"*[46] *and both form the one return to the Father.*[47] *But in the rest of the New Testament the exaltation comes after the humiliation of the cross.*

"Dying into God" is not something to be taken for granted, not a natural development, not a desideratum of human nature to be fulfilled at all costs. Death and resurrection must be seen as distinct, *not necessarily in time but objectively. This is also emphasized by the ancient, presumably less historical than theological reference: "on the third day he rose again," "third" being not a date in the calendar but a salvation date for a day of salvation. Death is man's affair, resurrection can only be God's. Man is taken up, called, brought home, and therefore finally accepted, saved, by God into himself as the incomprehensible, comprehensive ultimate reality. He is taken up in death or—better—from death as an event in itself, rooted in God's act and fidelity. It is the hidden, unimaginable, new act of the Creator, of him who calls into existence the things that are not.*[48] *And therefore—though not a supernatural "intervention" contrary to the laws of nature—it is a genuine gift and a true miracle.*

Do we need then expressly to insist on the fact that man's new life, involving as it does the ultimate reality, God himself, is *a priori* a matter of *faith?* It is an event of the new creation, which breaks through death as the last frontier and therefore the horizon of our world and thought as a whole. For it means the definitive breakthrough of one-dimensional man into the truly other dimension: the evident reality of God and the rule of the Crucified, calling men to follow him. Nothing is easier than to raise doubts about this. Certainly "pure reason" is faced here with an impassable frontier. At this point we can only agree with Kant. Nor can the resurrection be proved by historical arguments; traditional apologetics breaks down here. Since man is here dealing with God and this by definition means with the invisible, impalpable, uncontrollable, only one attitude is appropriate and required: believing trust, trusting faith. There is no way to the risen Christ and to eternal life which bypasses faith. The resurrection is not a miracle authenticating faith. It is itself the object of faith.

The resurrection faith—and this must be said to bring out the contrast with all unbelief and superstition—is not however faith in some kind of unverifiable curiosity, which we ought to believe in addition to all the rest. Nor is the resurrection faith a faith in the fact of the resurrection or in the risen Christ taken in isolation: it is fundamentally faith in God with whom the risen Christ is now one.[49]

> *The resurrection faith is not an appendage to faith in God, but a* radicalizing of faith in God. *It is a faith in God which does not stop halfway, but follows the road consistently to the end. It is a faith in which man, without strictly rational proof but certainly with completely reasonable trust, relies on the fact that the God of the beginning is also the God of the end, that as he is the Creator of the world and man so too he is their Finisher.*
>
> *The resurrection faith therefore is not to be interpreted merely as existential interiorization or social change, but as a radicalizing of faith in* God the Creator. *Resurrection means the* real *conquest of death by God the Creator to whom the believer entrusts everything, even the ultimate, even the conquest of death. The end which is also a new beginning. Anyone who begins his creed with faith in "God the almighty Creator" can be content to end it with faith in "eternal life." Since God is the Alpha, he is also the Omega. The almighty Creator who calls things from nothingness into being can also call men from death into life.*[50]

It is precisely in face of death that God's power hidden in the world is revealed. Man cannot work out for himself the resurrection from the dead. But man *may* in any case rely on this God who can practically be defined as a God of the living and not of the dead,[51] he may absolutely trust in his superior power even in face of inevitable death, may approach his death with confidence. The Creator and Conserver of the universe and of man can be trusted, even at death and as we are dying, beyond the limits of all that has hitherto been experienced, to have still one more word to say: to have the last word as he had the first. Toward this God the only reasonable and realistic attitude is trust and faith. This passing from death to

God cannot be verified empirically or rationally. It is not to be expected, not to be proved, but to be hoped for in faith. What is impossible to man is only made possible by God. Anyone who seriously believes in the living God believes therefore also in the raising of the dead to life, in God's power which is proved at death. As Jesus retorted to the doubting Sadducees: "You know neither the Scriptures nor the power of God."[52]

The Christian faith in the risen Jesus is meaningful only as faith in God the Creator and Conserver of life. But, on the other hand, the Christian faith in God the Creator is decisively characterized by the fact that he raised Jesus from the dead.[53] "He who raised Jesus from the dead," becomes practically the designation of the Christian God.[54]

Legends?

Anyone who perceives the real point of the resurrection message will regard some fiercely contested questions as peripheral. Only a person who attaches his faith to historical details will be upset by historical criticism. But the faith which is oriented to the new life of the Crucified with God and through God is able to recognize the relativity of historical questions. So anyone who is not interested in historical questions like the development of the Easter accounts, the empty tomb, the descent into hell and the appearances of the risen Jesus, may pass over the two following sections. Historical analysis cannot substantiate faith at its center, but it can interpret and clarify faith against unbelief and superstition.[55]

a. The history of the resurrection tradition reveals problematical *expansions, elaborations* and occasionally even gaps. The *oldest Easter testimony* of the New Testament—the ancient formula of faith in the first epistle to the Corinthians, already mentioned[56]—like other Pauline formulas of faith, has the brevity of recorded minutes, a minimum of information without any sort of description and without any indication of the place and time of the appearances. Even the oldest Easter account in the Gospels—which in their literary form are later than Paul's letters, but are themselves elaborations of earlier traditions—is amazingly jejune. This account in *Mark*[57]—to be distinguished from the supplement to Mark[58] (not known to Mark and Luke), which later also collected in catalogue form the traditions circulating about the resurrection—adds nothing new apart from the tradition of the empty tomb (perhaps originally independent) and the reference (not a narrative) to Jesus' appearance in Galilee.

The two longer Gospels however—partly for apologetic reasons—exhibit considerable changes and expansions. In *Matthew*, who makes a continuous narrative out of the appearance of Jesus to the women at the tomb and the Galilean appearance, there are several new features: the earthquake; the story of the guards at the tomb and the carrying out of the order of the angel and Jesus to go to Galilee; the appearance to the eleven on the mountain in Galilee with the order to go out into the world, to teach and baptize. In *Luke,* who simply omits the order to go to Galilee, passes over the Galilean appearance and concentrates the whole Easter event in place and time on Jerusalem which for him is theologically and ecclesially important, there are other additions: the artistically elaborated narrative about the Emmaus disciples; the appearance to the eleven in Jerusalem; a brief farewell discourse and a short account of an ascension of Jesus, which is taken up again and considerably expanded in the Lucan Acts of the Apostles.

In the later Gospels what has for a long time been the practice of the Church is ascribed to the action and mandate of the risen Christ: the mission to the Gentiles and baptism in Matthew, the breaking of bread (which in the Emmaus scene was bound to remind any reader of the Lord's Supper) in Luke, the status of Peter and authority to forgive sin (for *every* believer) in John. While no angel is mentioned in the Pauline Easter testimony, in Mark and Matthew there is one and in Luke and John even two. And while in Paul and Matthew the appearances of the risen Christ are simply for the sake of the mission to proclaim the message, in Luke and John the emphasis is on the authentication of the resurrection. In Luke there is a constant tendency to hypostasize. While Paul speaks paradoxically of a "spiritual," unimaginable, risen body, Luke insists—probably for apologetic reasons, against a spiritist interpretation of the resurrection—that the risen Jesus is not a ghost, that he has flesh and bones, eats grilled fish. And as the true corporality of the risen Jesus is more and more firmly emphasized for apologetic reasons, so too is the motif of overcoming doubt.

The considerably later Gospel of John, despite its many points of contact with Luke, likewise contains new elements and motifs: the conversation with Mary Magdalene, the wager of Peter and the unnamed beloved disciple, the gathering in the room in Jerusalem with the gift of the Spirit in the evening of Easter day, the story of the unbelieving Thomas with the motif of doubt particularly strongly developed. Later a further chapter was added, again for the sake of the experience of identity, with the appearance on the lake of Gennesaret, a miraculous draught of fishes with a meal and a special mandate to Peter. Here again there is the competition motif between Peter, as the first to whom Jesus appeared and whose precedence is confirmed, and the beloved disciple who is depicted in the fourth Gospel evidently as the true guarantor of the tradition.

The very development of the Easter tradition reveals some important details. Historically the Easter faith may quite probably have emerged in Galilee, where Jesus' followers gathered together again after their flight in order to go from there up to Jerusalem in expectation of the return of the exalted Son of Man. But the state of the sources alone rules out any *a priori* claim to historicity for the various expansions, displacements and elaborations of the Easter message: they may well have a largely legendary character. The diversity of the accounts is the result of the diversity of the communities, the bearers of the tradition and the settings of the tradition (missionary preaching, catechesis, worship). The decisive factor is not to be found in the varying individual features of the different narratives, the imaginative portrayals or the different intentions and theologies of the sources, authors and editors. What is decisive is the new life of Jesus from death through God and with God, affirmed by all the witnesses: God's life, which surpasses all statements and ideas, images, portrayals and legends.

b. What is to be made however of the narrative of the *empty tomb?* The reference already mentioned, found also in Paul and used as a kind of formula, "on the third day," may mean the discovery of the empty tomb by the women or the first Easter appearance to Peter; but it may also mean, as in Jewish apocalyptic literature, the term between the final disaster and the dawn of final salvation, the cross and resurrection being then marked in apocalyptic language as the end-event and the third day as day of salvation.[59] This reference, like the Lucan forty days between Easter and ascension, could be a theological code[60] word making clear the objective (not necessarily chronological) distinction between death and resurrection. In any case the "third day" after the death on Friday—and no longer the Sabbath—became the main day of assembly for the Christians: Sunday was to be the commemoration day of the resurrection of the Lord.

It is odd that the oldest testimony of the resurrection, reproduced in the first epistle to the Corinthians,[61] says nothing about an empty tomb and does not mention the women among the witnesses, perhaps because their testimony was not accepted in law anyway. *Paul,* like the rest of the New Testament writers outside the four Gospels, never mentions either the witnesses of the empty tomb or the empty tomb itself. He attaches importance only to the fact that Jesus "revealed" himself to his followers.[62] Paul could imagine the resurrection in the sense of being clothed with a new body already awaiting us in heaven[63] and thus in the case of the risen Jesus he might have assumed that the body remained in the tomb.

In Jewish Palestine of course people quite generally thought of the resurrection in material terms. But to Hellenistic Jewry this view was at least strange and for the Greeks scarcely intelligible at all. And even if Paul, the Hellenistic Jew educated in Jerusalem, with his conception of the unity of body and life-giving spirit, could not have imagined a resurrection without an empty tomb, his resurrection faith rests neither on the empty tomb nor on certain events on Easter morning. He attached no sort of significance to the empty tomb for the proclamation. It was not the empty tomb, but the proof of Jesus as a living person which was decisive for his proclamation.

The *differences* however are immediately apparent between the statements about the *appearances*—which, according to the first epistle to the Corinthians, may well go back to the very oldest phase of primitive Christendom and which for Paul are open to verification—and on the other hand the *stories of the tomb*—which acquire a literary form only in Mark about the year 70, decades after Paul, and are no longer verifiable at that time.[64] The stories of the tomb are concerned originally only with the women and not with the disciples, the appearance statements with the latter and not the former. The stories of the tomb describe appearances of angels and not of Christ, the appearance statements again the opposite. The stories of the tomb are narratives (artistically elaborated to some degree) about astonished listeners and were perhaps used in the readings at the eucharist; the appearance statements in their oldest versions are summaries in catechism form for learning by heart (probably in catechetical use). The angels, who announce the Christian creed,[65] function as apocalyptic interpreting angels and their appearance and activity are described in terms of contemporary apocalyptic. Perhaps the series of witnesses in its original form could even be reduced to that one woman whom all the Gospels unanimously present as a single witness and whom John makes the sole original witness: Mary Magdalene (Mary, the mother of Jesus, oddly enough, plays no part at all among the witnesses of the resurrection).

It is scarcely possible therefore to refute the assumption that the stories of the tomb are *legendary elaborations of the message of the resurrection.* They deviate greatly from one another and are considerably expanded in the later Gospels (guards at the tomb in Matthew, Peter running to the tomb in Luke and John, Jesus' appearance to the women in Matthew, to Mary Magdalene in John). The resurrection message as the message of the angels forms their center and has been shaped in accordance with the style of Old Testament epiphany stories. In any case, what is at the center even of this narrative is not the empty or—more precisely—opened tomb but the resurrection message. Even in the enigmatic, brief, original text of Mark, the intention is the proclamation while the form is legendary (miraculous opening of the tomb, flight of the women at the angels' appearance).

Did not the orientation of the resurrection message to Jerusalem however presuppose the fact of the empty tomb? Not necessarily. The disciples (returned from Galilee?), numbering no more than a hundred and twenty even according to Luke's possibly exaggerated and idealized estimate,[66] did not start at once to proclaim the risen Christ, but only several weeks after Jesus' death (the Lucan date for Pentecost assumes fifty days). All this made verification difficult, particularly since the proclamation can scarcely have created much of a stir at the beginning or called for public control in a city of perhaps twenty-five to thirty thousand inhabitants. The story of the empty tomb therefore must not be seen as the recognition of a fact. It can be understood as a probably relatively early expression in narrative form and a legendary development of the previous information about the resurrection as contained in the announcement of the angel or angels.

There are however a number of influential exegetes even today who hold that the empty tomb is historically probable: the women's testimony, being invalid in law at that time, would have been useless apologetically and therefore can scarcely have been invented; it can lead therefore to the conclusion—for what it is worth—that there was in fact an empty tomb, whatever the reasons for its being empty. But there should be agreement on the fact that the empty tomb alone even in the light of the stories *cannot provide any proof of the resurrection* or justify any hope of the resurrection. According to Luke, the Emmaus disciples expressly confirm this.[67] Even if the narrative of the empty tomb had a historical core, faith in the risen Christ would not be made any easier and for some people today it would even become more difficult. The simple fact of the empty tomb is ambiguous, open to misinterpretation. There are many possible explanations of an empty tomb, some of which are mentioned by the evangelists, admittedly to refute tendentious Jewish rumors: deception by the disciples, theft of the corpse, exchange, apparent death. But Jewish polemic, as far as we know, did not dispute the fact of the empty tomb.

The simple fact of the empty tomb provides no proof of the truth of the resurrection. As an argument it would beg the question. All that is conveyed by the empty tomb is: "He is not here."[68] We have to add: "He is risen."[69] And this is by no means self-evident. But the statement can be made without reference to the empty tomb. Nor was it the empty tomb which led the women to believe. According to the earliest account by Mark—noticeably changed by the other evangelists—the empty tomb creates not faith and understanding, but fear and terror, so that the women's lips are sealed.[70] Nothing is said about faith resulting from this encounter. But Matthew adds to the women's fear a "great joy" and turns their silence into "announcing the news."[71] There is a problem also about that strange final sentence of Mark's originally shorter ending[72] which was simply omitted throughout the centuries from the liturgical reading of the Easter Gospel. The abrupt ending, "for they were afraid," has led some exegetes to assume that the original conclusion has been lost: an opinion which cannot be proved, but cannot be *a priori* rejected, since such losses were only too frequent with books written on papyrus leaves or in the form of rolls. This conclusion, like Matthew's conclusion, may have mentioned an appearance of the risen Christ in Galilee.

To sum up our conclusions about the empty tomb:

Even according to the New Testament, the empty tomb never led anyone to faith in the risen Christ. As no one claims to have been present at the resurrection or to have known eyewitnesses of the resurrection, neither does anyone say that the empty tomb led him to faith in the risen Christ. The disciples never appeal to the evidence of the empty tomb in order to strengthen the faith of the Church or to refute and convince opponents.

Faith in the risen Christ therefore is independent of the empty tomb. The empty tomb is not a condition, but at best an illustration, of the Easter event. It is not an article of faith, it is neither the ground nor the object of the Easter faith. According to the New Testament message itself, we do not need to believe either because of or*—still less—*in *the empty tomb. Christian faith does not call us to the empty tomb but to encounter with the living Christ himself: "Why do you seek the living with the dead?"*[73]

At least at that time the narrative of the empty tomb, probably originally independent of the rest, could have fulfilled a function: as interpretation and confirmatory sign that the person risen is no other than the crucified Jesus of Nazareth. For that time at least it was an eloquent sign of identity. The risen person is not some other, perhaps a heavenly being, but the man Jesus of Nazareth who was laid in the tomb. He becomes anything but a vague, fluid reality, merged with God and the universe: even while living in God's life he remains the same particular, unique person as before.

*Today however historical criticism has made the empty tomb a dubious factor and the conclusions of natural science have rendered it suspect. To maintain the identity God does not need the relics of Jesus' earthly existence. We are not tied to physiological ideas of the resurrection. There can be identity of the person even without continuity between the earthly and the "heavenly," "spiritual" body. Resurrection is not tied to the substratum—*a priori *constantly changing—or the elements of this particular body. The corporality of the resurrection does not require the tomb to be empty. God raises the person in a new, different, unimaginable "spiritual corporality." As explained, the decisive thing is the new, eternal life in that ultimate, hidden reality which we call God.*

c. "Crucified, buried, descended into hell." In the Apostles' Creed, between the references to the death on the cross and those to the resurrection of Jesus, there is the statement about Jesus' *descent into hell.* This article first appeared as a very late addition in the second half of the fourth century.[74] There is perhaps no other statement in the creed which shows so clearly the uselessness of invoking isolated articles and the caution required when interpreting traditional teachings.

The question of the New Testament evidence is often prejudiced from the beginning as a result of its incorrect formulation. What is the meaning of "descended into hell," *descendit ad inferna* or *ad inferos?* The confusion arises from a *double meaning: inferna* or "lower regions" (like the word "hell" in West European literature into the early Middle Ages) means first of all simply the realm of the dead (Hebrew "Sheol," Greek "Hades"). After the rise of Scholasticism however it was assumed that all the devout reached their final state (paradise, heaven) immediately after death or purgatory. *Inferna* then became the place of those who had not attained eternal happiness: primarily for those who would never attain it, being finally damned (Hebrew "Gehenna," "hell"); but with three other areas of the lower regions—purgatory for the purification of the saved but still imperfect, the fringe of hell for the righteous of the Old Testament (limbo of the Fathers) and for infants who had died unbaptized (limbo of the children). Hence the ambiguity of the statement retained up to the present time in most versions of the Apostles' Creed: "descended into hell" (very recently "descended into the realm of the dead"). There is no problem about a descent into the realm of death, since it is no more than an affirmation of Jesus' death. But we might wonder why it is made into an article of faith after "died and was buried." There must obviously be a reference not merely to Jesus' death, to a journey to Hades. It must mean a special act *between* death and resurrection: a journey to hell, however it is understood. But can such a journey be substantiated from the New Testament?

Only in the late, inauthentic first epistle of Peter is there a text which can be cited for a proper activity of Jesus *between* death and resurrection: it speaks of the Christ put to death going in the Spirit to preach to the spirits in prison who had been disobedient at the time of the flood.[75] But there has been no consistent interpretation of this one text throughout the Church's history.

Cardinal Bellarmine and the Counter-Reformation theologians (with their interest in purgatory) thought that the soul (spirit) of Jesus, between death and resurrection, proclaimed the Gospel to the patriarchs and righteous of the Old Testament (limbo of the Fathers?). But the Greek distinction between "body" and "soul" by no means corresponds to the New Testament opposition between "flesh" and "spirit." Nor is there any mention of the Fathers here, but only of the disobedient at the time of Noah.

Long before Bellarmine, through the long centuries from Augustine's time through the medieval Scholastics it was assumed in Latin theology that the pre-existent Christ, according to his divine nature, preached through the mouth of Noah to the sinners before the flood. But this exegesis strays too far from the text and is not accepted by any modern exegetes.

The Greek Fathers from the time of Clement of Alexandria (who was the first to link the text with Christ's descent into hell) and the Latins before Augustine thought that Jesus preached in the realm of the dead in order to give the latter an opportunity of conversion. But here too there is an unbiblical opposition of body and soul. And Augustine's own theory was meant to exclude a conversion after death and judgment, which cannot be substantiated from the New Testament. It is perfectly possible to maintain the certainty of salvation for the righteous of the Old Testament who had fallen asleep in faith without assuming a special journey to hell on the part of Jesus.

Luther and Calvin maintained that the death of Jesus itself had to be understood as a passage through the torments of the damned, as the experience of God's anger in death and as a temptation to despair. But at best such an interpretation can be based on texts referring to Jesus' death on the cross which however say nothing of a journey to hell *after* his death.

A more fruitful approach to the text may have been discovered by two authors at the turn of the century. F. Spitta, a Protestant exegete, saw the "spirits," to whom Christ had to preach, as rebel angels,[76] and K. Gschwind, a Catholic, took the preaching to be an activity of the risen Christ.[77] There are parallels in the apocalyptic literature and particularly in the two versions of the book of Enoch which suggest that the most convincing solution is that the passage is concerned with the risen Christ, transformed by the Spirit, like a new Enoch announcing on his way to heaven their definitive condemnation to the fallen angels in the lower regions of heaven.[78] Under the influence of Hellenistic ideas, in early Christian times, the world picture had begun to change. The picture of a three-storied universe (heaven, earth, lower regions) was largely replaced by a picture of an earth moving freely in space, surrounded by the spheres of the planets, with the region above the moon being reserved to the gods and that below the moon to the spirits of men and the demonic powers. According to the Slavonic Enoch, which belongs to about the same time as the first epistle of Peter and may have been influenced in this form by Christianity, the fallen angels were imprisoned as a punishment in this "second heaven."[79] There are references elsewhere in the New Testament to the struggle against the spirits of wickedness in the heavenly regions.[80]

In view therefore of the exegetical conclusions, what is to be made of this article of faith? All that can be done here is to suggest a few reference points.

There is no unambiguous New Testament evidence of a descent of Jesus (or his soul) into hell after *death, if by this is meant more than the mere statement that Jesus died and thus—according to the contemporary Jewish view—would have gone to "Sheol."*

The New Testament says nothing at all about any activity of Jesus between *death and resurrection: neither about a final act of humiliation after death (a journey to hell as expression of his suffering) nor about a first act of exaltation before the resurrection (a journey to hell as ex-*

pression of his triumph). If death is understood as dying into God and the resurrection as being taken up from death into God's life, as explained above, then there is no point in asking about what happened in the "meantime."

The possibility of salvation for mankind before or outside Christianity (the righteous of the Old Covenant, those not reached by the Gospel, the unbaptized children) can be affirmed without appealing to the mythological idea of Jesus preaching in limbo. The universal significance of the vicarious suffering on the cross is not dependent on an unprovable journey of suffering or triumph on the part of Jesus to an a priori *inconceivable lower region.*

If however the "descent into hell" is supposed to be a real expression of Jesus' God-forsakenness in death, this is covered in the New Testament[81] *but does not need to be made into an article of faith distinct from death and burial. Relying only on the sources, it is scarcely possible to make a psychological analysis of Jesus' agony of conscience or even to produce a speculative interpretation of his spiritual suffering as victory over hell before the resurrection.*

Jesus' activity is quite generally seen in the New Testament within the mythological framework *of a victorious battle against the evil spirits,*[82] *graphically portrayed in the first epistle of Peter, insofar as the risen Christ ascending through the heavens to the Father encounters the ancient enemies of the human race. The patristic idea of the devils' rights or betrayal, or of the purchase of the release of the just from the power of Satan, belongs to this mythological framework.*

Evil as power, *as it finds expression in all its menace in the life and death of Jesus, is trivialized in two ways. On the one hand evil is personified in an army of individual spirits (mythological ideas of Satan with legions of devils which penetrated from Babylonian mythology into early Judaism and from there into the New Testament).*[83] *On the other hand evil is turned into a purely private affair of individuals. Evil as power in the light both of the New Testament ("authorities and powers") and of modern sociological findings ("anonymous powers and systems") is substantially more than the sum total of the wickedness of individuals.*[84]

Hell *in any case is not to be understood mythologically as a place in the upper or lower regions, but theologically as an exclusion—conveyed in many pictures although in fact non-visual—from communion with the living God as extreme, ultimate reality. The New Testament statements about hell are not meant to provide information to satisfy curiosity and fantasy about the hereafter. They are intended to put before us here and now the absolute seriousness of God's claim and the urgency of man's repentance. The "eternity" of the pains of hell ("fire") affirmed in a number of New Testament metaphors remains subor-*

dinated to God and his will. There are some New Testament texts, not balanced by others, which suggest that the consummation will bring about a reconciliation of all and mercy for everyone.[85]

These points bring out more clearly than what has been said elsewhere the fact that we have no intention here of providing a miniature book of dogmatics with solutions to all theological problems. On hell, death and the devil, it would be possible to fill not only pages but whole books.[86] But it is to be hoped that a direction has been given to the reader's thinking on the topics he might otherwise have missed in this introduction, even though they cannot be discussed in detail.

Origin of faith

If then the Gospel tradition about the empty tomb cannot be accepted as historical without more ado, does not the same question arise in regard to the *appearances* which are presented by the Gospels as the reason why the disciples came to believe in the risen Christ? Might it not be difficult to get at the origin of the Easter faith from the appearance stories of the Gospels with their numerous legendary features? Are these not perhaps merely confirmatory experiences? Is not the earliest Pauline testimony of the resurrection a form of authorization? The question of the appearances naturally raises also in a very much more fundamental way the question of the origin of the Christian Easter faith. In principle there are two possible explanations, but the objections to these must also be considered.

a. *Did faith originate in the reflections of the disciples?* Since the Enlightenment the question has constantly been raised in different forms as to whether the resurrection faith can be made psychologically and historically plausible even without assuming that the appearances took place.

Recently there has been a tendency to fall back especially upon the later Jewish resurrection expectation. Jewish traditions on the martyrdom and taking up of prophetic personalities of the end-time (Elijah, Enoch) and their application to the fate of John the Baptist could—it is thought—have provided categories which were not unfamiliar to Jesus' disciples or to Jesus himself: with the aid of these the disciples after Jesus' death could have understood and interpreted their Master's fate as martyrdom and divine justification, as death and resurrection. Faith in the resurrection of Jesus of Nazareth would then have originated in the disciples' reflections, based on contemporary material of the history of religion but definitely also on Jesus himself: his activity, his fate, his death, his person, the faith that he founded. Talk about his resurrection would be the expression of the perseverance of their faith and the profession of their faith in Jesus' decisive significance, mission and authority, despite his death.[87]

This explanation of the origin of the resurrection faith is not to be lightly set aside. Two points should be considered.

(i) Even from this standpoint the object of faith is more than merely the continuation of Jesus' cause. It is faith in the living Jesus, taken up out of death into the life of God, an exaltation which is not comparable to that of other just men or martyrs. Even according to this explanation, the disciples did not invent the Easter faith. Jesus himself established it by his whole destiny. The priority of God's action is secured in all the disciples' reflections. The new life of Jesus, on which the disciples reflected, is a reality in God and not merely the projection of disappointed hopes. It is therefore a question solely of the *origin* of the resurrection faith. It is important to note this, in order to avoid futile controversies.

(ii) In the last resort, as compared to the certainty of Jesus' resurrection, not only the empty tomb but also the appearances are of secondary importance. The Easter faith is oriented neither to the empty tomb nor to the "appearances," but to the *living Jesus himself*. Even someone who believes neither in the empty tomb nor in certain Easter "appearances," but does believe in Jesus himself as the living Christ, must be regarded as a Christian. This living Christ and through him the living God, who called him from death to life, are the object of the Easter faith. And this faith in the God of the living, who did not leave Jesus in death but took him up into his own life, was the presupposition for the coming into existence of the proclamation of Christ, for the foundation of the community of faith and the beginning of the Christian mission. On the basis of this faith, the one who called men to faith became the one who is believed, Jesus' proclamation of the kingdom of God became the Church's proclamation of Christ. And in this sense, according to Paul, Christian faith itself stands or falls with faith in Jesus' being raised to life but not simply with faith in certain appearances.

b. *Objections to a psychological, religious-historical reconstruction.* These objections have certainly more weight in the case of the appearances than in the case of the empty tomb.[88] There are several points to be considered.

(i) In view of a chain—and this must certainly be admitted—of largely hypothetical conclusions as a result of a psychological-historical deduction of the resurrection faith, the question can first of all be reversed. Would it not have been very much simpler for the primitive community to proclaim Jesus not as risen but merely as one of those *martyr-prophets* whose tombs for that very reason were being reconstructed and cared for at the time of Jesus and who were venerated as intercessors?[89] Why is it that, contrary to these tendencies of the time, no cult arose at the tomb of Jesus? Would not such a proclamation have been much better understood by his contemporaries than a proclamation about someone raised up before the general resurrection of the dead—which, after the preceding events, was bound to seem suspicious from the outset?

(ii) According to certain Old Testament texts God saves and exalts the devout sufferer,[90] but nothing is said of "revelations" by the people so exalted. Nowhere in the Old Testament is there any mention of raising an individual from death as something that takes place before the eschatological resurrection. Enoch and Elijah were regarded in Jesus' time as witnesses to the reality of the resurrection since tradition had it that they were taken up to God without dying or being buried.[91] The later expectation, not mentioned in the Old Testament itself, that Elijah would come again before the end-time, suffer the violent death of the prophets and then be raised up, appears to be too slightly attested, too disputed in its dating and too uncertain in its reconstruction to provide a firm basis on which to build an argument for belief in Jesus' resurrection. Nor is there a single instance in the New Testament of an argument for Jesus' resurrection making use of the examples of Enoch, Elijah or even John the Baptist. Neither are Enoch and Elijah anywhere assigned the function of an eschatological mediator of salvation, to whom as to the first of the resurrected we would have to belong.

(iii) The popular opinion mentioned but not shared by Mark of a supposed resurrection of the *Baptist*[92] has no historical support, particularly if it is ascribed to Herod Antipas, completely Hellenized and educated in Rome. It could have been made up by Mark, perhaps to form a contrast to the resurrection of Jesus. It can be adequately explained as a popular view of Jesus' own activity, in whose person the Baptist, who had recently been put to death, continued to work.

(iv) The idea of a resurrection of the *Messiah*—still more of a *failed Messiah*—was an absolute novelty in the Jewish tradition, breaking through the apocalyptic imagery and remaining unacceptable even today for Judaism, despite all faith in the resurrection of the dead. According to the New Testament sources Jesus alone has been expressly confirmed by his resurrection, so that his resurrection and establishment as Messiah, Lord, Son, cannot be compared with a possible exaltation of other righteous men and martyrs. In Judaism the resurrection of the righteous is the consequence of their righteous action, in Christianity it is the consequence of the resurrection of Jesus and of belonging to him.

With regard to this first attempt at a psychological-historical explanation of the origin of the Easter faith we must conclude that the original Christian faith in the resurrection obviously has a thoroughgoing Jewish character. Obviously the Jewish tradition offered the first disciples innumerable aids to understanding. Obviously then there can be no objections to the suggestion that the disciples reflected on the death of Jesus in the light of the Jewish faith. But hitherto at least it does not seem to have been conclusively proved that the disciples' reflections on Jesus' message and fate led them to deduce their faith in Jesus' resurrection directly from this Jewish faith. We cannot avoid the question, not only of new reflections, but also of new experiences. The further question may well be the most important: may a historical-psychological reconstruction of the origin of the resurrection faith rightly claim to be historically the "real" meaning of the New Testament testimonies, if the latter constantly say the opposite? Is it permissible to interpret them constantly in a way contrary to their real intention? It is all too easy to neglect the factor of the "new" attested in all the New Testament texts.

c. *Did faith originate in new experiences of the disciples?* If we do not indulge in historical speculation but keep strictly to the testimonies themselves, there can be no doubt about the unanimous agreement of the New Testament writings that the disciples did not conclude from Jesus' fate to his resurrection but in fact *experienced* after his death the living person himself.

A number of points must be considered.

(i) Neither the indisputable flight of the disciples before Easter[93] nor the equally indisputable new quality of their faith after Easter can be dismissed with hermeneutical slickness and replaced with a continuity of faith scarcely interrupted by the death of Jesus. It is only now that faith acknowledges him as the risen Messiah, the exalted Lord, the coming Son of Man, the Son of God. There is *no* mention of an immediate *continuation* of the cause of Jesus after his death, *but* the emphasis is on the *discontinuity*. The sources speak of Peter's weeping but not of his repentance before Easter;[94] there is nothing about isolated reflections of the disciples who had undoubtedly been mentally shattered by the death of their Master and had fled, but then became his witnesses and apostles.

(ii) All the Easter testimonies of the New Testament are characterized by an *opposition* which cannot be eliminated between what the *disciples* did and do and what *God* did in and through Jesus. Never do the disciples see themselves as more or less steadfast fellow warriors with God and Jesus, but as those who failed in their faith and were conquered by God through Jesus. This is the very opposite of the interpretation of the resurrection in Goethe's *Faust:*

In sunshine they will walk abroad
To keep the Raising of the Lord,
For they themselves are resurrected.[95]

(iii) The Easter faith is a new start which in the New Testament is unanimously ascribed, not to any sort of prototypes, not to the disciples' own conclusions, not to a secret perseverance in faith, but to *new experiences*—admittedly also lived and interpreted—and to true encounters with the crucified Jesus, now raised up. The witnesses report and interpret occurrences with the risen Jesus which have brought the confused and dispersed disciples with Peter at their head to repentance and of course to new reflection.

(iv) These occurrences were naturally interpreted *in the light of Jewish-Old Testament experience*, with the aid of current and sometimes older terminology. In the Old Testament Greek text, for instance, God's manifestation, his revelation, is described as "appearing," "revealing."[96] Even when Paul was persecuting the Christians, he knew about the resurrection faith though he did not share it. After his conversion he appealed to a revelation of Christ which came upon him quite personally and in which the risen Christ "was seen," "let himself be seen," "appeared," "revealed himself,"[97] in which Paul "saw" the risen Christ.[98] This "appearing" and the "seeing" that corresponds to it cannot be critically eliminated or played down. Using the language of Old Testament visions at the calling of the prophets, Paul speaks here of an experience which provides the basis for the surprising vocation of the persecutor of Christians to be an apostle of Jesus Christ and which he co-ordinates with the appearances to the other apostles.

(v) These appearances—quite unlike those in the infancy story in Matthew or those in the Acts of the Apostles—never occur at night, in sleep or dreams, but *in broad daylight, in the waking hours*. What was for Paul a unique and basic encounter and experience[99]—obviously distinguished from other "visions and revelations of the Lord"[100] which Paul had for himself personally and which do not form the content of his preaching[101]—is described by Luke at length in the style of a vision-legend.[102]

(vi) That ancient creed in the first epistle to the Corinthians certainly cites these "appearances" and uses the epiphany formula, "he appeared," in order to authorize the witnesses named there to be witnesses also in their vocation to proclamation. But it is only because Jesus has in fact "appeared" to them that they can be authorized and obliged to proclaim the message of the resurrection. This witness formula has more historical weight than a mere certificate of authorization. It is not only a declaration of the validity of certain authorities and their message, but shows also that the appearances are to be explained as the source from which the message originated. Paul's allusion to the main witnesses, whom he knows, and to other witnesses still living confirms the fact that he is dealing with a state of affairs which is both theological and historical. From this evidence it seems quite clear that the disciples acquired their faith, not as a result of their own reflections, but as a result of their experiences—of whatever kind—with the risen Christ. Hence it was not their faith which raised Jesus to life for them, but it was Jesus raised by God to life who led them to faith and the profession of faith. He does not live in any sense by grace of his disciples, but they live by him. Since the *resurrection testimonies* were genuine, they could also be *evidence of authorization*. The message of the resurrection is a testimony of faith, but not a product of faith. If then we want to keep to the New Testament evidence, however we explain them, we must start out one way or another from encounters of the living Jesus with his disciples: re-encounters and at the same time new encounters with the living, crucified Jesus, for which the initiative comes from God and not from the disciples and of which Paul's experience marks the close.

d. *Objections to a reception of new experiences.* All objections to the disciples' reception of new experiences with Jesus raised to life can in fact be reduced to one. Are we postulating here a supernatural intervention, the very thing that we tried to avoid in regard both to miracles[103] and to the empty tomb?[104] Three points may be considered.

(i) There would in fact be an *a priori* suspicious retrogression to superseded ideas if we were to attempt first to understand the numerous New Testament miracle stories without the unprovable assumption of a "supernatural intervention" in the laws of nature and then at the end to postulate for the miracle of the resurrection just such a supernatural intervention, which is contrary to both scientific thinking and the convictions and experiences of ordinary people. If then we want to speak of new experiences of the disciples after Jesus' death, they cannot be regarded as miracles canceling the laws of nature, in principle plain for all to see, but merely by accident not seen by the public at large. Even the New Testament texts themselves do not suggest that these were in any way spectacular miracles which could have been watched with amazement by the general public.

(ii) On the other hand, despite all the indisputable legendary, vivid-dramatic embellishments and enlargements, all the time- and environment-conditioned interpretations, historical criticism simply does not require us to regard the appearances *merely* as an expression of faith in the light of Jesus' death in his decisive significance, mission and authority. According to all the texts, the reason why the departed and dejected disciples became death-defying confessors was not simply Jesus' proclamation, life and death, but quite definite *experiences of him* as raised from the dead. The proclamation was occasioned, not by Jesus' death—which as such just did not manifest God's victory over death—but by new experiences. What are cited in the New Testament by way of psychological phenomena clearly exclude a psychological transformation as the initial spark for that Christian faith which was to prove a turning point in world history: an indisputable breakdown and dejection on the part of the disciples, one of whom betrayed, another denied and cursed him, all of whom forsook him in an ignominious flight after the arrest; afterwards sadness, consternation, fear, non-recognition, doubt, unbelief. What is described points, not to development, but to surprise: a closeness not opened up from within by rational reflection, but only broken down by a revealing encounter with another person. All the psychological explanations which seem so practical and yet so banal contradict what the texts themselves stubbornly assert: that the Crucified is living and has manifested himself to his disciples as Lord, that with him the new age has dawned for the world, that his cause and his person are not past but effectively present and that this is the reason why the disciples came to believe and to proclaim. From whatever text we start out, we are continually coming up against a radically new experience of the disciples with Jesus after his death: in these experiences the Crucified encounters them as a living person and in his insistent claim as the Lord.[105]

(iii) But can the *dilemma* revealed here be overcome? Are we to accept the experiences of the disciples with Jesus after his death and yet reject all supernatural interventions nullifying laws of nature?

e. *The appearances involve vocation.* The "appearances" certainly mean that the resurrection, the risen Christ are made known. But this is not all. For Paul and similarly for the apostles appearance and vocation, encounter and mission obviously go together. How is this to be understood?

(i) In the new experiences it is a question not simply of identifying Jesus, but of personal vocation, of mission for proclamation, not so much of looking back as of looking forward: the wholly *concrete enlistment of a person for this message*, which appeals for a commitment in faith and apparently also leaves scope for doubt.[106] It means the binding of a few to serve the many. As Paul's apostolic life exemplifies, this unique "revelation" had as its consequences a total seizure and utilization, vocation and mission, for life and death. What is recorded by the ancient creed and by Paul himself with the utmost brevity and with tacit respect in the presence of mystery is depicted in the resurrection stories of the Gospels in the form of pious legends, full of inconsistencies, but—compared, for instance, with the Apocrypha—with complete restraint. The older the account, the more prosaic it is. The resurrection message therefore points not to a distant mythical future, but to a clearly defined place in history.[107]

(ii) All *psychological or speculative interpretation is quickly brought to a halt* in face of such vocations. The form they take is not decisive. What is decisive is the fact, which is of course unanimously and emphatically asserted in the New Testament writings. These vocations of the first witnesses, the apostles, which are on each occasion unique and limited to a definite point of time, have nothing to do with experiences which can be repeated at will, like spiritualist materialization (spirits of the dead) or anthroposophical spirit-vision (of an invisible higher materiality of living people).

(iii) These vocations can be best understood if *compared with the callings of the Old Testament prophets* which, like the phenomenon of vocation as such, cannot be dismissed as hallucination. According to the Pauline statements, as with the prophetic vocation-visions, we have to regard these as experiences which cannot be tested by the neutral observer, which are guaranteed only by witnesses whose testimony is then confirmed by other witnesses—especially through the way their life has been transformed—but which can be verified only by faith. Our knowledge of spiritual experiences, ecstasies, visions, enlargements of consciousness, "mystical" experiences is still too limited to be able to clarify the reality which is ultimately concealed behind the New Testament vocation stories.

It is the same with the prophetic experience behind the vocation stories of the Old Testament, subsequently more or less stylized for public consumption: we cannot clarify this experience, but neither can we adopt a rationalistic, skeptical attitude to the experience as such. These accounts speak in the ninth century B.C. of the presence of the Spirit of Yahweh and in the eighth and seventh of a direct, personal approach by Yahweh, creating an entirely new status for the person concerned and enlisting him completely for a special service: visions and hearings of another person spontaneously and incalculably agitating the person affected mentally and often also corporeally and equipping him for his task. For these the expression "ecstatic" is misleading since the self-consciousness and free decision of the prophet are not only not excluded, but demanded in a way never before experienced in the whole of the ancient East.[108]

(iv) Everything will depend on our not imagining God's call within the supernaturalist system as a divine intervention from above or from outside. If God is the incomprehensible, comprehensive ultimate reality, if man is in God and God in man, if the *history of man is taken up in the history of God* and if the *history of God is worked out in the history of man*,[109] then *in the word of mission or vocation* there is a possibility of action and interaction, a constant intercommunication of God and man, of freedom that gives and freedom given, which in no way infringes laws of nature and yet is never to be surpassed in reality. If historical science, as a result of its philosophical presuppositions, considers man alone as creator of his history and *a priori* methodically excludes and is bound to exclude God, it obviously cannot verify God's action historically. If it could be historically verified it would not be God's action at all. The fact that God is at work in the history of the world and of the individual person is not an observation demonstrated by historical criticism, but—and this must constantly be stressed—a matter of trusting faith.

f. *Vocations involve faith.* If the appearances were meant as vocations, they could not simply be noted as historical facts: for a vocation there must be believing trust, which does not however exclude doubt. Linked as they are with the resurrection, these vocations demand that faith which entrusts everything to God, even and particularly the very last thing, victory over death.

(i) These vocations by their very nature culminate in an *experience of faith.* In these experiences the persons concerned freely allow themselves to be enlisted to follow and proclaim this crucified but still living Christ.

It is a question of a spontaneous happening which is not to be forced and which has to overcome resistance. The call becomes fully effective only when accepted in faith. Yet faith is neither prior to the call nor identical with it. It is in fact only the call which provides the occasion and opportunity for faith. The resurrection therefore is not merely an "objective" fact which can be understood as meaningful even apart from the resurrection faith. The resurrection cannot be observed as a simple, concrete fact, it cannot be "objectified." Easter experience and Easter faith are not merely externally linked with one another: not like a telephone connection which can be broken off as soon as the message gets through. Easter experience and Easter faith belong intrinsically and indissolubly together: there is no place for an objective, neutral observer.

The vocation event in particular is not a magical or mechanical happening which overpowers the person and automatically excludes any doubt. It is only through faith that this event ceases to be ambiguous: when the inviting, challenging call is accepted. Only if and as long as the disciple clings to the risen Christ does he know that he is being carried, just as Peter could confidently walk on the water as long as he kept his eyes on the Lord and not on the swell of the waves.[110] These experiences of faith therefore really amount to *vocations received in faith*. In this sense—as against a resurrection conceived in terms of concrete, solid, objective reality—Bultmann is right, though his statement can be misleading, in saying that Jesus rose into the faith of his disciples, into the word of proclamation, into the kerygma.[111] But we are not called because we believe. We believe because we are called.

(ii) Again as with the Old Testament prophets, for his new word to his people, God did not turn to any of the available institutions, but addressed the mind of *individuals*. This explains the fallacy in the old and glibly repeated objection that the "appearances," in order to be historically credible, ought to have taken place before neutral observers. They took place in fact, not in the presence of "believers" but of "unbelievers," who freely became believers as a result of these surprising experiences, a cognition that was a recognition and in that sense established a continuity. As they themselves testified, they came to believe as a result of God's action, despite all their fears and against all their doubts.

(iii) An isolated resurrection in itself would have little point, unless it were a resurrection *for us*. A revelation of this event would be irrelevant unless its proclamation meant something to *all*. Jesus' resurrection is the ground of hope in the resurrection for all who believe in him. Since he is risen, they too will rise. Their own hope is substantiated, guaranteed. But at the same time their obligation to follow him is clear. A meaning has entered into their life and death which excludes all that resigned hopelessness which finds expression in the merely apparently cheerful saying: "Eat, drink, for tomorrow we die."[112] Reality and significance are therefore one in the resurrection. The resurrection faith is not science or ideology, but an attitude of trust and hope in the light of the risen, crucified Jesus: an attitude which has to find expression in all personal and also socio-political decisions and which can be sustained throughout all doubts and despair.

g. *Faith today.* All questions about the historicity of the empty tomb and the Easter experience cease to count beside the question of the significance of the resurrection message.

(i) We moderns have neither the empty tomb nor an Easter experience on which to base our faith. These experiences of the first witnesses were—like those of the prophets—unique vocations. And we cannot expect a religious enlightenment and awakening which for us would be a repetition of those unique experiences of the first disciples. We are *thrown back on the testimony of the first, foundational witnesses* which—whatever may be the case with the tomb and the Easter experience—declares with the utmost clarity that the Crucified is not dead, but lives on and rules forever through and with God. We are always thrown back again on the word of proclamation.

The Easter stories are meant to be related as such and we should let them be told today. What is non-visual—and raising to life as the beginning of the consummation, like creation, is just that—cannot be made visual in concepts, but must be made so in the form of pictures which tell a story. New experiences, such as the vocation experiences of the first witnesses, cannot be made intelligible simply through arguments, but must be made so in the form of pictorial narratives. Terms like "raising" or "resurrection" are also pictorial, metaphorical terms. Even today most people are unwilling to dispense with visual images and perceptibility. That is why the Easter narratives are not to be eliminated from the proclamation, but interpreted with discriminating criticism and in such a way that they are not merely privately edifying but stir people to follow Christ in both personal and public life.

(ii) Is this indirectness more difficult for us moderns? Even the calling of the first witnesses, as we saw, seemed ambiguous and open to doubt, becoming unequivocal only by acceptance in faith. Even the first disciples did not manage without faith. Being preachers of the faith did not give them a direct insight nor dispense them from faith either at the beginning or—still less—subsequently. What was expected of them was not a disinterested observation but a perception in faith which could be brought simultaneously into service. And from us moderns too *no less and no more than faith* is required: to accept our own vocation, not indeed to give the first testimony, but—on the basis of the first testimony through the proclamation—to accept our vocation to faith, trustingly to commit ourselves to God and the message of the living Christ and to consider what this must mean in practice. Nothing compels us to believe, there is much that invites us: his words, his behavior and fate, authenticated by God. Every believer is thus called, in virtue of the apostolic testimony, to be himself a witness in word and still more in deed to the risen Christ.

(iii) More important than all the controversy about the sequence and explanation of the Easter events is *the shaping of one's own life* out of the effective power of the life of this Jesus as related in the Easter stories, out of faith in him. If someone still has no idea or very little idea of what to make of the miracle of the resurrection, of the new life, but regards this Jesus as the ultimate criterion of his mortal life and finite death and thus as living, then it cannot be denied that he is a Christian. And he is different from that other person who regards Jesus' resurrection as a great miracle, but draws no conclusions from it for his own life and death. Easter is the origin and goal of faith, but it should not be turned into a law of faith. The ultimate criterion of a person's Christian spirit is not theory but practice: not how he thinks of teachings, dogmas, interpretations, but how he acts in ordinary life. Paul severely reprimanded the early deniers of the resurrection and invited them to think again, but he did not excommunicate them.[113] The decisive thing about being a Christian is trying—as far as this is possible for human nature—to imitate Jesus and not to disown him as the Lord.[114]

(iv) Here again it becomes clear how closely *Jesus' person is linked with his cause.* No one believes in Jesus who does not acknowledge his cause by following him. On the other hand, it is impossible to support his cause without in some way joining his followers. It is possible therefore to speak credibly of Jesus' person and cause only by entering in practice on their way in the direction indicated by the resurrection faith.

Here too is the answer to the questions raised at the beginning of this chapter. According to the unanimous evidence of the New Testament, it is Jesus of Nazareth himself known and recognized as living, the new experiences of faith, vocations received in faith, knowledge by faith of Jesus of Nazareth, which can explain why his cause continued: why after his death there came into existence the Jesus movement with all its vast consequences, after Jesus' failure a new beginning, after the disciples' flight a community of believers. Here is the explanation why this heretical teacher, false prophet, seducer of the people and blasphemer, disowned and judged by God, was proclaimed—one might almost say, precipitately—Messiah, Christ, Lord, Saviour, Son of God. This is the reason why the disgraceful gallows could be understood as a sign of victory; why the first witnesses, sustained by a final confidence, fearless in the presence of contempt, persecution and death, brought to men as glad tidings such scandalous news of an execution. Here then is the explanation why Jesus was not only venerated, studied and followed as founder and teacher, but known as active in the present; why the mystery of God was seen as linked with his whole tense, enigmatic history and thus Jesus himself became the real content of their proclamation, the compendium of the message of the kingdom of God.

The historical riddle of the origin of Christianity appears to be solved here in a provocative way. According to the only testimonies we possess, the experiences of faith, vocations in faith, knowledge of faith of the disciples about the living Jesus of Nazareth form the initial spark for that unique world-historical development in which a "world religion" and perhaps more than that could arise from the gibbet of someone who ended in being forsaken by God and men. Christianity, inasmuch as it is a confession of Jesus of Nazareth as the living and powerfully effective Christ, begins at Easter. Without Easter there is no Gospel, not a single narrative, not a letter in the New Testament. Without Easter there is no faith, no proclamation, no Church, no worship, no mission in Christendom.[115]

2. *The criterion*

The proclamation of the risen, exalted, living Christ presented an enormous challenge. But, it should be noted, not the proclamation of the resurrection as such. In the Hellenistic and other religions there are many who are said to have risen. These include heroes like Hercules who were taken up into Olympus, gods and saviors like Dionysius who died and were revived. Their fate became the model and prototype for that of their devotees and they were continually venerated afresh in mystical participation in the Hellenistic mystery religions. These were nature cults in a new form: constructed out of the natural rhythms of sowing and growth, sunrise and sunset, coming to be and passing away, projected by the wishes and desires of men longing for immortality. Everywhere here myth is at the beginning and—somewhat as in the Old Testament—is given a historical form. With Jesus it is the other way round.

Justified

With Jesus history comes at the beginning. History was of course often interpreted mythologically, but here the dying and coming to be of the grain of seed[1] is not the beginning, but merely a metaphor. What is decisive for Christian faith is not that a dead man has risen as a model for all mortals. What is decisive is the fact that the very person who was crucified has been raised. If the risen one were not the Crucified, he would at best be an ideograph, an ideogram, a symbol.

The Easter event therefore may not be considered in isolation. It compels us to ask the further question about Jesus, his message, his behavior, his fate, and then too the preliminary question about ourselves and what is to be our lot. The "first-born from the dead" must not be allowed to suppress the Messiah of the weary and burdened. Easter does not neutralize the cross but confirms it. The resurrection message therefore does not call for the adoration of a heavenly cult god who has left the cross behind him. It calls for imitation: to commit oneself in believing trust to this Jesus, to his message, and to shape one's own life in accordance with the standard of the Crucified.

The resurrection message, that is, reveals the very thing that was not to be expected: that this crucified Jesus, despite everything, *was right*. God took the side of the one who had totally committed himself to him, who gave his life for the cause of God and men. God acknowledged him and not the Jewish hierarchy. He approved of his proclamation, his behavior, his fate.

In the concrete, Jesus was right in setting himself above certain customs, prescriptions, precepts, whenever this was for man's general well-being and thus in accordance with God's will. He was right in questioning the existing legal system and the whole religio-social system and relativizing in practice the existing norms and institutions, the established dogmas, ordinances and appointments, where these were not intended to serve men but to submit men to their service. He was likewise right when he questioned the established liturgy and the whole cult and in practice undermined the existing rites and customs, feasts and ceremonies, giving service to men priority over service to God.

His identification of God's cause with men's, God's will with the general well-being of man, was therefore right. He was right in surmounting the barriers between one's fellow countrymen and foreigners, party and non-party members, in his love of men, of neighbors, of enemies. His plea for endless forgiveness was right, for service regardless of rank, renunciation without return. He was right too in identifying himself with the weak, sick, poor, underprivileged, even with the moral failures, the irreligious and godless. And his plea for pardon instead of punishment was right, his assurance also of forgiveness in the particular, concrete case. Finally and above all he was right in the commitment of his life, in his perseverance and in continuing his way to the end.

All this is implied in the resurrection message. His claim, his faith in God's closeness, his obedience, his freedom, his joy, his whole action and suffering were confirmed. The one forsaken by God was justified by God. With his proclamation and his whole behavior he was in the right. Against all his scoffing opponents and fleeing friends, against his family, against the establishment and against the revolutionaries, against all parties, the man who has obviously failed with men and yet been put in the right by God has conquered. Jesus' assumption into God's glory means God's acknowledgment of him to whom the world—as is made clear constantly throughout John's Gospel—denied its acknowledgment.

His whole way was right, even though it became—had to become—the way of the cross. Here is a man of humble origin and insignificant family who—as we saw—seemed to be without education, possessions, office or title, called by no authority, authorized by no tradition, supported by no party. Yet through his very death his unparalleled claim was confirmed in an earth-shattering way and indeed finally justified. The innovator, who set himself above law and temple, above Moses, kings, prophets, family, who relativized marriage and nation, appears now as the great fulfiller. The heretical teacher turns out to be the authorized teacher who shows people the right way.[2] The false prophet is seen to be the true prophet.[3] The blasphemer is now the saint of God.[4] The seducer of the people will be the eschatological judge of the people.[5] Thus he was definitively authenticated as God's advocate and as advocate of man.

Jesus' assumption into the life of God therefore does not bring the revelation of additional truths, but the revelation of Jesus himself: he now acquires final credibility. In a wholly new way Jesus thus justified becomes the sign challenging men to decide. The decision for God's rule, as he demanded it, becomes a decision for himself. Despite the break, there is a continuity in the discontinuity. Already during Jesus' earthly activity the *decision for or against the rule of God* hung together with the *decision for or against himself*. Now they coincide. For in the Crucified raised to God's life God's presence, rule and kingdom are already realized, already present. In this sense the *immediate expectation had been fulfilled*.

The one who *called men to believe* has become the *content of faith*. God has forever identified himself with the one who identified himself with God. Faith in the future now depends on him and on him too depends the hope of a definitive life with God. Again the message of the coming kingdom of God rings out, but in a new form: since Jesus with his death and new life has entered it and now forms its center. Jesus as exalted to God has become the *personification of the message of the kingdom of God*, its symbolic abridgement, its concrete core. Instead of speaking generally of "proclaiming the kingdom of God," people begin to speak more particularly of "proclaiming Christ." And those who believe in him will be called briefly "Christians." Thus message and messenger, the "Gospel of Jesus" and the "Gospel of Jesus Christ," have become a unity.

Believers thus perceive more and more clearly that through him God's imminently expected new world has already broken into the world marked by sin and death. His new life has broken the universal dominion of death. His freedom has prevailed, his way has been proved. And there appears more and more clearly the whole relativity, not only of death, but also of the law and the temple, and the Christian community—at first the Hellenistic-Jewish community and then Paul with the Gentile Christians —will draw the conclusions to an increasing extent: called by Jesus to life and liberated for freedom.[6] Liberated from all powers of the finite world, from law, sin and death. What law and temple meant for the Jews, the Christ, who defended the cause of God and man, comes to mean more and more clearly for Christians. At the point where the Jews are waiting for fulfillment, it is already present in the one person. And for this one what does it mean?

Honorific titles

After Easter, Jesus' person became the concrete standard for God's kingdom: for the relationship of man to his fellow men, to society and to God. Jesus' cause could then no longer be separated from his person. In Christianity from the very beginning there was no question merely of permanently valid ideas. It has always been a question wholly and really of the concrete person who remains permanently valid: of Jesus the Christ. *The cause of Jesus, which continues, is first of all the person of Jesus,* who remains in a unique fashion significant, alive, valid, relevant, effective, for the believer. It is he himself who reveals the mystery of the history of this cause and so makes possible a profession of faith in it: the confession at baptism and in the eucharist, in preaching and teaching; the acclamation at worship and the proclamation before the world. And quite soon the confession before the tribunal was to follow: when required to confess "Kyrios Kaisar," Christians would answer: "Kyrios Jesous." The whole faith in Christ finds its wholly intelligible expression in the one phrase "Jesus is Lord."

This is a provoked and provocative *profession of faith in Jesus as the criterion.* To the first Christians no honorific title seemed too high-flown to express the unique, decisive and determinative significance of him who—as we saw—most probably never claimed any title for himself. For this very reason the community came to accept the titles only tentatively and hesitatingly. In this respect the individual title as such was not important. What was important was the way in which all these titles expressed the fact that this person himself, put to death and living, is and remains the *criterion:* authoritative in his proclamation, his conduct, his whole fate, in his life, his work, his person; authoritative for man, his relationship to God, world and fellow men, his thinking, action and suffering, living and dying.

The *individual titles,* although diversely tinted, are largely interchangeable and supplement one another with reference to Jesus. Each formula, however brief, is not a part of the creed but the whole creed. It is *only in Jesus himself* that the different titles have a *clear, common point of reference.*[7] It has been calculated that about fifty different names are used in the New Testament for the earthly and risen Jesus. The majestic titles still used to some extent today were not invented by the early Christians, but—in the early Palestinian primitive community, in Hellenistic Jewish Christianity and then in Hellenistic Gentile Christianity—taken over from the milieu and transferred to Jesus: Jesus as the coming "Son of Man," the imminently expected "Lord" ("Mar"), the "Messiah" established in the end-time, the "Son of David" and vicariously suffering "Servant of God," finally the present "Lord" ("Kyrios"), the "Saviour" ("Redeemer"), the "Son of God" ("Son") and the "Word of God" ("Logos").

These were the most important of the titles applied to Jesus. Some of them—as for instance the mysterious, apocalyptic title "Son of Man" (used particularly in Q)—were falling out of use in the Greek-speaking communities even before Paul and particularly with him (it was the same with "Son of David"), since they would be unintelligible or liable to be misunderstood in the new environment. Others, like "Son of God," enlarged their meaning in Hellenistic regions and acquired a greater significance; or they even came together in one, as "Messiah" translated by "Christ" formed together with the name "Jesus" a single proper name: "Jesus Christ." While the New Testament has about twenty references to Son of David, seventy-five to Son of God (Son), eighty to Son of Man, Lord (Kyrios) is used for Jesus about three hundred and fifty times and Christ a good five hundred times.

Thus an explicit New Testament Christology emerged from the implicitly Christological speech, action and suffering of Jesus himself. Or —better—very *diverse New Testament "Christologies"* emerged, varying with the different social, political, cultural, intellectual contexts, with the different types of people to be addressed and with the individuality of the author. There is not a single normative Christ image, but a variety of Christ images each with a different emphasis. The standard, the "Christological" significance of Jesus had to be made clear: what he really is and what is his decisive importance for men.

In the New Testament *letters*, especially those of Paul, this is brought out mainly in the light of the crucified and risen Christ; but in these letters, closely related to particular situations and frequently fragmentary, we can scarcely discover how much belongs to Paul's rudimentary preaching and catechesis, which itself must have contained a strong element of a Jesus tradition.[8] In the *Gospels*, produced in their final versions from about 70 but making use of very ancient material, of whose origin we already heard,[9] the significance of Jesus is brought out mainly with an eye on his earthly way of life. At the same time this earthly Jesus is seen in the light of the risen Jesus, so that—as we also saw[10]—even in the Gospels the Jesus proclaimed (=the kerygmatic Christ) may not simply be equated with the Jesus to be proclaimed (=the historical Jesus). Even the earliest evangelist declares his intention to announce "the message of salvation of Jesus Christ, the Son of God."[11] The Gospels attempt to proclaim Jesus as the man in whom God himself is at work and in whom therefore man's salvation is effected.

At the same time however the different New Testament authors, because of their different situations and diverse theological conceptions, see the same Jesus up to a point in a very *discriminating perspective*. While Mark sees him as the hidden Son of God in his earthly life and Matthew as the Messiah of God and Israel promised in the Old Testament Scriptures, explaining and fulfilling the law, Luke sees him mainly as the Saviour of the poor and abandoned and John finally as the Word existing from the beginning with God and the Son, revealed in his earthly life and revealing the Father. Paul can understand him as the obedient, new Adam and definitive human being, Hebrews as the great high priest bringing to an end the ancient cult, the Acts of the Apostles as the exalted Lord ruling the one Church through the Spirit, the Johannine writings as the one who came in the flesh and John's Revelation as God's victor.[12]

Within our context it is not necessary to work out how the complex history and significance of each honorific title in the New Testament is to be understood.[13] Through being applied to the one Jesus they not only became ultimately interchangeable but were *radically changed*. With the aid of the titles the attempt was made tentatively to reduce to the forms of human language what had been perceived in faith. At the same time the religious and political misunderstandings had to be removed which were involved in the Jewish-Hellenistic titles in their existing shape: a task that was all the more difficult as a result of the penetration of pagan influences, giving to the titles an alien stamp. But in any case Jesus did not get his authority from these ambiguous, misleading titles. He himself as the Crucified who is risen and the Risen who is crucified gave them authority and definite clarity. They were not simply transferred, but recoined. The titles did not determine what he was. He himself, his concrete, historical existence, his death and new life determined how they were to be freshly understood and gave them a new meaning.

"Son of Man." Early Jewish expectation saw the Son of Man as coming in the future for judgment. Jesus dissociated himself from this figure, speaking of him always in the third person. Possibly he is not to be identified with the Son of Man, although Jesus declares that acknowledgment of himself will be decisive and will be confirmed by the verdict to be delivered by the Son of Man coming for the last judgment.[14] *For the primitive Christian community however Jesus was undoubtedly identical with the Son of Man, since, after his exaltation to "the right hand of the Father," there was no place for any other in addition to himself.*[15] *Thus the coming Son of Man of early Judaism became the Son of Man who had* already come *and the Son of Man* coming again (*soon*) *as judge in the future consummation of the world.*

"Messiah-Christ." This title of the mandatory, bringing salvation expected in the end-time, could mean a great deal. In the most widespread political and Jewish-national conception, often mingled with the apocalyptic conception of the Son of Man, the "Messiah of God" meant the mighty war hero of the end-time and royal liberator of the people. But through Jesus the title of Messiah acquired a completely new interpretation and now meant a non-violent and unarmed and therefore misunderstood, persecuted, betrayed and finally suffering and dying Messiah: which, for the current Jewish understanding, must have sounded as scandalous as the title on the cross, "King of the Jews," which completely corresponded to it. In this completely recoined sense, the title of Christ according to the New Testament has also remained for Christendom until today the majestic name most frequently used for Jesus of Nazareth.

"Lord." Many who had authority to command were addressed in this way. It was the title of every superior (employers, officers, slaveowners) and particularly the holder of supreme authority to command and to legislate: in Greek-speaking Judaism Yahweh himself, in Hellenistic paganism the emperor. If the exalted Jesus was addressed as "Lord," the name was meant to express this exalted one's unique authority and also his closeness, as he is the one to come and at the same time present in worship. But, unlike other lords, unlike the Pharaohs and Caesars, this lord made himself slave, servant, friend, brother, and, exalted to the right hand of God, must now be seen forever together with God: as the Lord quite plainly, who tolerates no other lords—political or religious—alongside himself. In the course of time this claim was bound to lead to conflict with the Roman state as the latter became increasingly committed to emperor worship.

"Son of God." In the ancient East the king could be so designated. And in Hellenism many heroes and demigods were so named. What Jesus was certainly could not be deduced from the term "Son of God" as such. On the contrary, by contrast with all those sons of God in the Hellenistic-syncretist pantheon, by contrast with all those divinely begotten kings and emperors, heroes and geniuses, the believer had to learn from Jesus' person and history what "Son of God" really, decisively, incomparably means: the Son of God who is tempted like us, obedient, crucified.

"Logos." The Old Testament speaks just as emphatically as the Greek philosophers of the divine "Word," the Jewish-Hellenistic wisdom literature just as much as Philo and the Gnostic Hermetic corpus. The decisive thing was not that just this ambiguous term "Logos" was applied to Jesus—in John's prologue emphatically, elsewhere only exceptionally—but that it was Jesus in particular to whom the term was ap-

plied and from him acquired a wholly new precision and a "logic" entirely of its own: as the Word *of* God made flesh.

Thus a variety of contemporary titles of dignity and mythical symbols were—so to speak—baptized in the name of Jesus, to remain linked with his name but with a different content, to be at his service and to make his unique, decisive significance intelligible to men of that time and not only of that time. These names were not *a priori* intelligible means of identification, but pointers in his direction. They were not *a priori* infallible definitions, but *a posteriori* explanations of what he is and what he signifies.

Yet they are something more, as became evident just now in our examination of the individual titles. They do not merely define and explain theologically and theoretically Jesus' being, nature, person. They are not merely sedate liturgical formulas or innocuous missionary expressions, they are also supremely critical and polemical acclamations and proclamations. They are tacit or even explicit *challenges* to all who regard their own power and wisdom as absolute, who demand what belongs to God, *who themselves want to set the ultimate standards:* whether they are the Jewish hierarchs, the Greek philosophers or the Roman emperors, whether they are great or petty lords, rulers, autocrats, Messiahs, sons of the gods. All these are denied final, decisive authority, which instead is ascribed to that one person who exists, not for himself, but for God's cause and man's. In this sense the post-paschal, Christological, honorific titles have an indirect social and political significance. The twilight of the gods—of whatever kind—had set in. And as the emperors began increasingly to claim final authority, the threatened fatal conflict with the Roman state became a reality and lasted for centuries. Whenever Caesar demanded what was God's, Christians had to face the great either-or: "either Christ or Caesar."

It is clear therefore that *the titles as such* are *not* the decisive factor. The believer and the community of faith should not cling to the titles, *but* in faith and action *to Jesus* himself as the definitive criterion. What titles are used to express this authoritative character of Jesus was and is even today a secondary question, and both then and now dependent on the socio-cultural context. There is no need to repeat and recite all the titles of that time. These are marked once and for all by a quite particular world and society which for us has vanished and in the meantime—as always happens when language is conserved—their meaning has changed. There is no need to construct a single Christology out of the different titles and the ideas connected with them. It is not as if we had only a single Gospel instead of four, only one New Testament theology instead of many apostolic letters. Faith in Jesus permits many statements of faith about him. There is one faith in Christ and many Christologies. In the same way there is one faith in God and many theologies.

This is not a call to iconoclasm—neither images nor titles are to be broken down—but a call to *translate* the titles and ideas of former times into the outlook and language of our own. In fact this is the very thing we are trying to do in this book. Faith in Christ must remain the same, but terms and ideas which are unintelligible or even misleading today must not make it more difficult or—still less—impossible to accept and to live the message of Christ today. This sort of translation does not simply mean abolishing ancient titles and creeds, does not mean overlooking the long Christological tradition, still less their biblical source. On the contrary, any good translation must be oriented to the original text and learn from the mistakes and strong points of former translations. But any good translation may not merely mechanically repeat, but must creatively sense and seize upon the possibilities of the new language. We need have no more hesitation about new designations of Jesus than about the old, which frequently were not at all bad and even succeeded to a surprising extent in getting at the real meaning.

Anyone in Germany under the National Socialist regime who confessed publicly that there was still as formerly only one authoritative "leader" in the Church could be understood—if not by the Catholic or Lutheran episcopate, then at any rate by Karl Barth, the "Confessing Church" and the Synod of Barmen—just as well as those Christians who almost two thousand years earlier confessed before the Roman tribunals that "Jesus is Lord." Such confessions expressed in living as well as in words have to be paid for—often dearly—not only in times of martyrdom, but also in times when Christianity is prospering. We have to pay for it whenever we invoke Christ and refuse to worship the idols of the time—and there are many of them. The Christian does not need to pay with his sufferings, still less with his life, for Christological titles and predicates, formulas and propositions, but he must do so for this Jesus Christ himself and for what he authoritatively represents: the cause of God and man.

Representation

People gradually became more clearly aware of the whole significance of Jesus. At the same time, in the pious usage of the community, some of the ancient titles made history and developed an important dynamism of their own, thus creating quite considerable difficulties for the modern mentality. This is true particularly of the title "Son of God," which had been used, not only in Hellenism, but also in the Old Testament. In the Israelite ceremony of accession the king is installed as "Son of Yahweh," adopted as Son.[16] And a successor of David was expected, who as "Son" of God would ascend the ancestral throne and establish the Davidic rule over Israel forever.[17] This title is now applied to Jesus. He is acknowledged as the one installed, through resurrection and exaltation, as Son of God in power —as it says in the ancient creed at the beginning of the epistle to the Romans[18]—or "begotten"—to use the psalmist's expression[19]—on Easter day.

And yet the question could scarcely be avoided: is not the risen the same as the earthly Jesus? Must we not then say of the earthly what we say of the risen Jesus? Is not the earthly Jesus already the Son of God, even though his sovereignty is still hidden? Hence his installation into God's sonship is placed at an earlier stage in time in other New Testament writings: at the baptism as the beginning of his public activity[20] or at his birth[21] or even before his birth, in God's eternity.[22]

Originally therefore the title of "Son of God" had *nothing to do with Jesus' origin but with his legal and authoritative status*. It is a question of function, not of nature. Originally the title did not mean a corporeal sonship, but a divine election and authorization, it meant that this Jesus now rules in place of God over his people. "Son of God" therefore did not designate Jesus any more than the king of Israel as a superhuman, divine being, but as the appointed ruler in virtue of his exaltation to the right hand of God: the general plenipotentiary of God, so to speak, who should be venerated like God himself by all his subjects.

The earthly, historical Jesus of Nazareth already appeared as public advocate of God by proclaiming God's kingdom and will in word and deed.[23] And at the same time he was more than a mandatory, plenipotentiary, advocate, spokesman of God in the legal sense. Without any title or office, he appears in all his action and speech as advocate in the wholly existential sense: as personal messenger, trustee, indeed as confidant and friend of God. He lived, suffered and struggled in the light of an ultimately inexplicable experience of God, presence of God, certainty of God, and indeed of a singular unity with God which permitted him to address God as his Father. The fact that he was first of all called "Son" in the community might simply be the reflection which fell on his countenance from the Father-God whom he proclaimed. From then on the transition to the traditional usage of "Son of God" was understandable.

For the people of that time this title more than others made it clear how closely the man Jesus of Nazareth belongs to God, how closely he stands now at God's side, in face of the community and the world, subject only to the Father and to no one else. As finally exalted to God, he is now in the definitive and comprehensive sense—"once and for all"—*God's representative* to men. Titles like God's "mandatory," "plenipotentiary," "advocate," "spokesman," "representative," "deputy," "delegate" express for many today perhaps more clearly what the old names, "king," "shephard," "saviour," "God's Son," or even the traditional doctrine of the three "offices" of Jesus Christ (king, prophet, priest) attempted to express.

But even the earthly Jesus, for whom God's cause was man's cause, was the public advocate of men by the very fact of being God's advocate. By fulfilling God's will in his whole life, speech, action and suffering, he stood for the comprehensive well-being of man, he stood for man's freedom, his joy, his true life, his chance with God, for love. He was wholly absorbed in the cause of God and therefore also of man. And all this with absolute consistency and perseverance to the very end. In his death he only brought to an end what he had preached and lived from the beginning. He did not die merely for his "conviction." Nor merely for a "cause" in a general sense, but in fact he died wholly concretely for all the abandoned and despised, lawbreakers, outlaws, sinners of all kinds, with whom —to the scandal of his opponents—he had associated, combined, identified, and who really would have deserved the same fate as himself. He took on himself their lot and the curse that lay upon them. He died, not in the very worst sense (as his enemies thought), but in the very best sense (as his disciples perceived more and more clearly in the light of the resurrection), as representative of sinners—even, as Paul insisted, as sin personified.[24] And, in the sense that his death revealed the pious and righteous in their self-seclusion, self-assurance and self-righteousness as the real guilty ones and sinners, paradoxically he died also for them. He died, as became more clearly perceptible in the course of time, "for the many" without distinction of nation, class, race or culture: he died "for all," "for us." So the man Jesus of Nazareth, definitively God's representative, proved also to be in the most comprehensive and radical sense—"once and for all," transcending time and space—the delegate, deputy, *representative of men before God.*

It was however only after the disaster that Jesus was confirmed and justified as the representative of God and men. He first had to pay the price of death in order to make a radical breach in the law and to make possible a new freedom, a new existence, a new man. Only then did he come to be recognized as Son of Man and of God, as redeemer and reconciler, as sole mediator and high priest of the new covenant between God and man, indeed as the way, the truth and the life of God for men. He is all this not in a magical or mechanical way. He is not a substitute who occupies the position himself instead of leaving it open.[25] Being representative, delegate, deputy of God and man, he does not suppress God, but neither does he suppress man. He respects both God's will and man's responsibility. He calls men to freedom and awaits their consent. He goes ahead, involves himself and God, and provokes imitation.

Even as exalted to God, Jesus, who proclaimed not himself but God's kingdom, has not become an end in himself. Precisely as Son of God, as representative, delegate, deputy, he is in everything the living pointer to

God the Father, who is greater than he.[26] He is God's "precursor"[27] to men, before God himself reaches them. And at the same time he is the "precursor" of men to God, identifying himself with those who are running behind or hold back. His rule is not yet the definitive final state. It is for the time being, provisional. It is characterized by the "not yet" and "but even now," between fulfillment and consummation, time and eternity. Hence the goal of history, as Jesus proclaimed it, has not been changed by the fact that the proclaimer has become the proclaimed. The goal is and remains the kingdom of God, in which God's cause has prevailed, the absolute future has become present and the representative has given back his dominion to him whom he represented, so that God may be not only in all things, but all in all.[28]

The definitive standard

Throughout the New Testament Jesus is expected at the consummation of the reign of God in God's kingdom as *judge of the world,* coming to judge the living and the dead. Although this idea is firmly rooted in the creeds, it seems strange to some of our contemporaries. It may be easier to understand in the light of what has just been said.

The idea of a judgment of the dead—widespread even at that time—had been linked in both early Judaism and the Persian religion with the end-expectation: a judgment not only for the individual immediately after his death, but for all mankind at the end of time. We have already seen, in connection with Jesus' immediate expectation, how much this expectation of the consummation is expressed in the forms of early Jewish apocalyptic and how necessary it is to apply a discriminating demythologization when interpreting the beginning and the end of the history of mankind.[29] We must examine the problem a little more concretely.[30]

Church history from the first to the twentieth century shows that the history of the expectation of an early end is one of constantly repeated disappointments—even or more particularly in what are called "apocalyptic" times. But even conceptions like those of the second epistle to the Thessalonians (presumably not composed by Paul),[31] of a final accumulation of evil, a great apostasy before the end and the embodiment of anti-God and anti-Christian forces in an eschatological "lawless adversary," or —according to the Johannine letters[32]—of one or several "Antichrists" (individual or collective) are not, as is often assumed, special divine revelations about the end-time. They are images from Jewish apocalyptic,[33] making use partly of ancient mythological motifs and partly of historical experiences (King Antiochus IV Epiphanes who had to be worshiped as a visible god; Emperor Caligula, Nero *redivivus*). The "apocalyptic" (revelatory) images cannot be harmonized with each other and—despite their name—today at any rate cannot be understood as disclosures or information about the chronological sequence of the "last things" at the end of world history. They do not form a kind of script for the last act of the human tragedy. Despite the amazingly widespread curiosity even today, man does not learn here what will befall him and what will then happen. The picture of a great public gathering of all mankind—of billions and billions of people—for judgment is no more than a picture.

There is neither a clear scientific extrapolation nor an exact prophetical prognosis of the definitive future of mankind. In the history of freedom we must continually allow for the emergence of something utterly new, which could never have been deduced from the old. The end is not determined from the outset. Man should not simply await this end, but should take up his role creatively in world and history. In the interlacing of freedom giving and freedom given, man is the irreplaceable partner who should give a meaning to the irresistible evolution of the cosmos and set his stamp upon it. The coming of God's kingdom does not condemn man to passivity, but demands his fearless activity inspired by faith on behalf of his fellow men. There must be no flight into the future, but—resisting all rising skepticism and fatalism—action here and now inspired by hope. In view of the coming kingdom of justice, freedom and peace, there must be a tireless struggle for justice, freedom and peace: against all powers of evil, bondage, desolation, lovelessness, death. We do not need to repeat here what we have already said about turning the relative into the absolute, about the polarity of the future of God and the present of man.[84]

Both the end of mankind's history and its beginning, man's ultimate future and his ultimate origin, are matters of faith. In Scripture their meaning is conveyed in easily remembered but certainly time-conditioned poetic images which are meant to rouse alertness and confidence, but today more than ever must be examined closely to discover the essential message. Their purpose is not to describe the sequence of the end-events, but to point to the eschatological action of God himself and the co-responsibility of man for the end. But this promised *end* may *not* be equated without more ado with a cosmic disaster and a *breaking off* of the history of mankind. Although it is the end of the old and evil, it must be understood as an ending which is a *perfecting* and a consummation. It is the perfecting of the history of mankind by God who is faithful, creator and new creator, as is conveyed in the metaphors of the meal, the feast, marriage, the new earth and the new heaven, of a new world. The continuing future of the new world remains open for faith. It does not in any case mean rigidity, but the dynamism of eternal life: *vita venturi saeculi*, the life of the world to come, as it is expressed in the triumphal ending of the creeds.

Is it surprising that the *Gospels* and not the *apocalypses*—also widely propagated in the primitive Christian communities—became the characteristic form of literature for the early Church? Little apocalypses were incorporated—so to speak, domesticated—into the Gospels (and the great apocalypse attributed to John into the totality of the New Testament).[85] What does this mean except that apocalyptic is to be understood in the light of the Gospel and not vice versa.[86] As already noted, apocalyptic represents in a particular mental climate a framework of understanding and ideas which is to be clearly distinguished from the matter involved, from the message itself. To what are the apocalypses in the Gospels oriented? Wholly to the *manifestation of Jesus*, now unequivocally identical with the Son of Man: function and figure of the exalted Jesus, expected through the consummation of God's reign, have been fused at the latest here with function and figure of the apocalyptic Son of Man expected for the last judgment. The judge of the world is no other than Jesus and this very fact is the great sign of hope for all those who have committed themselves to Jesus.

Michelangelo's monumental painting in the Sistine Chapel makes an indelible impression of the "Last Judgment" of mankind. But artistic genius is not an answer to the question of a doubting faith: just *what* could *still* be *relevant* today in such a mythologically depicted assembly of all nations for judgment? Would it not be better to disregard this picture and speak of all men being gathered together in God, their creator and finisher? There are however some features which remain relevant. These may be listed first of all in a more or less negative form.

I cannot, in the last resort, judge myself, nor can I leave this judgment to any other human tribunal.

My opaque and ambivalent existence, like the profoundly discordant history of mankind as a whole, demands a final transparency and the revelation of a definitive meaning.

All that exists—including religious traditions, institutions, authorities—has a provisional character.

There is a true consummation and a true happiness for mankind only if these are shared by all mankind and not merely by the last generation.

The better future of a perfect society in peace, freedom and justice is something for which men can only strive: to suppose that it can ever be fully realized is to be the victim of an illusion or even of the terror of violent would-be benefactors of the people.

Other features may be listed in a more positive form.

Only in the encounter with the manifest ultimate reality of God will my life acquire its full meaning, will the history of mankind become transparent, will the individual and human society reach their true fulfillment.

> *On the way to the consummation, for the active and suffering realization of true human existence both in the life of the individual and in society, the crucified and yet living Jesus is the final judge, the reliable, permanent, ultimate,* definitive standard.[37]

He is the model of radical human existence, the standard by which all men—Christians and non-Christians—are measured and to which non-Christians, who are taken equally seriously in this respect, often correspond better than Christians.[38] It is a standard which will certainly be established only in the future of God's kingdom, but which even now brings about a decision, so that John's Gospel can insist that the judgment is already taking place.[39] The idea of a world judgment throws the Christian back forcefully onto this ultimate standard, making him aware of the provisional nature of each present moment, able to withstand the pressure of prevailing conditions and the temptations of the spirit of the age and to orient himself in accordance with God's will to the total mental and corporeal well-being of man (which is what is meant by the "corporal works of mercy" in the Gospel narratives of the judgment[40]).

What will be the outcome of it all? It must be stated at once that the *outcome of the whole is not obvious.* Not only are all ideas and opinions inadequate to cope with creation and new creation, but it appears to be impossible to answer ultimate questions like that of the salvation of all mankind (including the great evildoers throughout history up to Hitler and Stalin).

The greatest minds of theology—from Origen and Augustine, by way of Aquinas, Luther and Calvin, up to Barth—have wrestled with the obscure problems of the final destiny, the election, predetermination, *predestination* of man and of mankind, without being able to lift the veil of mystery. All that has become clear is that we cannot do justice to the beginning and the end of God's ways with the aid of simple solutions in the light either of the New Testament or of the questions of the present time. It was not possible either with the positive predetermination of a part of humanity to damnation—Calvin's idea of a *praedestinatio gemina,* a "double predestination"—or with the positive predetermination of all men to eternal bliss—Origen's *apokatastasis panton,* "universal restoration." To say that God *must* save all men (universal reconciliation) and *must* exclude the possibility of a final removal of man from his presence (hell) is to contradict the sovereign freedom of his grace and mercy. But it is likewise wrong to suppose that God *could not* save all men and—so to speak—leave hell empty.[41]

The accounts of the judgment in the New Testament announce a clear division of mankind. But other statements—particularly of Paul—suggest that there will be mercy for all.[42] The former statements are *never harmonized* with the latter in the New Testament. The question then—as many theologians today say—can only *remain open*. It must be noted, however, in view of the warning of a possible dual outcome, that no one should make light of the infinite seriousness of his personal responsibility. But this infinite seriousness of his personal responsibility need not lead him to despair: he can find encouragement in the opportunity of salvation for each and every human being, in the fact that there are no limits to the mercy of God. And the very fact that it is the man Jesus, our fellow man, friend of the oppressed and burdened, who is announced as judge, means that man has not to await tremblingly as in the medieval sequence for the dead a *dies irae*, a "day of wrath" (the dramatic climax in the Requiem Masses of Cherubini, Mozart, Berlioz and Verdi), but may await in the joy and composure of the ancient Christian *Maranatha* ("Our Lord, Come") his encounter and that of all men with God.

We are not required to master intellectually the highly complicated speculative details of this problem.[48] But neither can we be content with the individualistic-spiritualistic slogan: "Save your soul." We are required to struggle together with others for a better human world, preparing for the coming kingdom of God, to live in practice according to the standard of the crucified Jesus. According to the measure of the Crucified?

3. *The ultimate distinction*

"Alexamenos worships his God." This is the inscription under the oldest crucifix in existence: a sarcastic scribble representing the Crucified with an ass's head, probably from the third century, found on the Palatine, the imperial residential district in Rome. It would be impossible to bring out more clearly the fact that the message of the Crucified seemed anything but edifying, more like a bad joke, or—as Paul wrote to Corinth—"a scandal to the Jews and folly to the Gentiles."[1]

Revaluation

"The very name of the *cross* should never come near the body of a Roman citizen, nor even enter into his thoughts, his sight, his hearing." That is what Cicero declared in his speech on behalf of Rabirius Postumus in the Roman forum.[2] According to Cicero, Postumus could not be defended if the indictment were true that he had had Roman citizens crucified in the province. Crucifixion, he maintained, was the most cruel and repulsive, the most horrible form of death penalty.[3] Long after it was abolished by the Emperor Constantine, until into the fifth century, Christians hesitated to depict the suffering Jesus on the cross. To do this on a large scale became customary only in medieval Gothic.

So the cross was a harsh, cruel fact—anything but a timeless myth, still less a religious symbol or ornament. The sort of thing that Goethe heartily disliked: "a lightweight little ceremonial cross always adds to life's gaiety; no reasonable man should bother to dig up and replant the dismal cross of Calvary, the most repulsive thing under the sun."[4] Goethe speaks for secular humanism, but D. T. Suzuki, the prominent Zen Buddhist, speaks similarly for the world religions: "Whenever I see a crucified figure of Christ I cannot help thinking of the gap that lies deep between Christianity and Buddhism."[5] To no one—not to Jew, Greek or Roman—would it have occurred to link a positive, religious meaning with this outlaw's gibbet. The *cross of Jesus* was bound to strike *an educated Greek* as *barbaric folly, a Roman citizen* as *sheer disgrace*, and *a devout Jew* as *God's curse.*"

And it is this infamous stake which now appears in a completely different light. What was inconceivable for anyone at that time is achieved by faith in the still living Crucified: the *sign of disgrace* appears as a *sign of victory.* This disgraceful death of slaves and rebels can now be understood as a salvific death of redemption and liberation. The cross of Christ, the bloody seal on a life which made it wholly inevitable, becomes an appeal to renounce a life steeped in selfishness. As Nietzsche in his invectives against Christianity rightly sensed, a revaluation of all values is announced here. This does not mean constraint, feeble self-abasement, as Christians sometimes think and Nietzsche rightly feared. It means a brave life, undertaken by innumerable people, without fear even in face of fatal risks: through struggle, suffering, death, in firm trust and hope in the goal of true freedom, love, humanity, eternal life. The offense, the sheer scandal, was turned into an amazing experience of salvation, the way of the cross into a possible way of life.[6]

Obviously the early Christian community did *not* come to terms *at one stroke* with the monstrous offense of the crucified Messiah—it was vital first of all to establish Jesus' authority. Easter alone did not remove the embarrassment. Discussion of the cross runs right through the different New Testament writings—it is not necessary here to analyze the strata—and it is not for nothing that the Passion story is the oldest coherent Jesus story. It was only in the course of time that the cross came to be recognized as the very center and sum of Christian faith and life. Yet both discussion within the community and apologetic outside it necessitated a deeper reflection from which it became clear how the cross marks the parting of the ways for Christian community and Judaism, Hellenism and Romanism, and indeed for faith and unbelief.

In the light of the Easter experience, in place of the initial dejection and speechlessness, there emerged first of all the steadfast conviction that everything must have taken place in accordance with God's decree, that Jesus according to God's will "had to" go by this way. Examples from the

Old Testament—the persecuted prophet, the servant of God innocently and vicariously suffering for the many, the sacrificial animal symbolically taking away sin—helped gradually to give a positive meaning to the cruel, senseless event of the cross. Everything happened, it was said, "according to the Scriptures." By this was meant at first the Old Testament as a whole, which must have spoken everywhere about Jesus if he was the Messiah. A special exegesis was necessary to discover these references to Jesus. The Jewish tradition had not envisaged a suffering, still less a crucified Messiah even in the Servant Songs of Deutero-Isaiah.[7] But in this way the Old Testament was increasingly understood in the light of the cross and the cross increasingly interpreted in the light of the Old Testament, so that the fact emerged more and more clearly that God, the God of the Old Testament, had acted in Jesus. Such a developed "theology of the cross" is found on the grand scale on the one hand in the earliest of the four Gospels and on the other in the Pauline letters. In this connection it is clear that even titles like "Son of God," which are very often understood simply in the light of an "incarnation," can be rightly understood only in the light of the cross.

Mark makes no mention of the infancy story and lets it be seen in his Gospel that the Passion story in effect replaces it as the revelation of divine sonship.[8] Jesus is Son of God, as the superscription—presumably by Mark—of his Gospel records. But Mark does not base this claim on any wondrous birth or conception, which he does not even mention. He bases it on the mandate of God, calling Jesus to a particular way at baptism.[9] According to Mark, the fact that Jesus is Messiah and Son of God remained concealed from the public at large. It was known only to the devils[10] and finally also to Peter—the disciple who confessed his faith—but silence was imposed on these. Immediately after Peter's messianic confession there follows the first announcement of suffering: the path of the Messiah goes by way of the cross and no one who wants to follow him can escape his own cross. Hence Peter's misunderstanding is vehemently corrected: "Away from me, Satan."[11] It is only in the light of the cross that Jesus' messianic secret—introduced into the Gospel by Mark himself—is rightly understood. According to the Marcan view, Jesus never used the title "Son of God" and only accepted it as used by others at the Passion. Only after his death could someone—a pagan—for the first time spontaneously acknowledge that this man was God's son. Only after his death (and resurrection) can Jesus' secret be known and proclaimed.

Long before Mark, however, Paul—who likewise has no mention of an infancy story—sees the divine sonship as wholly and entirely oriented to Jesus' cross and resurrection.

Beyond fanaticism and rigidity

For the Apostle Paul,[12] regarding himself as chosen to preach the Gospel among the Gentiles, the Christian message is essentially the *message of the Crucified* and this crucified Jesus the concentration—so to speak—of the earthly Jesus as a whole. To put it briefly and epigrammatically, the Christian message is the word of the cross.[13] It is a word which may not be canceled or emptied of meaning, nor may it be suppressed or mythicized. If we compare the early first letter to the Thessalonians with his very different later work, it would seem that his opponents, particularly in Corinth and Galatia, with their curtailments and corruptions of the Gospel, had forced Paul to make his proclamation more concentrated and terse. It is in the light of the Crucified that Paul's theology comes to be marked by that pungent criticism which notably differentiates it from others. In the light of this center—even for Paul it is not the whole—he tackles all situations and problems. At the same time therefore he can produce an amazingly apt and also coherent ideological criticism of both left and right.

a. On the one side are the progressive, pneumatic *enthusiasts* in the proverbially infamous Greek seaport of *Corinth*[14] who imagine—because they are baptized, have received the Spirit, share in the agape—that they are already in secure possession of salvation and even perfect. They regard the wretched earthly Jesus as belonging to the past and prefer to invoke the exalted Lord and victor over the powers of fate. From the fact of possession of the Spirit and from their "superior" knowledge they deduce a self-assured freedom which permits them to indulge in all kinds of self-glorification, arrogance, uncharitableness, self-opinionatedness, violence, even drinking bouts and intercourse with sacred prostitutes (known as "Corinthianizing"). Paul refers these extravagant, utopian, libertinist, resurrection fantasts, who want to anticipate heaven on earth, to the *Crucified*.

From the very beginning he wanted to proclaim the Crucified and him alone. And how could anyone show off his religious talents and powers or boast of his superior wisdom and mighty deeds in view of this Crucified, who died in his weakness for the weak? How could anyone ruthlessly attain his objectives, misuse his freedom, seek to give himself airs before God, in order to set himself above weak men and the weakness of God himself? It is precisely in the weakness and folly of the Crucified—in which the weakness and folly of God himself seems to be manifested—that God's power to raise the dead and his overwhelming wisdom ultimately prevail. God's weakness, so obvious particularly on the cross, proves to be stronger than the power of men. His folly is shown to be wiser than their wisdom. It is indeed the cross, seen in the light of the new life, which means God's power and wisdom to all who trustingly commit themselves to it. In faith in the Crucified, that is, man becomes capable of using freedom, not as a libertine, but for others: able to apply the individual gifts of the Spirit for the benefit of the community, to proceed in everything boldly by way of active love. This crucified and living Jesus then is for believers the foundation which is already laid and which cannot be replaced by any other. The Crucified as living is the ground of faith. He is the criterion of freedom. He is indeed the center and norm for what is Christian.

The cross was the great question which was answered by the resurrection. Through Paul the cross itself became the great answer, *putting in question a false conception of the resurrection.* Against all pseudo-progressive resurrection and freedom enthusiasm, the cross therefore remains the warning sign which compels man to face its reality and *calls him to follow the Crucified.* The core of the Christian message, vigorously defended by Paul against its deniers, is no other than the Crucified, who is not dead and gone for the Christian community, but living now and into the future. The risen Christ rules only to serve the crucified. Easter does not cancel the cross. Easter confirms the cross, not indeed by approving its offensiveness, but by making the offensiveness good and meaningful. The resurrection message therefore may not for a moment obscure the message of the cross.[15] The cross is not merely a "transit station" on the way to glory, nor merely the way to the prize, nor merely one "salvation fact" in addition to others. It is the permanent signature of the living Christ. What would this Christ look like if he were not the Crucified? The exalted Jesus is rightly depicted always with the stigmata of the earthly. Easter is rightly understood only if the burden and strain of Good Friday are not forgotten. It is only by this means that the idea of eternal life will be something more than a mere consolation for the cross of the present time, the suffering of the individual and the problems of society. We cannot indulge in blissful dreaming of life after death instead of changing life and social conditions here and now *before* death.

b. On the other side however are the opponents on the right, those conservative devout *moralists* in the *Galatian* province of Asia Minor,[16] confused by Judaizing missionaries, who—unlike the Corinthian enthusiasts—do not anticipate the end but turn back to the past. They regard freedom from the law as an aberration. In addition to baptism and faith in Christ, they consider Jewish ritual, circumcision, Sabbath, calendar, other ordinances of Jewish life and even the "elements of nature"* as essential. And they now think that they can put themselves right with God by means of religious practices, moral achievements, pious works. They take God's

* Gal. 4:9. A difficult expression, probably meaning primitive usages now rendered obsolete, whether embodied in the Mosaic law or not. (Translator.)

promises as their privilege and God's commandments as means of their self-sanctification.

Paul also refers to the Crucified these legal pietists, reverting to the ancient cultic and moral legalism, for whom Jesus need never have come and died. He points to this crucified Jesus

who did not want to make the devout more devout, but turned to the abandoned, the irreligious, the lawbreakers, the godless;

who submitted to the law himself, but radically relativized it and in his proclamation opposed the God of love and mercy to the God of the law;

who therefore appeared to the guardians of law and order as the servant of sin and sinners and was crucified in the name of the law as a criminal;

who took on himself for the lawless and godless the curse of the law and in this very way, justified by the vivifying God against the law, liberated men finally from the curse of the law for freedom and true humanity.

If men look to this crucified Jesus, Paul thinks, they can no longer be subject to the Jewish law or ritual, or indeed to any religious conventions. They can only be really *free Christian men, entrusting to God* themselves and their whole fate, men who are "in Christ" and in that sense "Christians." This is the way of trusting faith which is practicable for Jews and Gentiles, masters and slaves, educated and uneducated, men and women, and even for both the religious and the irreligious. For it does not require any particular preconditions, any special lineage, religious proficiency, evidence of piety, ritual acts or preliminary moral achievements. Looking to Jesus all that is required is this simple entrusting of ourselves to God, regardless of all our weaknesses and faults, but also regardless of our prerogatives, merits, achievements or claims.

What does it mean to be truly a child of God and so truly human?

It means abandoning all pious dreams, ridding ourselves of illusions and admitting that no effort of ours counts when it comes to the final decision: admitting that we make no progress with God by observing the letter of the ritual and the moral law (which can never be completely fulfilled and therefore constantly create new feelings of guilt); that all our moral exertions and pious practices are inadequate to put in order our relationship with God and that no achievements of ours can merit God's love.

It means relying completely on this Christ and believing that God wants to help in particular the abandoned, irreligious, lawbreakers, ungodly, and out of sheer friendliness himself puts in order our relationship with him.

It means then seeing in the dark mystery of the cross the very essence of the grace and love of that God who does not judge men in a human way according to their deeds, but simply accepts, approves and loves them from the outset.

A person who accepts all this is no longer a bondsman or slave under the dominion of law and ritual and therefore of men. He is then truly a child of God and thus truly human.

As grown-up son or daughter of this Father, with believing trust, but without legal constraints or pressure to achieve results, such a person becomes capable in complete freedom of obedience to God and commitment to men. Instead of being wholly wrapt up in himself (which is sin), he can live for others who are around him and thus by being actively present, by love, can in fact abundantly fulfill the law which aims at man's well-being.

All this can be read in greater detail in Paul's letters to the Corinthians and Galatians. But the attentive reader cannot fail to notice a very considerable difference between Paul and Jesus.

By faith alone

Paul has sometimes been represented as the real founder of Christianity. Or was he—as Nietzsche claimed in *Antichrist*, developing the ideas of liberal theology (those of F. Overbeck?)—its great falsifier? Nietzsche displays sympathy for Jesus: "There was really only one Christian and he *died* on the cross. The 'gospel' died on the cross."[17] But he wildly misunderstands Paul and abuses the latter as the "disevangelist," the "forger out of hatred," the very "opposite of a bringer of glad tidings," "the genius in hatred, in the vision of hatred, in the stubborn logic of hatred."[18] And even some Christian theologians were superficial and foolish enough to make the rallying cry of "Back to Jesus" a demand for a break with Paul.

There is no doubt about the *significance of Paul* and his theology *for world history*. He opened the way theologically and practically for non-Jews to approach the Christian message in absolute freedom. They did not have to become Jews, to be circumcised, to be tied by the innumerable Jewish purity taboos, regulations about food and the Sabbath, observances which were all so alien to the Gentiles. It was only through Paul that the Christian mission to the Gentiles, as distinct from the Hellenistic Jews, became a success. Only through him did the community of Palestinian and Hellenistic Jews become a community made up of Jews and Gentiles. Only through him did the small Jewish sect finally develop into a world religion. It is obvious—but worth further consideration—that there is and must be an essential difference between the message of Jesus himself and the Jewish-Hellenistic interpretation, in the light of Jesus' death and resurrection, of the happenings connected with Jesus.

Nevertheless, only blindness to what Jesus himself willed, lived and suffered to the very roots or to what Paul urged with elemental force, in Jewish-Hellenistic terminology, moved—like Jesus—by the prospect of the imminent end of all things: only blindness to all this can conceal the fact that the call "Back to Jesus" runs right through the Pauline letters and frustrates all attempts to turn the message into a Jewish or Hellenistic ideology. At the heart of Paul's thinking is not man (anthropology), nor Church (ecclesiology), nor even salvation history in general, but the *crucified and risen Christ* (Christology understood as soteriology). This is a Christocentrism working out to the advantage of man, based on and culminating in a theocentrism: "God through Jesus Christ"—"through Jesus Christ to God." As the Holy Spirit came to be inserted in such binitarian formulas—as the one in whom God and Jesus Christ are present and active both in the individual and the community—they were turned by Paul at this early stage into trinitarian formulas, the basis for the later development of the doctrine of the Trinity, of the triune God who is Father, Son and Holy Spirit.

Paul's whole vision of *salvation history* from creation by way of the promises to Abraham and the law of Moses up to the Church and the imminent consummation of the world—the Abraham-Christ line[19] and the Christ-Adam parallel,[20] as well as the conception of the Church as community of Jews and Gentiles and as body of Christ,[21] all bring out the same thing—has its immovable critical *center* in the crucified and risen Jesus. This center may be designated "Christology," "kerygma," "theology of the cross" or "message of justification."[22] It is only in the light of this center that we can rightly understand both Paul's processing of the Christian tradition and his use of the Old Testament; all his epoch-making theological comments on law and faith, wrath and grace of God, death and life, sin and God's justice, spirit and letter, Israel and the Gentiles; his statements too about the proclamation, the Church, the gifts of the Spirit, baptism and eucharist, the new life in freedom and hope of fulfillment.[23]

The view of some liberal exegetes that Paul was not interested in the *historical Jesus*, adopted after the First World War by dialectical theology (K. Barth) and kerygmatic theology (R. Bultmann), has been shown by recent discussion to be untenable. Nowhere in Paul is there any deliberate depreciation of the Jesus tradition. But does not Paul say that he has no wish to know a "Christ according to the flesh"?[24] But by this he does not mean the earthly Jesus as distinct from the exalted, nor the crucified as distinct from the risen, and certainly not the "historical Jesus" discovered by historical research as opposed to the Christ who is the object of faith. He means the Jesus whom he had understood (or misunderstood) at the time when he was persecuting Christians in a natural way, without faith, that is, in a "fleshly" way. This was Christ as opposed to the Jesus Christ whom he now (after his conversion) knows (acknowledges) in a pneumatic-believing, that is, "spiritual" way. It is not a question then of another Jesus Christ but of a fundamentally changed relationship with him.[25]

In his letters—mostly, as we saw, fragmentary occasional writings which presuppose a rudimentary catechetical introduction to the Christian faith

—Paul only rarely has recourse to the Gospel tradition of Jesus. But his attitude to it is undoubtedly positive. And in the authentic Pauline writings there are at least twenty passages which could be cited where he clearly relies on the Gospel tradition of Jesus.[26] We may rightly conclude that, over and above what he had received in this very casual way, he had much more to tell the community of what he had heard in Jerusalem, Damascus, Antioch and elsewhere about the message, the behavior and the fate of this earthly and historical Jesus. In the eighteen months of preaching and catechizing in Corinth, for instance, Paul could scarcely have been constantly repeating with new variations an abstract kerygma of the crucified and risen Jesus.

The Old Testament too up to a point plays a surprisingly small part in the Pauline letters (no part at all in fact in 1 Thessalonians, in Philippians and in large sections of 1 and 2 Corinthians) and yet was constantly in the mind of Paul, the former Pharisee theologian. It comes to the fore expressly in the letters only where it becomes necessary—as in Galatians or Romans—as a result of controversy with Jews or Judaistic Christians. If then Paul stresses God's activity with reference to the historical Jesus and therefore the cross and resurrection, this must be because he knows and assumes that his readers know also Jesus traditions which do not find expression in his letters but whose range must not be underestimated. Nevertheless the sources do provide some quite important information.

Obviously the former *persecutor of the Christian community* was able to explain why Jesus was condemned to be crucified and why he himself thought he had to persecute the community. According to his own statement, he did this as a "Pharisee according to the law,"[27] "zealous for the traditions of my ancestors."[28] Paul, the Hellenistic diaspora Jew from Tarsus, had come up against Jesus' criticism of the law presumably in confrontation with the Jewish-Christian Hellenists of the Jerusalem community. As a result of the way in which the law (*Torah* and *halakhah*) had been put in question,[29] he had been so provoked in his genuine Pharisaic zeal for God and his law that he resolved on an active struggle against the community, "beyond measure," and even to bring about its "destruction."[30] The scandal created for any Jew by a crucified Messiah under the curse of the law could only have strengthened his immense persecuting zeal.[31]

All this explains very well how this model of Pharisaic legalist piety became a persecutor of the Christian community and its faith. But how did the fanatical persecutor of Christians become an *apostle of the Crucified?* No one has yet explained it in psychological or historical terms. Paul himself does not ascribe his radical change to human instruction, a new self-understanding, a heroic effort or a conversion achieved by his own resources. Instead, he speaks of a "revelation" ("seeing")—which he does not describe and which is not easy to explain[32]—of the crucified and now risen Christ, the result of which was a radical conversion.[33] Here too there is a vocation. But it is only when his position or his Gospel is contested that he speaks—and then in very few words—of this happening, on which his apostolate and his apostolic freedom are based.[34] Man and not the law is God's cause and this in the last resort is what counts for God. Paul now understands the death on the cross as a consequence of the law. But at the same time—because God himself justified Jesus against the law—he sees the cross as a liberation from the curse of the law.[35] If the right relationship between God and man (righteousness) came by the law, then Jesus would have died in vain.[36]

What Paul throughout his life understood by *"grace,"* as the completely unmerited friendliness of God, is based on this living experience of the Crucified who revealed himself to him as the living, the true Lord. From now on—except when considering the conscience of troubled brethren[37]—Paul defends uncompromisingly the basic significance of faith in Christ by pure grace against all tendencies to introduce an "and": salvation through Christ in faith *and* through works of the Jewish (or another) law? He expounds this Gospel of his in his longest, most compact, most comprehensive letter, written before getting to know them to the Christian community in *Rome.*[38] In the light of the whole course of salvation history from creation to consummation, starting out from the universal sinfulness of men, both Jews and Gentiles,[39] he explains how man's definitive well-being, his salvation, can be attained only on the basis of faith in Jesus Christ:[40] on this basis of faith he sketches in a striking way both the new life from the Spirit in freedom and hope[41] and God's great plan of salvation for Jews and Gentiles[42] and draws out the most important consequences for a Christian life.[43]

As in the earlier letter to the Galatians—although referring to God's law as good in itself but not leading to salvation, in a more balanced and less polemical manner—Paul denies that there are any further conditions for establishing man's right relationship with God, appealing simply to the Crucified and to God's grace. Man's salvation does not depend on any kind of prescribed works of the law, on devotional practices and moral efforts. It depends exclusively on trusting faith in Jesus Christ. As Paul expresses it in the juridically colored Jewish language of his time, guilty, sinful man is "released," "declared just," "justified," in the sight of God and his judgment, not on the basis of works of the law good in themselves, but through God's grace and friendliness, solely *on the basis of faith.*[44] The *locus classicus* from the epistle to the Romans can be paraphrased in a modern way: "We hold that man can enter into a right, a good relationship with God without satisfying any religious requirements, provided only that he trusts himself to God and so receives what God wants to give him."[45]

No other cause

So the conflict with the law and its understanding of God, which had brought death to Jesus, had also become Paul's conflict and a deadly threat to him. His teaching on the law—a basic continuity is apparent here—represents the continuation of Jesus' proclamation. It is of course a *radicalized continuation* in the light of the death of Jesus: in this sense there is not a simple continuity between Jesus and Paul, but only a continuity in discontinuity. There stands between the proclamation of the historical Jesus and the proclamation of Paul the death of Jesus: the death brought about by bringing the law into question, the meaning of which was revealed by the resurrection, and in which Paul perceived God's action in Jesus. That is why Paul sees as concentrated in the death on the cross everything that the historical Jesus brought, lived and endured to the end. The Crucified is obviously identical with the historical, earthly Jesus and in this sense the latter is the indispensable presupposition and a part also of Paul's faith: faith in the crucified and risen Jesus is thus prevented from being reduced to illusion or unhistorical myth. In the light of the cross Paul grasped and constantly maintained the reality and the meaning of Jesus' earthly existence.

For Paul the one "word of the cross" really said everything that had to be said about Jesus' proclamation, behavior and fate. In the light of the cross of the one who is alive for faith, Paul *as theologian* could make explicit what Jesus had simply done in fact and often said only implicitly. Not that Paul produced a comprehensive theoretical outline. Even in the letter to the Romans his theology—based on the crucified and risen Christ and essentially only on a few basic, main themes—is related to the whole concrete situation of this community. But in the particular context Paul expressly thought out and developed in theological terms consistently in the light of the death and resurrection what is found in non-theological terms and undeveloped in Jesus' proclamation. For this he made use both of his rabbinic training and in particular exegesis and of a number of terms and ideas from his Hellenistic environment. Hence for anyone who approaches it from the standpoint of the Gospel tradition of Jesus, Paul's presentation of Jesus' message is bound to appear at first in a very different light: reshaped into quite different perspectives, categories and ideas. Nevertheless, a closer examination cannot fail to reveal there very much more of Jesus' proclamation than is indicated by particular words or sentences and that its "substance" has entered completely into Paul's proclamation.

Like Jesus, Paul too lives in a state of intense expectation of the coming kingdom of God. *But Jesus looks to the future while Paul also looks back to the turning point involved in death and resurrection. He sees the intermediate period between resurrection and future consummation (and universal resurrection) as under the present rule of the exalted Christ.*

Like Jesus, Paul too starts out from the fact of the sinfulness *of man, even of the righteous, devout, law-abiding man. But Paul develops this insight theologically, by making use of Old Testament material and especially by the* Adam-Christ *contrast.*

Like Jesus, Paul too brings a message which thrusts man into a crisis, *calls for* faith, *demands* conversion. *But with Paul the message of God's kingdom is concentrated in the word of the cross which creates scandal and thus involves in a crisis the Jewish* and *the Greek way of self-assertion. This is the end of legal obedience* and *the end of human wisdom.*

Like Jesus, Paul too is not interested in a doctrine of demons or in the practice of exorcism, but sees himself engaged in the struggle with demonic forces of evil *whose dominion is reaching its end. But for Paul, even if these forces are still effective, they have in principle been deprived of power through Jesus' death and new life.*

Like Jesus, Paul too claims God *for his work. But Paul does this in the light of Jesus' cross and resurrection, the point at which for him God's activity made a definite breakthrough: from Jesus' implicit factual Christology there emerged after the death and resurrection the explicit, positive Christology of the community.*

Like Jesus, Paul too, for the sake of man, radically relativized the law with all its purity taboos, regulations about food and the Sabbath: the faith of Israel is now manifestly concentrated on its central and essential elements, the law reduced to a few valid and obvious fundamental requirements. But for Paul Jesus' death under the law means the end of the law itself as a way of salvation and the new way of salvation by faith in Jesus Christ.

Like Jesus, Paul too defended forgiveness of sins out of pure grace: the justification of the sinner. *But Paul's message of the justification of the sinner, of the ungodly (Jew or Gentile), presupposes Jesus' death on the cross, understood as death for sinners, for the ungodly.*

Like Jesus, Paul too went beyond the limits of the law, turning in quite a practical way to the poor, abandoned, oppressed, outsiders, outlaws, lawbreakers, and defended a universalism *in word and deed. But Jesus' universalism in principle in regard to Israel and his practical, virtual universalism in regard to the Gentile world became for Paul—in the light of the crucified and risen Jesus—a formal universalism in principle in regard to both Israel* and *the Gentile world which made necessary the mission to the Gentiles.*

Like Jesus, Paul too proclaimed love of God and neighbor *as the practical fulfillment of the law and lived this love radically in absolute obedience to God and in unselfish existence for his fellow men, even for enemies. But Paul perceived in the very death of Jesus the most profound revelation of this love on the part of God and of Jesus himself and this revelation became for him the ground of men's own love of God and neighbor.*

It can therefore be said that this message of justification, typical and central for Paul, is present already in the parables of Jesus and in the Sermon on the Mount, but that a decisive new light is thrown on it by Jesus' death and resurrection. The Pauline message of revelation therefore is rightly designated "applied Christology." As such it naturally becomes also the critical norm for the correct application of Christology as opposed to all attempts either to trivialize it and empty it of meaning or even to idealize and transfigure it.

Whenever in the course of Church history the essential importance of the crucified and living Jesus as the model for the relationship of man and God, man and man, has been obscured, then the question of justification solely by *faith* in Jesus Christ has suddenly acquired a new importance and led to a discernment of spirits. At that point too Paul's letter to the Romans together with that to the Galatians has again developed a veritable explosive force. So it was with Pelagianism in the time of Augustine. So it was with the medieval idea of sanctification through works and the Roman misuse of authority particularly at the time of the Reformers. So it was also with a cultural Protestantism which had become idealist-humanist and with the National Socialist ideology against which Karl Barth reacted after the First World War. And is it not so today at a time of a secularized piety of works, based on the principle of payment by results?

All this is not to say that "through faith alone"—which is an echo of "through Christ alone" or "through grace alone"—was ever meant to exclude good works. But the appeal to any sort of good works can never be the basis of being a Christian and the criterion for justification in the sight of God. All that counts is to cling to God absolutely firmly through Jesus the Christ in a believing trust, against which neither human failures nor any good works can prevail, but from which works of love obviously follow. This is an extraordinarily consoling message which provides a solid basis for a man's life through all the inevitable failures, errors and despair. And it frees that life also from the pressure to produce pious works, sustaining it through even the worst situations in freedom, wisdom, love and hope.

It is a message which need no longer be a matter of dispute between Catholic and Protestant theology.[46] After the long controversy about "faith alone," some of the more recent ecumenical translations of the Bible give clear expression to a common understanding particularly of the important text in Romans: "For we hold that man is justified *only* through faith, *independently* of the works of the law."[47] Of course, particular words and ideas are not the important thing in the "doctrine of justification." As we saw, Paul himself expressed it quite differently for the Corinthians, using terms like "wisdom" and "folly" of God and men—which can hardly be said to have legal implications. What is important is the reality, which every age must formulate again in its own words.

Paul then—a man not of hatred but of love, a genuine bearer of "glad tidings"—did not establish a new Christianity. He laid no new foundation. According to his own words, he built on what was already laid:[48] Jesus Christ who is source, foundation, content and norm of the Pauline proclamation, of his kerygma. In the light of a fundamentally different situation after Jesus' death and resurrection, he defended, not a different cause, but the same: the *cause of Jesus* which is no other than the *cause of God* and the *cause of man*—only now, after death and resurrection, it is understood as the cause of Jesus Christ.[49] Paul described himself modestly but also proudly as "apostle" of Jesus Christ. As such, as authorized ambassador he simply drew out the logical conclusions of the message first outlined in the proclamation, behavior and fate of Jesus. But he brought to bear on the decisive issue controlled passion, vigor, independence and originality, using different forms of language, different categories and different ideas. He thus rendered the message intelligible beyond Israel for the whole *oikoumene*, for the then known world. And throughout the ages, like no other except Christ, he remained a constant inspiration to Christendom to rediscover the true—but far from obvious—Christ in Christianity and to follow him.

As a result, not only of theological reflection, but of the most concrete, often most cruel experience[50] in imitation of Jesus, even finally in a similar, violent death (under Nero, probably in 66), Paul succeeded more clearly than anyone in expressing what is *the ultimately distinguishing feature* of Christianity. As far as we are concerned in this book, the circuit is completed here.

As we established at an early stage,[51] *the distinguishing feature of Christianity as opposed to the ancient world religions and the modern humanisms is this* Christ *himself. But what protects us against any confusion of this Christ with other religious or political Christ figures?*

We then defined[52] *more closely the distinctive feature of Christianity as opposed to the ancient world religions and the modern humanisms as the Christ who is identical with the real, historical Jesus of Nazareth, that is, as* Jesus *who is in the concrete this Christ. But what protects us against any confusion of this historical Jesus Christ with false images of Jesus?*

The distinguishing feature of Christianity as opposed to the ancient world religions and the modern humanisms—at the end of this chapter, after examining closely the proclamation, behavior and fate of Jesus, we can now give the answer—the ultimate *distinctive feature of Christianity is quite literally according to Paul "this Jesus Christ, Jesus Christ* crucified."[53]

It is not indeed as risen, exalted, living, divine, but as crucified, that this Jesus Christ is distinguished unmistakably from the many risen, exalted, living gods and deified founders of religion, from the Caesars, geniuses and heroes of world history. The cross then is not only example and model, but ground, strength and norm of the Christian faith: the great distinctive reality which distinguishes this faith and its Lord in the world market from the religious and irreligious ideologies, from other competing religions and utopias and their lords, and plunges its roots at the same time into the reality of concrete life with its conflicts. The cross separates the Christian faith from unbelief and superstition. The cross certainly in the light of the resurrection, but also the resurrection in the shadow of the cross.

Without faith in the cross, faith in the risen Christ lacks its distinctive character and decisiveness.

Without faith in the resurrection, faith in the crucified Jesus lacks confirmation and authorization.

John, although using a very different terminology, is speaking of the same distinctive Christian feature as Paul when he calls Jesus the way, the truth and the life[54] and illustrates this with images of Christ as the bread of life,[55] the light of the world,[56] the gate,[57] the true vine,[58] the good shepherd who gives his life for the sheep.[59] Jesus here is evidently not a name which must be constantly on our lips, but the way of life's truth which must be practiced. The truth of Christianity is not something to be "contemplated," "theorized," but to be "done," "practiced." The Christian concept of truth is not—like the Greek—contemplative-theoretical, but operative-practical. It is a truth which is not merely to be sought and found, but to be pursued, made true, verified and tested in truthfulness. A truth which aims at practice, which calls to the way, which bestows and makes possible a new life.

VI. Interpretations

The crucified and yet living Christ is the concrete summing up of the Christian message and the Christian faith. He is himself the wholly concrete truth of Christianity. And it was the concrete, living reality of his historical person and his fate which gave early Christianity its superiority over contemporary philosophical theories of salvation, Gnostic visions, over the mystery cults and their comparatively abstract figures unmoved by fate. "The picture of Jesus as the Christ conquered them through the power of a concrete reality."[1] And even today the individual historical concreteness of his person constitutes the strength of the Christian faith as opposed to universal religious world views, abstract philosophical systems and socio-political ideologies—which, however, for their own part, have been inclined to depend on a concrete hero in the person of a founder or leader (of the nation, of the party), of the head of a school, of a master, mystagogue or guru.

But there are some who will then ask: what about the different Christian "truths," articles of faith, dogmas, which—unlike the concrete figure of Jesus—are so difficult to understand and assimilate? How are they related to this one concrete truth of Christianity, which is Jesus Christ himself? These "truths" are to be understood as attempts to interpret the one truth.

1. Discriminating interpretation

Anyone who looks at the immense difficulties, both historical and systematic, of the stories for instance of the empty tomb, the descent into hell and ascension to heaven, world judgment and second coming, and also—as we shall see later—the infancy stories, may easily wonder if the message of the real Jesus of Nazareth has not become a narration of "stories of the gods," that is, a "mythology." Would not the simplest and best way to make the Gospels intelligible for modern man therefore be a radical demythologizing, an elimination of all mythical and legendary elements from the very roots? Ought not the Gospels to be purified from all this and rationally paraphrased?

Limits to demythologization

Purified and paraphrased, of course, the Gospels would no longer be what they are: any more than Dante's *Divine Comedy*, the French *Song of Roland*, Milton's *Paradise Lost* or Goethe's *Faust*. It is not only a question of cutting out a great deal from the beginning and end of the Gospels (both infancy and Easter and judgment stories). But between beginning and end also—for instance, in the miracle and epiphany stories—the message is interwoven with mythical and legendary elements. What would be left of the Old Testament narratives of the creation of the world and of man, still more of the Gospels, if they were reduced to the "essential" statements? Could we imagine such an excerpt being read aloud at Mass? Would these "essential theses" be read any more than, for instance, the propositions of pre-Socratic philosophers as they advance from myth to logos?

The Gospels were in fact written for people thinking mythologically at a time of mythological thinking, although in fact—as a result of its monotheistic faith being confronted with the pagan polytheistic faith—the process of demythologizing and historicizing is further advanced in the New Testament than in the Old. We cannot examine here the immense influence of myths—whether of the ancient East or of the Bible, those of India or those of Homer, those of ancient Rome, of the Middle Ages, or even the substitute myths of modern times—on the evolution of mankind and of individual nations. The comparative study of religions, anthropology, psychology and sociology have revealed in a variety of ways the power of myth to establish meaning and effect social integration: not only its function in a religious interpretation of the world or in cult, but also in man's individual and social development as a whole.

Certainly at that time, when the redaction of the Gospels was completed, a vivid, narrative form of proclamation, making use of myths, legends, symbols, was absolutely necessary. How are new experiences and particularly new experiences of faith to be communicated if not by storytelling? It is obvious that the biblical Christmas and Easter stories are more comprehensible and easier to remember than any amount of abstract propositions on divine sonship and passing through death to life. Even today, in the age of rational-causal and functional-technical thinking, might not a vivid, narrative form of proclamation still be absolutely necessary and certain ancient formulas—mythological in the widest sense—still be useful? The conclusions of the comparative study of religions[2] should be considered here, as also those of ethnopsychology.[3] Even in Freud's supposedly highly rational psychoanalysis Greek mythology plays a considerable part in the interpretation of scientific analyses, and C. G. Jung made an extensive study of myths in connection with the psychical growth of the individual.

Whatever we may think of Freud's use of myth—for instance, in connection with the Oedipus complex—or of Jung's theory of the collective unconscious, of archetypes as the expression of a superindividual meaning to life, and his psychological refunctioning of myths and symbols (even the Marian invocations of the Litany of Loreto), can there be any doubt about man's persistent need? Does not even modern man (and his mass media) live not only by arguments but also by *stories*, not only by concepts but also by *images*—often very primitive images—and does he not always need valid images and stories that can be retold? The Utopia of the kingdom of God, for instance, even in its secular form, proved immensely attractive up to the time of National Socialism and—in a very different, but still serious way—Marxism. And the messianic redeemer in the person of a child, isolated and exposed but still triumphant over his enemies, has demonstrably inspired not only Francis of Assisi and the medieval poverty movement but also modern movements for emancipation. Images from biblical protology and eschatology have their fascination even today.

Is then *demythologizing*—which logically had to have a place in this book—to be abandoned? No. But, together with the *necessity* of demythologizing, its *limits* must also be recognized. What has been suggested in various ways must now be treated systematically. The Christian message is not a myth and we do not live in a mythological-archaic world, but in a modern world bearing the imprint of science and technology, oriented not to the past but to the future. There is no question of presenting as historical facts in theology, preaching or catechesis, biblical happenings and ideas which have proved to be myth, saga, legend, symbol, image, still less of imposing them on the faithful as truths of faith, binding for all time. In this sense historical criticism may not remain shut up in the ivory tower of theological scholarship, but must extend its influence to the proclamation and practice of the Church and throw a critical light on these. Three points must be noted with reference to *myths, legends, images and symbols.*

a. Myths, legends, images and symbols *may not be taken literally*. For a long time it was typical of *Catholic* theology, Church and proclamation, more or less skillfully to avoid demythologizing and—especially in the Catholicism of the southern parts of Europe—even to cultivate myth in all possible biblical and post-biblical forms and shapes, the result being ignorance and obscurantism among the ordinary people and widespread de-Christianization and lack of faith among the educated classes. If therefore *the mythical element is simply preserved*, this is at the expense of the Christian message which is confused with the myth and *makes faith degenerate into superstition*. It must be repeated here: demythologizing is inescapable.

b. On the other hand, myths, legends, images and symbols may *not be criticized merely because they are myths, legends, images and symbols.* Was this not a danger for *Protestant* theology, Church and proclamation, especially in the German-speaking countries, which frequently practiced demythologization too thoughtlessly, hastily and arbitrarily? To a large extent pictorial, mythical, symbolical and sacramental elements were simply excluded from the Church. As if men had only ears and not eyes. As if the appeal had to be made to intellect and critical-rational discourse and not also to fantasy, imaginative power, emotions, to spontaneity, creativity, innovation. As if Christian faith were merely a matter of intellect and did not have to stir the whole man. As if being stirred could ever be replaced by intellectual comprehension, images by concepts, stories by abstract ideas, narrating by proclaiming and appealing. Paul Tillich has insistently reminded Protestantism that in the course of time its intellectual Gospel would appeal only to intellectuals.[4] The result has been a depopulation of the Church—already far advanced in certain areas—often linked with a susceptibility to new mythologizings. Thus, even when *the mythical element is simply eliminated*—as became evident in the theology of the Enlightenment and of liberalism—it is at the expense of the Christian message, which is then thrown out together with the myth. *Faith then hardens into a rational religion.*

c. Genuine *critical interpretation* avoids the extremes of traditionalism and rationalism: it dissociates itself from all forms of superstition (among which is also rational religion). Critical theology today sees the necessity *and* the limits of demythologization. It seeks—as Bultmann also admits in theory—neither to preserve nor to eliminate the mythical factor. It seeks, as we have repeatedly insisted, *to interpret the mythical element with discrimination.* If at the same time we want to avoid any narrowing down or undue reduction of the message, we must certainly not subscribe to any one-sided preconception: neither that of the existentialist philosophy of the early Heidegger nor that of the critical social theory of the New Left. The message must be introduced without dogmatic (existentialist, socialist or other) prejudice, without any "jargon of authenticity" (Adorno) or "jargon of unauthenticity," but with an understanding of reality as comprehensive as possible.

In such a discriminating interpretation the myths certainly cannot be taken literally, but neither can they be simply excluded. What counts then is the principle that the *mythical* must be *understood as mythical*, legends as legends, images and symbols as images and symbols.[5] That is not to say that everything mythical-legendary must mean for modern man what it meant in former times. Myths and legends too, images and symbols, can die and occasionally—not arbitrarily of course—be replaced, if in a new age they no longer have the power to express what they are supposed to express. Even for the men of the New Testament not everything in the Old

Testament meant the same as it had done to former generations in Israel. Giving up an image or symbol for a reality is not at all the same thing as giving up the reality. If, for instance, someone were to regard the Virgin Birth—of which there will be more to be said later—as a legend for divine sonship, he would not necessarily abandon the reality of the divine sonship in abandoning the reality of the virgin birth.

Truth is not simply facticity

The fact is often overlooked that, not only our images, but even our most carefully elaborated concepts, are never able to capture completely the ultimate reality which we call God. In the last resort they remain always symbolical, analogical, similar-dissimilar concepts, only pointing to the reality: we can merely hope that they are not too narrow to designate the incomprehensible, inconceivable, all-comprehending or to open up a living approach to him. The possibility certainly cannot be excluded that in any particular situation an apparently vague image or simple narrative may be able to say more of what is ultimately ineffable and lay bare more of the depth structure of reality than the apparently so precise and for that very reason so fixed, inflexible, restricted concept, than the supposedly clear and definite and for that very reason so one-sided and colorless argumentation or documentation. Just so does poetry occasionally come closer to the mystery of nature and of man than the most accurate description or photograph.

Here it must be remembered that truth is not the same as facticity and in particular not equivalent to historical truth. As there are *different forms and strata of reality*, so there are different forms of *truth:* and often different strata of truth in one and the same reality. A story of what has actually happened, for instance, can leave us completely cold; on the other hand, we can occasionally be deeply moved by a made-up (fictitious) story of something that never happened historically. A newspaper report of a traveler attacked on the way from Jerusalem to Jericho would perhaps leave us quite cold, even if it were true, historically true. On the other hand, the invented story of the good Samaritan on the same road stirs us immediately, since it contains more truth. The first story tells me a truth which does not concern me or at least does not seem to concern me, which has no importance for me: it is a pure fact, a purely historical truth. The other story tells a truth which, although not a fact, affects me deeply: a truth significant for me, a relevant ("existential") truth for me. With reference to a story like that of the good Samaritan or the prodigal son, the historian's question "what actually happened?" is out of place. The question of what is historically true or false is inadequate, without interest. The poem, the parable or the legend has its own rationality. It underlines, stresses, brings out, gives concrete shape: the truth announced can be more relevant than that which is contained in a historical account. The Bible is interested primarily not in historical truth, but in truth relevant for our well-being, for our salvation, in the "truth of salvation."

As we have observed at every step, in all the accounts particularly of Jesus, the question inevitably arises at least today and even for every child as to whether such events as walking on the lake, the transfiguration or the ascension really took place as they are reported, whether they are historical. And this question arises not only for scientific theology, but also for up-to-date proclamation. On the other hand however it has already become clear that even the stories of Jesus are not only to be dissected—a task with which historical-critical theology has often been solely concerned—into the different traditions and the historicity of their statements tested. Even an apparently straightforward account is meant to express more than one truth. These stories are never meant to convey mere information, leaving the hearer or reader uninvolved. They contain a *message*, carrying with it a promise or a threat.

Particularly in the Christmas, miracle, Easter and judgment stories, the main interest is not in what really happened or will happen at that point—of which we often know very little—but in the practical question of *what it means for us:* on which there is always scope for fresh critical thinking in each individual and social situation. Such stories often reveal more about the effect of a particular happening on people than about the happening itself. This occurs particularly when the event and the transmitted texts are separated by decades, as in the New Testament (for instance, with reference to the birth of Jesus and to the Easter vocational experiences), or centuries, as in the Old Testament (for instance, with reference to the exodus from Egypt or taking possession of the promised land). We know comparatively little about the historical fact and yet a great deal about its effect and how Israel or the Christian community coped with it. The stories then reveal the way through which Israel or the community passed, with their basic historical experiences, and which is also significant for the Christian way today.

Narrative presentation and critical reflection

Thus we are back again at the problem of *literary forms.*[6] Proclamation, preaching, catechesis are somewhat different from science, whether of theology or history. Although they must also constantly be open to the test of scholarship and neglect this only at their peril, their goal and therefore also their language are different. Thus a historical play like Shakespeare's *Henry* V has a different purpose and therefore a different literary form from that of a historical account of that sovereign. Our Gospels—obviously with essential differences—are closer to a Shakespearean play than to a chronicle or historical biography. In the Gospels as in the play what is offered is not meant to be history with the greatest possible accuracy and yet the essential tradition about the main personalities and events has to be reproduced as faithfully as possible. In both cases a message (of a better England or of Jesus Christ and the kingdom of God) is to be proclaimed as convincingly as possible and a new age addressed. In neither case is it a question of giving an objective orientation merely to a few scholars, but of capturing and stirring a large audience of the most varied origins. The presentation in both Gospel and play must be brief—even Luke's Gospel can be read within two hours. To this end and aim, in both Shakespeare and the Gospels, chronology and topography are considered only as far as they are necessary; there are shifts of emphasis, facts and persons are selected and—if necessary—even freely invented. To this end and aim sometimes everything is swept together and a long sequence of events summed up in a single sentence or on the other hand a whole scene is built up from a single sentence.

Would it not be ridiculous to try to replace Shakespeare's *Henry* V or Mark's Gospel with a "more exact" paraphrase? Are not both Mark and Shakespeare still read today as much as ever, given a public presentation (in church or theater) and understood spontaneously (if not always correctly) by a large audience, while much more exact chronicles and historical works are at best studied by specialists in libraries? In both the Gospels and Shakespeare it is a question, not of a presentation of the historical facts as such, but of a *dramatic presentation of history* which has its own style and which can gain its objectives more effectively than abstract ideals and dogmas. In both the Gospels and Shakespeare, despite their differences, there is a complex, interlacing action at many levels (with reference to space, time, audience), with epic, dramatic and even lyrical features, which vividly places the one totality before us.

From this standpoint, "narrative theology"[7] recently set out as a program, despite its justified polemic against too much abstract reflection, adopts an overnarrow approach. Certainly Christian theology should never be above adopting a narrative style in speaking of Jesus and his cause, something that has been too much neglected, not only by Neo-Scholastic, but also by existential and political theology. But even from a literary standpoint the Gospels are by no means pure narratives, but—as explained —dramatically composed, historical presentations with a diversity of narrative elements. Certainly the relativity of historical reason and of "argumentative" theology is freshly emphasized and the importance of narrative highlighted. But a theology of proclamation which tells stories, biblical or post-biblical, without taking account of the authenticity of the event itself would rightly not be taken seriously in either literary or theological terms by thoughtful people. The result would be a "narrative" biblicism or even merely aimless talk without any sort of criterion.

Has the literary scholar and particularly the theologian adequately considered this aspect of the problem? The question of historical authenticity is comparatively unimportant *for literary scholars*.[8] For the latter do not believe as a matter of life and death "in" Henry V or even Henry VIII, in Julius Caesar or William Tell. There is no question of "following" them. The literary scholar is concerned essentially with the text and its literary quality and only secondarily with the matter dealt with in the text. To him it is ultimately irrelevant whether William Tell really existed (Schiller) or is merely a legendary figure (Frisch), whether Caesar's murder was contrived by his murderers against his will (Shakespeare) or provoked and staged by Caesar himself to secure a glorious exit (Jens), whether St. Joan must be understood from the standpoint of Schiller, Shaw or Brecht. He very rarely goes to the authentic documents.

For the believer it is a different matter. For the person who believes in Jesus and makes him the concrete model for his behavior it is not a matter of indifference whether this Jesus is a historical figure, a legend or a myth, whether he acted as hierarch, monk or social revolutionary, whether his death was a just penalty or not. Perhaps to him it is not irrelevant whether Jesus was really born of a virgin, whether he performed miracles against the laws of nature, instituted baptism and eucharist, founded the papacy and literally went up to heaven. The man who believes—and even the literary scholar insofar as he is a believer—is primarily interested, not in the text and its literary quality, but in the reality itself, in the person depicted in literary form, his fate and the consequences of this for himself and his society. He wants to know whether and to what extent his faith is based on illusion or on historical reality. Any faith based on illusion is not really faith but superstition.

Nevertheless, it remains true that a theology of proclamation (whether Scholastically or Neo-Scholastically, existentially or politically oriented) which transformed all the traditional stories as far as possible into concepts, ideas, principles, systems, would be forgetting its own origins and would be really unable to capture men and lead them to the following of Christ. One way or the other, its result would be dogmatism and often also ritualism. *Narrative presentation and critical reflection* therefore must be united in Christian theology and proclamation.

The decisive thing for theology is not to stick to an ambiguous slogan which is then misunderstood in practice. Practical-theological deeds must follow the programmatic call. Obviously it is not sufficient merely to narrate the narrative, simply to commemorate the memory. We must take the trouble to return to the biblical narratives themselves, subject them to a historical-critical scrutiny and thus refresh our memory of them in a critical spirit. But, whatever is done in this respect, it is here that the justification of our own enterprise also lies. This introduction to being a Christian —for all the necessary systematization and critical reflection, which will be continued in what follows—has "narrated" as much as possible about Jesus, the story of his suffering and death, and has not only abstractly reasoned, argued, discussed and theorized about Christianity and being a Christian. It would be a source of encouragement to the author if as many readers as possible and especially preachers of the word were to be stirred by it to listen again to the texts of the New and the Old Testament, reflect on them and translate them into life. For this book itself would never have been written or at any rate not in this form without the continual preaching (*lectio et praedicatio continua*) among other things of Mark's Gospel, the Sermon on the Mount and large parts of the Old Testament.

2. *Interpretations of death*

With reference to beginning and ending, to the birth and death of Jesus Christ, insofar as these things transcend sense experience, the formation of myths is to be expected. It is just at these points—sacrificial death and sacrifice of the Mass, pre-existence and virgin birth—that the question becomes insistent: must we believe all this? But again is there not something wrong when we talk about having to believe? Is it not like asking if we are obliged to enjoy ourselves?

A slight warning in advance may be opportune—not to shock but to stimulate. We have to wrestle here with a two-thousand-year-old theological tradition which still determines every Sunday sermon and every religious lesson. While trying to make it all as intelligible as possible, we have to call on the reader to cope with a rather more complicated theology. We have already dealt with the essentials, of course. But various consequences are to be considered. Not that this—or any other theology—need be at all boring.

No uniform theory

The reflections, not only of the Apostle Paul, but of early Christendom as a whole, continually center on Jesus' death on the cross. How could it be otherwise? Even before Paul we find attempts at interpretation which vary with the different situations in which the proclamation is made and with the different character of the communities and authors. The question is always: how can Jesus' painful, repulsive, ignominious death be better understood in the light of his new life? How can it be understood, not as a disastrous, but as a salvific event? Understandably, these efforts to grasp the problem are very tentative. Would it ever have been right—as happened often in theology and the history of dogma from the Middle Ages onwards—to claim finality for any of these interpretations? Different categories of interpretation and often also mythological imagery belonging to the time are used to make this death and particularly *its permanent significance and effect* intelligible for men, "for us."

Neither in the New Testament nor in the works of the Fathers is there any exclusively normative model of interpretation. There is a *diversity of interpretations, shading into one another, at many levels*. Juridical categories of interpretation are needed for the *death* of Jesus, understood—as we have seen—as a declaration of the sinner's righteousness. But cultic categories too are needed to explain Jesus' death as vicarious, as a sacrifice and sanctification. And also financial, when Jesus' death is seen as the payment of a ransom. Finally even military categories are involved if Jesus' death is described as a struggle with the powers of evil.

Quite consistently with all this, *Jesus* himself can be seen then in very different ways: as the (rejected) teacher, the (misunderstood) prophet, the (betrayed) witness, the (judged) judge, the (self-sacrificing) high priest, the (thorn-crowned) king, the (crucified) victor. There is a corresponding diversity in the way that the *fruits* of what happened on the cross are described: for example, redemption, liberation, forgiveness of sin, purification, sanctification, reconciliation, justification.

The distinctions between some ideas—for instance, of ransom, representation, sacrifice (Passover, covenant, expiatory sacrifice)—are blurred. Nevertheless, the different and differently adapted motifs do not coalesce in the New Testament. Neither in the New Testament nor in subsequent patristic theology is there any uniform theory of the cross or of the death of Jesus. A definite theory was developed only from the Middle Ages onwards, from the time of Anselm of Canterbury (†1109), in Catholic theology and then also—in a modified way—in Protestant theology. And it is only from the time of Calvin that there has been a systematic development of the doctrine—likewise not without its problems—of the three offices of Jesus, as king, prophet, priest.[1]

Is it really surprising? *Not all* these concepts or images, which are meant to bring out in different ways the significance of Jesus' death for our salvation, are *equally intelligible* today. Some of the conceptual models of that time have become strange to us. Some can be directly misleading.

This must be remembered, not least with reference to the two ancient patristic ideas of the death of Jesus transmitted to the Middle Ages in the Latin West mainly by Augustine and Pope Gregory. The first sees Jesus' death as purchasing release ("redemption") by a ransom (Jesus' blood or his death) to be paid to the devil (understood as a person). The second sees the death of Jesus as an expiatory (atoning, reconciling) sacrifice offered to God—as it were—to propitiate him. Both ideas were bound to stimulate theological development in the Middle Ages, particularly in connection with the sacrament of penance and the sacrifice of the Mass. But the question arises as to whether the legendary-mythological ideas or ideological systems of a particular epoch were not sometimes confused with faith in Christ.

Slain for us

In contrast to the more philosophical-metaphysical outlook of Eastern theology, the *theology of the Latin West*—oriented to Rome and its mentality—was more concerned with the practical organization of life and with ecclesiastical discipline. For that reason jurist-theologians and juridical ideas had an unusually strong influence from an early date, beginning with Tertullian, the initiator of Latin theology. The influence continued by way of Cyprian and Gregory the Great up to the precursors of Scholasticism, to Anselm's teacher, Lanfranc, and to Anselm's contemporaries, Bernold of Constance and Ivo of Chartres, who established the connection between theology and canon law. Such a theology was inclined to make *legal relationship the model* for relations between God and man, according to the motto, *Do ut des* ("I give so that you may give"). Both parties have clearly defined rights and duties: *suum cuique* ("to each his own").

The *event of the cross* too was *interpreted* at an early date *with the aid of juridical concepts* associated more with moralist-legalistic trends in early Judaism than with Paul's understanding of justification. The juridically colored leading ideas which were used included law, guilt, penalty, reward, penance, expiation, ransom, satisfaction, reconciliation, restitution. In this theology the favorite title for Jesus—paradoxically enough in view of his criticism of the law—is the "new lawgiver." And the Gospel is known as the "new law." Can there be any doubt that this so moral and strict theory of redemption, based on achievement, amounts theoretically and practically to a re-Judaizing process in the name of Christianity?

The disparate elements contained in the work of the early Latin theologians and which were still treated separately and unsystematically by Augustine were brought together in the eleventh century by Anselm of Canterbury in a compact *theory of satisfaction*.[2] In practice this became normative both for the medieval-Tridentine and the Reformers' doctrine of redemption and still leaves its mark on the catechisms of the Church. The fact cannot be overlooked that Anselm as Archbishop of Canterbury was influenced by pastoral and apologetic motives when he wrote the first theological treatise on the redemption.[3] He wanted to explain incarnation, death and redemption in the spirit of the new age as rationally as possible: as not only in accordance with reason, but rationally necessary. Acutely aware of what could no longer be understood in a new age, he dissociated himself from the patristic ransom concept which permitted the devil a legal claim on man and in regard to God. Instead, in an epoch when the study of jurisprudence was flourishing, he attempted a grandiose and apparently solid *rational proof of the necessity of the incarnation and particularly of the redemption.* How does the argument run?

Anselm does not start out from the death on the cross and from our own situation: from below upwards, so to speak. He boldly argues from above downwards, explaining why—from God's standpoint, as it were—incarnation and death on the cross had to be. Through sin—*the* problem of the Anselmian theory of redemption—man has culpably disturbed God's just and rational world order (the *ordo universi*, a leading theme from Augustine to Aquinas). Thus God's honor has been infinitely offended. That is why it is absolutely necessary to restore God's honor, to make restitution. According to Anselm, this is not legally possible through sheer mercy (*sola misericordia*), but only by rendering appropriate *satisfaction.* But can man's infinite guilt in regard to God's infinite majesty be compensated by any expiation, however great, on the part of a man? It can be made good only through the undue, voluntary, infinitely valuable death of a God-man: that is, through the self-offering in death of God's Son who has become man for that reason and whose merits are applied to his fellow men.

This theory of redemption, with its formal clarity, juridical consistency and systematic compactness, was undoubtedly fascinating for that time. But it was fitted into an impersonal, juridical scheme of objective equivalence: guilt and atonement, achievement and counterachievement, injury and reparation. Elsewhere, for Anselm, God is "that than which nothing greater can be conceived"[4] or "greater than that which can be conceived."[5] But in his theory neither God's incomprehensibility nor his freedom (which is wholly tied to the world order now established once and for all) is involved.

Aquinas a little later corrected and reinterpreted the rational constraint, the narrowing down to the death on the cross and the juridical-cultic emphasis of the Anselmian theory of satisfaction. Instead of deducing *a priori* —like Anselm—a rational necessity, he sought to reflect *a posteriori* on a rational appropriateness (*convenientia*). In the light however of the modern theological approach, the alienation of the biblical message through Anselm's juridical system can be much more clearly discerned.[6] What is *questionable* about it?

a. The very *presupposition* of this theory of redemption is questionable. The *idea of an originally paradisiac-unspoilt world*, of a primal sin of the first human pair and above all the Augustinian theory of an *inherited sin*, transmitted through generation (belonging—so to speak—to the race), all seem problematic to us today.[7] The first pages of the Bible cannot and are not meant to explain *how*—historically and scientifically—the world, man and woman, sin, came to be. They are meant to announce *what* in their relationship to God—that is, theologically—world, man and woman, sin, are and should be. The paradisiac primal state is described, not for its own sake, but as a background to the story of the fall, to explain why world and man are as they are. These are the eternal questions about the grandeur and misery, destiny and responsibility, of man. The topics discussed—in a more popular way in the ancient Yahwist account of creation and at a deeper level in the later priestly account—include God's care for man, man's control over nature, the power of his love for woman, but also his guilt in the sight of God and his shame in the sight of other men, his arduous daily toil.[8] The dream of an initial golden age is no more than a dream. These narratives are not concerned with an imaginary—and to us, incidentally, wholly uninteresting—primal human couple, perhaps a good half-million years ago. They are concerned with "Adam," that is, with "man" as such: primarily with man here and now, who is also the object of the redemptive event. *Tua res agitur*—it is your cause—and mine—that is involved: in creation and redemption.

b. The *objectives* of this theory of redemption are also questionable. In the Anselmian theory what is sought as the goal of the redemptive event is in fact not attained by the death of Jesus. Or, if suffering, death, concupiscence, sin do not disappear, will the supposedly paradisiac-unspoilt world order of the beginning perhaps be restored? All that happens is that *satisfaction* is rendered *in a purely external fashion*—by the restoration of his "honor"—to this God infinitely offended by the sin of our first parents and its results. Man's debt is paid on a solid legal basis by God's Son. What is dominant here is not—as in the New Testament—grace, mercy and love, but—as in Roman law—justice understood in a very human way (*justitia commutativa*): this theory of redemption is in fact more or less dominated by a legalistic logic. For the sake of this logic, Jesus' death on the cross is isolated from his message and life and at the same time also from his resurrection: essentially Jesus came simply in order to die. The concrete proclamation, conduct, suffering and new life of the historical Jesus of Nazareth have no constitutive part in this theory. What we are offered instead is a deadly "illusory performance between Father and Son" or indeed between the divine and human nature in the Son, based on legal niceties.[9] Concrete human beings, for whom all this is supposed to be done, thus largely disappear behind the figure of God's Son; they are not inwardly affected and for the most part are simply put off with promises of the afterlife.

c. Is it perhaps because of this somber process of redemption that the redeemed—as Nietzsche critically observed—look so little redeemed? From all that has been said it must at least be obvious that the satisfaction theory in the form given to it by Anselm reflects not so much the New

Testament as the Middle Ages and the juridical-rational idea of order then prevailing. The theory originated with the completely laudable intention of making the *old tradition freshly intelligible to a new age* with a new background of experience, using forms of thought and language common to believers and unbelievers. But if this was permitted to medieval theology, can we forbid to modern theology its own fresh approach? We can no more commit ourselves now than in New Testament or patristic times to a particular conceptual framework—whether juridical, cultic, metaphysical, or even scientific, technical, psychological, sociological—for the interpretation of the highly complex event of the redemption. What has already been said here and what is still to be said as fully as possible within a brief space about the cross and the redemption amount to an attempt to test the tradition transmitted through the centuries and preserve the best of it, in order to gain a hearing for the original message of the cross and the redemption among modern men with a completely different mental horizon.

Sacrifice?

If an up-to-date understanding of redemption has to be freed from juridical and cultic constraints, must not the concept of sacrifice also be abandoned? Can there be any doubt about the fact that the concept of *expiatory sacrifice* in particular—in popular exposition at least—often creates really painful misunderstandings, linked as it is with pagan sacrifice? Is God so cruel, even sadistic, that his anger can be appeased only by the blood of his Son? Does an innocent person have to serve as scapegoat, whipping boy and substitute for the real sinners?

a. In the New Testament—apart from the letter to the Hebrews—the concept of expiatory sacrifice has nothing like the central importance assigned to it in theological systematizing. It cannot of course be disputed that the apostolic proclamation—perhaps following Jesus' own interpretation in anticipation of his death[10] and probably with reference to the Old Testament[11]—sees Jesus' *death as expiatory*: Jesus as sign of reconciliation,[12] as slaughtered Passover lamb,[13] as lamb of God who bears the sins of the world.[14] It seemed natural of course to make use of Old Testament sacrificial terminology, even in connection with the brief formula "blood of Christ." Up to a point—particularly for Jews—it could make the scandal of the death on the cross endurable and intelligible. But in fact it is largely a question of making use of set formulas and metaphors. Only in the comparatively late letter to the Hebrews, by an unknown Hellenistic author, partly utilizing Pauline motifs, is the theme of sacrifice broadly developed in cultic terminology: as a radical criticism of the Jewish cult.[15]

Jesus' "sacrifice" must in fact *not* be understood *in the Old Testament or the pagan sense*. In the New Testament sacrifice is not meant to be a conciliatory influence, putting an angry demon into a good mood. Man has to be reconciled, not God. And the reconciliation is entirely due to God's initiative:[16] what is removed is not God's personal animosity, but that real enmity between man and God which has its origin, not in an inherited sin, but in actual, personal guilt and the universal burden of sin.

Unlike the temple priests, Jesus offered not merely external, material gifts (fruits, animals), but himself:[17] a *voluntary, personal self-surrender* in obedience to God's will and in love for men. He, who was quite clearly not a priest, is now designated priest in a figurative sense and indeed as the real high priest who through his self-giving is at the same time also the victim sacrificed. In the letter to the Hebrews such a self-giving could not be understood merely as one "sacrifice" among others: it had to be seen as the perfect "sacrifice," the end of *all imperfect sacrifices of men.* With this self-giving the object always intended by animal sacrifices is actually attained: the reconciliation of man with God. The conclusion merely suggested in other parts of the New Testament is established in the letter to the Hebrews: that the perfect self-giving has permanent validity and that by it all other expiatory sacrifices have been rendered forever superfluous.

This one "sacrifice" has been offered "once and for all"[18] and abolishes the multiplicity of the former sacrifices, thus freeing the event from the restrictions of time and space and raising it beyond the limits of one generation or of one nation. Nor does the exalted Lord offer any further sacrifice. For he who was given up on the cross once and for all, who was "sacrificed," is now to be considered as the exalted Lord, the eternal high priest, who unceasingly pleads for his followers before God. He is therefore called "high priest" *not* as one who carries out a static *sacrificial cult* in a sacred place. But the reference is first of all to a *way of sacrifice* on which the Son proceeds in obedience: in death, through the curtain of his flesh, into the sanctuary, so that with him his covenant community too has access to the throne of God in the sanctuary. Thus it is only in the light of this historical path that the present pleading of Christ the high priest for his brothers until he comes again is to be understood: Jesus Christ the same today and yesterday and forever.[19] This is the teaching of the letter to the Hebrews.

b. But is it sufficient *today* simply to repeat these ancient words, concepts, images and ideas, even though meanwhile the horizon of man's experience has been almost completely transformed? With reference to the use of the concept of sacrifice today we may draw the following conclusions:

The idea of the death on the cross as an expiatory sacrifice, understandable enough for Jewish Christians at that time, is only one and not the most important model for the interpretation of that death.

Since in modern man's environment cultic sacrifices are no longer offered and there is no need to point to a Christian "sacrifice" in defending the faith against pagans (who, as late as Augustine's time, attributed the first conquest of Rome to the abandonment of sacrifices to the gods), the concept of sacrifice is not related to any experience and has thus become largely misleading and unintelligible.[20]

The term "sacrifice," understood in the sense of cult ("expiatory sacrifice"), is therefore avoided in practice as much as possible in modern proclamation and replaced by more intelligible terms like "reconciliation," "representation," "redemption," "liberation." If it is used, however, it is to be understood in a personal sense as "offering," "self-offering,"[21] *and not with reference only to Jesus' death, but for his whole way of life. The imagery of the cultic sacrifice in the letter to the Hebrews is also deeply marked by the uniquely obedient life and death of Jesus, offered to God and men (self-giving, sacrifice of life).*

The "for us" or "for our sake," "for our benefit," "for our advantage," expressed in the New Testament in a variety of relative terms,[22] *is essential to Christian faith in the Crucified. The death on the cross is certainly a historical event, but at the same time it is more than this. Jesus was not only crucified (once) and now lives merely in his influence, his example and our memory. But as the one raised to life with God he is and remains the Crucified for us (once and for all). So for believers he is present and living. The death on the cross is therefore a historical fact with universal significance: all men are affected by it and called to believe.*

The universal significance of the death on the cross "for us," "for the many," "for all," can however be expressed in different ways, today often more intelligibly—as attempted above—with the aid of the concept of representation.[23] *In any case what should be most prominent in the "for us" are not sins, as in Anselm's theory, but men.*

The permanent, definitive and irrevocable significance and effect of Jesus' death therefore must—as we have attempted in all the foregoing chapters—be freed from the restrictions of the older terminology and considered always in connection with the proclamation and activity of the historical Jesus, with the living presence of the risen Christ and obviously with modern man's horizon of experience. Only in this way can Christian faith in the Crucified transform man and his world.

c. If the concept of sacrifice itself is so problematic today, then still more the concept of the *sacrifice of the Mass,* which is deduced from the sacrifice of the cross. The comments in particular of the letter to the Hebrews make it clear that the community meal, the eucharistic celebration, can by no means be understood as repetition, extension or still less as a surpassing of the unique "sacrifice" of Jesus. The Last Supper—as we saw—is primarily a supper, a *meal.* The name "sacrifice of the Mass" is misleading and should be avoided. Certainly the meal must be understood in the sense that, by the (broken) bread and the (red) wine, a share is given in the body of Jesus which is given up and in his blood which is shed. This is the reason for the sacrificial terminology of the accounts of the Last Supper and for the outstanding importance of the "for us." As the community is given a share in this once-and-for-all self-giving of his, the sacrifice of his life, it is taken up into the new covenant which is established through his "sacrificial blood" for the many. Thus the meal gives believers a share in Jesus' unique sacrifice of the cross. But for that very reason it is itself *not a repetition of the "sacrifice" of the cross*. It is a *commemorative* (*anamnesis, memoria*) and *thanksgiving celebration*, carried out first in houses in great simplicity and lucidity: a sharing, in grateful, believing memory, in the effect of this unique, enduring life's sacrifice of Jesus.

If the meal of the community—the Last Supper, the Lord's Supper,[24] the eucharistic celebration[25]—is to be rightly understood, *three dimensions* must be seen at one and the same time:

> *The dimension of the* past. *The eucharistic celebration was always essentially a* commemorative and thanksgiving meal. *It should not therefore be a solemn mourning repast for the righteous, but may be celebrated as a joyous meal also for sinners.*
>
> *The dimension of the* present. *The eucharistic celebration was and is both* covenant and community meal. *Consequently it should be celebrated, not as the solitary meal of one individual (private* Mass), *but as a common love feast* (agape) *of the community together with their Lord, present among them.*
>
> *The dimension of the* future. *The eucharistic celebration from the very beginning was the* sign and image of the meal at the consummation *in the kingdom of God. It should therefore not be celebrated as a meal to satisfy hunger, oriented to the past, but as a meal of messianic hope pointing forward and calling to action.*[26]

These refinements of the concept of sacrifice with reference to the death on the cross and the Last Supper should serve to exclude any sadistic conception of God or any correspondingly masochistic conception of man (we may recall the criticism of Nietzsche and Freud).

But man's tremendous and insistent question, which lies behind the concept of sacrifice, is still not answered. What place has suffering in God's scheme? How is man to cope with his own and mankind's history of suffering? How is God, the all-powerful and all-good God, charged with the history of suffering, to be exonerated from this charge?

God and suffering

"Auschwitz": that one word sums it all up for T. W. Adorno,[27] R. L. Rubinstein[28] and others. But, looking around the world and over the course of history, many another name could be added. Human suffering: who can take in this *history of human suffering*, compared to which the millions of years of the pre-human history of nature scarcely count? This is a history of contradictions and conflicts, of injustice, inequality and social distress, all the incurable involvement in sickness and guilt, all the meaningless fate and senseless wickedness: an endless stream of blood, sweat and tears, pain, sorrow and fear, loneliness and death. It is a history in which all identity, significance and value of reality and human existence seem to be constantly radically called in question by non-identity, pointlessness and worthlessness. In this history of suffering the primal reason, primal meaning and primal value of reality and human existence also become constantly radically questionable through chaos, absurdity and illusion.

Even the suffering of one person for a single day raises at once the question, why? Why should I be afflicted, just at this moment? What is the point of it? Why is there all this terrible individual and collective suffering, crying to heaven—even against heaven? Is it not to be charged against the Creator of mankind: mankind overburdened with suffering? God is supposed to be the embodiment of all meaning and yet there is so much that is pointless in this world, so much meaningless suffering and senseless sin. Is this God perhaps what Nietzsche accused him of being: a despot, impostor, swindler, executioner? Are these blasphemies—or provocations of God?

From Epicurus to the modern rationalist Pierre Bayle—whom Feuerbach regarded as his teacher—the *answer of the skeptic* to the question why God did not prevent evil has scarcely changed. Either God cannot prevent evil—and then is he really all-powerful?—or he will not—and then is he still holy, just and good? Or he cannot and will not—and then is he not both powerless and resentful? Or, finally, he can and will: but then why is there all the wickedness in this world?

Mythological attempts at a solution cannot help us here. Not the dualistic assumption of a good primal principle alongside an evil principle of equal rank, so that the good God cannot be the one sole God (as in the ancient Persian religion and Marcionism in the second century). Nor by pushing back man's guilt to the beginning, attributing it to angelic powers fallen away from God: which merely means that the question is put back to God again (as in early Jewish apocalyptic). Attempts at a solution in terms of the history of philosophy have not been lacking. K. Löwith traces a line backwards—Burckhardt-Marx-Hegel-Proudhon, Comte, Turgot, Condorcet-Voltaire-Vico-Bossuet-Joachim of Flora-Augustine-Orosius—and points out: "that the modern philosophy of history corresponds to the biblical faith in a fulfillment and that it ends with the secularization of its eschatological model."[29] In modern times the abundantly gifted and diversely occupied philosopher and theologian Gottfried Wilhelm Leibniz attempted in a systematic-philosophical way to answer rationally the difficulties which result from the existence of evil and wickedness opposed to God's dominion over the world. This he did, sustained by an unshakable trust in the good God, in a *Justification of God* or *Theodicy* (1710).[30] But the optimism of the Enlightenment was followed in 1755 by the Lisbon earthquake and in 1789 the human upheaval of the French Revolution. In 1791 Immanuel Kant wrote "On the failure of all philosophical attempts in theodicy."[31] Then Hegel in his *Philosophy of World History* again made the great attempt at a justification of God. He translated Leibniz's ontological-static theodicy into a historical-dialectical and tried to explain the contradictions of world history as the evolution of the divine world spirit itself: "True theodicy, the justification of God in history, lies in the fact that world history is this evolutionary course and the real coming-to-be of the spirit, under the changing spectacles of its histories."[32] World history as God's justification and therefore as world judgment.

But can such rational or speculative arguments, such metaphysical systems or visions of the philosophy of history, can all the shrewd reasoning really give new heart to man, almost overwhelmed by suffering? Is it any help when someone he loves is taken away from him through death or infidelity or when he himself becomes incurably ill or is faced with imminent death? To explain all this existential suffering all that is offered is merely cerebral argumentation or speculation, about as helpful to the sufferer as a lecture on the chemistry of foodstuffs to a starving man. And can such rational argument or speculation do anything to change the suffering world, to transform oppressive and repressive structures and, if not to abolish suffering, at any rate to reduce it to a tolerable scale?

People thought for a long time that the course of the history of suffering could be changed, in the *modern process of emancipation*, by man's assuming responsibility for his own fate. Self-redeeming, self-emancipating man was to take the place of the redeeming God: man instead of God was to direct the course of history. But, as we have seen,[33] it is more questionable than ever today whether scientific-technological evolution or even politico-social revolution could of themselves bring about a decisive turn in mankind's history of suffering. Certainly the sufferings have changed but they have not thereby become less. And, instead of God, it is now man who is charged with being a perpetrator of misdeeds and thus compelled to justify himself: instead of a theo-dicy there has to be an anthropo-dicy. But, compelled to justify himself, emancipated man attempts to exonerate himself, to find an alibi and to shift the blame with the aid of a variety of excuse mechanisms. He practices the art of showing "that it was not him."[34] As if he were responsible only for the successes and not for the failures of technological evolution. As if all blame and all failure could be laid on the transcendental ego (Idealism) or on the reactionary, counterrevolutionary class enemy (Marxism). As if there were no one responsible for the suffering of history, but only man's environment, or his genetic pre-programming, or his instinctive urges, or quite generally individual, social, linguistic structures.

But should not emancipated man, in view of the equivocal results of emancipation, face the *question of his guilt and thus* also the question *of his real redemption*—and not merely his emancipation? Redemption and emancipation both mean liberation. But emancipation means liberation of man by man, it means man's self-liberation. And redemption means liberation of man by God, not any self-redemption on man's part. As the word "redemption" was for a long time overtaxed and emotionally overburdened, so too is the word "emancipation" today.[35]

Not that "emancipation" can be simply replaced by "redemption." Christians have been content for far too long with a premature reconciliation of God and suffering, simply declaring that it was his will that we should suffer, postponing liberation to the hereafter and consoling enslaved man with the promises to be fulfilled there. Man today is expected to liberate himself. Emancipation as man's self-determination as opposed to authority accepted in blind faith, to unauthorized dominion, is necessary: freedom from natural constraint, social constraint, from the self-constraint of the person who has not come to terms with himself. It means emancipation of groups and classes, of minorities, of women, of states; emancipation from tutelage, from underprivileged status, from social oppression.

But for this very reason the opposite is also true: "redemption" cannot simply be replaced by "emancipation." In modern times people thought for far too long that they could abolish the manifold suffering of man and mankind by their own power, by the application of science and technology. For far too long they thought they could leave aside the questions of man's identity, of the meaning of human life as a whole, of the reasons for morality, of the unconsoled suffering of the dead and vanquished, and also the question of guilt.

Redemption alone makes man free at a depth which emancipation cannot reach. Redemption alone can lead a person liberated from sin, aware that he is accepted for time and eternity, to a meaningful life, to an unreserved effort for his fellow man, for society, for the new men liberated from the misery of this world. For emancipation has by no means enabled man to escape his history of suffering, sin and death. And if he still wants to find a meaning in meaningless suffering and dying, in the suffering even of the dead and vanquished, he is thrown back on the ultimate reality: *confronted with God* from whom he certainly cannot demand an account, being himself no longer innocent but in need of justification. Emancipated man cannot bypass his substantial co-responsibility for the world and mankind as they are. In the light of this, his self-understanding is perhaps made easier today than it was for the non-emancipated Job, who apparently had nothing with which to reproach himself. Yet, in a fundamentally different situation from that of Job, he will never face God with his history of suffering. With intellectual arguments he gets no further than Job's friends. Suffering imposes a limit to all reasoning.

"Why do I suffer? This is the rock of atheism. The slightest throb of pain, even if it stirs merely in an atom, makes a rent in creation from top to bottom." Georg Büchner, in his play *Danton's Death*,[36] attributes these sentiments to Thomas Paine. Our attitude to suffering is connected at the deepest level with our attitude to God and to reality as a whole. In suffering man reaches his extreme limit, the decisive question of his identity, of the sense and nonsense of his life, of reality as a whole. *Suffering* constantly proves to be *the crucial test of trust in God and of basic trust*, provoking decisions. Where is trust in God more challenged than in wholly concrete suffering? For many a person concrete suffering has been the occasion of his unbelief, for many another the occasion of his faith. And where is basic trust in reality as a whole more challenged than in face of all the suffering and evil in the world and in one's own life? For many a person overwhelming suffering has been a stimulus to basic mistrust in regard to reality as a whole, but for many another a stimulus to basic trust.

In face of the overwhelming reality of suffering in the history of mankind and in the individual human life, for suffering, doubting, despairing man there is still an alternative to the rebellion, for instance, of an Ivan Karamazov against this world of God which he found unacceptable[37] or to the revolt of an Albert Camus, who points like Dostoevsky to the suffering of the innocent creature.[38] Instead of rising up defiantly against the power of the gods, like emancipated, autonomous Prometheus, or constantly rolling the rock up the mountain and seeing it roll down again, like Sisyphus, he can adopt the attitude of *Job*. Despite all the suffering of this world, he can place an *absolute, unshakable trust* in the incomprehensible God. Even for Job this had nothing to do with resignation and passivity. Certainly it is possible to say that we cannot believe in God when we see the immense suffering of the world. But can this not be reversed? It is only if there is a God that we can look at all at this immense suffering in the world. It is only in trusting faith in the incomprehensible, always greater God that man can stride in justifiable hope through that broad, deep river: conscious of the fact that a hand is stretched out to him across the dark gulf of suffering and evil.

Of course the question constantly recurs: what sort of a God is this, incomprehensible, unconcerned, aloof from all suffering, who leaves man sitting, struggling, protesting, perishing in his immense desolation? But this question too can be reversed. Is God really so aloof from all suffering—as we imagine in our human way and assume in all our protests—as philosophers in particular think he is? Does not the very suffering and death of *Jesus* make God appear in a different light?[39]

For Job all that had become clear was the *incomprehensibility* of the God who delivers men from suffering. Man is to place his believing trust in this incomprehensibility, even if he understands nothing and has to die anyway: an attitude which is so difficult to maintain in concrete suffering and which—to judge from the written records—found little support even in Israel. But in *Jesus'* suffering and death has there not been revealed by the incomprehensible God a *definitive delivery* from suffering which goes beyond all the incomprehensibility of God and which transforms suffering and death to life and to the fulfillment of longing? Does this not make possible a faith understanding reality in a very different way, even though this understanding faith always remains faith? The *fact* of the suffering of every man cannot be canceled even in the light of Jesus. Some remaining doubt is always possible. But from this standpoint the *right attitude* of man to suffering, the *relative value* and a hidden *meaning* of suffering may become clear.

Even Jesus did not explain suffering, but *endured* it as innocent in the sight of God, endured it however—unlike Job—*to the bitter end.* His story was different: real, not fictional. His end was different: not a "happy ending," not a restoration to a prosperous life. His suffering was different: the outcome of his life and definitive, up to death. In the light of Jesus' definitive Passion, his suffering *and* death, the passion of each and every man, the passion of mankind as a whole, could acquire a meaning which the story of Job—calling simply for absolute faith and trust—cannot convey.

Of course Jesus' suffering cannot be taken merely "existentially" as a symbol ("the fact of being dead") for our personal understanding of our existence as involved in death. Nor can it be understood purely "futuristically" as promise of a utopian freedom from suffering, sin and death, still lying completely in the future. Nor finally highly "speculatively" as an inner-trinitarian (eternal) history of suffering of a crucified God, enacted dialectically between God and God, God against God:[40] Jesus being directly instead of indirectly identified with God and the distinction between Father and Son played down in favor of the one divine "nature" or "substance" as understood in later Hellenistic and especially Latin speculation on the Trinity.[41]

The historical suffering and death of Jesus therefore may not be dissolved either by existential reduction or by utopian futurization, nor by lofty speculation on argumentative theology, but must constantly be narrated afresh as what it was.[42] But, unless we are content with a scarcely helpful naïve repetition of the biblical stories or even with a new acceptance of myths (like the descent into hell[43]), historical-critical reflection pursued with an eye on the present is also necessary. This sort of reflection has shown us[44] how Jesus' Passion was so shattering just because it was consistent with his whole action. From the standpoint of the official religion the condemnation of the heretic, pseudo-prophet, blasphemer and seducer of the people to an ignominious death was quite right and made it obvious that he had nothing to do with the true God. In his death he was forsaken by men and, as we saw, his abandonment by God was also unparalleled and boundless: left utterly alone by him on whose presence he had staked everything. It was all in vain: a pointless death, which cannot be made into a mystery.

This senseless death acquires a meaning only with the resurrection of Jesus to new life with God, as known by faith. Only in the light of this new life from God does it become clear that the death was not in vain. That God, who seemed to have left him without support in the public gaze, did in fact sustain him through death. That God had not forsaken him who felt God's abandonment as no one had ever felt it before. That God, while publicly absent, maintained his hidden presence. This senseless human suffering and death thus acquires a meaning which man as he suffers and dies simply cannot produce himself, which can only be given to him by someone who is wholly Other, by God himself.

Cannot the already *completed* suffering and death of this One also reveal a hidden meaning in the otherwise meaningless suffering and death of the many? Man's suffering remains suffering, death remains death, past suffering is not made not to have happened, present suffering is not rendered innocuous nor future suffering made impossible. Suffering and death remain as an attack on man's life. Suffering is not to be reinterpreted, belittled or glorified. Nor is it to be accepted stoically, apathetically, unemotionally. And certainly it should not be sought masochistically, making asceticism a source of pleasure. It is to be fought by every human means—as must be made clearer later—in both the individual and the social sphere, in both persons and structures.

In the light of the suffering and death of this One who senselessly suffers and dies only one thing can be said, but this is decisive: even manifestly senseless suffering and death *can* have a meaning, can *acquire* a meaning. A hidden meaning. Man cannot himself attach this meaning to suffering, but he can accept it in the light of the perfect suffering and dying of this One. A meaning is not given automatically: no wishful thinking is to be satisfied, no glorification of suffering proclaimed, no tranquilizers provided and no cheap consolation offered. But *a meaning is offered* which can be freely accepted. Man has to decide. He can reject this—hidden—meaning: in spite, cynicism or despair. He can also accept it: in believing trust in him who endowed the senseless suffering and death of

Jesus with meaning. Protest, rebellion or frustration then become superfluous. Despair is at an end.

The Christian, looking to the raising up of the One sufferer to life, has himself the resurrection not behind him, but before him. Suffering remains an evil. But with trust in God it is not absolute evil which—as in Buddhism—would have to be dissolved in a nirvana by denying the will to live. Only separation from God is absolute evil and apart from God evil has no meaning. Suffering belongs to man. It belongs in fact to the fullness of man's life in this world: even love is linked with suffering. Man is meant to reach life through suffering. Reason can never show why this is so, why this is good and appropriate for man, why things would not be better without suffering. But, with trust in God, in the certain hope of a revelation of its meaning at the consummation, it can be accepted as meaningful even at the present time in the light of the suffering, death and new life of Jesus.

Man then, still suffering, is involved in the dialectic of suffering (as a natural effect) and freedom from suffering (granted in faith). He must still suffer and must still die. But neither suffering nor death can make him fear that his hope will not be fulfilled. *In itself* suffering is mostly without meaning. *When we look to the One sufferer* a meaning is offered which—despite all absurdity—has only to be trustfully accepted in order to know that God is present, however bleak, meaningless, desperate the situation may be. I *can* encounter him, not only in light and joy, but also in darkness, sorrow, pain and melancholy. Suffering as such is not a sign of God's absence. In the light of the suffering of the One it has been clearly shown to be the way to God.

What is asserted by Leibniz and obscurely perceived by Dostoevsky is confirmed to Job and made definitively clear and certain in the light of the risen Crucified: suffering too is encompassed by *God*; suffering too, even though it seems like being forsaken by God, can *become* the point of encounter with God. The believer knows no way to avoid suffering, but he knows a way through it: unperturbed, actively indifferent in face of suffering and for that very reason prepared to struggle against suffering and its causes. He looks to the One sufferer in believing trust in him who is also secretly present particularly in suffering and who *himself sustains and maintains man in the utmost peril, meaninglessness, nothingness, abandonment, loneliness and emptiness:* a God who stands alongside men as also affected, a God who identifies himself with men. No cross in the world can refute the offer of meaning which was issued on the cross of him who was raised to life.

Nowhere has it been proved more clearly than here that this God is not only a God of the strong, healthy, successful, a God of the bigger battalions. It is in suffering particularly that God can be shown to be the One whom Jesus proclaimed: as we saw,[45] the Father of the lost. This God is himself the answer to the question of theodicy, to life's enigmas, to suffering, injustice, death in the world. As Father of the lost, he is no longer a God transcendent and remote, but a God close to man in incomprehensible goodness, generously and magnanimously pursuing him through history, in darkness, futility and meaninglessness, inviting him to dare to hope, mercifully sustaining him even in his remoteness from God.

Nowhere did it become more clearly visible than in Jesus' life and work, suffering and death, that this God is a God for men, a God who is wholly on our side. He is not a theocratical God, creating fear, "from above," but a God friendly to men, *suffering with men*, "with us below." It is scarcely necessary to insist that we are talking here in metaphors, symbols, analogies. But what is meant is understandable enough and it is now clearer than ever that the God manifested in Jesus is not a cruel, despotic, legal-minded God, but a God encountering man as redeeming love, identifying himself in Jesus with suffering man.

Where does this become clearer than in the cross, confirmed and endowed with a new significance by the resurrection? Nowhere did it become more clearly evident than in the cross that this God is in fact a God on the side of the weak, sick, poor, underprivileged, oppressed, even of the irreligious, immoral and ungodly. He is a God who—unlike the pagan gods—does not take his revenge on those who sin against him; who does not permit himself to be paid or bribed by those who want something from him; who does not envy men their happiness, who does not demand their love and then let them down in the end. He is a God who lavishes his grace on those who do not deserve it. Who gives without envy and never disappoints. Who does not demand love, but gives it: who himself is wholly love. It follows from all this that the cross is not to be understood as a sacrifice demanded by a cruel God. In the light of Easter it was understood as quite the reverse, as the deepest expression of his love. *Love,* by which God—not so much in an abstract "nature" as in his activity, his "style"—can be defined:[46] love not as feeling, but as "existing for," "doing good to" others. A love, that is, which cannot be defined abstractly but only with reference to this Jesus.

It was this God of love, according to Paul, who did not spare even his own Son but sacrificed him for us: in giving him, how could he fail to give us everything?[47] And this then is the reason why, according to Paul, nothing—absolutely nothing—can endanger the Christian, since nothing can separate him from this love of God manifested in Jesus Christ.[48] And Paul shows in his own life that this theodicy is not merely theological theory but can be lived and proved in practice.[49]

Man can revolt against a God aloof from all suffering, enthroned in undisturbed bliss or apathetic transcendence. But is it possible to revolt against the God who revealed all his com-passion in Jesus' Passion? Man can revolt against an abstract justice of God and against a universal harmony pre-established for the present or postulated for the future. But is it possible to revolt against the love of the Father of the lost, made manifest in Jesus, unconditionally and unreservedly embracing also my suffering, reducing my indignation to silence, overcoming my frustration, making it possible for me to endure continual distress and finally to be victorious?

God's love does not protect us *against* all suffering. But it protects us *in* all suffering. Thus what is admittedly to be completed only in the future does indeed begin in the present: the justification of God in the justification of man, of all men, even of the dead and vanquished, theodicy as anthropodicy. This is the harmony which is not simply given without expiation, but established in the cross. The definitive victory of the love of a God who is not an unconcerned, unloving being, whom suffering and injustice cannot move, but who himself has assumed and will assume men's suffering in love. The victory of the love of God as Jesus proclaimed and manifested it, as the final, decisive power: this is the kingdom of God. For Horkheimer's longing and the longing of innumerable people in the history of mankind for justice in the world, for genuine transcendence, for "the wholly Other," the desire "that the murderer will not be allowed to triumph over the innocent victim"[50]: all this longing and desire will be satisfied, as it is promised—beyond all critical theory and critical theology—on the last pages of Scripture: "God himself will be with them as their God. He will wipe away all their tears. There will be no more death and no more sadness, no mourning and no torment. What has once been is past forever."[51]

So much for the interpretations of Jesus' death. But do not the interpretations of his origin create still more difficulties?

3. *Interpretations of the origin*

There are still some today for whom Christmas counts as the main feast of Christendom and God's incarnation as the central dogma. It should however be clear from all the foregoing that it is not Jesus' birth, but his death and his new life with God which constitute the unmistakable center of the Christian message.

Become man

The three "holy nights" of the great world religions—the enlightenment of the Buddha, the descent of the Koran and the birth of Jesus—can certainly not—as sometimes happens—be placed on the same level. But can we fail to perceive that *extraordinary events are traditionally associated with the birth of the great founders* of religion and that, from this standpoint, it cannot be claimed that there is anything unique about Jesus of Nazareth. Virginal conception, marvelous birth, angelic appearances, temptations of the devil are also mentioned in connection with the founders of religion and cannot be regarded as solely characteristic of Jesus. Miracles form the framework also of the births of Buddha, Confucius, Zarathustra and Muhammad. The birth of the prophet Muhammad is promised to his mother by an angel. Zarathustra's conception is accompanied by miraculous circumstances. The Persian world savior, Saoshyant, arises from Zarathustra's seed in a virgin. Buddha too is associated with a virginal conception, emerging from his mother's right side ten months after Maya's left side had been pierced by the tusk of a mysterious white elephant. Angels appear at the birth of Muhammad and Confucius. All kinds of marvelous accomplishments are reported, not only of the boy Jesus—as in some apocryphal texts—but also of the young prince Siddhartha. And, like Jesus, Buddha and Zarathustra are also tempted by the evil spirit. If therefore Jesus' divine sonship is reduced to such extraordinary events at his birth or miraculous deeds in his life, he could simply be ranked with the founders of religions—not to speak of other heroes and more or less dubious miracle workers of antiquity.

a. The distinctively Christian reality is and remains the cross. But *the first witnesses look back from the cross of the risen Christ* to the beginning of Jesus' life. Even the statements about the Son of God *becoming man* would amount to a "story of the gods," would be pure mythology if they were not seen in connection with the message of the cross and resurrection. Originally they were meant in fact only to explain who it really was who suffered here, who was sacrificed, who had shown such obedience.[1] We saw how the primitive community already called Jesus the "Son" and the "Son of God": he was the advocate, plenipotentiary, spokesman, and indeed the personal legate, trustee, representative, deputy and delegate of God.[2] The ideas of the Son of God, of the one conceived by the Spirit, of the pre-existent, the mediator of creation, were used to interpret the person and cause of Jesus at first in the light of the Jewish tradition. But when these ideas were transferred into the very different environment and language of the Hellenistic world, they were bound to provoke quite different associations. In what follows we shall examine these far from simple associations.

The name and concept of "in-carnation" ("*en-sarkosis*," "becoming flesh," "becoming man") made a tremendous impact as a result of its use in John's Gospel. Here and here alone in the New Testament is found the idea of the divine "Logos" or "Word," pre-existing from eternity with God and as God, in God's nature: this word, according to Jewish wisdom literature (and pre-Christian gnosis?), was present in personal form and before time at the creation of the world and then found a place among men.[3] In Philo's speculations it appears as God's first-born Son and secondary God, as God's image and prototype of created things, as organ of creation and revelation.[4] Finally, in John's prologue, it is seen as a divine person who becomes "flesh" for men: Jesus' incarnation as God's *revelation* (life, light, truth) in the world.[5]

Before John's Gospel, however, in the Pauline and Deutero-Pauline writings, there are not a few statements about the incarnation of God's Son, composed as creeds[6] or hymns,[7] which may well go back to a large extent to pre-Pauline formulas.[8] The earliest statement is that pre-Pauline hymn, enlarged by Paul, in Philippians, about Jesus being in the form of God and not considering it "robbery" to be with God, but emptying himself, taking the form of a slave and becoming like men: found in the appearance of a man, he humbled himself and became obedient unto death, even to death on the cross.[9] Incarnation is here understood as *emptying and humiliation:* the reason for Christian love and unselfishness.

"Epiphany" is the word chosen in the Pauline pastoral epistles to describe Jesus Christ's becoming man.[10] As understood in its own time this is not merely a harmless liturgical expression. In Hellenistic times the "appearance" of the gods bringing blessings in the mystery cults and also the "appearance" of the ruler on a state visit were celebrated and announced in solemn tones in an ancient, sacral language. In the Christian communities there was now a similar proclamation of the "appearance" of Jesus, the "Saviour" (Greek *soter,* a Hellenistic title used for divine "saviors"), and his "grace," his "friendship for men," his "goodness," in his whole life from incarnation to death.

In the year 42 or 41 *before* Jesus' birth, at the beginning of the fifteen years of grievous civil war following on the murder of Caesar, the Roman poet Virgil in his famous Fourth Eclogue announced the birth of a world savior. Was this an expression of hope in Caesar's great nephew and adopted son Octavius and his house? In any case, when Octavius finally returned to Rome in the year 29, as sole ruler, after the victory over Antony and Cleopatra, his first official act was to close the temple of Janus, the double-faced god of war. And "Augustus Divi Filius"—"son of the divine one" (of Caesar elevated after his death to be a state god), translated in the Greek East as "Son of God"—did everything possible to realize the hopes nourished by Virgil of the Utopia of an imminent reign of peace: Pax Romana, Pax Augusta, sealed with the consecration of the gigantic Ara Pacis Augustae, the Augustan altar of peace, in the year 9 B.C. In the same year (according to the famous inscription found in 1890 in Priene in Asia Minor and later elsewhere) the "gospel" (*euangelion,* "good news") of the birthday of the "Saviour" and "God" who had now appeared—Caesar Augustus—was proclaimed in the East to the whole world: the savior who had brought to the broken world new life, happiness, peace, fulfillment of ancestral hopes, salvation.[11]

In the light of this political theology of the Caesars, do we not read

Luke's annunciation of a "Son of God" and "Saviour," composed as it was in a corner of the Empire—to which we shall have to return—rather less as a "Christmas" story? And do we not also see in a different light the proclamation in the pastoral epistles of the "appearance" of the "Saviour" and "God," Jesus Christ, in a wholly similar solemn style, likewise used in the Christmas liturgy?[12] According to the Priene inscription the birthday of the god-savior Augustus on 23 September was in future to be the official beginning of the year (and the time of admission to public office). From the fourth century Jesus' birthday has been celebrated on 25 December: "Natalis Christi"—presumably in deliberate opposition to "Natalis Solis Invicti" (birthday of the unconquered sun-god), recently officially introduced as a Roman imperial feast day on 25 December (winter solstice). For centuries then the beginning of the year was linked with this day, until it was postponed mainly for practical reasons to the first day of the next month, 1 January. This Roman feast of Christmas became established also in the East, where—for instance, in Jerusalem—the feast of the "Epiphany" or "Theophany" was taken as Jesus' birthday and not as the feast of the Magi (or of the three kings) or even of Jesus' baptism.

Of course the development starting out from the idea of the incarnation cannot be viewed without some misgivings. Can it be overlooked that an increasing concentration on the incarnation in Christian theology and piety caused a premature shift of emphasis? A shift of emphasis which was not covered by the original message and which makes an understanding of the Christian message considerably more difficult even today? A shift of emphasis from death and resurrection to eternal pre-existence and incarnation: the man Jesus of Nazareth overshadowed by the Son of God?

b. There can be no doubt that *exaltation Christology* (exaltation of the human Messiah to Son of God, two-stage Christology), starting out from below and centered on death and resurrection, was in fact increasingly *superseded by an incarnation theology starting out from above*. It begins with the incarnation of the Son of God, admitting of course that his emptying and humiliation are presupposed for his exaltation. Another way of describing the process would be to say that the "ascending," *ascendence Christology*, for which divine sonship means in Old Testament terms an election and assumption to the status of Son (in exaltation, baptism, birth), was supplemented or even replaced by a "descending," *descendence Christology*. For this divine sonship—to be more and more closely circumscribed in Hellenistic terms and ideas—meant an *ontological generation* of a higher kind. It is now a question less of the legal and authoritative status of Jesus Christ in the Old Testament sense than of his *descent* in a Hellenistic sense. It is a question less of function than of essence. Terms like essence, nature, substance, hypostasis, person, union, were to acquire increasing importance.

"Son of God" for Hellenistic hearers therefore did not mean advocate, plenipotentiary, spokesman, deputy and representative of God,[13] but quite obviously a divine being who is distinguished from the human sphere in virtue of his divine nature. A superhuman being of divine origin and with divine power! A being who pre-exists from eternity with God, but in the fullness of time assumes a human form and appears in the man Jesus. Thus the one term "Son of God" implies two things: the *distinction from God*, the Father (obedience, subordination), and the identification with God, the Father (unity with God, divinity).

From now on however importance is increasingly and often one-sidedly attached to this *unity with God*, no longer described in historical and personal but in ontological categories. In the New Testament itself of course the term "God" practically always means the Father. But the transference of the names both of God's Son and of the divine Kyrios (Lord Jesus) was bound in the Hellenistic world to bring with it the transference of divine attributes to Jesus, was bound to lead to reflection on his divine rulership, dignity, nature, in a word his divinity. This is clear from the earliest, still very vague and undeveloped statement on Jesus' pre-existence and incarnation in Philippians. Nevertheless, interest here is centered less on Jesus' divinity than on the happening started by God in Jesus.

With Paul himself Jesus is called "the Lord," in order to depose the many lords and gods, and this lordship is ascribed to him already in his pre-earthly existence. In one passage, in connection with the creation of the world, "the Lord" (Jesus) and "God" (the Father) are brought very close together.[14] God himself is less frequently called "Lord" in the New Testament, the name being generally used for Jesus. But on the other hand Jesus is scarcely ever directly called "God" and never by Paul himself. There is certainly an emphasis on the distinction, extending also to the use of the appropriate terms. There is no mention at all in the New Testament of an incarnation of God himself. These two most important predicates are clearly transferred together to Jesus only in John's Gospel, in the exclamation of the unbelieving Thomas, "My Lord and my God."[15] Outside John's Gospel, Jesus is directly designated as "God" only in a few, very late, exceptional cases under the influence of Hellenism.[16] But all this was soon to be changed in Greek theology.

Deification or humanization?

a. *Greek theology* subsequently drew very far-reaching and not unproblematic conclusions from the new Hellenistic conception of divine sonship. At the turn of the first century Ignatius of Antioch in quite a natural way calls Jesus "God."[17] And at the same time in the Hellenistic world it was no longer necessary to defend the divine power and authority of the Son of Man, as it had been in the Jewish world, but—with a change of front—to defend the true humanity and capacity for suffering of the Son of God (against Gnostic heretical teachers).[18] Neither Ignatius nor any of the later Christian writers wanted to give up Jewish monotheism: bitheism and tritheism were always rejected in principle. But the more Jesus as the Son was placed on one level of being with the Father and the more this was described in essential categories, so many more difficulties were created in the way of reconciling conceptually *monotheism* and *divine sonship*, the distinction from God and the unity with God.

Helpful and unavoidable as some of these ideas were in the Hellenistic world, this development involved almost insurmountable difficulties and in practice complete failure for the mission and preaching of the Gospel of Jesus Christ among the Jews and many centuries later among the Muslims. For the Christian community itself it led to unsuspected theological confusion and continual involvement in ecclesiastic politics. People had largely adapted themselves to the Hellenistic ways of thought and life-style, as determined by the schools of philosophy, the mystery cults and the Roman state. Philosophical terms became increasingly precise, differences between the schools more delicate, explanations more complicated, dogmas—now in the form of state laws—to protect orthodoxy more numerous. But misunderstandings, factions and even schisms also became more numerous. Even the great ecumenical councils of the post-Constantinian era could only partially overcome them.

Unlike that of the Latin West, Eastern teaching on the redemption[19] concentrated increasingly on the incarnation, on the Logos becoming man. In this theory the primary event of salvation is not so much the cross of the risen Jesus as the appearance of a divine being in human form, which was not regarded—as it had been by the Jews—as a scandal but as a mystery. From the time of Irenaeus—the first systematic theologian—in the second century the decisive principle for Greek systematic theology was that God himself entered history in Jesus and became man so that men might become God. That is, *God becomes man as the precondition for man to become God*. This deification of man was of course understood not as a pantheistic identification with the divinity, but as an ontological and completely dynamic participation with God.

Greek theology depicts the whole history of mankind in a most impressive way as a great, continuous, upward-leading educational process (*paideia*). God's image, shattered by guilt and sin, is restored and brought to perfection in man by the pedagogy of God himself. At the culmination of this progressive revelation and education of the human race, according to a preconceived plan (the economy of salvation), God himself in his Son and Logos enters into the world and assumes a human nature. Thus man is definitively freed from darkness, error and death and by teaching and example invited to follow: that is, to imitate (*mimesis*) and participate (*methexis*) in order in this way to reach God.

We cannot provide here an appreciation of this sublime Greek theology of redemption. Undoubtedly it represents a comprehensive Christianizing of the Hellenistic (and particularly Platonic-Stoic) conception of *paideia.* But at the same time it is a Hellenization of the Christian message of redemption and liberation with too many negative features. We saw how the Latin West's theory of redemption was weakened by a rationalistic, juridical and moralistic view of the God-man relationship and a theology of the cross isolated from Jesus' life and resurrection. The Greek theory is weakened in another way. Not infrequently it comes close to an unfruitful Christological mysticism of concepts and neglects the historical teaching, life and death of Jesus. There is a tendency often to get lost in cosmic speculations and to overlook personal relationships. In theory and practice there is an inclination to accept a dangerous matter-spirit dualism and to make this equivalent to the biblical sin-grace contrast.

More important however is the fact already mentioned that, according to this conception, redemption is essentially effected by the incarnation of the Logos. By comparison with Christmas and Easter, with the incarnation and with the resurrection understood as confirming the incarnation, Jesus' death on the cross loses its proper place and falls into the background. Its significance becomes accidental rather than constitutive: almost a kind of misfortune—although incomprehensibly great—incidental to the triumphal descent and ascent of the divine Logos. The effect of the redemption, even if it does not follow directly on the incarnation, is seen less in personal and historical terms than as something essential and natural. It means—and this is certainly not entirely wrong—imperishability and immortality, sonship and deification of man, calling back the whole cosmos to God. But both in theory and in practice not only do incarnation and resurrection very often supplant the cross, but the divine life often supplants the earthly, the deification of man supplants his humanization, the calling back of the world to God replaces the transformation of the world and society. But patristic theology was not yet aware of the later division into such disciplines as exegesis, dogmatics, moral theology and canon law. And thus its uniformity—not always a disadvantage when compared to the greater differentiation of Latin scholasticism—prevented extreme consequences.

b. But does a reasonable man *today* want to become God?[20] What were stirring patristic slogans at that time—like "God became man so that man might become God"—are almost completely unintelligible today. The theme of an exchange between God and man (or between the two "natures"), highly relevant for Hellenistic hearers, means nothing at all to an age so sensitive as ours to the absence of God and "God's darkness." Our problem today is not the deification but the *humanization of man*. Even in the New Testament what happened in and with Jesus of Nazareth is not interpreted everywhere as the incarnation of God or—more exactly—of

God's Son or God's Word. If this interpretation is to have any meaning at all for modern man it will only be in virtue of its implications for man's becoming man.

But, looking at it from the other side, in view of the enormous possibilities open to modern man, is there not a more serious temptation of wanting—in the process of emancipation—by his own power "to be like God"? Is he not faced with the ancient and primal temptation of mankind, as it is described in the biblical account of the dawn of human history?[21] Are not those "emancipated" men themselves, who are most militant in abolishing God, only too often the very ones who want to occupy the place apparently left empty, who want to replace God in order "to know what is good and what is evil" for themselves and society? Are there not numerous anonymous powers and systems particularly in modern society who would like to play at being God's providence? In view of the manifold individual and social dehumanizing of man in connection with the modern de-deification of God, in view of the substitute gods which dehumanize man (party, state, race, science, money, personality cult, power), shall we not be more ready perhaps again to accept the old truth that, without God, it is scarcely possible for man to become truly man in the individual and social sphere?

This process of becoming man certainly does not mean—as atheists constantly fear, under the influence of many bad sermons—that God is a kind of superpower keeping man small and suppressing his freedom, a God in fact made to our image and likeness. But—as it is sharply defined on the cross—it is a God of powerlessness who humanizes man and makes possible his freedom: as such he revealed himself from the beginning—and the Christmas story stresses this—in the child Jesus in his friendliness to men. In this Jesus therefore, as men have concretely experienced and as faith acknowledges, God himself is active. In him, as we have seen, God's word and will have become known, have become "flesh."

But this activity of God, this presence of his word and will, must not simply be linked to the mathematical or mystical point of the conception or birth of Jesus. As became clear through all the previous chapters, it was in Jesus' *whole* life, in his *whole* proclamation, behavior and fate, that God's word and will took on a human form. In his whole speech, action and suffering, in his whole person, Jesus *proclaimed, manifested, revealed* God's word and will. Indeed, it can be said that he, in whom word and deed, teaching and life, being and action, completely coincide, *is* the embodiment of God's word and will: *God's word and will in human form.*[22]

From this comprehensive—not speculative but historical—standpoint it can be seen even today that Jesus was understood from the beginning by Paul and then by Pauline tradition as the revelation of God's power and wisdom,[23] as head and lord of creation,[24] as image or likeness of God,[25] as God's yes.[26] It can be understood that by John he was described, not only as God's Word,[27] but indirectly as equal to God,[28] and even as Lord and God.[29] It is in this perspective too that a number of difficult and high-sounding statements can be understood: that God was in Christ reconciling the world to himself;[30] that in Christ the whole fullness of divinity lives corporeally;[31] that God's word became flesh.[32] These statements must of course be protected against misunderstanding.

True God and true man

Nowhere in the New Testament is a mythological two-gods doctrine (bitheism) developed: God is one and we may not talk of God simply as we talk of man, nor of man as we talk of God. But neither is the Son anywhere identified with the Father (as in the heresies of monarchianism and Sabellianism): the Son is not simply the Father and the Father is not simply the Son.

a. If neither a simple duality nor a simple identity is possible, how can Jesus' relationship to God be positively expressed? We might put it in this way: the *true man* Jesus of Nazareth is for faith the real *revelation* of the one *true God*.

This is what John's Gospel especially makes clear. Since the Father knows the Son and the Son the Father,[33] since the Father is in the Son and the Son is in the Father,[34] since therefore the Father and the Son are one,[35] it follows that whoever sees the Son sees also the Father.[36] Here we are presented with neither mythology nor mysticism, nor metaphysics, but with the plain but basic statement that God encounters us, manifests himself in the work and person of Jesus—admittedly not perceptibly for the neutral observer, but certainly for the person who commits himself trustfully to Jesus and believes.

In him therefore God shows himself, shows who he is. In him he shows his face, so to speak. The Old Testament God, as we saw at an earlier stage,[37] in contrast to the god of Greek metaphysics, is a God with qualities, with a human face. The man Jesus shows, manifests, reveals this human visage in his whole being, speech, action and suffering. He might almost be called the *visage* or *face of God* or—as in the New Testament itself—the *image* or *likeness of God*.[38] The same thing is expressed also in other terms: when Jesus is called the *Word of God* or even the *Son of God*. All these metaphors are meant to express both the unique relationship of the Father to Jesus and of Jesus to the Father as also the unique relationship of Jesus to men: his work and his significance as God's revealer for the salvation of the world. Hence it is obvious why talk *about* Jesus Christ always easily turned into talk *to* Jesus Christ, why faith and profession of faith were always accompanied by acclamation, invocation, prayer.

b. Before attempting some further summary definitions as an aid to interpreting the relationship between God and Jesus, it seems appropriate to reflect a little on the idea of *pre-existence:* that is, of the existence of the Son of God in God's eternity before the incarnation. This is a thought that is particularly difficult to grasp today. But we shall only understand this theological idea at all if we remember that it was quite the opposite at that time: the idea was in the air.[39] It had not only been fostered by Jewish and particularly Philo's speculations on God's eternal wisdom. It was familiar also from the apocalyptic ideas of the coming Son of Man, already existing, hidden, with God and from the rabbinic ideas of the pre-existence of the Torah, of paradise, of the Messiah's name. Finally there were the Gnostic speculations about pre-existing human souls, later immersed in matter, then gathered by the divine primal man, released from matter and led back into the world of God. But, particularly on this last point, the reconstruction of possible Gnostic ideas is difficult since it is impossible to exclude Christian influences in the texts.

In this mental climate similar ideas of a pre-existence of Jesus, God's Son and God's Word, in God's eternity must have seemed extremely plausible. There was no need to appeal to any kind of direct revelations of these things. The theological reflections were available. They were found not only in John's prologue but also in his Gospel.[40] And even much earlier they appeared in what was certainly the earliest statement about Jesus' pre-existence with God—in the pre-Pauline Christ hymn in Philippians[41]—and then in texts about the creation of the world in Christ in Paul's own words[42] and finally—in a slightly more developed form—in the Pauline tradition.[43]

Obviously here too thought was directed not from the beginning to the end, but *from the end to the beginning*. The question was asked: if the one who was crucified and raised up has from God's standpoint such a unique, fundamental, decisive importance, must he not always have been in God's thoughts? If he is the goal of creation and history, was he not therefore always in God's eternal plan of creation and salvation? And if as Son he is now with God, was he not as Son and Word with God from eternity? The Last is then also the First.[44] And he in whom the end of all things appeared is recognized as the beginning of all things, to whom all things are adapted, in whom they are created and hold together.[45] Times and generations, doctrines and leaders change in the Church, but Jesus Christ is the same yesterday and today, and forever.[46]

The difference between a real and an ideal pre-existence was of limited interest at a time when ideas—under Plato's influence—were regarded as real. *It was natural to think in Hellenistic physical-metaphysical categories*. An attempt was made to bring out the incomparable significance of what had happened with and in Jesus with the aid of the terms and ideas available in that mental climate. Mythical elements played a large part, but never became absolutely dominant. For any kind of cosmic system of laws stopped short at the concrete history of this man, Jesus of Nazareth, and broke down completely at his cross.

Even the most sublime speculative and mythological statements about the pre-existence of the divine Son could never be complete in themselves. *The reality of the cross always broke in* and could not be dismissed by any amount of discussion. John's prologue, formulated as a hymn, about the Word through which all things came to be, culminates in "and the Word was made flesh" and thus in his not being known and not being accepted.[47] The ancient hymn in Philippians about the one who was in the form of God does not stop at this point, but goes on in Paul's version to the emptying, humiliation and obedience up to death on the cross.[48] The sublime words of the letter to the Colossians about creation in Christ are linked with those on reconciliation and peace by a reference to Christ's blood.[49] And even the apparently idyllic Christmas story and Luke's sublime statements and songs about Mary and the child come under the shadow of the cross.[50]

Why then were theological conclusions drawn, even in New Testament times, about the pre-existence of God's Son in God's eternity? It was not in order to indulge in clever speculations about God and the world. The reason for it was to make clear and to justify in practice the *unique claim* of this crucified and yet living Jesus. We can no longer accept the mythical ideas of that age about a being descended from God, existing before time and beyond this world in a heavenly state; a "story of gods," in which two (or even three) divine beings are involved, is not for us. But we certainly have to consider in our very different mental climate just what the ideas of that time were meant to express.

c. What is the interest behind the ideas of pre-existence? The fact had to be expressed vividly that the *relationship between God and Jesus* did not emerge only at a later stage and—as it were—by chance, but *existed from the beginning* and *has its foundation in God himself*. Even if we express it differently today, we must not lose interest in this fact.[51] Difficult as it is for us today to conceive this pre-existence, there are a number of points which must be considered.

(i) *From eternity* there is *no God other* than the one who manifested himself in Jesus. The face he showed in Jesus is really his true and single face. He is not a God with a Janus face. Even in the Old Testament he is not a God other than the God of the New Testament. He is not an enigmatic God, not a sphinx. Behind the God we know as the Father of the lost ones there is not some kind of sinister abyss, as Gnosticism suggested. Nor is there a God of dark, inscrutable decrees, as Calvin's theory of double predestination assumed. No. God was from the beginning and always will be as he became known in Jesus Christ. His being and action from the very beginning bear—as we might formulate it retrospectively—a "Christological" imprint.

(ii) Since there is no God other than the one revealed in Jesus, *Jesus has a universal significance in the light of this universal God.* If God encounters men outside the proclamation of Christ (in a world religion or in secular life)—which cannot be dogmatically excluded—it is the one true God who encounters them. Even if men do not recognize his features and if for them he is the "unknown God,"[52] it is in reality the God with the countenance of Jesus: the God who encounters them in the sense and spirit of Jesus. In this one God the non-Christian too—wherever his lot is cast—can find his salvation. And then it is outside the Christian community, outside the Church: *extra ecclesiam.* But not outside that God who, although unrecognized by non-Christians, bears the face of Christ. But, so that men may also recognize this face and that God may not remain for them the unknown God, there is needed the Christian proclamation and mission announcing Jesus as God's Messiah, advocate and representative, as God's Son, Word, countenance. It is only through professing faith in Jesus as the Christ of God that the non-Christian is made a Christian.[53]

(iii) What happened in and with Jesus therefore is not explained for the believer merely from the course of history; in its *ultimate origin it is explained* for him *only from God.* According to Jesus himself it is in his own claim that God's claim is made known. In his word is God's word. In his will is God's will. Jesus' proclamation, behavior and fate, the origin and significance of his person, therefore, are not founded only in the social context which we discussed at the outset of this investigation. In fact they are founded in God's action, to which Jesus himself refers for his authority and to which our investigation finally led. The basis of all that happened in and with Jesus is the Creator's friendship, love and fidelity, given in advance and now making known the connection between creation and salvation. This Creator in his compassion does not permit his creature to fail even in suffering and guilt, but elevates and accepts him in Jesus.

(iv) Man for his part is summoned in *believing trust to rise above the world and its time into another dimension:* to transcend the present state of things, not in the sense of entering into a world beyond this, but in the sense of rising to that ultimate reality on which we can absolutely rely and which we call God. It is only in this truly other dimension that man can get to the roots of what Jesus is and means, can understand why Jesus in particular has a unique and decisive significance for himself and for mankind, why Jesus and no other can bind men to follow him. *In Jesus the one true God himself calls men on to the way.* Man's definitive and comprehensive well-being, his salvation, is therefore not simply a reality of this world, but also a gift of God: grace.

d. After these reflections on pre-existence it will be possible also to understand better the *relationship between God and Jesus.* In the New Testament, as we see, Jesus' divine dignity is conceived primarily functionally and not physically or metaphysically. It is certainly an essential characteristic of Jesus' person, but it is not attributed to him in the form of an abstract statement about his essence ("essence Christology"): the statement is about salvation for us men ("functional Christology"). Later of course it came to be interpreted with the aid of contemporary philosophical concepts and explained as a metaphysical statement. There was simply no other conceptual system available. From the modern perspective it must be said that the Hellenistic concepts were not very apt to express the original message.[54] But were they not unavoidable? Despite inadequate conceptual aids and the entanglements of imperial politics, the first ecumenical councils—occupied, unlike the later ones, not with marginal questions, but with the very center of the Christian message—succeeded in defending this center against underestimating either the divine or the human factor. We should be under no illusion. It was not joy in theological speculation or in development of dogma, but pastoral concern, which led to the definitions of these councils.[55]

The first, epoch-making *Council of Nicea* in 325, in its definition of the "consubstantiality" (*homo-ousia*) of Jesus with God his Father, against Arius, prevented a disguised introduction of polytheism into Christianity. In Jesus the one true God is present, not a second God or demi-God. Our whole redemption depends on the fact that in Jesus we are concerned with the God who is really God.

The Council of Ephesus, dominated by Cyril of Alexandria, by its ambiguous statements created the danger that the true humanity of Jesus would be swallowed up by the one all-absorbing nature of God. Twenty years later, in 451, the Council of Chalcedon, influenced by a theologically counterbalancing letter of Pope Leo the Great, in a series of paradoxical formulas, stressed both the "consubstantiality with us" and the "consubstantiality with the Father."[56] In this way it made sure that the full humanity of Jesus, although constantly threatened, would not in principle be sacrificed for the sake of his divine nature.[57]

The whole development of dogmatic Christology[58] from Chalcedon up to our own time has been dominated by the "God-man" formula: "truly God" (*vere Deus*) and "truly man" (*vere homo*). After the (significant) patristic and the (less significant) medieval development, in modern times it reached its final, grandiose climax and—so to speak—its recapitulation in Hegel's philosophy of religion.[59] All things considered, it was an essentially speculative Christology (from above) with the emphasis on Jesus' divinity. After Hegel's death—partly as a result of David Friedrich Strauss's *Life of Jesus*—it had to take a new turn and become a historical Christology (from below) with the emphasis on Jesus' humanity. Instead of "high" Christology we have now the "low" study of the historical Jesus.[60]

According to the New Testament we cannot have one without the other. There is not a Jesus of Nazareth who is not proclaimed as the Christ of God. There is not a Christ who is not identical with the man Jesus of Nazareth. Hence there cannot be either an untheological Jesusology or an unhistorical Christology. The coalescence of the name Jesus with the title of Christ makes it clear that, for the New Testament, the true Jesus is the Christ of God and the true Christ is the man Jesus of Nazareth: that both are one, "Jesus Christ." That God and man are truly involved in the story of Jesus Christ is something to be steadfastly upheld by faith even today. This faith must be maintained even—and particularly—if it is better—as originally—not to postulate and deduce theologically from above divine sonship, pre-existence, creation mediatorship, incarnation, but—as we are attempting to do here—to proceed by way of induction and interpretation from below.

In the light of the New Testament therefore no interpretation of the story of Jesus Christ can be justified which makes him out to be "only God": a God moving about on the earth, relieved of human defects and weaknesses. But neither must he be seen as "only man": a preacher, prophet or sage, symbol or cipher for universally human basic experiences. Perhaps after the negative demarcations, against the background of all that has been said about Jesus in this third main section, without any claim to infallibility, we may attempt an up-to-date positive paraphrase of the ancient formula, "truly God and truly man."

Truly God: *The whole point of what happened in and with Jesus depends on the fact that, for believers,* God himself *as man's friend was present, at work, speaking, acting and definitively revealing himself* in this Jesus *who came among men as God's advocate and deputy, representative and delegate, and was confirmed by God as the Crucified raised to life. All statements about divine sonship, pre-existence, creation mediatorship and incarnation—often clothed in the mythological or semi-mythological forms of the time—are meant in the last resort to do no more and no less than substantiate the* uniqueness, underivability and unsurpassability *of the* call, offer and claim *made known in and with Jesus, ultimately not of human but of divine origin and therefore absolutely reliable, requiring men's unconditional involvement.*

Truly man: *Against all tendencies to deify Jesus, it must constantly be stressed even today that he was* wholly and entirely man *with all the consequences of this (capacity for suffering, fear, loneliness, insecurity, temptations, doubts, possibility of error). Not merely man, but* true man. *In describing him as such we insisted on the truth which has to be made true, the unity of theory and practice, of acknowledging and following him, of faith and action. As true man, by his proclamation, behavior and fate, he was a* model of what it is to be human, *enabling each and everyone who commits himself to him to discover and to real-*

ize the meaning of being man and of his freedom to exist for his fellow men. As confirmed by God, he therefore represents the permanently reliable ultimate standard of human existence.

It has now become clear that nothing is to be deducted from the truth taught by the ancient Christological councils, so far as this is really covered by the New Testament, even though it must constantly be taken out of the socio-cultural Hellenistic context and transferred to the mental climate of our own time.

According to the New Testament, of course, the final test of *being a Christian* is not assent to this or that dogma—however sublime—about Christ, *nor* agreement with a *Christology* or *theory of Christ, but* the acceptance of *faith in Christ* and *imitation of Christ*. For the sake of faith in Christ and imitation of Christ we may and must speak today of Jesus more prosaically and less in the style of ancient festal inscriptions and festal forms of address, and also less in the style of Hellenistic professions of faith, but more in the style of the Synoptic Gospels and of present-day speech—which is what we have been trying to do in the preceding chapters.

Yet, with reference to Jesus' conception and birth especially, do not these very Synoptic Gospels contain so much that is mythological or semimythological, so much in the style of ancient legends and sagas, that they cannot simply be repeated at the present time any more than the highly theological Hellenistic incarnation formulas?

Born of a woman

If anyone, for any reason at all, were to take offence at this heading, he might recall from the start that it is a quotation from the oldest New Testament statement about Jesus' birth from Mary.[61]

a. In the *birth stories* of Matthew[62] and Luke[63] the divine sonship is portrayed in the popular form of individual stories. They became important for the later development of Christian piety and for the calendar of feasts. From Christmas, including the four weeks of Advent, we go back nine months to the Annunciation (25 March); we likewise connect with Christmas the feasts of the Holy Innocents (28 December), of the Circumcision (1 January), the Epiphany (6 January) and the Presentation in the Temple (2 February). Matthew and Luke provide the reader with information about things which had not interested Mark and which for John later did not seem relevant. But Matthew and Luke form these marvelous happenings into a grandiose prelude to the main part of their Gospels: Jesus' genealogy and parentage, begetting by the power of the Spirit and virgin birth, the events in Bethlehem and the youthful years in Nazareth.

Today of course it is admitted even by Catholic exegetes[64] that these stories are a collection of largely uncertain, mutually contradictory, strongly legendary and ultimately theologically motivated narratives, with a character of their own. Unlike the rest of Jesus' life, there are dream happenings here and angels constantly enter on the scene and leave it—as heavenly messengers of God announcing important events at a time when divine transcendence was strongly emphasized (cf. the Old Testament "angel of the Lord"). The contradictions (which cannot be harmonized) do not affect merely the two genealogies of Jesus, which agree only from Abraham to David (according to Jewish lists).[65] They affect also numerous other points. While Matthew seems to know nothing about Nazareth as the domicile of the mother of Jesus, Luke on the other hand has nothing about the sensational happenings (obviously legendary and not attested in any secular source) of the visit of the Magi, of the massacre of the children in Bethlehem and the flight into Egypt. Doubts may well be raised also about the historical basis of the relationship of Jesus to John the Baptist, of Bethlehem as birthplace, of the conveniently timed census.

Obviously these are not properly historical accounts, although the use of historical material cannot be excluded. But there is something more: these are stories as professions of faith, stories which form part of the proclamation, which may have emerged in the Jewish Christian communities, been adapted by Matthew and Luke and placed at the opening of their Gospels. Here—*retrospectively* in the light of the Easter faith—*Jesus' Messiahship is proclaimed and justified,* in two ways:

(i) Jesus as *son of David*. The providential descent and the justification of the title of David's son is presented in genealogies. The genealogy leads from David to Jesus' legal father, Joseph (not to Mary!) in the symbolical numbers scheme of 3 × 14 in Matthew and probably 11 × 7 (Jesus as the twelfth age of the world) in Luke.

(ii) Jesus as the *new Moses*. The providential destiny of the child is set out in the style of early Jewish stories of Moses (as in the legendary additions to the Old Testament, in the Haggadah). Both the motif of the rescue of Moses from Pharaoh (Jesus from Herod) and that of the Israelites from Egypt (the holy family into Egypt) entered into it. Against an indisputable background of historical experience, the story of the coming of the pagan Magi forms an effective counterpart to the story of Herod's massacre of the children: for the reactions of Israel and of the Gentiles to the message of Jesus the Messiah, proclaimed by the community, were opposed to one another. Matthew underlines this fact with the aid of Old Testament quotations which bring out the salvific character of the development. While Israel refuses the Messiah Jesus who was meant to be its second Moses, the pagans come to him. The very different Lucan infancy stories too are shaped entirely in accordance with Old Testament models: the annunciation scene even to the very words; also the three songs of Mary, Zechariah and Simeon, which could stem from Jewish Christian tradition and which reflect Old Testament-Jewish poetry.

Even if the stories of the birth are not historical accounts, they can—as we have already explained[66]—be true in their own way, can make a truth known.[67] The infancy stories as part of the proclamation and as professions of faith are meant to make known, *not primarily historical, but saving truth:* the message of the salvation of men in Jesus. And this can be achieved more graphically and therefore more impressively in the form of a Christmas story, legendary in its detail, of the child in the crib at Bethlehem than with the aid of documents giving completely accurate details of the time and place of birth.

It is not historical criticism, searching for the essential message, which has emptied the Christmas message and the Christmas feast of meaning, but on the one hand the trivializing of these things, reducing them to a romantic idyl, a cosy private affair, and on the other the superficial secularization and ruthless commercialization. As if the "holy infant so tender and mild"—not indeed in Luke and Matthew, but in the holy pictures—were always smiling and had never cried in his very human misery (which is indicated, without any social-critical protest, by the crib and the swaddling clothes). As if the Saviour of the needy, born in a stable, had not clearly revealed a partisanship for the nameless ones (shepherds) against the great ones who are named (Augustus, Quirinius). As if the Magnificat of the grace-endowed maid, about the humiliation of the mighty and the exaltation of the humble, about satisfying the hungry and sending away the rich, were not a militant announcement of a revision of priorities. As if the lovely night of the newborn child meant that we could ignore his work and his fate three decades later and as if the child in the crib did not already bear on his brow the mark of the cross. As if already in the announcement scenes (the center of the Christmas story) before Mary and the shepherds—as later in the process before the Jewish tribunal—the complete profession of faith of the community were not given expression by bringing together a number of majestic titles (Son of God, Saviour, Messiah, King, Lord) and by ascribing these titles to this child instead of the Roman emperor here named. As if here—instead of the illusory Pax Romana, bought by increased taxes, escalation of armaments, pressure on minorities and the pessimism of prosperity—the true peace of Christ were not being announced with "great joy," founded on a new order of interpersonal relationships in the spirit of God's friendship for man and the brotherhood of men.

It is in fact obvious that even the apparently idyllic Christmas story has very real *social-critical* (and, in the broadest sense, political) *implications and consequences.*[68] This is a peace opposed to the political savior and the political theology of the Imperium Romanum which provided ideological support for the imperial peace policy: it is a true peace which cannot be expected where divine honors are paid to a human being and an autocrat, but only where God is glorified in the highest and he is well-pleased with man. We need only compare Luke's Christmas Gospel with the Gospel already mentioned of Augustus at Priene to see how the roles here are exchanged. The end of wars, worthwhile life, common happiness—in a word, complete well-being, man's "salvation" and the world's—are expected no longer from the overpowerful Roman Caesars but from this powerless, harmless child.

Within the scope of the present work, these few references must suffice to confirm the fact that these infancy stories correctly understood are anything but innocuous, edifying accounts of the child Jesus. They are stories of Christ, based on profound theological reflection, to be used in a carefully planned proclamation, seeking to portray artistically, vividly and in a highly critical light the true significance of Jesus as Messiah for the salvation of all the nations of the world: as Son of David and new Moses, as consummator of the Old Covenant and initiator of the New, as Saviour of the poor and as true Son of God. Here then is obviously not the first phase of a biography of Jesus or a precious family history. It has much more the character of a Gospel: a message of invitation, according to which the Old Testament promises were fulfilled in Jesus, the chosen one of God, who did not provide any detailed political prescriptions and programs, but in his very existence, in his speech, action and suffering, set up an absolutely concrete standard at which man in his individual and social action can confidently aim.

b. The *virgin birth* presents a special problem which continues to be a subject of passionate discussion.[69] The virginal conception (without male procreation) of *Jesus* by the Virgin Mary, firstly and only mentioned in the infancy stories of Matthew and Luke, but taken up in numerous ancient creeds—among them the Apostles' Creed—has been understood in different ways in the Church's tradition. At first it was taken in a strictly Christological sense, as in Matthew and Luke, as virginity *before* the birth (*virginitas ante partum*=virginal conception). But from the fourth or fifth century, under the influence of somewhat dubious sources (the apocryphal Protoevangelium of James) and a strong ascetic movement, it was given a broader meaning to include virginity *in* the birth (*in partu*=without birth pangs and/or rupture of the hymen). Finally it came to be understood as virginity—likewise not attested in the New Testament—*after* the birth (*post partum*=no sexual relations and no further children). That is: *semper virgo*, for all time, perpetual virginity. Instead of the Christological approach, the Mariological becomes increasingly prominent. The term "virgin birth" is used instead of "virginal conception."

And even then this virginal conception or birth of *Jesus* himself is still frequently confused today with the "immaculate conception" of *Mary* by a mother who is not named in the New (or Old) Testament. Neither is the immaculate conception itself mentioned in the New Testament. In the West it was rejected by Bernard of Clairvaux and Thomas Aquinas, explicitly formulated only in the twelfth century and disputed up to the sixteenth, but taught with increasing clarity at the time of the Counter-Reformation and infallibly defined by Pius IX in 1854. It is claimed that Mary as Mother of Jesus was not merely purified from original sin, but preserved from it from the very beginning by the prevenient grace of God in anticipation of Christ's merits.[70] The declaration was rejected by the Orthodox and particularly by the Protestant churches (upholding the universal destiny of sin) as unscriptural and today it has largely become pointless as a result of increasing criticism of the Augustinian view of the transmission of "original sin" by the act of procreation. There can be no doubt however that in the Church's consciousness both doctrines had something to do with the negative valuation of the sexual act on the part of the Fathers of the Church and still propagated even in our own time. The sanctity (understood in a moral sense) of Jesus and Mary had to be protected from the evil influence of sex (according to Pope Siricius †398 even marital intercourse would have meant defilement for Mary[71]). But has all this much to do with the original view of the virgin birth attested in the New Testament?

A great deal of effort has been expended on the search for the *derivation* of this doctrine in Matthew and Luke. The passage of Isaiah quoted in the New Testament about the "young woman" (the Hebrew *almah* is rendered in the Greek Old Testament by *parthenos*) who will conceive and bear a son with the name of Emmanuel[72] may have been interpreted even in Judaism and in any case was subsequently understood in Christianity as referring to a "virgin." Did the idea of the virgin birth (and the translation, *parthenos*) perhaps originate in the Egyptian myth of the Pharaoh as the god-king miraculously begotten from the spirit-god Amon-Re in the form of the reigning king and his virgin queen? Or from Greek mythology where gods enter into "holy marriages" with daughters of men, from which emerge, not only sons of the gods like Perseus, Hercules, Iphicles, but also historical figures like Homer, Pythagoras, Plato, Alexander, Augustus? The common features cannot be denied, but neither can the differences be overlooked. The annunciation and acceptance of the conception event with Mary are effected in words, without any intercourse of God and man, in a completely unerotic and intellectualized context. The Holy Spirit is understood, not as procreating father, but as operative force, in the conception of Jesus. Thus the direct influence of particular mythologies can scarcely be proved, but neither can it be *a priori* disputed. All that is certain is that the myth of a virgin birth was widespread in the whole ancient world and is found even—as we noted—in Persia, India and South America. It is therefore by no means specifically Christian.

In the birth stories, which—as we saw—are not historically but theologically oriented, the virgin birth must obviously be understood *in the light of the divine sonship* and not vice versa. The Jesus of history had proclaimed God in a new way as Father and addressed him as his loving Father. As the exalted one after his death, he was given the titles of Son and Son of God, while the divine sonship was increasingly transferred from the exaltation to the baptism and even to the very beginning. In an area under Hellenistic influence was it not natural to understand such Old Testament statements as "Today I have begotten thee" (=the king's election and ascent of the throne)[73] as a definite reference to a generation from God and not from a human father? Was it not easily possible to portray vividly the divine sonship of Jesus by the use of the widespread symbol of the virgin birth (in Alexandria, for instance, there was an annual celebration on 6 January of the birth of the new year—Aeon—from the virgin—Core)? The double-meaning Greek text of Isaiah about the "young woman" or "virgin" could have been used in this way. There could also have been—for polemical reasons—an overemphasis on the story of the birth of John the Baptist[74] (interlaced by Luke with the story of Jesus), who, like Isaac,[75] Samson[76] and Samuel,[77] was born from an unfruitful but not virginal womb.

The Messiah now was not to be filled with the Spirit in the Old Testament sense (Spirit-bearer as, for instance, the Servant of God in Isaiah),[78] but conceived by the Spirit. Conception by the Creator Spirit of God originally meant, not a biological state of affairs, but the Christological dignity of the person so conceived. Nevertheless, this idea began almost immediately increasingly to acquire a *biological meaning*. The real humanity of Jesus is in fact always assumed in the New Testament. Apart from an occasional correction,[79] his parents too are mentioned as a matter of course.[80] The references also to his "brothers" and "sisters" come in quite naturally.[81] These terms have a wider sense in Hebrew, but cannot without positive reasons be simply taken to mean "cousins." One of Jesus' brothers, James (not to be confused with the James who belonged to the circle of the twelve), played the leading part with and after Peter in the Jerusalem community.[82] Would it have been possible to talk in this way if there had been any thought of a virgin birth in the early period? An early profession of faith states quite openly that Jesus according to the flesh came from David's seed.[83] As we observed above, Paul knows nothing of a virgin birth and declares forthrightly that the Son of God was born of a woman.[84] The idea of a marvelous birth—with which he was certainly familiar in the light of Isaac's birth from Sarah[85]—he applies, not to Jesus, but in a secondary, symbolic sense to Christians as heirs of the promises.[86] Similarly, in the much later Gospel of John—where again, surprisingly enough, there is no mention of the virgin birth—just before the statement on the incarnation of the Logos, all Christians are described as being born not of blood, nor of the will of the flesh, nor of the will of man, but of God.[87]

In the birth narratives, however, Jesus' creation by the Spirit and virgin birth are described in the form of historical-corporeal events. From Luke's own formulation[88] it is clear that this explanation provides a reason—an *aitia*—for the application to Jesus of the title "Son of God," widespread even before Luke's time. A narrative of this kind is called an aetiological legend or saga. The theologoumenon of the Son of God is thus vividly portrayed as history: the theologoumenon has been turned into a mythologoumenon.[89]

This is how the state of discussion is presented today, not only by Protestant, but also by Catholic theologians. Obviously the proceedings of the Roman authorities[90] against the somewhat vague forms of expression of the Dutch Catechism[91] did not stop the debate in Catholic theology, but exercised a critical influence upon it. The trend away *from the biological-ontological to the Christological-theological* is obvious.[92] In this question too only absolute truthfulness and not concealment, ambiguity or reinterpretation can contribute to the progress of theology and the Church. On this question, which is of course a matter of controversy even outside the Catholic Church, the following points could become acceptable.

The virgin birth, attested only in the pre-histories of Matthew and Luke, does not belong to the center of the Gospel. *As Mark, Paul, John and the other New Testament witnesses prove, the Christian message can be proclaimed even without these theological (aetiological) legends which are marginal to the New Testament. Jesus' divine sonship is not dependent on the virgin birth. He is God's Son, not because God instead of a man effected his origin, but because he is chosen and destined as God's Son. Neither Jesus' sonship nor God's fatherhood can be understood in terms of biological origin. There is no incompatibility between birth from God and human procreation.*

Although the virgin birth cannot be understood as a historical-biological event, it can be regarded as a meaningful symbol *at least for that time. It would symbolize the fact that, with Jesus who closes and surpasses the Old Covenant, God has made a truly new beginning; that the origin and meaning of his person and fate are ultimately to be understood, not from the course of the world's history, but from God's action in him. Admittedly, even then, a sign liable to be misunderstood. At first it was rejected by those who completely denied Jesus' humanity or human birth (Docetism, which taught that Jesus had only an apparent human body or an apparent human existence). But subsequently the birth was often used by those who saw in Jesus simply a god in human guise (Monophysitism, which held that there was only a single divine* physis *or nature of Jesus).*

The new beginning, *granted by* God *with Jesus, was given expression even* in the New Testament in other ways *besides the virgin birth:*
by tracing back the descent of Jesus through Adam *to* God;[93]
by the idea—prepared in the work of Philo, the Jewish philosopher of religion (and in the Gnostic myth of the primal man)—of the new Adam, *who is the beginning and head of the new humanity;*[94]
by the mythological pictures of the birth of the immediately exalted Messiah-child from the woman, threatened by the dragon ("serpent" in late Judaism meant "Satan"), clothed with the sun, moon and the twelve stars (the "woman" meant Israel and perhaps also the Church), often interpreted with reference to Mary;[95]
by the idea of the divine "Logos" or "Word," pre-existing from eternity with God, *the* Word *which becomes flesh.*[96]

This new beginning then can be proclaimed also today *without the aid of the legend of a virgin birth, which is more than ever liable to be misunderstood in modern times. No one can be obliged to believe in the biological fact of a virginal conception or birth. Christian faith is related —even without a virgin birth—to the crucified and still living Jesus manifested in his unmistakability and underivability.*

For public reading in church the story obviously does not need to be omitted. But, recalling what was said about the necessity and limits of demythologizing,[97] *it should be honestly and discriminatingly interpreted.*

Mary

In connection with the conception and birth of Jesus, there are many questions about Mary, his mother, which are discussed by theologians. Leaving aside the temporary schism occasioned by the unilateral definition of the "Mother of God" formulated to the great joy of the people of Ephesus, it is only in recent times with the dogmatic definitions of the immaculate conception (1854) and of the bodily assumption of Mary into heaven (1950) that Mariological statements have become burning controversial questions.

a. It will be possible to establish a solid foundation for Marian devotion —which is not the subject of any universally binding dogmatic definition even in the Catholic Church—and an ecumenical agreement in these questions only if on all sides we keep to the guidelines of the *New Testament data.*[98]

Oddly enough, Mary (late Greek form "Mariam," rendering the Hebrew "Miriam"), of whose descent we know nothing, plays no part at all in the early Christian testimonies. Paul, as we saw, is the first to mention her, but only once and in a very general way with reference to the human birth of Jesus "from a woman."[99]

The *Synoptic Gospels*, which are authoritative in this respect, mention *only one meeting with his mother* during his public life and this has a definitely negative character. His relatives were shocked by Jesus' public appearance, regarded him more or less as mad and tried to take charge of him.[100] When his mother and his brothers came to him, Jesus pointed to another family. Pointing to those around him, he said: "Look, these are my mother and my brothers. He who does the will of my Father is my brother and sister and mother."[101] In the oldest Gospel, apart from this story and the mention of her name together with the names of the four brothers and the sisters of Jesus,[102] there is nothing about Mary. It is odd that just this single scene could have been so thrust into the background and played down in the Christian proclamation. But it is incompatible with the dignity of the grace-endowed Mary only if the latter is supposed to be *a priori* relieved of all doubt and the need of faith. At the same time this scene confirms the blessing which in Luke is assured primarily not to his mother but to all who hear the word of God and keep it.[103] The mention, likewise by Luke, of the mother of Jesus in the Pentecost story of the Acts of the Apostles agrees with this: it is only after Easter that she awaits the Holy Spirit, together with Jesus' brothers and disciples, as a member of the believing community.[104]

In *John's Gospel* Mary appears twice. At the beginning of Jesus' public life, she is at Cana for the miracle of the wine, but clearly as believing, requesting and not entirely understanding, her plea at first rejected by Jesus. And at the end she stands at the foot of the cross. This scene on the whole does not count as historical, since Mary is not named among those at the foot of the cross mentioned by the Synoptics,[105] but it has its own profound significance. Mary and the outstanding witness of the faith (the disciple whom Jesus loved) represent the Church which reached complete faith at the hour of the death on the cross, the center of John's Gospel.[106] Since she is not present at the cross, according to the Synoptics, she is also notably absent in the Easter stories.

The *infancy stories* of Matthew and particularly of Luke therefore form the comparatively slender foundation for the essentials of Marian piety and Marian theology which began at an early date with the typological relationship between Eve and Mary and which has undoubtedly had an enormous if sometimes dubious significance for the Catholic Church in the past centuries. The statements there naturally provide little material for historical study but, as we have seen in the wider context of the Christmas story, quite a lot for the proclamation. Mary is presented here as the Virgin, full of humble faith, the object of God's gracious choice and blessing, and at the same time as the prophetic singer in whom the great deeds of God in the Old Testament are completed. Her bold Magnificat, of which we have already spoken, is woven out of texts from the Psalms and the prophets and can be interpreted as the song of Mary, of Israel or of the Church. It is with Luke[107] that the series begins of Mary's honorific titles, constantly augmented in later centuries (*de Maria nunquam satis*, "never enough about Mary," has been a favorite saying since the Middle Ages).

Two features of her image are solidly *founded in Scripture* and must not be neglected in proclamation.

> *Mary is the mother of Jesus. She is a human and not a heavenly being. As a human being and as a mother, she is a witness of his true humanity, but also of his origin from God. Hence, as a result of what was admittedly—as we shall shortly explain—a very problematic development both historically and objectively, she later came to be understood as Christ-bearer and indeed as God-bearer* (*Mother of God*).
>
> *Mary is the example and model of Christian faith. Her faith, which feels the sword of scandal, dissension and contradiction, and is required in face of the cross,*[108] *according to Luke, is typical for all Christian faith* (*for Matthew, although less noticeably, Joseph's obedience in faith forms the leitmotif*)*. There is nothing unique therefore about Mary's faith, nor has she any special insight into the mysteries of God. Her faith also has a history and so provides a pattern for Christian faith as a whole. Hence she was seen later—admittedly in a way frequently misunderstood—as mother of believers* (*in the same way that, for Paul,*[109] *Abraham was father of believers*) *and so as image and type of the Church.*

b. Apart from the fact that *Marian devotion*, stemming from scriptural sources, has both enormously influenced and been itself influenced by literature, art, custom, feasts and celebrations, its development has been shaped, like every important historical phenomenon, by a number of very *varied extra-biblical factors:*[110] the cult of the Near Eastern mother divinities and also of the Celtic and Germanic goddesses (associated with ancient mountain, water and tree sanctuaries and later often with miracle-working images of a marvelous origin); theological rivalries (Alexandrian and Antiochene Christologies); ecclesiastico-political antagonisms (between the patriarchates of Alexandria and Constantinople); sometimes very personal interventions by churchmen (Cyril of Alexandria's large-scale manipulation of the Council of Ephesus in 431 and his definition of "God-bearer" before the arrival of the other, Antiochene party at the council).

Marian devotion arose quite definitely in the *East* and in the form of a cult of the "perpetual virgin," the "Mother of God" and august "Queen of Heaven." It was in the East that Mary was first invoked in prayer ("We fly to thy patronage," third-fourth century) and the memento of Mary introduced into the liturgy. In the East legends of Mary were first related and hymns to Mary composed, churches were first named after Mary (fourth century), feasts of Mary introduced and images of Mary produced (fifth century). And, above all, it was in the East in the fifth century—as already mentioned—that Mary, regularly called "Mother of Jesus" in Scripture, was defined "Mother of God."[111] This was a new, post-biblical title, attested with certainty only in the previous century, but—after Cyril's intervention—taken up with enthusiasm by the people in the city of the ancient "Great Mother" (originally the virgin goddess, Artemis or Diana): a formula (like others of Cyril and that council) which might imply a Monophysite conception of divine sonship and incarnation, hypostasizing God (as if *God* could be born and not a man in whom as God's *son* God himself is *evident* to faith).

Eastern forms of devotion became established eventually in the *West*, but not without opposition. Even Augustine does not mention any hymns or prayers to Mary, nor does he speak of feasts of Mary. The first example of a Latin hymn addressed to Mary ("Salve sancta parens," Caelius Sedulius) appears only in the fifth century. But from the time of Venantius Fortunatus toward the end of the sixth century there develops an increasingly rich Latin and then German literature. In Rome it was only in the sixth century that Mary's name was introduced into the Canon of the Mass (that of Joseph by John XXIII in the twentieth century). Only in the seventh century were the Eastern feasts of Mary (annunciation, visitation, nativity, purification) taken over. And only toward the end of the tenth century did the legends start about the miraculous power of prayer to Mary.

This development continued in the *Middle Ages*. From the definition of "God-bearer" or "Mother of God" in the fifth century up to the twelfth century the emphasis came to be laid less on Mary's past action as mother of Jesus and more on her present role for Christians as the ever-virgin Mother of God and Queen of Heaven. While the older Church Fathers had still spoken of Mary's moral faults, she now began to be credited with perfect sinlessness and the doctrine of her sanctity even before birth, as a result of her preservation from original sin, began to be taught expressly here and there in the West from the twelfth century onwards. Yet at the same time in other respects, like Jesus himself, Mary was regaining more human features, especially under the influence of scripturally minded saints like Bernard of Clairvaux and Francis of Assisi. She was now seen more as the embodiment of compassion, close to men, as all-powerful intercessor with her Son (depicted in art as bringing men under the shelter of her cloak). The minnesingers introduced an erotic element into Marian devotion, perceptible also in visual art from the time of Renaissance painting. Scholasticism attempted a conceptual clarification of Mary's position in salvation history in relation to original sin (Duns Scotus †1308). Mysticism saw in her mainly the prototype of the pure soul spiritually receiving and bearing God. Going beyond the veneration of the saints (*doulia*), veneration of Mary (*hyper-doulia*) was in fact distinguished theologically from the adoration (*latria*) due to God. But in practice Mary's createdness and humanity often played a very slight role.

From the twelfth century the biblical Ave Maria—in the present form, with the plea for her aid at the hour of death, only from 1500—has become the most widespread form of prayer and is linked with the Our Father. The Angelus stems from the thirteenth century, the Rosary from the thirteenth to the fifteenth century, but it is only in the nineteenth and twentieth centuries that we have had May and October devotions, some apparitions of Mary and Marian pilgrimages to Lourdes and Fatima, national and international Marian conferences and associations.

On this question too the *reformers* were opposed to medieval developments and went back to the biblical roots. In his interpretation of the Magnificat in relation to Christ Luther venerated Mary as the model of faith and humility; Johann Sebastian Bach set the Magnificat to music. But Protestant veneration of Mary declined with the Enlightenment. During the Counter-Reformation Marian devotion was propagated mainly by the Jesuits in an anti-Protestant spirit. After a temporary setback through the Enlightenment it was again revived in Catholic Romanticism.

From the time of Pius IX—who, after the definition of the immaculate conception (1854), had papal primacy and infallibility defined at Vatican I—the *popes* have promoted Marian devotion by every means. From the nineteenth century Marianism and papalism have gone hand in hand and given each other mutual support. The peak of this "Marian" age was reached in the year 1950 when Pius XII, the last Pope to act as an absolute ruler, against all Protestant, Orthodox and even Catholic misgivings, defined solemnly the dogma of the bodily assumption of Mary into heavenly glory at the end of her life. There is nothing about this in Scripture or even in the tradition of the first five centuries. It appeared at first only in the apocryphal sources, in legends, pictures and feasts. But this age—reinforced by Pius XII's consecration of the whole human race to the immaculate heart of Mary in 1942 (under the influence of Fatima) and by the Marian Year of 1954—came to a surprisingly sudden end a few years later. The Second Vatican Council deliberately refrained from defining further dogmas, regarded as logically following on what was already defined (mediatrix, co-redemptrix), integrated its (moderately traditional) Mariology as the closing chapter in its teaching on the Church and unmistakably condemned the excesses of Marianism. During the time after the council this exaggerated Marian cult has completely lost its force also in theology and the life of the Church.[112]

c. An *ecumenical agreement* on this question will be achieved only as a result of certain efforts on both sides.

(i) On the *Catholic* side there must be a more decisive attempt than formerly to follow the guidelines of the biblical evidence and not to fear an honest, critical examination of the recent two Marian and two papal dogmas, which in various respects form a unity and which are not substantiated in a universally convincing way either in Scripture or in tradition, or by "intrinsic reasons" (=theological postulates); in any case ranking very low in the "hierarchy of truths."[113] In such an examination—we cannot undertake it here—we would have to distinguish between the possible intentions behind a definition, which could be approved, and its dubious formulation, which would be open to criticism.

(ii) On the *Protestant* side a purely apologetic and polemical attitude is not sufficient. The biblical material on Mary and the role of woman as a whole in the history of salvation must be examined without prejudice and utilized for proclamation. At the same time poetical statements in the Catholic tradition (songs, hymns, prayers) and forms of piety which suit individuals or nations must be distinguished from the strictly theological or still more official dogmatic utterances of a Church. Much more freedom should be conceded to the former than—in all tolerance—can be permitted to the latter.

In no case may a Church—as has happened—seek its own glorification in Mary, the humble maid. A Church, like Mary, has meaning only in adaptation and subordination to the event which has its immovable center, not in Mary and not in the Church, but solely in Jesus himself.

At the close of this third main section we must once more speak expressly of the Church, now that it has become sufficiently clear that the attempts to interpret the death of this Jesus have brought out his enduring significance and impact, the attempts to interpret the conception and birth of Jesus his unique, underivable origin and claim. The different interpretations illuminate and complement one another. But all are possible only in the light of the concrete history of this Jesus of Nazareth which they must never be allowed to supersede. The Church is indeed more than a community for interpretation and argument, but it is also more than a storytelling community: it is first and last a community of faith.

VII. Community of Faith

After two thousand years Jesus of Nazareth still lives for mankind. What has kept him alive? Who testified to him time after time before mankind? Would he have remained alive, merely living on in a book? Did he not remain alive because he lived for two thousand years in the minds and hearts of innumerable human beings? In the institution of the Church or outside it, or on its fringe, human beings at immense distances of time and place have been and are under his sway: in all their human weakness and in very varying degrees, stirred, moved, filled with his word and spirit and thus forming in their different ways a community of faith.

1. Inspired and inspiring word

Without this community of people who have committed themselves to his cause, Jesus would not have remained alive in mankind. And, without it, that little book would never have existed in which the oldest and best records of him are collected.

Inspiration?

This small book, the New Testament, did not drop out of heaven. As we saw, the Koran is supposed to have been kept in heaven, dictated sentence by sentence as God's direct word for man, and therefore to be infallibly true in every sentence. It is thus regarded in every respect (linguistically, stylistically, logically, historically) as a perfect, holy book which has to be literally believed and may not even be interpreted or provided with a commentary. And the Bible? The Bible, both of the New and of the Old Testament—as Paul's letters in particular and the beginning of Luke's Gospel openly testify—was written and collected on earth. Thus it is unequivocally *man's word:* collected, written down, given varied emphasis, sentence by sentence by quite definite individuals and developed in different ways. Hence it is not without shortcomings and mistakes, concealment and confusion, limitations and errors. So there emerged a highly complex collection of clear and less clear, stronger and weaker, primary and secondary documents of faith.[1]

But is not *God's word* supposed to be recorded in these writings? As so often, the important thing is to understand this sort of question in the right way: that is, how we can take seriously the human history of these writings while still believing in God's word. Here too we shall be compelled to examine ideas of former centuries, to take up the justified concerns which they express and make them our own, and—where necessary—critically but cautiously to correct their language and imagery if today these are misleading or liable to be misunderstood.

Even in the early Hellenistic Church, Scripture was regarded as "inspired" by the Spirit of God. But what was this "inspiration" supposed to mean? Under a variety of influences from outside Christianity a conception took shape which was rigorously systematized only much later by Lutheran and Reformed orthodoxy (and in the nineteenth century, with the inevitable difference of emphasis, also by Roman Catholic theology).[2] For Hellenistic paganism and for Judaism the spirit seized on a person in ecstasy. In ecstasy human individuality appeared to be extinguished under the divine frenzy (like Pythia in the Delphic Oracle). Early Christian theologians had similar ideas. They saw the biblical authors, not at all as the latter had seen themselves, but simply as instruments who had written wholly under the "inspiration," the "prompting" and even the dictation of the divine Spirit. They were then rather like secretaries. Or even like flutes or harps made to produce sound by a breath of air. God himself through his Spirit here plays the melody, decides content and form of the unity, so that—because of God's involvement—the whole Bible had to be free or be kept free by interpreters (by harmonizing, allegorizing or mystification) from contradictions, faults and errors. Everything therefore was inspired, right down to the last word ("verbal inspiration"). Consequently every word had to be accepted. All of which was bound to lead to serious and yet essentially unnecessary conflicts both with the natural sciences (after the Copernican turning point) and with history (after the "Enlightenment").

This *traditional view* of a kind of mechanical inspiration however has been increasingly *shaken* by the historical-critical study of the Old and New Testaments. In a way that could never have been suspected, over the last two hundred years, light has been thrown on the genuine human frailty, historicity and capacity for error of the authors of the biblical writings. Today there can be no reasonable doubt about this. But was the authority of these writings thus destroyed, as many at first feared? Or was it not at this very point that a link was again established with the ancient Church, which saw God himself at work in the biblical authors and yet took seriously—as the Old Testament had done—their human and historical peculiarities? What then counted was not the infallibility or inerrancy of the authors, but the truth of the content, the testimony, the message itself. The biblical authors do not appear here as unhistorical, shadowy essences, as almost superhuman and yet essentially inhuman, because ultimately instruments without will or responsibility through which the Holy Spirit directly effects everything. Here they are witnesses of faith who speak of the real ground and content of faith, but in all human frailty, relativity and limitedness, in frequently halting speech and with utterly inadequate terminology.

In the Jewish-Hellenistic region people spoke of "Holy Scripture" or of the "Holy Scriptures," which conveyed the idea of a more or less perfect, divine, "holy" writing. The New Testament on the other hand avoids almost completely any statement about holiness. Only in a single, late text of the pastoral epistles[3]—which, as is well-known, are not by Paul—do we find a statement in Hellenistic style to the effect that "all Scripture, inspired by God (or the Spirit of God)" is useful for instruction, correction, education—which anyway does not imply a mechanistic theory of inspiration.[4]

If today the misleading term "inspiration" of Scripture is to be used at all, it must certainly not be understood in the sense of that later theory of inspiration which conceives the activity of the divine Spirit as a miracle limited to certain particular acts of writing on the part of an apostle or a biblical author. Not only the recording, but the whole pre-history and post-history of the writing, the whole process of acceptance in faith and transmission of the message, all these have something to do with the divine Spirit. Properly understood, this process can be described as *Spirit-pervaded* and *Spirit-filled*. If—that is—the first witnesses think that they are moved by the divine Spirit, this will also determine their writing without having to prove to their hearers or readers that there is somewhere an act of inspiration which they must recognize. It is in fact simply taken for granted in the New Testament that every reception and proclamation of the Gospel happens *a priori* "in the Holy Spirit."[5]

Yet such mental happenings, according to the New Testament itself, definitely involve human historicity which for its own part not only makes biblical criticism possible but even requires it: textual and literary criticism, historical and theological criticism. Serious biblical criticism—and it is to be hoped that this has been made clear throughout these chapters—can help to prevent the good news from remaining closed up in a book and enable it to be proclaimed again as fresh and living in each new age. The first witnesses—and as such they are of fundamental importance—did not receive the Gospel dictated as a fixed formula or a rigid doctrine and did not slavishly transmit it; they received it in fact in their particular situation and with their special peculiarities and they proclaimed it in their own interpretation and theology. So too those who proclaim the message today can and should transmit *the old message in a new form* in their own locality, in their own time and in their own way.

Certainly the New Testament is and remains the record of the original testimony, which the early Church came to recognize and acknowledge in a long process of discussion. Here too the early Church had no need to issue an infallible decision on the subject. These writings prevailed particularly in the liturgy, primarily because of their content in contrast to other writings (=apocrypha). People constantly experienced their power afresh and could constantly boldly renew their confidence in them. The concrete standard (=canon) of the early Church has proved itself in the course of the centuries. The New Testament has continually proved its *irreplaceable normative authority and significance.* And we are thrown back on this norm as long as we remain authentic Christians and do not want to be anything else. The New Testament as the original written Christian testimony remains (fortunately) the unchangeable norm for all later proclamation and theology in the Church and provides protection against subjective whims and all kinds of fanaticism. But, despite everything, the freedom and variety of the New Testament documents, which have their unity and simplicity solely in virtue of the message of God's action in the history of Israel and in Jesus Christ, justify the freedom and variety of the testimonies today. But how far can these human testimonies of the New Testament be called God's word?

Word of God?

As we have said, Christianity is not a book religion. The Scriptures are not themselves divine revelation. They are merely the human testimonies of divine revelation in which the humanity, independence and historicity of the human authors always remain intact. I do not believe *first* in Scripture or even in its inspiration and *then* in the truth of the message it provides. I believe in God who revealed himself in the history of Israel for believers and finally in a liberating message in the person of Jesus, and who is authentically attested in the Scriptures of the Old and New Testament. My faith arises from Scripture in the sense that the latter provides me with external evidence in an authentic form of this God of Israel and of Jesus Christ. But my faith is not based on Scripture. It is not the book as such, but this God himself in Jesus who is the ground of my faith.

The *truth of Scripture* then reaches man without any violence *through the humanity,* historicity and frailty of the human authors. Over and above all true—or scientifically, historically, religiously less true—propositions, the truth of Scripture means "truth" in the originally biblical sense: the "fidelity," "constancy," "trustworthiness," of God himself who stands by his word and promises. There is not a single text in Scripture asserting its freedom from error. But every text in its wider or narrower context attests this unswerving fidelity of God to man, preventing God from ever becoming a liar.

It thus becomes possible to understand how Scripture can be called *God's word.* "It is written" can never mean "God's word lies before us in writing." It is not there to be recognized by any neutral observer, to be forced on man as it were. If we are not to speak naïvely about it as formerly, but in a way that is theologically justifiable, we must say:[6]

> *The Bible* is *not simply God's word: it is first of all and in its whole extent man's word, the word of quite definite individuals.*
>
> *The Bible does not simply* contain *God's word: there are not certain propositions which are God's word, while the rest are man's.*
>
> *The Bible* becomes *God's word: it becomes God's word for anyone who submits trustfully and in faith to its testimony and so to the God revealed in it and to Jesus Christ.*

It is God himself, revealed in the history of Israel and in the person of Jesus Christ, who calls through these testimonies for faith and provides for the message—despite all human weakness and all opposition—constantly to be truly heard, understood, believed and realized. The word thus becomes effective without being manipulated or controlled. But it can also be rejected if someone so desires: even then it remains effective, as condemnation and judgment. For someone who does not accept this invitation to believe, the Bible remains only an immensely problematical human word, however much he knows about it in terms of philology, history or theology. But for someone who accepts the invitation, even if he understands little of historical-critical exegesis, the Bible does not remain man's word, but—despite all the problems—becomes God's assisting, liberating, saving word. He knows then quite clearly and unequivocally what is decisive in the Christian message. In all words he grasps the word, in the different Gospels the one Gospel. He allows himself to be inspired by the Spirit of this Scripture, who is in truth the Spirit of God and the Spirit of Jesus Christ: the Spirit who in a wholly unmechanical way turns the documents themselves into Spirit-filled and Spirit-pervaded testimonies. And the question whether and how the Bible itself is inspired word is far less important—even for the text of 2 Timothy mentioned above—than the question of how *man himself allows himself to be inspired by its word.* For this word inspired by the Spirit is meant through the same Spirit to be an inspiring word.

But why do we speak here so insistently of the Spirit? To put the question in a more general way, why introduce a third factor alongside God the Father and Jesus Christ, so that in the end we come to a doctrine of the Trinity? Were not the original creeds—as we can easily see from the New Testament—binitarian and only at a later stage trinitarian?

2. *The one Spirit*

We cannot overlook the fact that any talk of the Holy Spirit is so unintelligible to many today that it cannot even be regarded as controversial. But there can also be no doubt that the blame for this situation may be laid to a large extent on the way in which the concept of the Holy Spirit has been misused in modern times both by the official Church and by pious individuals.[1]

Unholy and holy Spirit

When holders of high office in the Church did not know how to justify their own claim to infallibility, they pointed to the Holy Spirit. When theologians did not know how to justify a particular doctrine, a dogma or a biblical term, they appealed to the Holy Spirit. When mild or wild fanatics did not know how to justify their subjectivist whims, they invoked the Holy Spirit. The Holy Spirit was called in to justify absolute power of teaching and ruling, to justify statements of faith without convincing content, to justify pious fanaticism and false security in faith. The Holy Spirit was made a substitute for cogency, authorization, plausibility, intrinsic credibility, objective discussion. It was not so in the early Church or even in the medieval. This simplification of the role of the Holy Spirit is a typically modern development, emerging on the one hand from Reformation fanaticism and on the other hand from the defensive attitude of the great Churches, seeking to immunize themselves from rational criticism.

But we may look at the matter in another way. In primitive Christendom how was the fact to be expressed that God, that Jesus Christ, is truly close to the believer, to the community of faith: wholly real, present, effective? To this the writings of the New Testament give a unanimous response, but without regard to power claims for Church, theology and piety: God, Jesus Christ are *close in the Spirit* to the believer, to the community of faith; present in the Spirit, present through the Spirit and indeed as Spirit. It is not then through our memory, but through the spiritual reality, presence, efficacy of God, of Jesus Christ himself. What is the meaning of "Spirit" here?

Perceptible and yet not perceptible, invisible and yet powerful, real like the energy-charged air, the wind, the storm, as important for life as the air we breathe: this is how people in ancient times frequently imagined the "Spirit" and God's invisible working. According to the beginning of the creation account, "spirit" (Hebrew, *ruah*; Greek, *pneuma*) is the "roaring," the "tempest" of God over the waters.[2] "Spirit" here does not mean in the idealistic sense a capacity for knowledge or a psychological power, still less an immaterial, intellectual or ethical principle, and certainly not spiritual or mental reality in the modern sense as opposed to sensible, corporeal reality or to nature. "Spirit" as understood in the Bible means the force or power proceeding from God, which is opposed to "flesh," to created, perishable reality: that invisible *force of God* and *power of God* which is effective creatively or destructively, for life or judgment, in creation and in history, in Israel and in the Church. It comes upon man powerfully or gently, stirring up individuals or even groups to ecstasy, often effective in extraordinary phenomena, in great men and women, in Moses and the "judges" of Israel, in warriors and singers, kings, prophets and prophetesses.

But the age of the great prophets was long past in Israel. In early Judaism at the time of Jesus, according to rabbinical teaching, the Spirit had ceased to be active with the last prophetical writers. The Spirit was expected again only for the end-time and then, according to the famous prophecy of Joel,[3] he would be "poured out" not only over individuals but over the whole people. Is it surprising that the primitive Christian communities, who had seen Jesus as the great Spirit-bearer (at his baptism?), regarded this prophetic experience as having been fulfilled in the fact of their existence? The descent of the Spirit was therefore seen as the signal for the beginning of the end-time and indeed—as it was written in Joel—not only for the privileged few, but also for the non-privileged: not only for the sons, but also for the daughters; not only for the old, but also for the young; not only for the masters, but also for the menservants and the maids.[4]

This Spirit then is not—as the word itself might well suggest—the spirit of man, his knowing and willing living self. He is the Spirit of God, who as *Holy* Spirit is sharply distinguished from the unholy spirit of man and his world.[5] It is true that he has dynamistic and animistic features which are scarcely clearly separable: he appears sometimes as impersonal force (*dynamis*), sometimes as personal being (*anima*). But in the New Testament he is certainly not any sort of magical, substance-like, mysterious-supernatural aura of a dynamistic character or even a magical being of animistic character. The Spirit is no other than God *himself*: God close to man and the world, as comprehending but not comprehensible, self-bestowing but not controllable, life-giving but also directive power and force. He is then not a third party, not a thing between God and men, but God's personal closeness to men. Most misunderstandings of the Holy Spirit arise from setting him apart from God mythologically and making him independent. In this respect the Council of Constantinople itself in 381, to which we owe the extension of the Nicene Creed to include the

Holy Spirit, expressly emphasizes the fact that the Spirit is of one nature with the Father and the Son.[6]

Primitive Christendom's view of the Holy Spirit however is not uniform in its details. The operation of the Holy Spirit appears in a very different light particularly in the Lucan Acts of the Apostles and in Paul.[7]

Luke is very interested in the operation of the Spirit particularly in its extraordinary forms and, as we saw,[8] places an interval of time between Easter and a Christian Pentecost with the reception of the Spirit (is the "driving wind" of the Spirit meant to recall God's "tempest" before all creation?). In the Acts of the Apostles the Spirit appears frequently as the natural consequence of becoming a believer and receiving baptism.[9] But at the same time he appears also as the source of the extraordinary charismatic force which is ascribed in special cases to the Spirit of God, as a special gift for certain supplementary activities. It is the Spirit who gives a mandate, capability, power, authorization, continuity in the Church, and the imposition of hands is the sign of this.[10]

Paul was the first to reflect more closely on the nature and working of the Holy Spirit. With him the Spirit determines, not only individual, more or less extraordinary deeds, but the very existence of the believer as such.[11] Paul, that is, understands the Spirit quite definitely in the light of that great turning point of time which for him is constituted by Jesus' death and resurrection. Since it became evident at that point that God himself acted in Jesus, the *Spirit of God* can now be *understood also as the Spirit of Jesus as exalted to God*. God's Spirit therefore can no longer be misinterpreted as an obscure, nameless, divine power as understood by Hellenistic Gnosticism, but is completely unequivocally the Spirit of Jesus Christ, of the Son.[12] God and the exalted Jesus, although clearly distinct as "persons" also for Paul, are seen together in regard to their operation. God gives salvation through Jesus. God's power, force, spirit, have become so much his own as exalted Lord that he not only possesses and controls the Spirit, but, as a result of the resurrection, can himself be understood as Spirit: Jesus has become a life-giving spirit.[13] Indeed, Paul even says "the Lord is the Spirit."[14]

Just what does this enigmatic statement mean? As we have already indicated, not a straightforward identity of two personal factors. It means that *the Lord raised up to God is in the Spirit's mode of existence and operation*. He appears as identical with the Spirit as soon as he is considered, not in himself, but in his action on community and individual: the exalted *Jesus acts now through the Spirit, in the Spirit, as Spirit*. In the Spirit therefore the exalted Christ himself is present. The equation of the Son with the Spirit therefore and the subordination of the Spirit under the Lord can stand side by side;[15] the phrases "in the Spirit" and "in Christ" or even "the Spirit in us" and "Christ in us" can run parallel and in practice can be interchanged. The encounter of "God," "Lord" and "Spirit" with the believer is therefore in the last resort one and the same encounter: "May the grace of the Lord Jesus Christ and the love of God and the communion of the Holy Spirit be with you all."[16] Everywhere it is a question of an action of God himself. What then is the Holy Spirit?

The Holy Spirit is God's Spirit. He is God himself, as gracious power and force, gaining dominion over the mind and heart of man, in fact the whole man, becoming inwardly present to man and giving effective testimony of himself to man's spirit.

As God's Spirit he is also the Spirit of Jesus Christ *exalted to God: through him Jesus is the living Lord, the model for the Church and the individual Christian. No hierarchy, no theology, no fanaticism, seeking to invoke the "Spirit" without regard to Jesus, to his word, his behavior and his fate, can in fact lay claim to the Spirit of Jesus Christ. The spirits therefore are to be tested and discerned in the light of this Jesus Christ.*

As Spirit of God and of Jesus Christ for men *he is never identified with man's own possibilities, but is* force, power and gift of God. *He is not an unholy spirit of man, spirit of the age, spirit of the Church, spirit of office, spirit of fanaticism, but is and remains always the Holy Spirit of God who moves where and when he wills and does not permit himself to be used to justify absolute power of teaching and ruling, to justify unsubstantiated theology, pious fanaticism and false security of faith.*

It is the person who truly submits in faith *to the message and thus to God and his Christ who receives the Holy Spirit. He does not operate in a magical, automatic way, but allows a free consent. So far as baptism is sign and sacrament of faith, baptism and reception of the Spirit go together. For baptism is an expression of readiness wholly and entirely to submit to the name of Jesus, in fulfillment of the will of God for the well-being of our fellow men.*

As Christians we believe in *the Holy Spirit ("credo* in *Spiritum Sanctum") who is in the holy Church, but not* in *the Church. The Church is not God. We ourselves, the believers, are the Church. In the strict sense we believe, not in ourselves, but in God, who in his Spirit makes possible the community of believers. In the light of the sanctifying Spirit we believe* the *holy Church ("credo sanctam Ecclesiam").*[17]

The Spirit of God and of Jesus Christ is essentially a *Spirit of freedom:*[18] in the last resort freedom from guilt, law, death; freedom and courage to act, to love, to live in peace, justice, joy, hope and gratitude. The Pauline letters are full of it. But—in passing—the question may be asked: is this freedom real? It is.

From Paul's time up to the present day, the freedom of the sons and daughters of God has been continuously quite practically attested, experienced, lived, mostly unobtrusively and in a way only indirectly verifiable as part of world history, by small people more than by great. Despite all shortcomings and all failures of the Church, innumerable believers from apostolic times until today have constantly grasped this freedom in faith and obedience, lived it in love and joy, suffered it in hope and patience, fought for it, expected it. In this freedom innumerable unknown people, with their great or slight decisions, fears, perils, forebodings and expectations, have constantly found fresh courage, support, strength, consolation. The Spirit of freedom then as Spirit of the future directs men forward: not to the hereafter of empty promises, but to the here and now of probation in the midst of ordinary secular life until the consummation of which the Spirit is the pledge.[19]

Trinity

If we look at the question in the light of what we have just said, it is possible even today to understand the *relationship of Father, Son and Spirit* in non-mythological terms, to understand also the numerous three-membered, *triadic formulas* of the New Testament in their originally non-mythological sense. The theological teaching which in fact emerged out of all this of the immanent divine triunity ("Trinity"), attempting with the aid of Hellenistic terms to conceive Father, Son and Spirit in true diversity and undivided unity, has its own problems and unfortunately is scarcely understood by modern man.

The Greek word *trias* was first used by the apologist Theophilus of Antioch in the second century, the Latin *trinitas* by the African Tertullian in the third. The *Hellenistic formula*, which found its classical expression as a result of a highly complex, partly inconsistent and in any case protracted process of thought in the work of the three Cappadocians (Basil, Gregory of Nazianzen and Gregory of Nyssa) in the fourth century, is well-known. God is threefold in the "persons" (*hypostases, subsistences, prosopa*), but single in the "nature" (*physis, ousia, essence, substance*). An increasingly pretentious, intellectual *speculation on the Trinity* was built up on the basis of the originally straightforward triadic creedal statements, particularly the triadic baptismal formula of the Matthaean community tradition[20] which had itself been developed from the simple Christological baptismal formula.[21] It amounted almost to a kind of higher trinitarian mathematics, but—despite all striving for conceptual clarity—scarcely reached any lasting solutions. Was not this Greek speculation, remote from its biblical roots, attempting on the dizzy heights to catch sight of the mystery of God, in very much the same state as Icarus, son of Daedalus, the pioneer of Athenian craftsmanship, when he came too near the sun with his wings made of feathers and wax? At least in practical proclamation, while Father, Son and Spirit are mentioned, this doctrine of the Trinity is largely passed over in silence. The *liturgy of the Trinity* (propagated from the eighth century onwards on Gallic soil against persistent opposition from Rome) and the feast of the Trinity, first introduced by Pope John XXII in 1334, did little to change the situation. Incidentally, this was the first feast to celebrate a dogma and not a salvation event. The dogma was scarcely disputed—except by Unitarians—but it also scarcely made any impact.

The New Testament however, in the way we have described, affirms positively the unity of God, Jesus and Spirit. To this Spirit—particularly according to the Johannine farewell discourses[22]—pertain the personal characteristics of an "advocate" and "helper" (this and not "comforter" is the meaning of "the other paraclete"[23]). He is—so to speak—the representative on earth of the exalted Christ, sent by the Father in Jesus' name, not speaking of himself but only recalling what Jesus said.[24] But, although there are many triadic statements on Father, Son and Spirit in the New Testament, neither in John's Gospel nor in the later Apostles' Creed do we find any properly trinitarian doctrine of a God in three persons (modes of being). The clearest testimony, the famous Johannine Comma, defended as authentic by the Roman authorities up to the turn of the century, an "interpolation" into the first epistle of John,[25] about Father, Word and Spirit, who are one, is generally regarded today as a forgery (originating in North Africa or Spain in the third or fourth century). The original text refers to a very different "trinity" (which, incidentally, proves how little we can conclude to a particular unity from a triad as such): "There are three who bear witness, the spirit, the water (=baptism) and the blood (=the Lord's Supper); and these three amount to one" (both sacraments are testimonies in virtue of the one Spirit).[26]

Like the oldest dual formulas of Father and Son, in both the letters[27] and the Gospels[28] it is possible to find a respectable number of examples also of the more developed triple formula of Father, Son and Spirit.[29] But is not the really important thing the *mode of co-ordination* of these two or three factors with each other and with the one nature of God? Or is the triadic (or binitarian?) element as such supposed to be the distinctive Christian reality ("central mystery," "basic dogma" of Christianity)?

The distinctively Christian feature—as we have seen throughout this whole book—is this Christ himself and obviously in his decisive relationship to God, his Father, and thus also to God's Spirit. But this very number three, fascinating from time immemorial as the primal unity in variety, immensely important for religion, myth, art and literature and even for ordinary life, and the triple divinity (found from Rome and Greece to India and China) are anything but specifically Christian. They have no more to do with Christianity than life's three part time (an outgoing from identity with oneself and a returning to oneself) or the dialectical triad (thesis-antithesis-synthesis).

The Christological element is the specific feature and it is from this that everything about the Trinity appears to be deduced both in the Bible and in the history of dogma. In popular Christian belief of course, if only because of the change of meaning of the terminology, the Trinity is largely understood in a tri-theistic sense. Three "persons" are understood in modern psychological terms as three "self-consciousnesses," three "subjects": that is to say, essentially three Gods. This *de facto* tritheism is found, not only in some portrayals of the Trinity in Byzantine and Russian icons, Carolingian miniatures and medieval illustrations, in the form of three men with the same figure (against which Benedict XIV issued a warning in 1745), but also in theological and liturgical expressions. But it has little to do with the biblical unity of Father, Son and Spirit. As little as—on the other hand—*modalism*, where Father, Son and Spirit are seen merely as three modes of revelation, as three successive manifestations of the one God, or correspondingly in art the famous *trikephalos* or three-faced God who constantly turned up until the end of the eighteenth century (despite warnings of theologians like Antoninus of Florence and Robert Bellarmine).

According to the New Testament, as against tritheism on the one hand and modalism on the other, the unity of Father, Son and Spirit is a *unity of operation and revelation* in which they are involved as *three very diverse factors* (beautifully illustrated in artistic representations of Jesus' baptism), to be described at best in analogical terms. According to the New Testament, Father, Son and Spirit cannot be leveled down in an ontological scheme to one divine nature ("three persons in one nature"), in the sense developed in terms of formal logic by the Cappadocians and then worked out by Augustine—well aware of the innovation[30]—in anthropological-psychological terms. He uses an ingenious but questionable analogy with the three-dimensional spirit (*mens*) of man—memory (*memoria*), understanding (*intelligentia*) and will (*voluntas*)—to explain a self-unfolding of God. The Son is "begotten" by way of intellect (in the divine act of thought) from the substance of the Father as his likeness. The Spirit however "proceeds" from the Father (as loving) and the Son (as loved) by way of will (in a single breathing=*spiratio*) as love in person. In this way Father, Son and Spirit are understood in the last resort as three subsisting relations, really distinct from each other and yet at the same time one with the one divine nature. Aquinas later separated the treatise on the triune God from that on God as one and made use especially of Aristotelian categories to develop Augustine's thought and draw the necessary conclusions.

All this led also to an unnecessary *controversy between the Latin and the Greek Church* which has not been officially settled up to the present time. Augustine, because of his idea of the Trinity, asserted a procession of the Spirit from the Father *and* the Son (*filioque*). From the sixth century this *filioque* clause was gradually and by Pope Benedict VIII in 1014 definitively introduced into the Niceno-Constantinopolitan Creed. Thus what appeared to the East as a corruption of both the ecumenical creed and the ancient tradition and even as sheer heresy became a dogma for the West. The East maintained strictly the procession of the Spirit from the Father *through* the Son and—especially from the ninth century onward—protested against the Western development which now threw a theological burden on relations between Rome and Constantinople. Today this controversy is largely seen to be concerned with a merely apparent problem. For Western interpretation does not question the fact that the Father is the source of the innertrinitarian processions, so that the two interpretations are not necessarily mutually exclusive. But this is by no means the end of the problem.

The real difficulties of the specifically Western doctrine of the Trinity arise from the fact that Augustine, its founder, making use of the ideas of the other great Africans, Tertullian and Cyprian, *started out, not* like the Greeks, *from the triplicity of the persons, but from the unity of the divine nature.* In this respect Augustine had against him not only the Greeks and —for instance—Hilary of Poitiers in the West, but also the New Testament.[31] For the Greeks the source (*arche*) of the unity between Father, Son (Word) and Spirit was not the one nature. For them the one God and Father is the origin who reveals himself through the Word (Son) in the Spirit. Diagrammatically, not three stars alongside each other in a triangle as in the Western tradition (Augustine however had protested against the Manichees' trinitarian interpretation of the triangle), but three stars coming after each other with the first star giving its light to the second and finally to the third, so that these three stars appear as one to the human eye. Whoever sees the Son in the Spirit sees also the Father.

In the New Testament it is unequivocally a question of a *unity in the event of revelation,* in which the diversity of the "roles" must not be suppressed, the sequence must not be reversed, and Jesus' humanity in particular must not for a moment be disregarded. Even in John's Gospel none of the statements about Father, Son and Spirit or on God as spirit,[32] light[33] and love[34] are ontological statements about God in himself and his innermost nature, about the static, self-sustaining essence of a triune God. In the whole of the New Testament such statements are concerned with the manner of God's revelation: his dynamic activity in history, the relationship of God to man and man's relationship to God. The triadic formulas of the New Testament are meant to express, not an "immanent" but an "economic" theology of the Trinity, not an inner-divine (immanent) essential triunity in itself but a salvation-historical (economic) unity of Father, Son and Spirit in their encounter with us. The New Testament is not concerned with God in himself, but with God for us, as he has acted on us through Jesus himself in the Spirit, on which the reality of our salvation depends.[35]

We must always remember that the Trinity was not originally an object of theoretical speculation. It was the object of the profession of faith and of the act of praise (doxology). The expression which arose out of opposition to the Arians, placing the persons alongside each other, "Glory be to the Father *and* to the Son *and* to the Holy Spirit," is liable to be misunderstood. It would be better to keep to the classical form of the Roman collects, fortunately maintained up to the present time and corresponding to the original promise of Greek trinitarian theology, where the *Father* himself is addressed *"through" the Son "in" the Holy Spirit.*[36] This is throughout the perspective of the New Testament which should be taken up and thought out again. Again diagrammatically, it could be said: God the Father "above" me, Jesus as the Son and brother "beside" me, the Spirit of God and Jesus Christ "in" me.

The trinitarian confession of the early Church developed theologically through a long history into an increasingly expanded doctrine of the Trinity. The culminating points of this development came in the last century with Hegel's philosophy of religion[37] and in the present century with Karl Barth's *Church Dogmatics.*[38] It continues to play a significant role in worship and in hymns and also in the basis formula (accepted without coming to terms with Nicea and Chalcedon) of the World Council of Churches, which excludes Unitarians. Every attempt at a critical new interpretation will have to be justified in the light of this great tradition.[39] From the standpoint of the New Testament neither the *classical doctrine* of the Trinity nor the classical two-natures doctrine *are to be thoughtlessly repeated or thoughtlessly dismissed, but discriminatingly interpreted for the present time.* Before making any new statement on the Trinity a number of points would have to be considered.

The key question *with regard to the doctrine of the Trinity is not the trinitarian question—described as an impenetrable "mystery"—of how three can be one, but the* Christological *question of how the relationship of Jesus to God is to be defined in a way that is both rational and in accordance with Scripture. Both historically and objectively the Christological problem became the source of the often misunderstood trinitarian problem.*

The monotheistic faith *taken over from Israel and held in common with Islam must never be abandoned in any doctrine of the Trinity. There is no God but God.*

The New Testament itself forces us to reflect on the co-ordination *of God, Jesus (Word, Son, Christ) and Spirit and at the same time to bring out their true* diversity *and undivided* unity. *It is here that the legitimate basic intention of the traditional doctrine of the Trinity lies.*

The attempts at interpretation based on Hellenistic ideas *and the resultant dogmatic formulations of this co-ordination are however* time-conditioned *and not simply identical with this basic intention. Not that a doctrine of the Trinity can be rejected just because it makes use of Hellenistic categories. But neither can any future doctrine of the Trinity be tied to the use of such categories. The traditional formulas of the doctrine of the Trinity, defined in Hellenistic terms, however helpful they may have been, cannot be imposed as a timeless obligation of faith on all believers at all times.*

The unity of Father, Son and Spirit is to be understood as revelation event and revelational unity. *In considering the Trinity we must go beyond the Christological question and reflect on the relationship between God and Jesus with reference to the Spirit. Christology would be incomplete without pneumatology (theology of the Spirit). Christologically defined, "truly God" means that the true man Jesus of Nazareth is the real revelation of the one true God. Hence the question arises: how does he become this revelation* for us? *And the answer is: not physically or materially and yet truly, in the Spirit, in the Spirit's mode of existence, as spiritual reality. The Spirit is the presence of God and of the exalted Christ for the community of faith and the individual believer. In this sense God himself is manifested through Jesus Christ in the Spirit.*

In this brief section we have not attempted to develop a doctrine of the Trinity, but only to draw attention to some points which may be helpful to its understanding. And here too the discussion was deliberately restricted. In that sense we may add as a postscript to this all-too-brief interpretation of the dogma the words with which Augustine prefaced his treatise on the Trinity:

I ask my readers to make common cause with me
when they share my convictions;
to keep an open mind
when they share my doubts.
I ask them to correct me
if I make a mistake,
to return to my way of thinking
if they do.[40]

But now perhaps it is time to descend from these dogmatic heights to lower plains of ordinary Christian life where Christian faith must be mainly tested. Have we not hitherto taken it far too much for granted that we know what the Church is?

3. *The pluriform Church*

The Church might be briefly defined as the community of those who believe in Christ.[1] More precisely: not founded by Jesus, but emerging after his death in his name as crucified and yet living, *the community of those who have become involved in the cause of Jesus Christ and who witness to it as hope for all men.* Before Easter there was nothing more than an eschatological collective movement. A congregation, a Church, came into existence only after Easter and this too was eschatologically oriented: at first its basis was not a cult of its own, a constitution of its own, an organization of its own with definite ministries, but simply and solely the profession of faith in this Jesus as the Christ. The "Church of Jesus Christ" in the sense of a community confronting the ancient people of God is also a post-Easter factor according to the New Testament itself.[2]

The Church's one task today then would be to serve the cause of Jesus Christ: that is, at least not to obstruct it, but to defend it, give effect to it, itself to realize this cause in the spirit of Jesus Christ in modern society. The question that most readily occurs at this point is: is this what the Church is doing? It is a question which will have to be discussed and one which in fact every Christian as a member of the Church should put to himself at the same time as he puts it to others, as he—rightly—puts it to the institution. First of all, a systematic treatment of the meaning of the Church.

Assembly, congregation, Church

The *name* itself shows how much the Church would be committed, is committed, to the cause of its Lord.[3] The usual word *in the Germanic languages* (German *Kirche*, English "Church," Swedish *kyrka*, cf. Slav *cerkov*) fortunately is not derived from *curia*, as Luther thought (which had not a little to do with his dislike of the word "Church" and his preference for "congregation" or "community"). The word did not come from Rome, but was brought up the Danube and down the Rhine from the Gothic kingdom of Theodoric the Great. Its source was the Byzantine popular form *Kyrike* and thus means "belonging to the Lord" or, in a wider sense, "house of the Lord." A brief description might be Kyrios-congregation, the Lord's congregation. And this is all that is essential. In contrast to the Germanic, the *Romance languages* have preserved a direct connection with the word used in the New Testament: Latin *ecclesia*,

Spanish *iglesia*, French *église*, Italian *chiesa*. They all stem from the Greek *ekklesia*. But what is the meaning of this word?

In secular Greek usage *ekklesia* means the assembly, the political gathering of the people. But the model for the New Testament concept of *ekklesia* was the use of the word in the Greek translation of the Old Testament. There *ekklesia* stands almost always for the Hebrew term—in itself secular—*kahal*=the assembly called together. What is decisive is the explicitly or implicitly added qualification "of the Lord" or "of Yahweh." The ecclesia of God is more than the occasional event of gathering together. Ecclesia is the assembly of the group previously chosen by God which gathers round God as its center. The term is used in a religious and cultic sense and increasingly understood in an eschatological sense: ecclesia as the true eschatological congregation of God. When the primitive community adopted the designation of ecclesia, it was deliberating asserting a large claim: to be the true assembly of God, the true congregation of God, the true eschatological people of God which comes together in the name and spirit of Jesus Christ—that is, the "ecclesia of Jesus Christ."

Ecclesia—like "assembly"—means both the *actual process of assembling* and the *assembled congregation* itself. The former usage particularly must never be forgotten. There is not an ecclesia merely because something was once instituted, founded and then remains unchanged. There is an ecclesia only as a result of a constantly new concrete event of coming together, of assembling, and especially of assembling for worship. The concrete assembly is the actual manifestation, representation and indeed realization of the New Testament community. Conversely it is the community itself which permanently sustains the constantly recurring event of assembling.

"Assembly," "congregation," "Church" are not to be played off against one another, but must be seen in their context. The fact cannot be overlooked that, while we speak of assembly or congregation or Church, the New Testament always uses the same term "ecclesia." This alone should prevent us from contrasting these terms.

"Assembly" expresses the fact that the ecclesia never exists merely as a static institution, but only as a result of the constantly renewed event of actually coming together.

"Congregation" stresses the fact that the ecclesia is never merely an abstract and distant superorganization of functionaries over and above the concrete assembly, but always a community assembled at a definite place at a definite time for a definite action.

"Church" makes clear the fact that the ecclesia is never merely an unconnected juxtaposition of isolated and self-sufficient religious associations, but the members of a comprehensive community, united with one another in reciprocal service.

It is true that "assembly" stresses mainly the actual event of coming together, "congregation" mainly the local, permanent group, "Church" mainly the supra-local foundation. Hence in translating *ecclesia* different renderings will be preferred at different times. But in principle they are interchangeable. As we can speak of the local Church instead of the local congregation, so too we can speak of the universal congregation instead of the universal Church.

But how are *local Church and universal Church* related to one another? The brief answer is that each ecclesia (=each individual assembly, congregation, Church) *is not the* ecclesia (=the universal Church, congregation, assembly), but fully *represents* the ecclesia. This implies two things.

On the one hand Catholics today recognize that the local ecclesia is not merely a "section" or "province" of the universal Church. It is by no means a subdivision of the real "Church" which, as the more comprehensive structure, would have to be regarded as of higher rank and of primary importance. It is not a good thing to use the term "Church" exclusively of the universal ecclesia—this is the consequence of an abstract and idealist conception of the Church. It implies that the Church is not *wholly* present in every place; that the local Church has not been given the *whole* promise of the Gospel and the faith in *its entirety*; that the *whole* grace of the Father has not been assured to it, the *whole* Christ is not present in it and the Holy Spirit not *entirely* bestowed on it. No, the local Church does not merely *belong* to the Church. The local Church *is* the Church and can fully represent the cause of Jesus Christ. It is only in the light of the local Church and its concrete realization that the universal Church can be understood. But it is really the Church to which is promised and given in its own place everything it needs there for men's salvation: the proclamation of the Gospel, baptism, the eucharist, the different charisms and ministries.

On the other hand Protestants today recognize that the universal Church is not merely an "accumulation" or an "association" of the local ecclesiae. There is more than a common name uniting the individual local Churches, more than an external combination, more than an organization to which the individual Churches are subordinated. One and the same cause of Jesus Christ, the same Gospel, the same assurance and promise are given to all the individual Churches. They are all dependent on the grace of one and the same Father, they have the same Lord, they are moved by the same Spirit of charisms and ministries. They all believe the same faith, they are sanctified by the same baptism, they assemble for the same meal. Through all this—and what could be more important for them?—they are not merely externally linked, but inwardly united, they all form not only an ecclesiastical organization, but a Church of Jesus Christ. The Church is not an umbrella association of individual congregations. *The* ecclesia is not the sum total of the individual ecclesiae; the ecclesia cannot be broken down into the individual ecclesiae. But it is *the* ecclesia of God in different places.

Each ecclesia, each assembly, congregation, Church—however small, insignificant, mediocre, wretched—fully represents *the* ecclesia, *the* assembly, congregation, Church of God and of Jesus Christ. All this holds both for a lonely mission station in the African bush and for a large prosperous parish in the American Middle West or in Central Europe, both for a parish on a new housing estate and for the usual large city parish or for a regional parish uniting several former village parishes. This is true not only of the normal territorial congregations or parishes, but also of functional parishes like student and university parishes, the congregation of a hospital, a factory, a tourist center, of a linguistic minority; of parishes mainly in the form of a "service station" (a Mass center in the great railway stations, for instance) or mainly in the form of an "effective community" (involved in a quite definite enterprise); finally for congregations in the Catholic or Orthodox or in one or another Protestant tradition (with increasing integration and—we may hope—eventual mutual recognition). In all their diversity and multiplicity all these can truly be called "Church." And they must all be kept in mind—not only the great diocesan and national Churches, nor even the universal Church—when we go on now to talk about the "Church."

Is this all mere theory? This is a question to be answered later. For the moment, we shall continue quietly with our theorizing.

Community in liberty, equality, fraternity

A Church which represents the cause of Jesus Christ in great things or in small, bears his name, hears his word and is moved by his Spirit, however varied its appearance, can never be identified with a particular class, caste, clique, administration. Like Jesus himself, his Church also turns to the whole people and particularly to the underprivileged. The Church then is the *whole community* of those who believe in Christ, in which *all can see themselves as people of God, body of Christ, building of the Spirit.*[4] What really counts in this community is not any privilege of birth, class, race or office. The kind of "office" a person holds or even whether he holds office at all is not important. What matters is whether and to what extent a person is simply and solely a "believer": whether and how far he believes, serves, hopes and commits himself in the spirit of Jesus Christ in a wholly concrete way.

Unlike the pagan or Jewish worshiper, a Christian needs no priest in addition to Christ as mediator in the innermost center of the temple, with God himself. For in the last resort he has been given an immediate access to God which no ecclesiastical authority can disturb, still less take away from him. No one has any power to judge, control or order decisions which fall within this innermost sphere. It is true that the Christian faith does not drop directly out of heaven but is transmitted in the Church. But "Church," great or small, is the *whole* community of faith which proclaims the Gospel—often more through humble people than through the hierarchs and theologians, more by deeds than by words—in order to awaken faith in Jesus Christ, provoke commitment in his Spirit, make the Church present in the world in everyday Christian witness and so to carry on the cause of Jesus Christ. For it is to *all* in all the different forms of congregation and not to a few chosen ones that the Christian proclamation is committed. It is from all that an individual and social life based on the Gospel is required. To all baptism in the name of Jesus, the memorial, thanksgiving and covenant meal, the consolation of forgiveness of sins are entrusted. To all are committed everyday service and the responsibility for their fellow men, for the congregation, for society and the world. All these basic functions in the Church exist in a community of liberty, equality and fraternity.[5]

a. *Liberty:* Liberty is both a gift and a task for the Church. In great things and in small, the Church can and should be a *community of free* people. If it wants to serve the cause of Jesus Christ, it can never be an institution for domination, still less a Grand Inquisition. Its members should be liberated for freedom: liberated from servitude to the letter of the law, from the burden of guilt, from dread of death; liberated for life, for a meaning to life, for service, for love. They are people subject to God alone and therefore neither to anonymous powers nor to other human beings.

Where there is no freedom, the Spirit of the Lord is not present. Although it has to be realized in the existence of the individual, this freedom cannot remain merely a moral appeal in the Church (mostly addressed to others). It must have its effect on the formation of the ecclesial community, on its institutions and constitutions, so that these can never have an oppressive or repressive character.

No one in the Church has any right openly or secretly to manipulate, suppress or still less to abolish the basic freedom of the children of God and, instead of the rule of God, to set up the domination of men over men. This freedom should be manifested particularly in the Church in free speech (frankness) and the free choice of action or refraining from action (liberality and magnanimity in the widest sense of the terms); and it should be evident also in the Church's institutions and constitutions. The Church itself should be a *realm of freedom* and at the same time the *advocate of freedom in the world.*

b. *Equality:* In virtue of its freedom given and realized, the Church in great things and in small can and should be a *community of fundamentally equal people,* not equal as a result of leveling down the diversity of their gifts and services, but—despite essential differences—enjoying a fundamental equality of rights. If the Church wants to serve the cause of Jesus Christ, it can never be the Church of a class, race, caste or officials. It is by a free decision that individuals join or remain in the community of faith. Here unequals are to be brought together in a solidarity of love: rich and poor, prominent and obscure, educated and uneducated, white and non-white, men and women. Faith in the crucified Christ cannot and is not meant to abolish all social inequalities: the kingdom of perfect equality is still to come. But this faith can adjust and offset inequalities in society: inequalities of social (master and servant), cultural (Greeks and barbarians) and natural (man and woman) origin. In principle all members of the Church are equal: in principle they have equal rights and equal duties.

In the Church respect of persons should never be a deciding factor, in the body of Christ not even the humblest member should be despised. This fundamental equality, although largely a matter for the individual, may not remain merely a mental attitude in the Church without practical consequences. It must be preserved and protected by the established structures of the ecclesial community, so that these can never be used to aid and abet injustice and exploitation.

No one in the Church has the right to abolish, play down or inter the fundamental equality of believers in a domination of men over men. Such equality should be evident particularly in the Church, so that the person who wants to be foremost or first becomes slave and servant of all. And at the same time the structures of the Church should be established in such a way as to testify to the basic equality of the members. The Church itself should be both a *place of equality of rights* and an *advocate of equality of rights in the world*.

c. *Fraternity:* In virtue of its freedom and equality given and realized, in both great things and small, the Church can and should be a *community of brothers and sisters*. If it wants to serve the cause of Jesus Christ, it can never be a power structure under patriarchal rule. There is only one holy Father here, God himself. All members of the Church are his adult sons and daughters and they are not to be thrust back into tutelage. People in this community may set up only a truly fraternal and not a paternalistic authority. There is only one Lord and Master, Jesus Christ himself, and all members of the Church are brothers and sisters. In this community therefore the supreme norm is not the patriarch, but God's will, the object of which, according to the message of Jesus Christ, is the well-being of men—and indeed of all men.

In the freedom of Christian brotherliness, independence and obligation, power and renunciation, autonomy and service, mastery and servitude are united: an enigma of which the solution is love, whereby master becomes servant and servant master, independence becomes obligation and obligation independence. Even though democratic demands for the greatest possible freedom and the best possible equality are basically mutually opposed, they can be reconciled in a fraternity understood in this way. This brotherliness must be expressed in personal attitudes, but it cannot be produced in the Church by high-sounding appeals to the "spirit" of brotherhood (which often means in practice a spirit of subservience). In particular it must be given effect in the ordinances and social relationships of the ecclesial community, so that these do not alienate people.

No one in the Church has the right to replace this brotherliness by the paternalism and cult of persons which are the marks of a clerical system, thus continuing to promote the domination of men over men. Brotherliness should be evident in both the Church's ordinances and its social relationships and find there its concrete expression. The Church itself should be a *haven of brotherliness* and at the same time *an advocate of brotherliness in the world.*

Charisms, offices, ministries

Liberty, equality and fraternity in the Church therefore by no means imply conformity and uniformity. On the contrary, they positively stimulate pluriformity.

Diverse theologies and life-styles, social tensions and congregational structural problems were present from the beginning and often led to severe conflicts. Parties were constantly emerging.[6] In Jerusalem the "Hebrews" quarreled with the "Hellenists" and in Antioch there were struggles between the champions of a Christianity freed from the law and the upholders of circumcision. Paul implored the different groups at Corinth to maintain harmony and he himself had to deal quite firmly with Judaistic missionaries—for instance—in Galatia. There were then both Jewish and Gentile Christians; there was Paul on the one hand and the Corinthian enthusiasts on the other; besides the distinctively Catholic type of official structures existing at an early date, there was also the group associated with John the Evangelist who were very reserved in their attitude to office in any form.

So too even today the Church will take on a multiplicity of forms. There will not only be a Church with many congregations, but also Churches and congregations with many groups and wings, trends and tendencies, theologies and types of devotion. The only thing that matters is that no group should break off talks with the others and so become a heresy, that partisanship for Jesus Christ should transcend all party formations in the congregation.[7]

Here however we want to pursue only one aspect of pluriformity, which is admittedly decisive for all other aspects. What should be the structure of a congregation if it is to fulfill its mission with mobility and flexibility?

a. *Pluriformity instead of uniformity.* We may take it as obvious from the New Testament that there are innumerable differences on the basis of a fundamental liberty, equality and fraternity—differences not only of persons but also of functions. Inasmuch as there is an indeterminate multiplicity and differentiation of functions, tasks and services, it is misleading to speak in the singular of office in the Church.

Distinctions can be found even in the New Testament. There are the functions of apostles, prophets, teachers, evangelists, admonitors for proclamation. And as auxiliary services there are the functions of deacons and deaconesses, of alms distributers, of those who care for the sick and of the widows who devote themselves to the service of the congregation. And finally for leadership in the community there are the functions of the first fruits,* those who preside, the overseers, the shepherds. Paul—about whose congregations we have by far the most information—sees *all* these functions in the congregation (and not only certain "offices") as gifts of the Spirit, as ways of sharing in the authority of the exalted Lord of the Church: each is a *vocation given by God to a particular ministry in the congregation*—in a word, *charism.*[8]

A charism therefore is

(i) not primarily an extraordinary, but an ordinary phenomenon;

(ii) not a uniform, but a pluriform phenomenon;

(iii) not limited to a particular group of persons, but an absolutely universal phenomenon in the Church.

According to Paul, this means that *every* service which is de facto (permanently or not) performed for the building up of the congregation is a charism, is an *ecclesial* ministry: it deserves therefore to be recognized and given its due place. *Authority* therefore belongs to *every* ministry in its own way, whether official or not, if it is exercised in love for the benefit of the congregation. But how then are unity and order to be secured?

Paul does not expect to get *unity* and *uniformity* in the Church by smoothing out the differences, but by the operation of the one Spirit, bestowing on each one *his* charism (rule: to each his own) which he is to use for the benefit of the others (rule: with one another for one another) and to exercise in subordination under the one Lord (rule: obedience to the Lord).

Two criteria in particular are useful *for discerning the spirits:*

> *Genuine charism binds a person to Jesus and his rule. Anyone who has the Spirit from God confesses Jesus as Lord (this is the distinctive mark of being a Christian);*

* In this connection the first converts in a particular place who then go on to convert and lead others (cf. 1 Corinthians 16:15). (Translator.)

Genuine charism is related to the community. The sign of a true vocation is not a miracle, but service for the benefit of the community. Any kind of ministry in the Church therefore is of its nature dependent on solidarity, on collegial agreement, on discussion among partners, on communication and dialogue.

b. *Ministry instead of office.* Even though different functions are mentioned in the New Testament, there is no systematic discussion anywhere of the problem of office as such in the Church. "Office" is not a biblical term but one that has emerged from later reflection and created its own problems. It is obvious in the New Testament that the secular terms for "office" are deliberately and consistently avoided in connection with functions in the Church: they give expression to a relationship between ruler and subject.[9]

Instead of this another generic term is used which for Paul is frequently synonymous with "charism." This is an absolutely ordinary, non-religious word suggestive of inferiority, which for that very reason cannot awaken any associations with any kind of officialdom, authority, dominion, positions of dignity and power: *diakonia*, "service" (really "waiting at table"). Here obviously Jesus himself had set up a standard which was not to be set aside.[10]

Certainly there is authority in the Church. But authority is legitimate only if it is based on service and not on power brutally or subtly applied, not on old or new prerogatives or privileges which themselves would create an obligation to service. If we want to be exact in our theological terminology, it would be better to speak, not of "office," but of "ministry" in the Church. Not that the term itself counts so much as the way in which it is understood. Even to talk about "service" or "ministry" in the Church may be a form of false humility and may be misused to conceal the true state of affairs, unless at the same time the speaker renounces any exercise of ecclesiastical domination.

Unlike "office" however both the term "ministry" and its content

(i) are grounded in New Testament usage;

(ii) being functional, they are not likely to be misunderstood as referring to institutions;

(iii) even in the literal sense they imply a requirement to serve which in practice can be imposed on any functionary;

(iv) their misuse therefore is easily perceptible.

In this connection it is important to make exact conceptual distinctions both terminologically and theologically:

Power *can be used well or badly. Even in the Church power cannot simply be abolished. But it can be used intelligently in undertaking functions for the well-being of the whole.*

The exercise of power as domination *(by individuals or groups) is somewhat different from the unavoidable exercise of power. It is then a question of maintaining a privileged position or increasing one's own power and utilizing (or manipulating) human beings for personal or institutional ends.*

Exercise of power in the Church can be justified only in virtue of service and must be judged by its character as service. Such power, as it arises from service, is genuine (primarily intrinsic) authority.

There is no opposition therefore between power and service, but only between the exercise of power as domination and the exercise of power as service. Exercise of domination (especially through external power with the use of force in the last resort) is the opposite of service and is an abuse of power.

In the Church at least the term "sacred dominion" ("hierarchy"), introduced at a very late stage by Pseudo-Dionysius, should be abandoned as misleading. And certainly there must be a renunciation of the outward forms of domination.

c. *Ministry of leadership instead of priesthood.* More striking is the fact that in the New Testament, not only are expressions which correspond to "office" avoided, but also—in connection with congregational functions—the word "priest,"[11] understood as sacrificing priest (*hiereus*) as in the history of religions, and all sacral cultic titles; instead, designations of function are borrowed from the secular sphere. The word "priest" is used for Jewish and pagan dignitaries, but never for those who exercise a ministry in the Church. It is only in a late phase of the New Testament—as we have seen[12]—that Jesus himself, risen and exalted, is seen as a "priest." But here the Old Testament priesthood is totally overthrown: as the sole remaining high priest (representative, mediator), offering once and for all the sacrifice of his life, he both fulfills and abolishes all Old Testament priesthood (Hebrews). With the dissolution of the *special* priesthood by the priesthood of the *one* new and eternal high priest there emerges—as a reflection of the outlook of the primitive community[13]—the *universal* priesthood of *all* believers, which has as its concrete content the immediate access of everyone to God, spiritual sacrifices, proclamation of the word, carrying out baptism, eucharist, forgiveness of sins and interceding for one another.

In the light of the New Testament therefore—although we should not argue about words—terms like "priest," "clergyman," "clergy" or "Church" should be avoided as the specific and exclusive designation solely of those who have a ministry in the Church, since the New Testament itself regards all believers as "priests," "clerics," "clergy," "Church." The expression "priestly ministry" too, if it is not used of all Christians but only of certain people who have a ministry in the Church, obscures the real state of affairs in the New Testament. On one occasion only,[14] in connection with *proclamation* (and not with cult), Paul describes himself (and not overseers or presbyters) *figuratively* (and not literally) as a *leitourgos* offering sacrifice (like the pagans). But no conclusion can be drawn from this to justify a New Testament *cultic priesthood* of certain officeholders.

Instead of talking about "priesthood" (official priesthood, ordained priesthood and so on), it would be more correct here to choose functional designations. Even in the New Testament presiders, overseers, deacons, elders, pastors, leaders are mentioned. Some of these originally expressly non-cultic and non-sacral designations (bishops, pastors, presbyters, deacons), together with a number of later titles (*parochus*, for instance), have rightly been maintained up to the present time. If we want a general term for all these ministries, we might use "ministry of leadership" or "ministry of presiding" in the Church, the holder of the ministry being known as "leader" or "presider" (of the congregation, diocese or national Church and so on). It should also be remembered that the English word "priest" (*Priester, prêtre, prete, presbítero*), although traditionally referring to the cultic-sacral *sacerdotium*, stems originally from the non-cultic title of the congregational elder, so that in itself it can be appropriately replaced (as it is in a number of Churches) by "presbyter" or "elder," perhaps by *presbyter parochianus*—that is, "pastor."

The diverse constitutions

Not all ministries in the Church are of equal importance. For a start, a distinction arises in the New Testament itself from the fact that not all ministries or charisms are *permanent and public* congregational ministries. Some charisms—as, for instance, those mentioned by Paul of exhorting, consoling, wise speaking, knowledge, discerning the spirits—are obviously more or less private endowments and virtues bestowed by God, which can be put at the service of others and used as the occasion arises. But other charisms—those of the apostles, prophets, teachers, evangelists, deacons, presiders, overseers, pastors—are public, congregational functions set up by God, which are permanently and regularly carried out. In the former group the New Testament generally names the gift and the effect; in the latter the persons are designated. The titles of the persons can be given because the vocation obviously does not come and go arbitrarily, but remains associated more or less permanently with certain persons, in the sense that these people are "appointed" in the Church as apostles, prophets and so on.

In connection with this second type of *special* charismatic ministries—that is to say, with the structure of the permanent, public congregational ministries—we can speak of the "diaconal structure" of the Church, which represents a particular aspect of the general, basic charismatic dimension of the Church. Not that any importance is to be attached to this terminological distinction. The basic outlines are the really important thing, no matter what the structure is to be called.

a. *The basic apostolate.* According to the New Testament as a whole, among the permanent and public congregational ministries, apostleship has a *church-founding function* and significance for the Church at all times. The apostles (who, as we saw, are not simply identical with the Twelve) are the original witnesses and original messengers who precede all ecclesial ministries, to whom for that very reason the Church as a whole and each individual member remain indebted. As the first witnesses, they proclaimed the message of Christ, founded and led the first Churches and provided for the unity of the Church. On them therefore the Church is built.[15]

The *basic* "apostolic succession" therefore is not succession to certain offices, but that of the Church as a whole and of each and every individual Christian. It must consist in a positive concord with the apostles which is to be continually freshly renewed. What is required is the enduring agreement with the *apostolic testimony* (transmitted to us in the New Testament) and the continual implementation of the *apostolic ministry* (missionary advance into the world and building up of the congregation). Apostolic succession therefore is primarily a succession both in the apostolic faith and confession and in apostolic ministry and life. The question of a *special* succession of the ministries of leadership will be discussed shortly.

b. *Diversity of life-styles.* The model of service set up by Jesus himself was quite clearly defined for the young community of faith, but it could find expression in a great variety of concrete forms. In the light of this *model of Jesus* and on the foundation of the apostles—together with whom, according to Paul, the "prophets" and "teachers" had a special significance for the congregations—the organization of life in the different congregations could develop in very different ways, adapted to the circumstances of time and place.[16] The differences between the Pauline and the Palestinian congregational orders are striking.

As far as we can ascertain, the *congregations founded by Paul himself* with apostolic authority, which remained freely responsible to him as the minister of the Gospel, *set up whatever ministries of order and leadership seemed necessary* for their congregational life. These voluntary congregational ministries acquired an authority which could positively demand subordination. What proved the ministry to be genuine, however, was not the simple fact of possessing a certain function but the form in which the service was carried out. In the unquestionably authentic letters Paul never speaks of ordination or presbyters and obviously knows nothing of any institutionalized office to which a person is first appointed and only then obliged to perform a service. His Churches are communities of free charismatic ministries.

In the long run, especially after the apostle's death, even in the Pauline congregations institutionalization could not be avoided. The fact that very soon after Paul's time, even in the charismatic congregation of Corinth, the system of presbyter-overseers came to prevail—although, as it appears from Clement's first epistle, not without opposition—is *neither an accident nor a lapse*. After the time of the apostolic foundations, characterized by the expectation of Christ's imminent return, came the period of post-apostolic growth and expansion when everything that could help to preserve the original tradition was bound to acquire a special significance: not only the original written testimonies, but also the calling by imposition of hands (ordination) to the Church's ministry of leadership in the service of the apostolic tradition.

In the *Palestinian tradition institutionalization* had set in at a very early stage *as a result of taking over from Judaism the college of elders and ordination*. The Acts of the Apostles and the pastoral letters show that the Pauline congregations had also reached an advanced stage of institutionalization (ordination). Other congregations however (centered around Matthew or John) still exhibit expressly fraternal structures, so that even up to the end of New Testament times there is an immense variety—which cannot be harmonized—of both congregational constitutions and forms of the ministries of leadership (partly charismatic and partly already institutionalized). But the unity of the congregations with each other is maintained. The question however arises: under these circumstances is it still possible to uphold a special "apostolic succession" of the ministries of leadership?

c. *The special apostolic succession*. It *cannot* be maintained historically that the *bishops in a direct and exclusive sense are the successors of the apostles* (still less of the college of the Twelve). But this does not mean that the question of the special succession is settled. From the nature of the case, as the immediate witnesses and first envoys of Jesus Christ, the apostles could not be replaced or represented by any successors. But, even though there could be no new apostles, the apostolic mission and the apostolic ministry remained necessary. As we already observed, these are now undertaken primarily by the whole Church which—as a whole—can and should remain the apostolic Church.

Nevertheless, inasmuch as the ministries of leadership in particular—bishops and presbyters or pastors can be distinguished from each other in terms of law and discipline, but not in terms of theology and dogma—carry on in a special way the *apostolic mission of founding and leading Churches*, based on proclamation of the word, we can rightly speak of a *special apostolic succession in a functional sense* on the part of the manifold ministries of leadership. The *special* "apostolic succession" therefore consists in leading and founding the Churches, and is rooted in the proclamation of the Gospel.

There are however a number of developments which cannot be traced back exegetically and historically to a "divine institution" or an "institution by Jesus Christ," to a divine right (*jus divinum*), but must be seen as part of a long and *problematic historical process*.[17]

(i) Bishops (presbyters), as opposed to prophets, teachers and other charismatic ministries, prevailed as the main and finally as the *sole congregational leaders*. That is to say: the "collegiality" of *all* believers becomes increasingly a collegiality of certain ministerial groups *as distinct from* the congregation, so that a division emerges between "clergy" and "laity."

(ii) The monarchical episcopate of a single bishop, as opposed to a plurality of bishops (presbyters) in the congregations, becomes increasingly prominent. That is to say: the collegiality of the various bishops or presbyters now becomes the collegiality of the one bishop with his presbyters and his deacons, so that the division between "clergy" and "laity" definitively prevails.

(iii) With the spread of the Church from the cities to the country, the bishop, who had formerly presided over the congregation, now comes to *preside over a larger area of the Church*, of a diocese: he is a bishop in the modern sense, for whom the "apostolic succession" is now historicized, formalized and externalized by counting up the series of successions in lists of succession. That is to say: beside the collegiality of bishops with their presbyters, the collegiality of the individual monarchical bishops with each other and then—although only in the West—with the Bishop of Rome becomes increasingly important.

From such a functional and historical standpoint, it is possible to assert a special apostolic succession of the ministries of leadership for leading and founding Churches only if certain assumptions are made:

The Church leaders, as special successors of the apostles, are surrounded in the Church from the outset by the other gifts and ministries: in particular by the successors of the New Testament prophets and teachers who co-operate with the Church leaders in virtue of their own underived authority.

The apostolic succession of Church leaders does not follow automatically or mechanically on the imposition of hands. It presupposes faith and demands a faith which is active in the apostolic spirit. It does not exclude the possibility of failure and error and therefore needs to be tested by the believers as a whole.

The apostolic succession of the Church leaders must take place in the fellowship of mutual service for Church and world. In the light of the New Testament conception of the Church, entry into the apostolic suc-

cession of the ministries of leadership should normally take place—as is possible in the most varied ways—through co-operation on the part of presiders and congregations. Normally (but not exclusively) it could take the form of a calling by the congregational leaders with the participation of the congregation. Both the independent responsibility of the congregational leader in the service of the Gospel and a controlling function exercised in his regard by the congregation must be safeguarded.[18]

In addition to the Pauline or Gentile Christian Church constitutions, other ways of entry into ministry of leadership and apostolic succession must be left open—especially for emergencies. In principle anyone can become a Church leader as a result of a calling by other members of the congregation or in virtue of the spontaneous appearance of a charism for leading or founding a congregation.

The presbyteral-episcopal Church constitution, which de facto*—and rightly—prevailed in the Church in the post-apostolic era, must therefore leave room even today—at least, in principle—for other possibilities which existed in the New Testament Church. This observation has important implications*

for the missions: a valid eucharistic celebration, even without a presbyter, is possible in principle—for instance, in China or South America.

for ecumenism: an acknowledgment of the validity of ministries and sacraments is required even for the Churches whose leaders are not historically within the special "apostolic succession."

for internal Church affairs: an unbiased theological appraisal of oppositional groups which are in conflict with the Church's leaders cannot be refused (validity of ministries and sacraments).

d. *Constants and variables.* The decline into institutional ministry cannot be claimed as normative for the evolution of official structures in the Church, but neither can the change from the original order be regarded in itself as infidelity. The New Testament material reveals diverse types of congregational order and congregational leadership which cannot be related originally to one another, even though they have been amalgamated in the course of time. The New Testament therefore does not permit the canonization of any one congregational constitution. This is by no means simply a privation for the Church. On the contrary, it is a state of affairs which gives the Church freedom to move with the times and to be open to new developments and modifications of ecclesial ministry for the good of men and of the congregations. It is not necessary to imitate the individual New Testament models. But, as long as we claim to be Christian, the essential New Testament factors must be preserved and proved even under quite different conditions.

In the light of the New Testament certain elements are essential for the ministry of leadership. It must be service to the congregation,
according to the standard of Jesus—which permits no relationships of domination—and bound by the original apostolic testimony,
in the midst of a multiplicity of different functions, ministries and charisms.

This evidence from the New Testament enables us to give answers to three questions which are by no means so simple as they might appear to be.[19]

What are the constants *of the Church's ministry of leadership? Besides other ministries, every congregation or Church needs leadership which can be undertaken by individuals or collegially. Its task is public provision for the common cause at the local, regional or universal level: to lead the Christian community continuously in the spirit of Jesus Christ in virtue of a special vocation. That is, to stimulate, to co-ordinate, to integrate the community and to represent it to those outside and in regard to the individual members. This comes about basically through the proclamation of the word, together with the administration of the sacraments and active involvement in congregation and society.*

What are the variables *of the Church's ministry of leadership? The concrete organization of the Church's ministries must be functional in regard to each new situation and therefore flexible. And any particular form which has come into existence historically must be changed if it no longer corresponds to the function of the ministry in question. In the light of the particular tasks, circumstances and personal aptitudes, offices in the Church in each case can be exercised full time or part time, for a period or a lifetime, by men or women, by married or unmarried people, by graduates or non-graduates. The present breakdown of the clerical "state" does not mean a breakdown of the Church's ministry of leadership as a whole.*

What is ordination? *Ordination is a call to office, which is linked with the mission of the Church as a whole and must be understood as a participation in the mission of Christ, traditionally carried out with prayer and the imposition of hands. As distinct from the universal priesthood of believers, it authorizes a person publicly to carry out the one mission of Christ, of which the main tasks are proclamation and the administration of the sacraments. This authority can be exercised in a variety of specialized functions. In the individual case ordination for the person ordained and for the congregation can mean the confirmation of a charism or a calling with the promise of the charism. Whether ordination is to be described as a sacrament or not is a question of terminology.*

One question of the utmost importance and unfortunately more burdensome than any other for the *oikoumene* has however remained open up to now. In addition to all the other ministries of leadership, does Christendom need a universal ministry of leadership, a Pope?

A Petrine ministry?

It is now nine hundred years since the schism between the Eastern and Western Churches and four hundred and fifty since the outbreak of the Protestant Reformation, both involving the papacy. Should it not therefore be possible and even necessary to speak impartially and objectively about this question? In order to clarify the situation, we may first glance briefly back into history and then at the present and the future.[20]

a. *The ambivalence of history*. The services rendered by the Roman primacy to the unity of the Church, to its faith and to Western civilization are beyond question.[21] We can understand how the young Western peoples, at the time of the barbarian invasions, the general breakdown of the political system and the decline of the ancient imperial capital, were infinitely grateful for this ministry of the See of Peter which, almost alone, proved to be a firm rock, intact and unshaken. It needed a Pope Leo to preserve Rome from Attila and Genseric. In the confused and tempestuous times when the new Western community of nations was emerging, the Roman See performed an invaluable service for the young Churches. And this was not merely a cultural service for the preservation of the priceless heritage of antiquity, but also a genuine pastoral service for the building up and maintenance of these Churches, for their liturgy and their Church order. The Catholic Church, both at this time and later, owes it largely to the papacy that it did not simply come under the sway of the state and that it was able to secure its freedom better than other Churches against both the Caesaropapism of the Byzantine emperors and the German princes' proprietorial claims on the Church, as also against modern absolutist and totalitarian systems. All this amounted to a genuine service to the unity of Christendom.

We certainly cannot pass over the undoubted achievements of the Roman primacy for the unity of the Church in late antiquity, the early and late Middle Ages. But neither can we avoid the depressing observation that the expansion of the unified Church, increasingly achieved by means of centralism and absolutism, was purchased at the cost of the *division of Christendom*, which found it more and more difficult to cope with this absolutist system and its abuses. First it was the Orthodox East, then the Protestant North. How sad that these divisions were not avoided by a timely reflection on the origins, such as many people demanded at the time. But this was the very thing that was appreciated only to a limited extent even in the post-Tridentine Church and the Counter-Reformation papacy. The bulwarks of power were not brought down, but extended by every possible means. Admittedly, there were strong countercurrents even within the walls, even in Rome—we need only recall men like Contarini, other cardinals and the Viterbo circle with Michelangelo and Vittoria Colonna. Ancient ideas of the Church's constitution, although in all-too-politicized forms, continued to exercise an influence on the later Gallicans, the Episcopalians and finally in the nineteenth century on the Catholic Tübingen school—particularly on the young J. A. Möhler. But the attitude of the papacy became increasingly stubborn, even though its achievements for the unity and freedom of the Catholic Church—particularly as opposed to state absolutism—remained important.

From the Middle Ages onward and throughout modern times official Catholic ecclesiology (theology of the Church) was a defensive and reactionary theology. It was opposed to early Gallicanism and the French crown jurists and became therefore a theology of hierarchical and especially papal power and a theory of the Church as an organized kingdom. As opposed to conciliar theories, there was a renewed emphasis on the papal primacy. Against the Wycliffite and Hussite spiritual movements, the ecclesiastical and social character of the Christian message was stressed. Against the Reformers, the objective significance of the sacraments, the importance of the hierarchical powers, of the official priesthood, of the episcopal office and again of the primacy were asserted. Against Jansenism as linked with Gallicanism, there was a special emphasis on the papal teaching office. Against the state absolutism of the eighteenth and nineteenth centuries and against laicism, the Church was presented as a "perfect society" equipped with all the rights and means necessary to attain its end. All this led quite logically to the *First Vatican Council* and to its definition of papal primacy and infallibility which took place in 1870 under the influence of anti-Gallican and anti-Liberal attitudes.[22]

Would Vatican II have defined the primacy and infallibility of the Pope if these had not been defined by Vatican I? Unlike Vatican I, Vatican II had no desire for new dogmas, obviously because it was clear—as John XXIII had expressed it—that new definitions of ancient truths were of no use to the Church's proclamation of the faith in the modern world. Finally Vatican II was characterized by an alert sense of community, collegiality, solidarity and service. This awareness contrasted with the underlying mentality of the majority at Vatican I which, understandably enough, was dominated by the political-cultural-religious outlook of the Restoration period, of romantic traditionalism and political absolutism.

b. *The higher legitimacy*. In our context there would be little point in listing all the many objections raised by Protestantism and Eastern Orthodoxy against the biblical and historical arguments for a primacy of jurisdiction and teaching on the part of Peter and the bishops of Rome, objections which have scarcely been satisfactorily answered from the Catholic side. All the difficulties are centered on three questions, each of which presupposes the solution of the one before it. Can a primacy of Peter be justified? Must the primacy of Peter endure? Is the Bishop of Rome the successor to the Petrine primacy?

These are historical questions and we must not take refuge in dogmatic postulates which cannot be historically justified. But, if the vast amount of literature on the subject is anything to go by, it will not be at all easy to deprive these difficulties of their force.[23]

Whatever his attitude, however, even if he finds the Catholic arguments far from convincing, neither the Eastern Orthodox nor the Protestant theologian will dispute the fact that the ministerial primacy of a single individual in the Church is not *a priori* contrary to Scripture. Whatever the value of the arguments which may be adduced in its favor, there is nothing in Scripture to exclude such a ministerial primacy. This sort of primacy therefore is not *a priori* unscriptural. Indeed, the Eastern Orthodox or Protestant theologian could presumably admit even that such a primacy might be in accordance with Scripture, at any rate if it is substantiated, exercised, carried out, treated, in the light of Scripture. Most of the Reformers, from the young Luther by way of Melanchthon to Calvin, admitted this. And many Orthodox and Protestant theologians will also admit it today.

But the important thing about a Petrine ministry or any other ministry of leadership is not the historical evidence of a line of succession. *What really matters* is *succession in spirit:* that is, in the Petrine mission and task, in the Petrine testimony and service. To put it concretely, let us suppose that someone could provide irrefutable proof that his predecessor and the latter's predecessor and so on were "successors" of the one Peter, that he could even prove that the predecessor of a long line of his predecessors had been "appointed" by Peter himself as his successor with all his rights and duties. If such a person did not carry out this Petrine mission, did not fulfill his appointed task, did not give testimony or perform his service, what would be the use of the entire "apostolic succession" to him or to the Church? On the other hand, suppose there were someone whose ministry it was difficult to link with its source in the earliest period, since there could be no check on "appointments" made but not recorded two thousand years ago. If this other person lived up to the Petrine mission as described in Scripture, if he fulfilled mandate and task and performed this service to the Church, would it not then be a secondary—although still important—question whether the "genealogy" of this authentic servant of the Church was in order? Perhaps he would then not have an irreproachable line of succession, but he would have the charism of leadership (*kyberneseis*) and this would basically suffice.

Thus the important thing is not the claim, the "right," the "chain of succession," as such, but *the accomplishment, the exercise, the action, the service itself concretely realized.* When John XXIII took the great ecumenical initiatives for the Catholic Church, Christendom and the world, people were not very interested in his place in the chain of succession or whether he could furnish historical evidence of the legitimacy of his office. They were only too glad and relieved to see someone who—despite all human weaknesses—acted at this time as a true "rock," who could give support and a new integrity to Christendom.[24] Here was someone who was able in virtue of his strong faith "to strengthen and encourage his brethren."[25] Here was one who wanted to "guard the sheep," like his Lord, with unselfish love.[26] This did not lead everybody to become Catholic. But people felt spontaneously that this action and this spirit had *behind them the Gospel of Jesus Christ* and in any case were justified by that Gospel. And this legitimacy is higher than any other for the Petrine ministry.

c. *Petrine power and Petrine ministry.* This is not to say that discussion of the exegetical and historical questions is superfluous. But it should be seen from the proper angle, be put in the right perspective. The rocklike and pastoral function of the Petrine ministry exists, according to the Catholic view, precisely to preserve and strengthen the unity of the Church. Yet it has become an immense blockage—apparently immovable, unsurmountable, unavoidable—in the way of a mutual understanding between the Christian Churches. Even after the Second Vatican Council the blockage remains. This is an absurd situation which must provide abundant food for thought for anyone who is convinced of the advantage of a Petrine ministry. How could things have reached this stage? Is it simply the result of a lack of knowledge, an immature understanding or even a malicious obstinacy on the part of opponents of a Petrine ministry? No one will venture to assert this today. And even though we cannot by any means regard the guilt for the division of the Churches as being all on one side, we cannot avoid the question: Did not the distortion of the functions of the Petrine ministry come about also, and particularly, because this *Petrine ministry*—for a variety of historical reasons and certainly not because of the evil will of one or several individuals—was presented to men increasingly as *Petrine power?* It was a long process which turned the papacy into a world power and an absolutist ecclesiastical power.

It might have been otherwise. Whatever may be the exegetical and historical arguments, the divine or human authorization, for a permanent Petrine ministry in the Church, it would indeed have been possible—and the atmosphere in the pre-Constantinian era was certainly favorable to such a conception—for the Roman community with its bishop, endowed in fact with quite extraordinary gifts and possibilities of service, to have striven for a truly *pastoral primacy of spiritual responsibility, of moral guidance and active provision for the welfare of the Church as a whole.* It would then have qualified as a universal court of appeal in the Church, to mediate and arbitrate at the highest level. This would have been a primacy, not of domination, but of unselfish service, responsible to the Lord of the Church and acting in a spirit of humble brotherliness. A primacy, not in the spirit of Roman imperialism dressed up as religion, but in the spirit of Jesus Christ.

The question now thrust upon us, in view of the lost unity of Christ's Church and the frequent rigidity within the Catholic Church, is that of the future: is there a *way back* from this primacy of domination and—for that very reason—*forward* to the ancient primacy of service?

It is clear from history that the high points of papal power were always followed by periods of outward humiliation and restriction of power. But a *voluntary renunciation of spiritual power* is also possible. What seems politically unreasonable—even in terms of Church politics—may be required in the Church if it is to follow the example of Jesus. Surprisingly enough this sort of thing really does happen and it is a great sign of hope. Otherwise—leaving aside Hadrian VI or Marcellus II who made little impact on history, either because the time was not opportune or because of their early deaths—it would not have been possible for a Gregory the Great or again a John XXII to have arisen after a series of very power-conscious popes, or for Vatican II to have come after Vatican I.

Without the renunciation of "spiritual" power neither a reunion of the separated Christian Churches nor a radical renewal of the Catholic Church in the light of the Gospel is possible. There is nothing natural about the renunciation of power. Why should a person, an authority, an institution, give up something it already possesses without being assured of anything in return? Renunciation of power is in fact possible only for someone who has grasped something of the message of Jesus and the Sermon on the Mount. But even a brief reflection on that Peter on whose succession Rome sets so much store could be helpful.

d. *Three temptations.*[27] Would the real Peter have recognized himself in the picture built up of him in Rome? He was no prince of the apostles, but to the end of his life the modest fisherman, now a fisher of men, who wanted to serve in imitation of his Lord. But beyond that, as all the Gospels agree, he had another side which constantly displays the erring, sinning, failing and for that very reason human Peter. It seems almost scandalous that each of the three classical texts in Matthew, Luke and John, pointing to Peter's pre-eminence, should be followed immediately by a harsh reprimand in sharp contrast to the serene promise and providing at least a counterbalance to it. To the three lofty promises there correspond three profound lapses. And anyone who lays claim to the promises cannot avoid applying to himself also the three lapses, which for him anyway represent three temptations. The three promises in huge black letters against a gold background, surrounding the whole Church of St. Peter like a frieze, ought really to be complemented by the contrasting propositions in golden letters against a black background, if they are not to be misunderstood. Would not Gregory the Great, who is buried in this church, have appreciated the point as much as John XXIII?

The first temptation, according to Matthew,[28] was to place himself above his Lord, taking the Master on one side with an air of superiority, claiming to know better what was really to be done and how things would turn out, suggesting a way of triumphalism which would bypass the way of the cross. And these very brain waves of someone who thinks he knows better, these ideas of a *theologia gloriae*, are in fact human ideas which are directly opposed to what God thinks and wills: a pious *theologia satanae*, a theology of the Tempter par excellence. Whenever Peter simply takes it for granted that he is thinking God's thoughts, whenever—perhaps without noticing it—he ceases to confess his faith and begins to misunderstand and takes man's side instead of God's, then the Lord turns away from him and the harsh words strike him: "Get behind me, Satan! You are a scandal to me, for your thoughts are not those of God, but those of man."

The second temptation, according to Luke,[29] shows that special responsibility goes with a special position and special gifts, but that none of these things excludes trial and temptation. Here too Satan appears, determined to sift Jesus' disciples like wheat. Peter's faith is not to waver, but as soon as he becomes self-confident and assumes that his loyalty is unquestionable, his faith an infallibly secure possession, as soon as he forgets that he is dependent on the prayer of the Lord and must continually receive faith and loyalty as new gifts, as soon as he pretends that his readiness and his commitment are his own achievement, as soon therefore as he self-confidently overestimates himself and no longer places all his trust in the Lord, then the hour of cock-crow and denial is at hand: he no longer knows his Lord, he is capable of denying him, not once only, but three times—that is, completely: "The cock will not crow before you have denied three times that you know me."

The third temptation, according to John,[30] is linked with the request for Peter's love. Peter, the man who denied his Lord three times, is asked three times for his love: "Do you love me more than these?" Only in this way, only under this condition, will the leadership of the community be committed to him. He guards the lambs and feeds the sheep by following Jesus in love. But, instead of looking at Jesus, Peter turns round, sees the man whose love has always surpassed his own, and asks the irrelevant question as to that man's position and what is to happen to him. He then gets the answer, which seems to contradict his universal pastoral mandate: "What is that to you?" There are some things then that are no concern of Peter's. Whenever Peter is unwilling to cope with his own limited task, whenever he does not see that there are those whose fate he cannot decide, whenever he forgets that there are special relationships to Jesus in which he has no part, whenever he is unwilling to tolerate other ways besides his own, then he has to hear the word that must strike him harshly, but also calls him once again to follow Jesus: "What is that to you? Follow me!"

The greatness of the temptation corresponds to the greatness of the mission. Who could measure the enormous burden of responsibility, care, suffering and anguish which lies on the Petrine ministry if its holder *really* wants to be rock, really key-bearer, really shepherd at the service of the Church as a whole. For the time is long past when Leo X, contemporary of Luther, could talk about enjoying the papacy as a gift of God. In all the toil and tribulation involved in this ministry, in all the feeling of being misunderstood and in all the holder's awareness of his unsuitability, how often faith will be inclined to waver,[31] love to fail,[32] the hope of overcoming the gates of the underworld to fade.[33] This ministry more than any other is thrown back on the grace of the Lord. This ministry may also expect much from the brethren, more than is often given and more in a form that can be helpful: not servile obsequiousness, not uncritical devotion, not sentimental adoration, but daily intercession, loyal co-operation, constructive criticism, sincere love.

Perhaps the Eastern Orthodox or Protestant Christian will be able to sympathize a little with the Catholic in his conviction that something would be lacking in his Church and perhaps in Christendom as a whole if this Petrine ministry were suddenly to disappear: something that is not inessential to the Church.[34] How much it could mean for Christendom if this ministry were freshly understood dispassionately and unsentimentally in the light of Holy Scripture as what it ought to be: service to the Church as a whole. The complete biblical meaning of service cannot be confined within the legal categories of Vatican I.

> *This ministerial primacy is more than an honorary primacy* (primatus honoris), *which no one can bestow in a Church of service and which—being passive—can be of no use to anybody.*
>
> *This ministerial primacy is more than a primacy of jurisdiction* (primatus jurisdictionis) *which, understood as pure force and power, if it does not deny the essential thing—which is service—at least passes over it in silence.*
>
> *The Petrine ministry is rightly described in biblical terms as ministerial primacy in the whole Church, as pastoral primacy* (primatus servitii, primatus ministerialis, primatus pastoralis *at the service of the Church for the cause of Jesus Christ.*[35]

e. *No party programs.*[36] No one today knows what the Petrine ministry, the diaconal structure of the Church as a whole, or finally the reunion of the divided Churches will look like in the future. The present generation is charged with doing whatever is within its power. In this respect, it must be pointed out finally that each Church in virtue of its history has its own peculiarities which are not accepted in the same way by others: each has, so to speak, its "speciality." These "specialities" however are of varying importance. The Catholic "speciality" of course is the Pope. But Catholics are not alone in this. The Eastern Orthodox also have their "Pope": this is "tradition." For Protestants it is the "Bible." And finally "freedom" for the Free Churches. But as the "papacy" of the Catholics is not simply the Petrine ministry of the New Testament, neither is the "tradition" of the Orthodox simply the apostolic tradition, nor the "Bible" of the Protestants simply the Gospel, nor the "freedom" of the Free Churches simply the freedom of the children of God. Even the best password is misused if it becomes a *party program* with which men march out to fight for power in the Church. A party program which is often linked with the name of a leader. A party program which necessarily excludes others from their own Church.

In Corinth too there were parties from the very beginning. Each had its program—we do not know the details—which was attached to a leader whom they acclaimed and exalted above the others, thereby denying authority to the others: "For it has been reported to me, brothers, by Chloe's people, that there are disputes among you. What I mean is that each of you says: 'I am for Paul,' 'I am for Apollos,' 'I for Cephas,' 'I for Christ.' "[37]

If we were to permit ourselves an anachronism here, we should undoubtedly identify the Catholics with the party of Cephas, which would in any case be right as against all the rest in virtue of his primacy, his power over the keys and his pastoral power. The Eastern Orthodox would be the party of Apollos, explaining revelation in the light of the great tradition of Greek thought more spiritually, more thoughtfully, more profoundly and even "more correctly" than all the others. The Protestants would certainly be the party of Paul, who is in fact the father of their community, the apostle par excellence, the unique preacher of the cross of Christ, who labored more than all the other apostles. Finally the Free Churches would be the party of Christ himself, free from all the constraints of the other Churches, their authorities and confessions, relying solely on Christ as the one Lord and Master and in the light of this developing the fraternal life of their congregations.

And for whom did Paul decide? Surely for Peter, for Cephas is the rock on which the Church is built. But Paul passes over Peter's name in silence and tactfully omits also that of Apollos. Surprisingly enough, he even disowns his own party supporters. He will not have groups dependent on a human being and making a program out of a man who was not crucified for them, in whose name they are not baptized. Paul brought baptism to the Corinthians. They were not however baptized in his name, but in the name of the crucified Christ, and they also belong to him in whose name they are baptized. And for that reason even the name of Paul, who founded their Church, cannot become the name of a party.

It is clear that the (important) Petrine ministry may indeed be a "rock" for the Church, for its unity and cohesion; but it must not become the sole criterion for identifying the Church. Tradition (still more important) may be an excellent guideline for the Church, for its continuity and steadfastness; but it must not become a dividing line with "orthodoxy" all on one side and heterodoxy all on the other. The Bible (most important of all) may certainly be the "foundation" for the Church, for its faith and confession; but it must not become a quarry providing stones more for throwing than for building up. And that is not the end of it. The problem is not solved by invoking Christ directly, instead of the apostles. This would invite the question: "Is Christ divided?"[38] Christ the Lord must not be made to serve as the banner of a party which wants to launch an attack on others in one and the same Church.

The Bible as basic, liberating message, tradition as the faithful transmission of the original testimony, the Petrine ministry as unselfish pastoral service to the Church, the free assembly of the brethren under the guidance of the Spirit: all this is good if it is not understood in an exclusive sense, not turned against others, if it is at the service of the cause of Jesus Christ, who is and remains Lord over the Church and all that belongs to it. In the last resort no Church can pass judgment on itself. Each must pass through the Lord's testing fire. This will bring to light how much of its special character, its special tradition and its special teaching is wood, hay and straw, and how much is gold, silver and precious stones, what perishes as worthless and what will be perserved as of proven worth.[39]

4. *The great mandate*

Considered in this way, however, it is difficult to see where the differences lie between the Churches, particularly between the Catholic Church and the Protestant Churches. What do "Catholic" and "Protestant" really mean today?

Catholic-Protestant

From all that has been said up to now it is clear that the differences today are not the traditional doctrinal differences: for instance, in regard to Scripture and tradition, sin and grace, faith and works, eucharist and priesthood, Pope and Church. On all these specific issues a theoretical agreement is at least possible or has already been attained. All that is required is for the Church's machinery to put the theological conclusions into practice. The essential difference lies in traditional basic attitudes, which have developed since the Reformation, but which today can be overcome in their one-sidedness and integrated into true ecumenicity.

> *"Catholic" as a basic attitude means that special importance is attached to the Catholic—that is, to the* entire, *universal, all-encompassing, total —Church. In the concrete, to the* continuity *in time of faith and the community of faith enduring in all disruptions (tradition) and to the* universality *in space of faith and the community of faith embracing all groups (against "Protestant" radicalism and particularism, which are not to be confused with evangelical radicality and congregational attachment).*
>
> *"Protestant" as a basic attitude means that in all traditions, doctrines and practices of the Church special importance is attached to constant, critical recourse to the* Gospel *(Scripture) and to constant practical* reform *according to the norm of the Gospel (against "Catholic" traditionalism and syncretism, which are not to be confused with Catholic tradition and breadth of vision).*
>
> *And yet, correctly understood, "Catholic" and "Protestant" basic attitudes* are by no means mutually exclusive. *Today even the "born" Catholic can be truly Protestant in his outlook and even the "born" Protestant truly Catholic, so that even now in the whole world there are innumerable Christians who—despite the obstructions of the Church's machinery—do in fact live out an* evangelical Catholicity *centered on the Gospel or a* Catholic evangelicity *maintaining a Catholic breadth of vision: in a word, they realize a genuine* ecumenicity. *In this way a Christian today can be such in the fullest sense, without denying his own denominational past but also without obstructing a better ecumenical future. Being truly a Christian today means being an ecumenical Christian.*[1]

What should be the concern of the Church, of all the Churches? As we have seen from the beginning, essentially one thing only: the *cause of Jesus Christ*. And this means, as we now know, everything in one: God's cause and for that very reason man's cause, God's will and for that very reason man's total well-being.

The cause of Jesus Christ—this is the great *mandate* of the community of faith: critically and constructively, in theory and practice, to show Jesus to the individual and society as the criterion with all that he means for present and future. By proclaiming the message of Jesus as the model, the Lord, *the Church takes up Jesus' message of the rule of God in a concentrated form*. With the slogan "Jesus the Lord" it proclaims—or should proclaim—the same radical requirements which Jesus proclaimed with the slogan "kingdom of God" and fulfilled in an exemplary way to the very end. The Church is not the kingdom of God, but it is—or should be—*spokesman and witness* for the kingdom of God.

The Church is a *credible* spokesman and witness only if it tells Jesus' message first of all, not to others, but to itself, and at the same time does not merely preach but also fulfills Jesus' requirements. Like other "founder religions," Christianity has been accused of getting away from hard, absolutely faithful discipleship in its second phase by deifying its founder, thus making religion easier for the masses and acquiring absolute authority for itself: the Church is relieved of its burdens and exalted by the deification of Jesus. There is no doubt that it is easier to say "Lord, Lord" than "to do the will of the Father."[2] But cultic veneration and adoration can never replace the imitation of Christ in living discipleship. The Church as community of faith is living discipleship or it is not the Church of Jesus Christ. The cause of Jesus Christ is not only the reason and ground of the Church's existence, it is also God's judgment on the Church. The Church's whole credibility—and what is the use of preaching and organizing, of all rights, privileges and church collections, if it is not credible?—depends on its *fidelity to Jesus and his cause.* In this sense none of the present-day Churches—including the Catholic Church—is automatically and in every respect identical with the Church of Jesus Christ, still less is it the "still living Christ."[3] A Church is identical with the Church of Jesus Christ only to the extent that it keeps faith with Jesus and his cause.

Despite the distance in time, the Church is faced with the same religio-social basic positions and basic options, involved *in the same quadrilateral choice* between establishment, revolution, retreat and compromise, in which Jesus was involved. And it should find its bearings in the light of these orientation points. He remains then the authoritative standard: the Christological indicatives become the ecclesiological imperatives. A brief clarification of these points may be helpful.[4]

Provisional Church

Unlike the advocates of the religio-political establishment of his time, *Jesus* proclaims not only the permanent rule of God existing from the dawn of creation (as the Jerusalem hierarchs did) but the coming kingdom of God of the end-time. If the *Church* as community of faith following Jesus Christ wants to proclaim the coming kingdom of God, *it must face certain obligations.*

In these days the Church may never make itself the content of the proclamation, may never publicize itself. It must point away from itself to the presence of God which has already dawned in the living Jesus, which it also awaits as the critical consummation of its mission. Thus it is still only moving toward the universal and definitive revelation of God in the world. It may not therefore claim to be an end in itself, as if it could ever be a factor revolving around itself. As if man's basic decisions were related not primarily to God and his Christ, but to the Church and its announcements. As if *it* were the end and consummation of world history, the definitive reality. As if *its* definitions and declarations and not the word of the Lord remained forever. As if *its* institutions and constitutions and not God's rule outlasted all time. As if it were ever permitted to work with all methods of secular power politics, strategy and intrigue. As if, as a religious establishment, it could be permitted to indulge in secular pomp and display, to grant honorific titles and places of honor to right and left, pointlessly to heap up money and possessions beyond what is necessary. As if men had to exist for the Church and not the Church for men and, for that very reason, for God's cause.

A Church which forgets that it is something temporary, provisional, interim, celebrating victories which are really defeats, is overtaxed and must retire, since it has no genuine future. A Church however which remembers that it will find its end, not in itself, but in God's kingdom, can hold out through all historical upheavals. It knows that it has no need to construct a definitive system nor to offer a lasting home; being provisional, it also knows better than to be surprised when tempted by doubts, held back by obstacles, burdened with problems. If indeed it were the definitive reality, despair would be inevitable. But if it is merely provisional, hope may be sustained. The promise has been given that it will not be overcome by the "gates of hell."

Serving Church

Unlike the advocates of political revolution in his time, *Jesus* did not proclaim a religio-political theocracy or democracy to be established by force (as the Zealot revolutionaries did), but the direct, unrestricted world rule of God himself, to be awaited without violence but not inactively. If the Church as community of faith following Jesus Christ wants to proclaim this direct, unrestricted world rule of God, to be awaited without violence, then it *must accept a number of obligations*.

In these days the Church cannot want to strive either by revolution or evolution, openly or secretly, for a religio-political theocracy or any kind of seizure of power. Its vocation is active *diakonia* in every form. Instead of setting up an "empire" of spiritual-unspiritual power, it has the opportunity of exercising an unconstrained and non-violent "ministry." This it does by intervening constantly and effectively for the socially neglected or ostracized groups, for all despised, downtrodden, abandoned people in the world, and yet at the same time noting without prejudice the concerns of the ruling classes. How then could it set up new barriers (mental, ideological, denominational) to communication instead of breaking down the old, preach disorder and divide people into friends or enemies instead of preaching peace and justice? How could it fail to help men to control their defense-mechanisms, to abandon the roles they have adopted, to give way to one another, to understand one another? How could it link up with one power or another against other men? How identify itself *a priori* with any kind of secular party-political grouping, a cultural organization, an economic or social power group? How could it uncritically and unconditionally support a particular economic, social, cultural, political, philosophical or ideological system? On the other hand, how could it fail by its radical message constantly to upset, estrange, disturb, question all secular powers, parties, groupings, systems, and for that very reason have to face also their resistance and attack? How could it avoid suffering, contempt, calumny and even persecution, and choose the easy way of triumphalism instead of the way of the cross? In all this how could it regard outsiders always as its enemies to be hated and destroyed and not attempt to take them seriously as neighbors to be understood, borne with, spared, encouraged?

A Church must not overlook the fact that it exists for unselfish, active service to society, to individuals and groups and even to its opponents. If it does so, it loses its dignity, its claim and the reason for its existence, since it abandons discipleship. But if a Church remains aware of the fact that what is to come is not itself, but God's kingdom, "in power and glory," if it finds its true greatness in its littleness, then it knows that it is great precisely without display of power and application of force. It knows that it can rely only in a very relative sense and to a limited extent on the agreement and support of the influential people, that its existence is constantly ignored, neglected and merely tolerated or even deplored, blamed or wished out of the way by society. It knows that its activities are constantly ridiculed, suspected, disapproved and suppressed, but also that God's power rules unassailably over all other powers and can itself be actively effecting salvation among the nations and in the hearts of men. Indeed, if its strength had to lie in worldly power, the Church would be lost in the world. But if its strength lies in the cross of the risen Christ, then its weakness is its strength, and it can go on its way without fear of losing its identity. The promise has been made that, if it gives up its life, it will gain it.

Guilty Church

Unlike the advocates of a retreat from the world, *Jesus* does not proclaim an avenging judgment in favor only of an elite of the perfect (as the Essenes and the Qumran monks did), but the glad tidings of God's infinite goodness and unconditional grace for the abandoned and needy. If the *Church* as community of faith following Jesus Christ wants to proclaim the good news of this infinite goodness and unconditional grace, *it must again recognize its obligations.*

In these days, despite its opposition to the world and its powers, the Church must never appear to be an institution of threats and intimidation, preaching disaster and creating fear. It is there to announce the good news, not to issue threats; to spread joy in God, not to create a dread of God. For the Church exists not only for those whose religion and morals are irreproachable, but also for the moral failures, the irreligious and those who are ungodly for a variety of reasons. It should not condemn or anathematize, but—without ignoring the serious judicial implications of the message—should heal, pardon, save, and then leave the judgment to God. Exhortations and warnings are often unavoidable, but they should not be an end in themselves and they should point to God's merciful benevolence and to man's true humanity. Despite all the promises, it can never pose as a self-righteous caste or class of the pure, the holy, as an elite of the morally upright. Nor may it shut itself off from the world in a spirit of asceticism and delude itself that whatever is evil, unholy, ungodly, is outside. For there is nothing about the Church which is perfect, which is not imperiled, fragile, questionable, which is not constantly in need of correction, reform and renewal. The front between the world and God's rule, between good and evil, runs right through the Church, right through the heart of the individual.

A Church which will not accept the fact that it consists of sinful men and exists for sinful men becomes hardhearted, self-righteous, inhuman. It deserves neither God's mercy nor men's trust. But if a Church with a history of fidelity and infidelity, of knowledge and error, takes seriously the fact that it is only in God's kingdom that the wheat is separated from the tares, good fish from bad, sheep from goats, a holiness will be acknowledged in it by grace which it cannot create for itself. Such a Church is then aware that it has no need to present a spectacle of higher morality to society, as if everything in it were ordered for the best. It is aware that its faith is weak, its knowledge dim, its profession of faith halting, that there is not a single sin or failing of which it has not in one way or another been guilty. And though it is true that the Church must always dissociate itself from sin, it can never have any excuse for keeping any sinners at a distance. If the Church self-righteously remains aloof from failures, irreligious and immoral people, it cannot enter justified into God's kingdom. But if it is constantly aware of its guilt and sin, it can live in the joyous assurance of forgiveness. The promise has been given to it that anyone who humbles himself will be exalted.

Determined Church

Unlike the advocates of moral compromise in his time, *Jesus* does not proclaim a kingdom to be built up by exact observance of the law and a higher morality (as the Pharisees did), but the kingdom to be created by God's free act. If the *Church* as community of faith following Jesus Christ wants to proclaim this kingdom to be created by God, *it must be aware of the obligations involved.*

In these days it must not be concerned primarily with the observance of ritual, disciplinary and moral regulations, but with men being able to live and receive from one another what they need in order to live. In a time of excessive social and economic pressure for results, it may certainly not write off those who have failed to meet the various demands or dismiss the moral failures, as if they were forsaken by God, but must proclaim particularly to them the closeness of that God who is not primarily concerned with results. As community of faith, for all its involvement in day-to-day Church affairs and in society, it must not itself fall into the temptation of trusting in its own achievements and not in God. Nothing must be allowed to restrain the Church from a decision and firm commitment, made in faith and trust, for God and his kingdom. It will itself constantly have to turn away in a radical conversion from its own selfish interests and—for the sake of the coming kingdom of God—to turn to men with love: not in flight from the world, but in work on the world.

The Church cannot dispense itself from this radical obedience to God's will which has as its object the total well-being of man. It could not make up for obedience to God by obedience to itself, its own liturgical, dogmatic and juridical laws and prescriptions, traditions and customs. It could never declare time-conditioned social conventions, moral constraints, sexual taboos to be eternal norms and then adapt them to each new age with the aid of artificial and forced interpretations. When it comes to the great questions of peace and war, the welfare of the masses, classes, races and successive generations, the Church may not "swallow camels" while "straining out gnats" in its application of petty moral casuistry to secondary dogmatic and moral (most often sexual) questions. This would mean laying on men's shoulders the burden of innumerable commandments and prohibitions which they could not bear. The Church is not there to demand blind obedience in a spirit of fear, not as a result of understanding and approving the requirement but only because it is commanded and because people would act otherwise if it were not commanded. Obedience must be a responsible, justifiable obedience, based on love of God. The Church must never give the impression of preferring external legality to internal dispositions, the "tradition of the elders" to the "signs of the times," lip service to purity of heart, "commandments of men" to the absolute and uncurtailed will of God.

The Church which forgets to whom it owes obedience, which seizes power for itself and makes itself sovereign, becomes shut up within itself. But if—despite all its failures—the Church remains always intent on the kingdom coming through God's act and remembers to whom it belongs, for whom it has decided and must again and again uncompromisingly and unreservedly decide, it becomes truly free: free in imitating Christ in service to the world, free for the service of men in which it serves God and free for the service of God in which it serves men. It becomes free even for the conquest of suffering, sin and death, in the power of the cross of the living Jesus. It is free for the all-embracing creative love which does not merely explain but even now transforms the broken world in virtue of unshakable hope in the coming kingdom of complete justice, of eternal life, of true freedom, of endless love and of future peace; hope in the removal of all estrangement and in the final reconciliation of mankind with God. If then the Church, unfaithful to its mission, becomes involved in the world or too much concerned with itself, it makes men unhappy, wretched, enslaved. But if in its checkered history it clings constantly to God as its origin, its support and its goal, then it has an amazing way of making the unfree free, the sorrowful glad, the poor rich, the wretched hopeful, the unloving ready to help. The promise has been made that, if it is prepared and remains prepared, God himself will make *all things new* and be all in all.

Thus the close of this third main section has brought us back to its opening. On the long road we have traveled it should have become clear, intelligible and vivid what the Christian program is in the light of the fourfold choice in Jesus' own time and today. The content of what was outlined in the second main part on the distinguishing feature of Christianity has now been filled in. The Christian program is no other than this Christ Jesus himself with all that he means for the life and action, suffering and death of men and of humanity. Obviously many questions remain. But now only one of them matters: what has been made of the program in practice? Or, perhaps better: what is to be made of it in practice?

D. PRACTICE

The title of this section could be misleading. It might give the impression that we had not hitherto been concerned with practice. But to what are we to trace the whole Christian program if not to the practice (proclamation, conduct, suffering, dying) of this Christ? And to what is this whole Christian program oriented if not to the practice (living, acting, suffering, dying) of man in imitation of this Christ? So even before this we were concerned with the "theory" behind a certain practice. It is this practice which is now to be explained and given a definite outline—as well as possible within a brief space—for man and society at the present time. In what form is the Christian program to be realized and carried out today? This is the reason for the title of "Practice."

Even today, in both great things and small, in both the private and the social sphere, Jesus of Nazareth still affects in a quite practical way the expectations and habits, attitudes and decisions, requirements and finances of a not inconsiderable part of the world's population. The figure of Jesus of Nazareth is effective through all ages, in all camps and continents, significant for all who are involved in the history and fate of mankind and who are working for a better future. It sometimes seems as if Jesus were more popular outside than inside the Church and its government, where in practice dogma and canon law, politics and diplomacy—most of all, politics and diplomacy—frequently play a greater part than he does. "Here no one ever asks what Jesus did and said. The question of Jesus is so alien in this context that it would seem downright absurd to most people." This is the opinion of a member of the Roman Curia for many years on the Vatican, and he did not speak only for himself.[1] Does the question of Jesus play a greater part in other centers of ecclesiastical power or even sometimes of learning? In any case the diplomatic strategists and ecclesiastical politicians, the ecclesiastical bureaucrats and managers, the administrators, inquisitors and court theologians who conform to the system, are not to be found only in the Vatican, nor even only in the Catholic Church.

I. The Practice of the Church

Turning from the Christian program as worked out in our third main section to its realization, to Christian practice, from the message of Jesus Christ particularly to the Churches of the present time, even the Christian who is a committed member of the Church cannot avoid the question of whether the Church—and we are speaking here always of all Churches—has not in practice strayed a long way from the Christian program. Is this not the reason why many people decide for God and Jesus without being able to decide for the Church, for any Church?

1. *Decision for faith*

There are people, often with a religious education, who in practice never think of God for years and then discover—sometimes in very odd ways—that God could mean much, could even be decisive, not only at death, but for their life here and now. And there are people, put off or left cold by the dogmatisms and "fairy stories" of the Church's instruction, who for many years make nothing of Jesus in his mythological framework and then —again frequently in odd ways—reach the conclusion that he might mean much and even be decisive for their understanding of man, the world and God, for their existence, action and suffering. The decision for or against Jesus, for or against being a Christian, must be faced here before we turn —again quite practically—to the question of the Church.

A personal decision

If anyone takes even a little trouble to come to grips with the figure of Jesus, he will find that it faces him with a challenge. And if anyone has consistently attempted to follow our thought up to now, he might have learned how arguments centered on this figure turned naturally into appeals, how both brain and heart were involved. The enthusiasm inspired by the subject itself could not be wholly concealed. Not only—as intended—[2] did the characteristic basic features and outlines of Jesus' proclamation, conduct and fate become clear. On almost every page of this dispassionate, critical inventory the pressing consequences for one's own life have become palpable. Is this not sufficient for practice? In the theological sense is any more required? Fundamentally, what has been said is sufficient. Nevertheless, in view of the immense amount of material and the difficult and complex problems involved here, it may not be superfluous to outline a practical program for Christians to apply to the needs of the present time.

Here first of all, to effect the transition, are some preliminary thoughts which may summarize what has been said and provide a basis for what follows. All previous explanations of the Christian program have made clear *why* this Jesus in particular ought to be the standard for me. But *whether* he is in fact to be the model for me is a wholly personal question. It will depend on my wholly personal decision. No Church, no Pope, no Bible, no dogma, nor any pious assurance, any devout profession of faith, any testimony of another person, and not even any theological reflection—however serious—can extort an answer or a decision from me; it cannot even simply relieve me of the burden of answering or deciding. Ultimately the decision is made in complete freedom between him and me, without any intermediate agencies.

And, as we may recall,[8] theological study does not solve any problems of decision. It can only define the scope and the limits within which an answer is possible and appropriate. It can remove impediments, clarify prejudices, bring to a head the crisis of unbelief and superstition, arouse good will, set in motion what may turn out to be a time-consuming process of decision-making. It can examine whether an assent is not unreasonable, not too much to expect, whether it is the result of reflection and argument and therefore whether I can justify it in my own eyes or in those of others. It can help to guide the process of decision-making in a rational way. All this however must not be allowed to destroy free consent, but can and should stimulate it and to some extent even "cultivate" it.

In the last resort therefore man can say "No" to Jesus and nothing in the world can prevent him from doing this. He can find the New Testament interesting, beautiful, readable, edifying; he can call the man of Nazareth sympathetic, fascinating, moving, even a true Son of God—and yet get on without him in his daily life. But he can also attempt to organize his daily activities, his life, unobtrusively and yet decisively in the spirit of Jesus, can make Jesus his guideline in all his all-too-human humanity. This is not of course because he has been convinced by a conclusive argument. It is because of a trust completely freely bestowed, even though mostly conveyed by trusting and trustworthy men. Why is this? Because in these words and deeds, this life and death, man is able gradually to detect something more than merely an utterly human reality; because in all this he can perceive a sign of God and an invitation to faith and can say

"Yes" with complete freedom and yet with complete conviction. He has no mathematically certain proofs, but he is not without very good reasons. His trust is not blind, but it is not based on clearly established evidence; it is an understanding, absolute trust and thus absolutely certain. This is the faith of a free Christian man, so like love and often passing into love.

It does not however amount to a "No" of unbelief when someone doubts if one or a number of "salvific facts," attested in the New Testament, really took place. Not everything recorded actually happened, nor did it always happen in the way described. There is a "No" of unbelief if someone evades what is ultimately a clearly recognized claim of God in Jesus, if he refuses the clearly demanded acknowledgment of him and his message and is not prepared to see in Jesus God's sign, word and deed, to acknowledge him as the model for his own life. Certainly a banknote in one's hand seems more real than that most real reality which we call God. And a "Yes" to this most real reality, to which Jesus in person binds us, will always be accompanied by doubt. In honest doubt there can be more faith—more considered faith—than in the unhesitating and unthinking Sunday recital of the creed, which is no protection against heresy. And what a lot of things they believe in, these so unshakably certain "faithful": so often in ritual and ceremonies, apparitions and prophecies, miracles and mysteries, more than in the living, surprising, disturbing God who just is not identical with tradition and custom, with what is familiar, congenial and harmless. Tertullian in the third century, commenting on John's text, says: "Our Lord Christ adopted the name Truth (*Veritas*), not Custom (*Consuetudo*)."[4]

Innumerable people learn that faith ebbs and flows, has its day and its night. Nevertheless a once-living faith cannot simply be lost—as is sometimes naïvely suggested—just like a watch. But, stifled by suffering, pressure of work or self-indulgence—or even sheer thoughtlessness—it can grow cold, wither, cease to shape our life. In this sense a person, unfortunately particularly a young person, fascinated by the new possibilities of life (experience of the world, sexuality, money, career), "loses" his faith without any idea of the pain it may cost to find it, rouse it, revive it again. On the other hand a man can maintain his faith even in utter darkness. As a young Jew wrote on the wall of the Warsaw ghetto:

I believe in the sun, even if it does not shine.
I believe in love, even if I do not feel it.
I believe in God, even if I do not see him.

Are there not innumerable people even today who, like others in this world, see fear and suffering, hate and inhumanity, misery, hunger, oppression and war? And yet they believe that God has power also over these powers? And are there not people who, like the rest, see their lives ruled by other lords: aversions and aggressions, prejudices and desires, conventions and systems, and especially all kinds of selfishness? And yet they believe that Jesus is the true Lord. And are there not people who, like others, are aware of insecurity and inadequacy, doubt and rebellion, arrogance and indolence, in their thinking, willing and feeling? And yet they believe that the Spirit of God can determine our thinking, willing and feeling.

Innumerable people are seeking answers, looking for help and support in their existential questions and problems. All this *is* offered. It has only to be grasped. The wholly personal decision for God and for Jesus is the properly Christian basic decision: it is a question of Christian existence or non-existence, of being a Christian or not being a Christian.

There are however some for whom the question recurs: is this basic decision for faith or unbelief identical from the outset with the decision for or against a particular Church? Today more than ever there are Christians, often indisputably good Christians, outside the Church, outside all Churches. And this unfortunately—as we must now consider more closely —is at least partially the fault of the Church, of all Churches.

Criticism of the Church

It is particularly the Christian who is a committed member of the Church who has no reason for hesitating to criticize the Church in the light of the message of Jesus or for leaving criticism to those "outside." Criticism from "outside," however radical, can never replace, still less surpass criticism from within. The most severe criticism of the Church arises, not from the numerous historical, philosophical, psychological, sociological objections, but from the Gospel of Jesus Christ himself, which the Church is constantly invoking. And in this sense we cannot be required to refrain from criticism of the Church, not even from "within," not even by the Pope and still less by the many petty popes. All this with due reverence and charity.

The Church however—the Catholic Church in particular—is still admired by innumerable people. And why not? But it is equally blamed and rejected by innumerable people. And why not? This discordant reaction is due not only to the different attitudes of people, but to the *ambivalence of the phenomenon of the Church itself.*

Some admire the unique way in which the Church sustained and shaped two thousand years of history. Others see this shaping and mastery of history as a yielding and capitulation to history. Some are full of praise for the effective worldwide organization, rooted in a small space, with hundreds of millions of members and a rigidly organized hierarchy. Others see the effective organization as the machinery of power working with secular aids, the impressive numbers of the masses of Christians as a superficial, insubstantial traditional Christianity, the well-organized hierarchy as an administrative authority seeking pomp and power. Some extol the solemn liturgy, steeped in tradition, the doctrinal system based on carefully reasoned theology, the far-reaching secular cultural achievement of building up and shaping the Christian West. But others see in the cultic solemnity an unevangelical-externalized ritualism which is still tied to the medieval, baroque tradition; in the clear, coherent doctrinal system a rigid authoritarian, unhistorical, unbiblical textbook theology making use of traditional, hollow-sounding terms; in the Western cultural achievement a secularization and a deviation from the Church's proper task.

Thus the admirers of the Church's wisdom, power and achievement, its splendor, influence and prestige, are very clearly reminded of the persecution of Jews and the Crusades, trials of heretics and burning of witches, colonialism and "wars of religion," of wrong condemnations of men and wrong solutions of problems. They are reminded of the Church's involvement in particular systems of society, government and thought, of its frequent failures in coping with the problem of slavery, the problem of war, the question of women's rights, the social question, with the questions of science—the theory of evolution, for instance—and a number of historical questions.

Are all these only the all-too-often quoted mistakes of the past, which should be understood "in the light of the time"? Or are they all only charges of the past such as Heinrich Böll has to direct against the Catholic Church[5] and Alexander Solzhenitsyn against the Russian Orthodox Church?[6] Is such criticism not better than the frequently total lack of interest displayed by innumerable Christians and particularly Protestant Christians toward their Protestant Churches in Europe?

There is so much that can be brought against the Church by so many: natural scientists and medical experts, psychologists and sociologists, journalists and politicians, workers and intellectuals, practicing churchgoers and non-practicing Christians, young and old, men and women, against bad sermons, dull liturgy, repulsive piety, mindless tradition. Against authoritarian, unintelligible dogmatics and an impractical, narrow-minded casuistic moral theology. Against opportunism and intolerance, the legalism and arrogance of ecclesiastical functionaries and theologians at all levels, against the scarcity of creative minds in the Church and the boring mediocrity. Against the manifold complicity with the powerful and the neglect of the despised, downtrodden, oppressed, exploited; against religion used as opium of the people; against a Christianity wholly occupied with itself, at odds with itself, a divided *oikoumene*.

Despite all the efforts for reform and renewal described at the beginning of this book, does not the original fire of the Spirit seem to be extinguished in the Churches? Are not these institutionalized bearers of Christianity nervous of new experiments and experiences? For many people are they not hopelessly backward subcultures, organizations living in the past and unaware of the needs of our time? Where does *credibility* lie in all this? Not with those self-centered *Church leaders* who are continually attempting to put a ban on knowledge and curiosity and to immunize the faithful against criticism from inside and outside, who are ridden by fear for the system, for their influence and power and who are forever preoccupied with problems for which a theological solution was found long ago. Nor is credibility to be found among those *practicing Christians* who were never taught the meaning of critical freedom, who believe something simply because the parish priest, the bishop or the Pope has said it, who are not prepared for change in any form and wonder what or whether they can still believe when the slightest modification is introduced, say, in Catholic canon law or calendar of saints, in the Eastern Orthodox liturgy, in a Protestant translation of the Bible.

Is any more credibility to be attached to those moderately modern *theologians* who sometimes seem to be more concerned about formulas and their own petty systems, about opportunism and adaptation, than about Christian truth? These theologians have not yet liquidated the feuds of the sixteenth century nor yet digested the developments of the eighteenth and nineteenth centuries. They feel that their Christian faith is threatened if there should be mistakes in the Bible, if questions are raised about one of the traditional articles or dogmas and no one can say at once with absolute certainty what "must" be believed. Is there anything inviting in such Church leadership and theology, is such a faith infectious, can such a way of being a Christian rouse the curiosity of non-Christians? What a discrepancy there is between the Christian program and the Church's practice!

The fact that it is the *Catholic Church* in particular which is most affected by criticism is due not only to its age, its influence, its size far surpassing that of the rest of Christendom, its central importance for the *oikoumene* and the weight it carries even with political powers. More important is the fact that the Catholic Church particularly in the *Second Vatican Council* roused among its own members and outside very great hopes which however were sadly frustrated in the post-conciliar period.[7] The Council had offered a far-reaching program for a renewed Church of the future. And people set to work energetically to realize it in innumerable parishes and dioceses throughout the world. In a short time a new understanding of the Church (as people of God) and of office in the Church (as service to this people) came to prevail at least theoretically in the Catholic Church.

It is scarcely possible to overestimate the progress achieved by the reform of the liturgy and the introduction of the vernacular with a new arrangement of readings at Mass. Ecumenical collaboration both on the parish level (common campaigns and liturgy of the word) and on the level of the universal Church (through reciprocal visits and mixed study commissions) was strengthened. The Roman central administration was reformed by Pope Paul VI in a variety of ways and given a more pronounced international structure. Up to a point the reform of the priests' seminaries and religious orders was very energetically promoted. Diocesan and parish councils with the laity playing an important part were set up and began to be active. New life appeared in theology and it became evident that the Church was more open to the problems of modern man and society. Nothing was perfect, but everything was essentially good and gave ground for great hope.

There were however important internal Church problems which were not settled at the council, largely because Pope and bishops failed to protest about their neglect. It was the failure to deal with these problems which led straight into a crisis of leadership and of confidence at all levels. The same Church leadership which tackled old and new questions at the time of the council and went a surprisingly long way toward solving them appears in our *post-conciliar age* to be incapable of reaching concrete results in such urgent problems as birth control, justice and peace in the world, election of bishops and the crisis in the Church's ministry; the celibacy law, essentially a peripheral question, has undeservedly become a test question of renewal. But, while the Church authorities are content to issue charges or warnings or to impose arbitrary sanctions in face of these very diverse problems, priests are still abandoning their ministry in large numbers and vocations are declining both quantitatively and qualitatively. Many Christians are completely at a loss and many of the best pastoral clergy feel that they are being left in the lurch in their most vital concerns by the bishops and often too by the theologians. Admittedly some episcopates and individual bishops have become seriously involved in the cares of their Churches. But most bishops' conferences have managed to find constructive solutions only in secondary questions and have disappointed many expectations of clergy and people. Hence the credibility of the Catholic Church, higher at the beginning of the pontificate of Paul VI than perhaps at any time in the last five hundred years, has declined to an alarming extent. There are many who suffer in regard to the Church. There is widespread discouragement.

The reasons for the present crisis of leadership and confidence—which can only be briefly summarized here—are not to be found merely in connection with certain individuals or officeholders and certainly not in their lack of good will. It is the ecclesiastical system itself which has failed to keep abreast of the times and still displays numerous features of an outdated absolutism. Pope and bishops continue to behave largely as sole rulers over the Church, combining in their hands legislative, executive and judicial functions. Despite the councils set up in the meantime, they exercise their power in many places free from any effective control; conformity is the criterion for the choice of their successors.

Widespread complaints in different regions of the Church include: the appointment of bishops by a secret procedure without the co-operation of the clergy and people concerned; lack of openness in the processes of decision-making; continual appeals by the leaders to their own authority and to the obedience of others; insufficient explanation of the reasons for demands and directives; monocratic official style and disregard of genuine collegiality; reduction of the laity and "lower clergy" to a state of tutelage, unable to appeal effectively against the decisions of the authorities. Freedom is demanded for the Church in its dealings with the outside world, but not assured to its own members. Justice and peace are preached when this costs nothing to the Church and its leaders. There is a struggle for things of secondary importance, but there is no evidence either of great conceptions for the future or of clear priorities for the present. Even timid attempts on the part of theology to help the Church in this situation are met with distrust and rejection. The results can be seen in the passivity of many members of the Church and the increasing apathy of the public at large toward those who speak for the Church.

Today it is not only a question of what might be called "democratization" of the Church. If we get down to the reason for the present lack of leadership and ideas in the Church, we constantly find that the Church is *not only far behind the times, but has also and more importantly fallen far short of its own mission.* In so many things—in the opinion of friends and enemies—it has not followed the example of him whom it constantly invokes. That is why we see today a strange contrast between the interest in Jesus himself and the lack of interest in the Church. Whenever the Church wields power over men instead of performing a service to men, whenever its institutions, doctrines and laws become ends in themselves, whenever its spokesmen hand out personal opinions and requests as divine precepts and directives: whenever these things happen, the Church's mission is betrayed, the Church dissociates itself from both God and men, it reaches a crisis.

2. *Decision for the Church*

What is to be done? Rebel? Reform? Resign? Friends and foes alike—complaining or accusing, depressed or triumphant—are continually bringing up against any committed Christian the failure of the Church. But, instead of forever writing up the ecclesiastical *chronique scandaleuse,* we could look at the more interesting question as to why a committed Christian in particular, an "insider" wholly free from illusions, who has scarcely anything new to learn about scandals in the Church, nevertheless remains in this Church, in his Church. The question comes from both sides: from those who are outside and think that such a person is wasting his energies in a rigid ecclesiastical institution and could achieve more outside it; and from those who are inside and think that radical criticism of conditions in the Church and of the authorities is not compatible with staying in the Church.[8]

Why stay?

This is not at all an easy question to answer convincingly when so many social motivations have ceased to count as a result of the secularization of modern life and knowledge, when the Church is no longer linked with the state, part of the life of the nation, bound up with tradition. For the Christian, as for Jew or Muslim, it cannot—or at any rate hitherto could not—be unimportant that he was born into this community and in one form or another, for good or ill, whether he wanted or not, has remained conditioned by it. Similarly, it is not unimportant whether a person remains in touch with his family or has parted from it in anger or indifference.

This at least today is a reason for some Christians to remain in the Church and also for many engaged in the Church's ministry a reason for staying in it.

They want to attack rigid ecclesiastical traditions which make it difficult or even impossible to be a Christian. But they do not want to give up living by the great Christian tradition, which is also the Church's tradition, of two thousand years.

They want to submit the Church's institutions and constitutions to criticism whenever personal happiness is sacrificed to them. But they do not want to dispense with these insofar as they are necessary in the long run for the life even of a community of faith, insofar as they are necessary to prevent too many people being left unaided particularly in their most intimately personal problems.

They want to resist the arrogance of ecclesiastical authorities when these rule the Church according to their own ideas and not according to the Gospel. But they do not want to dispense with the moral authority which the Church can exercise in society whenever it acts truly as the Church of Jesus Christ.

Then why stay? Because, despite everything, in this community of faith critically but jointly we can affirm a great history on which we live with so many others. Because, as members of this community, we ourselves are the Church and should not confuse it with its machinery and administrators, still less leave the latter to shape the community. Because, however serious the objections, we have found here a spiritual home in which we can face the great questions of the whence and whither, the why and wherefore, of man and the world. We would no more turn our backs on it than on democracy in politics, which in its own way is misused and abused no less than the Church.

Obviously there is the other possibility, and those who have chosen it often enough were not the bad Christians. This is to break with the Church because of its decline, for the sake of higher values, perhaps even for the sake of being a genuine Christian. There are Christians—and, at least as borderline cases, Christian groups—outside the Church as institution. Such a decision is to be respected, it can even be understood. More than ever in the present phase of depression in the Catholic Church. And any committed and informed Christian could certainly list as many reasons for leaving as those who have in fact gone.

And yet? They jumped ship as an act of honesty, of courage, of protest, or even simply as a last resource, because they could endure no more. But for us would it not be finally an act of despair, an admission of failure, a capitulation? We were with it in better times: are we now to abandon the boat in the storm and leave others, with whom we used to sail, to steer against the wind, to bale out the water and perhaps to fight for survival? We have received so much in this community of faith that we cannot so easily get out of it. We have become so involved in change and renewal that we cannot disappoint those who have shared our commitment. We should not provide this joy for the opponents of renewal nor inflict this sorrow on our friends. We are not to dispense with efficiency *in* the Church.

The alternatives—another Church, no Church—are not convincing. Breaking away from the Church leads only to the isolation of the individual or even to new institutionalizing. All fanaticism proves this. There is little point in an elite Christianity which seeks to be better than the masses of Christians, in ecclesiastical Utopias which presuppose an ideal community of pure like-minded people. In the last resort would it not be more challenging and, throughout all the suffering, more pleasant and fruitful to fight the battle for a "Christianity with a human face" *in* this concrete Church of human beings where we know at least with whom we are dealing? Here is a constantly new invitation to responsibility, to critical solidarity, to stubborn endurance, vigilant freedom, loyal opposition.

And now, when the authority, unity, credibility of this Church have been shaken in a variety of ways as a result of the evident failure of its leaders, when it is increasingly seen to be weak, erring, searching for directions, there are not a few who will say what they never said in former times of triumph: "We love this Church, as it is now and as it could be." They love it, not as "mother," but as the family of faith, for the sake of which the institutions, constitutions, authorities exist at all and sometimes simply have to be endured. It is a community of faith which even today, despite all its shocking deficiencies, cannot only open wounds but still work miracles among men. This it can do where it "functions": where it is not only the place where Jesus is remembered—although this too counts for something—but where it truly defends the cause of Jesus Christ in word and deed. And this too it certainly does, at least in addition to other things, admittedly more before small groups than before the public at large, more through humble people than through the hierarchs and theologians. But it does happen, daily, hourly, through the innumerable witnesses who as Christians in ordinary life make the Church present in the world. And therefore the decisive answer is: we should, we may remain in the Church because we are convinced of the cause of Jesus Christ and because the community of the Church, despite and in all its failings, has remained and will still remain in the service of the cause of Jesus Christ.

The large number of those who call themselves Christian did not get their Christianity from books, not even from the Bible. They got it from this community of faith, which has kept going reasonably well for two thousand years, despite all weaknesses and errors, and constantly in one way or another awakened faith in Jesus Christ and issued a challenge to commitment in his Spirit. This call of the Church does not ring out unmistakably as the pure word of God. It is a very human, often too human call. But, even distorted by false notes and crooked actions, the real meaning of the message can be perceived and has in fact continually been perceived. Even opponents admit this when they—rightly—accuse the Church of playing a role which often ill accords with its message: Grand Inquisitor, tyrant, trading in the cause instead of defending it.

Whenever the Church privately and publicly advocates the cause of Jesus Christ, whenever it champions his cause in word and deed, it is at the service of man and becomes credible. It can then be a center where individual and social need can be met at a deeper level than the efficiency-oriented, consumer society can reach with its own resources. For all this does not come about of itself or by chance. There is a reciprocal relationship and a reciprocal causality between these achievements and what happens—modestly enough, but today perhaps in greater freedom than in the past—in the Church, in its proclamation and in its worship. New possibilities arise whenever a priest in the pulpit, on the radio or in a small group preaches this Jesus; when a catechist or parents give Christian instruction; an individual, a family or parish prays seriously without a lot of words. They arise when a baptism is carried out in the name of Jesus Christ, when the memorial or thanksgiving meal is celebrated in a community committed to drawing the conclusions for everyday life; when in the power of God the forgiveness of sin is incomprehensibly assured. New opportunities arise therefore whenever in the service of God and the service of men, in instruction and pastoral care, in conversation and charitable service, the Gospel is truthfully proclaimed and life lived and seen to be lived in accordance with it. In brief, the following of Christ takes place when the cause of Jesus Christ is taken seriously. The Church as community of faith, therefore, can help men—and who should do this *ex professo* if not the Church?—to be human, Christian, to be Christian men and remain so in deed.

It depends on the Church itself how it gets over the crisis. There is nothing wrong with its program. Why stay in the Church then? Because from faith we can draw *hope* that the program, the cause of Jesus Christ himself, as hitherto, is stronger than all the mischief which has been created in and with the Church. That is why a decisive effort in the Church is worthwhile, why also a special effort in the Church's ministry is worthwhile—despite everything. I am not staying in the Church *although* I am a Christian. It is *because* I am a Christian that I am staying in the Church.

Practical suggestions

Once more however: what is to be done? A basic theological reflection on staying in the Church is not in itself an answer to the question. Least of all for difficult transitional phases like ours. What indeed can be done particularly in this situation, which may of course pass more quickly but then return more quickly than we think?

The essential outlines of a practical policy should be clear without long explanations. There is only one way to overcome any crisis in the Church, any polarization between Catholics and Protestants, between conservative and progressive Christians, between "pre-conciliar" and "post-conciliar" Catholics, between old and young, men and women; in the Catholic Church between bishops and clergy, bishops and people, Pope and Church. We must renew our awareness of the *center and foundation:* the *Gospel* of Jesus Christ from which the Church started out and which it has to grasp again and relive in each new situation. We cannot work out here what this means in principle and practice in the different Churches, countries, cultures, spheres of life, what it means for the individual and for the community. We can only indicate some immediate possibilities.

It is not enough for the whole *oikoumene,* both Rome and the World Council of Churches, to address fine speeches to the "outer world," to society at large, and "inside," between the Churches, merely to set up everlasting mixed commissions, arrange polite mutual visits, indulge in endless academic dialogue without practical consequences. There must be genuine, increasing integration of the different Churches:

through reform and reciprocal recognition of the ecclesial ministries;
through a common liturgy of the word, open communion and increasingly frequent common eucharistic celebrations;

through common construction and common use of churches and other buildings;
through a common fulfillment of service to society;
through increasing integration of theological faculties and of religious instruction;
through concrete plans for union worked out by the leaders of the Churches at national and universal levels.

For the *Catholic Church* especially a settlement of what was left unsettled at Vatican II must be demanded with increasing urgency, fought for and finally effected by both congregations and their leaders. Once again we must insist here on a number of reforms in the Catholic Church. Some of them have been demanded by many for a long time and all of them are based on the Gospel.[9]

Church leaders *should carry out their tasks as a whole not hierarchically but competently, not bureaucratically but creatively, not with regard to their office but with regard to men; they should summon up the courage to involve themselves more with people than with the institution; they should provide for more democracy, autonomy, humanity among all ranks in the Church and strive for better collaboration between clergy and laity.*

Bishops *especially should not be appointed for their conformity by secret procedures in the style of* Roman *absolutism (with the "papal secret" secured by oaths), but should be elected for a limited time in the light of the needs of the diocese concerned by representative bodies of the clergy and laity.*

The Pope *too, if he claims to be more than Bishop of Rome and Primate of Italy, should be elected by a body consisting of bishops and laypeople which—unlike the college of cardinals, nominated solely by the Pope—would be representative of the* whole Church, *not only the different nations, but especially the different mentalities and generations.*

"Priests" *(leaders of congregations and also of dioceses), in the light of the freedom that the Gospel assures them on this point, should decide—each according to his personal vocation—whether they want to marry or not.*

"Laypeople" *(parishes and dioceses) should have the right, not merely to offer advice, but also to share with their leaders in a well-balanced system with spheres of authority clearly marked out (checks and balances); they should exercise the right to object whenever Jesus himself would raise an objection.*

Women *should have at least that dignity, freedom and responsibility in the Church which they are guaranteed in modern society: equal*

> *rights in canon law, in the Church's decision-making bodies, and also practical opportunities of studying theology and being ordained.*
>
> *In questions of* morality *freedom and conscience should not again be replaced by a law and a new slavery set up (in the Church); in particular there should be understanding in the light of the Gospel for a new attitude to sexuality, remembering that the younger generation can find more ways than one of maintaining purity of heart.*
>
> *The question of* birth control, *even by artificial methods, should be left to the married parties to decide conscientiously in the light of medical, psychological and social criteria; the leaders in the Catholic Church should revise the present teaching (the encyclical* Humanae Vitae) *on this point.*

And so on. The fulfillment of these and similar desiderata must be vigorously demanded and fought for until it is achieved: for the sake of the people who suffer from the present unhappy state of affairs in the Church.

Against discouragement

The question however constantly recurs: does not the excessive power and the tight structure of the ecclesiastical system itself prevent any serious reform? In the difficult times of the Church's history is there any midway between revolution and merely putting up with the situation? But the question may be stated in another way: could not the situation particularly of the Catholic Church quickly change again, if the present credibility gap, the crisis of leadership and confidence, were to be overcome? In this respect it would be stupid to wait every time simply for a change at the top and for a new generation. We may therefore set down here some orientation points for dealing with such situations in practice. What can be done to prevent discouragement?[10]

> We must not be silent. *The requirements of the Gospel and the needs and hopes of our time are in many outstanding questions so unambiguous that silence out of opportunism, lack of courage or superficiality can involve guilt just as much as the silence of many responsible people at the time of the Reformation.*

Therefore: Those bishops—often a strong minority or even the majority in national bishops' conferences—who regard certain laws, regulations and measures as disastrous should state this quite publicly and insist forthrightly on change. The size of the majority at any decision of the bishops' conferences can no longer be withheld from the public in the Church. Nor can the theologians avoid questions concerning the life of the Church by claiming to be occupied with pure scholarship. They too have to take an appropriate stand whenever the interests of the Church, with consequences for theology, are involved. Everyone in the Church, whether holding office or not, man or woman, has the right and often the duty of saying what he thinks of the Church and its leaders and what he thinks ought to be done. Tendencies to disintegration of course must be resisted just as much as tendencies to become rigid.

> We must act ourselves. *Too many Catholics complain and grumble about Rome and the bishops without doing anything themselves. If in a particular congregation today the liturgy is boring, pastoral care ineffective, theology sterile, awareness of the needs of the world limited, ecumenical collaboration with other Christian communities minimal: if this is the state of affairs, the blame cannot simply be shifted off to Pope and episcopate.*

Therefore: Whether parish priest, curate or layman, every member should do something for the renewal of the Church in his own sphere, small or great. Many great things have come about in the parishes and in the Church as a whole through the initiative of individuals. In modern society especially the individual has opportunities of exercising a positive influence on the life of the Church. In a variety of ways he can press for a better liturgy, more intelligible sermons, more up-to-date pastoral care, ecumenical integration of congregations and a Christian involvement in society.

> We must advance together. *One member of the parish who goes to the parish priest does not count, five can be troublesome, fifty can change the situation. One parish priest does not count in the diocese, five are given attention, fifty are invincible.*

Therefore: The officially established parish councils, priests' councils, pastoral councils can become powerful instruments of renewal in parishes, dioceses and nations whenever individuals aim at specific goals in their own sphere and in the Church as a whole. But today also the voluntary associations of priests and laypeople are indispensable if certain issues in the Church are to be brought to a head. Priests' associations and solidarity groups have achieved quite a lot in various countries. They deserve more publicity, among other forms of support. The collaboration of the different groupings should not be disturbed by sectarian isolation, but must be strengthened for the sake of the common goal. Priests' groups especially must maintain contact with the numerous married priests who have lost their ministry, with a view to their return to full ministry in the Church.

We must seek provisional solutions. *Discussions alone do not help. It is often necessary to show that we are serious. Pressure on the ecclesiastical authorities in the spirit of Christian fraternity can be legitimate when officeholders fall short of their mandate. The mother tongue in the whole Catholic liturgy, changes in the rules for mixed marriages, the approval of tolerance, democracy, human rights, and so many other things in the history of the Church have been achieved only as a result of continual pressure from below in a spirit of loyalty.*

Therefore: When a measure is adopted by higher authority in the Church which quite obviously does not correspond to the Gospel, resistance can be permitted and even required. When an urgent measure is intolerably delayed by higher authority in the Church, provisional solutions can be introduced with prudence and moderation while maintaining the unity of the Church.

We must not give up. *The greatest temptation or often the convenient alibi in the renewal of the Church is the excuse that there is no point in it all, that we can make no headway and we had better get out of it: we leave altogether or withdraw into ourselves. But if there is no hope, there can be no action.*

Therefore: Particularly in a phase of stagnation the important thing is to endure it and hold out in confident faith. Opposition can be expected. But there is no renewal without a struggle. It is essential therefore not to lose sight of the goal, to act calmly and resolutely and continue to hope for a Church which is more committed to the Christian message and which is then more open, more kindly, more credible—in a word, more Christian.

Why can we hope?

Because the Church's future has already begun, because the desire for renewal is not restricted to certain groups, because the new polarizations within the Church can be overcome, because many—notably, the best—bishops and priests, superiors—men and women—of religious orders approve and promote a profound and radical transformation.

But also because the Church cannot hold up the development of the world and because the history of the Church itself also goes on.

Finally—or, better, first of all—because we believe that the power of the Gospel of Jesus Christ constantly proves to be stronger than all human incapacity and superficiality, stronger than our own sloth, folly and discouragement.[11]

II. Being Human and Being Christian

It is evident from the history of the Christian Church, of theology and spirituality, that being Christian has meant all too often being less than human. But is this really being Christian? For many then the only alternative was to be human and therefore less Christian. But is this being truly human? In the light of our new understanding of the evolution of human society and new awareness of the Christian message, we have to find a new definition of the relationship between being human and being a Christian, particularly with reference to action. Once again the question of origins recurs here as a leitmotif.

1. *Norms of the human*

To many a non-Christian it seems that the Christian is so intent on self-denial and self-renunciation that he neglects his *self-development*.[1] The Christian may indeed want to live for men, but he is often not enough of a man himself. He is very ready to save others, but he has never learned properly to swim himself. He proclaims the salvation of the world, but does not perceive the relativity of his own environment. He devises fine programs to give effect to love, but does not see through his own pre-programming. He is troubled about the souls of others, but does not recognize the complexes of his own psyche. By attaching too much importance to and making too many demands on love of neighbor, service, self-sacrifice, he is very likely to break down, become discouraged and frustrated.

In fact is it not the failure to be fully human which so often makes being a Christian seem inadequate? Is not the lack of genuine, complete humanity particularly with official representatives and exponents of the Churches the reason why being a Christian is disregarded or rejected as an authentically human possibility? Must we not strive for the best possible development of the individual: a humanization of the whole person in all his dimensions, including instinct and feeling? Being human ought to be complementary to being a Christian. The Christian factor must be made effective, not at the expense of the human, but for the benefit of the latter.

Today more than ever this human factor must be seen as a *social reality*. Formerly Christian moral theology deduced the criteria for being human and the norms of human action apparently demonstrably and conclusively from the simple concept of an immutable, universal human nature. And these criteria and norms, assumed to be eternally valid, were then dogmatically asserted. But moral theologians have come to see more and more that this attitude is impossible in our history of a dynamic society increasingly planned and shaped by man himself with reference to the future.[2] We can no longer start out from a traditional and passively accepted system of eternal, rigid, immutable moral norms. We must constantly make a new start with the concrete, dynamic, changeable, complex reality of man and society. We must accept this manifold reality, as much as possible without prejudice, as it has been investigated today according to strict *scientific methods* with reference to its objective laws and possibilities for the future. Modern life has become too complex for us to be able blindly and naïvely to ignore the scientifically established empirical data and insights when we are defining ethical norms (in regard, for instance, to economic power, sexuality, aggressiveness). No ethic is possible without close contact with the human sciences: with psychology, sociology, behavior study, biology, history of civilization, philosophical anthropology. These sciences offer an increasing abundance of assured anthropological conclusions and information relevant to action: aids to decision-making which can be tested, although of course they cannot replace the ultimate ethical foundations and norms.

Human autonomy

In a *totalitarian coercive system*—whatever its color—it is decided from above in an official, doctrinaire way what must count as socially relevant truth, what are the essential priorities and values, the appropriate models and norms for society, what are self-realization and humanization for the individual. Under these conditions clear limits are set to freedom of conscience and tolerance in ideological questions. But there is also no lack of orientation: people know what line they must follow. To a large extent criteria for right and wrong, good and evil, for the official way of life, are decreed. It is exclusiveness that counts here, tolerating no other truths but its own. Freedom to choose values and norms is limited strictly to private life and creates no public danger. But we may wonder whether an orientation is not possible which provides quite a different scope for man's freedom.

In a *system where there is openness and freedom* official doctrinaire decisions cannot be made in regard to truth, meaning and style of life, self-realization and humanization, in regard to values, priorities, models, ideals and norms. Here political tolerance, freedom of conscience, of religion, information, research and teaching are constitutionally guaranteed and institutionalized. This system is built on the imperishable dignity and freedom of man as man and seeks to guarantee the human rights or democratic liberties involved in being a man. These provisions however should not be ends in themselves, but only the institutional conditions for each man to claim his wholly personal freedom, free from compulsion by state or party, to aim at a suitable goal, at a life worth living, at values, norms and ideals, to pursue his self-realization and complete humanization.[3]

But this is only the beginning of the problems of the ideologically neutral constitutional state. It just cannot justify in terms of a philosophy or religion the very thing which it must unconditionally assume: man's dignity and freedom. Does it not therefore leave man completely without bearings? Is there not a danger of an arbitrary pluralism which easily ends in nihilism and disorder, where just about everything is permitted?[4] Can this system of openness (to learning, to the future, to truth) and freedom still enable men to live together at all?

As history shows, man's freedom cannot be secured either solely through improving social conditions or solely through giving the individual an absolute value. Consciously or unconsciously, man has an elementary need of a basic spiritual bond, a bond with meaning, truth, certainty, with values and norms. If this need is not satisfied in the free play of intellectual forces which is prior to the state; if, that is, there is nothing or no one at all to convey an orientation, a scale of values, a bond with truth, a meaning to life; if the one institutionalized religion which provides an ultimate interpretation of things (the Church) has lost its credibility for many: out of all this a dangerous spiritual vacuum emerges. Men and particularly young people then live perhaps without any ultimate ties: with all the dangers of human breakdown. Or they commit themselves to an ideology, a totalitarian ideology—the color is not important—which promises and all too quickly provides what they are looking for. They abandon their former freedom—not even unwillingly—since they acquire in its place truth and meaning, values, ideals and norms to which they can cling.

But could not truth, meaning, values, ideals and norms also be conveyed in a free system, without the individual having to sacrifice freedom of thought, speech and action, to an ideological system, whether irreligious or even religious? Could it not provide an orientation for all the innumerable, unavoidable, relevant decisions of life, not abolishing freedom but making it possible? For it is a question here of a spiritual bond, not with a finite, relative, properly speaking casual (contingent), rigidly determining factor, but with an infinite, absolute, truly necessary liberating factor.

Theological ethics now seeks to overcome the former monistic fixation by pluralistic open-mindedness, without however abandoning the quest for what is morally right and good. We can only touch marginally here on the fundamental problems of the justification of *ethical norms*—that is, of universally binding rules of human conduct and common life, of being genuinely human—which have recently been the subject of intense discussion and which are so difficult for non-specialists to understand.[5] It is obvious from the discussion how much even Catholic ethics has recently avoided the traditional, categorical, brief formulas for what is permitted or not permitted and the primitive, apodictic dogmatism which brought so many discriminating thinkers into disrepute.[6] In fact it is of little use to appeal to absolute norms and simple rules, deduced from natural law or Scripture, in order to solve the apparently almost insoluble problems and conflicts of humanity: questions like overpopulation and birth control, economic growth and environment protection, political power and its control, aggressiveness and sexuality.

In all these questions man *cannot simply bring down fixed solutions from heaven* or deduce them theologically from an immutable essential nature of man. He must try them out in rough sketches and models and put them into practice and test them often for generations. From a historical standpoint the concrete ethical norms and views have normally been formed in a highly complicated process of group dynamics and social dynamics. When life's requirements which had to be satisfied, human pressures and needs became evident, there also appeared rules of action, priorities, conventions, laws, morals—in a word, definite norms—for human behavior. After periods of adaptation and acclimatization such established norms were finally universally recognized and sometimes too—when times had completely changed—undermined and dissolved.

In all the difficult problems and conflicts of modern humanity man "on earth" and—so to speak—"by the sweat of his brow" must *seek and work out for himself specific solutions*. He must start out from the diversity and complexity of life and keep to the facts, acquire assured information and knowledge and make use at every turn of relevant arguments. In this way he will discover aids to test and reconsider decisions and finally reach practicable solutions. No appeal even to the highest authority can deprive man of his *autonomy* in this world, of his moral power to *legislate for himself* and of his *responsibility to himself* for developing the world in the state in which the modern process of secularization for better or worse has brought it to him.[7]

Of course, in view of the complex and partly conflicting specific problems and in view of man's enormously increased responsibility, *the question of the ultimate grounds and norms* of his action becomes more urgent than ever before. The difficult empirical and technical problems themselves raise deeper questions. In this secular world where are the arguments to be found for that joint responsibility which is assumed in any individual, social and most of all global planning and direction toward the mastery of the problems of mankind? We are faced with the vast problems of population policy, of economic, social, cultural and foreign policy, of education, marriage and the family, of occupation and work, of consumer behavior. Where in all this are we to find a basis for determining priorities of values and goals? Yet without these priorities neither operative planning nor even meaningful organization is possible. Where can we find arguments for the rationality of reality assumed in all individual and social planning, guidance, organization and enterprise? Where shall we find an answer to those who are continually asking if it all makes sense?

Man's theonomy

At least it has become clear that we are not by any means facing entirely new questions here. All that we are doing is to bring out again with reference to practical action the basic problems already discussed. And inasmuch as it is a question of the practical attitude to the same questionable reality from which we started out in a more theoretical (but by no means unpractical) reflection, we can revert to what was said in the first chapters:

a. Any assumption of meaning, truth and rationality, of values and ideals, priorities and preferences, models and norms, presupposes a *basic trust in reality*: in which man rejects nihilism, accepts reality in principle and keeps up his acceptance; he accepts its identity, meaningfulness and values, accepts also the basic rationality of human reason.[8]

b. This fundamental trust in the identity, meaningfulness and values of reality, in the basic rationality of human reason, is justified only if all this is itself not groundless, unsupported and aimless, but is rooted in a primal source, primal meaning and primal value: in that most real reality which we call God. As we saw, there is no *justified* basic trust without trust in God, without *belief in God*.[9]

This fundamental context of justification holds therefore also for the justification of binding, normative rules of human action, behavior and fellowship: that is, for the justification of ethical norms.

But if reality and man are characterized by an ultimate identity, meaningfulness and value, then we can reasonably deduce individual norms of genuinely human action and existence from the essential human requirements, pressures and needs, as these latter can be experienced in ordinary life and ascertained in a new way scientifically-empirically today with the aid of the human sciences. The *morally good* then is what "works" for man, what permits human life in its individual and social dimensions to succeed and to work out happily in the long run, when freedom and love are engendered.[10] In the light of this primary and autonomous norm of morality two modes of behavior can be distinguished and as such tested by experience: ways in which human life is aided in its identity, meaningfulness and values, in which man gains a meaningful and fruitful existence; and ways in which human life is impeded in its identity, meaningfulness and values, in which man misses a meaningful and fruitful existence. Norms and structures are right "if and as long as they provide a cover under which mankind advances on its way toward the complete development of its values and possibilities."[11] Here the autonomy of morality is confirmed. Man should realize, not simply a principle or a universal norm, but himself in all his dimensions: this realization means humanization, means that he really becomes man.

Of course it is scarcely possible to deduce an *absolute claim* from all these human pressures and necessities. Why indeed should we? Anthropological certitudes prove to be relativities, to be dependent on all kinds of factors. Man—man in the concrete, determined by his environment, preprogrammed, driven by instinct—is a very finite, very relative being and cannot be made absolute either individually or collectively. And yet for ethics—Kant was right in this respect—it must be possible to impose an absolute obligation, an unconditional "ought": that is, not merely a hypothetical "You should," but an absolute "You shall." But how can such a categorical demand be deduced from the sheer finiteness and relativity of human life?

The unconditional ethical demand, the unconditional "ought" can be substantiated only in the light of an *unconditioned reality* (which of course cannot be proved by pure reason[12]): an *absolute* which can impose a meaning and which cannot be man either as individual or as society. Any demand based—for instance—only on the human fellowship of communication and argumentation remains hypothetical in the sense that it presupposes a will to participate and so the human "ought" is ultimately deduced from a human "will." It is therefore a hypothetical imperative, based on interest. "In principle an immanent humanism can lead only to a hypothetical requirement."[13]

The sole absolute in all that is relative is that primal reason, primal support and primal meaning of reality which we call *God*. God is the unconditioned in all that is conditioned, whose reality however can be accepted only in an act of trusting faith. This anchorage in an ultimate ground, not identical with man but surpassing him, enables man truly to exist for himself and to act for himself, gives him a genuine moral autonomy. And whenever, even in a purely immanent humanism, something like unconditionality is postulated in the light of man's freedom, his existing for himself, his openness to the future, there is in fact a reference to that ultimate dimension of unconditionality as the condition of possibility, even though it is not named.[14] This much is correct about Kant's postulate of God's existence on the ground of man's morality, that God must be presupposed if in the last resort man wants to lead a meaningful moral life. *Theo-nomy* is the *condition of the possibility of the moral auto-nomy of man* in secular society.[15]

In the last resort an unconditional demand in a world where everything is conditioned can be justified only in theological terms. The problem of the relation between the conditioned and the unconditioned is in fact no more and no less than an aspect of the basic theological problem of transcendence and immanence.[16] Only the bond with an infinite bestows freedom in regard to all that is finite. Only such an ultimate justification of ethics goes beyond a mere critical comparison of ethical systems and the separation which it presupposes between "objective-neutral" science and subjective value judgments. Only such an ultimate justification of ethics brings out the justification of that dignity and freedom of man which—as we saw—must be presupposed by a free society, if the latter is not to decline in the nihilism of permitting everything to count and/or break down into totalitarianism.

The unconditioned in the conditioned

If we speak of man's theonomy as authenticating his state of being under obligation, are we not turning into an absolute the *particular norm*, the individual (material, specific) moral precept or prohibition? Quite the contrary. It does not mean making the individual moral directive absolute, even if it is meant to impose a universally binding rule on concrete human action. And, despite all the dangerously abstract dissociation of Kant's purely *a priori* categorical imperative from experience and history, this much is correct about his formal ethics: no material norms can be directly deduced by human reason from man's theonomy. In this sense man is thrown back on himself: in the ascertaining and application of norms there is no heteronomy but a genuine autonomy of man.

It is true that individual interpersonal norms of all kinds (priorities, rules of action, conventions, laws, customs) can claim intersubjective, universal validity and can provide a binding interpretation in the particular situation of a demand justified in the last resort in terms of theonomy. Nevertheless the individual norms for interpersonal relationships *cannot claim any absolute validity:* they are not unconditionally valid, without exception, in every situation.[17]

Admittedly, an unconditional validity, permitting no exceptions, can be ascribed to purely *analytic-explicative* ("deontological") propositions (for example: "Never act unjustly!" "Never kill unjustly!"). But such tautological propositions scarcely occur in practice. They do not tell us just what to do here and now. "You must never kill unjustly" is merely a tautology: "unjust killing is always unjust." No answer is given to the concrete question: is it unjust, against morality, to kill a hostile aggressor, an embryo or myself? What is the concrete meaning of "just," "good," "moral"? But the genuinely *synthetic* propositions, which therefore embody concrete experience, are in fact always based (consciously or not) on a consideration of the relevant arguments, on a judgment of preference: that this particular good (life, truth) is more important than another. This also holds for lying and contraception which moral theology for a long time regarded as contrary to nature and therefore made their prohibition into an absolute norm. In that case, we would have to tell the truth under all circumstances, even if it involved the death of an innocent person (to say nothing at all of contraception for the good of marriage and family).

The fact that particular norms cannot claim any absolute validity in interpersonal relationships does not however justify the demand for absolute freedom from norms. If norms have no absolute validity, this certainly does not imply *an absolute non-validity*. The alternative of life without norms or life with norms and the corresponding distinction between ethics and morality (ethics demanding a changed awareness—morality meaning the regulation of behavior by external norms) are not only false, but—as we saw—also fatal, particularly in modern society. They would lead to the nihilistic tolerance of anything and everything.

Between absolute validity and absolute non-validity there is the *relative validity* of norms. Everywhere in interpersonal relationships—it is otherwise in regard to God as the "absolute good"—it is a question of *relative values* which may not be declared absolute (unconditional), but must be balanced against other (relative) values. All these precepts and prohibitions are valid therefore, not however for their own sake, but for the sake of realizing the greater good. They are essentially hypothetical imperatives: not infallible norms holding without exception and in every case, but always merely conditionally (the expression of a *moralitas conditionata*). If we talk about the "universal validity" of moral norms, we mean therefore that they are "generally valid." The norms are valid insofar as they express the general rule and in any particular situation take into account fully and precisely the necessary conditions and empirical data.

Relative validity means therefore nothing more than *validity appropriate to the situation.* It has nothing to do with an unprincipled *libertinism,* with living only for the present moment and adapting oneself exclusively to the situation (we may recall the enthusiasts at Corinth[18]). It does not mean behavior wholly suited to the occasion, regardless of any principles or tenets, guidelines or demarcation points, maxims or regulations. Validity appropriate to the situation therefore does not mean antinomianism, opposition to the law as such. Norms are not valid only as oriented to a particular case, related purely to the present moment, directed solely to the situation which is always wholly and entirely special.[19]

Still less of course has situational validity to do with an unfree, heteronomous *legalism*, keeping strictly to the law, regardless of the situation (we may recall the moralizers in Galatia[20]): the letter of the law simply has to be obeyed; clauses have to be applied regardless of their content; principles and tenets, guidelines and demarcation points, maxims and regulations are turned into laws which hold unconditionally and without exception. Validity appropriate to the situation then does not mean "nomism," "legality." It is not a question of solutions which can simply be looked up in the statute book of natural law (in the sense of discovering by reason alone what is in accordance with nature) or in the statute book of Sacred Scripture (in the sense of deciding what is lawful solely in the light of the Bible).

Ethics does not merely assert principles nor does it merely devise tactics. Neither the law alone nor the situation alone should be the dominant factor. The norms should illuminate the situation and the situation determine the norms. What is good and moral is not simply good and right in the abstract, but concretely good and right: what is appropriate. It is only in the determining situation that the obligation becomes concrete, but in a particular situation the obligation—to be judged of course only by the person concerned—can become unconditional. What we ought to do is related to the situation, but in a particular situation we may be absolutely bound to do it. Each situation is therefore characterized by a factor which is unconditional and another which must be weighed and considered: a universal normative constant linked with a special variable related to the situation.

It should have become clear in the meantime that the discussion of the problems of ascertaining and establishing norms involves the application of the conclusions reached at the beginning of this book after examining the problems of the knowledge of God and of reality. Retrospectively the parallels may be formulated as follows:

The assumption that there are autonomous norms of human behavior is the ethical expression of basic trust in the identity, meaningfulness and especially the values of reality and of human life. Without this basic trust autonomous ethical norms cannot reasonably and justifiably be accepted.[21]

The assumption that there are autonomous norms of human behavior imposing an unconditional and therefore theonomous demand is the ethical expression of justified basic trust in reality (and human life), so far as this is determined by an ultimate primal reason, primal meaning and primal value: it is thus the ethical expression of belief in God.

Without this trust in God an unconditional demand of autonomous ethical norms cannot reasonably and justifiably be accepted.[22]

Uncertainty of norms

From this standpoint is it not clear all along the line that norms are very uncertain? What is moral is seen in a plurality of forms and thus appears to be uncertain. From the empirical-rational standpoint it cannot be denied that there are obviously several ways and not merely one in which a person may find moral fulfillment, several ways of living a life worthy of man, which is right and good, according to conscience.

Cannot the obligations resulting from the demands of reality be very diversely articulated? Cannot human needs and pressures be defined in a great variety of ways? Are not all conclusions, even scientific-"objective" conclusions, influenced by interests? Do not even the much-invoked human sciences, for all their empirical investigations, always see man only from a quite definite viewpoint? Has not ethics even as a science always a limited perspective, so that it can scarcely grasp simultaneously or even successively in their historical forms all aspects of what is morally right? Is not human life particularly today so varied and complex that pluralism in moral convictions is only too understandable? In concrete life do not abstract-ideal norms everywhere come up against the limits of what can be effected? And is not the individual conscience aware only in varying degrees of their binding character?

It must be admitted that what is truly human and humane is not at all obvious. And if people were not at least tacitly oriented to Christian standards of value, it would be even less obvious. Why in fact are dominating and domineering not supposed to be genuinely human, as the *Herrenmensch* or master-race morality of all ages (and of Nazism in particular) maintained? Is not the prevailing morality mostly the morality of the rulers, as Marx and Marxism declare in their criticism of the morality of a class society? Why are sheer pleasure and material consumption not supposed to be truly human, as hedonism has claimed with more or less ingenuity in every age (and particularly in the age of the welfare society)?

Are then the norms deduced from human needs and pressures so obvious that they have a compelling intrinsic clarity? Are they not probabilities rather than transparent certainties, even though several arguments for their necessity coincide and converge and thus give it some plausibility? As historical studies show, even in Christian ethics, opinions have varied greatly in the course of centuries. Opinions have changed and are changing about the lawfulness of war, resistance and revolution, about the limits of freedom and obedience, about ownership, work and occupation, freedom of conscience and tolerance, sexual behavior, marriage, divorce and celibacy. For instance, is the "golden rule," accepted by many religions and philosophies and not least by Kant, so obvious that we all know what to do even when the person I must treat as I want to be treated myself stands clearly in my way, in the way of my plans, my policy? How do we know which policy is moral as a whole, which science is truly human, which civilization or form of economy is humane?

Even in such fundamental questions as love and hate it is difficult to explain why I should love and not hate. Scientifically considered, is hatred simply worse than love? "There is no logically stringent reason why I should love and not hate, as long as this hatred does not put me at a disadvantage in my social life."[23] Why should not war be as good or as bad as peace, freedom as good or as bad as oppression? "For how can it be proved exactly that I should not hate if I feel like it? Positivism knows of no authority transcending man which might distinguish between helpfulness and greed for gain, kindness and cruelty, cupidity and self-denial. Logic too is dumb, it gives no preference to moral dispositions."[24]

As with the understanding of God which is gained from the reality of this world and of man, the norms which are deduced from this reality are also ambivalent. They too are never immediately obvious, never objectively explicit. And so they remain ambiguous, *in the last resort indeterminate*, both for every individual and for society. It is particularly difficult to perceive how far these obviously conditional norms can give expression to an unconditional obligation.

In view then of the non-evidence, uncertainty and vagueness of the norms and of the pluralism of the ethical systems resulting from this, we may wonder where we should get if each person in isolation had to find the norms for himself. Where would we be if there were not always people who had tested, exemplified and experienced in a variety of ways the meaning, the concrete function and the human value of these norms? If the child were not constantly told what it must do, what is really human? Where would the family, the social group and even the state be if it were not possible to make use of every means and all the media to *say* what we ought to do, to what we must cling unreservedly, which is the right, the good, the truly human way?

2. *The criterion for deciding what is Christian*

Only relatively few people—of this we can be quite certain—are capable of using the many modern opportunities of information and communication in such a way as to be able to adopt a completely independent, critical attitude in society. And even the most critical and independent person is not guided simply by the norms which he has himself discovered and substantiated by reason. For no one begins at zero. Nor is this only because he is determined by his environment, pre-programmed and driven by instinct. He belongs to a community, to a tradition. Even before him, people in very diverse conditions tried to live in a manner befitting human dignity. Normative human conduct is essentially made known by human beings, in a genuinely human way by words, deeds, achievements and attitudes, which cannot be deduced from general truths but emerge in a very concrete way out of a complex tension between intellectual reflection and immediate involvement. A risk is always taken with an ethos which can be proved by its results to be sustainable, which can be measured by its "fruits." We might have gone into a lengthy and complex analysis at this point, but we must be content to say briefly that *knowledge of the good, its norms, models, signs, is conveyed to the individual by society.*

Hence neither philosophical nor theological ethics can simply create an ethos and impose it as binding on a large group of people. As a science, theological ethics—like theological science as a whole[25]—can define scope and limits, remove impediments, utilize experiences, clarify prejudices, bring out the true or false, genuine or hypocritical ethos. It can help to give rational guidance to the reception of new ethical norms. By integrating the multifarious conclusions of the human sciences it can offer new impulses, questions and opportunities, as a result of which a human ethos acquires new dimensions, becomes better and more quickly adapted to the present and the imminent future. But, through all this, freedom of consent, strength of experience and particularly the power of convincing speech should not and cannot be replaced, but in fact stimulated.

Would it not therefore be a good thing for someone to make use of the experiences and maxims of a community, of the great human and religious traditions, of the wealth of experience of his own ancestors, in order to illuminate his own problems, the questions raised by the organization of his own life, his own norms and motivations? It is true that he can never get out of his personal responsibility for his actions and the maxims which govern his life. But for that very reason it is extraordinarily important for him to decide *who* is to tell him anything, to whom he will listen on *decisive issues.* From all the foregoing it is completely clear that the Christian lets *Christ* tell him what is essential even for practical action. But does this solve all problems in practice?

Specifically Christian norms?

As with the ambiguous understanding of God, it might also be said of the ambiguous ethical norms that they cease to be ambiguous in the light of the biblical proclamation. We may recall the Old Testament, especially the Ten Commandments (Decalogue), which are important also for the

Christian tradition: "You shall honor your father and mother. You shall not kill, not commit adultery, not steal, not bear false witness . . ." But precisely at this point it becomes obvious that at least a brief elucidation is necessary. Even the biblical precepts and prohibitions are norms conveyed by human means. What was said about norms in general still holds.

a. The *distinguishing feature* even *of the Old Testament ethos* did not consist in the individual precepts or prohibitions, but in the *Yahweh faith* which meant that all the individual precepts and prohibitions were subordinated to the will of the God of the Covenant.

The ethical requirements of the Old Testament—here we may rely on the results of Old Testament studies[26]—did not fall from heaven either in content or in form. What can be proved for the ethos of the prophets and correspondingly for that of the wisdom literature holds most of all for the earlier ethos of the law. The whole, lengthy Sinai story[27] contains some very complex material in the form of divine ordinances which reflect the different phases of time. Yet even the Ten Commandments—the "Ten Words,"[28] which are extant in two versions[29]—passed through a long history. The directives of the "second tablet" for interpersonal relationships go back to the moral and legal traditions of the pre-Israelite semi-nomadic tribes and have numerous analogies in the Near East. There was a long period during which they were put into practice, shaped and tested until the Decalogue had become so general and concise in content and form that it could be regarded as an adequate expression of the will of Yahweh.

These fundamental minimal requirements then are not specifically Israelite and they originated before faith in Yahweh. All that is specifically Israelite is the fact that these requirements are subordinated to the authority of Yahweh, the God of the Covenant, who is the "object" of the "first tablet" (duties to God). The new faith in Yahweh[30] had its effect on the former ethos: like other sets of precepts incidentally, these requirements insofar as they are compatible with faith in Yahweh outline as succinctly as possible Yahweh's will in regard to men. Now it is Yahweh himself who makes provision in the Ten Commandments for the rudiments of authentic human existence, as in the "second tablet" with reference to honoring parents, protecting life, to marriage, ownership and one's neighbor's honor. The peculiarity of Old Testament morality therefore consists not in finding out new ethical norms, but in placing traditional directives under the authority and protection of Yahweh and his covenant: in the assumption of the existing ethos into the new association with God. This theonomy presupposes the autonomous development of ethical norms and at the same time starts them on a new course: the existing norms undergo a further development and correction—admittedly, not consistently in all fields (marriage and the position of woman, for example)—in the light precisely of this God and his covenant.

The *consequences* of giving the Decalogue a religious setting within the covenant scheme are plain to see.[31]

Moral behavior acquires a new motivation: gratitude, love, the prospect of long life, the gift of freedom become decisive motives.

At the same time *moral life gains a new dynamism:* ancient pre-Israelite and recent extra-Israelite norms are increasingly if not completely adapted to the new relationship with God; new moral and legal norms are developed and there is a significant concentration and unification insofar as the "Ten Words" cease to be merely minimal ethical requirements and become pithy statements of God's will possessed of absolute validity and applying in principle to wider areas.

Finally, *moral obligation becomes more clearly defined.* It is true that the precepts and prohibitions retain their social meaning and remain indispensable postulates of a genuinely human existence. But at the same time they acquire a new religious character: Yahweh himself appears as advocate of humanity. Thus the fulfillment of the law becomes an expression of a union in faith and love with the divine Partner to the Covenant. And, although the norms have arisen autonomously out of the evaluation of human experiences, Israel has not now an impersonal law, but simply requirements of the God of the Covenant speaking and acting in history. Just like the ethos of the law, the existing (now Israelite) ethos of the prophets awaiting the eschatological reign of God and of the wisdom literature is taken up into the individualistic theological idea of wisdom.

b. The *distinguishing feature* in particular *of the Christian ethos* does not consist in the individual precepts or prohibitions, but in *faith in Christ* for which all the individual precepts or prohibitions are subordinated to Jesus Christ and his rule.

The ethical requirements of the New Testament—here we may rely on the results of New Testament studies[32]—did not fall from heaven either in content or in form. What holds for the ethos of the New Testament as a whole can be made clear particularly from the ethical requirements of the Apostle Paul. Not that we can really speak of a Pauline "ethic," since Paul did not develop either a system or a casuistry of morality. What he did was to draw his admonitions (paraenesis)—and this is important here—largely from Hellenistic and especially Jewish tradition.

Of course we cannot ascribe to him the "house tablets" with exhortations to the different classes, current in contemporary popular Graeco-Roman ethics (Epictetus, Seneca), as they are found first in the epistle to the Colossians[33] and in the epistle to the Ephesians dependent on it, as also in the pastoral epistles and the works of the Apostolic Fathers. But Paul certainly makes use of concepts and ideas from the Hellenistic popular philosophy of the time. And, although he uses only once the term "virtue" which is central to that ethic, he places it in this one text of Philippians in the midst of so many Greek—especially Stoic—ethical terms that the whole thing reads almost like a summary of current Greek ethics: "Whatever is true, whatever is noble, whatever is just, whatever is pure, whatever is lovable, whatever is reputable, if there is any virtue, anything worthy of praise—think over these things."[34] In the other lists of virtues and vices[35] Paul keeps to the Jewish more than to the Hellenistic tradition.

The consideration in the New Testament of some particular ethical requirement does not mean that this is specifically Christian[36] and as such without parallel. The ethical requirements taken over by Paul from Jewish or Hellenistic tradition can be justified for other reasons. Paul has no special principle of synthesis or selection, but justifies his ethical demands with a variety of motives: kingdom of God, imitation of Christ, eschatological kerygma, body of Christ, Holy Spirit, love, freedom, being in Christ. Although he uses catchwords like obedience or freedom, these are not meant to be systematic main themes but simply express the wholeness and indivisibility of the obligation on the part of the believer and the believing community to its Lord.

What is specifically Christian therefore is the fact that all ethical requirements are understood in the light of the rule of the crucified Jesus Christ. It is then not a question merely of what is moral. The gift and the task coincide under the rule of Jesus Christ; the indicative already contains the imperative. Jesus, to whom we *are* subordinated once and for all in baptism by faith, *must* remain Lord over us. "In following the Crucified it is a question of manifesting the rule of the risen Christ. Justification and sanctification go together in the sense that both mean assimilation to Christ. They are distinguished, since this does not happen once and for all, but must constantly be freshly experienced and endured in varying situations from the time when it all began with baptism."[37] Thus Pauline ethics is nothing but "the anthropological reverse side of his Christology."[38]

In these basic questions of ethical action, therefore, we are brought back to the central issue of this book: the proclamation and conduct, the suffering, death and new life of this Christ Jesus. And it is now confirmed retrospectively in the light of ethics how right it was, in determining what is Christian, to start out from this concrete Jesus Christ.

Concrete person instead of abstract principle

Christian proclamation and Christian action remain tied to his person, not merely historically but also essentially. Platonism as a doctrine can be separated from Plato and his life, Marxism as a system from Marx and his death. With Jesus of Nazareth, however, as we saw from beginning to end, his teaching forms such a unity with his life and death, with his fate, that an abstract system of universal ideas does not reproduce what was really involved. Even for the earthly Jesus and most of all for the Jesus who has entered into God's life and been confirmed by God, person and cause completely coincide. If the end of his proclamation, his action, his person, had been simply a fiasco, nothingness and not God, his death would have been the disavowal of his cause: nothing then would have been left of that cause which, it is claimed, is God's cause (and only as such man's cause). But if his end is eternal life with God, then he himself is and remains in person the living sign of the fact that his cause has a future, demands effort, deserves to be followed. No one then can claim to believe in the living Jesus without expressing in deeds his allegiance to that cause. Nor, on the other hand, can anyone support his cause without in practice entering into a bond of discipleship and fellowship with him.

The *following* of Christ is what distinguishes Christians from other disciples and supporters of great men, in the sense that Christians are ultimately dependent on this person, not only on his teaching, but also on his life, death and new life. No Marxist or Freudian would want to claim this for his teacher. Although Marx and Freud personally composed their works, these can be studied and followed even without a special commitment to their authors. Their works, their doctrines, are separable in principle from their persons. But we understand the real meaning of the Gospels, the "teaching" (message) of Jesus only in the light of his life, death and new life: in the New Testament as a whole his "teaching" cannot be separated from his person. For Christians then Jesus is certainly a teacher, but at the same time also essentially more than a teacher: he is *in person the living, archetypal embodiment of his cause.*

As long as Jesus remains in person the living embodiment of his cause, he can never become—like Marx and Engels, for instance, in totalitarian systems—a vacant, impassive portrait, a lifeless mask, the tamed object of a personal cult. This living Christ is and remains Jesus of Nazareth as he lived and preached, acted and suffered. This living Christ does not call merely for inconsequential adoration or even to mystical union. Nor of course does he call for literal imitation. But he does call for practical, personal discipleship.

For this it is notable that only the verb is used in the New Testament: "following" means "walking behind him."[39] It is a question of being active, no longer visibly accompanying him around the countryside as in Jesus' lifetime, but of binding oneself to him in the same spirit of allegiance and discipleship, of joining him permanently and making him the measure of one's own life. This is what following means: *getting involved with him and his way and going one's own way*—each of us has his own way—*in the light of his directions*. This possibility was seen from the beginning as the great opportunity: not a "must," but a "may." It is there-

fore a genuine vocation to such a way of life, a true grace, which requires us only to grasp it confidently and *adapt our lives* according to it.

The important thing is one's *attitude to life*. People so often have difficulty in finding convincing reasons for a particular decision. Why? Because no decision is ever explained merely in the light of immediate dispositions and motivations, but is rooted in a certain basic attitude, a basic approach, a basic orientation. In order to give a completely rational justification of a decision we would have to set out, not merely all the principles on which it was based, but also all the consequences which might result from it. This would mean giving a detailed description of our attitude to life (life-style, way of life), of which this one decision is part. But how can this be done in practice? "This complete specification is impossible in practice to give. The nearest attempts are those given by the great religions, especially those which can point to historical persons who have carried out the way of life in practice."[40]

The Christian faith is one of those great religions the strength of which lies in being able to justify and substantiate in detail an attitude to life, a way of life and a life-style, by pointing to a quite definite, authoritative, historical figure. In the light of Jesus Christ—with complete justification, as we saw—the basic attitude and basic orientation of a person, his form of life, life-style and way of life, can be described both comprehensively and concretely. In fact there is no doubt that the whole Christian message aims not merely at certain decisions, enterprises, motivations or dispositions, but at a wholly new approach to life: at an awareness transformed from the roots upward, a new basic attitude, a different scale of values, a radical rethinking and returning (*metanoia*) of the whole man.[41] And in this respect a historical figure is undoubtedly convincing in a way that is impossible to an impersonal idea, an abstract principle, a universal norm, a purely ideal system. Jesus of Nazareth is himself the *personification* of this new way of life.

a. As a concrete, historical person, Jesus possesses an *impressiveness* which is missing in an eternal idea, an abstract principle, a universal norm, a conceptual system.

Ideas, principles, norms, systems lack the turbulence of life, the vivid perceptibility and the inexhaustible, inconceivable richness of empirical-concrete existence. However clearly defined, simple and stable, however easy to conceive and express, ideas, principles, norms, systems appear to be detached, abstracted from the concrete and individual, and therefore colorless and remote from reality. Abstraction results in uniformity, rigidity, relative insubstantiality: all "sicklied o'er with the pale cast of thought."

A concrete person however does not merely stimulate thinking, critical-rational conversation, but also continually rouses fantasy, imagination and emotion, spontaneity, creativity and innovation: in a word, appeals to the whole man, of flesh and blood. We can depict a person,[42] but not a principle. We can enter into an immediate existential relationship with him. We can talk about a person and not only reason, argue, discuss, theologize. And just as a story cannot be replaced by abstract ideas, neither can narrating be replaced by proclaiming and appealing, images replaced by concepts, the experience of being stirred replaced by intellectual apprehension.[43] A person cannot be reduced to a formula.

Only a living figure and not a principle can *draw* people, can be "attractive" in the most profound and comprehensive sense of the term: *verba docent, exempla trahunt*, words teach, examples carry us with them. It is not for nothing that people speak of a "shining" example. The person makes an idea, a principle, visible: he gives it flesh and blood, "embodies" this idea, this principle, this ideal. Man then not only knows about it, he sees it in a living shape before him. No abstract norm is imposed on him, but a concrete standard is set up for him. He is not only given a few guidelines, but is enabled to take a concrete, comprehensive view of his life as a whole. He is not therefore expected merely to undertake a general "Christian" program or merely to realize a general "Christian" form of life, but he can be confident in this Jesus Christ himself and attempt to order his life according to his standard. Then Jesus, with all that he authoritatively is and means, proves to be far more than simply a "shining example,"[44] proves in fact to be the true "light of the world."[45]

b. As a concrete, historical person, Jesus possesses an *audibility* which makes ideas, principles, norms and systems appear to be mute.

Ideas, principles, norms and systems have neither words nor voice. They cannot call, cannot appeal. They can neither address us nor make demands on us. In themselves they have no authority. They are dependent on someone to give them their authority. Otherwise they remain unnoticed and ineffective.

A concrete, historical person has his unmistakable proper name. And the name Jesus—often uttered only with an effort and hesitatingly—can signify a power, a protection, a refuge, a claim. For this name is opposed to inhumanity, oppression, untruthfulness and injustice, and stands for humanity, freedom, justice, truth and love. A concrete, historical person has words and a voice. He can call and appeal. And the following of Christ is based essentially on being summoned by his person and way, that is, on a vocation—today conveyed by human words. A concrete, historical person can address us and make demands on us. And the following of Christ means being required by his person and his fate to commit ourselves to a specific way. Through the transmitted word a historical person can make himself heard even over the span of the centuries. And man with his perceptive reason is called, led by the words of Jesus in understanding faith, to attempt an interpretation of human life and to develop this human life.

Only a living figure and not a principle can make sweeping *demands*. Only such a figure can invite, summon, challenge. The person of Jesus

Christ is characterized, not only by impressiveness and luminosity, but also by practical direction. He can reach a man's personal center and stir him to enter on a free, existential encounter; he can activate that basic trust, that trust in God, in virtue of which man is capable of giving his heart to this person with his invitation and demands. He rouses the desire to act according to his will and shows the way in which this desire can be realized in ordinary life. And he provides that authority and assurance which enable us to act in accordance with his will even if it cannot always be proved completely rationally that such behavior is meaningful and worthwhile. So Jesus, with all that he is and means, then proves to be not only "the light," but the "Word" of God dwelling with men.[46]

c. As a concrete, historical person, Jesus displays a *realizability* which makes ideas often appear to be unattainable ideals, norms unrealizable laws, principles and systems unrealistic Utopias.

Ideas, principles, norms and systems are not themselves the reality which they exist to regulate and set in order. They do not offer realization, they demand it. Of themselves they have no reality in the world, they are dependent on someone to realize them.

A historical person however is indisputably real, even though this personality is open to different interpretations. There is no doubt that Jesus Christ existed, that he proclaimed a very definite message, displayed a particular attitude, realized certain ideals, suffered and survived a very specific fate. With his person and his way we are dealing, not with a vague possibility, but with a historical reality. And, unlike an idea or a norm, one historical person cannot simply be rendered obsolete by another: he is irreplaceably, once and for all, himself. In the light of the historical person of Jesus man can know that he *must* go on his way and keep to it. There is no question therefore of an imperative being simply imposed on us: you shall go on this way and be justified, liberated. An indicative is presupposed: he went by this way and—in view of this—you *are* justified, liberated.

Only a living figure and not a principle can be *encouraging* in this comprehensive fashion. Only such a figure can attest in this way the possibility of realization. Only he can stimulate people to follow him: inspiring and strengthening their confidence that they too can go his way, dispelling doubts about their ability to do good. All this means of course that a new standard is set: not only an external goal, a timeless ideal, a universal norm of conduct, but a reality, a promise fulfilled, which only has to be trustfully accepted. Norms tend to require a minimum, Jesus a maximum —but the way remains always within man's power and in accordance with his nature. So Jesus himself, with all that he is and means, then proves to be not only "light" and "word" for man, but quite plainly "the way, the truth and the life."[47]

Jesus therefore acts as the authoritative concrete person: in his impressiveness, audibility and realizability, attracting, demanding, encouraging. And do not these very words—"light," "word," "way," "truth," "life"—themselves clearly state what is essential for Christian action, for Christian ethics: the criterion of what is Christian, the distinctively Christian reality, the much discussed "Proprium Christianum"?[48]

The distinctive Christian element in ethics

In ethics too we shall not find the distinctive Christian feature in any abstract idea or in a principle, not simply in a special mentality, a background of meaning, a new disposition or motivation. And others too—Jews, Muslims, humanists of all types—can act out of "love" or in "freedom," in the light of a "creation" or "consummation." The criterion of what is Christian, the distinctive Christian feature—this holds both for dogmatics and consequently also for ethics—is not an abstract something nor a Christ idea, not a Christology nor a Christocentric system of ideas: it is *this concrete Jesus as the Christ, as the standard.*

It is quite legitimate, as we saw, to track down the autonomous discovery or even acceptance of ethical norms and establish the different connections with other systems of norms. It is also legitimate therefore to follow up different traditions within the ethos of Jesus and to note what they have in common with the ideas of other Jewish or Greek teachers. Jesus was not by any means the first to put forward simple ethical instructions (for example, rules of prudence) or even certain higher ethical requirements (for example, the golden rule): all these are found elsewhere.[49] But, in examining all this, it is easy to overlook the unique context of Jesus' ethical requirements, which are not to be regarded as isolated peaks and lofty statements in a wilderness of ethically worthless propositions, allegorical and mystical speculations and trivialities, sophisticated casuistry and ossified ritualism. And it is particularly easy to overlook the radicality and totality of Jesus' requirements: the reduction and concentration of the commandments to a simple and final statement (Decalogue, basic formula of love of God and neighbor); the universal and radical significance of love of neighbor shown in service regardless of precedence; endless forgiving; renunciation without a quid pro quo; love of enemies.[50] The important thing however is that we shall never see the full meaning of all this if we do not see it in the *totality of Jesus' person and fate.* What does this mean?

In the music of Wolfgang Amadeus Mozart we can observe the roots of his style and all the points at which he is dependent on Leopold Mozart, on Schobert, Johann Christian Bach, Sammartini, Piccinni, Paisiello, Haydn and so many others; but we have not thereby explained the phenomenon of Mozart. Although he was intensely occupied with the whole musical environment and the whole available musical tradition, we find in amazing universality and differentiated balance all styles and genres of music of his time; we can analyze "German" and "Italian" elements, homophony and polyphony, the erudite and the courtly, continuity and contrast of themes, and nevertheless lose sight of the new, unique, specific Mozartean feature: this is the *whole* in its higher unity rooted in the freedom of the spirit, it is *Mozart himself* in his music.

So too in Jesus' ethos all possible traditions and parallels can be detected and again brought together in unity, but this does not explain the phenomenon of Jesus. And we can emphasize the pre-eminence and universality of love in Jesus' message and bring out the radicality of the theocentrism, of the concentration, intensity, spiritualizing of the ethos of Jesus by comparison—for instance—with Jewish ethics; we can distinguish also the new background of meaning and the new motivations: but we are still far from grasping clearly what is new, unique, about Jesus. What is new and unique about Jesus is the *whole* in its unity; it is this *Jesus himself* in his work.

Yet even then we have only begun to define what is distinctive about Jesus and have not even begun—and here the analogy with Mozart ends—to define what is the distinctively Christian feature, although this is based of course on what is different about Jesus. Nor do we catch sight of this *distinctive Christian element*, particularly with reference to Christian ethics, if we look merely at Jesus' proclamation, the Sermon on the Mount (ethos), and then transfer this directly to the present day—as if nothing had happened in the meantime. Between the historical Jesus of the Sermon on the Mount and the Christ of Christendom however there are death and resurrection, which come within the dimension of God's action and without which the Jesus proclaiming would never have become the Jesus Christ proclaimed.[61] Just what is distinctively Christian therefore is the *whole* in its unity, it is this *Christ* Jesus himself as proclaiming and proclaimed, as crucified and living.

Any attempt to reduce the cause of Jesus Christ to a cause understood exclusively as that of Jesus, assuming that God's dimension in this event can be disregarded, must lack any final binding force. Christian ethics too is then exposed to arbitrary ethical pluralism. And even an "Ethics of the New Testament" acquires a unity only with difficulty[62] if it treats successively Jesus, primitive community, Paul, the rest of the New Testament, as if there were—so to speak—four new Gospels, as if there could ever be any talk in this respect of a juxtaposition—theological or historical. And Christian ethics too must be worked out in the light of the fact that its foundation *is* laid and that this foundation is not simply the commandment of love or the critical relationship to the world, or the community, or eschatology, but solely Jesus the Christ.[63]

It has been shown repeatedly throughout this book that the reference to this name is anything but an empty formula even and indeed particularly for the working out of human action. We may be permitted therefore to dispense with concrete details and be content to refer back in general and in principle to all that has been said. It is all summed up in the words of Dietrich Bonhoeffer, who not only taught discipleship but practiced it to the very end. On the meaning of the following of Christ he says: "It is nothing else than bondage to Jesus Christ alone, completely breaking through every program, every set of laws. No other significance is possible, since Jesus is the only significance. Beside Jesus nothing has any significance. He alone matters."[54]

The basic model

At this point, however, we must preclude two possible misunderstandings.

First: We have depicted Jesus Christ as a historical figure in his impressiveness, audibility and realizability. But, however impressive, audible and realizable, Jesus' person and cause are not from the outset so unmistakably discernible and so conclusively evident to anyone that it is simply impossible to reject them. On the contrary. This very impressiveness is so attractive, this audibility so demanding, this realizability so encouraging, that man finds himself faced with a clear and inescapable decision which in fact can only be a *decision of faith:* a decision to trust this message, to commit himself to Jesus' cause, to follow Jesus' way.

Second: Even for someone who has decided in the light of faith for him, for his cause and his way, Jesus does not become an easy, universal answer to all the ethical questions of ordinary life: methods of birth control, education of children, control of power, organizing co-determination and assembly-line production, environment pollution. He is not an optional model simply to be copied in every detail, but a *basic model* to be realized in an infinite variety of ways according to time, place and person. Nowhere in the Gospels is he described in terms of his virtues, but always in his actions and in his relations with others. What he is, is shown in what he does. This Jesus Christ permits discipleship in response and in relation to himself, but no imitation, no copies of himself.

If someone commits himself to Jesus as the standard, if he lets himself be determined by the person of Jesus Christ as the *basic model for a view of life and a practice of life*, this means in fact the transformation of the whole man. For Jesus Christ is not only an external goal, a vague dimension, a universal rule of conduct, a timeless ideal. He determines and influences man's life and conduct, not only externally, but from within. Following Christ means not only information, but formation: not merely a superficial change, but a change of heart and therefore the change of the whole man. It amounts to the fashioning of a *new man:* a new creation within the always diverse, individually and socially conditioned context of each one's own life in its particularity and singularity, without any attempt to impose uniformity.

We might then summarily define Jesus' unique significance for human action in this way: with his word, his actions and his fate, in his impressiveness, audibility and realizability, he is himself *in person* the *invitation,* the *appeal,* the *challenge,* for the individual and society. As the standard basic model of a view of life and practice of life, without a hint of legalism or casuistry, he provides inviting, obligatory and challenging *examples, significant deeds, orientation standards, exemplary values, model cases.* And by this very fact he impresses and influences, changes and transforms human beings who believe and thus human society. What Jesus quite concretely conveys and makes possible both to the individual and to the community who commit themselves to him may be described as follows:[55]

A *new* basic orientation *and* basic attitude, *a new approach to life, to which Jesus summoned men and whose consequences he indicated. If a man or a human community has in mind this Jesus Christ as concrete guiding principle and living model for their relations with man, world and God, they may and can live differently, more genuinely, more humanly. He makes possible an identity and inner coherence in life.*

New motivations, *new motives of action, which can be discovered from Jesus' "theory" and "practice." In his light it is possible to answer the question why man should act just in one way and not in another: why he should love and not hate; why—and even Freud had no answer to this*[56]*—he should be honest, forbearing and kind wherever possible, even when he loses by it and is made to suffer as a result of the unreliability and brutality of other people.*

New dispositions, *new consistent insights, tendencies, intentions, formed and maintained in the spirit of Jesus Christ. Here readiness to oblige is engendered, attitudes created, qualifications conveyed, which can guide conduct, not only for isolated and passing moments, but permanently. Here we find dispositions of unpretentious commitment for one's fellow men, of identification with the handicapped, with the fight against unjust structures; dispositions of gratitude, freedom, magnanimity, unselfishness, joy, and also of forbearance, pardon and service; dispositions which are tested in borderline situations, in readiness for complete self-sacrifice, in renunciation even when it is not necessary, in a readiness to work for the greater cause.*

New projects, *new actions on a great or small scale, which in imitation of Jesus Christ begin at the very point where no one wants to help: not only universal programs to transform society, but concrete signs, testi-*

> *monies, evidence of humanity and of humanizing both the individual and human society.*
>
> A *new* background of meaning *and a new* definition of the goal *in the ultimate reality, in the consummation of man and mankind* in God's *kingdom, which can sustain not only what is positive in human life, but also what is negative. In the light and power of Jesus Christ the believer is offered an ultimate meaning, not only for man's life and action, but also for his suffering and death; not only for the story of man's success, but also for the story of his suffering.*

In a word: for both the individual human being and the community Jesus Christ in person, with word, deed and fate, is
invitation ("you may"),
appeal ("you should"),
challenge ("you can"),
basic model therefore of a *new way of life, a new life-style, a new meaning to life.*

III. Being Christian as Being Radically Human

All theological talk, all Christian programs, about a "new man," a "new creation," have no effect on society and in fact are often calculated only to perpetuate inhuman social conditions, as long as Christians today fail to struggle against unjust structures and so to make convincingly clear to the world what is this "new man," this "new creation." Is there anyone who does not suffer daily in one way or another under these often anonymous and opaque structures in marriage and family, in work or in training, in living or economic conditions, on the labor market, in associations, parties, organizations? "Under certain social conditions a liberated or liberating attitude is practically impossible. There are living quarters which systematically destroy the mother-child relationship; there are ways of organizing labor which define the relations between the strong and the weak in Darwinistic terms and thus leave dispositions regarded as useless for production—like helpfulness, sympathy or fairness—to atrophy. If conditions are changed—that is, if living conditions are made fit for human beings and co-operative forms of organization established—then conditions exist which offer the possibility of a different life: no more than this, but also no less."[1]

1. *Social relevance*

But we should be able to change human beings! This is the plaint of all those who want to make great structural changes, the educators and politicians, technocrats and revolutionaries. Nevertheless they have had only a partial success in changing man inwardly, in his innermost core, in changing his "heart," with the aid of environment technology or psychoanalysis or even political revolution. For how can we change man's heart without depriving him of dignity and freedom, without some sort of manipulation (of the genes, perhaps)? How can we change man in such a way that a new man emerges from the roots? It has now become clear that the message of Jesus Christ is aimed precisely at this change, at this new man. It is aimed, as we continually stressed, at man as entangled in the social structures. All that we now have to do is to bring out a little more clearly the fact that the Christian message and man's social situation must be seen as interdependent.

No political short cuts

First of all it must be repeated that Jesus, despite his fearless advocacy of a radical change, his criticism of the ruling classes and outstanding grievances, was not a politico-social revolutionary. His message of the kingdom of God which was to change everything, liberating man from all evil and for all good, was not a program of politico-social action.[2] If then we take him as the standard, we cannot even today turn the Christian message directly into a program of politico-social action.

But it also remains true that Jesus, despite his rejection of violence, hatred and revenge, was not a man of the establishment or an apologist of the existing order. In the light of God's claim on man he questioned the very basis of the religio-social system and in this sense—but only in this sense—his message had political implications.[3] If then we take him as the standard, we must even today take seriously the political implications of the Christian message.

Christian practice therefore may not by any means be restricted to the private or non-political sphere, nor to purely ecclesiastical affairs. Under no circumstances can it disregard society and the world. Even the separation in theological theory of dogmatics (teaching of faith) from ethics (moral teaching), which emerged only gradually and for technical reasons to permit a division of labor, presents a number of problems in this respect. The result has often been a practically ineffective dogmatics on the one hand and a dogmatically unsubstantiated ethics on the other. The classical works of the Reformation period—Melanchthon's *Loci communes* and Calvin's *Institutio*—still treat dogmatics and ethics in one, not to mention the medieval *summas* (notably that of Aquinas which provided the foundation for the systematizing of ethics). If today for technical reasons it is scarcely possible to avoid a division of labor between dogmatics and ethics and even between individual and social ethics, the link must be established—as we are trying to do here—of dogmatics with individual and social ethics and vice versa. Christian faith and Christian action cannot be separated either in the individual or in the social sphere.

Jesus—wholly within the horizon of immediate expectation of the kingdom of God—did not produce any program for the renewal and transformation of social structures. He did not raise in principle either the question of slavery or that of woman, still less the universal emancipation of man. Nor did he outline any commercial, political or cultural ethics. He did not bother in any way about large areas of social life like law and politics, learning and culture as a whole. Neither did he found the Church as a "perfect society" nor claim for it authority ("direct" or "indirect power") over "temporal matters." The fact cannot be overlooked that the Sermon on the Mount and all Jesus' ethical requirements were addressed primarily to the individual or to groups.[4]

But after the horizon of the apocalyptic immediate expectation had been submerged and Christendom had to prepare for a longer period of existence, the social and political implications of the Christian message needed to be developed—always with a view to the coming of God's kingdom—quite differently from what had seemed right at the beginning. The danger of a direct identification of the Christian message with a political program was present even in the first centuries. Naturally the change of power in the Roman Empire under Constantine was an invitation to hand over theology uncritically and without control to the dominant social-political ideology. The first great outline of a Christian "*political theology*," that of the Constantinian court bishop, Eusebius of Caesarea, developed as a model for many a religio-political imperial theology according to the program: "One God, one Logos, one emperor, one empire." The term *theologia politike* (or *theologia civilis*, distinguished in Stoicism from "mythical" or "natural" theology) in the historical context means the direct theologizing of the existing forms of state and society and an intertwining of the religious and the political factors in a way that was first severely criticized at length by Augustine in his *City of God*. For Christian "political theology" was the immediate successor of the religious state ideology of ancient Rome and thus itself a pure ideology of the state. Its theological sanctioning of the primacy of politics and its authorization of the absolute claim of the state influenced not only Byzantine Caesaropapism and in the Renaissance period Machiavelli's and Hobbes's theories of state and society, but also even the political romanticism and the French traditionalism of the last century (and in another way the absolutist religio-political papacy).

The concept of "political theology" is thus burdened with the two-thousand-year tradition of an integralist theory of state and society, aiming at the restoration of the old order. Even after the distinction between state and society and the new conception of political order as a variable and changeable order of freedom had come to prevail as a result of the political "Enlightenment," the concept retained its own historical gravitation. It can scarcely be given a new function by decree as a critical-revolutionary concept without misunderstandings, particularly since it has gained a new and dubious publicity in the present century through the work of Carl Schmitt, the Catholic political theorist who involuntarily prepared the way for National Socialism.[5] His views were attacked at an early stage by the theologian Erik Peterson, who tried to prove in a well-known study of monotheism as a political problem "the theological impossibility of a 'political theology.'"[6]

Despite all the demarcations and dissociations put forward by recent advocates of a new "political theology,"[7] it is liable to be understood, not as a critical theological awareness of the social and political implications and tasks of Christianity, but—as the name itself implies—constantly in theory and practice as "politicizing theology." The term itself is an invitation to load on to "political theology" from behind—so to speak—a political ideology (now of course "left wing"). It is no longer a question of providing religious grounds for an absolutist order in state and society, but of supporting "changes of democratic political systems and constitutions," "emancipation," "democracy" or "socialism" by directly deducing from the Christian message in a spirit of political partisanship every possible political demand: from the nationalization of key industries to the possibility of voting out of office at any time every one of the people's representatives.

Instead of an anti-Communism and anti-socialism directly based on "Christianity," we now have a criticism of capitalism and a socialist theory also directly based on "Christianity." Certain political thought schemes of a modern critique of society are claimed to be categories of the Christian message. As a counterpart to the reactionary politicizing of faith from the right (in the sense of an establishment theology), the danger is now evident of a revolutionary neo-politicizing of faith from the left (in the extreme case a theology of revolution).[8] Formerly God was directly and unequivocally involved in the political order and represented by the absolute ruler (or Pope); now people think they can find his traces directly in the history of social freedom and in the socialist revolution (but not of course in the National Socialist seizure of power or in military putsches). Now as before politicizing theology claims to be an awareness of God in political systems and movements.

But is there not lacking in *both* conceptions a critical dissociation from and a genuine respect for the modern secular autonomy of politics, state and society, which are part of the worldliness of the world and have no need of neo-integralist theologizing? Do not *both* conceptions fail to see the true political relevance of the Christian message, from which it is impossible directly to deduce a particular policy and particular detailed solutions for questions of law and constitution, for economic, social, cultural and foreign policy?

If however it is better not to use the historically loaded and now misleading term "political theology," because of the dubious terminology and uncertain content, its positive implications—as we insisted at the very beginning of our long road[9]—should be accepted. We do in fact need what had better be called a *social-critical theology* which is not simply identified with the present social order, with the status quo, but has a critical-dialectical relationship with it. Little as a particular program of socio-political action has to do with the Christian message, still less can an interiorization, spiritualization and individualization find support in that message. Whenever this happens—and it has happened continually up to the present time—there is a failure to understand the social-ethical potency and social relevance of the Gospel, the primarily (and not subsequently) public character of the Christian message and also the social-critical function and practical import of Christian theology and the Church.

Social consequences

If Christians with their theology wish to undertake a critical function in society—in certain respects and within certain limits—they must know and be able to explain the basis of their criticism. If both their negative and positive criticism amount to no more than what society itself is constantly saying, then their specifically Christian criticism is superfluous. It is not sufficient to call for justice, peace and freedom, like all the rest, merely using a biblical label like "Kingdom of God." After all that has been said, it is clear that a critique of society can be described as specifically Christian only if its authorization comes from *this Jesus Christ*.

The author of the best book on Jesus from the Marxist-atheist standpoint, the Czech Milan Machoveč, rightly draws attention to the fact—typical of the situation—that "polemicists and critics practically never reproach Christians for being followers of Christ, but on the contrary for *not* being such, for betraying the cause of Jesus, for showing all the characteristics which Jesus attributed to the Pharisees, for falling under the condemnation: 'These people honor me with their lips, but their hearts are far from me.' This may be a criticism of Christianity at any particular time, but not of the real ideals of Jesus."[10] And at the same time he recalls in particular the charges laid by Karl Marx against bourgeois Christianity with the slogan: "Does not every moment of your practical lives give the lie to your theories?"

Despite all necessary distinctions, in the light of this Christ Jesus, it is not possible simply to separate theory and practice, private and public, religious and political. But might there not be an enormous significance for both the individual and secular society, for the whole field of public and political life, for people in every position, in every office and in all ranks, as also for structures and institutions, in what has been said in all the different chapters in the light of Jesus Christ

on the identification with the weak, sick, poor, underprivileged, oppressed and even the moral failures?

on forgiveness without end, mutual service regardless of rank, renunciation without a quid pro quo?

on the removal of barriers between associates and non-associates, distant

people and neighbors, good and bad, in a love which does not exclude good will even to the opponent and enemy?
on the norms, precepts and prohibitions, which exist for the sake of men, and on the men who do not exist for the sake of the norms, precepts and prohibitions?
on the institutions, traditions and hierarchs, to be relativized for man's sake?
on God's will as supreme norm, which aims at nothing but man's well-being?
on this God himself who identifies himself with the needs and hopes of men, who does not demand but gives; who does not oppress but raises up; who does not punish but liberates; who establishes the absolute rule, not of law, but of grace?
on this death finally and its forsakenness and on the hope of new life and the consummation in God's kingdom?

Does it need much imagination to see that things would look different, not only in man's heart, but also in society, its structures and institutions, if this message were really lived? Or indeed that things look different even now whenever this message *is* lived? We do not really lack a fundamental Christian program, there is nothing wrong with this Christ Jesus himself: it is entirely the fault of Christians if too little is changed in the world. *Christians* themselves are the strongest *argument against Christianity:* Christians who are not Christian. *Christians* themselves are the strongest *argument for Christianity:* Christians who live a Christian life. Faced with the familiar and hardly pleasant history of the Church, we often forget the very much more encouraging history of Christians—unfortunately only to a very limited extent an object for the historian.

Naturally we cannot make any *law* applicable to everyone out of the Christian program, which is Jesus Christ himself. And whenever anything of the kind has been attempted, even in particular issues—for instance, in matrimonial legislation (divorce)—the result has been an un-Christian totalitarian oppression of men by men. And when people wanted to carry through such a program quite consistently and universally—as with the religio-political fanaticism of the Anabaptist revolutionaries of Münster (1534–35)—and, absolutely intent on justice, freedom and peace, to bring about the kingdom of God by force in this society (the "kingdom of Zion"), it ended in the cruel reign of terror of a Christian integralism. Finally, whenever the Church itself turned the Gospel into an infallible law (of teaching, dogma, morals, discipline), unspiritual force and bondage inevitably replaced Christian freedom and spiritual service: there had to be burnings at the stake (made of wood or other material) and people had to suffer; the Church had to become a Grand Inquisitor and Jesus himself silently departed.

Jesus himself—this much has become abundantly clear—did not act like a new lawgiver. He neither inculcated a natural moral law[11] nor set up a positive revealed law:[12] no directions for all areas of life, no all-embracing moral principles, no new ethical system. Following him does not mean carrying out a number of regulations. Even the Sermon on the Mount[13]—as is well known, a redactional collection of scattered texts—is not a summary of precepts and prohibitions to be literally observed: it is not a code of conduct, not a compendium of moral theology and certainly not a basic law of a new society from which all evil would be abolished and where state power, police, courts and army would no longer be needed. The Sermon on the Mount does not replace a juridical and legal system. What it does is to give expression to what cannot be legally and juridically regulated. And at least indirectly it leads to the changing and humanization of the juridical and legal system.

Without norms of course, without a minimal consensus on norms of political, economic, social and individual action, no society would be viable. But Jesus' instructions are not new norms, not abstract, universally binding rules of human behavior and human fellowship, the limits of which are exposed by the concrete case. And in particular the much-quoted "*commandment*" *of love*[14] is not meant to be a new law: nor a compendium, a summary, a collection of many laws. We cannot love just because we must. The "commandment" of love is not so much a commandment as the quintessence, the main issue, the whole meaning, and according to Paul the "fulfilling" of the law. Understood from Jesus' standpoint, love is not simply one virtue among others, not one principle among similar principles. It is really the basic criterion of all virtues, principles, norms, forms of human behavior. The commandment always exists for the sake of love and not love for the sake of the commandment.

As we saw,[15] Jesus had reduced all the commandments with unprecedented simplicity and concreteness to the double commandment of love of God and neighbor: a requirement which can embrace unreservedly the whole life of man and yet applies quite precisely to each particular case. Love is understood, not as sense or feeling, as sentimentality, but as the deliberately decided attitude and act of good will toward one's neighbor, even toward one's opponent: an alertness, an openness, a helpfulness in creative conduct, in productive imagination and in decisive action in each case in the light of the situation. It involves man and wife, boy and girl, colleagues, neighbors, acquaintances and strangers.

According to Jesus then love is good *in all situations*. It must be decisive when one good is weighed against another. It cannot be pinned down to certain actions but is the essential regulating factor for all actions. The commandments acquire a uniform meaning from love, but they are also limited and on occasion—as Jesus' infringements of the law in practice show—even suspended, for man's sake. This does not mean morality without norms, not antinomianism or libertinism, not a license for the subjectivist whims of obstinate and frequently uninformed individuals. Love requires supreme responsibility of conscience, which has to make use of all opportunities of information and communication (the "well-informed conscience"). In his practical life man is expected to abide entirely by the norms, precepts and prescriptions, without which the one society or a particular community or even in the last resort the individual cannot live: beginning with traffic lights and going on to the country's constitution and God's Ten Commandments. But all norms—including the Ten Commandments—must serve man: according to Jesus, they exist for the sake of man and not man for the sake of the norms.

That is why in each and every case action is required, not according to the letter of the law, but in a form that does justice to the situation.[16] And it is love which *directs this action in the light of the situation*, which provides an all-embracing and yet concrete, final criterion. It facilitates the settlement of conflicts of duties which inevitably occur when particular commandments are understood as laws to be literally observed. Man no longer follows mechanically the particular precept or prohibition, but responds to the demands and possibilities of reality: every norm, every precept or prohibition, has its intrinsic criterion in love of neighbor.

Love then, active good will to our fellow man, from Jesus' standpoint is that which makes equivocal norms[17] become unequivocal in the concrete case. In this sense we can understand Paul's saying: love does not hurt our neighbor and so is the fulfilling of the law.[18] But the opposite is also true: if someone had all knowledge and all faith and if he were even to surrender his body to be burnt, it would be of no avail without love.[19] Anyone who behaves with good will toward his neighbor fulfills God's law even if he acts against a particular commandment: for the meaning of God's law is love. Love therefore means an appeal, not for adaptation or possession, but for freedom, which is measured by the freedom of the other person.

In modern society man can live less than ever without norms. But in practice the Christian will interpret and carry out (or not carry out) these norms in loving good will to the advantage of his neighbor.

That which helps the other person who needs me here and now is therefore good, that which harms or hurts him is bad.

What is it then in the concrete situation which renders unequivocal norms so menacingly equivocal in themselves? How do the obligations become unequivocal when they are so often far from evident and can be articulated and defined in so many ways in the light of the claim of reality, of human pressures and needs? We saw that it is not at all easy to decide what is genuinely human, what is humane: why we should not simply domineer and consume; why we should love and not hate, none of which is at all easy to prove by pure reason. The direction can be seen in Jesus

Christ: there it is quite clear why man should love and not hate; why he should not domineer over other people, but serve them; why he should not simply take possession of things but also renounce them; why he should opt for helpfulness against greed for profit, for kindness against cruelty, for self-sacrifice against avarice. In brief, no matter what the situation, *love makes the norms unequivocal.* Through love the supreme norm remains the will of God, who wants man's total well-being: what helps man, our neighbor or our neighbors, is right.

It is a question of neighbors—the plural must be stressed more than ever in the modern mass society. As modern group study[20] has frequently shown, it is a question, not only of the relationship of one individual to another, but of the relationship of individuals to groups, of groups to individuals, and especially of *groups to groups.* We need only recall racial discrimination, nationalism, social oppression, the selfishness of groups, classes and parties. Love of neighbor then has also a social, collective aspect and is required especially by the weaker, handicapped, oppressed groups.

This becomes more clearly evident in the underdeveloped countries of Asia, Africa and Latin America than in the highly developed industrial states. Even on a large scale love is relative to the situation and experiences in particular countries and continents can be generalized only with difficulty, but they can certainly be made indirectly fruitful for situations elsewhere. A special challenge to active Christian involvement is presented by *"Christian" Latin America,* where not only relatively small groups, but whole nations, subcultures and social classes are suffering poverty and exploitation and can scarcely make use even of the most rudimentary human rights. Problems of essential human self-realization, which exist only to a relatively slight extent in Europe and North America, have a quite different degree of urgency here and form a test case of what it is to be human and to be Christian which must be taken very seriously by Europeans and North America.

Commitment to liberation

Since the Latin American bishops' conference at Medellín in 1968—for that continent, comparable in significance to the Second Vatican Council —the Latin American Church and theology also have become aware in a new way of the social, political, cultural and religious situation: "Latin America appears to live still under the tragic sign of underdevelopment, which makes it impossible for our brothers not only to enjoy material goods, but also to fulfill themselves. Despite all the efforts that are made, we are faced with hunger and poverty, massive disease and infant mortality, illiteracy and marginalism, profound inequalities of income and tensions between the social classes, outbreaks of violence and a scanty participation of the people in the management of the common good."[21]

In face of such *structural inhumanity and "violence,"* described by South American Christians as a state of "collective" sin and as a scandal crying to heaven, Christians cannot, the Churches cannot and may not be silent, cannot ignore their share of responsibility and remain inactive.[22] Indeed, with their own program, with this Jesus Christ and the Old Testament prophets in mind, ought they not to be the first to register their prophetic protest and jointly actively oppose any sort of political, economic or cultural oppression? There must be a commitment to liberation for all who are legally destroyed as human beings and who have no real opportunity to be Christians: for the forsaken of a continent, whose poverty is not a natural necessity but the side effect of a cruel social system; for the classes of people directly or indirectly exploited, cultures despised, races (Indians, for instance) suffering from discrimination. A commitment to liberation so that an underdeveloped people may obtain basic food and basic culture and the underprivileged full equality before the law; so that the unbalanced international division of labor, the constantly new sources of dependence of the underdeveloped peoples on the industrial nations, are removed and the unjust economic conditions internally and externally abolished. A commitment to liberation so that in all this a new way of being human and being Christian becomes possible: not only an inactive sympathy or magnanimous acts of mercy, nor only superficial reforms, but really a "new man" in a changed, truly just, fraternal and free social order.

Under these specific Latin American conditions *theology* has a special function. Still less than elsewhere can it be merely scholarly preoccupation with the past, merely repetition of ancient dogmas and teachings or even merely critical-historical exegesis of Scripture. In these countries the contrast between Christian program and human opportunities in the broad masses of the people is so great that theology is faced with the problem of speaking about God and his love for men, not only as elsewhere before non-Christians, but more or less before non-humans or sub-humans in an inhuman world. In such a theology the start should be made, not from what theologians have said about theology, but from what reality itself says today directly of man and society. This would not be merely a "theology of earthly things" or a "theology of question," such as we had a short time ago in Europe, nor merely a variety of a "political theology" regarded by South Americans as all-too-academic, noncommittal, ineffective and concentrated on one part of the world. It would have to be a *teología de la liberación*, a "theology of liberation" presented in the form of a program with great spiritual depth and evangelical immediacy: theology as consistent critical reflection in the light of living experience there today of the liberation movement and liberation praxis in confrontation with the very concretely understood Christian message.[23]

Under these circumstances theology will be understood as something more than an abstract theology of secularization, as "a theological reflection born of the experience of shared efforts to abolish the current unjust situation and to build a different society, freer and more human," where "people can live with dignity and be the agents of their own destiny."[24] A theology, that is, which is ethically oriented and wholly concentrated on practice: to be more exact, on "liberation praxis." It would be a theology turned in these countries against all brutal oppression, whether politico-social (the poor, downtrodden, weak), erotic-sexual (woman as sex object) or pedagogical (children educated in an oligarchic-repressive educational system).[25] This theology would seek to present a historical project of political, economic, cultural, sexual liberation, as a true sign and anticipation of the definitive eschatological project of complete freedom in the kingdom of God.

Not only theology, however, but also the *Church*—which so often in the centuries of colonial Christendom and right up to the present time betrayed its own program—may no longer misuse the Gospel of Jesus Christ to justify a social situation clearly contradicting the requirements of that Gospel. The Gospel must no longer be distorted and turned into an ideology, sanctioned by the Church, useful to a thin, excessively wealthy upper stratum for satisfying the religious needs of the masses and so securing a social order which is set up and dominated only by a few and is of service and advantage only to a few. The Church, for which the claim to universal liberation in Christ cannot be restricted solely to the religious plane, must identify itself differently from what it has done hitherto with the wretched condition of large masses of the people, with their hopes and struggles for a better human existence. And so the fact cannot be overlooked that Christians—from workers up to priests and bishops—are getting involved to an increasing extent in the liberation process: "liberation *from* an overall system of oppression and liberation *for* the self-realization of the people, enabling them to determine for themselves their political, economic and cultural destiny."[26]

"Commitment for liberation" then along the whole line! But here we must be cautious about slogans. For this expression and a number of things said and demanded in this context are *vague and ambiguous*. "Even today in Latin America it can be utilized for ideological or party political ends."[27] Cannot "theology of liberation" easily become a mere shell of a word, filled with the most violently contrasted political contents: from the opinions of relatively conservative theologians to the explicitly Marxist arguments of revolutionaries?[28] Most leading advocates of a "theology of liberation" of course see the great danger: that the Christian message, which cannot be identified with any existing or future social order, might be reduced to a political program or a political campaign. It is fully recognized that the participation of Christians in the liberation process "varies in radicalism," using tentative expressions in "a process of searching and advancing 'by trial and error.' "[29] Those involved would like to keep "several options" open, not only for directly political, but also educational, cultural, economic, pastoral-prophetic activity. The main interest of this theology is not socio-political or economic to satisfy party selfishness. Here too man should not live by bread alone, although many would be glad if they were able to do just this. There is an intense search for a new synthesis of the "militant-committed" and the "religious-contemplative" factors, of action and prayer, mysticism and politics, and an attempt to bring this to life.[30] And the living testimony of poverty in particular—as expression of love of neighbor and testimony against injustice, not as an ideal of life valuable in itself or as glorifying the inhuman reality—acquires a special significance in the specific social conditions of the poor countries.[31]

In practice, for Latin-American Christians, the discussion on the political-social realization of the impulse to liberation centers on the question: does not the commitment to liberation necessarily mean a political option for *socialism* against *capitalism?* The widespread sympathy for socialism particularly among active Christians is often the only political way out of the outrageous conditions set up in this continent as a result of the capitalist economic system (but also of other factors often overlooked like climate, cultural historical development, prevailing mentality, attitude to life and work, established religion) and which are comparable only with those caused in the last century in Europe by the exploitation of Manchester Liberalism. And at this point the universal significance and supreme relevance of the Latin American statement of the theological question also becomes evident not least for Asia, Africa and even North America.[32] The same question however arises also in Europe, even if leading advocates of "political theology" largely avoid it and for that reason are severely criticized by their Latin American colleagues.

No uncritical identifications

Even theologians however must take the terms involved here at their face value, if the confusion of language and reality is not to increase. If "*left*" means simply the permanent openness of society to its future and "*socialism*" standing up for the abolishing of poverty, for democracy and a more just society, would not any intelligent, fair-minded person be "left" and a "socialist"? But this sort of usage obscures the true state of affairs: "socialism," in its exact sense, does not in fact mean merely any kind of social democracy to which even conservative European bishops' conferences could no longer seriously object any more than to definite "Christian" parties, which also support social democracy. "Socialism" in its exact sense means socialization, collectivization, in fact nationalization of the means of production and hence the abolishing of private ownership. And this precisely is the socialism of which many Latin American Christians decidedly approve.

But in the light of the Gospel of Jesus Christ itself can there be any serious objection to this kind of socialism, at least as long as elementary, basic human rights (freedom of opinion and religion, for instance) are not infringed? No. But there might be objections for other reasons: economic, social or political. Is nationalization of the means of production with all its consequences—excessive power of the state (or the state party) and the threat to individual freedom—the great panacea for Latin America? This remains a matter of serious dispute among Latin Americans themselves, both Christians and non-Christians, more than ever after so many decades of scarcely credible socialism in Eastern Europe and recent experiences of socialism in Cuba and Chile. All agree about the goal of a more just order in society. What is questionable is the fundamental means of establishing such a society. With all the insistence on a realistic approach, there is surprisingly little reference on the part of liberation theology to the concrete models of a socialist society: at best there is a very vague and general demand for a specifically Latin American way to socialism. At the same time the political-social reality also in Latin America (Cuba, Chile) imperatively demands an explanation of how these aims are to find concrete expression, if well-meant Christian involvement is not once more to be either overrun by Communism or strangled by military dictatorships. The fact that this theology is concerned about relating its principles to practice ought to lead to further reflection on a fact only sketchily described in our introductory chapter. "Capitalism" (like "socialism" frequently a mythological factor for theologians) has proved to be reformable to a large extent ("social market economy," with stronger state control and guidance). At the same time, neither in the West nor in the East, neither in scientific theory nor in political practice, has any other economic and social system been developed which eliminated the defects of a liberal economic system without producing other, worse evils, and which consequently would be better able to guarantee freedom and democracy, justice and prosperity.[83]

But we are not going to attempt here an undiscriminating and uncritical defense of private ownership and still less the "capitalist system" in the light of the Gospel, nor are we going to present either socialization or socialism as un-Christian. Not only are the elements of truth and the liberation potential in socialism and especially in Marxist socialism to be recognized. It was also admitted from the outset that there are circumstances in which a Christian can be a (critical!) "Marxist," that is, a socialist in the strict sense.[84] But even then there was added a reservation which must now be repeated: it is possible to be a Christian without being a Marxist or a socialist. Even the formula, often understood as indicative instead of imperative, "no socialism without democracy and no democracy without socialism" (Rosa Luxemburg against Lenin) cannot be sustained either in its first part (the socialist peoples' republics, from the German Democratic Republic to China) or in its second (the non-socialist Western democracies). And the formula, Christianity=socialism, in particular conceals the fact that today also there are convinced Christians who are not socialists and that consequently there is in practice a Christianity without socialism, just as there is obviously a socialism without Christianity. We must therefore again insist (regardless of any unpopularity to left or right) that a *Christian can be a socialist* (against the "right"), but a *Christian is not bound to be a socialist* (against the "left"). A Christian can take quite seriously his commitment to liberation, as outlined at the beginning of this section, and yet need not see the remedy in the socialization of industry, rural economy and wherever possible also of education and culture.

Why is this distinction important, in Europe and North America as much as in South America? Not because of any bourgeois prejudices or of thinking on party lines. But for objective reasons which must now be explained more thoroughly:

a. Only in this way will individual Christians avoid being coerced by party politics, whether socialist or anti-socialist in any form. If the "hierarchy" in a particular country expressly or tacitly favors one party, Christians and even Christians in the Church's ministry cannot be forbidden to publicize and organize their support for the opposite party.

b. Only in this way will the polarization of the Church into socialist and non-socialist members or possibly even parishes be avoided. Parties of every kind should be avoided as much as possible within the fellowship of the Church, which in fact in the light of its Christian program deliberately seeks to be above parties.[35]

c. Only in this way will the Gospel avoid being theologically burdened, as it were, from behind and reinterpreted as a "left" or—according to the spirit of the age—"right" or even "center" political party program. It would then be useless to look for the distinctive Christian reality.

A general *examination of the Church's involvement* in society on the national or regional plane seems to be called for, not only in Latin America. In this respect voluntary renunciation of time-conditioned and obsolete privileges (for instance, in the matter of Catholic schools) should be considered in certain, especially Catholic countries (not to speak of Northern Ireland). If we want to provoke the right commitment of the Church in society, if we want to avoid excessive involvement in some public fields and defective involvement in others, we shall have to recall the special mandate of the Church—the cause of Jesus Christ—and define the *criteria* in the light of this:

The individual Christian must take a stand on all outstanding questions. The Church as community of faith and its representatives must not, cannot and may not take a stand on all outstanding questions.

The Church and its representatives may, should and must take a stand publicly even on controversial social questions where, *but* only where, *it is empowered to do so by its special mandate:* wherever *and* as far as *the Gospel of Jesus Christ itself (and not just any sort of theory) unambiguously (and not only obscurely) demands this.*

This public commitment of the Church has to take different forms in different continents and countries. Hence no general prescriptions can be laid down here: we may recall the section on "Uncertainty of norms." The Latin American, Asian and African Christians and Churches too have the right to work out Latin American, Asian and African solutions to their own questions without being impeded by any central authority in the Church. In accordance with the above principles the Churches could be socially involved—for instance, in questions of overpopulation, peace and disarmament, apartheid, social grievances—perhaps more often than those on the right would wish, and rather less often than those on the left would urge. Frequently, because of the complexities of the essential problem, in the light of the Gospel it will be impossible to do more than provide the relevant criteria for action and it will be necessary to refrain from suggesting definite, ready-made solutions. All the Church's proclamations and projects of course should be related as far as possible to the matter in hand, unpretentious and realistic. But today less than ever can there be any question of institutionalizing as quickly as possible every kind of initiative and project of the Church in the social field or of developing it into a position of power. The Churches should act as a mobile "fire brigade" wherever and as long as no one else renders help and where consequently there is a need for a special intervention outside the normal rules. From this standpoint there is one principle of Catholic social teaching, the principle of subsidiary function ("help for self-help"), which might acquire a new significance. In the course of the centuries the Churches to their credit have performed indisputable and immense services in the fields of health and education and indeed in the whole social field. These tasks however have largely been taken over by the state or specialist organizations. But is it likely that there will ever be a shortage of new and perhaps more essential tasks for the Church in the service of man?

In Latin America too any uncritical identification of the Churches with political parties must be avoided at all costs. There are several options. In the light of the Gospel of Jesus Christ there can certainly not be any neutrality on decisive issues: "Today in Latin America . . . the oppressed have wakened up to their needs and sufferings and their conditions must be improved." With reference to the concrete solution the Church cannot be pinned down to a particular program of political action, but in principle must remain open for a variety of options: "The Church respects all that we do to help them . . . provided it meets the appeal for liberation of the oppressed, the poor and the afflicted which Christ himself left alive among us in his own person."[36]

The appeal of which Jesus Christ in person is the living embodiment, the distinctively Christian reality, must be the criterion everywhere. Christians may never identify themselves *totally* with any party, institution or even Church. Only totalitarian systems demand total identification. Christians may never join uncritically in every cry of the age. Only *partial* identification can be justified: *insofar as* this party, institution or Church corresponds to the Christian criterion or at least does not clearly contradict it.

In the concrete life of the individual and of society of course, particularly in the harsh confrontation where one life has to be balanced against another, there are extraordinarily difficult cases, impossible to disentangle in the whole mass of problems; there are exigencies and emergencies in which all general rules of conduct and even a final appeal to the example of Jesus Christ seem to break down. What is to be done, for instance, when *violence* takes over and lands people in disaster? What is to be done when countless individuals have to suffer under the "structural," "institutionalized" violence of an externally (politically and economically) functioning, but clearly inhuman, cruel system? Could not an attempt on Hitler's life seem like a duty particularly to earnest Christians like Dietrich Bonhoeffer? Are there not social and political emergencies, as in certain Latin American states, in which violent revolution seems to be the only way out? This may well be so, but who would want to decide in the abstract before the emergency actually arises?

The rule of violence, arbitrary or institutionalized, sooner or later produces counterviolence. In some states then, on grounds of reason and the common good, there remains perhaps no solution except consistent revolution, deprivation of power and expropriation of inhuman rulers, even envisaging their death, if more just, more democratic, more human conditions are to be established or at least made possible. By these criteria, in a borderline situation, violence as self-defense may be barely justified, if there is any prospect of success: for the individual, a group or a nation. The challenge however remains for anyone who takes to violence: he cannot in this respect appeal to the example of Jesus Christ. Anyone who takes violent measures is involved in the vicious circle between violence and counterviolence. The sacrifices and risks are incalculable. For the most part oppression and the rule of violence are still more severe after revolutions have failed. Not only that, but even if the revolution succeeds, there is often no more than a change of rulers, while the problems and the oppression remain unchanged.

It will be better then not to propagate a "theology of revolution" or any theological glorification of violent revolution. Since Jesus' time it has become difficult to find God in the event of such a liberation, which is simultaneously an event of violence. In a borderline situation violence as self-defense may still be barely justified: for the individual, a group or a nation. But in such cases, where blood—even if it is solely guilty blood—"had to" flow, there will be more reason to seek forgiveness than to celebrate the revolution. The occasional use of violence is not to be justified as something to be positively sought, but at best as a barely permissible reaction of self-defense. And even then—in the "just" war or in the "just" revolution—there will always be Christians who invoke the name of Jesus Christ as a reason for rejecting the use of violence: "I would prefer a thousand times to be killed than to kill" (Helder Camara, Archbishop of Olinda and Recife, Brazil[87]).

No strategy of violence, but only one of non-violence, can be deduced from the example of Jesus Christ, as not only Helder Camara and Martin Luther King, but also Mahatma Gandhi and many others have very clearly understood and made politically effective.[88] *Non-violence* can always find support in *Jesus Christ*, the *use of violence* perhaps in an emergency can find support in reason. Violence, revenge, oppression, irreconcilability, hatred: all this is not humane, but human, all-too-human. Renunciation of violence, renunciation of the desire for revenge, readiness to spare opponents, readiness for all-round pardon, resolute action for reconciliation and unselfish good will: this is the real challenge which Jesus presents. It is a challenge to be truly human, to be humane. And it is in fact a challenge for both sides: for both the guarantors of the status quo of repressive "structural" violence and likewise for the rebels who include violence as an instrument of policy.

Could not this very appeal for non-violence, forbearance and indeed love open up once more other possibilities in the great social conflicts in Berlin, Rio de Janeiro and Santiago de Chile? We may leave the last word to a voice of the Latin American "theology of liberation": "These Christians see in the practice of their faith the guarantee that their options are governed by love, and that they preserve the ethical values and feeling for persons. It is also a guarantee of freedom from pragmatism and from Machiavellian political methods, but it in no way diminishes the intensity of their commitment, or their clarity of vision. Their Christian experience enables them to encounter more creative, human, brotherly ways in liberation, beyond the watchwords of the politicians."[89]

2. *Coping with the negative side*

The positively loaded, stimulating expressions used in liberation theology make a splendid sound: love, sense, personal dignity, values, liberation, human, creative, fraternal. And yet they are no more than sound and fury if they are not thoroughly tested and proved by what must be called the seamy side of life: hatred and nonsense, indignity and worthlessness, constraint and inhumanity, rigidity and hostility, the banality of the ordinary routine of public and private life. What is involved here is no more and no less than the question of man and human existence, humanity and humanism. Here commitment and political enthusiasm reach depths unattainable by a routine-pragmatic superficiality. Here we are at the very roots of the question of being human and being Christian. Coping with the negative side of life is the acid test of Christian faith and non-Christian humanisms.

Misused cross

We have already considered how inscrutable is the enigma presented by suffering, the history of the suffering of mankind and of each individual. We have also seen the multifarious, often radical mythological, philosophical, theological blueprints for solving the enigma.[40] The importance in this connection of the modern process of emancipation or liberation, as we also saw, has been made concretely and brutally clear in the example of Latin America. Man must accept responsibility for his own fate and try to liberate himself by reshaping human society. Emancipation cannot be replaced by redemption.

The opposite of course is also true: redemption cannot be replaced by emancipation. No one can evade the question of the unrequited suffering of the living and the dead, the question of his guilt and his death, and thus of a final liberation of man: a liberation by God (redemption), as opposed to which the liberation of man by man (emancipation) can never have more than a provisional character. How is he to know otherwise that he is liberated from sin, accepted for time and eternity, liberated for meaningful life and unreserved involvement for his fellow man and society? How is he still to find a meaning in meaningless suffering and death, in the suffering even of the innocent and unfortunate?

What do we say to the defeated revolutionary, to the prisoner wanting to preserve his freedom even in chains, to the person condemned to death but still looking for reasons to hope? Or, less dramatically but no less seriously, what do we say to the person who is indissolubly bound by certain social structures in which revolutions have no prospect of success? What do we say to the incurably sick, to the person tied by a single wrong decision, to the professional, moral or human failures?

Against all temptations to rebellion, revolt, discouragement and cynicism, is it possible to say any more than Job ventured to say: "Yes," "Yes" to the incomprehensible God, despite everything, in unshakable, absolute trust? It is possible to say a little more:

that everything negative in this life *can* have a positive meaning;
that there need not be any *absolutely* bleak, meaningless, desperate situation;
that encounter with God is *possible*, not only in success and joy, but also in failure, in melancholy, in sorrow and pain.

All this I venture to say in the light of the passion of him from whom the passion of each and every man, just as the passion of mankind, can acquire a meaning. I say this looking to the Crucified with faith and trust in him who also—as the resurrection attests—sustains and supports man in the utmost peril, futility, triviality, abandonment, loneliness and emptiness: a God who identifies himself with man as one who is also affected. But there is no need to repeat here what has already been discussed at length.[41] It is the cross of the living Christ in the light of which the believer can resolve on the venture of hope in the midst of darkness and futility: on following in the way of the cross.

The following of the cross: unfortunately just this most profound and strongest aspect of Christianity has been discredited by the "pious," the "obscurantists and mumblers and stay-at-homes," as Nietzsche called them, who bend down and "crouch to the cross," who have grown old and cold and lost their "morning valor."[42]

In modern usage "crouching to the cross" then means something like taking things lying down, lacking self-confidence, yielding, knuckling under in silence, cringing, complying, capitulating. And "bearing the cross" likewise means surrendering, humbling oneself, cowering, not making a sound, lowering one's fists. . . . The cross thus becomes a sign for weaklings and yes men. This is certainly not what Paul meant when he called the cross folly to the Gentiles, a scandal to the Jews, but the "power of God" for believers.[43]

Official preachers of the word must bear part of the blame if the "pious" misunderstand the cross as a degradation of man. How much dirty work has been done with the cross? Why was the cross made to bear everything in the Churches? People have by now got used to the cross, borne not as a burden on the back, but as a decoration on the chest ("pectoral cross," the bishop's cross, worn on the chest at least from the twelfth century; prescribed for Mass from 1572, but now used also outside the liturgy; growing ever larger and more spectacular from the baroque age onwards); they have got used to seeing this central Christian sign of shame and victory used in routine fashion as an episcopal gesture of blessing. But there is one thing to which we should not become accustomed: hierarchs, who like to identify their own words with the word of Christ and of God, eulogizing the cross as "God's great and mysterious design," as a heavy burden imposed on men for penance and other undiscoverable purposes, and thus projecting the "will to suffer" onto God and Jesus. Why do they say this and what is behind it? It is an attempt to discredit modern values (living standards, maturity, structural change, acceptance of the world, intellectual honesty) and active involvement in society for these values. They want to justify in this connection such burdens of ecclesiastical tradition as celibacy and other things as a cross willed by God. It is a way of casting suspicion on their opponents, claiming that their own parish priests, curates, laypeople and the theologians with whom these associate are "making void the cross of Christ."[44] The cross as a sledge hammer? What would Paul—who of course was not at that time a cardinal—have said about this way of preaching the cross? Certainly we have no wish to hurt anyone's feelings or to question the sincerity of his pastoral intentions. In this serious connection, however, where so much thoughtlessness affects practice, we must also very resolutely—in season and out of season—demand reverence for the cross.

Misunderstood cross

It is to be hoped that the author will not be blamed—as so often happens—for citing this one typical example of misuse of the cross. But it may suffice. We cannot hold up the reader by listing the countless crude distortions of the following of the cross, however serious their consequences may be both for the individual and for whole areas of the Church. But, for the sake of a genuine following of the cross, we must point out three more sublime misunderstandings of the message of the cross which have often been criticized.[45]

a. Following the cross does *not* mean *cultic adoration*. As we have already seen, the cross of Jesus cannot be confined within the systematic theology of sacrifice nor within the scheme of cultic practice.[46] The very profaneness of his cross bars any cultic appropriation or liturgical glorification of the Crucified.

Naturally we cannot withhold respect for the symbol of the cross and for a veneration of the cross rightly understood, in accordance with the Gospel, as for example in the Good Friday liturgy. Nor of course for the great works of art which bear the marks of a serious attempt to wrestle with this central Christian theme—admittedly after centuries of hesitation.[47]

But the test must be applied:

In the light of the cross of Jesus Christ is there not something questionable about that shrunken, often purely ritual gesture of making a crosslike sign which is thoughtlessly repeated a thousand times and often degraded to a more or less magical symbol?

In the light of this cross is there not something questionable even about the crucifix on the wall, if it has no effect on practice and people think that they can escape the burden of Christ's cross with the aid of these traditional and ornamental bits and pieces?

In the light of this cross is there not something questionable about the manufacture of devotional objects by shrewd speculators in faith and superstition and about the surrender of the cross to cheap commercialism?

It remains true that, for someone who enters seriously on the way of Jesus, the cross of Jesus cannot be appropriated cultically or piously for just any sort of interests. The cross of Jesus remains the scandal, the sign that the barriers between the profane and the sacral are finally down. This is and remains a challenge for anyone who celebrates Mass, the eucharist, the memorial of the Passion, in this sign. The liturgical celebration in the sign of the cross may not remain ineffective. Practical following of the cross must correspond to the commemoration.

b. Following the cross does *not* mean *mystical absorption:* no convulsive, privatized sharing in suffering on the same level, becoming united in prayer and meditation with Jesus' mental and physical pains. This would be a wrongly understood mysticism of the cross.

Yet here too:

Respect for the great mysticism of suffering and the cross of a Francis of Assisi, Bonaventura, a John of the Cross, a Teresa of Avila.

Respect too for the critical-emancipatory impulse which lay piety, inspired by the cross, brought into Church and society: from the medieval poverty movements to the Negro spirituals of the black slaves in the Southern states of America, the suffering, poor, defenseless Christ was set up against Christ the heavenly ruler, the Christ of the wealthy and powerful.

Respect for that genuine religious usage which—for instance—in the Stations of the Cross activates the memory of this Jesus Christ in uninhibited, liberating meditation without any self-torment.

But here too the test must be applied:

In the light of this cross of Jesus Christ is there not something questionable about that mysticism which renders innocuous the radicalness of Jesus' suffering, his abandonment by God and men, by making it all seem cosy and tawdry?

In the light of this cross is there not something questionable about that mysticism which amounts to pious self-pity, sentimentally associating one's own often well-merited suffering with the suffering of Christ or playing the hero by assimilating one's own pains to the pains of Jesus?

In the light of this cross then is there not something questionable about that mysticism which has no longer a sense of distance and reverence before the cross and the suffering of this one person, which all too rapidly smooths over the unique distance and, by passively submitting to suffering, neglects any action to remove its causes in one's own life and in society?

It remains true that, for someone who seriously enters on the way of

Jesus, it is impossible to match up to the cross of Jesus Christ by pious ingratiation or cosiness, turning it into a private affair and smoothing out its roughness. The cross is and remains a challenge to faith in God, even in his absence: in a God however who does not sadistically torture man, but suffers with him. It is a challenge to faith in Jesus Christ who was not the weak, patient sufferer, but the courageous brother of all the poor, tormented and terrified, in whose fellowship the humiliated find exaltation, respect, recognition, human dignity. In his light the cross is ambivalent: expression of misery and at the same time of protest against misery, sign of death and sign of victory.

c. Following the cross does *not* mean *ethical imitation* of Jesus' course of life; it does not mean producing a faithful copy of the model of his living, preaching and dying.

Yet here too:

Respect for the great individuals, from Francis of Assisi to Leo Tolstoy and Martin Luther King, who, by renouncing possessions or force, directly followed this Jesus as model and gave the lead for vast programs of Christian action.

Respect for the tradition of great martyrs of Christianity, seeking to be like this Jesus in his suffering, by their self-denial, their courage and their utter consistency to the end.

Respect for the great tradition of monasticism, inspired by the idea of the imitation of Christ, especially in the Middle Ages, to achieve far-reaching reforms in Church and society, and deducing directly from Christ its principles of life: homelessness, celibacy and poverty.

But here too the test must be applied:

In the light of the cross of Jesus Christ is there not something questionable about that imitation which means that devout self-sacrificing souls seek to reproduce exactly his physical suffering and which leads to a more than dubious cult of the wounds and the stigmata (as in the example of Therese of Konnersreuth[48])? Is not any kind of canonization within a person's lifetime more than dubious, when the attempt is made to amass merits in heaven and to secure salvation in advance?

In the light of this cross is there not something questionable about that imitation which means that someone arrogantly assumes that he can carry his cross behind Jesus the great leader, giving himself credit for the achievement and in admiration and blind enthusiasm trying to escape the confines of his time and situation to share his sufferings with Christ's?

It remains true that, for someone who enters seriously on the way of Jesus Christ, the cross is set apart from any cheap copy, any heroic imitation, which might be supposed to produce security. His cross remains incomparable, his abandonment by God and man unique, his death unrepeatable. Even for Paul[49] imitation of Christ does not simply mean "copying the individual features or the total impression of the earthly

Jesus"[50] in order to become more and more like him. For Paul imitation of Christ means obedience to the heavenly Lord which has to be proved in concrete action: an imitation which means, not copying, but following him. To be an imitator means for Paul nothing other than being a disciple. Following the cross then does not mean being forsaken in exactly the same way by God and men, suffering the same pains, bearing the same wounds. On the contrary. When the cross is set apart from the copy and precisely then, it is and remains a challenge to take up one's own cross, to go one's own way in the midst of the risks of one's own situation and uncertain of the future.

Understood cross

There are many who hang on the cross: not only unsuccessful revolutionaries, prisoners, those condemned to death; not only the incurably sick, the complete failures, those who are weary of life and those who despair of themselves and of the world. There are many who hang on the cross: tormented by cares and oppressed by their fellow men, overwhelmed by demands and worn out by boredom, crushed by fear and poisoned by hatred, forgotten by friends and ignored by the media. Is not everyone in fact hanging on his own cross?

In the presence of inarticulate suffering often only silence is appropriate. In face of sickness and death, in face of all the questions of the why and wherefore, we have all known in our own lives how often the answers stick in one's throat, how difficult it is to spell out words of consolation. And yet the very experience of these extreme human situations demands expression in words, presses for clarifying, consoling, constructive language. We have to work to respond to sorrow and any material or spiritual help of its nature is clothed in speech. In the light of the cross of Christ, the Christian does not merely stand there dumb, without an answer, although at this point especially any trite formulas are to be avoided. The Christian does not stand there in silence, when he lets the Crucified speak.

What has he to say? How far is he to help? If cultic adoration, mystical union, ethical imitation, are of no avail, what is left? To put it quite plainly: following the cross, a following in the form of correlation, of correspondence. What does this mean?

a. *Not seeking, but bearing suffering.* Jesus did not look for suffering, it was forced on him. Anyone who indulges in self-torture, plainly longing for pain and suffering or even inflicting these on himself, is not truly following the cross of Jesus. Pain is and remains pain. Suffering is and remains suffering. We must not try to find a new interpretation of this fact, still less seek a masochistic pleasure in suffering. Suffering and pain are and remain an assault on man. But the Christian cannot cultivate sadness, as the sensualist can easily do in an odd reversal of attitudes when he abandons his outspoken pursuit of life and its pleasures.

Following the cross does not mean copying the suffering of Jesus, it is not the reconstruction of his cross. That would be presumption. But it certainly means enduring the suffering which *befalls me* in my inexchangeable situation—in *conformity* with the suffering of Christ. Anyone who wants to go with Jesus must deny *himself* and take on himself, not the cross of Jesus nor just any kind of cross, but his cross, his own cross; then he must follow Jesus.[51] Seeking extraordinary suffering in monastic asceticism or in romantic heroism is not particularly Christian. But what is required of the person who believes in the crucified Jesus is something that frequently recurs and is therefore mostly more difficult than a single heroic act: it is the endurance of ordinary, normal, everyday suffering, which is then most likely to prove excessive. The cross to be borne is therefore the cross of everyday life.[52] That this is far from being obvious or edifying is apparent to anyone who has seen how often a person tries to get away from his own cross, all his daily obligations, demands, claims, promises in his family or his calling; how he tries to shift his cross onto others or suppress it altogether. In the light of all this the cross of Jesus becomes a criterion for self-critical knowledge and self-critical action.

b. *Not only bearing, but fighting suffering*. It is likewise not a true following of the cross to adopt the Stoic ideal of apathy toward suffering, enduring our own suffering as unemotionally as possible and allowing the suffering of others to pass by while we remain aloof and refuse to be mentally involved. Jesus did not suppress his pain either at his own or at others' suffering. He attacked these things as signs of the powers of evil, of sickness and death, in the still unredeemed world.[53] The message of Jesus culminates in love of neighbor,[54] unforgettably instilled in the parable of the good Samaritan[55] and in the critical standard of the Last Judgment: involvement with the hungry, thirsty, naked, strangers, sick and imprisoned.[56]

In this light the young community of faith from the very beginning recognized active care for the suffering as a special task. Hence systematic care for the sick became a specifically Christian affair, distinguishing that religion from the world religions: from the nursing organized by the bishop and his deacons and practiced in the early congregations and the *nosocomia* emerging in the fourth century, by way of the medieval care of the sick in monasteries, especially after the Cluniac reform, by the Knights Hospitalers and the civilian Hospitalers, up to modern nursing by Catholic and Protestant religious orders and congregations. At the same time it was a logical historical development that the secularization process should take away from the Church many of these tasks, which it had taken up out of necessity.

So much the more is it the task and duty of Christians and the

Churches in modern society to collaborate vigorously in the many-sided fight against suffering, poverty, hunger, social grievances, sickness and death. The modern world has produced a great deal of fresh suffering, but has also created immense opportunities for mastering suffering, as the successes of medicine, hygiene, technology, social welfare demonstrate. The Christian then will never look to his faith for arguments enabling him to dispense himself from active collaboration in society or to console himself with promises of the hereafter instead of changing the present social reality. Faith in God, prayer, which must always be the basis of his work, can never be used as a refuge for the Christian who is simply discouraged by suffering or merely dreams of heaven. A sober and realistic estimate of the always limited personal and social opportunities for changing conditions is necessary in order to preserve Christians in the fight against suffering from a pragmatism forgetful of suffering and from illusory activism.

c. *Not only fighting, but utilizing suffering*. In the light of the cross of Jesus Christ the opportunity is laid open to men, not only of breaking down and removing suffering and its causes bit by bit, but also positively to transform and utilize them. This presupposes experience in perceiving causes and conditions, connections and structures of human suffering. It also presupposes imagination in devising opportunities for a less unhappy human condition in the future, in giving consolation, in entering into the needs and the mental state of the person who needs me here and now, of my neighbor, of my neighbors. This imagination finds expression in speech and is thus able to break down the crust which so often covers suffering, leaving it muffled, dumb, inarticulate. Entering closely into conversation with the other person makes it possible to become aware of all that is spontaneous and elemental in pain, the groaning and screaming, the whimpering and sighing, the discouragement and powerlessness, to perceive connections and analyze causes. It is able to make people aware that suffering is relative and therefore frequently variable, not merely decreed by fate or simply imposed by God.

Consolation gets the individual out of the isolation and fixation of his purely personal experience of suffering and makes him capable of utilizing it in the fellowship of all who are involved in suffering. But utilization means also positive, active acceptance and integration of suffering into the total meaning of life. "It is impossible completely to refuse suffering without refusing to accept life as a whole, without ceasing to enter into any relationships, without making ourselves invulnerable. Pains, losses, amputations exist even in the smoothest-running life which can be conceived, if not desired: separation from parents, fading of youthful friendships, the death of people who have figured in our lives, with whom we have identified ourselves, the death of relatives and friends, finally our own death. The more strongly we insist on reality, the more we are immersed in it, and the more deeply we are affected by these processes of dying surrounding us and pressing in upon us."[57]

We are faced here with a phenomenon which has been widely attested by countless Christians who have lived out their Christian and human existence without looking for any cheap consolation. Countless incurably sick who discovered through their sickness a new awareness of themselves. Countless individuals for whom a new dimension in their lives was opened up through their own misfortune, through the loss or even the treachery of someone they had loved. Countless people who, through all disappointments, separations, mis-hits, failures, humiliations, setbacks and disregard, transformed their lives and acquired a new personal quality: through suffering becoming more mature, more experienced, more modest, more genuinely humble, more open for others—in a word, more human.

Suffering then—particularly for the Christian—does not need to be a fate to be borne passively, a destiny to which we have to submit. "Suffering is a change experienced by man, it is a mode of coming to be."[58] It is a growth toward a greater, higher, freer, final goal. But what is the source of the vast certainty of the Christian, rising above empty promises and trivialization, neither ignoring suffering nor revolting against it?

d. *Freedom in suffering.* If someone looks to Jesus, while fighting suffering by every means, he will remain a realist. He will never cherish the illusion that technological developments or social-revolutionary changes, change of environment, psychical stabilization or even genetic manipulation could ever succeed in abolishing the uncertainty of reality, neutralizing the dialectic of the negative, breaking through the vicious circle of human self-destruction, restraining the power of the trivial, of chaos, of the meaningless in the world, in creating by themselves a paradise on earth, a golden age, a kingdom free from all suffering. As we saw, even if modern man seems to be coping with the world and with himself, he has not really done so—as is evident from the experience of each and every individual. Do we need to point it out once more? The unparalleled external progress and prosperity of the technological society have themselves produced for man an equally unparalleled internal void and boredom. And psychical illnesses seem to increase almost at the same rate as physical diseases decline. Man is expected to fight suffering by every means. But it is not granted to him to be finally victorious.

Even if someone commits himself to the way of Jesus and takes up his cross without fuss in ordinary life, he cannot simply conquer and remove suffering. But in faith he can endure and master it. He will never then break down, simply crushed by suffering and despairing in suffering. If Jesus did not break down in the utmost suffering of abandonment by men and God, then neither will that person break down who clings to him with trusting faith. For with faith he is also given hope: faith and hope that suffering is not simply the definitive, the ultimate reality. For him too the ultimate is a life without suffering, which of course neither he himself nor human society will ever realize but which he can expect from the consummation, from the mysterious wholly Other, from his God: all suffering definitively dissolved in eternal life.[59]

But the promise of a future untouched by suffering is not a prophecy intended to satisfy curiosity, to put people off with hopes of the future. It is a summons, not simply to make the best of the present in a spirit of resignation, but actively to stand up to it: it is a call to endure present suffering as the way to an ultimate future without suffering, a future revealed even now to the believer in the experiences of present suffering. For if anyone has committed himself to this Christ and his way, if Christ therefore lives in him,[60] then for him the old man with his selfishness is already crucified,[61] for him the new man has already become living reality: the old is past, the new has come to be.[62]

Unconquered suffering and the constant threat of death are of course signs that man is not yet perfected, that he is ultimately to rely not on himself but on God, that he is never to be presumptuous but to trust in God's power. For it is just in our weakness that God's power is at work, it is just when we are weak that we are strong.[63] Dialectical trickery? No. The expression of *being untouched by suffering* even in the midst of suffering: the freedom of the believer who refuses to be crushed in all his misery and affliction, who never despairs in all his doubts, is not forsaken even in solitude, not without cheerfulness even in grief, not destroyed by any defeat, not lacking fulfillment even in a total void. Paul not only wrote, but exemplified what everyone can experience in his own way:

harassed on all sides, but not crushed;
plunged in doubt, but not despairing;
persecuted, but not forsaken;
struck down, but not destroyed;
as dying, but see, we live;
as punished, but not put to death;
as poor, yet making many rich;
as having nothing and yet possessing everything.[64]

Man's life in any sort of economic system is crisscrossed, it consists of events determined by the cross—by pain, care, suffering and death. But it is only in the light of the cross of Jesus that man's crisscrossed existence acquires meaning. Discipleship is always—sometimes in a hidden way, sometimes openly—a discipleship of suffering, a following of the cross. Does a man submit to this? It is under his cross that he comes nearest to Jesus, his crucified Lord. His own passion is set within the Passion of Christ.[65] And this very fact makes it possible for him ultimately to rise supreme above all suffering. For there is no cross in the world—we may recall here all that was said in connection with the question of theodicy—which can refute the offer of meaning issued on the cross of the one raised to life: that even suffering, even extreme peril, futility, triviality, abandonment, loneliness and emptiness are encompassed by a God who identifies himself with man; that a way is thus opened to the believer, not indeed bypassing, but going right through suffering, so that his active indifference to suffering itself prepares him for the struggle against suffering and its causes both in the life of the individual and in human society.

We spoke of mastering the negative as the acid test of Christian faith and non-Christian humanisms. Is it not clear now that the negative can be mastered in the light of the Crucified in a way that seems scarcely possible for non-Christian humanisms? Nowhere is the challenge more unmistakably returned than at this point.

3. *Liberated for freedom*

Suffering makes it clear how essentially stationary is the history of mankind. Have all the indisputable technological evolutions and politico-social revolutions made much difference in this respect? There scarcely seems to have been any serious evolution or revolution in mankind's history of suffering. Was it harder for the slave working on the Egyptian pyramids at the time of the Middle Kingdom two thousand years before Christ than it is for a South American mineworker today two thousand years after Christ? Was there greater misery in the proletarian settlements of Nero's Rome than in the slums of modern Rome? Were the mass deportations of whole nations by the Assyrians worse than the mass liquidations in the present century by Germans, Russians and Americans? The vast modern opportunities of fighting suffering appear to correspond more or less exactly to the opportunities of creating suffering. In this respect it is only relatively speaking that there is anything "new under the sun." The sole consolation is that great responses and hopes are also maintained and that not only the history of the suffering, but also the history of the hope, of mankind, despite all the vast upheavals, exhibits a certain stability. This holds too and not least for the question to which an answer intelligible and acceptable today must be given: what ultimately is the point of human life?

Justification or social justice?

It has rightly been observed that the question most disputed at the time of the Reformation now leaves people in the Protestant Churches just as cold as those in the Catholic Church—not to mention the fact that an agreement is being sought on this point. Justification by faith? Does anyone still ask with Luther: "How does God's rule come about in man?" Or with the Council of Trent: "How does sinful man reach a state of grace?" Apart from theologians, who regard all old questions as eternal questions, who is there to argue about these things? Is grace God's good will or an intrinsic quality of man? Is justification God's external verdict or man's inward sanctification? Justification by faith alone or by faith and works? Are not all these questions obsolete, without any basis in real life? Are even Lutherans any longer secure in their *articulus stantis et cadentis Ecclesiae*, in the article of faith by which the Church stands or falls?[66]

Against this contemporary background it is not surprising that people in all Churches today talk, not about "Christian justification," but about "social justice."[67] Not that they would simply deny the former. But they are passionately interested only in the latter. And, after all that we have said here positively about the social relevance of the Christian message and the commitment to social liberation, we certainly have not the slightest excuse for raising doubts about the supreme importance and urgency of social justice. We shall not take back a word of what we said on this point. But there is one thing which must be examined here and it leads directly to the answer to the really essential question: is it so easy to have the one without the other?

If we set out schematically the old and the new statement of the problem, it looks like this:[68]

Formerly the question was asked in great cosmic and spiritual anguish: how do I get a gracious God?

But now the question is asked with no less cosmic and existential anguish: how does my life acquire a meaning?

Formerly this God was seen as God the judge who acquits man from his sin and declares him just.

Now he is seen as God the partner who calls man to freedom and to responsibility for world and history.

Formerly it was a question of individual justification and of "saving our souls" in a purely personal sense.

Now it is a question of the social dimension of salvation and of all-round care of our fellow men.

Formerly people were concerned in a spiritual sense with salvation hereafter and peace with God.

Now they are concerned wholly and entirely with social conditions and the reform or even revolution of structures.

Formerly man was constrained to justify his life before God.

Now he is constrained to justify his life to himself and his fellow men.

It has become clear from this whole book how much of the new statement of the problem is right and important. We need not repeat it here. Undoubtedly Luther did not appreciate the social consequences of his conception of justification, for instance, in regard to the misery of the peasants. And Ernst Bloch has rightly compared and contrasted Thomas Münzer with Luther on this point.[69] Luther's doctrine of the two kingdoms decisively simplified the problem and it has exercised a negative influence up to recent times, particularly on the question of resistance to National Socialism. The Catholic tradition too undoubtedly saw the consequences of the doctrine of justification more in pious works within the Church than in the reorganization of society. The papal states with their monsignorial economy were largely regarded as the most socially backward in Europe and until their fall those in Rome successfully opposed any sort of Catholic social teaching. A great deal could therefore be said in the light of history for the turning of the Church to the world and society, on the lines indicated in our introductory chapter.[70]

Now, however, as we approach the end of this book, there is something more important: it is just this which shows that the antitheses just mentioned do not bring out the essential point.

What is not ultimately important

The important thing in modern life is a person's achievement. We do not ask so much, "Who is he?", as "What is he?" By this we mean his calling, his work, his achievements, his position and his standing in society. This is what matters.

This statement of the question is not as obvious as it seems. It is typically "Western," although it is to be found today also in the socialist countries of the Eastern bloc (Second World) and in the developing countries (Third World). But it originated in the First World, in Western Europe and North America, where *modern industrial society* first took shape. It was only there that a rationally organized science with qualified experts had existed for a long time. And it was only there that the firm had a rational organization of free labor based on earning power. There alone was a middle class properly so called and a specific form of rationalization of the economy and finally of society as a whole, with a new economic mentality. But why only there?

Max Weber examined this process more closely in his classical study, already mentioned, *The Protestant Ethic and the Spirit of Capitalism* (1905). Western rationalization was certainly hastened by special economic conditions (as Marx rightly stated). But on the other hand the Western economic rationalization as a whole came about only as a result of a new practical-rational economic mentality which had its roots in a particular religio-moral way of life (as Weber rightly maintained). What decisively produced this new approach in life and economy were certain beliefs and ideas of duty. To what extent? Surprisingly enough, the roots are to be found in the now supposedly irrelevant questions of the Reformation period. The unintended consequence of the strict Calvinistic doctrine of a double predestination (of some to eternal happiness, of others to damnation) was that in the Churches influenced by Calvin stress was laid on "sanctification," on works in everyday life, the duties of one's calling as fulfillment of love of neighbor and on success in these things: all were understood as visible signs of a positive election to eternal happiness. The spirit of unceasing work, of success in one's calling and of economic progress arose therefore, not out of rationalist, but out of religious motives. There was a supremely effective combination of intensive piety and capitalistic business acumen in historically important Churches and sects, with the English, Scottish and American Puritans, the French Huguenots, members of the Reformed Churches and Pietists in Germany.

The more secularization took a hold on all spheres of life and the more the modern economic system came to prevail, so much the more did unremitting diligence, strict discipline and a lofty sense of responsibility become the virtues of secular man now come of age in the "*industry society*." All-round "ability" became the virtue par excellence, "profit" the way of thinking, "success" the goal, "achievement" the law, of this modern *efficiency-oriented society* where each has his part to play (the main part in his calling and mostly a variety of secondary parts).[71]

In a dynamically developing world and society man attempts then to realize himself through his own achievements, not as in the former static society—although man at all times must be concerned with his self-realization.[72] Now it is only by achieving something that a person is something. The worst thing that can be said of anyone is that he has achieved nothing. Work, career, earning money—what could be more important? Industrializing, producing, expanding, consuming on a large or small scale, growth, progress, perfection, improvement in living standards in every respect: is not this the meaning of life? How is man to justify his existence if not by achievements? The economic values rank uppermost in the scale of values, profession and ability determine social status. By being oriented to prosperity and achievement the industrial nations can escape the pressure of primitive poverty and establish the welfare society.

But in fact this highly successful way of *thinking in terms of efficiency* finally becomes a serious *threat to man's humanity*. Not only does man lose sight of the higher values and a comprehensive meaning to life, but he also loses himself in the anonymous mechanisms, techniques, powers, organizations of this system. For the greater the progress and perfection, so much the more firmly is man incorporated into the complex economic-social process. Discipline tightens until man becomes imprisoned by it. Increasing involvement and effort make it impossible for man to become aware of himself. Increasing responsibility absorbs man completely in his task. The network of norms created by society itself becomes increasingly finely meshed and mercilessly encompasses and controls man, not only in his calling and in his work, but also in his leisure, his entertainment, his vacations, his traveling. Traffic arrangements in every city with thousands of prohibitions, precepts, signals, indicators, none of which were formerly needed and which we must now scrupulously observe if we are to survive: this is the picture of ordinary life today, thoroughly organized, fully regulated, bureaucratized and rapidly becoming computerized from morning to night. There is a new *secular system of laws* in all sectors of human life to an unparalleled extent, beyond the comprehension of individual jurists, in comparison to which the Old Testament (religious) legal system and the interpreting skill of the legal experts at that time seem utterly innocuous.

But the more man fulfills the requirements of this legal system, so much the more does he lose his spontaneity, initiative, autonomy, so much less scope has he for himself, for being human. He often has the feeling that he exists for the laws (clauses, regulations, directions for action and use) and not the laws for him. And the more he gets lost in this network of expectations, regulations, norms and controls, so much the more does he cling to them in order to reassure himself. The whole of life becomes an "achievement game," under constant controls, which is terribly taxing and rapidly induces weariness: from professional to sexual life without any decline and wherever possible with an increase in achievement. This is basically a fatal closed system in which achievement drives man into a perpetual state of dependence from which he thinks he can escape only by new achievements: a great *loss of freedom.*

Man then experiences in a modern form what Paul called the *curse of the law.* Modern life constrains him to keep up his achievements, to continue to make progress, to be successful. He must constantly *justify his own existence:* no longer as formerly before the judgment seat of God, but before the forum of his milieu, before society, before himself. And it is only by achievement that he can justify himself in this efficiency-oriented society: only by achievement is he something, does he keep his place in society, does he gain the esteem he needs. He can assert himself only by providing evidence of achievements.

Is there not now a very obvious danger that this tremendous pressure—even mania—for achievement, the milieu's assignment of his role and the competition on all sides threatening to overwhelm him, will lead man to submit only to external guidance and to be completely lost in his own role: to be merely manager, businessman, scientist, official, technician, worker, professional man and no longer—man? This is what E. H. Erikson calls "diffusion of identity" in the diverse roles, resulting in a crisis and even a loss of identity: man is no longer himself, he is alienated from himself. He must nevertheless assert himself with the aid of his own resources, against the others and so often at the expense of others. Essentially he lives only for himself and tries to use all the others for his own ends.

The only question is: will man become happy in this way? Will the others permit themselves to be used and appropriated by him in this way? Under the law of achievement can he himself really fulfill all the demands which are constantly being made on him? And, more especially, with all his achievements can he really justify his existence? Is he not in this way really justifying only the part or parts he has to play, but not his being? Is he then really what he seems to be in his action? A man can indeed be a marvelous manager, scientist, official or skilled workman, be generally credited with playing his part brilliantly, and yet fail completely as a human being. He revolves around himself and yet never becomes aware of himself. He does not even notice that he has lost himself in all his achievements, that he must find himself again and that he will not find himself unless he begins again to think about himself. With all his achievements, all his activity, the man does not by any means acquire being, identity, freedom, personality; he does not gain any confirmation of his self or discover the meaning of his existence. If someone only wants to confirm himself, to justify himself, life will elude him. We are reminded of the saying that anyone who wants to save his life will lose it.[73] But has he any choice except to assert himself, to justify himself, by his achievements?

There is also another way. Not to do nothing. Not to refrain from achievement on principle. Not suddenly to refuse to play one's part in society, still less to abandon one's calling. But to know that the whole man is not absorbed in his calling and in his work, that achievements good and bad are important but not decisive. In a word, that *achievements are not what counts in the last resort.*

What is ultimately important

How can we venture to say anything so monstrous, contrary to the whole spirit of the modern age, in face of the efficiency-oriented society which in fact exists and is solidly established in different ways both in the West and in the East? But perhaps it may not seem so monstrous after all that we have said. In the light of this Jesus Christ it can in fact be claimed that what counts in the last resort are not man's achievements. *In the light of this Jesus Christ* it should even be possible *to adopt a different basic attitude,* to reach a different awareness, to find another approach to life, in order to perceive the limitations of thinking in terms of achievement, to avoid the mania for achievement and to break through the pressure for achievement, to become really free. So the tendency to dehumanization involved in the law of achievement must be dispassionately and realistically examined, for the sake of the men who cannot now opt out of the efficiency-oriented society, but must live and work here, find assurance in it and still long for a qualitatively different freedom.

We may recall[74] that *Jesus* did not reject achievements as such, whether legal, ritual or moral. But he was firmly opposed to making achievements in themselves the measure of being human. What did he say of that Pharisee who was proud of his achievements and thought that these made him count for something in the sight of God and men, to be something and therefore to be completely justified in his whole existence, in his position and his reputation? Jesus said that he did not go home justified. And what did Jesus say of that man who had never achieved anything, who could produce no achievements or at best only morally inferior ones, but who also made no attempt to claim justification in the sight of God and placed himself in all his failure before God and placed all his hope in God's mercy? Jesus said that this one went home justified.

Thus something else becomes clear. Not only are man's positive, fine and good achievements unimportant in the last resort. The consoling aspect of the same message is that there are also negative, evil and ugly "achievements" of man—and how much does everyone "accomplish" in this respect, even if he is not precisely a sinful tax collector—which, fortunately, are equally irrelevant in the last resort. Ultimately, with all man's unavoidable deeds and omissions, what counts is something different: *that, in both good and evil, man never under any circumstances gives up his absolute trust*. He knows therefore in his great and good deeds that he has nothing which he did not receive and that he has no occasion to be conceited, to boast, to try to make an impression. From the first to the last moment of his life he is a recipient, he is thrown back on others, he receives his life afresh each day; he owes all that he has and is to others. But at the same time it is important that man, even in his failure, however disgraceful, should know that he never has any excuse to give up and despair. He should also know that even and particularly in all his sin he is always sustained by him who is rightly understood and taken seriously only as the God of mercy. How can a person gain this certainty? The Crucified, absolutely passive, incapable of achievement, and yet in the end justified by God in the face of the defenders of pious works, is and remains God's living sign that the decision depends not on man and his deeds, but—for man's welfare in both good and evil—on the merciful God who expects an unshakable trust from man in his own passion.

We need only recall[75] that, in the light of the Crucified, it is not at all surprising if *Paul* proclaims precisely as the central point of his message that a person is not justified in the sight of God or men in virtue of his achievements. Paul too did not reject achievements. He could boast of having achieved more than all the other apostles and he expected deeds, fruits of the Spirit, expressions of love, from his Christians: faith is active through love.[76] But achievements are not decisive. What is decisive is faith, this absolute, unshakable trust in God, regardless of all one's own lapses and weaknesses, regardless also of one's own positive achievements, advantages, merits and claims. Man should entrust himself to God in *all* things and take what God wants to give him.

Only theologians who have not understood the Pauline message of justification and who try to adapt themselves to the efficiency-oriented society speak of attending to the "operational" factor and thus to the epistle of James with its doctrine of "justification by works."[77] As if Paul did not understand the "operational" factor very much better than that Hellenistic Jewish Christian, unknown to us, who at the end of the first century in good faith made use of the name of James, the brother of the Lord, in order to defend orthopraxis to the best of his knowledge and ability against an inactive orthodoxy. By comparison with him—and comparisons cannot be avoided here—Paul did not merely produce a better defense of orthopraxis. He also understood and substantiated much more comprehensively what is decisively important in being human and being Christian.

Obviously we are not going to make a sweeping attack here on achievements, good deeds, work, professional advancement, as if the Christian were not expected to make the most of his "talents." The Christian message of justification does not provide justification for doing nothing. Good deeds are important. But the foundation of Christian existence and the criterion for facing God cannot be an appeal to any kind of achievement, cannot be any self-assertion or any self-justification on man's part. It can only be absolute adherence to God through Jesus in a trust inspired by faith. What is proclaimed here is an extraordinarily encouraging message which provides human life with a solid basis, despite all inevitable failures, errors and despair, and which at the same time can liberate it from secular pressure for achievement, bestowing a freedom which can sustain it even through the worst situations.

We stressed at an early stage in this book the fundamental importance of trust for human life, how man can accept the identity, value and meaningfulness of reality and of his own existence in particular only with a "basic trust."[78] But now something even more fundamental has become clear: that if man wants to realize himself at all, if as a person he wants to gain freedom, identity, meaning, happiness, he can do so only in absolute trust in him who is able to give him all this. Man's basic trust seems in the best sense to be "sublimated" in trust in God, inspired by faith, as it was made possible by Jesus Christ. This is a trust in God in the light of Jesus which cannot be demonstrated but which, if it is attempted and achieved, proves of itself its meaningfulness and its liberating power.

Where is this *freedom* to be seen? Not in an illusory total autonomy, complete independence, absolute release from all obligations. For every man has his God or gods, whose authority he accepts, by whom he is guided, to whom he sacrifices everything. True freedom then means that man is liberated from dependence on and obligations to the false gods who drive him on mercilessly to new achievements: money or career, prestige or power, or whatever is the supreme value for him.

If man binds himself solely to the one true God, who is not identical with any finite reality, he becomes free in regard to all finite values, goods, powers. He then perceives also the relativity of his own achievements and failures. He is no longer subject to the merciless law of having to achieve something. Not that he is dispensed from all achievement. But he is liberated from the constraint and frenzy of achievement. He is no longer absorbed in his role or roles. He can be the person he is.

Anyone then who does not live for himself will truly become aware of himself, will be truly human, will gain meaning, identity, freedom. We are reminded of the saying that anyone who loses his life "for my sake"—for Jesus' message and his person—will gain it.[79] Man can receive meaning, freedom, identity, the justification of his existence only as a gift. And without a previous conception there is no action. Without grace, which makes it possible, there is no achievement. Without true humility toward the one God we can never really be superior to the many pseudo-gods. It is only by the one true God that man is given the great sovereign freedom which opens up to him new fields of freedom and new opportunities of freedom in regard to the many things which can enslave him in this world.

Man is then justified, not only in his achievements and roles, but in his whole existence, in his being human, quite independently of his achievements. *He knows that his life has a meaning*: not only in successes but also in failures, not only with brilliant achievements but also with faulty achievements, not only with heightened but also with declining achievement. His life then makes sense even if, for any reason, he is not accepted by his milieu or by society: if he is destroyed by opponents and deserted by friends; if he has supported the wrong side and come to grief; if his achievements slacken and are replaced by others; if he is no more use to anyone. Even the bankrupt businessman, the utterly lonely divorcé, even the overthrown and forgotten politician, the unemployed middle-aged man, the aged prostitute or the hardened criminal in the penitentiary: all these, even no longer recognized by anyone, are still recognized by him for whom there is no respect of persons and whose judgment follows the standards of his goodness.

What then is it that ultimately counts in human life? That, healthy or sick, able to work or unable to work, strong in achievement or weak in achievement, accustomed to success or passed over by success, guilty or innocent, a person clings unswervingly and unshakably, not only at the end but throughout his whole life, to that trust which always in the New Testament goes by the name of *faith*. If then his "Te Deum" is addressed to the one true God and not to the many false gods, he can make bold also to refer the end of this hymn in all circumstances as a promise to himself: *In te Domine speravi, non confundar in aeternum*, "In you, Lord, I have hoped; I shall never be brought to shame."[80]

4. Suggestions

In every situation, in every place and at all times Christian freedom must constantly be realized afresh, both individually and socially. If we take Jesus Christ in his impressiveness, audibility and realizability as the basic model, we can find countless opportunities of putting the Christian program into practice. Many practical consequences have already become clear, not only for the First and Second, but also for the Third World. In this final chapter we shall not attempt to develop systematically a program of Christian action. We shall only illustrate by the example of some basic problems of modern man and his society what the following of Jesus Christ can change and has really changed—wherever it is taken seriously. What Christian freedom in principle means in this connection has been brought out, not only in the previous chapter, but throughout this whole book. Here we shall merely point out how Christian freedom can reveal a new way, not only in extraordinary situations, but more especially in many contradictory situations—both individual and social—in ordinary life, by establishing different standards, scales of values and connections of meaning, in the light of Jesus Christ. Here then are some brief suggestions for reflection, to stimulate thought and action.

Freedom in the legal order

Jesus expects his disciples voluntarily *to renounce rights without compensation.*[81] If any individual or group today wants to take this Jesus Christ as a guide to behavior, no renunciation of rights will be required in principle. But in the wholly concrete situation for the sake of the other person the possibility of renouncing one's rights will be offered as an opportunity.

The *problem of peace and war* may be taken as an example. For decades it has proved impossible to establish peace in certain areas of the world: in the Near East, in the Far East, but also in Europe. Why is there no peace? It is easy to say, because "the other side" does not want it. But the problem lies deeper. Both sides assert claims and rights, rights to the same territories, nations, economic opportunities. Both sides can also substantiate their claims and rights: historically, economically, culturally, politically. The governments on both sides have the constitutional duty to uphold and defend the rights of the state. It used to be said that they had the right even to extend them.

The power blocs and political camps have based and still base their foreign policy on stereotypes of the enemy which are supposed to justify their own positions. Hostile images which are shaped psychologically both by the individual's fear of everything foreign and by his prejudices against whatever is different, disparate, unusual. Hostile images which also have an identification and stabilization function in internal politics for society as a whole. Such hostile images and prejudices in regard to other countries, nations and races are congenial because they are popular. Just because they are rooted in man's deepest psychical strata, they are extraordinarily difficult to correct. The political situation of the power blocs is thus characterized by an atmosphere of suspicion and of collective insinuations: a vicious circle of mistrust which renders any intention of peace and any readiness for reconciliation dubious from the very outset, since these will be regarded as weakness or mere tactics on the part of the other side.

Seen globally the consequences are of considerable relevance: armaments competition against which all negotiations and treaties already contracted on the limitation and control of armaments remain ineffective. Spirals of violence and counterviolence in international crises in which each side tries to outmaneuver the other power-politically, economically, militarily-strategically. Thus in different parts of the world there is no genuine peace, because no one sees why just he and not the other person should renounce his legal rights and power. No one sees why he should not occasionally make his standpoint prevail even brutally, if he has the power to do so. No one sees why he should not subscribe to a Machiavellian foreign policy which involves the least possible risk to himself. But what can Christians do? Here are some brief suggestions:

The Christian message provides no detailed information as to how—for instance—the Eastern frontiers of Germany, the borders between Israel and the Arab states or the international fishing limits should be drawn; how certain conflicts in Asia, Africa or South America, how in particular the East-West conflict should be settled. It makes no detailed suggestions for disarmament conferences and peace conversations. The Gospel is neither a political theory nor a method of diplomacy.

But the Christian message says something fundamental, something that statesmen could not so easily demand from their peoples, but which Catholic, Protestant and Orthodox bishops, Christian Church leaders, theologians, pastors and laypeople in the whole world very well could say and certainly ought to say: that renouncing rights without expecting anything in return *is not necessarily a disgrace; that Christians at least should not despise a politician who is prepared to make concessions. In fact, in very special cases—not as a new law—a renunciation of rights without recompense can constitute the great freedom of the Christian: he is going two miles with someone who has forced him to go one.*

The Christian who lives in this freedom becomes critical of all those—on whatever side—who constantly protest verbally their peaceful intentions, who are always promising friendship and reconciliation for the sake of propaganda, but in practical politics are not prepared for the sake of peace occasionally to give up obsolete legal positions, to take a first step toward the other person, publicly to struggle for friendship with other nations even when this is unpopular.

The Christian who takes this great freedom as the standard and determining factor of his life is also, in his small or large sphere of influence, a challenge to all who do not want to understand why it is appropriate in certain situations to renounce rights and advantages for the sake of men and for the sake of peace. He is a challenge to all who think that the use of power and violence, getting one's own way and exploiting others, whenever this is possible without risk to oneself, is the most advantageous, the most shrewd and even humanly speaking the most rational policy.

The Christian message is decidedly opposed to this logic of domination which gambles with men's humanity for the sake of legality, profitability and violence. It is an offer to see something positive, authentically human, in renunciation: a guarantee of one's own freedom and the freedom of others.

Anyone who suspects the Christian message of naïve, unrealistic neutralism or of having a purely individual-private appeal on this point has not understood how great is the explosive force of this Christian challenge, particularly for changing the structures of a whole society, the approaches, attitudes and prejudices of whole nations. But this succeeds only if there are increasing numbers in any party who are oriented to this demand; if there are increasing numbers of politicians who are guided by this demand without constantly invoking, in their speeches and negotiations, public appearances and programs, the name of him who in the last resort sets the standard for their policy.

What is gained by all this? Apparently nothing. Or—better—"only" peace. And perhaps in the long run we win over the other person. This is not to say that the Christian message provides simple solutions to all problems. This message—in particular the Sermon on the Mount—is not meant to abolish the legal order. It is not meant to render the law superfluous. But it is meant radically to relativize the law. Why? So that the law may serve men and not men the law.

Wherever individuals or whole groups forget that the law exists for men and not men for the law, they contribute—as is proved by the history of states and also of Churches, of congregations, of families and of individual human lives—to the establishment of the merciless legal standpoint in both the social and individual spheres and to turning the *summum jus* (supreme law) into the *summa injuria* (supreme wrong). In this way inhumanity is continually spread afresh among men, groups and nations.

But wherever individuals or whole groups remember that in every case the law exists for man, they promote the humanization of the now essential legal order and in the particular situation make satisfaction, forgiveness and reconciliation possible within the existing legal system. Within the legal sphere itself therefore they spread humanity between men, groups and nations. They may apply to themselves the promise that those who renounce force will receive the earth as their possession.[82]

Freedom in the struggle for power

Jesus appeals to his disciples voluntarily *to use power for the benefit of others*.[83] Any individuals or groups who take Jesus Christ as their model will not today be required to do the impossible: to renounce all use of power. But in the particular situation they will see how they are called to use power for others.

We may recall, for example, the *problem of economic power*. Since the problems here are analogous to those already discussed in connection with war and peace, we can be more brief and confine ourselves to what is absolutely essential. The facts are well-known. There seems to be no way of halting rising prices and inflation. They continue to rise, affecting most seriously the poorest members of the community. The employers blame the unions and the unions the employers, and both blame the government. A vicious circle? What is to be done? Here too we can only offer some brief suggestions:

The Christian message does not give any detailed information as to how the problem should be tackled technically, how therefore the riddle of the magic square is to be solved: how full employment, economic growth, price stability and a favorable trade balance can be simultaneously achieved. Supply and demand, home market and foreign market seem to obey iron economic laws. And each and every one enters into the merciless struggle for power, trying to exploit them as far as possible to his own advantage.

The Christian message says something which is not normally found in any economics textbook, either of the left or of the right, and which is extraordinarily important for the present context: namely, that in all the inevitable conflicts of interests it is no disgrace either for the industrialist or for the trade union leader if he does not always exploit to the full his power over the other. It is not a disgrace if the employer does not pass on every increase in production costs to the consumers, merely to keep his profit constant or if possible to increase it. Nor is it a disgrace if the union leader occasionally does not insist on an increase in wages even if he could do so and the union members are perhaps expecting him to do so. In brief, despite all the tough discussions, it is no disgrace if those who have power in society do not always use it to their own advantage, but in certain situations are prepared completely freely —again, not as a universal law—to use that power for the benefit of others: *being ready for once in the individual case to "give away" power, profit, influence, and to give his coat in addition to his cloak.*

What is the point of all this? Not to provide a screen for an ideology of partnership. Nor because there is something to be got out of it for our own advantage. It is for the benefit of others, so that man (and often even the state) is not sacrificed to the power struggle, but power is used to the advantage of men. Power cannot, as some demand, simply be abolished. That is an illusion. But in the light of the Christian conscience power can be radically relativized for the benefit of men. Power can be used for service instead of domination.

In this way something is made possible in the individual case which seems too much to demand of men belonging either to the capitalist or to the socialist society and which is nevertheless infinitely important for all human life together, of individuals and of nations, of different language groups, classes and even Churches: being able endlessly to forgive instead of off-setting the blame; to be able to make concessions unconditionally instead of maintaining positions; the better justice of love instead of continual litigation; peace surpassing all reason instead of the merciless struggle for power. A message of this kind does not become the opium of empty promises. It involves a much more radical commitment than other programs do to the present world. It aims at change where the rulers threaten to crush the ruled, institutions to overwhelm persons, order to exclude freedom, power to suppress law.

Wherever individuals or whole groups forget that power exists not for domination but for service, they contribute to the prevalence of power thinking and power politics in both the individual and the social sphere: to the dehumanization of man in the now unavoidable struggle for power.

But wherever individuals or whole groups remember that power exists for service and not for domination, they contribute to the humanizing of the all-round human competitive struggle and even in the midst of this struggle make possible mutual respect, respect for men, reconciliation and forbearance. They may then believe in the promise that mercy will be shown to those who show mercy.[84]

Freedom from the pressure of consumption

Jesus invites his disciples *to practice inward freedom from possessions (consumption)*.[86] If anyone wants his behavior to be inspired in the last resort by Jesus Christ, he will not be forced to renounce in principle possessions and consumption. But in the wholly concrete case he will be offered the opportunity to make this renunciation for the sake of his own and others' freedom.

We may recall, for example, the *problem of economic growth*. Despite all progress, our efficiency-oriented and consumer society is increasingly entangled in contradictions. Supported by an economic theory extolled on all sides, the slogan runs: increase production so that we can increase consumption, so that production does not break down but expands. In this way the level of demand is always kept above the level of supply: through advertising, models and bellwethers of consumption. Wants continue to increase. New needs are created as soon as the old are satisfied. Luxury goods are classified as necessary consumer goods, in order to make way for new luxury goods. The targets of our own living standard are raised with the improvement of the supply situation. There is now a dynamic expectation of prosperity and a satisfying life. The surprising result is that, with constantly increasing real income, the average citizen feels that he has scarcely any means completely at his disposal, that he is really living at a minimum of existence.

At the same time the industrial welfare society and the economists too to a large extent start out from the assumption that increasing prosperity creates increasing happiness, that the capacity to consume is the essential proof of a successful life. The consumption of goods becomes a demonstration of one's own status to oneself and to society, so that expectations mount up on all sides in accordance with the law of herd instinct, prestige and competition. We are what we consume. We are more when we have reached a higher standard. We are nothing if we remain below the standardized position of the generality of people. All things considered, if we want to reach a better future, production and consumption must continually increase: everything must become bigger, more speedy, more numerous. This is the strict law of economic growth.

On the other hand it is increasingly recognized today that the assumptions behind this law are largely out of date in the industrial nations. Our first and most important concern is no longer the conquest of poverty and shortage of goods: for these preconditions of a genuinely human life are normally fulfilled in the highly industrialized countries. So for many people the call for bread alone, for possessions and consumption alone, is no longer convincing. On the one hand efforts to eliminate poverty have now given way to the spiral of infinitely increasing demand (on the part of consumers) and continual stimulation of demand (on the part of producers). On the other hand certain groups in our society are making it increasingly clear that, in addition to the hitherto primary economic needs, there are now secondary and tertiary wants which can no longer be satisfied from the goods provided by the national economy. Even the propertied classes are no happier as a result of material prosperity alone. And, among young people particularly, habituated to consumption, there is a widespread feeling of boredom and profound disorientation, together with uneasiness about the one-sided orientation to constantly increasing consumption.

The law of uncontrolled economic growth however creates a continually widening gap between rich and poor countries and strengthens among the underprivileged part of mankind feelings of envy, resentment, deadly hatred, but also of sheer despair and helplessness. And, as outlined at the opening of this book, it is turned in the end against the well-to-do themselves. We are suffering increasingly from the apparently endless growth of cities, proliferating traffic, noise on all sides, pollution of rivers and lakes, bad air; we are worried about the disposal of butter and meat mountains, we are crushed under the waste and lumber of our own prosperity. The world's raw materials, ruthlessly and more and more extensively exploited, are becoming increasingly scarce; the problem of an ever more widely expanding world economy is becoming incomprehensible. But what is to be done? Again we give a brief summary:

The Christian message provides no technical solutions: not for environment protection, distribution of raw materials, town and country planning, noise abatement, elimination of waste; nor for any kind of structural improvements. Nor do we find in the New Testament any instructions about the possibilities of bridging the gap between rich and poor, between the industrialized and the industrially underdeveloped nations. Least of all can the Christian message offer any decision models or devices for solving the enormous problems which a change of policy would create: for instance, the problem of freezing the national and international economy to zero growth, without causing a breakdown of the different branches of industry, loss of jobs, chaotic consequences for the social security of whole population groups and for the underdeveloped countries.

But the Christian message can make something clear which is apparently not envisaged at all either in the economic theory or in the practical scale of values of the modern consumer- and efficiency-oriented society, but which perhaps could have a part to play: replacement of the compulsion to consume by freedom in regard to consumption. In any case there is some point in not constructing one's happiness on the basis of consumption and prosperity alone. But in the light of

Jesus Christ it also makes sense not to be always striving, not always to be trying to have everything; not to be governed by the laws of prestige and competition; not to take part in the cult of abundance; but even with children to exercise the freedom to renounce consumption. This is "poverty in spirit" as inward freedom from possessions: *contented unpretentiousness and confident unconcernedness as a basic attitude. All this would be opposed to all fussy, overbold presumption and that anxious solicitude which is found among both the materially rich and the materially poor.*

What is the point? Not asceticism or an urge to self-sacrifice. Not a new, stringent law. But so that the normal cheerful consumer may remain free, may become free. So that he does not give himself up to the good things of this world, whether money or a car, alcohol or cigarettes, cosmetics or sex. So that he does not give way to the addictions of the welfare society. In other words, so that man in the midst of the world and its goods—which he must use and may use—in the last resort remains human. Here too then it is not a question of possessions, growth, consumption, for their own sake. And certainly not men for the sake of possessions, growth, consumption. But everything for the sake of men.

Wherever individuals or whole groups overlook the fact that all good things of this world exist for the sake of man and not man for the sake of these things, they are not worshiping the one true God, but the many false gods—Mammon, power, sex, work, prestige—and they surrender man to these merciless gods. They intensify the humanly destructive dynamism in which our economic processes are involved today. They strengthen the thoughtlessness with which the economy today is run at the expense of the future. They strengthen the inhuman selfishness with which the forces of the world economy assign too much to one half of mankind and too little to the other. Even if they are not aware of it, they are spreading inhumanity in the welfare and consumer society.

But wherever individuals or whole groups insist that the good things of this world in any case exist for the sake of man, they are contributing to the humanization of the now unavoidable welfare and consumer society. They are creating the necessary new elite, not tied to one class, which is learning to live with a new scale of values in this society and in the long run can initiate a process of reorientation. Even in this new age they make possible for themselves and others independence, supreme simplicity, an ultimate, carefree superiority, true freedom. To these also the promise applies that all those who are poor in spirit will possess the kingdom of God.[86]

Freedom to serve

Jesus demands from his disciples a voluntary *service regardless of precedence.*[87] Wherever an individual or a group enters on the way of Jesus Christ, they are not in fact required to do the impossible: to abolish all superordination and subordination in society. But the mutual service of all is offered as a new opportunity of social life.

We may recall the *problems of education.* Educational programs, educational methods, educational goals and educational personnel are involved today in a far-reaching crisis. Educational authorities and those responsible for socialization (family, school, university, but also institutions and businesses) and likewise educational personnel (father, mother, teacher, educator, instructor) find that they are exposed to harsh criticism and impatient accusations from right and left: for some they are too conservative, for others too progressive; for some too political, for others too unpolitical; for some too authoritarian, for others too anti-authoritarian. Perplexity and disorientation are widespread. We can only outline the causes and conditions, symptoms and consequences of this crisis.

In the family: the acceleration of the rate of change in society means that parents not only grow older but often quickly lose touch with the situation. The criteria for educating their children are no longer certain. The result is a lack of understanding and knowledge. There is a profound insecurity which often leads to insistence on the wrong things and thus to disastrous conflicts of authority for children and family.

In school and university: the discrepancy between pretension and reality, between often unrealistic theory and heightened practical expectations and requirements, the conflict of roles between teachers and pupils, professors and students, turn school and university into objects of political-educational controversy between all socially relevant groups and a field of experiment for more and more new educational-didactic projects and plans of study. After a planning euphoria we are now threatened with a planning lethargy, after excessive organization we are faced with disorganization, after the optimism of a future equality of opportunity we are uncertain about the future as a result of increasing restriction of studies; after conjuring up an educational emergency and the exhaustion of the last educational reserves we now have an educational glut and the "academic proletariat."

And the young people themselves? At the center of the conflicts and contradictions of the educational scene, they are reacting increasingly with apathy, indifference and weariness and often enough break down completely. Taken seriously by society as consumers and pampered in their self-awareness also as consumers, at home and in school they are often made to feel irresponsible and dependent. Influenced by adults, by school attendance and the continual raising of the school-leaving age to think in terms of social prestige, they must see how dubious are the criteria of achievement, how remote from life their training has often been, and how uncertain are their future chances of an occupation.

And the adults? Educational virtues, absolutely sacred and unquestioned yesterday, have apparently become obsolete today: adult authority, obedience to older people, subordination to the parents' will, adaptation to the existing order. But now there are some who question not only the contents and methods but the very idea of education. Those who identified education with determination by others, manipulation, imposition of the teacher's will, now go to the other extreme and advocate anti-authoritarian education, absolute self-determination, unrestricted freedom; aggression is to be cultivated, frustrations worked out, instincts satisfied, conflicts encouraged. Relationships are reversed: young people are no longer subject to the will of adults, but the claims of adults are subordinated to the claims, needs and requirements of young people.

A significant trend is emerging. A false conception of authority on both sides, fear and uncertainty in reaction to the others produce an atmosphere of pressure and counterpressure, of refusal or self-assertion, of stronger destructive tendencies, of brutality and aggression. The school passes on the responsibility to the family and society, society to school and family, family to school and society. There is a vicious circle. What is to be done? Here again are some brief suggestions:

The Christian message gives no detailed information as to how the scholastic and vocational training system is to be better and more effectively organized, how curricula are to be worked out, training and educational programs implemented, educational problems solved, institutions governed and children educated.

But the Christian message has something essential to say about the attitude and approach of the teacher to the child and the child to the teacher, and also about the reason for commitment even in the face of disappointments and failures: that in the light of the person of Jesus education can never be for the sake of my own prestige, repute, interest, but for the sake of the one who is entrusted to me. Education is understood therefore as non-repressive, as mutual service regardless of precedence. *This means that the children never exist simply for the sake of the teachers, nor indeed the teachers simply for the sake of the children; that the teachers may never exploit their children, nor indeed the children their teachers; that the teachers may never impose their will in an authoritarian spirit on their children, nor however may the children impose their will in an anti-authoritarian spirit on their teachers. Mutual service regardless of precedence in a Christian spirit means for the teacher unconditional trust, goodness, giving, loving good will, in advance and without any compelling reasons. And in all this he will refuse to let anything deter him.*

The requirement of service regardless of precedence is also something which does not imply any new legalism. It is essentially an invitation to both sides. On the teacher's side service is not to be understood as pious camouflage for what remains authoritarian practice or as weakness on the part of adults toward children. But neither should the children understand service as an invitation to exploit the adults' readiness to serve as a sign of weakness. Service regardless of precedence really means mutual frankness, readiness to learn and to be corrected.

This service regardless of precedence, motivated by the figure of Jesus, puts in question the pragmatism of those teachers who always simply react to the wishes, needs and demands of the children and do for these children no more than their duty. It puts in question a rigid, comfortable way of life which the children may not disturb beyond a certain point fixed in advance. This service also puts in question the moralism, largely accepted by society, of those who want to pin down the children to their own ideas of morality and feel that they are right even in dropping the children who are not prepared to accept this. This service also puts in question the apparently rational commercial spirit of those who at least tacitly attach to their efforts for the children the condition that they will later be reimbursed and who are surprised when their moralizing meets with a brusque rejection.

Christians understand mutual service also in the educational process as trust, goodness, giving, commitment to the other person, in advance, without any compelling reasons but certainly to be justified in the light of the person of Jesus. They will not let themselves be deterred when the other person—the child—does not correspond to their ideas, images and hopes; when they do not gain the self-assurance they expect or need; when they are certain that they are really giving more than they will ever get back; when, according to all rational, human calculation, they know that no commitment to a particular child will ever produce visible results. Anyone who tries to satisfy this Christian demand for service regardless of precedence as his educational maxim knows that Christian love of neighbor in its most radical form is up for discussion here.

In the light of all this there emerge a new scale of values of human fellowship for education, new check points for teachers and children, a new horizon of meaning. We may never set up ourselves as absolute, but must always consider others regardless of ourselves, showing that we can share, can forgive, can care, can voluntarily renounce rights and advantages and give without expecting anything in return.

What then is the point of such service? It is not the result of weakness but of strong conviction: a conviction based not only on an understanding of the necessity of partnership, of a co-operative relationship between teacher and taught, but on the unselfishness which gladly goes beyond the essential requirements of co-operation. It is thus possible to create an atmosphere of trust and understanding, of genuine aids to orientation and guidance, a non-repressive education above the extremes of authoritarianism and anti-authoritarianism. It is possible also to exemplify to a young person the real meaning of life: that my life has a meaning only if I live it not merely for myself but for others and if my life and the life of others is sustained, guided, given a name, by a reality greater, more enduring, more perfect than ourselves—the reality, that is, which mysteriously encompasses us and which we call God.

Wherever individuals or whole groups forget that education is not for controlling man, but for mutual service regardless of precedence, they share the blame for the fact that in both the social and the individual sphere the rights of the stronger and more powerful, the laws of determination by others and of superior force prevail and that in this very way the preconditions for inhumanity and loss of dignity are created.

But wherever individuals or whole groups remember that education does not mean controlling man, but mutual service regardless of precedence: by trust, concession, assistance, even good will and love, in advance, over and above all spontaneous interaction and co-operation, they contribute to the humanization of human relationships and thus make possible a meaningful and fulfilled life even in a phase of uncertainty and disorientation. To those who see education in this sense as service regardless of precedence the promise is given that receiving a child, not only in his own name but in Jesus' name, means receiving Jesus himself.[88]

But these suggestions may suffice and stimulate further reflection. If we wanted to write down all that Jesus did, the world could "not contain the books that would be written."[89] Could the world contain the books which would be written if we wanted to record all that was done, is done and—above all—could be done in Jesus' following?

Human existence transfigured in Christian existence

We began this book with the direct question: *Why should one be a Christian?* And the answer is equally direct: *In order to be truly human.* What does this mean?

Being Christian cannot mean ceasing to be human. But neither can being human mean ceasing to be Christian. Being Christian is not an addition to being human: there is not a Christian level above or below the human. The true Christian is not a split personality.

The Christian element therefore is neither a superstructure nor a substructure of the human. It is an elevation or—better—a transfiguration of the human, at once preserving, canceling, surpassing the human. Being Christian therefore means that the other humanisms are transfigured: they are affirmed to the extent that they affirm the human reality; they are rejected to the extent that they reject the Christian reality, Christ himself; they are surpassed to the extent that being Christian can fully incorporate the human, all-too-human even in all its negativity.

Christians are no less humanists than all humanists. But they see the human, the truly human, the humane; they see man and his God; see humanity, freedom, justice, life, love, peace, meaning: all these they see in the light of this Jesus who for them is the concrete criterion, the Christ. In his light they think they cannot support just any kind of humanism which simply affirms all that is true, good, beautiful and human. But they can support a truly radical humanism which is able to integrate and cope with what is untrue, not good, unlovely, inhuman: not only everything positive, but also—and here we discern what a humanism has to offer—everything negative, even suffering, sin, death, futility.

Looking to the crucified and living Christ, even in the world of today, man is able not only to act but also to suffer, not only to live but also to die. And even when pure reason breaks down, even in pointless misery and sin, he perceives a meaning, because he knows that here too in both positive and negative experience he is sustained by God. Thus faith in Jesus the Christ gives peace with God and with oneself, but does not play down the problems of the world. It makes man truly human, because truly one with other men: open to the very end for the other person, the one who needs him here and now, his "neighbor."

So we have asked: why should one be a Christian? The answer will certainly be understood now if we reduce it to a brief recapitulatory formula:

By following Jesus Christ
man in the world of today
can truly humanly live, act, suffer and die:
in happiness and unhappiness, life and death,
sustained by God and helpful to men.

Basic Theological Literature

A book like this must take account of an immense amount of published work in the different fields of theology: not only books, but many thousands of articles scattered in a variety of specialist reviews.

To enable the reader to keep his head above water in this flood of literature, here is a brief survey of the more important recent works which can be regarded as fundamental at least for consultation and which have been used frequently in the present book, their titles being given mostly in an abbreviated form. For this edition the author has added a number of titles of books likely to be particularly useful to English-speaking readers.

1. *Dictionaries and Encyclopedias*

Bibellexikon, edited by H. Haag, Einsiedeln/Zürich/Cologne, 1968 (=BL).
Catholicisme. Hier–aujourd'hui–demain, edited by G. Jaquemet, Paris, 1948ff.
Concise Theological Dictionary, edited by Karl Rahner and Herbert Vorgrimler, London/New York, 1965.
Dictionary of the Bible, by J. L. McKenzie, Milwaukee/London, 1968.
Dictionnaire de la Bible, Supplement, Vols. I–VIII, edited by L. Pirot, continued by A. Robert, Paris, 1928ff. (=DBS).
Dictionnaire de Théologie Catholique, Vols. I–XVI, edited by A. Vacant and E. Mangenot, continued by E. Amann, Paris, 1903ff.
Encyclopedia of Biblical Theology, edited by J. B. Bauer, New York/London, 1970.
Evangelisches Kirchenlexikon. Kritisch-theologisches Handwörterbuch, edited by H. Brunotte and O. Weber, Göttingen, 1955ff. (=EKL).
Lexikon für Theologie und Kirche, Vols. I–X, edited by J. Höfer and K. Rahner, Freiburg, 1956ff. (=LThK).
New Catholic Encyclopedia, Vols. I–XV, New York, 1967.
Die Religion in Geschichte und Gegenwart. Handwörterbuch für Theologie und Religionswissenschaft, Vols. I–VI, edited by K. Galling, Tübingen, 1957 (=RGG).
Sacramentum Mundi. An Encyclopedia of Theology, Vols. I–VI, edited by A. Darlap, London/New York, 1968–70.
Theologisches Wörterbuch zum Neuen Testament, Vols. I–VIII, edited by G. Kittel, continued by G. Friedrich, Stuttgart, 1933ff. (=ThW). This work,

with the title of *Theological Dictionary of the New Testament*, is now available in English in ten volumes, Grand Rapids/London, 1971ff.

2. *Bible Commentaries*

The International Critical Commentary on the Holy Scriptures of the Old and New Testament, edited by S. R. Driver, A. Plummer and C. A. Briggs, Edinburgh, 1895ff.

The Jerome Bible Commentary, edited by R. E. Brown, J. A. Fitzmeyer and R. E. Murphy, Eaglewood Cliffs, 1968/London, 1969.

A New Catholic Commentary on Holy Scripture, edited by R. C. Fuller, L. Johnston and C. Kearns, London/New Jersey, 1969.

Peake's Commentary on the Bible, edited by M. Black and H. H. Rowley, London/New York, 1975 (latest edition).

The Anchor Bible, Vol. Iff., edited by F. M. Cross, R. E. Brown and J. C. Greenfield, Garden City, 1965ff.

The Interpreters' Bible, edited by G. A. Bullrick, New York, 1951.

The New Century Bible, Vol. Iff., edited by R. E. Clements and M. Black, London, 1967ff.

The Cambridge Bible Commentary on the New English Bible, Vol. Iff., edited by P. R. Ackroyd, A. R. C. Leaney and J. W. Packer, London, 1965ff.

Kritisch-exegetischer Kommentar über das Neue Testament, started by H. A. W. Meyer, 16 volumes, frequently revised, Göttingen, 1932ff. (*Meyers Kommentar*).

Handbuch zum Neuen Testament, edited by H. Lietzmann, continued by G. Bornkamm, 22 sections in different editions, Tübingen, 1906ff. (*Lietzmanns Handbuch*).

Das Neue Testament Deutsch. Neues Göttinger Bibelwerk, edited by P. Althaus and J. Behm, 12 volumes in different editions, Göttingen, 1932ff. (*NT Deutsch*).

Das Neue Testament, übersetzt und kurz erklärt, edited by A. Wikenhauser and O. Kuss, 9 volumes with an index volume in different editions, Regensburg, 1938ff. (*Regensburger NT*).

Herders Theologischer Kommentar zum Neuen Testament, edited by A. Wikenhauser and A. Vögtle, Freiburg, 1953ff. (*Herders theologischer Kommentar*).

Études Bibliques, Paris, 1907ff.

Commentaire du Nouveau Testament, edited by P. Bonnard and others, Neuchâtel/Paris, 1949ff.

3. *New Testament Theologies and Christologies*

R. Bultmann, *Theology of the New Testament*, 2 vols., London/New York, 1951–55.

H. Conzelmann, *Outline of the Theology of the New Testament*, London/New York, 1969.

J. Jeremias, *New Testament Theology*, Part I, London/Philadelphia, 1971.
W. G. Kummel, *Theology of the New Testament According to Its Major Witnesses, Jesus–Paul–John*, Nashville, 1973/London, 1974.
K. H. Schelkle, *Theologie des Neuen Testaments*, 4 vols., Düsseldorf, 1968ff.

O. Betz, *What Do We Know About Jesus?*, London, 1968.
O. Cullmann, *The Christology of the New Testament*, London/Philadelphia, 1963.
R. H. Fuller, *The Foundations of New Testament Christology*, New York, 1965.
F. Hahn, *Christologische Hoheitstitel. Ihre Geschichte im frühen Christentum*, Göttingen, 1963.
J. Knox, *The Humanity and Divinity of Christ*, Cambridge, 1967.
W. Pannenberg, *Jesus–God and Man*, Philadelphia/London, 1968.

4. *Works on Dogmatics and Systematic Theology*

H. Denzinger, *Enchiridion symbolorum, definitionum et declarationum de rebus fidei et morum*, edited by A. Schönmetzer, Barcelona/Freiburg/Rome/New York, 1963 (=DS). This work was first published in 1854 and has gone through more than thirty editions since then.

P. Althaus, *Die christliche Wahrheit. Lehrbuch der Dogmatik*, Gütersloh, 1962 (sixth edition).
K. Barth, *Church Dogmatics*, 4 vols., Edinburgh/Naperville, 1936–69.
E. Brunner, *Dogmatics*, London, 1949–52.
The Common Catechism. A Christian Book of Faith, edited by J. Feiner and L. Vischer, London/New York, 1975.
H. Diem, *Theologie als kirchliche Wissenschaft*, 3 vols., Munich, 1951ff.
Mysterium Salutis. Grundriss heilsgeschichtlicher Dogmatik, 5 vols., edited by J. Feiner and M. Löhrer, Einsiedeln/Zürich/Cologne, 1965ff.
H. Ott, *Die Antwort des Glaubens*, Stuttgart/Berlin, 1972.
K. Rahner, *Theological Investigations*, 14 vols., London/vols. 1–6, Baltimore, 1961–69; vols. 7–14, New York, 1972–76.
M. Schmaus, *Dogma*, 4 vols., New York/London, 1968–72.
P. Tillich, *Systematic Theology*, 3 vols., Chicago, 1951–63/London, 1968.
O. Weber, *Grundlagen der Dogmatik*, 2 vols., Neukirchen/Moers, 1959–62.

5. *Introductions to Christianity or to the Apostles' Creed*

H. U. von Balthasar, *Who Is a Christian?*, London, 1968.
G. Ebeling, *The Nature of Faith*, London/Philadelphia, 1961.
A. Harnack, *What Is Christianity?*, London, 1901/Philadelphia, 1908.
W. Kasper, *Einführung in den Glauben*, Mainz, 1972.
A New Catechism. Catholic Faith for Adults, commissioned by the Hierarchy

of the Netherlands (The "Dutch Catechism"), London/New York, 1967; second edition, New York, 1969.

K. Barth, *Credo*, London, 1964.
W. Pannenberg, *The Apostles' Creed in the Light of Today's Questions*, London/Philadelphia, 1972.
Joseph Ratzinger, *Introduction to Christianity*, London, 1969.

6. *Books by Hans Küng* (cited with abbreviated titles)

Justification. The Doctrine of Karl Barth and a Catholic Reflection, New York, 1964/London, 1965.
Structures of the Church, New York, 1964/London, 1965.
Menschwerdung Gottes. Eine Einführung in Hegels theologisches Denken als Prolegomena zu einer künftigen Christologie, Freiburg/Basle/Vienna, 1970.
Why Priests? A Proposal for a New Church Ministry, New York/London, 1972.

Notes

Editor's Note: *A superior number after the year of publication indicates the edition of the work.*

A I: The Challenge of Modern Humanisms

1 On the history of the concept see H. Lübbe, *Säkularisierung. Geschichte eines ideenpolitischen Begriffs*, Munich, 1965. Basic reading on the problematic is provided by F. Gogarten, *Verhängnis und Hoffnung der Neuzeit. Die Säkularisierung als theologisches Problem*, Stuttgart, 1953; H. Cox, *The Secular City*, New York/London, 1965; H. Blumenberg, *Die Legitimät der Neuzeit*, Frankfurt, 1966.
2 M. Greiffenhagen, art. "Emanzipation" in *Historisches Wörterbuch der Philosophie*, Vol. II, Darmstadt, 1972, Coll. 448–49; the same author, "Ein Weg der Vernünft ohne Rückkehr. Ist die Emanzipation in eine neue Phase getreten" in *Die Zeit*, 22 June 1973.
3 M. Weber, *The Protestant Ethic and the Spirit of Capitalism*, New York, 1958/London, 1967.
4 J. Kahl, *Das Elend des Christentums oder Plädoyer für eine Humanität ohne Gott*, Reinbeck bei Hamburg, 1968; cf. the more recent work of C. Amery, *Das Ende der Vorsehung. Die gnadenlosen Folgen des Christentums*, Hamburg, 1972.
5 For instance, F. Gogarten, op. cit., and H. Cox, op. cit. On the discussion, see D. Callaghan (ed.), *The Secular City Debate*, New York/London, 1966.
6 H. Blumenberg, op. cit.
7 D. von Hildebrand, *The Trojan Horse in the City of God*, Chicago, 1970.
8 J. Maritain, *The Peasant of the Garonne. An old man questions himself about the present time*, New York/London, 1969.
9 H. U. von Balthasar, *Cordula oder der Ernstfall*, Einsiedeln, 1966.
10 L. Bouyer, *The Decomposition of Catholicism*, Chicago/London, 1970.
11 R. Augstein, "Das grosse Schisma" in *Der Spiegel* (1969), No. 18; cf. also R. Altmann, "Abschied von den Kirchen" in *Der Spiegel* (1970), No. 28.
12 *Newsweek*, 4 October 1971.
13 The concept became popular as a result of the publications of J. B. Metz, J. Moltmann, D. Sölle (see discussion in D III, 1).
14 C. Schmitt, *Politische Theologie. Vier Kapitel zur Lehre von der Souveränität*, Munich/Leipzig, 1922, 1934[2].

15 Our analysis and basic conclusions largely coincide with what Jürgen Moltmann says about the identity and relevance of the Christian faith ("Identity-Involvement Dilemma"). Cf. J. Moltmann, *The Crucified God. The Cross of Christ as the Foundation and Criticism of Christian Theology*, London, 1974, Ch. I, 1–2, pp. 7–25.

16 A. Toffler, *Future Shock*, New York/London, 1970, p. 15.

17 D. L. Meadows, *The Limits to Growth*, New York, 1972.

18 G. R. Taylor, *The Doomsday Book*, London, 1970/New York, 1971; S. Kirban, *Die geplante Verwirrung*, Wetzlar, 1972; G. Ehrensvärd, *Nach uns die Steinzeit. Das Ende des technischen Zeitalters*, Berne, 1972; D. Widener, *Kein Platz für Menschen. Der programmierte Selbstmord*, Frankfurt, 1972; E. E. Snyder, *Todeskandidat Erde. Programmierter Selbstmord durch unkontrollierten Fortschritt*, Munich, 1972; M. Lohmann (ed.), *Gefährdete Zukunft*, Munich, 1973.

19 K. Steinbuch, *Falsch programmiert*, Stuttgart, 1968.

20 K. Steinbuch, *Kurskorrektur*, Stuttgart, 1973, p. 9.

21 K. Lorenz, *Civilized Man's Eight Deadly Sins*, New York/London, 1974.

22 Out of the extensive work of all these authors, cf. especially the basic studies: M. Horkheimer/T. W. Adorno, *Dialectic of Enlightenment*, London/New York, 1974; T. W. Adorno, *Negative Dialektik*, Frankfurt, 1966; M. Horkheimer, *Zur Kritik der instrumentellen Vernunft*, Frankfurt, 1967; the same author, *Kritische Theorie. Eine Dokumentation*, Frankfurt, 1968; H. Marcuse, *The One-Dimensional Man. Studies in the Ideology of the Advanced Industrial Society*, Boston/London, 1964; E. Bloch, *Das Prinzip Hoffnung*, Frankfurt, 1959. A. Schmidt provides a good introduction to the above in a special issue of *Nachrichten aus dem Kösel-Verlag*, Munich, 1970: "Die 'Zeitschrift für Sozialforschung.' Geschichte und gegenwärtige Bedeutung."

23 Cf. especially Marcuse, op. cit., on the one-dimensional society and one-dimensional thinking.

24 On the discussion with critical rationalism cf. H. Küng, *Existiert Gott?*, Munich, 1975.

25 Cf. the French Structuralists' interpretation of Marx: L. Althusser, *For Marx*, New York, 1970/London, 1972; L. Althusser/E. Balibar, *Reading "Capital,"* London, 1970/New York, 1971.

26 K. Marx, *Early Writings*, New York/London, 1963. Among these *The German Ideology* (also published separately London, 1965/New York, 1970) and *Theses on Feuerbach* are particularly important.

27 K. Marx, *Capital*. English translations published by Encyclopedia Britannica, Chicago, 1952/London, 1954–59.

28 Basic for orthodox *Marxism* (Marxist-Leninism) are K. Marx/F. Engels, *Communist Manifesto*, New York, 1968/London, 1969; F. Engels, *Anti-Dühring*, London 1955/New York, 1966; W. I. Lenin, "Materialism and Empirio-Criticism" in Lenin, *Selected Works*, London, 1936–39, Vol. xi, part 2; J. Stalin, *Dialectical and Historical Materialism*, New York, 1940/London, 1940.

29 Particularly informative are S. Stojanović, *Between Ideals and Reality. A Critique of Marxism and Its Future*, New York/London, 1973; P. Vran-

icki, *Geschichte des Marxismus*, Frankfurt, 1972–74. Notable among Hungarian publications are those of Andreas Hegedüs and Agnes Heller, representatives there of the New Left.

30 Cf. H. Pross, "Überleben des Kapitalismus? Mitwirkung der Unternehmer an der Verbesserung der Wirtschaftsverfassung" in the report of the annual conference of the study group of independent employers in Munich, 31 May to 2 June 1973, published under the title *Der Angriff auf den Unternehmer–Herausforderung und Chance*, pp. 15–20.

31 At an early date H. Marcuse produced his *Soviet Marxism. A Critical Analysis*, New York/London, 1958. On the conditions in the Soviet Union, Eastern Germany, Czechoslovakia, Cuba and North Korea, see likewise the five reports of the left-wing socialists R. Rossanda, B. Rabehl, S. Plogstedt, G. Maschke, H. Kurnitzky and K. D. Wolff, in *Kursbuch*, edited by H. M. Enzensberger, Berlin, 1972, No. 30.

32 M. Djilas, *The New Class*, New York, 1957/London, 1966. The same author, *The Unperfect Society*, New York/London, 1970. Djilas had been Tito's comrade in arms for many years and from 1945 to 1954 general secretary of the Communist Party of Yugoslavia, deputy prime minister and authoritative theorist of the party. His book brought him six years of captivity. In 1962 he was condemned to a further nine years in prison because of his book *Conversations with Stalin* (New York, 1962).

33 Cf. the publications of prominent Russian critics of the regime, which have become known in the West, especially the letter of the professors A. D. Sakharov, W. F. Turtshin and R. A. Medvedev in 1968 to the Central Committee of the Communist Party of the Soviet Union, printed in the *Neue Zürcher Zeitung*, 22 April 1970; A. D. Sakharov, *Wie ich mir die Zukunft vorstelle*, Zürich, 1969; the same author, "Ein Memorandum an den General-sekretär der KPdSU, L. I. Breschnew," 1971, printed in *Die Zeit*, 21 July 1972; the same author, interview in *Der Spiegel*, 1973, No. 28; A. Amalrik, *Will the Soviet Union Survive until 1984?*, London, 1970/New York, 1971; P. I. Jakir, *Kindheit in Gefangenschaft*, Frankfurt, 1972; A. Solzhenitsyn, *Letter to Soviet Leaders* (5 September 1973), London, 1974/"Live Not by Lies," 12 February 1974, in Leopold Labetz (ed.), *Solzhenitsyn: A Documentary Record*, London/Baltimore, 1974, pp. 375–79. Also informative is the investigation by R. Bernheim, formerly Moscow correspondent of the *Neue Zürcher Zeitung*, *Die sozialistische Errungenschaften der Sowjetunion*, Zürich, 1972.

34 Cf. the book by some of the participants, U. Bergmann, A. Dutschke, W. Lefevre, B. Rabehl, *Rebellion der Studenten oder Die neue Opposition. Eine Analyse*, Hamburg, 1968. For a critical treatment see E. K. Scheuch (ed.), *Die Wiedertäufer der Wohlstandsgesellschaft*, Cologne, 1968; W. Fikentscher, *Zur politischen Kritik an Marxismus und Neomarxismus als ideologische Grundlage der Studentenunruhen 1965/69*, Tübingen, 1971. On the controversial identification of "brown" and "red" see H. Grebing, *Linksradikalismus gleich Rechtsradikalismus. Eine falsche Gleichung*, Stuttgart, 1971; M. Greiffenhagen, R. Kühnl, J. B. Müller, *Totalitarismus. Zur Problematik eines politischen Begriffs*, Munich, 1972.

35 M. Horkheimer, preface to his miscellany, *Kritische Theorie*, Frankfurt, 1968.

36 H. Marcuse, *One-Dimensional Man*, Boston/London, 1964, pp. 253, 255, 257.

37 J. Habermas, *Legitimationsprobleme im Spätkapitalismus*, Frankfurt, 1973; cf. the same author's postscript to *Erkenntnis und Interesse*, Frankfurt, 1973.

38 On the relations between Christianity and Marxism, first from the Christian side: J. L. Hromádka, *Evangelium für Atheisten*, Berlin, 1957; H. Gollwitzer, *Christian Faith and the Marxist Criticism of Religion*, New York/Edinburgh, 1970; E. Kellner (ed.), *Christentum und Marxismus–heute* (especially the contributions by W. Dantine, G. Girardi, J. B. Metz, K. Rahner, M. Reding, D. Schreuder and G. A. Wetter), Vienna/Frankfurt/Zürich, 1966; R. Garaudy (Introduction by K. Rahner, Epilogue by J. B. Metz), *From Anathema to Dialogue: The Challenge of Marxist-Christian Cooperation*, New York, 1966/London, 1967; M. Stöhr (ed.), *Disputation zwischen Christen und Marxisten*, Munich, 1966; G. Girardi, *Marxism and Christianity*, New York, 1968; F. J. Adelmann, *From Dialogue to Epilogue. Marxism and Catholicism Tomorrow*, The Hague, 1968; W. Post, *Kritik der Religion bei Karl Marx*, Munich, 1969; J. Fetscher/W. Post, *Verdirbt Religion den Menschen? Marxistischer und christlicher Humanismus. Ein Interview*, Düsseldorf, 1969; J. Kadenbach, *Das Religionsverständnis von Karl Marx*, Munich/Paderborn/Vienna, 1970; H. Apthecker, *The Urgency of Marxist-Christian Dialogue*, New York, 1970; J. M. Lochman, *The Church in a Marxist Society. A Czechoslovak View*, New York, 1970; D. Sölle, "Christentum und Marxismus. Bericht über den Stand des Gesprächs" in *Das Recht ein anderer zu werden*, Neuwied/Berlin, 1971; F. v. d. Dudenrijn, *Kritische Theologie als Kritik der Theologie. Theorie und Praxis bei Karl Marx–Herausforderung der Theologie*, Munich/Mainz, 1972; J. P. Miranda, *Marx y la Biblia Crítica a la filosofía de la opresión*, Salamanca, 1972.

On the relations between Christianity and Marxism, from the Marxist side: E. Bloch, *Das Prinzip Hoffnung*, Frankfurt, 1967; the same author, *Thomas Münzer als Theologe der Revolution*, Frankfurt, 1962; the same author, *Atheism in Christianity*, New York, 1972; M. Machovec, *Marxismus und dialektische Theologie. Barth, Bonhoeffer und Hrodmádka in atheistisch-kommunistischer Sicht*, Zürich, 1965; the same author, *Jesus für Atheisten*, Stuttgart, 1972; R. Garaudy, *Marxism in the Twentieth Century*, New York/London, 1970 (especially the chapter on "Marxism and Religion," pp. 106–63); V. Gardavsky, *God Is Not Yet Dead*, Baltimore/London, 1974; L. Kolakowski, *Geist und Ungeist christlicher Traditionen*, Stuttgart, 1971; cf. also in the above-mentioned volume, *Christentum und Marxismus–heute*, the contributions of R. Garaudy, R. Havemann, L. Lombardo-Radice.

39 "Ohne Geschichte leben?" Opening address at the 29th Conference of German Historians before the Association of the History Teachers of Germany in Regensburg, in *Die Zeit*, 13 October 1972.

40 M. Weber, "Politik als Beruf" (October 1919) in *Gesammelte politische Schriften*, Tübingen, 1971, pp. 505–60 (quotation, p. 560).
41 R. Jungk, *Die Zukunft hat schon begonnen*, Stuttgart, 1952.
42 R. Jungk, *Der Jahrtausendmensch. Bericht aus den Werkstätten der neuen Gesellschaft*, Munich/Gütersloh/Vienna, 1973.
43 H. Pross, op. cit., p. 17.
44 H. Pross, op. cit., p. 19.

A II: The Other Dimension

1 E. Ionesco, "The Threat to Culture." Address at the opening of the Salzburg Festival, 1972. French original and German translation, Munich, 1972, p. 22.
2 E. Ionesco, op. cit., pp. 21–22.
3 Cf. A I, 3: "Humanity through technological evolution?"
4 Cf. A I, 3: "Humanity through politico-social revolution?"
5 For the discussion with nihilism, omitted here because of pressure of space, see H. Küng, *Existiert Gott?*, Munich, 1975.
6 M. Horkheimer, *Die Sehnsucht nach dem ganz Anderen*. An interview with commentary by H. Gumnior, Hamburg, 1970, esp. pp. 67–69.
7 H. F. Steiner, *Marxisten-Leninisten über den Sinn des Lebens. Eine Studie zum kommunistischen Menschenbild*, Essen, 1970; cf. esp. the documents, translated from Russian, on the discussion in Soviet periodicals, pp. 309–63.
8 A. Schaff, *Marxismus und das menschliche Individuum*, Vienna/Frankfurt/Zürich, 1965; M. Machoveč, *Jesus für Atheisten*, Stuttgart/Berlin, 1972, pp. 15–30; cf. the same author, *Vom Sinn des menschlichen Lebens*, German translation from Czech (original, 1965), Freiburg, 1971; E. Bloch, *Religion im Erbe* (a selection from his writings on the philosophy of religion), Munich/Hamburg, 1967.
9 P. Berger, *Invitation to Sociology. A Humanistic Perspective*, New York, 1963, pp. 174–75/London, 1966, p. 197; the same author, *A Rumor of Angels*, New York, 1969/London, 1970, esp. Chapter 3.
10 W. Heisenberg, *Der Teil und das Ganze. Gespräche im Umkreis der Atomphysik*, Munich, 1969, pp. 116–30; cf. also pp. 279–95; the same author, "Naturwissenschaftliche und religiöse Wahrheit," Address on the occasion of the award of the Guardini prize, in *Zur Debatte. Themen der Katholischen Akademie in Bayern* 3 (1973), No. 3/4. Cf. also P. Jordan, *Der Naturwissenschaftler vor der religiösen Frage. Abbruch einer Mauer*, Oldenburg/Hamburg, 1963.
11 Cf., outside the school of Freud, particularly C. G. Jung, *Psychology and Religion*, Princeton, 1970/London, 1970. On the problems: J. Rudin, *Psychotherapy and Religion*, Notre Dame, 1968. See also the founder of logotherapy, V. E. Frankl, *The Doctor and the Soul: From Psychotherapy to Logotherapy*, New York, 1965/London, 1969; the same author, *The Will to Meaning*, New York, 1969/London, 1971; the same author, *Der unbewusste Gott. Psychotherapie und Religion*, Munich, 1974[2].

12 Within the Freudian school, cf. especially E. H. Erikson, *Identity and the Life Cycle*, New York, 1957; the same author, *Insight and Responsibility*, New York, 1964; the same author, *Identity: Youth and Crisis*, New York, 1968/London, 1971; R. May, *The Meaning of Anxiety*, New York, 1950; the same author, *Man's Search for Himself*, New York, 1953; the same author, *Power and Innocence*, New York, 1972.

13 M. Machoveč, op. cit., p. 25.

14 P. Nobile (ed.), *The Con III Controversy: the Critics Look at the Greening of America*, New York, 1971.

15 T. Roszak, *The Making of a Counter Culture. Reflections on the Technocratic Society and Its Youthful Opposition*, New York, 1968/London, 1970.

16 C. Reich, *The Greening of America*, New York, 1971, p. 327/London, 1971, p. 223.

17 A. J. Toynbee, *Surviving the Future*, London/New York/Toronto, 1971, pp. 44–45, 66–67. Cf. also M. Mead, *Twentieth Century Faith. Hope and Survival*, New York, 1972, esp. p. 3.

18 Cf. the evidence given by the patriarchate of Moscow, *Der Spiegel*, 1974, No. 17.

19 Cf. A I, 1: "Secular world."

20 Cf. on the criticism of the secularization thesis and on the whole complex of the endurance of religion, A. M. Greeley, *Religion in the Year 2000*, New York, 1969; the same author, *The Persistence of Religion*, New York, 1972/London, 1973; O. Schatz (ed.), *Hat die Religion Zukunft?*, Graz/Vienna/Cologne, 1971, with contributions from A. Toynbee, P. Berger, T. Luckmann, A. Gehlen, K. Löwith, M. Horkheimer, E. Bloch, H. Cox, O. Schatz, among others; G. Baum, *New Horizon*, New York, 1972; finally the issue of *Concilium*, January 1973, edited by Gregory Baum and A. M. Greeley, with contributions by M. Marty, J. Brothers, W. and N. McCready, J. Remy, E. Servais, B. van Iersel, D. Power, J. Shea, E. Kennedy, D. Tracy, R. Ruether, R. Laurentin. Among earlier publications on the sociology of religion see E. A. Tiryakian (ed.), *Sociological Theory, Values and Sociocultural Change, Essays in Honor of P. A. Sorokin*, London, 1963, particularly the contributions by T. Parsons and T. F. O'Dea; likewise, D. R. Cutler (ed.), *The Religious Situation: Nineteen Sixty Eight*, Boston, 1968, especially the contributions by H. Smith, J. Campbell, C. Geertz, T. Parsons, G. E. Swanson.

21 H. Cox, the author of *The Secular City*, has now written *The Seduction of the Spirit. The Use and Misuse of People's Religion*, New York, 1973/London, 1974. Particularly illuminating as evidence of the new trend is Chapter 5, "Beyond Bonhoeffer," with the sentence: "In short, the question of the future of religion is open again." The question was never really closed.

22 O. F. Bollnow, *Wesen und Wandel der Tugenden*, Frankfurt/Berlin, 1958.

23 Cf. T. Luckmann, "Verfall, Fortbestand oder Verwandlung des Religiösen in der modernen Gesellschaft?" in O. Schatz (ed.), op. cit., pp. 69–82.

24 A. M. Greeley, *Religion in the Year 2000*, Chapter 3: "The Data."

25 H. Blumenberg, *Die Legitimität der Neuzeit*, Frankfurt, 1966, pp. 41–42.

26 On the problem of God as discussed in recent *philosophy*: K. Jaspers, *Der philosophische Glaube*, Munich, 1948; W. Schulz, *Der Gott der neuzeitlichen Metaphysik*, Pfullingen, 1957; M. E. Marty, *Varieties of Unbelief*, New York/Chicago/San Francisco, 1964; W. Strolz, *Menschsein als Gottesfrage. Wege zur Erfahrung der Inkarnation*, Pfullingen, 1965; E. Fontinell, *Toward a Reconstruction of Religion. A Philosophical Probe*, New York, 1970; E. Coreth/J. B. Lotz (eds.), *Atheismus kritisch betrachtet*, Munich, 1971; W. Weischedel, *Der Gott der Philosophen. Grundlegung einer philosophischen Theologie im Zeitalter des Nihilismus*, 2 vols., Darmstadt, 1971–72; G. Hasenhüttl, *Gott ohne Gott. Ein Dialog mit J-P. Sartre*, Graz/Vienna/Cologne, 1972; G. D. Kaufman, *God the Problem*, Cambridge, 1972; J. Splett, *Gotteserfahrung im Denken. Zur philosophischen Rechtfertigung des Redens von Gott*, Freiburg/Munich, 1973; R. Schaeffler, *Religion und kritisches Bewusstsein*, Freiburg/Munich, 1973; the same author, *Die Religionskritik sucht ihren Partner. Thesen zu einer erneuerten Apologetik*, Freiburg/Basle/Vienna, 1974. On the history of atheism see particularly F. Mauthner, *Der Atheismus und seine Geschichte im Abendland*, 4 vols., Stuttgart, 1921–23; H. Ley, *Geschichte der Aufklärung und des Atheismus*, 3 vols., Berlin, 1966–71. On the *proofs of God* in particular: W. Cramer, *Gottesbeweise und ihre Kritik. Prüfung ihrer Beweiskraft*, Frankfurt, 1967; K. Riesenhuber, *Existenzerfahrung und Religion*, Mainz, 1968; Q. Huonder, *Die Gottesbeweise. Geschichte und Schicksal*, Stuttgart, 1968; Hans Küng, *Menschwerdung Gottes*.

27 Emil Brunner and Karl Barth, *Natural Theology*, London, 1966, containing Emil Brunner's "Nature and Grace" and Karl Barth's reply "No"; K. Barth, *Church Dogmatics* II, 1, Edinburgh, 1957 (on Vatican I, see especially pp. 79–85); but see also how Barth corrected himself in his theology of creation in *Church Dogmatics* III, 1–3, Edinburgh, 1958, especially III, 3 §69, 2.

28 R. Bultmann, *Faith and Understanding. Collected Essays* I, London, 1969, pp. 28–52, 53–65, 313–31.

29 On the lines of Barth, see recently H. Gollwitzer in discussion with W. Weischedel, *Denken und Glauben. Ein Streitgespräch*, Stuttgart, 1965; J. Moltmann, *The Crucified God. The Cross of Christ as the Foundation and Criticism of Christian Theology*, London, 1974, especially Chapters I, 3 and VI, 2. On the lines of Bultmann, see especially G. Ebeling, *Das Wesen des christlichen Glaubens*, Tübingen, 1959; the same author, *Wort und Glaube*, Tübingen, 1960.

30 St. Thomas Aquinas, *Summa contra Gentiles* I, 3–14; *Summa Theologiae* I, q. 2.

31 First Vatican Council, Dogmatic Constitution, *De fide catholica*, especially DS 3004, 3015–20; cf. Pius XII, encyclical *Humani generis*, 12 August 1950 in Acta Apostolicae Sedis, 42 (1950), pp. 561–78 (excerpts in DS 3875–99).

32 St. Thomas Aquinas, *Summa Theologiae* I, q. 2, aa. 1–2.

33 A discriminating renewal of "natural theology" can be found in W. Pannenberg, *Was ist der Mensch?*, Göttingen, 1962; the same author, *Reve-*

lation as History, New York/London/Sydney, 1969; the same author, *Grundfragen systematischer Theologie*, Göttingen, 1967; the same author, "Brief an W. Weischedel" in J. Salaquarda (ed.), *Philosophische Theologie im Schatten des Nihilismus*, Berlin, 1971, pp. 176–80, with W. Weischedel's answer, pp. 180–81.

34 Cf. H. Küng, *Existiert Gott?*, Munich, 1975.

35 *Kant's Critique of Practical Reason*, translated by T. K. Abbott, Longmans Green, London/New York/Toronto, 1909, Book II, Chapter II, 5, pp. 220–29, especially 223.

36 There is an enormous *theological* literature on the *question of God*. Among the manuals and comprehensive works on dogmatics on the *Catholic* side may be mentioned Michael Schmaus, *Dogma*, 6 vols., New York/London, 1970–74; J. Feiner/M. Löhrer (eds.), *Mysterium Salutis*, 5 vols., Einsiedeln/Zürich/Cologne, 1965ff.; Karl Rahner, *Theological Investigations*, Baltimore/London (the first volume of these collected essays and articles appeared in 1961, others at frequent intervals afterwards and further volumes will appear in the coming years: at the time of writing twelve volumes have been published, corresponding to nine of the *Schriften zur Theologie*, Einsiedeln/Zürich/Cologne). On the Protestant side are Karl Barth's *Church Dogmatics*, Edinburgh, 1955ff. and the works of E. Brunner, H. Ott, H. Thielicke, P. Tillich.

Monographs include H. U. von Balthasar, *The God Question and Modern Man*, New York, 1967; H. de Lubac, *Sur les chemins de Dieu*, Paris, 1956; H. Gollwitzer, *Die Existenz Gottes im Bekenntnis des Glaubens*, Munich, 1963; J. A. T. Robinson, *Honest to God*, London, 1963; J. C. Murray, *The Problem of God. Yesterday and Today*, New Haven/London, 1964; E. Jüngel, *Gottes Sein ist im Werden. Verantwortliche Rede vom Sein bei Karl Barth. Eine Paraphrase*, Tübingen, 1965; S. M. Ogden, *The Reality of God and Other Essays*, New York, 1966; H. Engelland, *Die Wirklichkeit Gottes und die Gewissheit des Glaubens*, Göttingen, 1966; H. Zahrnt, *The Question of God. Protestant Theology in the Twentieth Century*, New York/London, 1970; the same author, *What Kind of God?*, London, 1972; F. Leist, *Nicht der Gott der Philosophen*, Freiburg/Basle/Vienna, 1966; C. H. Ratschow, *Gott existiert. Eine dogmatische Studie*, Berlin, 1966; J. Macquarrie, *God and Secularity*, Philadelphia, 1967/London, 1968; J. B. Cobb, Jr., *God and the World*, Philadelphia, 1969; F. Gogarten, *Die Frage nach Gott*, Tübingen, 1968; G. Ebeling, *Wort und Glaube*, Vol. II, Tübingen, 1969; E. Schillebeeckx, *God the Future of Man*, New York/London, 1970; E. Balthazar, *God Within Process*, New York, 1970; W. Kaspar, *Glaube und Geschichte*, Mainz, 1970, especially pp. 101–43; R. G. Smith, *The Doctrine of God*, London, 1970; H. Ott, *God*, New York/London, 1973; W. Pannenberg, *Gottesgedanke und menschliche Freiheit*, Göttingen, 1972; E. Biser, *Theologie und Atheismus*, Munich, 1972; J. Moltmann, *The Crucified God*, London, 1974.

From the aspect of linguistic philosophy the following should be noted: F. Ferré, *Language, Logic and God*, London/Glasgow, 1961; P. van Buren, *The Secular Meaning of the Gospel. Based on an Analysis of Its Language*,

New York/London, 1963; A. Gilkey, *Naming the Whirlwind. The Renewal of God-language*, Indianapolis/New York, 1969; E. Castelli (ed.), *L'analyse du langage théologique. Le nom de Dieu*, Paris, 1969.

Finally, among volumes of collected essays on the question of God, the following should be noted: A. Schaefer (ed.), *Der Gottesgedanke im Abendland*, Stuttgart, 1964; N. Kutschki (ed.), *Gott heute. Fünfzehn Beiträge zur Gottesfrage*, Mainz/Munich, 1967; H. Zahrnt (ed.), *Gespräch über Gott*, Munich, 1968; T. C. de Kruijf and others, *Zerbrochene Gottesbilder*, Freiburg/Basle/Vienna, 1969; H. J. Schultz (ed.), *Wer ist das eigentlich–Gott?*, Munich, 1969; A. Grabner-Heider (ed.), *Gott*, Mainz, 1970; J. Blank and others, *Gott-Frage und moderner Atheismus*, Regensburg, 1972; J. Ratzinger (ed.), *Die Frage nach Gott*, Freiburg/Basle/Vienna, 1972; J. Kopperschmidt (ed.), *Der fragliche Gott. Fünf Versuche einer Antwort*, Düsseldorf, 1973; K. Rahner (ed.), *Ist Gott noch gefragt? Zur Funktionslosigkeit des Gottesglaubens*, Düsseldorf, 1973.

37 *Immanuel Kant's Critique of Pure Reason*, translated by Norman Kemp Smith, Macmillan, New York/Toronto/London, 1964 (first edition, 1929; revised, 1933), III, ii, 2, p. 635.

38 We cannot discuss here the basic problems of the emptiness of reality and the free but not arbitrary choice which it involves between basic mistrust and basic trust, between nihilism and trust in being, which are presupposed in the question of God. They are discussed particularly with reference to Nietzsche in H. Küng, *Existiert Gott?*, Munich, 1973.

39 W. Weischedel, *Der Gott der Philosophen*, Darmstadt, 1971–72, Vol. II, §127. He is consistent in reaching God only as a "whence of uncertainty" (*Vonwoher der Fraglichkeit*): §128–31.

40 It was possible to discuss here only the argument from philosophy of history on the necessary emergence of atheism and the replacement of religion by science (cf. A II, 1). The refutation of the psychological argument for atheism–God as projection of man or illusion of the psyche–would require a discussion of Ludwig Feuerbach's humanistic atheism, Karl Marx's social revolutionary atheism, Friedrich Nietzsche's nihilistic atheism and Sigmund Freud's psychoanalytical atheism. On all this, see Hans Küng, *Existiert Gott?*

41 Cf. H-E Hengstenberg, "Wahrheit, Sicherheit, Unfehlbarkeit: zur 'Problematik' unfehlbarer kirchlicher Lehrsätze" in H. Küng (ed.), *Fehlbar? Eine Bilanz*, Zürich/Einsiedeln/Cologne, 1973, pp. 217–31.

42 M. Buber, "Betrachtungen zur Beziehung zwischen Religion und Philosophie" in *Werke*, Vol. I, Munich/Heidelberg, 1962, pp. 509–10.

43 W. Weischedel, *Der Gott der Philosophen*, Vol. I.

44 Ibid., Vol. II, pp. 494–95.

45 Answer to the question: "What is Enlightenment?" in *Werke*, edited by W. Weischedel, Vol. VI, Darmstadt, 1964, p. 53.

46 The very informative books by H. Zahrnt, already quoted, are related to the modern horizon of the question of God: *Die Sache mit Gott* (English translation: *The Question of God*, New York/London, 1969); *Gott kann nicht sterben*; and the source book, *Gespräch über Gott*. In what follows we are making use of *Gott kann nicht sterben*, Chapter 1.

47 C. F. von Weizsäcker, *Die Verantwortung der Wissenschaft im Atomzeitalter*, Göttingen, 1957, pp. 11–12.
48 Cf. the bibliographical data under A II, 1: "Proofs of God?"
49 Cf. the bibliographical data under A II, 1: "Proofs of God?"
50 Cf. H. Albert, *Plädoyer für kritischen Rationalismus*, Munich, 1971. On the basic discussion see H. Küng, *Existiert Gott?*, Munich, 1975.
51 H. Albert, op. cit., pp. 11–15.
52 W. Weischedel, "Was heisst Wirklichkeit" in G. Ebeling/E. Jüngel/G. Schunack (eds.), *Festschrift für Ernst Fuchs*, Tübingen, 1973, pp. 343–44.
53 Cf. H. Küng, *Infallible? An Inquiry*, New York/London, 1971, Chapter IV, 11: "A teaching office?" Cf. also H. Küng (ed.), *Fehlbar? Eine Bilanz*, Chapter E VII: "Die Chancen eines fehlbaren Lehramts."

A III: The Challenge of the World Religions

1 D. Bonhoeffer, *Letters and Papers from Prison*, London, 1973, pp. 359–62.
2 K. M. Panikkar, *Asia and Western Dominance*, New York/London, 1959[2].
3 Shusaku Endo, *Silence*, Rutland, Vermont/Tokyo, 1969.
4 Second Vatican Council, *Declaration on the Relationship of the Church to Non-Christian Religions*, 1965; *Declaration on Religious Freedom*, 1965.
5 Cf. H. J. Margull and S. J. Samartha (eds.), *Dialog mit anderen Religionen. Material aus der ökumenischen Bewegung*, Frankfurt, 1972. The Addis Ababa document of 1971 is particularly important: "Der Ökumenische Rat der Kirchen und der Dialog mit Menschen anderer Religionen und Ideologien."
6 See the short collection of texts in H. Küng, *Christenheit als Minderheit*, Einsiedeln, 1965.
7 On this point see the pioneer work of Karl Rahner, "History of the World and Salvation-History," "Christianity and the Non-Christian Religions," in *Theological Investigations*, Vol. V, London/Baltimore, 1966, pp. 97–134.
8 J. Neuner, "Missionstheologische Probleme" in *Gott in Welt*, Vol. II, Festschrift for Karl Rahner, Freiburg/Basle/Vienna, 1964, pp. 401–2.
9 H. R. Schlette, *Die Religionen als Thema der Theologie. Überlegungen zu einer "Theologie der Religionen,"* Freiburg/Basle/Vienna, 1963, p. 39; cf. the same author, *Colloquium salutis—Christen und Nichtchristen heute*, Cologne, 1965.
10 As against the Christian exclusiveness of Karl Barth (together with R. Bultmann and K. Heim), which is to be understood in the light of the history of theology, the truth content of the world religions is acknowledged also by Protestant theologians: on the one hand, on the basis of conclusions from the history of religion, especially by E. Troeltsch (and other theologians in the field of history of religion, belonging to the school of Ritschl); on the other hand, in the light of the Old and New Testament,

by A. Schlatter (and W. Lütgert), and–later–P. Tillich, P. Althaus, C. H. Ratschow, W. Pannenberg. For a useful survey of the problems see P. Althaus, *Die christliche Wahrheit*, especially §5 and 16. On recent trends cf. P. Knitter, "What is German Protestant Theology Saying About the Non-Christian Religions?" in *Neue Zeitschrift für systematische Theologie und Religionsphilosophie*, 50 (1973), pp. 38–64. We have already explained that none of this involves a "natural theology" (cf. A II).

11 For information about the world religions, out of the vast literature on the subject, a number of recent encyclopedias may be mentioned: M. Gorce/R. Mortier (eds.), *Histoire générale des religions*, Vols. I–V, Paris, 1947–52; C. Clemen (ed.), *Die Religionen der Erde*, Munich, 1949[2]; F. König (ed.), *Christus und die Religionen der Erde. Handbuch der Religionsgeschichte*, Vols. I–III, Vienna, 1951; C. M. Schröder (ed.), *Die Religionen der Menschheit*, Stuttgart, 1960ff. (36 volumes planned).

Less extensive but useful studies include A. Berthelot/H. von Campenhausen, *Wörterbuch der Religionen*, Stuttgart, 1952; H. von Glasenapp, *Die nichtchristlichen Religionen*, Frankfurt, 1957; G. Günther (ed.), *Die grossen Religionen*, Göttingen, 1961; H. Ringgren/A. V. Ström, *Die Religionen der Völker. Grundriss der allgemeinen Religionsgeschichte*, Stuttgart, 1959; R. C. Zaehner, *The Concise Encyclopedia of Living Faiths*, Boston, 1959/London, 1971; E. Dammann, *Grundriss der Religionsgeschichte*, Stuttgart, 1972; E. Brunner-Traut (ed.), *Die fünf grossen Weltreligionen*, Freiburg/Basle/Vienna, 1974. All these works provide abundant bibliographies on the individual religions.

Larger works include P. D. Chantepie de la Saussaye, *Lehrbuch der Religionsgeschichte*, Vols. I–II, Tübingen, 1925[4]; G. Mensching, *Allgemeine Religionsgeschichte*, Heidelberg, 1949[2]; J. Finegan, *The Archeology of World Religions*, Princeton, 1957; H. von Glasenapp, *Die fünf grossen Religionen*, Düsseldorf/Cologne, 1951/1952.

The most important non-biblical texts–especially of Indian and Chinese wisdom–have been translated into several languages and are mostly available in paperback.

12 On the history of the axiom, "No salvation outside the Church," see H. Küng, *The Church*, New York/London, 1967, D II, 2; the same author on the modern interpretation of the formula, *Truthfulness*, London/New York/Sydney, 1968, B VIII.

13 DS 1351. Cf. Fulgentius of Ruspe, *De fide, ad Petrum*, Chapters 37–39, nn. 78–80 (PL 65, coll. 703–704).

14 Second Vatican Council, Constitution on the Church, 1964, art. 16.

15 K. Rahner, "Anonymous Christians" in *Theological Investigations*, Vol. VI, London/Baltimore, 1969, pp. 390–98. Cf. A. Röper, *Anonymous Christians*, New York/London, 1965. In regard to this theory, which has become very popular, and to R. Panikkar's views in *The Unknown Christ of Hinduism* (London, 1964), H. J. Margull (op. cit., p. 85) has recently expressed some critical reservations, based on his concrete experiences of conversations with Hindus, Buddhists and Muslims.

16 K. Barth, *The Epistle to the Romans*, London, 1933, Chapter 7; the same

author, *Church Dogmatics*, Vol. I, pt. 2, Edinburgh, 1956, §17; but see his modifications in Vol. IV, pt. 3, Edinburgh, 1962, §69, 2.

17 D. Bonhoeffer, op. cit., pp. 279–82.

18 F. Gogarten, *Despair and Hope for Our Time*, Philadelphia, 1970.

19 E. Brunner, *Philosophy of Religion*, Cambridge, 1958; the same author, *Die Christusbotschaft im Kampf mit den Religionen*, Stuttgart/Basle, 1931; the same author, *Revelation and Reason. The Christian Doctrine of Faith and Knowledge*, London, 1947, especially Chapters 14–17.

20 H. Kraemer, *The Christian Message in a Non-Christian World*, Grand Rapids, 1961; the same author, *Religion and the Christian Faith*, London, 1956.

21 On the *phenomenology* of religion, in addition to earlier important works by R. Otto, H. Pinard de la Boullaye and N. Söderblom, cf. G. van der Leeuw, *Phänomenologie der Religion*, Tübingen, 1933, 1956[2]; the same author, *Einführung in die Phänomenologie der Religion*, Haarlem, 1948/Darmstadt, 1961[2]; G. Mensching, *Vergleichende Religionswissenschaft*, Heidelberg, 1949[2]; the same author, *Die Religion. Strukturtypen und Lebensgesetze*, Stuttgart, 1959; H. von Glasenapp, *Die Religionen der Menschheit. Ihre Gegensätze und Übereinstimmungen*, Vienna, 1954; M. Eliade, *Patterns in Comparative Religion*, New York/London, 1971; J. Wach, *The Comparative Study of Religions*, New York, 1958; K. Goldammer, *Die Formenwelt des Religiösen*, Stuttgart, 1960; F. Heiler, *Erscheinungsformen und Wesen der Religion*, Stuttgart, 1961; G. Lanczkowski, *Begegnung und Wandel der Religionen*, Düsseldorf/Cologne, 1971.

22 A. J. Toynbee, *An Historian's Approach to Religion*, London, 1956; the same author, *Christianity Among the Religions of the World*, London, 1958.

23 J. Ratzinger, "Der christliche Glaube und die Weltreligionen" in *Gott in Welt* (Festschrift for Karl Rahner), Freiburg/Basle/Vienna, 1964, Vol. II, pp. 287–305, especially 294–95.

24 Chinua Achebe's novel, *Things Fall Apart*, London, 1958, is informative in this respect.

25 Cf. the recent series of articles–admittedly one-sided, but informative–in *Der Spiegel*, 1973, Nos. 39–43, "Asiens kranker Riese" ("Asia's Sick Giant").

26 S. Radhakrishnan, *Eastern Religions and Western Thought*, London, 1939, pp. 308–9. Cf. the criticism of Indian Christian theologians in M. M. Thomas, *The Acknowledged Christ of the Indian Renaissance*, Naperville, 1969/London, 1970, Chapter VII.

27 Cf. G. Lanczkowski, op. cit., pp. 111–12, 115–16; cf. G. Mensching, *Toleranz und Wahrheit in der Religion*, Munich/Hamburg, 1966[2].

28 Cf. K. Jaspers, *Die massgebenden Menschen*, Munich, 1971[4] (reprinted from *Die grossen Philosophen*, Vol. I, Munich, 1964).

29 K. Jaspers, op. cit., p. 206.

30 Cf. H. Dumoulin, *History of Zen Buddhism*, New York/London, 1963; the same author, *Östliche Meditation und christliche Mystik*, Freiburg/Munich, 1966. There is a good summary comparison in P. Kreeft, "Zen

Buddhism and Christianity: An Experiment in Comparative Religion" in *Journal of Ecumenical Studies* 8 (1971), pp. 513–38.

31 Cf. Adelheid Krämer's study, *Christus und Christentum im Denken des modernen Hinduismus*, Bonn, 1958.

32 An excellent example of this is provided by a work produced by Christian and Buddhist experts, edited by H. Dumoulin, with contributions by E. Benz, H. Bechert, H. Dumoulin, A. Fernando, A. M. Fiske, H. Hoffmann, J. M. Kitagawa, H. Nakamura, Y. Raguin, F. Reynolds, D. K. Swearer, Vu Duy-Tu, H. Welch, *Buddhismus der Gegenwart*, Freiburg/Basle/Vienna, 1970. For fruitful Hindu-Christian discussion in India, in addition to the book by M. M. Thomas already mentioned, see especially K. Baago, *Pioneers of Indigenous Christianity*, Bangalore, 1969; the same author, *Bibliography of Indian Christian Theology*, Madras, 1969; R. H. S. Boyd, *An Introduction to Indian Christian Theology*, Madras, 1969; Robin Boyd, *What Is Christianity?*, Madras, 1970. Among Indian Christian theologians the following should be mentioned: Joshua Marshman, Nehemiah Goreh, M. C. Parekh, C. F. Andrews, S. K. Rudra, P. D. Devanandan, P. Chenchiah, D. G. Moses, J. R. Chandran, Surjit Singh, M. Sunder Rao.

33 See again note 11 above, on information about the world religions.

34 Cf. W. Schilling, *Einst Konfuzius–Heute Mao Tse-tung. Die Mao-Faszination und ihre Hintergründe*, Weilheim, Upper Bavaria, 1971.

35 On the relations between Christianity and the world religions, in addition to the works already mentioned by K. Barth, E. Brunner and H. Kraemer as also by K. Rahner, H. R. Schlette, H. Küng, see E. Troeltsch, *The Absoluteness of Christianity and the History of Religion*, Richmond, 1971/London, 1972; O. Karrer, *Das Religiöse in der Menschheit und das Christentum*, Frankfurt, 1934; F. Heiler, "Die Frage der 'Absolutheit' des Christentums im Lichte der vergleichenden Religionsgeschichte" in *Eine heilige Kirche* 20 (1938), pp. 306–36; W. Holsten, *Das Evangelium und die Völker. Beiträge zur Geschichte und Theorie der Mission*, Berlin, 1939; the same author, *Das Kerygma und der Mensch*, Munich, 1953; T. Ohm, *Die Liebe zu Gott in den nichtchristlichen Religionen*, Munich, 1950; the same author, *Asiens Nein und Ja zum westlichen Christentum*, Munich, 1960[2]; H. H. Farmer, *Revelation and Religion. Studies in the Theological Interpretation of Religious Types*, London, 1954; E. Benz, *Ideen zu einer Theologie der Religionsgeschichte*, Mainz, 1960; S. Neill, *Christian Faith and Other Faiths. The Christian Dialogue with Other Religions*, London, 1961; R. C. Zaehner, *At Sundry Times. An Essay in the Comparison of Religions*, London, 1958; the same author, *The Catholic Church and World Religions*, London, 1964; P. Tillich, *Christianity and the Encounter of World Religions*, New York, 1963; J. A. Cuttat, *Hemisphären des Geistes. Der spirituelle Dialog von Ost und West*, Stuttgart, 1964; the same author, *Asiatische Gottheit–Christlicher Gott. Die Spiritualität der beiden Hemisphären*, Einsiedeln, 1971 (new, revised edition); R. Panikkar, *Religionen und die Religion*, Munich, 1965; G. Thils, *Propos et problèmes de la théologie des religions non chrétiennes*, Tournai, 1966; J. Heislbetz, *Theologische Gründe der nichtchristlichen*

Religionen, Freiburg/Basle/Vienna, 1967; G. Rosenkranz, *Der christliche Glaube angesichts der Weltreligionen*, Berne/Munich, 1967; J. Neuner (ed.), *Christian Revelation and World Religions*, London, 1967; O. Wolff, *Anders an Gott glauben. Die Weltreligionen als Partner des Christentums*, Stuttgart, 1969; U. Mann, *Das Christentum als absolute Religion*, Darmstadt, 1970; M. Seckler, *Hoffnungsversuche*, Freiburg/Basle/Vienna, 1972, pp. 13–46; W. Kasper, "Der christliche Glaubeangesichts der Religionen. Sind die nichtchristlichen Religionen heilsbedeutsam?" in H. Feld and J. Nolte (eds.), *Wort Gottes in der Zeit. Festschrift für K. H. Schelkle*, Düsseldorf, 1973, pp. 347–60.

Further literature up to 1960 may be found in E. Benz/M. Nambara, *Das Christentum und die nichtchristlichen Hochreligionen. Begegnung und Auseinandersetzung. Eine internationale Bibliographie*, Leyden, 1960. In addition to the work of G. Rosenkranz already cited, recent summaries of the solutions of Protestant and Catholic theology are provided by P. Beyerhaus, "Zur Theologie der Religionen im Protestantismus," and W. Bühlmann, "Die Theologie der nichtchristlichen Religionen als ökumenisches Problem" in *Freiheit in der Begegnung. Festschrift für Otto Karrer*, Frankfurt/Stuttgart, 1969, pp. 433–78.

36 A particularly informative comparison from the morphology of cultural groups is provided by W. S. Haas, *The Destiny of the Mind*, London, 1956.

37 Cf. the book by M. M. Thomas (n. 26 above), in the chapters on Rammohan Roy, Keshub Chunder Sen, P. C. Mozoomdar, Brahmobandhav Upadhyaya, Vivekananda, Radhakrishnan, Mahatma Gandhi.

38 W. Johnston in his introduction to Shusaku Endo, *Silence*, p. 16.

39 I am grateful to Professor Julia Ching (National University of Australia, Canberra/Columbia University, New York) for important suggestions with regard to the whole of this chapter.

B I: *What Is Special to Christianity?*

1 Acts 11:26; cf. 26:28; 1 Pet. 4:16.

2 Pliny, *Letters* X, 96 (English translations of these and other early documents will be found in either Henry Bettenson (ed.), *Documents of the Christian Church*, London/New York, 1943, or C. K. Barrett (ed.), *The New Testament Background. Selected Documents*, London, 1956, or both).

3 Tacitus, *Annals* XV, 44.

4 Suetonius, *Claudius* XXV, 4.

5 Cf. Josephus, *Antiquities* XX, 9 n. 1.

6 P. L. Berger, *Invitation to Sociology*, New York, 1963, pp. 85–87, London, 1966, pp. 101–4.

7 H. Marcuse, *One-Dimensional Man*, Boston/London, 1964, p. 98.

8 J. B. Metz, "Zur Präsenz der Kirche in der Gesellschaft" in *Die Zukunft der Kirche* (Report of the Concilium Congress, 1970), Zürich/Einsiedeln/Cologne, 1971, pp. 86–96. Cf. the same author, *Reform und*

Gegenreformation heute. Zwei Thesen zur ökumenischen Situation in den Kirchen, Mainz, 1969, pp. 40–41, and "Glaube als gefährliche Erinnerung" in A. Exeler/J. B. Metz/K. Rahner, *Hilfe zum Glauben*, Zürich/Einsiedeln/Cologne, 1971, pp. 23–37.

9 Cf. A III.

10 Cf. A I.

11 K. Jaspers, *Die massgebenden Menschen*, Munich, 1964, 1971[4].

12 It is only in this way that an unequivocal answer can be given to the question of the "essence of Christianity" in the new form in which it has been raised since the Enlightenment. Otherwise, as emerges indirectly from the work of H. Wagenhammer, *Das Wesen des Christentums. Eine begriffsgeschichtliche Untersuchung* (Mainz, 1973), the essence of Christianity "can never be absolutely concretely grasped" (p. 256).

13 On what follows cf. H. Küng, *Menschwerdung Gottes*, Freiburg/Basle/Vienna, 1970, Chapter II, 5: "Das Christusbild der Modernen."

14 H. Spaemann (ed.), *Was ist Jesus von Nazareth–für mich? 100 zeitgenossische Zeugnisse*, Munich, 1973. A. M. Carré (ed.), *Pour vous, qui est Jésus-Christ?*, Paris, 1970, served as a text for Spaemann's survey.

15 On the concept of the teaching office see H. Küng, *Infallible? An Inquiry*, New York/London, 1971, Chapter IV, 11.

16 DS 125.

17 DS 302.

18 Cf. H. Küng, *Fehlbar? Eine Bilanz*, Zürich/Einsiedeln/Cologne, 1973, Chapter E VI: "Die wahre Autorität der Konzilien" (with reference to the studies of H.-J. Sieben).

19 As an introduction to the historical and theological problems see H. Küng, *Menschwerdung Gottes*, Excursus I–IV. In addition see the great works on the history of dogma by L.-J. Tixeront, T. de Régnon, J. Lebreton, J. Rivière, etc., and, on the Protestant side, by A. Harnack, R. Seeberg, F. Loofs, W. Koehler, M. Werner, A. Adam. On the Christological problems see especially A. Grillmeier, "Die theologische und sprachliche Vorbereitung der christologischen Formel von Chalkedon" in *Das Konzil von Chalkeldon. Geschichte und Gegenwart*, Vol. I, Würzburg, 1951, pp. 5–202; A. Gilg, *Weg und Bedeutung der altkirchlichen Christologie*, Munich, 1955[2]; B. Skard, *Die Inkarnation*, Stuttgart, 1958; J. Liébaert, "Christologie. Von der apostolischen Zeit bis zum Konzil von Chalcedon" (with a biblical-Christological introduction by P. Lamanche) in M. Schmaus/A. Grillmeier, *Handbuch der Dogmengeschichte*, Vol. III, 12, Freiburg/Basle/Vienna, 1965; A. Grillmeier, *Christ in Christian Tradition*, New York/London, 1965.

20 Cf. especially H. Küng, *Menschwerdung Gottes*, Excursus II: "Kann Gott leiden?" Also W. Elert, *Der Ausgang der altkirchlichen Christologie. Eine Untersuchung über Theodor von Pharan und seine Zeit als Einführung in die alte Dogmengeschichte*, Berlin, 1957.

21 Cf. H. Küng, *Menschwerdung Gottes*, Excursus V: "Neuere Lösungsversuche der alten Problematik" (especially K. Rahner, H. U. von Balthasar, K. Barth, E. Jüngel, D. Bonhoeffer, J. Moltmann). Important for the

discussion on traditional Christology is P. Schoonenberg's recent book, *The Christ*, New York/London, 1971, especially Chapter II.

22 K. Rahner, "Current Problems in Christology" in *Theological Investigations*, Baltimore/London, 1961, p. 150.

23 The classic formulation of the objections is to be found—even before the histories of dogma which followed on the work of A. Ritschl (especially A. Harnack)—in F. Schleiermacher, *Christian Faith*, New York/London/Edinburgh, 1928 (German original, Berlin, 1831), §96, pp. 391–98. Recent formulations are found—on the Protestant side—in W. Pannenberg, *Jesus: God and Man*, Philadelphia/London, 1968, §8, and—on the Catholic side—P. Schoonenberg, op. cit., pp. 50–105.

24 Cf., for example, W. Pannenberg, op. cit., 6, I.

25 It is good to see this plea confirmed by J. Ratzinger in his *Introduction to Christianity* (London, 1969) where he caricatures dogmatically "from above" the conclusions of the modern quest for the historical Jesus (cf. especially pp. 157–59: "A modern stock idea of the 'historical Jesus'"). More recently however Ratzinger has expressed a wish for a book "which takes account of the present state of our knowledge as a whole of Jesus of Nazareth, of the Jesus tradition of the New Testament and of the development of the Christological dogma, and in it makes clear today the presence of Jesus Christ, the positive content of our faith in him. In saying this, I assume that the Christ in whom the Church believes and the Jesus of history, the Jesus newly discovered today (as long as it is a question of an authentic discovery), are really one and that it must be possible in principle also to describe the connection" ("Im Dienst der Durchsichtigkeit des Glaubens" in *Notwendige Bücher. Heinrich Wild zum 65. Geburtstag*, Munich, 1974, p. 134). In the same volume Karl Rahner—with a somewhat different orientation—asks for a "small catechism for adults" (pp. 129–32). I cannot entirely agree with the arguments of H. R. Schlette, who asks for a book "providing reasons or motives, at the present level of scholarship, to explain why Jesus—particularly Jesus—as distinct from others is still of interest" ("Warum gerade Jesus," op. cit., pp. 136–39).

26 On Enthusiasm historically and in principle see H. Küng, *The Church*, London/New York, 1967, C II, 4.

27 "The Jesus Revolution" in *Time*, 21 June 1971; "Jesus Christ Superstar" in *Time*, 25 October 1971; likewise as front-page story "Jesus im Schaugeschäft" ("Jesus in Show Business") in *Der Spiegel* (1972), No. 8. Out of the immense flood of articles and books in different languages the following particularly have a documentary value: H. Hoffmann, *Gott im Underground. Die religiöse Dimension der Pop-Kultur*, Hamburg, 1971; *Jesus People Report*, Wuppertal, 1972[2]; W. von Lojewski, *Jesus People oder die Religion der Kinder*, Munich, 1972[2]; W. Kroll (ed.), *Jesus kommt! Report der "Jesus-Revolution" unter Hippies und Studenten in USA und anderswo*, Wuppertal, 1972[2]. G. Adler attempts a discriminating analysis in *Die Jesus-Bewegung. Aufbruch der enttäuschten Jugend*, Düsseldorf, 1972.

28 Cf. A I, 3: "Humanity through technological evolution?"

29 C. Reich, *The Greening of America*, New York, 1970/London, 1971, especially Chapters XI–XII.

30 J. Frenzel, "Killer Nummer eins" in *Die Zeit*, 27 August 1971.

31 F. J. Sheen, *Life of Christ*, New York/London, 1959.

32 *Letters of Fyodor Michailovitch Dostoevsky to His Family and Friends*, New York/London, 1962, p. 71.

33 I am grateful to Walter Jens, my colleague in Tübingen, for his firm grasp of the problems raised in this chapter and for numerous suggestions in detail. I obtained important information from K.-J. Kuschel, my collaborator in the Institute for Ecumenical Studies, who is preparing a dissertation on the image of Jesus in recent literature; cf. also P. K. Kurz, "Der zeitgenossische Jesus-Roman" in F. J. Schierse (ed.), *Jesus von Nazareth*, Mainz, 1972, pp. 110–34. Also K. Marti, "Jesus–der Bruder. Ein Beitrag zum Christusbild in der neueren Literatur" in *Evangelische Kommentare* 3 (1970), pp. 272–76.

34 Cf. G. Benn's poems "Requiem" and "Gedichte" in *Gesammelte Werke*, edited by Dieter Wellershoff, Vol. I, Wiesbaden, 1960, pp. 10 and 196; R. M. Rilke, "Der Brief des jungen Arbeiters" in *Sämtliche Werke*, Vol. 6, Frankfurt, 1966, pp. 1111–27 (for an English translation see "The Young Workman's Letter" in *Rainer Maria Rilke, Selected Works*, Volume I Prose, translated by G. Craig Houston, with an introduction by J. B. Leishman, published by The Hogarth Press, London/Clarke, Irwin and Co., Toronto, 1954, pp. 67–77).

35 G. Papini, *The Story of Christ*, London, 1923.

36 J. Dobraczyński, *Listi Nikodema*, 1952 (German translation: *Gib mir deine Sorgen. Die Briefe des Nikodemus*, Freiburg, 1962).

37 P. Lagerkvist, *Barrabas*, London, 1952/New York, 1968.

38 M. Brod, *Der Meister*, Gütersloh, 1952.

39 J. Schlaf, *Jesus und Mirjam. Der Tod des Antichrist*, 1901; G. Frenssen, *Hilligenlei*, 1905; G. Hauptmann, *Der Narr in Christo Emanuel Quint*, Berlin, 1910.

40 Cf. L. C. Douglas, *The Big Fisherman*, New York, 1948/London, 1949; R. Graves, *King Jesus*, London, 1960²/New York, 1967.

41 G. Herburger, *Jesus in Osaka*, Neuwied/Berlin, 1970; F. Andermann, *Das grosse Gesicht*, Munich, 1970.

42 P. Huchel, "Dezember 1942" in K. Marti (ed.), *Stimmen vor Tag. Gedichte aus diesem Jahrhundert*, Munich/Hamburg, 1965, p. 31; P. Celan, "Tenebrae" in *Sprachgitter*, Frankfurt, 1959, p. 23.

43 F. Dürrenmatt, "Weihnacht" and "Pilatus" in *Die Stadt 1952*, Zürich, 1962, pp. 11 and 169–93; P. Handke, "Lebensbeschreibung" in A. Gräbner-Haider (ed.), *Jesus N. Biblische Verfremdungen-Experimente*, Zürich/Einsiedeln/Cologne, 1972, pp. 14–15; G. Grass, *The Tin Drum*, London, 1962 (especially the chapter on the imitation of Christ); F. Arrabal, *Autofriedhof* (produced in Tübingen, 1973: no published text yet).

44 Cf. especially K. Marti (ed.), *Stimmen vor Tag*; J. Hoffmann-Herreros (ed.), *Spur der Zukunft. Moderne Lyrik als Daseinsdeutung*, Mainz, 1973.

45 W. Jens, *Herr Meister. Dialog über einen Roman*, Frankfurt/Berlin/Vienna, 1974, p. 58; cf. also pp. 291–96.

46 "Today is Friday" in *The Short Stories of Ernest Hemingway*, New York, 1954, pp. 357–58; E. Hemingway, *Men Without Women*, London, 1961, pp. 198–204, especially p. 201.

47 W. Borchert, "Jesus macht nicht mehr mit" in *Das Gesamtwerk*, Hamburg, 1959, pp. 178–81.

48 H. de Balzac, *Jésus-Christ en Flandre*, 1831; F. M. Dostoevsky, *The Brothers Karamazov*, Chapter 5, 5: "The Grand Inquisitor"; G. Hauptmann, "Hanneles Himmelfahrt" (1893) in *Das gesammelte Werk* 1st Section, Vol. II, Berlin, 1942, pp. 253–300, and *Der Narr in Christo Emanuel Quint*, Berlin, 1910; R. M. Rilke, "Christus. Elf Visionen" in *Sämtliche Werke*, Vol. III, Frankfurt, 1966, pp. 127–69; R. Huch, *Der wiederkehrende Christus. Eine groteske Erzählung* (1926). G. Herburger, *Jesus in Osaka*, Neuwied/Berlin, 1970.

49 H. Hesse, "Jesus und die Armen," quoted by K. Marti, *Jesus der Bruder*, p. 273; cf. R. M. Rilke, *Das Stundenbuch* III, *Das Buch von der Armut und vom Tode*, 1903 (English translation: *Rainer Maria Rilke. Selected Works*, Vol. II Poetry, translated by J. B. Leishman, The Hogarth Press, London/Clarke, Irwin and Co., Toronto, 1960, pp. 88–104); B. Brecht, "Maria" in *Bertolt Brecht. Selected Poems*, edited by K. Wölfel, Oxford University Press, 1965, p. 64.

50 Cf. A. Holz, who in his *Buch der Zeit* (1885) called Jesus the "first socialist"; E. Kästner, "Dem Revolutionär Jesus zum Geburtstag" in *Das Erich Kästner Buch*, edited by R. Hochhuth, Zürich (n.d.); C. Einstein, "Die schlimme Botschaft" (1921) in *Gesammelte Werke*, edited by E. Nef, Wiesbaden, 1962, pp. 353–419.

51 J. Paul, "Siebenkäs" in *Werke*, Vol. II, edited by G. Lohmann, Munich, 1959, pp. 7–565; pp. 266–71: "Rede des toten Christus vom Weltgebäude herab, dass kein Gott sei."

52 *The Diary of Dostoevsky's Wife*, edited by R. Fülop-Miller/F. Eckstein, London, 1928, p. 419.

53 F. M. Dostoevsky, *The Idiot*, Heinemann, London, 1913, p. 212.

54 H. Böll, "Blick zurück in Bitterkeit" (on R. Augstein's book, *Jesus Menschensohn*) in *Der Spiegel* (1973), No. 15.

55 John 12:24.

56 Cf. the ideas noted down from the years 1880 and 1881, shortly before his death: F. M. Dostoevsky, *Tagebuch eines Schriftstellers*, Munich, 1972[2], p. 620.

57 M. L. Kaschnitz, "Auferstehung" in *Stimmen vor Tag*, pp. 74–75; K. Marti, "Ihr fragt wie ist die Auferstehung der Toten" in *Leichenreden*, Neuwied/Berlin, 1969, p. 26, and in *Spur der Zukunft*, p. 82; cf. also the text by K. Tucholsky printed in K. H. Deschner (ed.), *Das Christentum im Urteil seiner Gegner*, Vol. II, Wiesbaden, 1971, p. 220.

58 N. Kazantzakis, *The Greek Passion*, New York, 1954.

B II: *The Real Christ*

1 Mahatma Gandhi, *Freiheit ohne Gewalt*, introduced, translated and edited by K. Klostermeier, Cologne, 1968, p. 118.
2 G. Janouch, *Gespräche mit Kafka*, Frankfurt/Hamburg, 1961, p. 111.
3 A. Drews, *The Christ Myth*, London, 1910.
4 J. M. Allegro, *The Sacred Mushroom and the Cross*, New York/London, 1970.
5 Cf. the Introductions to the New Testament by Paul Feine, first revised by J. Behm, then re-edited by W. G. Kümmel (English trans., Nashville/London, 1966); A. Wikenhauser (English trans., London/New York, 1958); W. Marxsen (English trans., Oxford/Philadelphia, 1968); originally in English, A. H. McNeile, *An Introduction to the Study of the New Testament*, Oxford, 1953; R. Heard, *An Introduction to the New Testament*, London, 1951; T. Henshaw, *New Testament Literature in the Light of Modern Scholarship*, London, 1952/New York, 1966.
6 Albert Schweitzer, *The Quest of the Historical Jesus. A Critical Study of Its Progress from Reimarus to Wrede*, London/New York, 1911[2].
7 See the Introductions to the New Testament above-mentioned.
8 The main methodical defect of R. Augstein's book on Jesus lies in the fact that Mark alone is assumed to be authentic and thus the greater part (including among other things the Sermon on the Mount) of Matthew and Luke are considered–without any sort of argument (cf. pp. 59–60)–as not authentic. See the criticism of this book in R. Pesch/G. Stachel (eds.), *Augsteins Jesus. Eine Dokumentation*, Zürich, 1972.
9 Cf. K. L. Schmidt, *Der Rahmen der Geschichte Jesu. Literarkritische Untersuchungen zur ältesten Jesus-Überlieferung*, Berlin, 1919; M. Dibelius, *From Tradition to Gospel*, London, 1934; R. Bultmann, *The History of the Synoptic Tradition*, Oxford/New York, 1963. On form-criticism see G. Lohfink, *Jetzt verstehe ich die Bibel*, Stuttgart, 1973.
10 Cf. especially the published correspondence with A. von Harnack in K. Barth, *Theologische Fragen und Antworten*, Zollikon/Zürich, 1957, pp. 7–31.
11 R. Bultmann, "Liberal Theology and the Latest Theological Movement" in *Faith and Understanding*, New York, 1968/London, 1969, pp. 28–52.
12 Paul Tillich, *Systematic Theology*, Vol. II, Chicago, 1957/London (three vols. in one), 1968, Chapter II A.
13 First published in German, edited by G. Kittel and G. Friedrich, the *Theological Dictionary of the New Testment* in nine volumes plus an index volume is now available in English (Eerdmans, Grand Rapids/SCM Press, London).
14 C. H. Dodd, *The Parables of the Kingdom*, London/New York, 1961[2]; *The Interpretation of the Fourth Gospel*, London/New York, 1953; *The Founder of Christianity*, New York, 1970/London, 1971; W. Manson, *Jesus the Messiah*, London, 1943; T. W. Manson, *The Sayings of Jesus, as Recorded in the Gospels According to St. Matthew and St. Luke ar-*

ranged with Introduction and Commentary, London/Naperville, 1949; *The Servant-Messiah. A Study of the Public Ministry of Jesus*, Cambridge, 1953; the same author, "Some Tendencies in Present Day Research" in the *Festschrift* for C. H. Dodd, *The Background of the New Testament and its Eschatology*, Cambridge, 1956, pp. 211–21; R. H. Fuller, *The Mission and Achievement of Jesus. An Examination of the Presuppositions of New Testament Theology*, London/Naperville, 1954; V. Taylor, *The Life and Ministry of Jesus*, London/Nashville, 1954; *The Person of Christ in New Testament Teaching*, London/New York, 1958; *The Names of Jesus*, London/New York, 1953; *The Cross of Christ*, London/New York, 1956; *Forgiveness and Reconciliation. A Study in New Testament Theology*, London/New York, 1956[2]; J. L. McKenzie, *The Power and the Wisdom*, Milwaukee/London, 1965; N. Perrin, *Rediscovering the Teaching of Jesus*, London/New York, 1967; A. Greeley, *The Jesus Myth*, New York, 1971/London, 1972; J. A. T. Robinson, *The Human Face of God*, London/Philadelphia, 1973.

15 X. Léon-Dufour, *The Gospels and the Jesus of History*, London/New York, 1968; L. Cerfaux, *Jésus aux origines de la tradition. Matériaux pour l'histoire évangélique*, Louvain, 1968; L. Evely, *L'Evangile sans mythes*, Paris, 1970, provided an occasion for further discussion.

16 E. Käsemann, "The Problem of the Historical Jesus" in *Essays on New Testament Themes*, London/Philadelphia, 1964, pp. 15–47; but see also, at an earlier date, E. Fuchs, "Jesus Christ in Person," published in the Festschrift for Rudolph Bultmann (1949), pp. 48–73; more recently "Zur Frage nach dem historischen Jesus" in *Gesammelte Aufsätze*, Vol. II, Tübingen, 1960, pp. 21–54. For the subsequent development cf. J. M. Robinson, *A New Quest of the Historical Jesus*, London/Naperville, 1959; J. Roloff, "Auf der Suche nach einem neuen Jesusbild" in *Theologische Literatur-zeitung*, 98 (1973), pp. 561–72; P. Grech, "Recent Developments in the Jesus of History Controversy" in *Biblical Theology Bulletin*, I, 2 (1971), pp. 190–213. On the recent discussion as a whole, see the extensive collection of essays in H. Ristow and K. Matthiae (eds.), *Der historische Jesus und der kerygmatische Christus*, Berlin, 1960.

Among recent books produced in the English-speaking world, see L. E. Keck, *A Future for the Historical Jesus*, Nashville, 1971/London, 1972.

17 The basic works on Jesus are R. Bultmann, *Jesus and the Word*, New York, 1934/London, 1958, and M. Dibelius, *Jesus*, New York, 1939/London, 1963. Works by authors of the Bultmann school include G. Bornkamm, *Jesus of Nazareth*, New York/London, 1960; H. Conzelmann, art. "Jesus Christ" in RGG III, Tübingen, 1959, pp. 619–53; H. Braun, *Jesus. Der Mann aus Nazareth und seine Zeit*, Stuttgart/Berlin, 1969; E. Fuchs, *Jesus. Wort und Tat*, Tübingen, 1971.

The following deal with the question as formulated by Bultmann: E. Schweizer, *Jesus*, London/Philadelphia, 1971; K. Niederwimmer, *Jesus*, Göttingen, 1968; R. Schäfer, *Jesus und der Gottesglaube*, Tübingen, 1970.

The following deal with the subject in their own way: E. Stauffer, *Jesus and His Story*, New York, 1960; the same author, *Die Botschaft Jesu damals und heute*, Berne, 1959; M. Craveri, *Das Leben des Jesus von Nazareth*, Stuttgart, 1970.

Recent Catholic books on Jesus include J. Gnilka, *Jesus Christus nach frühen Zeugnissen des Glaubens*, Munich, 1970; G. Schneider, *Die Frage nach Jesus. Christus-Aussagen des NT*, Essen, 1971; J. Blank, *Jesus von Nazareth. Geschichte und Relevanz*, Freiburg/Basle/Vienna, 1972; H. Zimmermann, *Jesus Christus. Geschichte und Verkündigung*, Stuttgart, 1973.

The following are openly opposed to R. Bultmann: *Theology of the New Testament*, 2 vols., New York/London, 1951 and 1955; H. Conzelmann, *An Outline of the Theology of the New Testament*, Philadelphia/London, 1969; W. G. Kümmel, *The Theology of the New Testament According to Its Major Witnesses, Jesus-Paul-John*, Nashville, 1973/London, 1974; J. Jeremias, *New Testament Theology*, Vol. I, Philadelphia/London, 1971; K.-H. Schelkle, *Theologie des Neuen Testaments*, Vols. I–III, Düsseldorf, 1968f. Among New Testament Christologies the following are important: G. Seventer, *De Christologie van het Nieuwe Testament*, Amsterdam, 1948[2]; the same author, "Christologie im Urchristentum" in *RGG* I, Tübingen, 1957, pp. 1745–62; O. Cullmann, *The Christology of the New Testament*, Philadelphia/London, 1963[2]; and particularly F. Hahn, *Christologische Hoheitstitel. Ihre Geschichte im frühen Christentum*, Göttingen, 1963.

The following are more pastoral-instructive in character: K. Schäfer, "Rückfrage nach der Sache Jesu" in N. Greinacher and others (eds.), *In Sachen Synode*, Düsseldorf, 1970, pp. 150–69; R. Baumann, *2000 Jahre danach. Eine Bestandsaufnahme zur Sache Jesu*, Stuttgart, 1971; M. Müssle (ed.), *Die Humanität Jesu*, Munich, 1971; N. Scholl, *Jesus—nur ein Mensch?*, Munich, 1971; J. Schierse (ed.), *Jesus von Nazareth*, Mainz, 1972; A. Läpple, *Jesus von Nazareth. Kritische Reflexionen*, Munich, 1972; F. Kerstiens, *Der Weg Jesu*, Mainz, 1973; R. Schwager, *Jesus Nachfolge*, Freiburg/Basle/Vienna, 1973; H. Spaemann (ed.), *Wer ist Jesus für mich? 100 zeitgenossiche Zeugnisse*, Munich, 1973.

From the philosophical standpoint the figure of Christ is examined closely in K. Jaspers, *Die massgebenden Menschen*, Munich, 1971[4], pp. 165–207; E. Brock, *Die Grundlagen des Christentums*, Berne/Munich, 1970;

and from the Marxist standpoint in E. Bloch, *Das Prinzip Hoffnung*, Vol. III, Frankfurt, 1971, pp. 1482–1504; the same author, *Atheismus im Christentum*, Frankfurt, 1968, pp. 115–243; V. Gardavský, *God Is Not Yet Dead*, Baltimore/London, 1973, pp. 34–52; E. Kolakowski, *Geist und Ungeist christlicher Traditionen*, Stuttgart, 1971; M. Machoveč, *Jesus für Atheisten*, Stuttgart/Berlin, 1972.

A certain amount of sensation was created by J. Lehmann, *Jesus-Report. Protokoll einer Verfälschung*, Düsseldorf, 1970; A. Holl, *Jesus in Bad Company*, New York/London, 1972; R. Augstein, *Jesus Menschensohn*, Munich/Gütersloh/Vienna, 1972.

18 Cf. B I, 2: "The Christ of dogma?"

19 Cf. H. Küng, *Menschwerdung Gottes*, II, 3 (Kant), IV, 1–3 (Fichte/Schelling), VIII, 3 (Hegel).

20 Cf. A. Schweitzer, *The Quest of the Historical Jesus*, London/New York, 1911².

21 For a criticism of "consistent eschatology" (J. Weiss, A. Schweitzer, M. Werner, F. Buri) see for example J. M. Robinson, op. cit., and more recently W. Trilling, "Geschichte und Ergebnisse der historisch-kritischen Jesus-Forschung" in F.-J. Schierse (ed.), *Jesus von Nazareth*, Mainz, 1972.

22 E. Jüngel, "Thesen zur Grundlegung der Christologie" in his collection of essays, *Unterwegs zur Sache*, pp. 274–95.

23 H. Ott, *Die Antwort des Glaubens*, Stuttgart/Berlin, 1972, p. 82.

24 Cf. Augustine on the distinction between *Credere Deum, Deo, in Deum: In Joannem* 29, 6; 48, 3 (*Corpus Christianorum, Series Latina*, Vol. 36, pp. 287, 413).

B III: Christianity and Judaism

1 The range of Christian-Jewish literature is immense. Worthy of mention are the series of specialist works (*Judaica, Studia Delitzschiana, Studia Judaica*) and periodicals (*Freiburger Rundbriefe, Der Zeuge, The Bridge, The Hebrew Christian, Cahiers sioniens*). Particularly important are the collections: *The Christian Approach to the Jew. Addresses Delivered at the Pre-Evanston Conference at Lake Geneva, Wisconsin*, New York, 1954; H. J. Schultz (ed.), *Juden-Christen-Deutsche*, Stuttgart/Olten/Fribourg, 1961; W. D. Marsch/K. Thieme (eds.), *Christen und Juden. Ihr Gegenüber vom Apostelkonzil bis heute*, Mainz, 1961; D. Goldschmidt/H. J. Kraus (eds.), *Der ungekündigte Bund. Neue Begegnung von Juden und christlicher Gemeinde*, Stuttgart, 1962; O. Betz, M. Hengel, P. Schmidt (eds.), *Abraham unser Vater. Juden und Christen im Gespräch über die Bibel* (Festschrift for O. Michel), Leyden/Cologne, 1963; W. P. Eckert/E. L. Ehrlich (eds.), *Judenhass–Schuld der Christen? Versuch eines Gesprächs*, Essen, 1964; K. T. Hargrove (ed.), *The Star and the Cross. Essays on Jewish-Christian Relations*, Milwaukee, 1966; K. H. Rengstorf/S. von Kortzfleisch (eds.), *Kirche und Synagoge. Handbuch zur Geschichte von Christen und Juden. Darstellung mit Quellen*, 2 vols., Stuttgart, 1968, 1970; W. Strolz (ed.), *Jüdische Hoffnungskraft und christlicher Glaube*, Freiburg/Basle/Vienna, 1971; C. Thoma (ed.), *Judentum und Kirche. Volk Gottes*, Zürich/Einsiedeln/Cologne, 1974. The October issue of *Concilium*, 1974 (No. 10, vol. 8) is devoted to the theme of Christians and Jews, with an introduction by H. Küng and parallel contributions from Jews and Christians: L. Jacobs-W. D. Davies, J. Heinemann-C. Thoma, R. Gradwohl-P. Fiedler, S. Sandmel-J. Lochman, A. Neher-A. T. Davies, J. J. Petuchowski-J. Moltmann, D. Flusser-B. Dupuy, U. Tal-K. Hruby.

Recent works on the problems: K. Barth, *Church Dogmatics*, Edinburgh/New York, II, 2, 1957, §34, pp. 195–305; III, 3, 1961, pp.

210–28; IV, 3, 1962, pp. 876–78; C. Journet, *Destinées d'Israël*, Paris, 1944; H. Schmidt, *Die Judenfrage und die christliche Kirche in Deutschland*, Stuttgart, 1947; J. M. Oesterreicher, *The Apostolate to the Jews*, New York, 1948; J. Jocz, *The Jewish People and Jesus Christ*, London, 1949/Naperville, 1954; A *Theology of Election. Israel and the Church*, London, 1958; P. Démann, *La catéchèse chrétienne et le peuple de la Bible*, Paris, 1952; G. Dix, *Jew and Greek*, London/Chester Springs, 1953; W. Maurer, *Kirche und Synagoge. Motive und Formen der Auseinandersetzung der Kirche mit dem Judentum im Laufe der Geschichte*, Stuttgart, 1953; L. Goppelt, *Christentum und Judentum im 1. und 2. Jahrhundert*, Gütersloh, 1954; G. Hedenquist and others, *The Church and the Jewish People*, London/Edinburgh, 1954; F. Lovsky, *Antisémitisme et mystère d'Israël*, Paris, 1955; E. Sterling, *Er ist wie Du. Aus der Frühgeschichte des Antisemitismus*, Munich, 1956; H. U. von Balthasar, *Einsame Zwiesprache. M. Buber und das Christentum*, Cologne/Olten, 1958; H. Gollwitzer, *Israel–und wir*, Berlin, 1958; G. Jasper, *Stimmen aus dem neureligiösen Judentum in seiner Stellung zum Christentum und zu Jesus*, Hamburg, 1958; F. W. Foerster, *Jews–A Christian View*, New York, 1962; W. Sulzbach, *Die zwei Wurzeln und Formen des Judenhasses*, Stuttgart, 1959; E. Peterson, *Frühkirche, Judentum und Gnosis*, Freiburg, 1959; M. Barth, *Israel and the Church*, Richmond, 1969; K. Kupisch, *Das Volk der Geschichte*, Berlin, 1960; H. Diem, *Das Rätsel des Antisemitismus*, Munich, 1960; D. Judant, *Les deux Israël*, Paris, 1960; *Israel en de Kerk* (a study commissioned by the general synod of the Dutch Reformed Church), Gravenage, 1959 (German translation: *Israel und die Kirche*, Zürich, 1961); G. Dellinger, *Die Juden im Catechismus Romanus*, Munich, 1963; G. Baum, *Die Juden und das Evangelium*, Einsiedeln, 1963; W. Seiferth, *Synagoge und Kirche im Mittelalter*, Munich, 1964; Augustine Cardinal Bea, *Die Kirche und das jüdische Volk*, Freiburg, 1966; F.-W. Marquardt, *Die Entdeckung des Judentums für die christliche Theologie. Israel im Denken Karl Barths*, Munich, 1967; C. Thoma, *Kirche aus Juden und Heiden*, Vienna, 1970; J. Brosseder, *Luthers Stellung zu den Juden im Spiegel seiner Interpreten*, Munich, 1972; P. E. Lapide, *Ökumene aus Christen und Juden*, Neukirchen/Vluyn, 1972. Cf. also the numerous manuals and books on the history of the Jews and the works of Jewish authors outstanding for their interpretation of the Jewish position (L. Baeck, S. Ben-Chorin, M. Buber, H. Cohen, E. L. Ehrlich, A. Gilbert, J. Klausner, F. Rosenzweig, H. J. Schoeps, P. Winter); finally the articles on Judaism and Judaeo-Christianity in the encyclopedias. On the whole question of the relationship between the Church and the Jews see the author's *The Church*, C I, 1 and 4.

2 *Memorandum of the First Assembly of the World Council of Churches on the Christian Approach to the Jews*, Amsterdam, 1948; since then the World Council has repeatedly expressed its views on the Jewish question.

3 Second Vatican Council, *Declaration on the Relationship of the Church to Non-Christian Religions*, 1965. A declaration of the French Bishops' Committee for relations with Judaism on the position of Christians in

regard to Judaism (1973) goes much further. It was published with a commentary by Kurt Hruby in *Judaica*, 29 (1973), pp. 44–70.

4 J. Oesterreicher, *The Rediscovery of Judaism*, South Orange, New Jersey, 1971.

5 J. J. Petuchowski, in an introduction to the German translation of Oesterreicher's book, *Die Wiederentdeckung des Judentums durch die Kirche*, Meitingen/Freising, 1971, p. 34.

6 Cf. P. E. Lapide, *Jesus in Israel*, Gladbeck, 1970; W. P. Eckert, "Jesus und das heutige Judentum" in F. J. Schierse (ed.), *Jesus von Nazareth*, Mainz, 1972, pp. 52–72. See also the work by G. Lindeskog, *Die Jesusfrage im neuzeitlichen Judentum*, reprinted Darmstadt, 1974 (especially the postscript to this reprint); R. Gradwohl, "Das neue Jesus-Verständnis bei jüdischen Denkern der Gegenwart" in *Freiburger Zeitschrift für Philosophie und Theologie*, 20 (1973), pp. 306–23. A survey of the image of Jesus in Jewry over the ages is given by Schalom Ben-Chorin in *Jesus im Judentum*, Wuppertal, 1970.

7 S. Sandmel, *We Jews and Jesus*, New York, 1965, p. 112; cf. the same author, *A Jewish Understanding of the New Testament*, Cincinnati, 1956.

8 Cited as in S. Ben-Chorin, *Bruder Jesus. Der Nazarener in jüdischer Sicht*, Munich, 1967.

9 C. G. Montefiore, *The Synoptic Gospels*, London, 1927[2]; revised edition, two vols., New York, 1968.

10 J. Klausner, *Jesus of Nazareth* (originally in Hebrew), London, 1925.

11 M. Buber, *Zwei Glaubensweisen*, Zürich, 1950, p. 11.

12 D. Flusser, "In what sense can Jesus be a question for Jews" in *Concilium*, 1974, No. 10, Vol. 8; cf. the same author, *Jesus*, New York, 1969.

13 S. Ben-Chorin, *Bruder Jesus. Der Nazarener in jüdischer Sicht*, p. 14.

14 Ibid., p. 12.

15 E. Käsemann, *Perspectives on Paul*, Philadelphia/London, p. 53.

C I: The Social Context

1. *Establishment?*

1 On the different religious movements in Judaism at the time of Jesus see: E. Schürer, *History of the Jewish People in the Age of Jesus Christ*, Edinburgh, 1973; H. L. Strack and P. Billerbeck, *Kommentar zum Neuen Testament aus Talmud und Midrasch*, I–VI, Munich, 1922–61; J. Bonsirven, *Le judaïsme palestinien au temps de Jésus-Christ*, Paris, 1950; E. Stauffer, *Jerusalem und Rom im Zeitalter Jesu Christi*, Berne, 1957; M. Simon, *Les sectes juives au temps de Jésus*, Paris, 1960; K. Schubert, "Die jüdischen Religionsparteien im Zeitalter Jesu" in *Der historische Jesus und der Christus unseres Glaubens*, Vienna/Freiburg/Basle, 1962, pp. 15–101; J. Jeremias, *Jerusalem in the Time of Jesus*, Naperville/London, 1969; J. Leipoldt/W. Grundmann, *Umwelt des Christentums* Vol. I: *Darstellung des neutestamentlichen Zeitalters*, Berlin, 1965, Vol. II: *Texte zum neutestamentlichen Zeitalter*, 1967, Vol. III: *Bilder zum*

neutestamentlichen Zeitalter, 1966; B. Reicke, *Neutestamentliche Zeitgeschichte*, Berlin, 1968; W. Foerster, *Neutestamentliche Zeitgeschichte*, Hamburg, 1968; J. B. Bauer, *Die Zeit Jesu. Herrscher, Sekten und Parteien*, Stuttgart, 1969; E. Lohse, *Umwelt des Neuen Testaments*, Göttingen, 1971; G. Baumbach, *Jesus von Nazareth im Lichte der jüdischen Gruppenbildung*, Berlin, 1971.

2 In addition to the above works by G. Baumbach, J. Bonsirven, J. Jeremias, E. Lohse, E. Schürer, M. Simon, cf. especially J. Wellhausen, *Die Pharisäer und die Sadduzäer*. Hanover, 1924, new impression Göttingen, 1967; R. Meyer, art. "Sadduzäer" in *ThW* VII, 1964, pp. 35–54; J. de Fraine, art. "Sadduzäer" in *Bibel und Liturgie*, pp. 1502–3; J. Le Moyne, *Les Saducéens*, Paris, 1972; K. Müller, "Jesus und die Sadduzäer" in H. Merklein/I. Lange (eds.), *Biblische Randbemerkungen* (Festschrift for R. Schnackenburg), Würzburg, 1974, pp. 3–24.

3 Lk. 2:41–52.

4 Mk. 6:2; cf. Jn. 7:15.

5 Mk. 9:1 par.; 13:30 par.; Mt. 10:23.

6 Mk. 1:9–11 par.

7 Mk. 1:10.

8 Cf. Jn. 1:35–51.

9 Mk. 1:15 par.

10 Mk. 12:33–34.

11 Mk. 13:2 par.

2. *Revolution?*

1 In addition to the Lexicon articles and the works above-mentioned by G. Baumbach, J. Bonsirven, J. Jeremias, E. Lohse, E. Schürer, M. Simon, cf. especially M. Hengel, *Die Zeloten*, Leyden/Cologne, 1961; the same author, *Was Jesus a Revolutionist?*, Philadelphia, 1971; S. G. F. Brandon, *Jesus and the Zealots*, Manchester, 1967; O. Cullmann, *Jesus and the Revolutionaries*, New York, 1970; G. Baumbach, "Zeloten und Sikarier" in *Theologische Literaturzeitung* 90 (1965), pp. 727–40; the same author, "Die Zeloten–ihre geschichtliche und ihre religionsgeschichtliche Bedeutung" in *Bibel und Liturgie* 41 (1968), pp. 2–25; Baumbach rejects the connection asserted by Josephus between the Zealots and the *sicarii* and seeks to establish a connection between priestly Zealots and Essenes. Against Baumbach see M. Hengel, op. cit., pp. 30, 32; cf. O. Cullmann, op. cit., pp. 3f. See also the discussion with S. G. F. Brandon in Hengel's and Cullmann's books.

2 H. S. Reimarus, *Vom Zwecke Jesu und seiner Jünger*, edited by G. E. Lessing, Brunswick, 1778.

3 K. Kautsky, *Der Ursprung des Christentums*, Stuttgart, 1908.

4 R. Eisler, *Jesous basileus ou basileusas*, Vols. I–II, Heidelberg, 1929–1930.

5 J. Carmichael, *The Death of Jesus*, London, 1963.

6 S. G. F. Brandon, op. cit.

7 Lk. 6:15; Ac. 1:13.

8 Mk. 3:17; Lk. 9:51–56.

9 Cf. Mk. 15:2, 9, 12, 18; Mt. 27:11, 29, 37; Lk. 23:3, 37, 38; Jn. 18:33, 37, 39; Jn. 19:3, 12, 14–15.
10 Mk. 11:1–11 par.; Mk. 11:15–19 par.; cf. Jn. 2:12–17.
11 Lk. 2:1–2.
12 Josephus, *Jewish Antiquities*, 17:285. Loeb translation: Heinemann, London/Harvard University Press, 1963.
13 Lk. 13:1.
14 Mk. 15:7 par.; cf. Jn. 18:40.
15 Y. Yadin, *Masada. Herod's Fortress and the Zealots' Last Stand*, London/ New York, 1966.
16 Mt. 11:8.
17 Lk. 22:25.
18 Lk. 13:32.
19 Lk. 9:62.
20 Lk. 14:18–20; Mt. 22:5; 8:21–22; Lk. 9:59–60.
21 Lk. 12:49.
22 Lk. 12:4; Mt. 10:28.
23 Lk. 22:35–38.
24 Cf. M. Hengel, op. cit.; O. Cullmann, op. cit.
25 Mt. 6:33; Lk. 12:31.
26 Lk. 13:31–33.
27 Lk. 13:1–5.
28 Lk. 22:35–38, 49–53; 6:29–30.
29 Mk. 1:12–13 par. On the story of the temptations cf. P. Hoffmann, "Zur Versuchungsgeschichte in der Logienquelle. Zur Auseinandersetzung der Judenchristen mit dem politischen Messianismus" in *Biblische Zeitschrift* NF 13 (1969), pp. 207–23.
30 Mk. 8:33.
31 Mt. 11:12.
32 Mk. 4:26–29.
33 Mk. 13:22 par.
34 Mk. 11:1–10 par.
35 Mk. 11:15–19 par.; cf. Jn. 2:12–17.
36 Cf. Is. 56:7: "My house shall be called a house of prayer for all peoples."
37 Mt. 10:34–37; Lk. 12:51–53.
38 Che Guevara, *Brandstiftung oder Neuer Friede*, Hamburg, 1969, pp. 147, 160.
39 Cf. J. Elull, *L'autopsie de la révolution*, Paris, 1969, p. 325.
40 Mk. 12:13–17 par.
41 Lk. 12:31.
42 Mk. 10:42–45 par.
43 Mt. 26:52.
44 Mt. 5:39.
45 Mt. 5:44; cf. Lk. 6:27–28.

3. *Emigration?*

1 On political and "unpolitical" radicalism see the Hungarian theologian,

E. Vályi-Nagy, "Lob der Inkonsequenz. Über Glauben und Radikalismus" in *Evangelische Kommentare* 4 (1971), pp. 509–13.

2 Mk. 6:3; Mt. 13:55.

3 Mk. 3:21; cf. Jn. 10:20.

4 W. E. Phipps spreads himself over 239 pages in *Was Jesus Married?*, New York, 1970.

5 Mt. 19:12 may well be–like Rv. 14:1–5–a late construction.

6 In addition to the works above-mentioned by G. Baumbach, J. Bonsirven, J. Jeremias, E. Lohse, E. Schürer, M. Simon, cf. especially S. Wagner, *Die Essener in der wissenschaftlichen Diskussion*, Berlin, 1960; H. Kosmala, *Hebräer, Essener, Christen*, Leyden, 1961; A van den Born, art. "Essener" in *Bibel und Liturgie*, pp. 439–40.

Out of the enormous amount of Qumran literature–for which there are several extensive bibliographies and study reports and, since 1958, a special periodical, *Revue de Qumran*–the following may be mentioned: H. Bardtke, *Die Handschriftenfunde am Toten Meer*, Vols. I–II, Berlin, 1953; M. Burrows, *The Dead Sea Scrolls*, New York, 1955/London, 1956; M. Burrows, *More Light on the Dead Sea Scrolls*, New York/London, 1958; F. Bruce, *Second Thoughts on the Dead Sea Scrolls*, London, 1961; Y. Yadin, *The Message of the Scrolls*, London/New York, 1957; K. Schubert, *The Dead Sea Community*, London, 1959; A. Dupont-Sommer, *The Jewish Sect of Qumran and the Essenes*, London, 1954; E. Sutcliffe, *The Monks of Qumran*, London, 1960; O. Betz, *Offenbarung und Schriftforschung in der Qumransekte*, Tübingen, 1960; J. Hempel, *Die Texte von Qumran in der heutigen Forschung*, Göttingen, 1962; J. Jeremias, *Die theologische Bedeutung der Funde am Toten Meer*, Göttingen, 1962; H. Haag, *Die Handschriftenfunde in der Wüste Juda*, Stuttgart, 1965; G. R. Driver, *The Judean Scrolls*, Oxford, 1965; C. Rabin and Y. Yadin, *Aspects of the Dead Sea Scrolls*, Jerusalem, 1965; J. van der Ploeg, art. "Qumran" in *Bibel und Liturgie*, pp. 1430–40 (with additional bibliography).

The texts have been translated into a number of languages. English translations are found in T. H. Gaster, *The Scriptures of the Dead Sea Sect*, Doubleday, New York/Secker and Warburg, London, 1957; G. Vermes, *The Dead Sea Scrolls in English*, Penguin Books, Baltimore/Harmondsworth, 1962 (frequent reprints); and in E. Sutcliffe, *The Monks of Qumran*, Burns Oates, London, 1960.

Particularly important for the connections between Qumran and the New Testament are: J. Carmignac, *Le Docteur de justice et Jésus-Christ*, Paris, 1957; J. Daniélou, *Les manuscrits de la Mer Morte et les origines du christianisme*, Paris, 1957; H. Braun, *Spätjüdisch-häretischer und frühchristlicher Radikalismus. Jesus von Nazareth und die essenische Qumransekte*, Vols. I–II, Tübingen, 1957; the same author, *Qumran und das Neue Testament*, Vols. I–II, Tübingen, 1966; H. H. Rowley, *The Dead Sea Scrolls and the New Testament*, London, 1957; K. Stendahl and others, *The Scrolls and the New Testament*, New York, 1957; E. Stauffer, *Jesus und die Wüstengemeinde am Toten Meer*, Stuttgart, 1957; A. Vögtle, *Das öffentliche Wirken Jesu auf dem Hintergrund der*

Qumranbewegung, Freiburg, 1958; J. van der Ploeg, *La secte de Qumran et les origines du christianisme*, Paris, 1959; M. Black, *The Scrolls and the Christian Origins*, Edinburgh, 1961; A. Steiner, *Jesus–ein jüdischer Mönch?*, Stuttgart, 1971.

7 K. Baus, art. "Koinobitentum" in *LThK* VI, p. 368.

8 Among them A. Dupont-Sommer, *Aperçus préliminaires sur les manuscrits de la Mer Morte*, Paris, 1950, p. 121.

9 Cf. especially M. Burrows, *The Dead Sea Scrolls*, pp. 246f., 273f., and *More Light*, pp. 64–73. Dupont-Sommer corrected the views he had formerly expressed: *The Jewish Sect of Qumran and the Essenes* (translation of *Nouveaux Aperçus sur les manuscrits de la Mer Morte*, Paris, 1953), London, 1954, pp. 160–63. The journalists continued as before: E. Wilson, *The Scrolls from the Dead Sea*, London, 1955; J. Lehmann follows Wilson in *The Jesus Report. The Rabbi J revealed by the Dead Sea Scrolls*, New York, 1971/London, 1972. A number of criticisms of this book appeared soon after its original publication in German: E. Lohse, "Protokoll einer Verfalschung?" in *Evangelische Kommentare* 3 (1970), pp. 652–54; K. Müller/R. Schnackenburg/G. Dautzenberg, *Rabbi J. Eine Auseinandersetzung mit Johannes Lehmanns Jesus-Report*, Würzburg, 1970. See also the special issue of *Bibel und Kirche* 26 (1971), No. 1, on the theme "Jesus von Nazareth und der Rabbi J."

10 Mk. 10:17–22 par.

11 Isaiah 40:3 is quoted in the Rule of the Community 1 QS VIII, 14.

12 IQS IV, 22.

13 Mt. 24:26.

14 Mk. 7:14–23 par.

15 Mk. 2:18–28 par.

16 Mt. 6:16–18.

17 Mt. 11:18–19.

18 Lk. 18:1.

19 Mt. 6:5–8 par.

20 Cf. Mk. 1:15.

4. *Compromise?*

1 In addition to the works already mentioned on the Sadducees and the lexicon articles in *BL* (J. de Fraine), *DBS* (A. Michel/J. Le Moyne) and *ThW* (R. Meyer/H. F. Weiss), see the monographs: R. Herford, *Die Pharisäer*, Leipzig, 1928; D. C. Ridelle, *Jesus and the Pharisees*, Chicago, 1928; L. Baeck, *Die Pharisäer*, Berlin, 1934, reproduced in *Paulus, die Pharisäer und das Neue Testament*, Frankfurt/Main, 1961, pp. 39–98; L. Finkelstein, *The Pharisees*, Philadelphia, 1938; the same author, *The Pharisees and the Men of the Great Synagogue*, New York, 1950; S. Zeitlin, *The Pharisees and the Gospels*, New York, 1938; W. Beilner, *Christus und die Pharisäer*, Vienna, 1959; A. Finkel, *The Pharisees and the Teacher of Nazareth*, Leyden, 1964; H. F. Weiss, *Der Pharisäismus im Lichte der Überlieferung des Neuen Testaments*, Berlin, 1965; R. Meyer, *Tradition im antiken Judentum. Dargestellt an der Geschichte des Pharisäismus*, Berlin, 1965.

2 Cf. Lk. 18:12.
3 Cf. Ex. 19:6.
4 DS 1501.
5 Mt. 5:21–22.
6 Mt. 5:27–28.
7 Lk. 15:11–32.
8 Lk. 8:10–14.
9 Lk. 15:4–6, 8–9.
10 Lk. 7:36; 11:37; 14:1.
11 Lk. 13:31.
12 Mt. 5:17.
13 Cf. especially D. Flusser's contributions to the study of the historical Jesus.
14 Cf. K. Niederwimmer, *Jesus*, pp. 66–70; H. Braun, *Jesus*, pp. 72–75, 78–83.
15 Mk. 7:15; Mt. 15:11.
16 Cf. E. Käsemann, "The Problem of the Historical Jesus" in *Essays on New Testament Themes*, Naperville/London, pp. 15–47 (especially p. 39).
17 Mk. 2:19 par.
18 Lk. 18:12, 14.
19 Mk. 2:23 par.
20 Mk. 3:1–6 par.; Lk. 13:10–17; 14:1–6.
21 Mk. 2:27.
22 Mk. 3:4 par.; cf. Lk. 14:5.
23 Mk. 2:25–26 par.; Mt. 12:5.
24 Mk. 2:28 par.
25 Especially in the great "Woes discourse" Mt. 23:13–36; cf. Lk. 11:37–52.
26 Mt. 23:23–24.
27 Mt. 23:25–28.
28 Mt. 23:15.
29 Mt. 6:1–18.
30 Mt. 23:1–4.
31 Mt. 23:5–12.
32 Mt. 23:29–36.
33 Cf. J. Jeremias, *New Testament Theology*, Pt. I, Philadelphia/London, 1971, pp. 147–51.
34 Mk. 3:28–29.
35 Cf. Mt. 11:20–24.
36 Lk. 17:10.
37 Mt. 20:1–15.
38 Mt. 6:3–4.
39 Mt. 25:37–40.
40 Lk. 15:11–32.
41 Lk. 7:36–50.
42 This is the title of Chapter II of E. Schweizer, *Jesus*, London/Philadelphia, 1971, p. 13.
43 Cf. K. Jaspers, *Die massgebenden Menschen*, Munich, 1964, p. 203.

C II: *God's Cause*

1. *The center*

1 Origen, *Contra Celsum* VII, 9. English translation: *Origen, "Contra Celsum"* translated with an introduction and notes by Henry Chadwick, Cambridge University Press, 1953, p. 402.

2 In addition to the books on Jesus and works on New Testament theology quoted above, cf. the lexicon articles on the Kingdom of God (*Reich Gottes*) in *LThK* (H. Fries, R. Schnackenburg), *RGG* (H. Conzelmann, E. Wolf, G. Gloege), *EKL* (L. Goppelt, J. Moltmann), also in *BL* (P. van Imschoot) and *ThW* (H. Kleinknecht, G. von Rad, K. G. Kuhn, K. L. Schmidt). More recent monographs include O. Cullmann, *Königsherrschaft Christi und Kirche im NT*, Zollikon/Zürich, 1941; K. Buchheim, *Das messianische Reich. Über den Ursprung der Kirche im Evangelium*, Munich, 1948; H. Ridderbos, *De komst van het Koninkrijk*, Kampen, 1950; A. N. Wilder, *Eschatology and Ethics in the Teaching of Jesus*, New York, 1950[2]; R. Morgenthaler, *Kommendes Reich*, Zürich, 1952; W. G. Kümmel, *Verheissung und Erfüllung*, Zürich, 1953[2]; T. F. Glasson, *His Appearing and His Kingdom*, Naperville/London, 1953; R. H. Fuller, *The Mission and Achievement of Jesus*, Naperville/London, 1954; H. Roberts, *Jesus and the Kingdom of God*, London, 1955; J. Bonsirven, *Le Règne de Dieu*, Paris, 1957; E. Grässer, *Das Problem der Parusieverzögerung in den synoptischen Evangelien und in der Apostelgeschichte*, Berlin, 1957; R. Schnackenburg, *God's Rule and Kingdom*, Edinburgh/London, 1963; H. Conzelmann, *Die Mitte der Zeit*, Tübingen, 1960[3]; T. Blatter, *Die Macht und Herrschaft Gottes*, Fribourg (Sw), 1961; F. Mussner, *Die Botschaft der Gleichnisse Jesu*, Munich, 1961; W. Trilling, *Das wahre Israel*, Munich, 1964; H. Flender, *Die Botschaft Jesu von der Herrschaft Gottes*, Munich, 1968; R. H. Hiers, *The Kingdom of God in the Synoptic Tradition*, Gainesville, 1970; A. Vögtle, *Das Neue Testament und die Zukunft des Kosmos*, Düsseldorf, 1970. On the development of the idea of the kingdom of God in the Church's tradition see the work in several volumes by F. Staehelin, *Die Verkündigung des Reiches Gottes in der Kirche Jesu Christi*, Basle, 1951 foll.

3 M. Dibelius, *Jesus: A Study of the Gospels and an Essay on "The Motive for Social Action in the New Testament,"* Philadelphia/London, 1963, p. 60.

4 Mt. 6:9–13 par.

5 Lk. 6:20–22; Mt. 5:3–10.

6 Cf. C I, 1.

7 Cf. especially Mk. 1:15 par.

8 Mk. 13:4–6, 32 par.; Lk. 17:20–21.

9 Mk. 9:1 par.; 13:30 par.; Mt. 10:23.

10 Mk. 13:30 par.; Mt. 10:33.

11 Mk. 9:1 par.

12 Lk. 4:18–21.
13 Cf. Lk. 22:29 with Mk. 14:62 and Mt. 26:64.
14 Jn. 5:25–29; 6:39–40, 44–54; 12:48.
15 2 P. 3:8–10.
16 Mt. 6:25–34.
17 Mt. 7:7–8 par.
18 Mt. 17:20.
19 Lk. 9:62.
20 Mt. 13:44–46.
21 Mt. 13:47–50.
22 Mt. 13:24–30; cf. 13:36–43.
23 Mk. 4:26–29.
24 Mk. 4:30–32.
25 Mt. 13:33.
26 The following are the more important works on the parables of Jesus: A. Jülicher, *Die Gleichnisreden Jesu*, 2 vols., Tübingen, 1910; P. Fiebig, *Die Gleichnisreden Jesu im Lichte der rabbinischen Gleichnisse des neutestamentlichen Zeitalters*, Tübingen, 1912; T. W. Manson, *The Sayings of Jesus*, London, 1957²; C. H. Dodd, *The Parables of the Kingdom*, London/Glasgow/New York, 1961²; J. Jeremias, *The Parables of Jesus*, London, 1963²/New York (revised edition), 1971; E. Linnemann, *Parables of Jesus: Introduction and Exposition*, Naperville/London, 1966; G. Eichholz, *Gleichnisse der Evangelien*, Neukirchen/Vluyn, 1971.
27 Heb. 4:15.
28 "Per omnia nobis assimilari voluit praeter peccatum (cf. Heb. 4:15) et ignorantiam" *Schema Constitutionis Dogmaticae de Fontibus Revelationis*, Vatican City, 1962, Cap. IIn. 14 (p. 14). A later version has only "absque peccato (Heb. 4:15)." A still later version omits all reference to Hebrews.
29 Cf. K. Rahner (-W. Thüsing), *Christologie–systematisch und exegetisch*, Freiburg/Basle/Vienna, 1972, pp. 28–30.
30 Mk. 13.
31 Mk. 13:14.
32 The basic contribution to the *demythologizing* debate was R. Bultmann's "The New Testament and Mythology" in H.-W. Bartsch (ed.), *Kerygma and Myth*, Vol. I, London, 1953, pp. 1–44. Further contributions will be found in later volumes of *Kerygma and Myth* (Vol. II, London, 1962), in the miscellanies of E. Castelli (ed.), *Il problema della demitizzazione*, and of C. A. Braaten and R. A. Harrisville (eds.), *Kerygma and History*, Nashville, 1962. Important monographs include K. Barth, "Rudolf Bultmann. An Attempt to Understand Him" in H.-W. Bartsch (ed.), *Kerygma and Myth*, Vol. II, pp. 83–132; E. Buess, *Die Geschichte des mythischen Erkennens. Wider sein Missverständnis in der "Entmythologisierung,"* Munich, 1953; F. Gogarten, *Entmythologisierung und Kirche*, Stuttgart, 1953; H. Ott, *Geschichte und Heilsgeschichte in der Theologie R. Bultmanns*, Tübingen, 1955; R. Marlé, *Bultmann et l'interprétation du NT*, Paris, 1956; L. Bini, *L'intervento di Oscar Cullmann nelle discussione Bultmannia*, Rome, 1961; G. Hasen-

hüttl, *Der Glaubensvollzug. Eine Begegnung mit R. Bultmann aus katholischem Glaubensverständnis*, Essen, 1963; G. Greshake, *Historie wird Geschichte. Bedeutung und Sinn der Unterscheidung von Historie und Geschichte in der Theologie R. Bultmanns*, Essen, 1963; E. Hohmeier, *Das Schriftverständnis in der Theologie R. Bultmanns*, Berlin/Hamburg, 1964; A. Anwander, *Zum Problem des Mythos*, Würzburg, 1964; F. Vonessen, *Mythos und Wahrheit. Bultmanns "Entmythologisierung" und die Philosophie der Mythologie*, Einsiedeln, 1964; R. Bultmann, "Zum Problem der Entmythologisierung" in *Glauben und Verstehen*, Vol. IV, Tübingen, 1965, pp. 128–37. Subsequently, in addition to a variety of articles, there appeared K. Prümm's *Gnosis an der Wurzeln des Christentums? Grundlagenkritik der Entmythologisierung*, Salzburg, 1972. A critical notice of this was published by H. Häring, "Autoritativ verfasste Kirche?" in *ThQ* 154 (1974).

33 Mk. 4:11–12.

34 On what follows cf. G. Bornkamm, *Jesus of Nazareth*, London /New York, 1960, pp. 69–75.

35 Mk. 4:33.

36 Mk. 4:3–8 par.

37 Lk. 17:21.

38 Cf. W. G. Kümmel, *Promise and Fulfilment*, London/Naperville, 1957.

39 After the shock of the new discovery by J. Weiss and A. Schweitzer of the strange *basic eschatological feature* in Jesus' proclamation, it was K. Barth who gave theology once again an appreciation of the eschatological element. After the Second World War, presentist eschatology in the form of Bultmann's existential interpretation was dominant. Then in the sixties in different fields there was a great revaluation of the future: thinking in terms of the future, prognoses, planning, futurology. In addition to P. Teilhard de Chardin and under the influence of E. Bloch, it was mainly J. Moltmann with his *Theology of Hope*, London, 1967, who made the theological breakthrough to a new understanding of futurist eschatology. On this discussion and for further details of the literature on the subject see H. Küng, *Menschwerdung Gottes*, VII, 6.

40 On the history of the diverse interpretations of the kingdom of God in antiquity, the Middle Ages and modern times, cf. H. Küng, *The Church*, B III, 2.

41 J. Moltmann, "Die Zukunft als neues Paradigma der Transzendenz" in *Internationale Dialog-Zeitschrift* I (1969), pp. 2–13.

42 Mt. 13:45.

43 Mt. 13:44.

44 Lk. 17:33; Mt. 10:39.

45 Mt. 17:20; cf. Lk. 17:6.

46 Mk. 9:24.

47 Mk. 1:15.

2. *Miracles?*

1 On the state of the problem of *miracles* cf. M. Seckler, "Plädoyer für Ehrlichkeit im Umgang mit Wundern" in *ThQ* 151 (1971), pp. 337–45.

This article reviews recent books on miracles, in particular R. Swinburne, *The Concept of Miracle*, London/New York, 1971, and R. Pesch, *Jesu ureigene Taten? Ein Beitrag zur Wunderfrage*, Freiburg/Basle/Vienna, 1970. The problem was examined in two articles in *ThQ* 152 (1972): "Zur theologischen Bedeutung der 'Machttaten' Jesu. Reflexionen eines Exegeten" by R. Pesch (pp. 203–13) and "Die Gretchenfrage des christlichen Glaubens? Systematische Überlegungen zum neutestamentlichen Wunder" by H. Küng (pp. 214–23). The latter article served as a basis for the present chapter.

In addition to the New Testament commentaries see the lexicon articles by A. Vögtle in *LThK* X, 1255–61, and by E. Käsemann in *RGG* VI, 1835–37. The books on Jesus are particularly important, outstanding among them being those by R. Bultmann, M. Dibelius, G. Bornkamm, E. Schweizer, K. Niederwimmer, H. Braun, E. Fuchs, C. H. Dodd, J. Blank. There are also important discussions of the question in the New Testament theologies of J. Jeremias (§10, 1) and K. H. Schelkle (Vol. II §6).

Indispensable among the older works are O. Weinreich, *Antike Heilungswunder*, 1909, new impression Berlin, 1969, and P. Fiebig, *Jüdische Wundergeschichten des neutestamentlichen Zeitalters*, Tübingen, 1911. The works on form-criticism by M. Dibelius and R. Bultmann should be consulted and especially the articles in Kittel's *Theological Dictionary of the New Testament* (on miracles, devils, cures). Recent monographs include R. H. Fuller, *Interpreting the Miracles*, London/Naperville, 1963; L. Monden, *Signs and Wonders*, New York, 1963; H. van der Loos, *The Miracles of Jesus*, Leiden, 1965; G. Schille, *Die urchristliche Wundertradition*, Berlin, 1966; F. Mussner, *The Miracles of Jesus*, Notre Dame, 1969/Shannon, 1970; K. Tagawa, *Miracles et Évangile. La pensée personelle de l'évangéliste Marc*, Paris, 1966; K. Kertelge, *Die Wunder Jesu im Markusevangelium*. Munich, 1970; O. Böcher, *Christus Exorcista*, Stuttgart, 1972; E. and L. M. Keller, *Miracles in Dispute*, Philadelphia, 1969; A. Fridrichsen, *The Problem of Miracle in Primitive Christianity*, Minneapolis, 1972.

2 Cf., e.g., Mk. 8:12; Lk. 11:29–30.

3 Mk. 1:32–34; 3:7–12; Mt. 9:35.

4 Mk. 6:5a; in both the supplement of 6:5b and the recasting of Mt. 13:58 the offensive character of the text is toned down.

5 Cf. Mk. 5:34; Lk. 7:50.

6 Cf. Mk. 9:14–29.

7 Mk. 1:26 par.

8 Mk. 9:18 par.

9 Lk. 10:18.

10 Cf. the material in R. Bultmann, *The History of the Synoptic Tradition*, Oxford/New York, 1963; M. Dibelius, *From Tradition to Gospel*, London, 1934/New York, 1935; L. J. McGinley, *Form-Criticism of the Synoptic Healing Narratives*, Woodstock, 1944; H. van der Loos, op. cit.; E. Käsemann, op. cit.; J. Jeremias, *New Testament Theology*, Pt. I, §10, 1.

11 Tacitus, *Historia* 4, 81; Suetonius, *Vespasianus* 7.
12 Lucian, *Philopseudes* 11.
13 Philostratos, *Vita Apollonii* 4, 45.
14 Lk. 7:11–17.
15 Cf. 4 Q Mess ar. My colleague in Tübingen, O. Betz, drew my attention to this.
16 Mk. 9:2–9 par.
17 Mk. 6:45–52 par.
18 Mk. 6:34–44 par.; 8:1–9 par.
19 Mk. 5:21–43 par.
20 Lk. 7:11–17.
21 Jn. 11:1–44.
22 Mk. 1:35–38, 44.
23 Mk. 1:30–31.
24 The sober, factual account of the healing of the blind man in Mark 10:46–52 should be compared with the stylized account in Mark 8:22–26.
25 Mk. 3:20–21, 22–30 par., 31–35 par.; also Jn. 7:20; 8:48, 52; 10:21.
26 Mk. 2:1–12 par.
27 4 Q Dam b; cf. 1 Q Sa 2:3–9. The translation is from G. Vermes, *The Dead Sea Scrolls in English*, Penguin Books, Harmondsworth/Baltimore, 1962, p. 109.
28 Mt. 11:5.
29 Cf. Mt. 12:28.
30 Cf. Lk. 17:21.
31 Mk. 8:11–12 and frequently elsewhere.
32 Cf. Jn. 2:23–25; 4:48; 20:29.
33 Mt. 11:5.
34 Mt. 11:6.
35 Jn. 6:27, 35.
36 Jn. 9:5.
37 Jn. 11:25.
38 Jn. 20:29.
39 Mk. 1:22.
40 Mk. 1:27.

3. *The supreme norm*

1 Mt. 7:12; Lk. 6:31.
2 Cf. H. Limbeck, *Die Ordnung des Heils. Untersuchungen zum Gesetzesverständnis des Frühjudentums*, Düsseldorf, 1971; R. J. Zwi Werblowski, "Tora als Gnade" in *Kairos* (N.F.) 15 (1973), pp. 156–63.
3 J. Jeremias, *New Testament Theology*, Pt. I, London/Philadelphia, 1971, §19, 1 (pp. 204–11).
4 Cf. Lv. 11; Dt. 14:3–21; cf. Mt. 15:11–20.
5 Dt. 5:12–14; cf. Mk. 2:27 par.
6 Mk. 10:2–9, 11–12 par.; cf. Dt. 24:1–4.
7 Mt. 5:33–37.
8 Lk. 6:28.
9 Mt. 5:44 par.

10 Mk. 13:2 par.
11 Cf. Mk. 14:58 par.
12 Mk. 12:33.
13 Mt. 5:23–24.
14 Mt. 5:20.
15 Mk. 1:22.
16 Mt. 26:42; cf. Lk. 22:42.
17 Mk. 3:35 par.
18 Mt. 7:21; cf. the parable of the obedient and the disobedient son (Mt. 21:28–32).
19 Cf. the bibliography on God's rule (C II, 1, n. 2).
20 For an interesting account of Jesus' understanding of the law from the standpoint of a jurist see P. Noll, *Jesus und das Gesetz. Rechtliche Analyse der Normenkritik in der Lehre Jesu*, Tübingen, 1968.
21 Cf. R. Bultmann, *Theology of the New Testament*, Vol. I, London, 1952, pp. 11–22; G. Bornkamm, *Jesus of Nazareth*, London/New York, 1960, pp. 96–100; K. Niederwimmer, *Jesus*, Chapter VII.
22 On the Sermon on the Mount see G. Bornkamm, *Jesus of Nazareth*, pp. 100–17, 222–26; H. Conzelmann, *An Outline of the Theology of the New Testament*, London, 1969, §15, pp. 115–27. I am particularly grateful to my colleague in Zürich, Eduard Schweizer, for his generosity in putting at my disposal the manuscript of his commentary on Matthew 5–7, shortly to appear in the Göttingen series of commentaries on the Bible, *Neues Testament Deutsch*. In addition to H. D. Wendland, *Ethik des Neuen Testaments*, Göttingen, 1970, Chapter I, 4, and other works on the ethics of the New Testament, a number of recent monographs may be consulted: J. Staudinger, *Die Bergpredigt*, Vienna, 1957; E. Thurneysen, *The Sermon on the Mount*, Atlanta, 1964/London, 1965; W. D. Davies, *The Setting of the Sermon on the Mount*, Cambridge, 1964; G. Eichholz, *Auslegung der Bergpredigt*, Neukirchen, 1965; H.-T. Wrege, *Die Überlieferungsgeschichte der Bergpredigt*, Tübingen, 1968; P. Pokorný, *Der Kern der Bergpredigt. Eine Auslegung*, Hamburg, 1969; G. Miegge, *Il Sermone sul Monte. Commentario esegetico*, Turin, 1970.
23 Cf. Mt. 5:18–19.
24 Cf. W. Trilling, *Das wahre Israel. Studien zur Theologie des Matthäus-Evangelium*, Munich, 1964, Chapter 9: "Die Gesetzfrage nach Mt. 5: 17–20."
25 Mt. 5:17–20.
26 Mt. 5:39–41.
27 Lk. 6:43–44; Mt. 7:16, 18.
28 Cf. H. Braun, *Jesus*, Chapter 7.
29 Mt. 5:22a.
30 Mt. 5:22b.
31 Mt. 5:34a, 37.
32 Mt. 5:34b–36.
33 Lk. 17:3.
34 Mt. 18:15–17.
35 Lk. 16:18; Mk. 10:11.

36 Mt. 5:32; 19:9.
37 Cf. H. Braun, *Jesus*, Chapter 8.
38 Dt. 24:1–4; cf. Mk. 10:9.
39 1 Co. 7:10–16.
40 Lk. 16:18; Mk. 10:11–12.
41 Mt. 5:32; 19:9.
42 Mk. 10:21.
43 Lk. 19:8.
44 Lk. 6:34–35.
45 Mk. 12:41–44.
46 Mk. 15:41.
47 Mk. 14:3–9 par.

C III: *Man's Cause*

1. *Humanization of man*

1 Mt. 6:19–21, 24–34; Mk. 10:17–27.
2 Mt. 5:38–42; Mk. 10:42–44.
3 Lk. 14:26; Mt. 10:34–37.
4 Lk. 17:33; Mt. 10:39.
5 Mk. 1:15 par. Cf. on *metanoia* in the New Testament, among the New Testament theologies, particularly R. Bultmann, pp. 4–22; J. Jeremias, pp. 151–58; K. H. Schelkle, Vol. III, §5. Among the books on Jesus, especially G. Bornkamm, pp. 82–89; H. Braun, §5; J. Blank, B V; also A. Hulsbosch, *De bijbel over bekering*, Roermond, 1963 (German translation, *Die Bekehrung im Zeugnis der Bibel*, Salzburg, 1967). Among the lexicon articles, see especially J. Behm/E. Würthwein, art. "metaneo" in *ThW* IV, 972–1004.
6 Lk. 9:62.
7 Cf., on faith in the New Testament, in addition to the above-mentioned New Testament theologies and books on Jesus, particularly A. Schlatter, *Der Glaube im Neuen Testament*, Stuttgart, 1927, new impression Darmstadt, 1963; R. Bultmann/A. Weiser, "pisteuo" in *ThW* VI, 174–230; E. D. O'Connor, *Faith in the Synoptic Gospels*, Notre Dame, U.S.A., 1961; H. Ljungman, Pistis, *Lund*, 1964.
8 Mt. 13:44–46.
9 Lk. 17:10.
10 Mk. 10:15 par.
11 Lk. 15:29.
12 Mt. 10:42.
13 Mt. 12:36.
14 Mt. 5:3–12.
15 Cf. Mt. 6:16–18.
16 Mt. 20:15.
17 Lk. 15:32.
18 Mt. 11:30.

19 Cf. especially K. Niederwimmer, *Jesus*, Chapter 7, and J. Blank, *Jesus*, B VI.
20 Cf. Mk. 2:27.
21 Mt. 5:23–24.
22 Cf. K. Jaspers, *Die massgebenden Menschen*, pp. 178–80.
23 Lk. 11:46.

2. *Action*

1 Mt. 22:37–38.
2 Lk. 10:30–35.
3 Mt. 25:31–46.
4 Lv. 19:18.
5 Mt. 22:39.
6 Mt. 7:12 par.
7 Lk. 10:29–37.
8 Mt. 25:31–46.
9 Cf. the recent detailed treatment of the history of the transmission by D. Löhrmann, "Liebet eure Feinde (Lk. 6:27–36/Mt. 5:39–48)" in *Zeitschrift für Theologie und Kirche* 69 (1972), pp. 412–38.
10 Cf. Mt. 15:24.
11 How much discussion–theological, philosophical and literary–can be stimulated by a parable is evident from W. Jens (ed.), *Der barmherzige Samariter*, Stuttgart, 1973, with contributions from C. Amery, G. Bornkamm, H. Braun, T. Brecher, W. Dirks, I. Fetscher, W. and R.-E. Schulz, among others.
12 Mt. 5:43–44.
13 Lk. 6:27–28.
14 Cf. Mt. 5:45.
15 On *eros* and *agape*–apart from philosophers like M. Scheler–see A. Scholz, *Eros und Caritas. Die platonische Liebe im Sinn des Christentums*, Halle, 1929, and especially A. Nygren, *Agape and Eros*, Philadelphia, 1953, which gave rise to an intensive discussion and roused severe criticism. Cf. K. Barth, *Church Dogmatics*, Vol. III, 2, Edinburgh, 1960, §45, 2, pp. 279–80; IV, 2, 1958, §68, 1, pp. 727–51; G. Bornkamm, *Jesus of Nazareth*, pp. 115–17; K. H. Schelkle, *Theologie des Neuen Testaments*, Vol. III, §8–9 (which lists earlier works on love of God and neighbor in the Old Testament by J. Ziegler and N. Lohfink, in the New Testament by K. Rahner, C. Spicq, W. Warnach and R. Völkl). In addition, see the corresponding articles in *ThW*: "agapao" (G. Quell/E. Stauffer), "plesion" and "phileo" (H. Greeven/J. Fichtner). An important theological work on the subject is H. U. von Balthasar, *Glaubhaft ist nur Liebe*, Einsiedeln, 1963.
16 Pr. 7:18; 30:16 (Septuagint).
17 Mt. 5:43–46.
18 Mk. 10:13–16.
19 Lk. 7:36–50; Mk. 14:3–9; cf. Jn. 11:2; 12:1–8.
20 Lk. 10:38–42; cf. Jn. 11:3–5, 28–29, 36; on John, who rested on Jesus'

breast, Jn. 13:23, and whom Jesus loved, Jn. 19:26; 20:2; 21:7, 20: the words *agape* and *philia* are used as synonymous.

21 Lk. 12:4; cf. Jn. 15:13–15; also the question addressed to Peter about his love, Jn. 21:15–17.
22 Cf. Bornkamm, *Jesus of Nazareth*, pp. 115–17. Bornkamm rightly rejects an overrigid separation.
23 Mt. 5:47.
24 Lk. 14:7–11.
25 Lk. 6:36–37; Mt. 7:1.
26 Mt. 5:37.
27 Mt. 6:12; cf. Lk. 11:4.
28 Cf. Mt. 18:21–35.
29 Mt. 18:22; cf. Lk. 17:4.
30 Mt. 7:1 par.
31 Lk. 14:11 par.
32 Mk. 10:43–44 par.
33 Mt. 23:25 par.; Mk. 12:40.
34 Mk. 9:43 par.
35 Mt. 5:41.
36 Mt. 5:40.
37 Mt. 5:39.
38 Ex. 20:1–17.
39 Mt. 5:20.
40 Cf. Rm. 13:8–10.

3. *Solidarity*

1 Jesus' way of acting as the real framework of his proclamation forms a key concept for the understanding of Jesus in E. Fuchs (as opposed to R. Bultmann), *Zur Frage nach dem historischen Jesus*, Tübingen, 1960, pp. 155–56.
2 Cf. C II, 2: "Miracles?"
3 Cf. Jn. 9:1–3.
4 *Against Apion*, 2, 201; cf. J. Jeremias, *New Testament Theology*, Vol. I, London, 1971, pp. 225–26.
5 Mk. 15:40–41 par.; Lk. 8:1–3; cf. Ac. 1:14.
6 Lk. 10:38–42; cf. 11:3, 5, 28–29, 36.
7 Mk. 15:40–41 par.; 15:47 par.
8 Lk. 16:18.
9 Mk. 10:13–16 par.
10 Mk. 10:15.
11 Cf. Mt. 11:25 par.; 21:16.
12 Cf. Mk. 9:42 par.; Mt. 18:10, 14; Mt. 10:42.
13 Cf. Mt. 25:40, 45; Mt. 11:11 par.; Lk. 9:48.
14 Mt. 5:3. Jesus' position in regard to the "poor" and poverty is thoroughly discussed in all the books about him. Particularly illuminating are G. Bornkamm, pp. 75–81, and H. Braun, Chapter 9; also the New Testament theologies of J. Jeremias, §12, pp. 108–21, and K. H. Schelkle, Vol. III, §23.

15 Lk. 6:20.
16 Lk. 6:20–23.
17 Mt. 5:3, 4, 6.
18 E. Bloch, *Das Prinzip Hoffnung*, Frankfurt, 1967, p. 1482.
19 For example, Mk. 9:42; Mt. 10:42.
20 Mt. 11:25 par.
21 On this see the interesting comments in M. Weber, *Gesammelte Aufsätze zur Religionssoziologie*, Vol. III, "Das antike Judentum," Tübingen, 1920, especially the appendix, "Die Pharisäer," pp. 401–42.
22 Mt. 6:19–21 par.
23 Lk. 14:11 par.
24 Mt. 6:24.
25 Cf. Lk. 6:24.
26 Mk. 10:25 par.
27 Lk. 19:8.
28 Mk. 10:17–22 par.
29 Lk. 8:1–3; cf. Mk. 15:40–41 par.
30 Cf. H. Braun, *Jesus*, pp. 104–13; M. Hengel, *Eigentum und Reichtum in der frühen Kirche. Aspekte einer frühchristlichen Sozialgeschichte*, Stuttgart, 1973, Chapter 3.
31 Mt. 6:25–34 par.
32 Mt. 6:11 par.
33 B. Brecht, *Die Dreigroschenoper*, Interlude (between Acts II and III): "Erst kommt das Fressen, dann kommt die Moral."
34 Cf. Mt. 6:33.
35 Mt. 18:23–35.
36 Lk. 19:10.
37 Mk. 2:17 par.
38 Mt. 11:9. On sin and grace (forgiveness) see the books on Jesus and the New Testament theologies, *passim*, especially H. Braun, Chapter 11, and K. H. Schelkle, Vol. III, §3. On the theological notion of grace as graciousness see H. Küng, *Justification. The Doctrine of Karl Barth and a Catholic Reflection*, New York, 1964/London, 1965, Chapter 27.
39 Lk. 19:1–10.
40 Mk. 2:13–17 par.
41 Lk. 15:2; cf. Mk. 2:16 par.
42 Lk. 7:36–50, probably identical with the woman of Mk. 14:3–9 and Mt. 26:6–13, but–despite Jn. 12:1–8, where the name "Mary" occurs–scarcely the same as Mary Magdalene.
43 Jn. 7:53–8:11.
44 Lk. 7:47; Jn. 8:7.
45 For all its one-sidedness, A. Holl's book, *Jesus in Bad Company*, London, 1972, brings out a very important point.
46 Lk. 18:10–14.
47 Lk. 15:11–32.
48 Lk. 10:30–37.
49 Mt. 20:1–16.
50 Lk. 15.

51 Lk. 15:4–7, 8–10.
52 Mt. 21:31.
53 Mt. 8:11–12.
54 Mt. 20:16.
55 Mt. 18:21–22.
56 Mt. 12:31.
57 Cf. Mt. 18:21–35.
58 Lk. 16:1–9.
59 Mt. 10:39 par.; 16:25; cf. Jn. 12:25.
60 Mt. 7:13–14; Lk. 13–24.
61 Mt. 22:14.
62 Mt. 19:26.
63 Lk. 14:15–24; Mt. 22:1–10.
64 Mk. 2:15–17, 19; Mt. 8:11; 22:1–14; Lk. 14:16–24.
65 Lk. 18:9–14.
66 Lk. 7:47.
67 Lk. 15:25–32.
68 Mt. 21:28–31.
69 Lk. 14:16–24.
70 Mt. 18:23–27.
71 Lk. 7:41–43.
72 Lk. 15:1–7.
73 Lk. 15:8–10.
74 Lk. 15:11–32.
75 Lk. 18:9–14.
76 Mt. 20:1–15.
77 Mt. 6:12 par.
78 Cf., for example, H. Braun, *Jesus*, p. 145.
79 Mk. 2:1–12 par.
80 Mk. 2:7.
81 Mk. 3:6.

C IV: The Conflict

1. *The decision*

1 Mk. 6:34 par.; cf. Mt. 14:14; 15:32.
2 On "following" and discipleship see G. Kittel, ant. "akoloutheo" in *ThW* I, 210–16; K. H. Rengstorf, art. "manthano" in *ThW* IV, 392–465; E. Schweizer, *Erniedrigung und Erhöhung bei Jesus und seinen Nachfolgern*, Zürich, 1962[2]; G. Bornkamm, *Jesus of Nazareth*, pp. 144–52; M. Hengel, *Nachfolge und Charisma*, Berlin, 1968.
3 Mk. 1:16–20; 2:14; Mt. 4:18–22; Lk. 5:9–11; cf. Jn. 1:35–51.
4 Jn. 15:16.
5 Mt. 23:8–10.
6 Mt. 19:12.
7 Mt. 12:30; Lk. 11:23.
8 Mk. 9:40; cf. Lk. 9:50.

9 Mk. 5:18–20.
10 Mk. 6:7–13; Mt. 10:1–11:1; Lk. 9:1–6; 10:1–16.
11 Mk. 1:17.
12 Lk. 5:10; cf. 5:1–9.
13 Mt. 10:40.
14 Cf. Mk. 3:14–15.
15 Mt. 8:20 par.
16 Cf. Mt. 10:7–22.
17 Mt. 10:24–25.
18 Lk. 14:28–33.
19 Lk. 9:59–62; cf. Mt. 8:21–22.
20 Mk. 10:35–40.
21 Lk. 12:8–9; cf. Mk. 8:38.
22 Cf. Mt. 8:23–27 with Mk. 4:35–41 par.
23 Jn. 14–16.
24 Cf. Mk. 9:33–35; 10:42–45.
25 Cf. Mt. 23:2–12.
26 Mk. 10:43–44 par.
27 Jn. 13:1–17.
28 On the "twelve" and the "apostles" cf. first of all the lexicon articles in *LThK* ("Apostel" by K. H. Schelkle; "Zwölf" by A. Vögtle), *RGG* (H. Riesenfeld), *EKL* (H.-D. Wendland), *ThW* (K. H. Rengstorf). In addition the more recent monographs: C. H. Dodd, *The Apostolic Preaching and Its Developments*, London, 1944[2]; H. von Campenhausen, *Kirchliches Amt und geistliche Vollmacht in den ersten drei Jahrhunderten*, Tübingen, 1953; K. H. Schelkle, *Jüngerschaft und Apostelamt. Eine biblische Auslegung des priesterlichen Dienstes*, Freiburg, 1957; B. Rigaux, "Die 'Zwölf' in Geschichte und Kerygma" in H. Ristow/K. Matthiae (eds.), *Der historische Jesus und der kerygmatische Christus*, Berlin, 1960, pp. 468–86; G. Klein, *Die zwölf Apostel. Ursprung und Gehalt einer Idee*, Göttingen, 1961; W. Schmithals, *Das kirchliche Apostelamt. Eine historische Untersuchung*, Göttingen, 1961; S. O. Barr, *From the Apostles' Faith to the Apostles' Creed*, New York, 1964; H. Küng, *The Church*, Chapter D IV; S. Freyne, *The Twelve. Disciples and Apostles*, London, 1968; G. W. Ittel, *Jesus und die Jünger*, Gütersloh, 1970; C. K. Barrett, *The Signs of an Apostle*, London, 1970/Philadelphia, 1972.
29 1 Co. 15:5.
30 Mk. 3:14 par.
31 Mt. 19:28.
32 Ac. 1:15–26.
33 Mk. 3:16–19; Mt. 10:2–4; Lk. 6:14–16; Ac. 1:13.
34 Mk. 2:14 par.
35 Mk. 3:18.
36 Mk. 3:16.
37 Lk. 22:28, 31–32.
38 Mt. 13:47–50; 13:24–30.
39 Mt. 19:28 par.

40 Mk. 3:14; in Mark 6:30 "apostle" does not seem to be meant as a permanent title, but merely designates the occasional activity of an "emissary."
41 Lk. 6:13.
42 Today this is no longer a matter of dispute between the denominations. On the *Protestant side* see W. G. Kümmel, *Kirchenbegriff und Geschichtsbewusstsein in der Urgemeinde und bei Jesus,* Uppsala, 1943; *Verheissung und Erfüllung. Untersuchungen zur eschatologischen Verkündigung Jesu,* Zürich, 1953; "Jesus und die Anfänge der Kirche" in *Studia Theologica* 7 (1953), pp. 1–27; "Die Naherwartung in der Verkündigung Jesu" in *Zeit und Geschichte, Festschrift für R. Bultmann,* Tübingen, 1964, pp. 31–46. See also A. Oepke, "Der Herrenspruch über die Kirche in der neueren Forschung" in *Studia Theologica* 2 (1948), pp. 110–65; P. Nepper-Christensen, *Wer hat die Kirche gestiftet?,* Uppsala, 1950; O. Cullmann, *Peter,* London/Philadelphia, 1953; F. G. Downing, *The Church and Jesus,* London/Naperville, 1968.
On *the Catholic side* see A. Vögtle, "Ekklesiologische Auftragsworte des Auferstandenen" in *Sacra Pagina* II, Paris/Gembloux, 1959, pp. 280–94; "Jesus und die Kirche" in *Begegnung der Christen. Festschrift für O. Karrer,* Stuttgart/Frankfurt, 1959, pp. 54–81; "Der Einzelne und die Gemeinschaft in der Stufenfolge der Christusoffenbarung" in *Sentire Ecclesiam. Festschrift für H. Rahner,* Freiburg, 1961, pp. 50–91; "Exegetische Erwägungen über das Wissen und Selbstbewusstsein Jesu" in *Gott in Welt. Festschrift für K. Rahner,* Freiburg, 1964, I, pp. 608–67. See also J. Betz, "Die Gründung der Kirche durch den historischen Jesus" in *ThQ* 138 (1958), pp. 152–83; O. Kuss, "Bemerkungen zum Fragenkreis: Jesus und die Kirche im NT" in *ThQ* 135 (1955), pp. 28–55; R. Schnackenburg, *God's Rule and Kingdom,* London, 1963, pp. 215–49; art. "Kirche" in *LThK,* VI, 167–72; H. Riedlinger, *Geschichtlichkeit und Vollendung des Wissens Christi,* Freiburg, 1966; H. Küng, *The Church,* D II, 3; F. J. Schierse, *Was hat die Kirche mit Jesus zu tun? Zur gegenwärtigen Problemlage biblischer Exegese und kirchlicher Verkündigung,* Düsseldorf, 1970.
On *New Testament ecclesiology in general,* for pre-conciliar literature see H. Küng, *The Church,* A I, 3. Among more recent monographs may be mentioned D. M. Stanley, *The Apostolic Church in the New Testament,* Westminster, Md., 1965; N. J. Bull, *The Rise of the Church,* London, 1967; B. Gherardini, *La Chiesa nella storia della teologia protestante,* Turin, 1969; R. McKelvey, *The New Temple. The Church in the New Testament,* London, 1969; J. Hainz, *Ekklesia. Strukturen paulinischer Gemeinde-Theologie und Gemeinde-Ordnung,* Regensburg, 1972.
43 Mt. 16:18.
44 The present Catholic consensus in the *Petrine* question can be seen in a number of recent contributions: A. Vögtle, "Messiasbekenntnis und Petrusverheissung. Zur Komposition Mt. 16:13–23 par." (1957–58), reprinted in *Das Evangelium und die Evangelien. Beiträge zur Evangelienforschung,* Düsseldorf, 1971, pp. 137–70; B. Rigaux, "St. Peter in Contemporary Exegesis" in *Concilium,* September 1967, pp. 72–86. See also

R. Pesch, "The Position and Significance of Peter in the Church of the New Testament" in *Concilium*, April 1971, pp. 21–35; J. Blank, "The Person and Office of Peter in the New Testament" in *Concilium*, March 1973, pp. 42–55; W. Trilling, "Zum Petrusamt im Neuen Testament. Traditionsgeschichtliche Überlegungen anhand von Matthäus, 1 Petrus und Johannes" in *ThQ* 151 (1971), pp. 110–33. The agreement among these three authors is brought out by H. Küng in *Fehlbar? Eine Bilanz*, Zürich/Einsiedeln/Cologne, 1973, pp. 405–14; R. E. Brown/K. P. Donfried/J. Reumann (eds.), *Peter in the New Testament. A Collaborative Assessment by Protestant and Roman Catholic Scholars*, Minneapolis, 1973.

45 Mk. 7:27; Mt. 15:24; 10:6.
46 Mk. 16:15; Mt. 28:18–20.
47 Is. 25:6–9.
48 Mt. 8:11–12 par.; cf. Mt. 25:32–40; 5:14. On the idea of the pilgrimage of the nations see J. Jeremias, *Jesus' Promise to the Nations*, London/Naperville, 1958.
49 Mk. 8:27–28 par.
50 Cf. B II, 3: "Historical criticism–an aid to faith?"
51 On the messianic titles cf. V. Taylor, *The Names of Jesus*, London, 1953; R. Fuller, *The Mission and Achievement of Jesus*, Naperville, 1954/London, 1955², pp. 79–117; O. Cullmann, *The Christology of the New Testament*, London, 1963/Philadelphia, 1964; F. Hahn, *Christologische Hoheitstitel. Ihre Geschichte im frühen Christentum*, Göttingen, 1963; L. Sabourin, *Les noms et titres de Jésus*, Bruges/Paris, 1963; B. van Iersel, *"Der Sohn" in den synoptischen Jesusworten*, Leiden, 1961. Among the books on Jesus, see G. Bornkamm, pp. 169–78, 227–32; J. Blank, pp. 77–86. Among the theologies of the New Testament R. Bultmann, §7, 12; H. Conzelmann, §10; J. Jeremias, pp. 250–76; K. H. Schelkle, Vol. 2 §11. See also the corresponding articles in *Theological Dictionary of the New Testament* and the theological lexicons.
52 Mk. 8:29 par.
53 Mk. 14:61 par.
54 Mt. 11:27; Mk. 13:32.
55 So, for example, J. Jeremias, pp. 250–51.
56 Dn. 7:13–14.
57 Ethiopic Enoch, 37–71; 4 Ezr. 13.
58 Cf. J. Jeremias, op. cit., §23.
59 On the question of the "Son of Man" cf., in addition to the above-mentioned works on the messianic titles, E. Sjöberg, *Der verborgene Menschensohn in den Evangelien*, Lund, 1955; E. Schweizer, "Der Menschensohn" in *Neotestamentica*, Zürich, 1963, pp. 56–84; H. E. Tödt, *Der Menschensohn in der synoptischen Überlieferung*, Gütersloh, 1959; P. Vielhauer, "Gottesreich und Menschensohn in der Verkündigung Jesu. Jesus und der Menschensohn" in *Aufsätze zum Neuen Testament*, Munich, 1965, pp. 55–140, 145–46; C. Colpe, art. "hyios tou anthropou" in *ThW*, Stuttgart, 1969, 403–81.
60 Cf., from Q, especially Lk. 12:8–9.

61 Mk. 15:14 par.
62 Cf. Mt. 5:21–48; cf. Mk. 10:5 par.
63 Cf. Mt. 12:42; cf. 12:6.
64 Mt. 12:41 par.
65 Jn. 1:46.
66 Mk. 11:28–33.
67 Mt. 11:6 par.
68 Lk. 24:21.

2. *The debate on God*

1 Cf. A II; "The Other Dimension."
2 In addition to the theologies of the Old and New Testaments (on the New see B II, on the Old see below) and the relevant literature on the comparative study of religions (A III), cf. especially the theological literature cited on the question of God (A II).
3 A. Görres, "Glaube und Unglaube in psychoanalytischer Sicht" in the international Catholic review, *Communio* I (1973), pp. 481–504.
4 For more precise explanations see H. Küng, *Menschwerdung Gottes*, Freiburg, 1970, Chapter VIII, 2: "Die Geschichtlichkeit Gottes." On the understanding of God in the Old Testament see the theologies of the Old Testament by W. Eichrodt, P. Heinisch, E. Jacob, P. van Imschoot, L. Köhler, G. von Rad, T. Vriezen. There is a useful survey of the question in "The God of Israel" in *The Common Catechism*, London/New York, 1975, Chapter VI.
5 Mk. 12:29–31 par.
6 Cf. the introductions to the Old Testament, particularly by J. A. Bewer, O. Eissfeldt, A. Feuillet, G. Fohrer, W. O. E. Oesterley, R. H. Pfeiffer, A. Robert, T. H. Robinson, A. Weiser.
7 Dt. 26:8.
8 Ex. 15:1–21.
9 Is. 40–55.
10 Mk. 15:37.
11 Is. 52:13–53:12.
12 Cf. E. Conze, *Buddhism. Its Essence and Development*, Oxford, 1953, p. 40.
13 Ps. 94:9.
14 There is a fine analysis of "being a person" ("reciprocity," "being able to say 'Thou,'" "being able to answer," "between") and its application to God in H. Ott, *God*, Edinburgh, 1974, Chapters IV and V. A discussion with defenders of a "post-theistic" understanding of God is also included here. In this connection see the same author's *Wirklichkeit und Glaube*, Vol. II, "Der persönliche Gott," Göttingen/Zürich, 1969, especially Chapters III–VI. Cf. also P. Tillich, *Systematic Theology*, Vol. I, Chicago, 1951/London, 1953, pp. 270–72.
15 On what follows cf. H. Küng, *Die Menschwerdung Gottes*, VIII, 2: "Die Geschichtlichkeit Gottes."
16 On the *anthropomorphisms* see P. van Imschoot, *Théologie de l'Ancien Testament*, Vol. I, Paris/Tournai, 1954, pp. 28–30; W. Eichrodt,

Theology of the Old Testament, Vol. I, London, 1961, pp. 211–20; E. Jacob, *Theology of the Old Testament*, London, 1958, pp. 39–42; T. C. Vriezen, *An Outline of Old Testament Theology*, Oxford, 1966, pp. 171–75; G. von Rad, *Old Testament Theology*, London/Edinburgh, Vol. I, 1962, p. 219.

17 Cf. A II, 2: "Ambiguity of the concept of God."

18 This is the aim of the whole discussion of Hegel's philosophy of God as developed in H. Küng, *Menschwerdung Gottes* (cf. especially Chapter VIII, 2).

19 M. Heidegger, *Identität und Differenz*, Pfüllingen, 1957, p. 70.

20 Cf. F. K. Mayr, "Patriarchalisches Gottesverständnis? Historische Erwägungen zur Trinitätslehre" in *ThQ* 152 (1972), pp. 224–55.

21 Ex. 4:22–23; Jr. 31:9; Is. 63:16.

22 Ps. 2:7.

23 Si. 4:10; Ws. 2:16–18.

24 Book of Jubilees 1:24.

25 Mt. 5:44–48.

26 Mt. 10:29–31.

27 Mt. 6:8.

28 Mt. 6:32.

29 Lk. 15:11–32.

30 Cf. especially J. Jeremias, *The Prayers of Jesus*, London/Naperville, 1967, pp. 11–65; *New Testament Theology*, Part I, London/Philadelphia, 1971, pp. 63–68.

31 Cf. also Ps. 89:27 (the royal prerogative of addressing God as "my Father"; cf. Si. 51:10), likewise the cries of despair in Is. 63:16; 64:8; Jr. 3:4.

32 Mk. 14:36.

33 Ga. 4:6; Rm. 8:15; cf. in this connection Mt. 23:9.

34 Mt. 6:9.

35 Mt. 6:9–13.

36 Lk. 11:2–4.

37 Mk. 11:25; Mt. 6:14–15; 18:35.

38 Mt. 6:7–8.

39 Lk. 11:5–8.

40 Lk. 18:1–5.

41 Mt. 7:7–11; Lk. 11:9–13.

42 Mt. 6:10; cf. Mk. 14:36.

43 Mt. 6:6.

44 Lk. 5:16; 6:12; 9:18, 28–29.

45 Mk. 1:35; 6:46 par.; 14:32–39.

46 Mt. 11:25.

47 H. Conzelmann, *An Outline of the Theology of the New Testament*, London, 1969, pp. 101–5.

48 G. Bornkamm, *Jesus of Nazareth*, p. 129.

49 J. Jeremias, *New Testament Theology*, Part I, §6, pp. 56–67. The reconstruction of the text is on p. 59. The first mention of the "thunderbolt

from the Johannine sky" is in Karl von Hase, *Die Geschichte Jesu*, Leipzig, 1877, p. 422, quoted by Jeremias, p. 56.

50 Mk. 10:18 par.

3. *The end*

1 Mk. 3:6.

2 Cf. K. L. Schmidt, *Der Rahmen der Geschichte Jesu. Literarkritische Untersuchungen zur ältesten Jesus-Überlieferung*, Berlin, 1919; new impression, Darmstadt, 1964.

3 Mt. 5:35.

4 Lk. 19:11; 24:21; Ac. 1:6.

5 Mk. 8:31 par.; 9:31 par.; 10:33–34 par.

6 Jn. 7:52.

7 Mk. 2:24; 3:6.

8 Mk. 6:17–29.

9 Josephus, *Antiquities*, 18, 118–19.

10 Lk. 13:31.

11 Cf. Mt. 23:35; Lk. 13:33.

12 Is. 53:12.

13 Mk. 10:45.

14 Mk. 14:24.

15 To this extent at least the material provided by J. Jeremias, *New Testament Theology*, Part I, pp. 276–86, must be taken seriously.

16 Mk. 9:31.

17 Mk. 8:33.

18 According to John 4:2, the disciples baptized.

19 Mark 16:15 belongs to the supplementary chapter; the evidence for John 3:5 is uncertain; Matthew's conclusion in its trinitarian form goes back to a community tradition or a community practice.

20 On the interpretation of baptism cf. H. Küng, *The Church* C III, 1: "Members through baptism" (with extensive bibliography up to 1965). Other recent works include G. R. Beasley-Murray, *Baptism in the New Testament*, London, 1962/Grand Rapids, 1973; W. Bieder, *Die Verheissung der Taufe im Neuen Testament*, Zürich, 1966; K. Barth, *Church Dogmatics*, Vol. IV, 4: "The Christian Life" (Fragment). "Baptism as the Foundation of the Christian Life," Edinburgh, 1969; N. Gäumann, *Taufe und Ethik. Studien zu Römer 6*, Munich, 1967; O. Böcher, *Christus Exorzista. Dämonismus und Taufe im Neuen Testament*, Stuttgart, 1972.

21 1 Co. 11:23–25; Mk. 14:22–25; Mt. 26:26–29; Lk. 22:15–20.

22 1 Co. 11:23–25.

23 Mk. 6:30–44; 8:1–10 par.; cf. Mk. 2:18–20.

24 Mk. 14:25.

25 1 Co. 11:25.

26 Ex. 24:8–11.

27 Jr. 31:31–34.

28 Cf. especially Is. 53:4–10.

29 Mk. 14:22.

30 On the interpretation of the eucharist see H. Küng, *The Church*, C III, 2: "United in the fellowship of the Lord's Supper" (extensive bibliography up to 1965). Other recent works include J.-J. von Allmen, *Essai sur le Repas du Seigneur*, Neuchâtel, 1966; C. O'Neill, *New Approaches to the Eucharist*, Staten Island, 1967; G. N. Lammens, *Het commemoratieve Aspect van de Avondmaalsviering*, Kampen, 1968; J. M. Powers, *Eucharistic Theology*, New York, 1972; J. P. de Jong, *Die Eucharistie als Symbolwirklichkeit*, Regensburg, 1969; B. Sandvik, *Das Kommen des Herrn beim Abendmahl im Neuen Testament*, Zürich, 1970; H. Schürmann, *Jesu Abendmahlshandlung als Zeichen für die Welt*, Leipzig, 1970; R. Feneberg, *Christliche Passafeier und Abendmahl. Eine biblisch-hermeneutische Untersuchung der ntl. Einsetzungsberichte*, Munich, 1971; H. Fries, *Ein Glaube. Eine Tauffe. Getrennt beim Abendmahl?*, Graz, 1971; H. Patsch, *Abendmahl und historischer Jesus*, Stuttgart, 1972; A. Gerken, *Theologie der Eucharistie*, Munich, 1973.

31 In this connection the commentary by E. Schweizer, *Das Evangelium nach Markus*, Göttingen, 1968, can be recommended.

32 Cf. G. Schneider, *Die Passion Jesu nach den drei älteren Evangelien*, Munich, 1973 (includes a summary of recent work on the exegesis of the Passion story). K. H. Schelkle, *Die Passion Jesu in der Verkündigung des Neuen Testaments*, Heidelberg, 1949. On the fourth Gospel cf. the recent work by A. Dauer, *Die Passionsgeschichte im Johannesevangelium*, Munich, 1972.

33 Is. 53.

34 Zc. 9:9.

35 Mk. 14:21.

36 Lk. 24:26–27.

37 Mk. 14:47; Lk. 22:49–51; Jn. 18:10–11.

38 Lk. 22:44 (a controverted text, possibly an interpolation).

39 Mk. 14:51–52.

40 Mk. 15:21.

41 Cf. Mt. 27:32; Lk. 23:26.

42 Mk. 15:40 par. by contrast with Jn. 19:25.

43 Mk. 15:24 par.

44 Mk. 15:27–28.

45 Mk. 15:29–30.

46 Cf. the Marcan apocalypse Mk. 13; cf. Mt. 24; Lk. 21:5–36.

47 Mk. 11:27–33 par.

48 Cf. Mk. 13:2 with Mk. 14:58.

49 Cf. C. H. Dodd, *The Parables of the Kingdom*, New York/London-Glasgow, 1961, pp. 100–1.

50 Mk. 14:1–2.

51 Jn. 19:42; Mk. 15:42.

52 Mt. 26:15; cf. Jn. 12:6.

53 Mt. 27:9; cf. Zc. 11:12–13.

54 Cf. Mk. 14:10–11 with Mt. 26:14–16; 27:3–10.

55 Mk. 14:17–21 par.

56 Mk. 14:32–42 par.

57 Jn. 18:4–9.
58 Cf. H. Lietzmann, *Der Prozess Jesu*, Berlin, 1931; J. Blinzler, *Der Prozess Jesu*, Stuttgart, 1951, new, revised edition Regeneburg, 1969; D. R. Catchpole, *The Trial of Jesus. A Study in the Gospels and Jewish Historiography from 1770 to the Present Day*, Leyden, 1971. Among the books on Jesus see particularly G. Bornkamm, *Jesus*, pp. 163–64.
59 Mk. 14:55–64.
60 Mk. 14:62.
61 Ps. 110:1 and Dn. 7:13.
62 Mk. 14:58 par.
63 Josephus, *The Jewish War*, 6, 301–3.
64 This is particularly clear in Lk. 23:2; Jn. 19:12, 15; but also in Mk. 15:9–10.
65 Cf. Mk. 15:2, 9, 12, 18, 26, 32 and parallels.
66 Mt. 19:27.
67 Lk. 23:6–12.
68 Jn. 18:33–38; 19:6–16.
69 Jn. 19:19–22.
70 Mk. 15:15–20 par.
71 Mk. 15:24 par.
72 Cf. J. Schneider, art. "stauros" in *ThW* VII, 572–84.
73 Mk. 15:33; cf. Am. 8:9–10.
74 Jn. 11:49–50.
75 C I, 2: "Revolution?"
76 Despite a large measure of agreement with J. Moltmann's intentions, we must disagree here with his systematization in *The Crucified God*, pp. 126–45.
77 Mk. 12:17 par.
78 Jn. 19:7.
79 Dt. 21:23. Jewish law imposed on idolaters and blasphemers, as an additional penalty (not a death penalty) after stoning, hanging on a tree.
80 Cf. Ga. 3:13.
81 Justin, *Dialogue with Tryphon*, 89–90.
82 Mk. 15:28.
83 2 Co. 5:21.
84 Cf. Mk. 15:40–41.
85 Lk. 23:39–43.
86 Jn. 19:26–27.
87 Mk. 15:37; Mt. 27:50.
88 Mk. 14:34 par.
89 Lk. 22:43.
90 Lk. 23:46; cf. Ps. 31:6.
91 Jn. 19:30.
92 Ps. 22:2; Mk. 15:34; Mt. 27:46.
93 J. Moltmann, op. cit., pp. 146–49.
94 Mk. 15:42–47.
95 Mk. 15:44–45.
96 1 Co. 15:35.

C V: *The New Life*

1. *The beginning*

1 E. Bloch, *Das Prinzip Hoffnung*, 1959, Frankfurt, 1967, p. 1297; cf. pp. 1297–1391.

2 Even Luke, who suppresses the flight of the disciples and tones down the death of Jesus with consoling and edifying details, speaks clearly of the broken hopes of the disciples (Lk. 24:21).

3 H. Grass has thoroughly worked over the older literature on the resurrection in *Ostergeschehen und Osterberichte*, Göttingen, 1956 (fourth edition, 1970). Fundamental to more recent discussion are K. Barth, *Die Auferstehung der Toten*, Munich, 1924; *Church Dogmatics*, Vols. IV, 1 §59, 3; IV, 2 §64, 2–4; R. Bultmann, *Theology of the New Testament*, §7 and 33; the same author, *Das Verhältnis der urchristlichen Botschaft zum historischen Jesus*, Heidelberg, 1962; W. Marxsen, *Die Auferstehung Jesu als historisches und theologisches Problem*, Gütersloh, 1964; the same author, *The Resurrection of Jesus of Nazareth*, London, 1970 (a translation of *Die Auferstehung Jesu von Nazareth*, Gütersloh, 1968).

In addition to the relevant comments in the books on Jesus, the following are important in recent discussion: H. von Campenhausen, *Der Ablauf der Osterereignisse und das leere Grab*, Heidelberg, 1966; G. Koch, *Die Auferstehung Jesu Christi*, Tübingen, 1959; W. Künneth, *Glauben an Jesus? Die Begegnung der Christologie mit der modernen Existenz*, Munich/Hamburg, 1969; J. Kremer, *Das älteste Zeugnis von der Auferstehung Jesu Christi. 1 Kor. 15:1–11*, Stuttgart, 1967; the same author, *Die Osterbotschaft der vier Evangelien*, Stuttgart, 1970; P. Seidenstücker, *Die Auferstehung Jesu in der Botschaft der Evangelisten*, Stuttgart, 1967; L. Schenke, *Auferstehungsverkündigung und leeres Grab*, Stuttgart, 1968; H. Schlier, *Über die Auferstehung Jesu Christi*, Einsiedeln, 1970; K. Lehmann, *Auferweckt am dritten Tag nach der Schrift*, Freiburg, 1968; J. Blank, *Paulus und Jesus. Eine theologische Grundlegung*, Munich, 1968, pp. 133–248; the same author, "The God of the Living" in J. Feiner/L. Wischer (eds.), *The Common Catechism*, London/New York, 1975, Chapter 8, especially pp. 162–85; F. Mussner, *Die Auferstehung Jesu*, Munich, 1969; G. Kegel, *Auferstehung Jesu–Auferstehung der Toten. Eine traditionsgeschichtliche Untersuchung zum Neuen Testament*, Gütersloh, 1970; U. Wilckens, *Auferstehung*, Stuttgart/Berlin, 1970; X. Léon-Dufour, *Résurrection de Jésus et Message pascal*, Paris, 1971; K. H. Schelkle, *Theologie des Neuen Testaments*, Vol. II, especially §9: "Auferweckung und Erhöhung–Geschichte und Deutung," pp. 128–50; R. H. Fuller, *The Formation of the Resurrection Narratives*, New York, 1971/London, 1972.

The following miscellanies provide important material: W. Marxsen/U. Wilckens/G. Delling/H. G. Geyer, *Die Bedeutung der Auferstehungsbotschaft für den Glauben an Jesus Christus*, Gütersloh, 1968; *Auferstehung heute gesagt. Osterpredigten der Gegenwart*, Gütersloh, 1970;

J. Delorme and others, *La résurrection du Christ et l'exégesè moderne*, Paris, 1969; A. Jaubert/X. Léon-Dufour/E. Floris/J. Cardonnel/M. Oraison/R. Dulong/M. de Certeau/J.-L. Afchain, *Dossier sur la résurrection-Lettre Nr. 163–164*, Paris, 1972.

4 Cf. the basic texts on the resurrection of Jesus: Mk. 16:1–8; Mt. 28; Lk. 24; Jn. 20; 1 Co. 15:3–8.

5 Gospel of Peter, Chapter 8:35–44.

6 1 Co. 15:5–8; cf. Ga. 1:16; 1 Co. 9:1.

7 Mt. 16:18.

8 Lk. 22:32.

9 Jn. 21:15–17.

10 Cf., however, the early writing, 1 Th. 4:14.

11 Cf. Rm. 6:4; 8:11, 34; 10:9; 1 Co. 6:4; Ep. 1:20; 2 Tm. 2:8; Ac. 2:24; 3:15; 4:10; 5:30; 10:40; 13:30, 37.

12 Ac. 2:24.

13 Mk. 12:25; cf. Lk. 20:36.

14 1 Co. 15:44.

15 1 Co. 15:43.

16 1 Co. 15:52.

17 Cf. K. Barth, *Church Dogmatics*, IV, 1, Edinburgh, 1956, pp. 351–52.

18 Cf. R. Bultmann, "New Testament and Mythology" in H. W. Bartsch, *Kerygma and Myth*, Vol. I, London, 1953, pp. 41–42.

19 This is the view of W. Marxsen in *Die Auferstehung Jesu als historisches und theologisches Problem*, Gütersloh, 1967, p. 25. In a later work, translated into English, *The Resurrection of Jesus of Nazareth*, London, 1970, Marxsen makes it clear that more than Jesus' cause is involved in the resurrection. Cf. P. Schoonenberg, *The Christ*, London/New York, 1971, pp. 156–66.

20 R. Bultmann, *Das Verhältnis der urchristlichen Christusbotschaft zum historischen Jesus*, Heidelberg, 1960, p. 27.

21 Cf. E. Schweizer, *Erniedrigung und Erhöhung bei Jesus und seinen Nachfolgern*, Zürich, 1972; W. Thüsing, *Erhöhungsvorstellung und Parusieerwartung in der ältesten nachösterlichen Christologie*, Stuttgart, 1969; G. Lohfink, *Die Himmelfahrt Jesu. Untersuchungen zu den Himmelfahrts- und Erhöhungstexten bei Lukas*, Munich, 1971; the same author, *Die Himmelfahrt Jesu. Erfindung oder Erfahrung*, Stuttgart, 1972.

22 Especially Ps. 110:1; 68:19.

23 Ac. 2:36.

24 Cf. Rm. 1:3–4.

25 Ga. 1:15–16.

26 On this whole question cf. especially G. Lohfink in the two works above-mentioned.

27 Lk. 24:50–52; Ac. 1:9–14.

28 2 K. 2:11.

29 Ps. 110:1.

30 Ac. 1:11.

31 Cf. E. Lohse, art. "pentekoste" in *ThW* VI, 44–53, and the articles on

Pentecost in the biblical and theological encyclopedias. A recommended recent monograph is J. Kremer, *Pfingstbericht und Pfingstgeschehen. Eine exegetische Untersuchung zu Apg.* 2:1–13, Stuttgart, 1973.

32 Jn. 20:22.

33 Ac. 8:14–17; 19:1–7; cf. 10:44–48.

34 Cf. H. Küng, "Die Firmung als Vollendung der Taufe" in *ThQ* 154 (1974), 26–47. The complex problems have been examined exegetically, historically and systematically, and expounded in detail by a student of mine, J. Amougou-Atangana, in *Ein Sakrament des Geistempfangs? Zum Verhältnis von Taufe und Firmung*, Freiburg/Basle/Vienna, 1974.

35 Ac. 17:32.

36 Dn. 12:1–2.

37 Cf. W. Pannenberg, *Jesus–God and Man*, Philadelphia/London, 1968 §3; the same author, *The Apostles' Creed*, London, 1972, pp. 106–9.

38 1 Co. 15:20.

39 Col. 1:18; cf. Rv. 1:5.

40 Mk. 5:21–43 par.

41 Lk. 7:11–17.

42 Jn. 11.

43 On dying "into" God see especially Karl Rahner on the theology of death, most recently in K. Rahner/W. Thüsing, *Christologie–systematisch und exegetisch*, Freiburg/Basle/Vienna, 1972, Chapter IV.

44 This is W. Marxsen's opinion. But he deserves our gratitude for his clearer view (following Bultmann) of the problems involved in the resurrection and of the importance of faith in this connection.

45 Cf. G. Bertram, "Die Himmelfahrt vom Kreuz aus und der Glaube an seine Auferstehung" in *Festgabe für A. Deissmann*, Tübingen, 1927, pp. 187–217.

46 Jn. 3:14; 8:28; 12:32, 34.

47 Jn. 17:4–5. Cf. W. Thüsing, *Die Erhöhung und Verherrlichung Jesu im Johannesevangelium*, Münster, 1970.

48 Rm. 4:17.

49 Cf. Rm. 4:24; 2 Co. 1:9; 4:14; Ga. 1:1; 1 Th. 1:10; 4:14; 1 P. 1:21.

50 Rm. 4:17.

51 Mk. 12:26–27; cf. 2 Co. 1:9.

52 Mk. 12:24.

53 Rm. 4:24.

54 Cf. Rm. 8:11; 2 Co. 4:14; Ga. 1:1; Ep. 1:20; Col. 2:12.

55 Cf. B II, 3: "Historical criticism–an aid to faith?"

56 1 Co. 15:3–5.

57 Mk. 16:1–8.

58 Mk. 16:9–20.

59 Cf. especially K. Lehmann, who attempts to throw light on the meaning of the formula from Targum and Midrash texts (especially pp. 262–90).

60 Cf. J. Gnilka, *Jesus Christus nach frühen Zeugnissen des Glaubens*, Munich, 1970, pp. 54–55.

61 1 Co. 15:4.

62 1 Co. 15:5–8.

63 2 Co. 5:2–4.
64 Cf. G. Ebeling, *The Nature of Faith*, London, 1961/Philadelphia, 1967, pp. 66–67.
65 Mk. 16:5–6.
66 Ac. 1:15.
67 Lk. 24:22–24.
68 Mk. 16:6.
69 Mk. 16:6.
70 Mk. 16:8.
71 Mt. 28:8.
72 Mk. 16:8.
73 Lk. 24:5.
74 Cf. DS 10–41; also 76, 801, 852; other references in DS 738, 1077.
75 1 P. 3:18–20.
76 F. Spitta, *Christi Predigt an die Geister*, Göttingen, 1890.
77 K. Gschwind, *Die Niederfahrt Christi in die Unterwelt*, Münster, 1911.
78 After B. Reicke, *The Disobedient Spirits and Christian Baptism*, Copenhagen, 1946, and W. Bieder, *Die Vorstellung von der Höllenfahrt Jesu Christi*, Zürich, 1949, cf. especially the convincing solution suggested by W. J. Dalton, after surveying the whole state of recent investigations, in *Christ's Proclamation to the Spirits*, Rome, 1965, which is also summarized in the article, "Interpretation and Tradition. An Example from 1 Peter" in *Gregorianum* 49 (1968), pp. 11–37. The commentaries on the first letter of Peter should also be consulted—especially those by U. Holzmeister, E. G. Selwyn, B. Reicke, C. Spicq and K. H. Schelkle. See also the section on this theme in the explanations of the Apostles' Creed by K. Barth, W. Pannenberg and J. Ratzinger.
79 Slavonic Enoch, 7:1–3.
80 Cf. Ep. 6:12; 1 Co. 2:8; Col. 2:15; Lk. 10:18.
81 Cf. C IV, 3: "In vain?"
82 Cf. C II, 2: "What really happened."
83 Cf. H. Haag, *Abschied vom Teufel*, Zürich/Einsiedeln/Cologne, 1969.
84 See H. Haag's large work on the devil: *Teufelsglaube*, Tübingen, 1974.
85 1 Co. 15:24–28; Rm. 5:18; 1 P. 4:6.
86 On Jesus' descent into hell cf. the thought-provoking chapter of H. U. von Balthasar, "Der Gang zu den Toten" in *Mysterium Salutis*, III/2, Einsiedeln/Zürich/Cologne, 1969, pp. 227–55.
87 Cf. R. Pesch, who goes beyond U. Wilckens and accepts the hypotheses of Wilckens' disciple, K. Berger, in "Zur Entstehung des Glaubens an die Auferstehung Jesu" in *ThQ* 153 (1973), pp. 201–28.
88 See in the same issue of *ThQ*, pp. 229–69, the answers to R. Pesch by W. Kasper, K. H. Schelkle, P. Stuhlmacher and M. Hengel. In addition, looking back at the controversy, H. Küng, "Zur Entstehung des Auferstehungsglaubens. Versuch einer systematischen Klärung" in *ThQ* 154 (1974), pp. 103–17. For the further context of the controversy: W. Kasper, *Einführung in den Glauben*, Mainz, 1972, especially pp. 57–61; K. H. Schelkle, *Theologie des Neuen Testaments*, Vol. II, Düsseldorf, 1973, §9; P. Stuhlmacher, "Das Bekenntnis zur Auferweckung Jesu von

den Toten und die Biblische Theologie" in *Zeitschrift für Theologie und Kirche*, 70 (1973), pp. 365–403; M. Hengel, *Nachfolge und Charisma. Eine exegetisch-religionsgeschichtliche Studie zu Mt. 8:21f. und Jesu Ruf in die Nachfolge*, Berlin, 1968; the same author, "Christologie und neutestamentliche Chronologie" in *Neues Testament und Geschichte. Festschrift für O. Cullmann*, Zürich/Tübingen, 1972, pp. 43–67; the same author, "Die Ursprünge der christlichen Mission" in *New Testament Studies* 18 (1971/1972), pp. 15–38.

89 J. Jeremias, *Heiligengräber in Jesu Umwelt*, Göttingen, 1958.

90 Ps. 16:8–11; Is. 52:13.

91 Gn. 5:24; 2 K. 2:11.

92 Mk. 6:14–16; cf. Mk. 9:9–13.

93 Cf. C IV, 3: "Stages."

94 Even Luke, 22:31–32 speaks of a future conversion. Luke spares the disciples and–in contrast to Mark and Matthew–passes over their flight in silence.

95 Goethe, *Faust*, Part One. Translation by Philip Wayne, Penguin Books, Harmondsworth, Middlesex, 1949, p. 61.

96 Ex. 3:2, 16; 6:3; 1:7, 10.

97 1 Co. 15:8; Ga. 1:16.

98 1 Co. 9:1.

99 Ga. 1:11–17.

100 2 Co. 12:1.

101 2 Co. 11:17; 12:1.

102 Ac. 9:1–9; 22:3–11; 26:9–20.

103 Cf. C II, 2: "Miracles?"

104 Cf. C V, 1: "Legends?"

105 Cf. G. Bornkamm, *Jesus*, pp. 180–86; J. Blank, *Jesus*, pp. 91–92; the same author in *The Common Catechism*, pp. 162–85.

106 Mt. 28:17; Jn. 20:24–29; cf. also Lk. 24:11, 34.

107 Cf. G. Ebeling's penetrating analyses in *The Nature of Faith*, pp. 58–71.

108 Cf. G. von Rad, *Old Testament Theology*, Vol. II, Edinburgh/London, 1965, pp. 50–69 ("The Prophets' Call and Reception of Revelation").

109 Cf. C IV, 2: "Revolution in the understanding of God."

110 Mt. 14:28–31.

111 Cf. K. Rahner (-W. Thüsing), *Christologie–systematisch und exegetisch*, pp. 38, 40–42; the same author, "Experiencing Easter" in *Theological Investigations*, Vol. VII, pp. 159–68.

112 1 Co. 15:32.

113 Cf. 1 Co. 15:12, 33–34.

114 Cf. E. Käsemann, *Der Ruf der Freiheit*, Tübingen, 1972, Chapter 3; the same author, *Perspectives on Paul*, London/Philadelphia, 1971, Chapter 2.

115 For a systematic study in depth of the *problems connected with the resurrection* cf. P. Althaus, *Die christliche Wahrheit*, §47; K. Barth, *Church Dogmatics*, Vols. IV/1 §59, 3; IV/2 §64, 2–4; H. U. von Balthasar, "Mysterium Paschale" in *Mysterium Salutis*, Vol. III, 2, Chapter 9; H. Ott, *Die Antwort des Glaubens*, art. 24; P. Tillich, *Systematic Theology*, Vol.

II, pp. 175–90; J. Blank, "The God of the Living" in *The Common Catechism*, Chapter 8; also the articles on the resurrection in the books on the Apostles' Creed by K. Barth, W. Pannenberg and J. Ratzinger.

2. *The criterion*

1 Cf. Jn. 12:24.
2 Cf. Mt. 23:8.
3 Cf. Lk. 7:39; 24:19; Jn. 1:25.
4 Cf. Mk. 1:24; Jn. 6:69.
5 Cf. Mt. 25:31–45.
6 Ga. 5:13.
7 On the dogmatic interpretation of the Christological titles see C. Duquoc, *Christologie. Essai dogmatique*, Paris, 1968, pp. 131–328.
8 We shall return to this.
9 Cf. B II, 2: "More than a biography."
10 Cf. B II, 3: "Counterquestions about Jesus."
11 Mk. 1:1.
12 A comprehensive survey of the different New Testament Christologies is provided by E. Schweizer in *Jesus Christus im vielfältigen Zeugnis des Neuen Testaments*, Munich/Hamburg, 1968.
13 On this cf. the above-listed works on the titles of Jesus, especially those by V. Taylor, O. Cullmann, F. Hahn, K. Sabourin, the New Testament theologies and the corresponding articles in *ThW*. J. Gnilka provides a good, brief historical-critical outline of the genesis of New Testament Christology in *Jesus Christus nach frühen Zeugnissen des Glaubens*, Munich, 1970.
14 Cf. Mk. 8:38; Lk. 9:26; 12:8.
15 Cf. especially Mt. 10:32 with Lk. 12:8: in the former "Son of Man" has been replaced by "I."
16 Cf. Ps. 2:7; Ps. 89:27–28.
17 2 S. 7:12–16.
18 Rm. 1:3–4.
19 Ac. 13:33; cf. Ps. 2:7.
20 Mk. 1:9–11.
21 Lk. 1:32, 35.
22 Ga. 4:4; Jn. 3:16.
23 Cf. C IV, 1: "The advocate."
24 2 Co. 5:21.
25 D. Sölle throws considerable light on the meaning of representation in *Stellvertretung. Ein Kapitel Theologie nach dem "Tod Gottes,"* Stuttgart/Berlin, 1965. For a critical study see H. Gollwitzer, *Von der Stellvertretung Gottes. Christlicher Glaube in der Erfahrung der Verborgenheit Gottes. Zum Gespräch mit Dorothee Sölle*, Munich, 1967.
26 Jn. 14:28.
27 D. Sölle, op. cit., pp. 142–50.
28 1 Co. 15:28.
29 Cf. C II, 1: "Demythologizing inevitable."
30 On the question of the *consummation* and the *last* judgment cf., in addi-

tion to the articles in the encyclopedias, especially P. Althaus, *Die christliche Wahrheit*, §68–70; E. Brunner, *Dogmatik*, Vol. III, pp. 464–97; H. Ott, *Die Antwort des Glaubens*, art. 49; M. Schmaus, *Dogmatik*, Vol. IV/2; C. Schütz, "Consummation," *The Common Catechism*, Chapter 22; P. Tillich, *Systematic Theology*, Vol. III, pp. 420–52; O. Weber, *Grundlagen der Dogmatik*, Vol. II, pp. 718–59. See also the interpretations of judgment and eternal life in the expositions of the Apostles' Creed by K. Barth, W. Pannenberg and J. Ratzinger. Recent monographs include P. Schütz, *Parusia. Hoffnung und Prophetie*, Heidelberg, 1960; G. C. Berkouwer, *De Wederkomst van Christus*, 2 vols., Kampen, 1961–63; A. L. Moore, *The Parusia in the New Testament*, Leyden, 1966.

31 2 Th. 2:3–12.

32 1 Jn. 2:18, 22; 2 Jn. 7.

33 Cf. also Rv. 13.

34 Cf. C II, 1: "Between present and future."

35 Cf. especially Mk. 13:24–32; Mt. 24:29–36; 25:31–46; Lk. 21:25–53; Jn. 5:25–29; 6:39–40, 44, 54; 11:24; 12:48.

36 Cf. C. Schütz, op. cit., pp. 533–34.

37 Cf. W. Pannenberg, *The Apostles' Creed*, pp. 118–22.

38 Cf. Mt. 25:37–40.

39 Jn. 5:24–25.

40 According to Mt. 25:35–36.

41 This dual demarcation is very clearly indicated in K. Barth, *Church Dogmatics*, II, 2, especially pp. 457–58.

42 1 Co. 15:24–28; Rm. 5:18; cf. 1 P. 4:6.

43 These are set out most impressively by K. Barth in *Church Dogmatics*, II, 2, Chapter 7: "The election of God" (developed in three stages as "the election of Jesus Christ," "the election of the community," "the election of the individual"). For the present state of the discussion see K. Schwarzwäller, *Das Gotteslob der angefochtenen Gemeinde. Dogmatische Grundlegung der Prädestinationslehre*, Neukirchen, 1970.

3. *The ultimate distinction*

1 1 Co. 1:23–24.

2 Cicero, *Pro C. Rabirio*, V, 16.

3 Cf. Cicero, *Second Speech Against Gaius Verres*, V, 64, 165; V, 66, 169.

4 On the different attitudes of Goethe and Hegel to the cross cf. H. Küng, *Menschwerdung Gottes*, pp. 376–78.

5 D. T. Suzuki, *Mysticism: Christian and Buddhist*, London, 1957: especially "Crucifixion and Enlightenment," pp. 129–39 (quotation, p. 129).

6 On the *theological interpretation of Jesus' death* see G. Bornkamm, *Das Ende des Gesetzes. Paulusstudien. Gesammelte Aufsätze* I, Munich, 1963; E. Lohse, *Märtyrer und Gottesknecht. Untersuchungen zur urchristlichen Verkündigung vom Sühnetod Jesu Christi*, Göttingen, 1963; the same author, *Die Geschichte des Leidens und Sterbens Jesu Christi*, Gütersloh, 1964; L. Morris, *The Cross in the New Testament*, Grand Rapids, 1965; E. Güttgemanns, *Der leidende Apostel und sein Herr.*

Studien zur paulinischen Christologie, Göttingen, 1966; W. Popkes, *Christus traditus*, Zürich, 1967; P. Viering (ed.), *Das Kreuz Christi als Grund des Heils*, Gütersloh, 1967; the same editor, *Zur Bedeutung des Todes Jesu*, Gütersloh, 1967, with exegetical contributions by H. Conzelmann, E. Flesseman, van Leer, E. Haenchen, E. Käsemann, E. Lohse; B. Klappert (eds.), *Diskussion um Kreuz und Auferstehung. Zur gegenwärtigen Auseinandersetzung in Theologie und Gemeinde*, Wuppertal, 1967; A. Fohrer/G. Strobel/W. Schrage/P. Rieger, *Das Kreuz Jesu. Theologische Überlegungen*, Göttingen, 1969; E. Käsemann, *Perspectives on Paul*, London/Philadelphia, 1971; H. Kessler, *Die theologische Bedeutung des Todes Jesu. Eine traditionsgeschichtliche Untersuchung*, Düsseldorf, 1970; G. Delling, *Der Kreuzestod Jesu in der urchristlichen Verkündigung*, Göttingen, 1972; J. Moltmann, *The Crucified God. The Cross of Christ as the Foundation and Criticism of Christian Theology*, London, 1974.

7 Is. 53.

8 It is not necessary to refer every time to the numerous commentaries on the Bible. The more important commentaries on the basic Gospel of Mark may be noted: P. Carrington, C. E. B. Cranfield, F. C. Grant, W. Grundmann, E. Haenchen, S. E. Johnson, E. Klostermann, E. Lohmeyer, D. E. Nineham, A. Schlatter, J. Schmid, J. Schniewind, V. Taylor, M. de Tuya, F. M. Uricchio/G. M. Stano. We have already stressed the value of the commentary by E. Schweizer, *Das Evangelium nach Markus*, Göttingen, 1967, the excursus on divine sonship (pp. 206–8) being particularly important in this connection.

9 Mk. 1:9–11.

10 Mk. 3:11; 5:7.

11 Mk. 8:27–33.

12 On Pauline studies see the early important articles by W. Wrede, A. Schlatter, A. Schweitzer, K. Holl, R. Bultmann, R. Reitzenstein, H. Lietzmann, A. Oepke and others, collected by K. H. Rengstorf: *Das Paulusbild in der neueren deutschen Forschung*, Darmstadt, 1964. Cf. also the account by B. Rigaux, *St. Paul et ses lettres. État de la question*, Paris/Bruges, 1962. More recent critical works on the person and work of Paul include M. Dibelius, *Paul* (edited and completed by W. G. Kümmel), London/Philadelphia, 1953; H. J. Schoeps, *Die Theologie des Apostels Paulus im Lichte der jüdischen Religionsgeschichte*, Tübingen, 1959; P. Seidenstücker, *Paulus, der verfolgte Apostel Jesu Christi*, Stuttgart, 1965; G. Bornkamm, *Paul*, London/New York, 1971; O. Kuss, *Paulus. Die Rolle des Apostels in der theologischen Entwicklung der Urkirche*, Regensburg, 1971. The New Testament theologies by R. Bultmann, H. Conzelmann, W. Kümmel, already mentioned, should also be consulted. On the theological problems E. Käsemann, *Perspectives on Paul*, London/Philadelphia, 1971, is important.

13 1 Co. 1:18.

14 In addition to the commentaries on 1 Corinthians–especially those by H. Lietzmann and H. Conzelmann–cf. R. Baumann, *Mitte und Norm des Christlichen, eine Auslegung von 1 Kor. 1:1–3, 4*, Münster, 1968.

15 On this section cf. the impressive treatment of the subject by E. Käsemann, *Der Ruf der Freiheit*, Tübingen, 1968, Chapter 3; the same author, *Perspectives on Paul*, London/Philadelphia, 1971, pp. 54–59.
16 Among the commentaries on Galatians cf. especially H. Lietzmann and H. Schlier; more recently F. Mussner, *Der Galaterbrief*, Freiburg/Basle/Vienna, 1974.
17 F. Nietzsche, *Werke*, edited by K. Schlechta, Vol. II, Munich, 1955, p. 1200.
18 F. Nietzsche, *Werke*, Vol. II, p. 1204. Cf. also K. Schlechta, *Nietzsche-Index*, under the headings of "Jesus," pp. 172–73, and "Paul," pp. 280–81.
19 Ga. 3–4; Rm. 4.
20 Rm. 5:12–25; 1 Co. 15:42–49.
21 1 Co. 1:13; 10:16–17; 12:12–31; Rm. 12:4–8; cf. Ga. 3:26–29; Rm. 1:18–3:28; Rm. 9–11.
22 Cf. Rm. 3:21–29 and the anthropological application in Rm. 6 (baptism); Rm. 7 (man's conflict situation); Rm. 8 (experience of the Spirit) and also the paraenesis in Rm. 12–15.
23 On the relationship between Jesus and Paul cf. R. Bultmann, "Die Bedeutung des geschichtlichen Jesus für die Theologie des Paulus" in *Glauben und Verstehen*, Vol. I, Tübingen, 1954, pp. 188–213; E. Jüngel, *Paulus und Jesus. Eine Untersuchung zur Präzisierung der Frage nach dem Ursprung der Christologie*, Tübingen, 1962; and especially J. Blank, *Paulus und Jesus. Eine theologische Grundlegung*, Munich, 1968; H.-W. Kuhn, "Der irdische Jesus bei Paulus als traditionsgeschichtliches und theologisches Problem" in *Zeitschrift für Theologie und Kirche* 67 (1970), pp. 295–320.
24 2 Co. 5:16; a main source for K. Barth and R. Bultmann.
25 Cf. J. Blank, op. cit., Chapter 6. What is said here is confirmed and developed further in the report on recent discussion by R. Pesch, "'Christus dem Fleisch nach kennen' (2 Kor. 5:16)? Zur theologischen Bedeutung der Frage nach dem historischen Jesus" in *Kontinuität in Jesus. Zugänge zu Leben, Tod und Auferstehung*, Freiburg/Basle/Vienna, 1974, pp. 9–34.
26 Cf. J. Blank, op. cit., pp. 129, 323–24. Among such passages are those on the central message (kerygma) of crucifixion and resurrection (1 Co. 15:3–8), the Last Supper tradition (1 Co. 11:23–25), the position on marriage and divorce (1 Co. 7:10–11), instruction on the livelihood of the preacher (1 Co. 9:14), the outstanding position of the commandment of love (1 Th. 4:9; Ga. 5:13; Rm. 13:8–10; 1 Co. 13), the Davidic descent of Jesus (Rm. 1:3), Christ from Israel according to the flesh (Rm. 9:5), sonship from Abraham (Ga. 3; Rm. 4), human birth and subordination to the law (Ga. 4:4), human existence, self-abasement, obedience to death (Ph. 2:6–8), weakness (2 Co. 13:4), poverty (2 Co. 8:9), passion (1 Co. 11:23); to these might be added 1 Co. 4:12; 13:2; Rm. 16:19.
27 Ph. 3:5–6.
28 Ga. 1:13–14.
29 Cf. C II, 3: "The supreme norm."

30 Ga. 1:13–14.
31 Cf. 1 Co. 1:17–31; Ga. 3:1–14.
32 Cf. C V, 1: "Origin of faith."
33 Cf. 1 Co. 15:8–10; 9:1; Ga. 1:15–16; Ph. 3:4–11. See also J. Blank, *Paulus und Jesus*, Chapter 4.
34 Ga. 1:1, 11–12.
35 Ga. 3:13; cf. 2:17–19; Rm. 7:4.
36 Ga. 2:21.
37 1 Co. 10:23–33; 8:7–13; Rm. 14.
38 After the commentaries on Romans by O. Michel and O. Kuss the commentary by E. Käsemann appeared: *An die Römer*, Tübingen, 1973. In this the earlier literature is subjected to a thoroughly critical examination.
39 Rm. 1:18–3:20.
40 Rm. 3:21–5:21.
41 Rm. 6–8.
42 Rm. 9–11.
43 Rm. 12–15.
44 Rm. 3:28; Ga. 2:16.
45 The German translation of the text is by J. Zink and is one of many felicitous renderings in his translation of the New Testament (Stuttgart, 1965).
46 I developed this view in *Justification. The Doctrine of Karl Barth and a Catholic Reflection*, New York, 1964/London, 1965. In the meantime it has largely come to prevail, as can be seen from the document of the study committee agreed to between the Lutheran World Federation and the Roman Catholic Church at its session in Malta 21–26 February 1970. The text is in *Herder-Korrespondenz* 25 (1971), pp. 536–44. My student C. Hempel has written a critical account of the literature on the discussion on justification: *Rechtfertigung als Wirklichkeit. Ein katholisches Gespräch. Karl Barth–Hans Küng–R. Bultmann und seine Schule*, Essen, 1974. On the biblical substantiation from the Catholic side see K. Kertelge, *Rechtfertigung bei Paulus. Studie zur Struktur und zum Bedeutungsgehalt des paulinischen Rechtfertigungsbegriffs*, Münster, 1967. Cf. also H. Küng, "Katholische Besinnung auf Luthers Rechtfertigungslehre heute" in *Theologie im Wandel. Festschrift zum 150jährigen Bestehen der Katholisch-theologischen Fakultät an der Universität Tübingen*, Munich/Freiburg, 1967, pp. 449–68.
47 Rm. 3:28.
48 1 Co. 3:11.
49 Ph. 2:21: "For all seek their own and not the cause of Jesus Christ." Cf. 1 Co. 7:32–34: "the affairs of the Lord."
50 Cf. 2 Co. 10–12.
51 Cf. B I, 1: "Taking concepts at their face value."
52 Cf. B II, 1: "Not a myth."
53 1 Co. 2:2.
54 Jn. 14:6.
55 Jn. 6:35, 48, 51.
56 Jn. 8:12.

57 Jn. 10:7.
58 Jn. 15:1, 5.
59 Jn. 10:11.

C VI: *Interpretations*

1. *Discriminating interpretation*

1 P. Tillich, *Systematic Theology*, Vol. II, p. 174.
2 The complete works of W. F. Otto, K. Kerenyi, M. Eliade, R. Pettazzoni should be mentioned in this connection, also the Scandinavian "Myth and Ritual School" and the "Uppsala School."
3 In this connection L. Levy-Bruhl and W. Wundt should be mentioned.
4 P. Tillich, *The Protestant Era*, Chicago, 1948, Chapter 15: "The End of the Protestant Era?", especially pp. 227–28; cf. *Systematic Theology*, Vol. II, pp. 175–76, 189–90.
5 Cf. P. Tillich, *Systematic Theology*, pp. 175–76, 189–90.
6 I owe these views to a report by R. M. Frye, the American literary historian, in which he put forward some important ideas which have been too much neglected in the European debate on demythologizing. The report was published under the title "A literary perspective for the criticism of the gospels" in D. G. Miller/D. Y. Hadidian, *Jesus and Man's Hope*, Vol. II, Pittsburgh, 1971, pp. 193–221. I would like to record here my gratitude to the Pittsburgh Theological Seminary for permitting me to take part in this very informative "Congress of the Gospels."
7 Cf. H. Weinrich, "Narrative Theology" in *Concilium*, May 1973, pp. 46–56; J. B. Metz, "A Short Apology of Narrative," ibid., pp. 84–96.
8 This holds for both Frye and Weinrich.

2. *Interpretations of death*

1 The finest systematic treatment in recent times is to be found in K. Barth, *Church Dogmatics*, Vol. IV, 1–3, 1956–69. Barth unites not only the doctrines–traditionally separated–of Jesus Christ's person (Christology) and work (soteriology), but also those of the two natures (divine and human) and the two states (humiliation and exaltation). Thus he deals with the five great groups of themes of the Christian doctrine of reconciliation, according to the classical scheme of the three-office doctrine, in three continuous perspectives (Volumes IV, 1; IV, 2; IV, 3):
Christology: Jesus Christ as true God–true man–God-man; priestly–royal–prophetic office.
Theology of sin: man's arrogance–sloth–falsehood.
Soteriology: man's justification–sanctification–vocation.
Ecclesiology: the Church's gathering–establishment–mission.
Pneumatology: awakening to faith–life in love–enlightenment to hope.
The three-office doctrine is systematized in very different ways: D. Bonhoeffer, *Wer ist und wer war Jesus Christus?*, Hamburg, 1962, pp. 35–50; F. Buri, *Das dreifache Heilswerk Christi und seine Aneignung*

im Glauben, Hamburg/Bergstedt, 1962; the same author, *Dogmatik als Selbstverständnis des christlichen Glaubens*, Vol. II, Berne/Tübingen, 1962, pp. 375–433; W. Pannenberg, *Jesus–God and Man*, Philadelphia/London, 1968, pp. 212–25; H. Ott, *Antwort des Glaubens*, pp. 266–75.

A comparison of the very diverse systems admittedly shows that there is comparatively little foundation for the systematically convenient three-office doctrine and that it leads, not only to the pressure of a formal system, but also to a certain arbitrariness and neglect of the complexity of the New Testament.

2 Anselm of Canterbury, "Cur Deus Homo" in *S. Anselmi Opera Omnia*, edited by F. S. Schmitt, Vol. II, London/Melbourne/Toronto/New York, 1946, pp. 37–133.

3 Cf. H. Kessler, *Die theologische Bedeutung des Todes Jesu. Eine traditionsgeschichtliche Untersuchung*, Düsseldorf, 1970, summing up and taking further earlier work on the history of dogma. The main emphasis of this work–important for the whole complex of problems in soteriology–lies in the careful and balanced criticism of Anselm's theory of satisfaction (pp. 83–167) and its further development by Aquinas (pp. 167–226). To supplement this cf. G. Greshake, "Erlösung und Freiheit. Zur Neuinterpretation der Erlösungslehre Anselms von Canterbury" in *ThQ* 153 (1973), pp. 323–45; the same author, "Der Wandel der Erlösungsvorstellungen in der Theologiegeschichte" in L. Scheffczyk (ed.), *Erlösung und Emanzipation*, Freiburg/Basle/Vienna, 1973, pp. 69–101.

4 Anselm of Canterbury, "Proslogion" in Schmitt, Vol. I, 1946, pp. 89–124, quotation from Chapters 2 and 3, pp. 101–3.

5 Ibid., Chapter 15, p. 112.

6 The contrast between Anselm's conception and the New Testament is brought out very clearly by H. Kessler, op. cit., pp. 227–337; compare the systematic continuation by the same author, *Erlösung als Befreiung*, Düsseldorf, 1972. There is also a surprisingly clear criticism in J. Ratzinger, *Introduction to Christianity*, London, 1968, pp. 172–74; 213–15.

7 Cf. H. Haag, *Biblische Schöpfungslehre und kirchliche Erbsündenlehre*, Stuttgart, 1966; U. Baumann, *Erbsünde? Ihr traditionelles Verständnis in der Krise heutiger Theologie*, Freiburg/Basle/Vienna, 1970. On the most recent discussion cf. H. Haag, "Die hartnäckige Erbsünde. Überlegungen zu einigen Neuerscheinungen" in *ThQ* 150 (1970), pp. 358–66, 436–56.

8 G. von Rad, Old Testament Theology, Vol. I, Edinburgh/New York, 1962, pp. 139–65; the same author, *Genesis*, London/Philadelphia, 1961.

9 Cf. A. von Harnack, *History of Dogma*, Vol. VI, London/Edinburgh/Oxford, 1899, pp. 76–77.

10 Cf. Mk. 10:45 par.; 14:24 par.

11 Cf. especially Is. 53.

12 Cf. especially Rm. 3:24–26: a formula of faith, interspersed with Old Testament motifs, presumably taken over by Paul.

13 1 Co. 5:7.

14 Jn. 1:29; cf. Rv. 5:6 and frequently.

15 Cf. especially Heb. 2:17; 7–10.

16 2 Co. 5:18.
17 Cf. Ph. 2:7–8; Heb. 9:14.
18 Rm. 6:10; Heb. 7:27; 9:12; 10:10.
19 Heb. 13:8.
20 Cf. H. Kessler, op. cit., pp. 186–87, 330–35.
21 Cf. Ph. 2:7–8; Heb. 9:14.
22 Cf. in *ThW* the articles on the prepositions "anti" (F. Büchsel), "dia" (A. Oepke), "peri" and "hyper" (H. Riesenfeld).
23 Cf. above C V, 2: "Representation."
24 1 Co. 11:20.
25 *Eucharistia* is first used in the *Didache* 9, 10, and by Ignatius and Justin.
26 Cf. *The Church*, C III, 2.
27 T. W. Adorno, *Negative Dialektik*, Frankfurt, 1966, pp. 352–59.
28 R. L. Rubenstein, *After Auschwitz*, New York, 1966.
29 K. Löwith, *Weltgeschichte und Heilsgeschehen. Die theologischen Voraussetzungen der Geschichtsphilosophie*, Stuttgart, 1953, pp. 11–12.
30 G. W. Leibniz, "Essais de théodicée sur la bonté de Dieu, la liberté de l'homme et l'origine du mal" in *Werke*, edited by C. J. Gerhardt, Vol. VI, Berlin, 1885, pp. 3–15.
31 I. Kant, "Über das Misslingen aller philosophischen Versuche in der Theodizee" in *Werke*, edited by W. Weischedel, Vol. VI, Darmstadt, 1964, pp. 103–24.
32 G. F. W. Hegel, *Vorlesungen über die Philosophie der Weltgeschichte* in Lasson-Hoffmeister's critical collected edition, Vol. VIII, p. 938. Cf. H. Küng, *Menschwerdung Gottes*, Chapter VII, 2: "Christus in der Weltgeschichte."
33 Cf. A I, 3: "No abandonment of hope."
34 Cf. O. Marquard, "Wie irrational kann Geschichtsphilosophie sein?" in *Philosophisches Jahrbuch*, 79 (1972), pp. 241–53. Quotation pp. 246, 249.
35 On the problems connected with emancipation and redemption cf. H. Kessler, *Erlösung als Befreiung*, Düsseldorf, 1972, pp. 95–130; J. B. Metz, "The Future in the Memory of Suffering" in *Concilium*, June 1972, pp. 9–25; the same author, "Erlösung und Emanzipation" in L. Scheffczyk (ed.), *Erlösung und Emanzipation*, Freiburg/Basle/Vienna, 1973, pp. 120–40.
36 G. Büchner, *Dantons Tod*, Act III, Scene 1.
37 F. M. Dostoevsky, *The Brothers Karamazov*, Heinemann, London, 1912, Book V, Chapter 4: "Rebellion."
38 Cf. A. Camus, *Le Mythe de Sisyphe*, Paris, 1942; English translation, *Myth of Sisyphus and other Essays*, Knopf, New York/Hamish Hamilton, London, 1955; the same author, *L'homme révolté*, Paris, 1951; English translation, *Rebel. An Essay on Man in Revolt*, same publishers, 1954. Camus's views on the suffering of children in an address to the Paris Dominicans may be found on p. 59 of *Fragen der Zeit*, Hamburg, 1970.
39 On the question of theodicy see H. Küng, *Gott und das Leid*, Zürich/Einsiedeln/Cologne, 1967; J. Moltmann, "Gott und Auferstehung. Aufstehungsglaube im Forum der Theodizeefrage" in *Perspektiven der*

Theologie. Gesammelte Aufsätze, Munich/Mainz, 1968, pp. 36–56; the same author, *The Crucified God*, London, 1974, especially Chapter VI, 3; H. Gollwitzer, *Krummes Holz—aufrechter Gang. Zur Frage nach dem Sinn des Lebens*, Munich, 1970, especially Chapters VII and XI; J. B. Metz, "The Future in the Memory of Suffering" in *Concilium*, June 1972, pp. 9–25; the same author, "Erlösung und Emanzipation" in L. Scheffczyk (ed.), *Erlösung und Emanzipation*, Freiburg/Basle/Vienna, 1973, pp. 120–140. Cf. also the June 1972 issue of *Concilium* on the "Question of God," edited by J. B. Metz.

40 Cf. J. Moltmann, *The Crucified God*, pp. 149–53; 184–87; 195–96; 235–49.

41 Cf. also the criticism of Moltmann's trinitarian interpretation of the history of salvation by J. B. Metz, "A Short Apology of Narrative" in *Concilium*, May 1973, pp. 91–93; largely identical with this is the same author's *Erlösung und Emanzipation*, pp. 135–37. The transition from the speculative problems to a different statement of the question in my *Menschwerdung Gottes*, Chapter VIII, has been overlooked by Metz. In what follows we shall attempt to define the relationship between God and Jesus.

42 In this we must agree with J. B. Metz.

43 Cf. J. B. Metz, *Erlösung und Emanzipation*, pp. 132–33. See also C V, 1: "Legends?"

44 Cf. C IV, 3: "In vain?"

45 Cf. C IV, 2: "Revolution in the understanding of God."

46 1 Jn. 4:8–9.

47 Rm. 8:32.

48 Rm. 8:38–39.

49 Cf. the autobiographical details in 2 Co. 11:16–12:10.

50 Cf. M. Horkheimer, *Die Sehnsucht nach dem ganz Anderem* (an interview with commentary by H. Gumnior), Hamburg, 1970, pp. 61–62.

51 Rv. 21:4.

3. *Interpretations of the origin*

1 Cf. Ph. 2:8; Rm. 5:19.

2 Cf. C V, 2: "Representation."

3 Pr. 8:22–30; Si. 24:8–12.

4 Philo, *On Husbandry*, 51; *Allegorical Interpretation*, 2, 86; 3, 96; 3, 177.

5 Jn. 1:1–14.

6 Rm. 1:3–4; cf. 2 Tm. 2:8.

7 Ph. 2:6–11; cf. 1 Tm. 3:16.

8 Cf. what is probably the earliest recorded text on the incarnation, Ga. 4:4; then 2 Co. 8:9; Rm. 8:3 and finally Tt. 2:11; 2:4. For an analysis of these texts see K. H. Schelkle, *Theologie des Neuen Testaments*, II, pp. 151–68.

9 Ph. 2:5–8.

10 Cf. 2 Tm. 1:10; Tt. 2:11; 2:13; 3:4.

11 Text and commentary in W. Schmithals, "Die Weihnachtsgeschichte Lk. 2, 1–20" in G. Ebeling/E. Jüngel/G. Schunack (eds.), *Festschrift für*

Ernst Fuchs, Tübingen, 1973, pp. 281–97. See also K. H. Schelkle, op. cit., II, pp. 166–68.
12 Cf. the texts cited from Titus and 2 Timothy.
13 Cf. again C V, 2: "Representation."
14 1 Co. 8:5–6.
15 Jn. 20:28.
16 Jn. 1:1: the pre-existing Logos, and Jn. 20:28 in Thomas' confession; probably also in 2 Th. 1:12; Tt. 2:13; 2 P. 1:1.
17 Ignatius, *To the Trallians*, 7:1; *To the Smyrnaeans*, 1:1; 10:1; *To the Ephesians*, 15:3; 18:2; and elsewhere.
18 Cf. H. Küng, *Menschwerdung Gottes*. Excursus II, "Kann Gott leiden?"
19 In addition to the great works on the history of dogma by A. Harnack, R. Seeberg, J. Rivière, cf. H. Kessler's recent book, *Die theologische Bedeutung des Todes Jesu*, Düsseldorf, 1970, §1–2. G. Greshake has a different emphasis in his article in L. Scheffcyk (ed.), *Erlösung und Emanzipation*, Freiburg/Basle/Vienna, 1973, pp. 72–83.
20 On this question see F.-J. Schierse, "Niemand will mehr Gott werden. Gedanken zu Weihnachten einmal anders" in *Publik*, 25.12.1970.
21 Gn. 3:5.
22 The Fathers, under the overwhelming influence of the Johannine Logos-Christology, scarcely attempted a systematic development of a Christology based on the *will*, such as is suggested by Jesus' proclamation of the will of God and by the frequent emphasis on his obedience. And yet–as H.-J. Vogt, my colleague in Tübingen, has pointed out–there are some hints of a Christology of the will–for example–in Christological utterances of the Emperor Constantine (cf. H. G. Opitz, ed., *Urkunden zur Geschichte des arianischen Streites* 318–28=Athanasius, *Werke* III, 1, Berlin/Leipzig, 1934, pp. 58–59, 69–70). There are hints of such a Christology also in Irenaeus, Clement of Alexandria and especially Athanasius.
23 1 Co. 1:24.
24 Cf. 1 Co. 11:3; 8:6; cf. Col. 1:15–18; 2:10; Ep. 4:15–16; 5:23.
25 Cf. 2 Co. 4:4, 6; Rm. 8:29; cf. Col. 1:15.
26 2 Co. 1:20.
27 Jn. 1:1–14.
28 Jn. 5:18–19; 10:33–38; 19:7.
29 Jn. 20:28; cf. 1 Jn. 5:20.
30 1 Co. 5:18–19.
31 Col. 2:9.
32 Jn. 1:14.
33 Jn. 10:15, 38.
34 Jn. 10:38; 14:10–11, 20; 17:21–23.
35 Jn. 10:30.
36 Jn. 14:9; 12:45; 5:19.
37 Cf. C IV, 2: "Not a new God."
38 2 Co. 4:4; Col. 1:15; cf. also Ph. 2:6.
39 On the *idea of pre-existence* see the extensive exegetical literature on the concept of wisdom (*sophia*) and the commentaries on John's prologue. On Paul see E. Schweizer, "Die Herkunft der Präexistenzvorstellung bei

Paulus" in *Neotestamentica*, Zürich, 1963, pp. 105–9. On John see R. Schnackenburg, *The Gospel According to St. John*, Vol. I, London/ New York, 1968, pp. 494–506: Excursus on pre-existence in Judaism, Gnosticism and in John. In general: P. Benoit, "Préexistence et incarnation" in *Revue Biblique* 77 (1970), pp. 5–29; F. Krist, *Jesus Sophia*, Zürich, 1970; K. H. Schelkle, op. cit., II, §10, 6. Obviously also the sections in the works on dogmatic theology (among the Protestants especially P. Althaus, K. Barth, W. Ott and O. Weber; among the Catholics especially M. Schmaus and D. Wiederkehr in *Mysterium Salutis*) and on Christology (O. Cullmann, F. Hahn, W. Pannenberg).

40 Cf. Jn. 1:30; 6:62; 8:58; 17:5, 24. On the idea of pre-existence in John's Gospel see R. Schnackenburg, loc. cit.

41 Ph. 2:6–11.

42 1 Co. 8:6; cf. 10:4.

43 Col. 1:15; Heb. 1:2; 13:8. On the idea of pre-existence in Paul see E. Schweizer, loc. cit.

44 Rv. 1:17.

45 1 Co. 8:6; Col. 1:15–18.

46 Heb. 13:8.

47 Jn. 1:1–14.

48 Ph. 2:5–8.

49 Col. 1:15–20.

50 Cf. Lk. 2:34–35.

51 Cf. here especially H. Ott, *Antwort des Glaubens*, art. 26.

52 Ac. 17:23.

53 Cf. B I, 1: "Taking concepts at their face value."

54 Cf. B I, 2: "The Christ of dogma?"

55 Cf. H. Küng, *The Living Church*, London/New York, 1963, Part 4, Chapter 3: "What is and what is not the theological task of this council?"

56 DS 301.

57 Cf. A. Grillmeier/H. Bacht (eds.), *Das Konzil von Chalkedon. Geschichte und Gegenwart*, Vols. I–III, Würzburg, 1951–54, 1959.

58 Cf. the books mentioned on the history of dogma.

59 That is why a survey of the whole development of Hegel's Christology is worthwhile: cf. H. Küng, *Menschwerdung Gottes. Eine Einführung in Hegels theologisches Denken als Prolegomena zu einer künftigen Christologie.*

60 Cf. H. Küng, *Menschwerdung Gottes*, Chapter VIII, 3.

61 Ga. 4:4.

62 Mt. 1–2.

63 Lk. 1–2.

64 Cf. A. Vögtle, "Offene Fragen zur lukanischen Geburts- und Kindheitsgeschichte" and "Die Genealogie Mt. 1, 2–16 und die matthäische Kindheitsgeschichte" in *Das Evangelium und die Evangelien. Beiträge zur Evangelienforschung*, Düsseldorf, 1971, pp. 43–102; the same author, *Messias und Gottessohn. Herkunft und Sinn der mattäischen Geburts- und Kindheitsgeschichte*, Düsseldorf, 1971; A. Smitmans, *Maria im Neuen Testament*, Stuttgart, 1970, especially pp. 13–34; K. H. Schelkle,

op. cit., Vol. II, pp. 168–75. With these may be compared H. Schürmann, *Das Lukasevangelium*, Vol. I, Freiburg/Basle/Vienna, 1969, pp. 18–145; R. Laurentin, *Structure et théologie de Luc I–II*, Paris, 1957.

65 Cf. Mt. 1:1–17 with Lk. 3:23–28.

66 Cf. C VI, 1: "Truth is not simply facticity."

67 Cf. on the further interpretation particularly of the Christmas story M. Dibelius, "Jungfrauensohn und Krippenkind" (1932) in *Botschaft und Geschichte*, Vol. I, Tübingen, 1953, pp. 1–78; W. Schmithals, "Die Weihnachtsgeschichte Lukas 2, 1–20" in *Festschrift für Ernst Fuchs*, op. cit., pp. 281–97; H. Schüngel-Straumann, "Politische Theologie im Weihnachtsevangelium" in *Neue Zürcher Zeitung* 22.12.1973.

68 H. Schüngel-Straumann, art. cit.

69 On the virgin birth cf. G. Delling, art. "parthenos" in *ThW* V, pp. 824–35; T. Boslooper, *The Virgin Birth*, London, 1962; H. von Campenhausen, *Die Jungfrauengeburt in der Theologie der alten Kirche*, Heidelberg, 1962; H. J. Brosch/J. Hasenfuss (eds.), *Jungfrauengeburt gestern und heute*, Essen, 1969; R. Ruether, "The Collision of History and Doctrine. The Brothers of Jesus and the Virginity of Mary" in *Continuum* 7 (1969), pp. 93–105; A. Smitmans, op. cit., pp. 24–34; R. E. Brown, "The Problem of the Virginal Conception of Jesus" in *Theological Studies* 33 (1972), pp. 3–24; the same author, *The Virginal Conception and the Bodily Resurrection of Jesus*, London, 1973; W. Pannenberg, *The Apostles' Creed*, pp. 71–77; K. H. Schelkle, op. cit., Vol. II, pp. 175–82.

70 DS 2803.

71 This text is omitted from Schönmetzer's edition of Denzinger. It will be found in editions before 1963: H. Denzinger, *Enchiridion Symbolorum*, 91.

72 Is. 7:14.

73 Ps. 2:7.

74 Lk. 1:5–25, 57–66.

75 Cf. Gn. 17:15–22; 18:9–16.

76 Cf. Jg. 13:3–5.

77 Cf. 1 S. 1:4–20.

78 Is. 11:2; 42:1.

79 Cf. Lk. 3:23.

80 Cf. Lk. 4:22; Jn. 6:42.

81 Mk. 3:31–35 par.; cf. Mk. 3:21.

82 Cf. Mk. 6:3; Mt. 13:55; Ac. 12:17; 15:13; 21:18; 1 Co. 15:7; Ga. 1:19; 2:9, 12.

83 Rm. 1:2–4.

84 Ga. 4:4.

85 Cf. Gn. 17f.

86 Ga. 3:29.

87 Jn. 1:12–13.

88 Lk. 1:34–35.

89 Cf. K. H. Schelkle, op. cit., Vol. II, pp. 178, 180.

90 Cf. the report on the Dutch Catechism published Freiburg, 1969, p. 226.

91 Cf. the English translation of the Dutch Catechism: A *New Catechism. Catholic Faith for Adults*, New York/London, 1967, p. 75.
92 The more recent Catholic literature above-mentioned (especially R. E. Brown and K. H. Schelkle) should be compared with the traditional view.
93 Cf. Lk. 3:38.
94 Rm. 5:14–19.
95 Rv. 12:1–5.
96 Jn. 1:1–14.
97 Cf. C VI, 1: "Limits to demythologization."
98 For the historical-critical basis as treated by Catholic scholars see K. H. Schelkle, *Die Mutter des Erlösers*, Düsseldorf, 1967; A. Smitmans, op. cit.
99 Ga. 4:4.
100 Mk. 3:21.
101 Mk. 3:31–35.
102 Mk. 6:3; Mt. 13:35.
103 Lk. 11:27–28.
104 Ac. 1:14.
105 Cf. Mk. 15:40 par.
106 Cf. Jn. 2:1–11 and Jn. 19:25–27.
107 Cf. Lk. 1:28.
108 Cf. Lk. 1:38; 2:34–35.
109 Rm. 4:11–12, 16–18.
110 On the history of Marian devotion, besides the lexicon articles of F. Heiler (RGG) and H. M. Köster (*LThK*), see especially the work—which provides a comprehensive survey of the literature on the subject—by H. Graef, *Mary: A History of Doctrine and Devotion*, 2 vols., London/New York, 1963–65. On the links with popular devotion in the history of religion cf. J. Leipoldt, *Von Epidauros bis Lourdes. Bilder aus der Geschichte volkstümlicher Frömmigkeit*, Hamburg, 1957.
111 DS 251.
112 The new trend in theology is illustrated by recent publications on Mariology, for instance, by K. Riesenhuber, *Maria im theologischen Verständnis von K. Barth und K. Rahner*, Freiburg/Basle/Vienna, 1973; W. Beinert, *Muss man heute von Maria reden? Kleine Einführung in die Mariologie*, Freiburg/Basle/Vienna, 1973.
113 Second Vatican Council, Decree on Ecumenism, n. 11.

C VII: Community of Faith

1. Inspired and inspiring word

1 Cf. B II, 2: "The documents."
2 Cf. the different theories of *inspiration* in the lexicon articles by A. Bea in *LThK* V, 703–11; by G. Lanczkowski/O. Weber/W. Philipp in RGG III, 773–82; likewise in the manuals of dogmatic theology, on the Catholic side—for instance—by S. Tromp, M. Nicolau, L. Ott, M. Schmaus, and on the Protestant side by P. Althaus, K. Barth, E. Brunner, O. Weber, H. Diem. More recent publications include (from the standpoint of the

history of dogma) J. Beumer, *Die Inspiration der Heiligen Schrift*, Freiburg/Basle/Vienna, 1968; and (from the exegetical-systematic standpoint) B. Vawter, *Biblical Inspiration*, Philadelphia/London, 1972.

3 2 Tm. 3:16.

4 Cf. G. Schrenk, art. "grapho, graphe" in *ThW* I, 742–73, especially 750–52; E. Schweizer, art. "pneuma," "theopneustos" in *ThW* VI, 394–453, especially 452–53.

5 1 Co. 7:40; 1 P. 1:12.

6 K. Barth, *Church Dogmatics*, I, 2, §19–21.

2. *The one Spirit*

1 Cf. W. Pannenberg, *The Apostles' Creed*, pp. 128–31.

2 Gn. 1:2.

3 Jl. 2:28–32.

4 Jl. 2:28–32, taken up in Peter's address at Pentecost, as edited by Luke, in Ac. 2:17–21.

5 On this whole section cf. H. Küng, *The Church*, C II, 2: "The Church of the Spirit."

6 DS 150.

7 On the biblical *conception of the Spirit* see among the lexicon articles H. Kleinknecht, F. Baumgärtel, W. Bieder, E. Sjöberg and especially E. Schweizer, *ThW* VI, 330–453; E. Käsemann, *RGG* II, 1272–79; F. Mussner, *LThK* VIII, 572–76; among the theologies of the New Testament R. Bultmann's is particularly important on this subject; important among recent monographs are C. K. Barrett, *The Holy Spirit and the Gospel Tradition*, London, 1947; E. Schweizer, *Geist und Gemeinde im NT*, Munich, 1952; S. Zedda, *L'adozione a figli di Dio e lo Spirito Santo*, Rome, 1952; H. von Campenhausen, *Kirchliches Amt und geistliche Vollmacht in den ersten drei Jahrhunderten*, Tübingen, 1953; N. Q. Hamilton, *The Holy Spirit and Eschatology in Paul*, London, 1957; I. Hermann, *Kyrios und Pneuma*, Munich, 1961; K. Stalder, *Das Werk des Geistes in der Heiligung bei Paulus*, Zürich, 1961; M.-A. Chevallier, *Esprit de Dieu, paroles d'hommes. Le rôle de l'esprit dans les ministères de la parole selon l'apôtre Paul*, Neuchâtel, 1966; H. Küng, *The Church*, C II, 2; E. Brandenburger, *Fleisch und Geist. Paulus und die dualistische Weisheit*, Neukirchen, 1968.

8 Ac. 2; cf. C V, 1: "Clarifications."

9 Cf. Ac. 2:38–39; 9:17; 10:44; 19:6.

10 Ac. 6:6; 13:2–3; cf. 15:28; 20:28.

11 Cf. especially Rm. 8:14–17.

12 2 Cor. 3:18; Ga. 4:6; Rm. 8:9; Ph. 1:19.

13 1 Co. 15:45.

14 2 Co. 3:17.

15 2 Co. 3:17–18.

16 2 Co. 13:13; cf. 1 Co. 12:4–6; Ga. 4:4–6; Rm. 5:1–5; Mt. 28:19.

17 Cf. DS 11, 12, 30, 150, etc. On the development of this article of faith see P. Nautin, *Je crois à l'Esprit Saint dans la Sainte Église pour la résurrection de la Chair. Études sur l'histoire et la théologie du symbole*, Paris,

1947. For literature on the Spirit and the Church see H. Küng, *The Church*, pp. 163–64, 181, and above (n. 7) on the biblical conception of the Spirit.
18 2 Co. 3:17; Rm. 8:2–11.
19 2 Co. 1:22.
20 Mt. 28:19.
21 Ac. 2:38; 8:16; 10:48; cf. 1 Co. 1:13–15; Ga. 3:27; Rm. 6:3.
22 Jn. 14–16.
23 Jn. 14:16.
24 Jn. 14:26.
25 1 Jn. 5:7.
26 1 Jn. 5:7–8. On the interpretation cf. R. Bultmann, *Die drei Johannesbriefe*, Göttingen, 1967, pp. 83–84.
27 Rm. 1:3; 8:9–11; 1 Co. 12:3–6; 2 Co. 13:13; Ga. 4:6; Ph. 3:3; 2 Th. 2:13–14; Ep. 1:3; 4:4–6; Tt. 3:5; Heb. 9:14; 1 P. 1:2; Jude 20–21.
28 Mk. 1:9–11 par.; Mt. 28:19.
29 See K. H. Schelkle, *Theologie des Neuen Testaments*, II, §21, 3–6.
30 Cf. the introduction to his great work, *De Trinitate* I, 3:5–6.
31 Cf. K. Rahner, "Theos in the New Testament" in *Theological Investigations*, Vol. I, London/Baltimore, 1961, pp. 79–148.
32 Jn. 4:24.
33 1 Jn. 1:5.
34 1 Jn. 4:8.
35 The real import of a doctrine of the "immanent" Trinity was discussed in the section on Christ's pre-existence. Cf. C VI, 3: "True God and true man."
36 On the historical development cf. J. A. Jungmann, "Die Abwehr des germanischen Arianismus und der Umbruch der religiösen Kultur im frühen Mittelalter" in *Liturgisches Erbe und pastorale Gegenwart*, Innsbruck/Vienna/Munich, 1960, pp. 3–86.
37 Cf. H. Küng, *Menschwerdung Gottes*, VII, 4: "Christus in der Religion."
38 K. Barth, *Church Dogmatics*, Vol. I, 1.
39 See the works on dogmatic theology on the Catholic side by M. Schmaus and—in *Mysterium Salutis* II—F. J. Schierse, A. Hamman, L. Scheffczyk, K. Rahner; on the Protestant side P. Althaus, E. Brunner, H. Ott, P. Tillich, O. Weber.
40 Augustine, *De Trinitate* I, 3:5.

3. *The pluriform Church*

1 Cf. B I, 1: "Taking concepts at their face value."
2 Cf. C IV, 1: "A Church?" (with bibliography on the New Testament teaching on the Church). For the systematic theology of the Church, in addition to the manuals of fundamental and dogmatic theology (P. Althaus, K. Barth, E. Brunner, F. Buri, H. Diem, W. Elert, Heppe-Bizer, A. Lang, L. Ott, R. Prenter, C. H. Ratschow, J. Salaverri, M. Schmaus, F. A. Sullivan, P. Tillich, W. Trillhaas, O. Weber, T. Zapalena) and the lexicon articles in *LThK* (J. Ratzinger, K. E. Skydsgaard), *RGG* (R. Prenter), *EKL* (J. Koukouzis, K. G. Steck, G. F. Nuttall), *DTC*

(E. Dublanchy), *Catholicisme* (M. J. Le Guillou), see the following recent monographs which have appeared during or after the period of the council: H. Küng, *Structures of the Church*, New York, 1964/London, 1965; P. Touilleux, *Réflexion sur le Mystère de l'Église*, Tournai, 1962; B. C. Butler, *The Idea of the Church*, Baltimore/London, 1962; Y. Congar, *Sainte Église. Études et approches ecclésiologiques*, Paris, 1963; A. Hastings, *One and Apostolic*, New York/London, 1963; H. Fries, *Aspekte der Kirche*, Stuttgart, 1963; P. Glorieux, *Nature et mission de l'Église*, Tournai, 1963; G. Wingren, *Evangelium und Kirche*, Göttingen, 1963; A. Winklhofer, *Über die Kirche*, Frankfurt, 1963; G. Baraúna (ed.), *De Ecclesia. Beiträge zur Konstitution "Über die Kirche" des 2. Vatikanischen Konzils*, 2 vols., Freiburg/Frankfurt, 1966; H. Fries, *Das Mysterium der Kirche*, Würzburg, 1966; H. Lutz, *Die Wirklichkeit der Kirche. Sein und Sollen*, Stuttgart/Berlin, 1966; A. Dulles, *The Dimensions of the Church. A Postconciliar Reflection*, Westminster, Md., 1967; H. Küng, *The Church*, London/New York, 1967; the same author, *Truthfulness. The Future of the Church*, London/New York, 1968; the same author, *Was in der Kirche bleiben muss*, Zürich/Einsiedeln/Cologne, 1973; G. Baum, *The Credibility of the Church Today*, New York/London, 1968; J. L. McKenzie, *The Roman Catholic Church*, New York, 1971; L. Bouyer, *L'Église de Dieu, corps du Christ et temple de l'Esprit*, Paris, 1970; J. Collantes, *La Iglesia de la palabra*, 2 vols., Madrid, 1972; F. Buri/J. M. Lochman/H. Ott, *Dogmatik im Dialog*, Vol. I: "Die Kirche und die letzten Dinge," Gütersloh, 1973.

3 Cf. H. Küng, *The Church*, B III, 1. In regard to the Church there exists a distinct and very complex group of problems. Since the author has produced a number of monographs on this theme, we must necessarily refer to these publications here. Extensive references to Scripture texts and further bibliographies will be found there. The reader may also be referred to the book edited by H. Häring and J. Nolte, *Diskussion um Hans Küng, "Die Kirche,"* Freiburg/Basle/Vienna, 1971. Despite all the differences, this book provides evidence of a clearly emerging ecumenical consensus.

4 The basic structure of the Church as people of God, creation of the Spirit, body of Christ, is not discussed here. For this see H. Küng, *The Church*, C I–III.

5 On what follows see H. Küng, *Why Priests?*, New York/London, 1972, Chapter I.

6 Cf. E. Käsemann, "Unity and Multiplicity in the New Testament Doctrine of the Church" in *New Testament Questions of Today*, London/Philadelphia, 1969, pp. 252–59; R. Pesch, "Were there parties in the New Testament Church?" in *Concilium*, October 1973.

7 Cf. the above-mentioned issue of *Concilium* which is wholly devoted to the theme of "The Danger of Parties in the Church," with a summary of the discussion by H. Küng.

8 In addition to the articles on "Charisma" or "Spirit" in the biblical and theological dictionaries and encyclopedias, see especially F. Grau, *Der ntl Begriff* χάρισμα. *Seine Geschichte und seine Theologie* (disserta-

tion), Tübingen, 1946; J. Brosch, *Charismen und Ämter in der Urkirche*, Bonn, 1951; E. Lohse, *Die Ordination im Spätjudentum und im NT*, Berlin, 1951; H. von Campenhausen, *Kirchliches Amt und geistliche Vollmacht in den ersten 3 Jahrhunderten*, Tübingen, 1953; K. Rahner, *The Dynamic Element in the Church*, London, 1964; E. Schweizer, *Gemeinde und Gemeindeordnung im NT*, Zürich, 1959; R. Bultmann, *Theology of the New Testament*, London/New York, 1951–55; E. Käsemann, "Ministry and Community in the New Testament" in *Essays on New Testament Themes*, London/Naperville, 1964, pp. 63–94; G. Eichholz, *Was heisst charismatische Gemeinde?* 1 Kor. 12, Munich, 1960; O. Perels, "Charisma im NT" in *Fuldaer Hefte* 15, Berlin, 1964, pp. 39–45; H. Schürmann, "Die geistlichen Gnadengaben" in G. Baraúna (ed.), *De Ecclesia. Beiträge zur Konstitution "Über die Kirche" des 2. Vatikanischen Konzils*, Freiburg/Frankfurt, 1966, pp. 494–519; H. Küng, *The Church*, C II, 3: "The continuing charismatic structure"; M. Hengel, *Nachfolge und Charisma. Eine exegetisch-religionsgeschichtliche Studie zu Mt. 8, 21f. und Jesu Ruf in die Nachfolge*, Vienna, 1968; G. Hasenhüttl, *Charisma. Ordnungsprinzip der Kirche*, Freiburg/Basle/Vienna, 1969; U. Brockhaus, *Charisma und Amt. Die paulinische Charismenlehre auf dem Hintergrund der frühchristlichen Gemeindefunktionen*, Wuppertal, 1972; J. Hainz, *Ekklesia–Strukturen paulinischer Gemeinde-Theologie und Gemeinde-Ordnung*, Regensburg, 1972.

9 Cf. H. Küng, *The Church*, E II, 1; in what follows I have kept mainly to the summary in *Why Priests?*, II.

10 Cf. C III, 2: "True radicalism."

11 In addition to the sections on the priesthood in the manuals of dogmatic theology, cf. especially the article by G. Schrenk in *ThW* 221–84, and also the articles on the same theme in the other biblical and theological dictionaries and encyclopedias. And, in addition to the biblical theologies, O. Cullmann, *The Christology of the New Testament*, London/Philadelphia, 1963, pp. 83–107; T. F. Torrance, *Royal Priesthood*, Edinburgh/London, 1955; H. Küng, *The Church*, E I: "The Priesthood of All Believers."

12 Cf. C VI, 2: "Sacrifice?"

13 Cf. 1 P. 2:4–5, 9–10; Rv. 1:5–6; 5:10.

14 Rm. 15:16.

15 Cf. C IV, 1: "A Church?"

16 Cf. C IV, 1: "A Church?"

17 Cf. H. Küng, *The Church*, E II, 2, and *Why Priests?*, II, 6.

18 On the problems of democratization in the Church cf. H. Küng, *Why Priests?*, I, 1; IV, 6–7.

19 The following three paragraphs reproduce theses 12, 13 and 15f. of the memorandum of the study group of the inter-university ecumenical institutes, *Reform und Anerkennung kirchlicher Ämter*, Munich/Mainz, 1973, pp. 18–19. Cf. H. Küng, *Why Priests?*, IV, 2–6. On the function and image of the Church leader today, ibid., 7–10.

20 The historical studies in H. Küng, *Structures of the Church*, New York, 1964/London, 1965, VII–VIII, are presupposed in H. Küng, *The Church*,

1967, E II, 3, which in turn largely provides the material for the following pages.

21 In addition to the histories of the popes (E. Caspar, J. Haller, L. von Pastor, J. Schmidlin, F. X. Seppelt), cf. on the historical development outlined here especially Y. Congar, "Geschichtliche Betrachtungen über Glaubensspaltungen und Einheitsproblematik" in M. Roesle/O. Cullmann (eds.), *Begegnung der Christen*, pp. 405–29; the same author, "Conclusion" in *Le concile et les conciles*, Paris, 1960, pp. 329–34; *Lay People in the Church*, New York, 1965; "Bulletin d'ecclésiologie" (1939–46) in *Revue des sciences philosophiques et théologiques* 31 (1947), pp. 77–96, 272–96.

22 On the pre-history, results and problems of this definition cf. H. Küng, *Infallible? An Inquiry*, New York/London, 1971. The "inquiry" may largely be regarded as settled. Cf. my summing up of the debate on infallibility in H. Küng (ed.), *Fehlbar? Eine Bilanz*, Zürich/Einsiedeln/Cologne, 1973. This contains a detailed bibliography on the debate, drawn up by B. Brooten and K.-J. Kuschel, pp. 515–24.

23 Cf. H. Küng, *The Church*, E II, 3: "The Petrine power and the Petrine ministry." A new ecumenical consensus on the Petrine question—which admittedly does not confirm Vatican I—seems to be emerging with reference to the exegetical basis. The evidence for this can be found in the works of Catholic exegetes like A. Vögtle, J. Blank, R. Pesch, W. Trilling, which largely agree with the conclusions of Protestant exegesis (most recently, for example, G. Bornkamm). The consensus is worked out (with references to the literature on the subject) in *Fehlbar? Eine Bilanz*, pp. 405–14.

24 Cf. Mt. 16:18.

25 Cf. Lk. 22:32.

26 Cf. Jn. 21:15–17.

27 Cf. H. Küng, *The Church*, E II, 3.

28 After Mt. 16:18–19 there follows Mt. 16:22–23.

29 After Lk. 22:32 there follows Lk. 22:34.

30 After Jn. 21:15 there follows Jn. 21:20.

31 Cf. Lk. 22:32.

32 Cf. Jn. 21:17.

33 Cf. Mt. 16:18.

34 Cf. *Concilium*, April 1971, on the theme "The Petrine Ministry in the Church," particularly the responses by S. Harkianakis, P. Evdokimov, A. Allchin and H. Ott to the question "Can a Petrine Office be meaningful in the Church?" and the Catholic answer by H. Häring. The effort to reach an ecumenical consensus on this question, which has been going on since the publication in German (1962) of *Structures of the Church*, has been considerably helped by the document of the mixed Catholic-Lutheran commission of theologians in the United States: "Ministry and the Church Universal. Differing Attitudes Toward Papal Primacy" (1974). Cf. the New York *Times*, 4 March 1974.

35 Further literature on the Petrine question: C. Journet, *Primauté de Pierre*, Paris, 1953; O. Karrer, *Um die Einheit der Christen. Die Petrus-*

frage. Ein Gespräch mit E. Brunner, O. Cullmann, H. von Campenhausen, Frankfurt, 1953; O. Cullmann, art. "petra," "petros" in *ThW* VI, 99–112; *Peter. Disciple–Apostle–Martyr*, London/Philadelphia, 1953; P. Gaechter, *Petrus und seine Zeit*, Innsbruck, 1958; J. Pérez de Urbel, *San Pedro, príncipe de los apóstoles*, Burgos, 1959; contributions by J. Ringer and J. Schmid in M. Roesle/O. Cullmann (eds.), *Begegnung der Christen*, Stuttgart/Frankfurt, 1959. Additional literature listed in the important articles on Peter by A. Vögtle and O. Perler in *LThK* VIII, 334–41 and by E. Dinkler in *RGG* V, 247–49; see also other lexicon articles on Pope and papacy. There are two very informative accounts of the present state of studies on the meaning of Matthew 16:18–19, with very full reading lists, by J. Ludwig, *Die Primatworte Mt. 16, 18f. in der altkirchlichen Exegese*, Münster, 1952, and by F. Obrist, *Echtheitsfragen und Deutung der Primatstelle Mt. 16, 18f. in der deutschen protestantischen Theologie der letzten dreissig Jahre*, Münster, 1960. An informative work from the Orthodox standpoint is F. Anassieff/N. Koulomzien/J. Meyendorff/ A. Schmemann, *Der Primat des Petrus in der Orthodoxen Kirche*, Zürich, 1961.

36 Cf. H. Küng, *The Church*, E II, 3.
37 1 Co. 1:11–12.
38 1 Co. 1:13.
39 Cf. 1 Co. 3:12–15. Cf. H. Küng, "Parties in the Church? A Summary of the Discussion" in *Concilium*, October 1973.

4. *The great mandate*

1 On the distinguishing marks of the Church (*notae Ecclesiae*)–unity, holiness, catholicity, apostolicity, from the Catholic standpoint; pure teaching of the Gospel and right administration of the sacraments from the Protestant standpoint–cf. H. Küng, *The Church*, D I–IV: "The Dimensions of the Church."
2 Mt. 7:21.
3 Cf. H. Küng, *The Church*, C III: "The Church as the Body of Christ."
4 On what follows see H. Küng, *The Church*, B III, 3: "In the service of the reign of God."

D I: The Practice of the Church

1 A. Hasler, in a discussion in *Der Spiegel*, 10 January 1972. For a better understanding see the great histories of the popes by L. von Pastor, J. Schmidlin, J. Haller, F. X. Seppelt-G. Schwaiger, C. Falconi and for the modern situation F. Leist, *Der Gefangene des Vatikans. Strukturen päpstlicher Herrschaft*, Munich, 1971 (reviewed by Edward Quinn in *New Blackfriars*, Oxford, November 1972); L. Waltermann, *Rom, Platz des Heiligen Offizium Nr. 11*, Graz/Vienna/Cologne, 1970; A. Mühr, *Das Kabinett Gottes. Politik in den Wandelgängen des Vatikan*, Vienna/ Düsseldorf, 1971. There is a more personal touch about Hieronymus, *Vatikan intern*, Stuttgart, 1973.

2 Cf. B II, 3: "Counterquestions about Jesus."
3 Cf. B II, 3: "Justifiable faith."
4 Tertullian, *De virginibus velandis* I, 1 in *Corpus Christianorum* II, 1209.
5 Cf. H. Böll, *Brief an einen jungen Katholiken*, Cologne/Berlin, 1961; the same author, *The Clown*, New York, 1965/London, 1973.
6 A. Solzhenitsyn, "Lenten Letter to Pimen, Patriarch of All Russia," published in New York *Times*, 9 April 1972, *Sunday Telegraph*, London, 9 April 1972, *Tablet*, London, 15 April 1972. An abridged version appears in Leopold Labedz, *Solzhenitsyn, A Documentary Record*, London/Baltimore, 1974, pp. 296–98.
7 The following analysis keeps literally to the declaration of the thirty-three theologians, "Against discouragement in the Church," on which the author substantially collaborated. The original German version appeared in *Publik-Forum*, 24 March 1972. English versions appeared in *The Tablet*, 25 March 1972 and *National Catholic Review*, 31 March 1972. (The translation in the present book is original.)
8 The following remarks keep to the answer given for the collection of essays edited by W. Dirks and E. Stammler, *Warum bleibe ich in der Kirche? Zeitgenossische Antworten*, Munich, 1971, pp. 117–24. English versions of the author's contribution, "Why I am staying in the Church," appeared in *The Tablet*, London, 1 May 1971, and *America*, 20 March 1971. (Again the translation in the present book is original.)
9 Cf. especially H. Küng, *The Council and Reunion*, London/New York, 1961; *The Living Church*, London/New York, 1963; *Truthfulness*, London, 1968; *Infallible? An Inquiry*, New York/London, 1971; *Why Priests?*, New York/London, 1972.
10 These orientation points also follow closely the declaration "Against discouragement in the Church."
11 The declaration was signed by the following Catholic theologians: Jean-Paul Audet (Montreal), Alfons Auer (Tübingen), Gregory Baum (Toronto), Franz Böckle (Bonn), Günther Biemer (Freiburg), Viktor Conzemius (Lucerne), Leslie Dewart (Toronto), Casiano Florestán (Madrid), Norbert Greinacher (Tübingen), Winfried Gruber (Graz), Herbert Haag (Tübingen), Franz Haarsma (Nijmegen), Bas Van Iersel (Nijmegen), Otto Karrer (Lucerne), Walter Kasper (Tübingen), Ferdinand Klostermann (Vienna), Hans Küng (Tübingen), Peter Lengsfeld (Münster), Juan Llopis (Barcelona), Norbert Lohfink (Frankfurt), Richard McBrien (Boston), John L. McKenzie (Chicago), Johann Baptist Metz (Münster), Johannes Neumann (Tübingen), Franz Nikolasch (Salzburg), Stephan Pfürtner (Fribourg), Edward Schillebeeckx (Nijmegen), Piet Schoonenberg (Nijmegen), Gerard S. Sloyan (Philadelphia), Leonard Swidler (Philadelphia), Evangelista Villanova (Montserrat), Hermann-Josef Vogt (Tübingen), Bonifac Willems (Nijmegen).

D II: Being Human and Being Christian

1 Cf. G. Szczesny, "Worauf ist Verlass?", Report to the fifteenth Evan-

gelical Church Congress, Düsseldorf, 1973, published (with abbreviations) in *Herder-Korrespondenz* 27 (1973), pp. 402–4. The same author, *Das sogenannte Gute. Vom Unvermögen der Ideologen*, Hamburg, 1971, especially Chapter 18.

2 Cf., for example, A. Auer, "Die Aktualität der sittlichen Botschaft Jesu" in A. Paus (ed.), *Die Frage nach Jesus*, Graz, 1973, pp. 273–80.

3 On the ethical aspect of the problems of religion and society see W. Korff, *Norm und Sittlichkeit. Untersuchungen zur Logik der normativen Vernunft*, Mainz, 1973, pp. 191–92.

4 Ibid., pp. 189–94.

5 Obviously we shall not attempt an ethics here, nor even a foundation of ethics. On this the larger works on Christian ethics should be consulted.

Among the recent *Catholic* works on ethics may be mentioned: F. Tillmann (ed.), *Handbuch der katholischen Sittenlehre*, Düsseldorf, 1953; J. Stelzenberger, *Lehrbuch der Moraltheologie. Die Sittlichkeitslehre der Königsherrschaft Gottes*, Paderborn, 1965; B. Häring, *The Law of Christ*, New York, 1966; J. de Finance, *Ethica generalis*, Rome, 1959; J. Mausbach/G. Ermecke, *Katholische Moraltheologie*, Vols. I–III, Münster, 1959–61; F. Böckle, *Grundbegriffe der Moral. Gewissen und Gewissensbildung*, Aschaffenburg, 1967. A philosophical treatment is found in H. E. Hengstenberg, *Grundlegung der Ethik*, Stuttgart, 1969.

Among recent *Protestant* works on ethics may be mentioned: E. Brunner, *Das Gebot und die Ordnungen. Entwurf einer protestantisch-theologischen Ethik*, Tübingen, 1932; A. de Quervain, *Ethik*, 2 vols., Zollikon-Zürich, 1945–56; D. Bonhoeffer, *Ethics*, edited by E. Bethge, London/New York, 1955; W. Elert, *Das christliche Ethos. Grundlinien der lutherischen Ethik*, Hamburg, 1961; N. H. Soe, *Christliche Ethik*, Munich, 1965; P. Ramsey, *Basic Christian Ethics*, New York, 1952; H. van Oyen, *Evangelische Ethik*, 2 vols., Basle, 1952–57; K. Barth, *Church Dogmatics*, II, 2 (§36–39); III, 4; H. Thielicke, *Theologische Ethik*, 3 vols., Tübingen, 1958–64; W. Trillhaas, *Ethik*, Berlin, 1959; P. L. Lehmann, *Ethics in a Christian Context*, New York, 1963; O. A. Piper, *Christian Ethics*, London, 1970; N. H. G. Robinson, *The Groundwork of Christian Ethics*, London, 1971/Grand Rapids, 1972.

6 On this whole chapter see the important works: by A. Auer, *Autonome Moral und christlicher Glaube*, Düsseldorf, 1971; the same author, "Die Aktualität der sittlichen Botschaft Jesu" in A. Paus (ed.), *Die Frage nach Jesus*, Graz, 1973, pp. 271–363; F. Böckle, "Was ist das Proprium einer christlichen Ethik?" in *Zeitschrift für Evangelische Ethik* 11 (1967), pp. 148–57; the same author, "Theonomie und Autonomie der Vernunft" in W. Oelmüller (ed.), *Fortschritt wohin? Zum Problem der Normenfindung in der pluralen Gesellschaft*, Düsseldorf, 1972, pp. 63–86; the same author, "Unfehlbare Normen?" in H. Küng (ed.), *Fehlbar? Eine Bilanz*, Zürich/Einsiedeln/Cologne, 1973, pp. 280–304; J. Fuchs, "Gibt es eine spezifisch christliche Moral?" in *Stimmen der Zeit* 185 (1970), pp. 99–112; J. Gründel/H. van Oyen, *Ethik ohne Normen? Zu den Weisungen des Evangeliums*, Freiburg/Basle/Vienna, 1970; W. Korff, *Norm und Sittlichkeit. Untersuchungen zur Logik der normativen Vernunft*, Mainz,

1973; the same author, "Wie kann der Mensch glücken? Zur Frage einer ethischen Theorie der Gesellschaft" in *ThQ* 153 (1973), pp. 305–22; D. Mieth, "Die Situationsanalyse aus theologischer Sicht" in A. Hertz (ed.), *Moral*, Mainz, 1972, pp. 13–33; B. Schüller, "Zur Problematik allgemein verbindlicher ethischer Grundsätze" in *Theologie und Philosophie* 45 (1970), pp. 1–23; the same author, *Die Begründung sittlicher Urteile. Typen ethischer Argumentation in der katholischen Moraltheologie*, Düsseldorf, 1973.

7 Cf. A I, 1: "Secular world."

8 Cf. A II, 2: "The hypothesis."

9 Cf. A II, 2: "Reality."

10 Cf. A. Auer, *Die Aktualität der sittlichen Botschaft Jesu*, p. 281 (with reference to H. Rombach and G. Meyer).

11 Ibid.

12 Cf. A II, 1: "Proofs of God?"

13 F. Böckle, *Unfehlbare Normen?*, p. 291.

14 Cf. W. Korff, *Wie kann der Mensch glücken?*, p. 3.

15 Cf. A II, 1: "More than pure reason."

16 Cf. A II, 2: "Ambiguity of the concept of God"; C IV, 2: "The God with a human face."

17 Cf. B. Schüller, "Zur Problematik allgemein verbindlicher ethischer Grundsätze," art. cit.

18 Cf. C V, 3: "Beyond fanaticism and rigidity."

19 Even explicitly situation ethics must not be understood in this way. Cf. J. Fletcher, *Situation Ethics. The New Morality*, Philadelphia, 1966.

20 Cf. C V, 3: "Beyond fanaticism and rigidity."

21 Cf. A II, 2: "The hypothesis."

22 Cf. A II, 2: "Reality."

23 M. Horkheimer, *Die Sehnsucht nach dem ganz Anderen*, edited by H. Gumnior, Hamburg, 1970, p. 60.

24 Ibid., pp. 60–61.

25 Cf. B II, 3: "Historical criticism–an aid to faith?"

26 For the Old Testament theologies cf. especially W. Eichrodt, *Theology of the Old Testament*, Vol. II, London, 1967, §22; G. von Rad, *Theology of the Old Testament*, Edinburgh/London, Vol. I, 1962, pp. 190–202; W. Zimmerli, *Grundriss der alttestamentlichen Theologie*, Stuttgart, 1972, p. 11. In addition H. van Oyen, *Ethik des Alten Testaments*, Gütersloh, 1967. On the Decalogue A. Alt, *Die Ursprünge des israelischen Rechts*, Leipzig, 1934, is still basic reading; then, in addition to the lexicon articles, H. Haag, "Der Dekalog" in J. Stelzenberger (ed.), *Moraltheologie und Bibel*, Paderborn, 1964, pp. 9–38; G. O. Botterweck, "The Form and Growth of the Decalogue," in *Concilium*, May 1965, pp. 33–44; N. Lohfink, "Die zehn Gebote ohne den Berg Sinai" in his miscellany, *Bibelauslegung im Wandel*, Frankfurt, 1967, pp. 129–57.

27 Ex. 19–Nb. 10.

28 Ex. 34:28; Dt. 4:13; 10:4.

29 Ex. 20:2–17; Dt. 5:6–21.

30 Cf. C IV, 2: "Not a new God."

31 A. Auer, *Autonome Moral*, pp. 63–68, deduces these consequences clearly from the Old Testament material.
32 Cf. C V, 3 on the literature relating to Pauline studies. On the problems discussed here see also L. Nieder, *Die Motive der religiös-sittlichen Paränese in den paulinischen Gemeindebriefen. Ein Beitrag zur paulinischen Ethik*, Munich, 1956; W. Schrage, *Die konkreten Einzelgebote in der paulinischen Paränese. Ein Beitrag zur neutestamentlichen Ethik*, Gütersloh, 1961; A. Grabner-Haider, *Paraklese und Eschatologie bei Paulus. Mensch und Welt im Anspruch der Zukunft Gottes*, Münster, 1968. On New Testament ethics as a whole, among the New Testament theologies, see especially K. H. Schelkle's systematic treatment in Vol. III, "Ethos." As typical historical-systematic presentations may be cited on the Catholic side R. Schnackenburg, *The Moral Teaching of the New Testament*, London/New York, 1964, and on the Protestant side H.-D. Wendland, *Ethik des Neuen Testaments. Eine Einführung*, Göttingen, 1970.
33 Col. 3:18–4:1.
34 Ph. 4:8.
35 Lists of virtues in Ga. 5:22–23 and Ph. 4:8. Lists of vices in Rm. 1:29–31; 1 Co. 6:9–10; 2 Co. 12:20–21; Ga. 5:19–21.
36 On what follows see E. Käsemann, *An die Römer*, Tübingen, 1973.
37 Ibid., p. 166.
38 Ibid.
39 In addition to the exegetical literature mentioned in C IV, 1, see D. Bonhoeffer, *The Cost of Discipleship*, London/New York, 1959; K. Barth, *Church Dogmatics*, IV, 2 §66, 3; A. Schulz, *Nachfolgen und Nachahmen*, Munich, 1962; E. Larsson, *Christus als Vorbild*, Uppsala, 1962; G. Bouwmann, *Folgen und Nachfolgen im Zeugnis der Bibel*, Salzburg, 1965; H. D. Betz, *Nachfolge und Nachahmung Jesu Christi im Neuen Testament*, Tübingen, 1967; M. Hengel, *Nachfolge und Charisma*, Berlin, 1968.
40 R. M. Hare, *The Language of Morals*, Oxford, 1952, p. 69; cf. also P. W. Taylor, *Normative Discourse*, Englewood Cliffs, N.J., 1961, pp. 151–58.
41 Cf. C III, 1: "The changed awareness."
42 Cf. B I, 2: "The Christ of piety?"
43 Cf. C VI, 1: "Limits to demythologization."
44 Even the English expression, "The Paradigmatic Individuals," is not an adequate translation of Karl Jaspers' term, *die massgebenden Menschen*. Cf. the otherwise very sound article by A. S. Cua, "Morality and the Paradigmatic Individuals" in *American Philosophical Quarterly*, 6 (1969), pp. 324–29.
45 Jn. 8:12.
46 Jn. 1:14.
47 Jn. 14:6.
48 Cf. the works above-mentioned, especially by A. Auer and F. Böckle.
49 Cf. C III, 2: "Even enemies."
50 Cf. C III, 2: "True radicalism."
51 Cf. C V, 2: "The criterion."

52 This holds with some reserve even for H. D. Wendland's very thorough "introduction" to the "Ethics of the New Testament."

53 1 Co. 3:11.

54 D. Bonhoeffer, *The Cost of Discipleship*, p. 49.

55 For a number of the following points I gained some valuable ideas from a conversation with J. M. Gustafson on the occasion of his lecture in Pittsburgh, "The Relation of the Gospels to the Moral Life," published in D. G. Miller/D. Y. Hadidan (eds.), *Jesus and Man's Hope*, Pittsburgh, 1971, Vol. II, pp. 103–17. Cf. the same author, *Christ and the Moral Life*, New York/London, 1968.

56 "When I ask myself why I have always aspired to behave honourably, to spare others and to be kind wherever possible, and why I didn't cease doing so when I realized that in this way one comes to harm and becomes an anvil because other people are brutal and unreliable, then indeed I have no answer." Sigmund Freud, Letter to J. J. Putnam, 8.7.1915, in *Letters of Sigmund Freud 1873–1939*, edited by Ernst L. Freud, London, 1961, p. 315.

D III: *Being Christian as Being Radically Human*

1 D. Sölle, *Politische Theologie. Auseinandersetzung mit Rudolf Bultmann*, Stuttgart/Berlin, 1971, p. 78.

2 Cf. C I, 2: "Not a social revolutionary."

3 Cf. C I, 2: "Non-violent revolution."

4 Cf. C II, 3: "The meaning of the Sermon on the Mount."

5 C. Schmitt, *Politische Theologie. Vier Kapitel zur Lehre von der Souveränität*, Munich/Leipzig, 1922, new edition, 1934, especially pp. 47–66. The same holds for the term "political Christ."

6 E. Peterson, "Der Monotheismus als politisches Problem" (1935) in *Theologische Traktate*, Munich, 1951, pp. 45–147.

7 Among the leading exponents of "political theology" in recent times is J. B. Metz, *Theology of the World*, London, 1970; "The Church's Social Function in the Light of 'Political Theology'" in *Concilium*, June 1968, pp. 3–11; art. "Political Theology" in *Sacramentum Mundi*, Vol. V, London/New York, 1970, pp. 34–38. In addition J. Moltmann, "Theologische Kritik der politischen Religion" in *Kirche im Prozess der Aufklärung. Aspekte einer neuen "politischen Theologie,"* Munich/Mainz, 1970, pp. 11–51; D. Sölle, *Politische Theologie. Auseinandersetzung mit Rudolf Bultmann*, Stuttgart/Berlin, 1971. On the discussion cf. H. Peuckert (ed.), *Diskussion zur "politischen Theologie,"* Munich/Mainz, 1969; note particularly the contributions of H. Maier, D. A. Seeber, W. Oelmüller, H. R. Schlette, H. Schürmann, F. Böckle, K. Lehmann, T. Rendtorff, W. Pannenberg, K. Rahner. See also in the same book (p. 268) the answer of J. B. Metz, who again dissociates himself from a "politicizing theology."

8 Cf. R. Shaull, "Revolutionary Change in Theological Perspective" in *Christian Ethics in a Changing World*, edited by J. C. Bennett, New

York/London, 1966, pp. 23–43; the same author, *Befreiung durch Veränderung. Herausforderung an Kirche, Theologie und Gesellschaft*, Munich/Mainz, 1970. On the discussion cf. T. Rendtorff/H. E. Tödt, *Theologie der Revolution. Analysen und Materialien*, Frankfurt, 1968; E. Feil/R. Weth (eds.), *Diskussion zur "Theologie der Revolution,"* Munich/Mainz, 1969; C. H. Grenholm, *Christian Social Ethics in a Revolutionary Age. An Analysis of the Social Ethics of J. C. Bennett, H. D. Wendland and R. Shaull*, Uppsala, 1973.

9 Cf. A I, 2: "No return."

10 M. Machoveč, *Jesus für Atheisten*, Stuttgart, 1972, p. 254.

11 Cf. C II, 3: "No natural law."

12 Cf. C II, 3: "No revealed law."

13 Cf. C II, 3: "The meaning of the Sermon on the Mount."

14 Cf. Jn. 13:34.

15 Cf. C III, 2: "Both God and man."

16 Cf. D II, 1: "The unconditioned in the conditioned."

17 Cf. D II, 1: "Uncertainty of norms."

18 Rm. 13:10; cf. Ga. 5:14.

19 1 Co. 13:2–3.

20 Cf. H. E. Richter, *Die Gruppe*, Hamburg, 1972; the same author, *Lernziel Solidarität*, Hamburg, 1974.

21 In what follows we are keeping mainly to the very informative and impressive issue of *Concilium* of June 1974 on "Liberation and Faith," edited by C. Geffré, containing articles exclusively by Latin American theologians. The quotation from the Medellín document is on pp. 137–38.

22 Cf. R. Muñoz, *Nueva Conciencia de la Iglesia en América Latina*, Santiago, 1973; the same author, "Two Community Experiences in the Latin American Liberation Movement," *Concilium*, June 1974, pp. 137–47.

23 Basic reading for the theology of liberation is the work of G. Gutierrez, the result of deep involvement and careful reflection, *Teología de la liberación*, Lima, 1971; American translation: *A Theology of Liberation*, Maryknoll, 1973/London, 1974. Cf. the same author, "Liberation, Theology and Proclamation" in *Concilium*, June 1974.

24 Cf. G. Gutierrez, *A Theology of Liberation*, pp. ix–x.

25 Cf. E. Dussel, "Domination-Liberation: A New Approach" in *Concilium* June 1974, pp. 34–56; P. Freire, *Pedagogy of the Oppressed*, New York, 1971.

26 L. Boff, "Salvation in Jesus Christ and the Process of Liberation" in *Concilium*, June 1974, pp. 78–91. Quotation from p. 78.

27 S. Galilea, "Liberation as Encounter with Politics and Contemplation" in *Concilium*, June 1974, pp. 19–33. Quotation p. 19.

28 Cf. H. Assmann, "Evaluation critique de la 'Théologie de la libération'" in *Lettre*, Paris, No. 187, March 1974, pp. 23–28. Assmann dissociates himself from J. Moltmann and J. Alfaro, whom he describes as advocates of a "reformistic progressivism."

29 G. Gutierrez in *Concilium*, June 1974, p. 58.

30 Cf. S. Galilea, loc. cit.
31 Cf. G. Gutierrez in *Concilium*, June 1974, pp. 59–60.
32 Cf. J. H. Cone, *A Black Theology of Liberation*, Philadelphia/New York, 1970; R. Radford Ruether, *Liberation Theology. Human Hope Confronts Christian History and American Power*, New York/Toronto, 1972.
33 Cf. A I, 3: "Humanity through politico-social revolution?"
34 Ibid.
35 Cf. *Concilium*, October 1973, "The Danger of Parties in the Church" and especially the summary of the discussion by H. Küng, "Parties in the Church?", pp. 133–46.
36 Observations on the communiqué of the student leaders by the university assessors of Sucre, Sucre, 1970 (photocopied), quoted in *Concilium*, June 1974, p. 143.
37 Address to Latin American Catholics in Paris, 25 April 1968. English translation in Helder Camara, *Church and Colonialism*, London/Sydney, pp. 101–11.
38 Cf. H. Goss-Mayr, *Die Macht der Gewaltlosen. Der Christ und die Revolution am Beispiel Brasiliens*, Graz, 1968; H. J. Schultz (ed.), *Von Gandhi bis Camara. Beispiele gewaltfreier Politik*, Stuttgart/Berlin, 1971.
39 S. Galilea, in *Concilium*, art. cit., p. 23.
40 Cf. C VI, 2: "God and suffering."
41 Ibid.
42 F. Nietzsche, *Thus Spake Zarathustra*, New York/London, 1933, p. 161.
43 1 Co. 1:23–24. Cf. C V, 3: "Revaluation."
44 The preaching of Cardinal A. Bengsch, Archbishop of Berlin, runs on these lines. Someone whom I regard as an exemplary parish priest in the German Democratic Republic (with his colleagues) scrutinized the cardinal's Passion sermon critically but with the utmost good will and reached some disturbing conclusions. Cf. K. Herbst, "Zur Verkündigung von Alfred Kardinal Bengsch" in the bulletin of the study group of the priests' and solidarity groups in the Federal Republic. *SOG-Papiere*, 5 (1972), pp. 81–103. This article refers also to the cardinal's sermon during the invasion of Czechoslovakia by East German troops in which every attempt at a critical reaction was offset by an invitation to "prayer to Christ." The study by K. Herbst was made available to the ordinaries and the pastors in East Germany.
45 Cf. most recently J. Moltmann, *The Crucified God*, Chapter 2.
46 Cf. C VI, 2: "Sacrifice?"
47 Cf. B I, 2: "The Christ of piety?" (cf. C V, 3).
48 Cf. J. Hanauer, *Konnersreuth als Testfall. Kritischer Bericht über das Leben der Therese Neumann* (with an appendix containing unpublished documents from the episcopal archives in Regensburg), Munich, 1972.
49 1 Co. 11:1; 1 Th. 1:6; Ep. 5:1.
50 Cf. W. Michaelis, art. "mimeomai" in *ThW* IV, 661–78; quotation p. 676.
51 Mk. 8:34.
52 Luke 9:23 has the variant "daily."
53 Cf. C II, 2: "Miracles?"
54 Mk. 12:31 par.

55 Lk. 10:25–37.
56 Mt. 25:34–46.
57 D. Sölle, *Leiden*, Stuttgart/Berlin, 1973, p. 112.
58 Ibid., p. 124.
59 Rm. 6:5–9; 1 Co. 15:20–22.
60 Ga. 2:20.
61 Rm. 6:6; Ga. 5:24; 6:14.
62 2 Co. 5:17; Rm. 6:11.
63 Cf. 2 Co. 12:7–10.
64 2 Co. 4:8–9; 6:9–10. Cf. 2 Co. 11:23–30; 1 Co. 4:10–13.
65 1 P. 2:20–21.
66 This became evident at the fourth plenary assembly of the Lutheran World-Federation in Helsinki in 1963, where the message of justification was discussed under the heading "Christ Today" by twenty-six groups, without adopting an agreed document. Cf. *Rechtfertigung heute. Studien und Berichte*, published by the theological commission of the Lutheran World-Federation, Stuttgart/Berlin, 1965.
67 See on the Catholic side N. Greinacher, *Christliche Rechtfertigung–gesellschaftliche Gerechtigkeit*, Zürich/Einsiedeln/Cologne, 1973. Cf. also C. Mayer, "Rechtfertigung durch Werke? Praxisbezug und politische Dimension des Glaubens" in *ThQ* 154 (1974), 118–36.
68 Cf. N. Greinacher, op. cit., pp. 7–13.
69 Cf. E. Bloch, *Thomas Münzer als Theologe der Revolution*, Berlin, 1960.
70 Cf. A I, 1: "Opening out of the Churches"; A I, 2: "No return."
71 A pioneer work on the interpretation of the message of justification in the secular world was F. Gogarten's *Despair and Hope for Our Time*, Philadelphia, 1970 (German original, 1953). More recently H. Zahrnt has made an impressive contribution to the same theme, with reference to the ideas of E. H. Erikson, in *Wozu ist das Christentum gut?*, Munich, 1972, Chapter 6.
72 Cf. D II, 1: "Human autonomy."
73 Mt. 16:25 par.
74 Cf. C I, 4: "Against self-righteousness"; C II, 3: "The supreme norm"; C III, 3: "The law of grace."
75 Cf. C V, 3: "By faith alone." Cf. H. Küng, *Justification*, Chapters 31–32.
76 Ga. 5:6; cf. 5:22–23.
77 Jm. 2:14–26.
78 Cf. A II, 2: "The hypothesis."
79 Mt. 16:25 par.
80 At this point especially it becomes clear how closely faith and prayer are linked and how far prayer is an essential part of being a Christian. As a logical continuation of the reflections on prayer in Part C, I had planned to devote a special section here to prayer, meditation and Christian worship (in particular, the Sunday act of worship). The tiresome disputes forced on me afresh by Rome cost me at least two months of working time and working energies in the final, decisive phase of producing this book, which could not be made up in view of the tight schedule. The

section planned therefore had to be dropped: a victim of the policy of the Roman Inquisition.

81 Cf. C III, 2: "True radicalism."
82 Mt. 5:5.
83 Cf. C III, 2: "True radicalism."
84 Mt. 5:7.
85 Cf. C III, 3: "Which poor?"
86 Mt. 5:3.
87 Cf. C III, 2: "True radicalism."
88 Mk. 9:37 par.
89 Jn. 21:25.

Index